Please Leave us a Review on Amazon

Ancient Patericon

or

A Thematic Collection of Sayings - Apophthegms
of the Desert Fathers

Compiled by Saint Paisos,
Revised by
Saint Theophan the Recluse

Other Orthodox Works Published by Based Books

The Lives of the Saints for Orthodox Christians

The New Testament Commentaries of Saint Theophylact of Ohrid

The Complete Discourses of Saint Symeon the New Theolgian

The Sayings of the Desert Fathers: The Patericon of Saint Ignatius Brianchaninov

The Arena - Saint Ignatius Brianchaninov

Unseen Warfare – Saint Theophan the Recluse

History of the Byzantine Empire – Fyodor Uspensky

Philokalia: Volumes 1-5

ST.
THEOPHAN
THE
RECLUSE

Ancient Patericon

or

A Thematic Collection of Sayings - Apophthegms
of the Desert Fathers

Compiled by Saint Paisos,
Revised by
Saint Theophan the Recluse

Table of Contents

From the Publisher

The *Ancient Patericon* presented here is a significant work by Saint Theophan the Recluse, who translated an ancient manuscript preserved in the Russian St. Panteleimon Monastery on Mount Athos. This edition marks its first publication.

In our current era—which might fairly be called a time of monastic renewal in Rus' following prolonged persecution that severely disrupted monastic traditions—the spiritual wisdom of the early Egyptian desert fathers holds particular relevance for those seeking authentic instruction in the ascetic life of early Christianity.

Saint Theophan's translation work represents a continuation of the great efforts begun by Saint Paisius (Velichkovsky). Yet their approaches differed considerably. Whereas Saint Paisius emphasized strict fidelity to the Greek original, Saint Theophan prioritized conveying the spiritual substance of the ancient texts in accessible language, valuing clarity and internal coherence over literal precision. His style is distinctive—neither purely literary nor conforming to the standard ecclesiastical language of his day. This edition, based directly on the manuscript, preserves those characteristic features that earlier editors sometimes smoothed over, whether for stylistic uniformity or to satisfy censorial concerns regarding difficult passages (which exist in the Greek as well). Saint Theophan himself, anticipating such scrutiny, occasionally modified or removed particularly challenging sections.

The authentic voice of Saint Theophan's translations thus proves richer and more distinctive than the synodal editions, which often simplified, abbreviated, or diminished the clarity of his work.

This publication offers readers access to the Athonite copy in its original form. The faithfully rendered text reveals the beauty of the Greek source while standing as an independent literary achievement within nineteenth-century Russian spiritual literature.

It should be noted that this translation does not claim academic precision in rendering the Greek original. Its value lies rather in its nature as the work of a renowned ascetic. The publishers have not undertaken textual analysis or source identification—a separate scholarly endeavor to which this edition may contribute. Preliminary observation suggests the translation drew from a collection resembling the well-known *Great Patericon*, though it includes material absent from that work. The precise manuscripts or printed editions consulted remain uncertain.

The *Ancient Patericon* addresses not only monastics, for whom it serves as practical guidance in emulating the struggles of the ancient fathers, but also laypeople. Its vivid depictions of authentic Christian relationships make it an invaluable resource for any Orthodox Christian striving to live according to God's commandments.

Preface:
On the Life and Asceticism of the Blessed Holy Fathers

The Word of God, eternally existing with God, who by His great goodness wisely created the world out of nothing, stretched out the heaven over all that is visible and established lights upon it, that they might illumine all creation and assist men in their labors. This Only-begotten Son and Word of the Father, in the last days born for our salvation through the Holy Spirit from the Virgin Mary, and through His incarnation having become like us in all things save sin, has fashioned for us another heaven, invisible and incomparably more beautiful than this visible one. For this visible heaven, being itself sensible, serves chiefly sensible ends, while that invisible one, being spiritual, raises the spirit to God. The visible heaven has moving and unmoving stars, as those who study such things say, but in that invisible one, all are unmoving, ever-bright, and unchanging. This sensible heaven, according to the divine decree, *will be rolled together as a scroll* (Isaiah 34:4), and the stars upon it shall fall like leaves on the last day, but that one will not only preserve its stars then, but will reveal them shining more brightly than the sun.

One of the hosts of this pure and life-giving firmament is the divine host of ascetics wounded with divine love, of whom our present discourse treats. Having accomplished with fortitude and beyond nature every form of virtue, they now shine in heaven with unwaning light and ceaselessly illumine mystically those who dwell upon the earth. The luminaries and teachers of the Church, having described for our edification their deeds, teachings, and rules of life, have thus shown forth a divine paradise, nourishing with every beauty of virtue the souls of those who read them with faith. And what virtue has not been cultivated in this divine paradise by Christ, our true God? Here we behold blessed stillness, and strict self-control in all things with chastity, and non-possessiveness that gives wings to the soul. There we see exemplary patience and courage, secret good works known to God alone, saving non-judgment of others, radiant discernment, sober and unceasing prayer, merciful hospitality, patience in imitation of Christ, lofty humility of mind, gifts of wonderworking, and examples of every virtuous life.

For all these virtues, the pattern, the rule, the guide, and the teacher is Christ Himself, our true God, as the word of God, Holy Scripture, reveals to us.

On Stillness

The Gospel testifies that after His baptism, the Lord *was in the wilderness forty days, tempted by Satan,* and ate nothing during those days, and *was with the wild beasts* (Mark 1:13; Luke 4:1–

2). And again: *And seeing the multitudes, He went up on a mountain, and when He was seated His disciples came to Him. Then He opened His mouth and taught them, saying: "Blessed are the poor in spirit, for theirs is the kingdom of heaven"* ...and so forth (Matthew 5:1–3). Likewise: *And when He had sent the multitudes away, He went up on the mountain by Himself to pray. Now when evening came, He was alone there* (Matthew 14:23). And again: *the Lord departed to a deserted place, and there He prayed* (Mark 1:35; Luke 4:42). So also John the Baptist *was in the deserts till the day of his manifestation to Israel* (Luke 1:80). And the Apostle says: *Therefore I exhort first of all that supplications, prayers, intercessions, and giving of thanks be made for all men, for kings and all who are in authority, that we may lead a quiet and peaceable life in all godliness and reverence* (1 Timothy 2:1–2). And in another place: *but we urge you, brethren, to increase more and more; and to aspire to lead a quiet life, to mind your own business, and to work with your own hands* (1 Thessalonians 4:10–11). Likewise: *Now those who are such we command and exhort through our Lord Jesus Christ that they work in quietness and eat their own bread* (2 Thessalonians 3:12). And again: *"Come out from among them and be separate"* (2 Corinthians 6:17), and: *seek those things which are above... Set your mind on things above, not on things on the earth* (Colossians 3:1–2).

On Self-Control

The Lord said: *"Enter by the narrow gate... narrow is the gate and difficult is the way which leads to life"* (Matthew 7:13–14). The Twelve Apostles in the desert *had only five loaves and two fish* (Matthew 14:17), and at another time the Apostles *had forgotten to take bread, and did not have more than one loaf with them in the boat* (Mark 8:14), and on another occasion: *His disciples plucked the heads of grain and ate them, rubbing them in their hands* (Luke 6:1). And the Apostle says in his epistle: *And everyone who competes for the prize is temperate in all things* (1 Corinthians 9:25). And again: *To the present hour we both hunger and thirst, and we are poorly clothed* (1 Corinthians 4:11). And again: *But food does not commend us to God* (1 Corinthians 8:8), and *Foods for the stomach and the stomach for foods, but God will destroy both it and them* (1 Corinthians 6:13), and there also: *Therefore, if food makes my brother stumble, I will never again eat meat, lest I make my brother stumble* (1 Corinthians 8:13). And in another place: *I know how to be abased, and I know how to abound. Everywhere and in all things I have learned both to be full and to be hungry, both to abound and to suffer need* (Philippians 4:12), and *we endure all things lest we hinder the gospel of Christ* (1 Corinthians 9:12). And in another epistle: *No longer drink only water, but use a little wine for your stomach's sake and your frequent infirmities* (1 Timothy 5:23).

On Chastity

The Lord said: *"there are eunuchs who have made themselves eunuchs for the kingdom of heaven's sake"* (Matthew 19:12). And in another place: *"But I say to you that whoever looks at a woman to lust for her has already committed adultery with her in his heart"* (Matthew 5:28). The harlot, the thief, and the tax collector, who had fallen into unchastity, the Lord received and calls all: *"Come to Me, all you who labor and are heavy laden"* (that is, with lusts and sins), *"and I will give you rest. Take My yoke upon you"* ...and so forth (Matthew 11:28–29). And the Apostle says: *Flee sexual immorality* (1 Corinthians 6:18), and *Pursue peace with all people, and holiness, without which no one will see the Lord* (Hebrews 12:14). Likewise: *Therefore put to death your members which are on the earth: fornication, uncleanness, passion, evil desire* (Colossians 3:5), and *Do you not know that you are the temple of God and that the Spirit of God dwells in you? If anyone defiles the temple of God, God will destroy him* (1 Corinthians 3:16–17). In another place: *lest there be any fornicator or profane person like Esau* (Hebrews 12:16), and *Do not be deceived. Neither fornicators, nor idolaters, nor adulterers, nor effeminate, nor sodomites... will inherit the kingdom of God* (1 Corinthians 6:9–10), for *the grace of God that brings salvation has appeared to all men, teaching us that, denying ungodliness and worldly lusts, we should live soberly, righteously, and godly* (Titus 2:11–12). Likewise he instructs: *Flee also youthful lusts* (2 Timothy 2:22), *exhort the young men to be sober-minded* (Titus 2:6), *But fornication and all uncleanness... let it not even be named among you* (Ephesians 5:3). The same Apostle mercifully receives the one who committed fornication in Corinth and afterward, upon being delivered to Satan, repented, and writes: *I urge you to reaffirm your love to him... lest perhaps such a one be swallowed up with too much sorrow* (2 Corinthians 2:7–8), but at the end of the epistle he warns: *For I fear lest, when I come, I shall not find you such as I wish... and that I shall mourn for many who have sinned before and have not repented of the uncleanness, fornication, and lewdness which they have committed* (2 Corinthians 12:20–21).

On Non-Possessiveness

The Lord said: *"Do not worry about your life, what you will eat or what you will drink; nor about your body, what you will put on"* (Matthew 6:25), and *"But seek first the kingdom of God and His righteousness, and all these things shall be added to you"* (Matthew 6:33). Likewise: *"Provide neither gold nor silver... nor two tunics"* (Matthew 10:9–10); and *"If you want to be perfect, go, sell what you have and give to the poor... and come, follow Me, taking up the cross"* (Matthew 19:21; Mark 10:21). And in another place: *"Foxes have holes and birds of the air have nests, but the Son of Man has nowhere to lay His head"* (Matthew 8:20). And John the Baptist *had his garment of camel's hair, and a leather belt around his waist* (Matthew 3:4). And the Apostle teaches: *For we brought nothing into this world, and it is certain we can carry nothing out. And having food and clothing, with these we shall be content. But those who desire to be rich fall into temptation and a snare, and into many lusts* (1 Timothy 6:7–9). He also says of all the Apostles that they are *as poor, yet making many rich; as having nothing, and yet possessing all things* (2 Corinthians 6:10).

On Patience and Courage

The Lord said: *"Let your waist be girded and your lamps burning; and you yourselves be like men who wait for their master"* (Luke 12:35–36). And again: *"By your patience possess your souls"* (Luke 21:19). And again: *"But he who endures to the end shall be saved"* (Matthew 24:13); and also: *"No one, having put his hand to the plow, and looking back, is fit for the kingdom of God"* (Luke 9:62). Finally: *"But you are those who have continued with Me in My trials. And I bestow upon you a kingdom, just as My Father bestowed one upon Me, that you may eat and drink at My table in My kingdom"* (Luke 22:28–30). And the Apostle says: *Stand therefore, having girded your waist with truth... and having shod your feet with the preparation of the gospel of peace... For we do not wrestle against flesh and blood, but against principalities, against powers, against the rulers of the darkness of this age... Therefore take up the whole armor of God* (Ephesians 6:12–15). Likewise: *be steadfast, immovable* (1 Corinthians 15:58); and *the sufferings of this present time are not worthy to be compared with the glory which shall be revealed in us*

(Romans 8:18). Again: *Who shall separate us from the love of Christ? Shall tribulation, or distress, or persecution, or famine, or nakedness, or peril, or sword?* (Romans 8:35). And in other places: *For whatever things were written before were written for our learning, that we through the patience and comfort of the Scriptures might have hope* (Romans 15:4); *No one engaged in warfare entangles himself with the affairs of this life... and also if anyone competes in athletics, he is not crowned unless he competes according to the rules* (2 Timothy 2:4–5). *Tribulation produces perseverance; and perseverance, character; and character, hope. Now hope does not disappoint* (Romans 5:3–5); and *in all things we commend ourselves as ministers of God: in much patience, in tribulations, in needs...* (2 Corinthians 6:4); *I take pleasure in infirmities, in reproaches... for Christ's sake* (2 Corinthians 12:10).

On Doing Nothing for Show

The Lord said: *"Take heed that you do not do your charitable deeds before men, to be seen by them... But when you do a charitable deed, do not let your left hand know what your right hand is doing"* (Matthew 6:1, 3). Likewise: *"But you, when you pray, go into your room, and when you have shut your door, pray to your Father who is in the secret place; and your Father who sees in secret will reward you openly"* (Matthew 6:6). The Lord Himself, after healing the man who had been infirm thirty-eight years, *withdrew, a multitude being in that place* (John 5:13); and to the healed leper He said: *"See that you say nothing to anyone"* (Matthew 8:4); likewise to the Apostles after the Transfiguration He commanded: *"Tell the vision to no one until the Son of Man is risen from the dead"* (Matthew 17:9), and on another occasion He asked the Jews: *"How can you believe, who receive honor from one another?"* (John 5:44). The Apostle Paul in his epistles instructs: *Let nothing be done through selfish ambition or vainglory* (Philippians 2:3), but *If we live in the Spirit, let us also walk in the Spirit. Let us not become vainglorious, provoking one another, envying one another* (Galatians 5:25–26), for from vainglory is born envy, and those who do things for show are *deceitful workers, transforming themselves into apostles of Christ* (2 Corinthians 11:13).

On Not Judging

The Lord said: *"Judge not, that you be not judged. For with what judgment you judge, you will be judged; and with the measure you use, it will be measured back to you"* (Matthew 7:1–2); and *"Condemn not, and you shall not be condemned. Forgive, and you will be forgiven"* (Luke 6:37). And in another place: *"For if you forgive men their trespasses, your heavenly Father will also forgive you"* (Matthew 6:14). Likewise: *"Our Father in heaven... forgive us our debts, as we forgive our debtors"* (Matthew 6:9, 12). And again He instructs: *"And why do you look at the speck in your brother's eye, but do not perceive the plank in your own eye?... Hypocrite! First remove the plank from your own eye, and then you will see clearly to remove the speck from your brother's eye"* (Matthew 7:3, 5). And the Apostle says: *But why do you judge your brother? Or why do you show contempt for your brother? For we shall all stand before the judgment seat of Christ... So then each of us shall give account of himself to God. Therefore let us not judge one another anymore* (Romans 14:10–13), *For each one shall bear his own load* (Galatians 6:5), and *he is bound by the cords of his sins* (Proverbs 5:22). Likewise: *But with me it is a very small thing that I should be judged by you or by a human court... He who judges me is the Lord. Therefore judge nothing before the time, until the Lord comes* (1 Corinthians 4:3–5).

On Discernment

The Lord said: *"Beware of false prophets, who come to you in sheep's clothing, but inwardly they are ravenous wolves. You will know them by their fruits"* (Matthew 7:15–16). Likewise: *"Not everyone who says to Me, 'Lord, Lord,' shall enter the kingdom of heaven, but he who does the will of My Father in heaven"* (Matthew 7:21). Again: *"No one can serve two masters"* ...and so forth (Matthew 6:24). And also: *"Do not labor for the food which perishes, but for the food which endures to everlasting life"* (John 6:27). And the Apostle says: *Therefore I run thus: not with uncertainty. Thus I fight: not as one who beats the air. But I discipline my body and bring it into subjection, lest, when I have preached to others, I myself should become disqualified... So run, that you may obtain* (1 Corinthians 9:24–27); and *Beware of dogs, beware of evil workers* (Philippians 3:2). Likewise: *Therefore whoever eats this bread or drinks this cup of the Lord in an unworthy manner will be guilty of the body and blood of the Lord. But let a man examine himself, and so let him eat of the bread and drink of the cup* (1 Corinthians 11:27–28). And there also: *For if we would judge ourselves, we would not be judged. But when we are judged, we are chastened by the Lord, that we may not be condemned with the world* (1 Corinthians 11:31–32). And in another place: *For godly sorrow produces repentance leading to salvation, not to be regretted; but the sorrow of the world produces death* (2 Corinthians 7:10). And again: *be transformed by the renewing of your mind, that you may prove what is that good and acceptable and perfect will of God* (Romans 12:2); and of himself he says: *forgetting those things which are behind and reaching forward to those things which are ahead, I press toward the goal for the prize of the upward call of God in Christ Jesus* (Philippians 3:13–14). And he instructs: *Be ready in season and out of season* (2 Timothy 4:2); *Therefore take heed to yourselves and to all the flock* (Acts 20:28), and *Test all things; hold fast what is good* (1 Thessalonians 5:21).

On Sober and Unceasing Prayer

The Lord said: *"But take heed to yourselves, lest your hearts be weighed down with carousing, drunkenness, and cares of this life... Watch therefore, and pray always"* (Luke 21:34, 36); *"Watch and pray, lest you enter into temptation"* (Matthew 26:41). Likewise: *"And what I say to you, I say to all: Watch!"* (Mark 13:37). And again: *"Ask, and it will be given to you; seek, and you will find; knock, and it will be opened to you. For everyone who asks receives, and he who seeks finds, and to him who knocks it will be opened"* (Matthew 7:7–8). The Lord also spoke a parable, *that men always ought to pray and not lose heart, saying: There was in a certain city a judge...* (Luke 18:1–6). And also: *"Therefore you also be ready, for the Son of Man is coming at an hour you do not expect"* (Matthew 24:44). And the Apostle Paul instructs: *Rejoice always, pray without ceasing, in everything give thanks* (1 Thessalonians 5:16–18), *work out your own salvation with fear and trembling* (Philippians 2:12), and again: *Be anxious for nothing, but in everything by prayer and supplication, with thanksgiving, let your requests be made known to God* (Philippians 4:6). Likewise of himself: *without ceasing I make mention of you always in my prayers* (Romans 1:9–10). In Acts it is related: *But at midnight Paul and Silas were praying and singing hymns to God* (Acts 16:25). And the Apostle Peter warns: *Be sober, be vigilant; because your adversary the devil walks about like a roaring lion, seeking whom he may devour* (1 Peter 5:8).

On Hospitality

The Lord said: *"He who receives you receives Me... And whoever gives one of these little ones only a cup of cold water... shall by no means lose his reward"* (Matthew 10:40, 42). And also: *"Come, you blessed of My Father, inherit the kingdom prepared for you from the foundation of the world: for I was hungry and you gave Me food..." and so forth* (Matthew 25:34–36). Likewise: *"When you give a dinner or a supper, do not ask your friends, nor your brethren... But when you give a feast, invite the poor, the maimed, the lame, the blind. And you will be blessed"* (Luke 14:12–14). And in other places: *He who has two tunics, let him give to him who has none; and he who has food, let him do likewise* (Luke 3:11), and *It is more blessed to give than to receive* (Acts 20:35). Likewise the Apostles instruct: *Do not forget to entertain strangers, for by so doing some have unwittingly entertained angels* (Hebrews 13:2); *Be hospitable to one another without grumbling* (1 Peter 4:9); *But do not forget to do good and to share, for with such sacrifices God is well pleased* (Hebrews 13:16); *he who gives, with liberality... he who shows mercy, with cheerfulness* (Romans 12:8). And also: *He who sows sparingly will also reap sparingly, and he who sows bountifully will also reap bountifully. So let each one give as he purposes in his heart, not grudgingly or of necessity; for God loves a cheerful giver* (2 Corinthians 9:6–7); and *For if there is first a willing mind, it is accepted according to what one has, and not according to what he does not have* (2 Corinthians 8:12), *that your good deed might not be by compulsion, as it were, but voluntary* (Philemon 1:14).

On Obedience

Our Lord Jesus Christ said: *"I have come down from heaven, not to do My own will, but the will of Him who sent Me"* (John 6:38). Likewise: *"He who loves father or mother more than Me is not worthy of Me"* (Matthew 10:37). And again: *"If anyone comes to Me and does not hate his father and mother... yes, and his own life also, he cannot be My disciple"* (Luke 14:26). And in other places: *"If anyone loves Me, he will keep My word"* (John 14:23), and *"If you keep My commandments, you will abide in My love, just as I have kept My Father's commandments and abide in His love"* (John 15:10). Likewise the Lord said to Peter and Andrew, to James and John, to Matthew and Philip: *"Follow Me,"* and they, leaving all, immediately followed Him (Matthew 4:18–22; 9:9; John 1:43). *Then another of His disciples said to Him, "Lord, let me first go and bury my father."* But Jesus said to him: *"Follow Me, and let the dead bury their own dead"* (Matthew 8:21–22). And the Apostle says: *Paul, a bondservant of Jesus Christ, called to be an apostle* (Romans 1:1), *for if I preach the gospel, I have nothing to boast of... for woe is me if I do not preach the gospel!* (1 Corinthians 9:16). Again: *Let this mind be in you which was also in Christ Jesus, who, being in the form of God, did not consider it robbery to be equal with God, but made Himself of no reputation, taking the form of a bondservant...* and so forth (Philippians 2:5–7). And in another place: *But you have carefully followed my doctrine, manner of life, purpose, faith, longsuffering...* (2 Timothy 3:10). And also: *bringing every thought into captivity to the obedience of Christ, and being ready to punish all disobedience when your obedience is fulfilled* (2 Corinthians 10:5–6).

On Humility of Mind

Our Lord said: *"So likewise you, when you have done all those things which you are commanded, say, 'We are unprofitable servants'"* (Luke 17:10), and that *"what is highly esteemed among men is an abomination in the sight of God"* (Luke 16:15), and *"everyone who exalts himself will be humbled, and he who humbles himself will be exalted"* (Luke 18:14). Likewise: *"Yet I am among you as the One who serves"* (Luke 22:27). And in another place: *"whoever desires to become great among you, let him be your servant. And whoever desires to be first among you, let him be your slave"* (Matthew 20:26–27). Or also: *When Simon Peter saw it, he fell down at Jesus' knees, saying, "Depart from me, for I am a sinful man, O*

Lord!" (Luke 5:8), and John the Forerunner said to the Pharisees: *I indeed baptized you with water... There comes One mightier than I after me, whose sandal strap I am not worthy to stoop down and loose* (Mark 1:7–8). The Lord Himself, giving us an example of humility, *rose from supper and laid aside His garments, took a towel and girded Himself. After that, He poured water into a basin and began to wash the disciples' feet, and to wipe them with the towel with which He was girded* (John 13:4–5). Likewise the Apostle also says: *For I am the least of the apostles, who am not worthy to be called an apostle, because I persecuted the church of God* (1 Corinthians 15:9); and also: *Christ Jesus came into the world to save sinners, of whom I am chief* (1 Timothy 1:15). Likewise: *I, therefore, the prisoner of the Lord, beseech you to walk worthy of the calling with which you were called, with all lowliness and gentleness, with longsuffering* (Ephesians 4:1–2). And again he instructs: *For not he who commends himself is approved, but whom the Lord commends* (2 Corinthians 10:18); and *Therefore, as the elect of God, holy and beloved, put on tender mercies, kindness, humility, meekness, longsuffering* (Colossians 3:12). And also: *For if I still pleased men, I would not be a bondservant of Christ* (Galatians 1:10).

On Guilelessness

The Lord said: *"Love your enemies, bless those who curse you, do good to those who hate you, and pray for those who spitefully use you and persecute you... And if anyone strikes you on your right cheek, turn the other to him also. And if anyone wants to sue you and take away your tunic, let him have your cloak also"* (Matthew 5:39–40, 44). Again: *"Father, forgive them, for they do not know what they do"* (Luke 23:34). Likewise, when at the time of Judas' betrayal in the garden of Gethsemane, *one of the disciples struck the servant of the high priest and cut off his right ear. But Jesus answered and said, "Permit even this." And He touched his ear and healed him* (Luke 22:50–51). And the Apostle instructs: *Bless those who persecute you; bless and do not curse... If it is possible, as much as depends on you, live peaceably with all men. Do not avenge yourselves* (Romans 12:14, 18–19). And he testifies of those who follow the Lord: *being reviled, we bless; being persecuted, we endure; being defamed, we entreat* (1 Corinthians 4:12–13). The Lord Himself, *when He was reviled, did not revile in return; when He suffered, He did not threaten, but committed Himself to Him who judges righteously* (1 Peter 2:23).

As for the wonder-working Fathers, he who does not believe them or does not accept what was said or done by them, disbelieves even more Christ Himself and His Apostles. For as our Lord Jesus Christ restored sight to the blind with clay, cast out demons, raised the dead, turned water into wine, fed five thousand with five loaves, and performed other countless and unfathomable miracles, which *the world itself could not contain* (John 21:25), so also He granted them power to heal *every sickness and every disease among the people* (Matthew 10:1), as He Himself, our true God, said: *"He who believes in Me, the works that I do he will do also; and greater works than these he will do"* (John 14:12), for where God is present, who is above nature, works above nature are also accomplished. But why speak much of this?

Thus the whole divine Scripture of the Old and New Testaments pours forth life-bearing and God-bearing teachings, which the blessed ascetics fulfilled in deed and word, *having been built on the foundation of the apostles and prophets, Jesus Christ Himself being the chief cornerstone* (Ephesians 2:20), our Lord, in whom, having established themselves through prayer (in which lies the whole mystery of the Christian life), they drew their souls out of the depths of sin and, ascending to the image and likeness of God, even here entered spiritually into the blessed paradise, a foretaste of the future unending blessedness. But what remains for us to do, except to weep bitterly, to sigh from the depths of our souls, and to grieve over our negligence and carelessness? Let us humble ourselves at least, for even from this we will receive no small benefit, as the Lord showed in the parable of the Publican and the Pharisee; and at the same time, let us at least a little compel ourselves to soften the stony insensibility of our souls by contemplating the virtues of the holy Fathers, these true forcers of their own nature for the sake of the kingdom of heaven, which, according to the Lord's word, *only the violent take by force* (Matthew 11:12). Come then, brethren, let us partake of this spiritual, soul-saving fragrance of Christ and, disdaining all that is earthly and human, as disciples of Christ, gentle and humble of heart, and of His holy Apostles, let us run with patience according to the commandments of the Lord, on the narrow and sorrowful path, in repentance, confession, and humility of mind, that we may attain to the city of God, the heavenly Jerusalem, *from which sorrow and sighing shall flee away* (Isaiah 35:10; 51:11), where is the dwelling of all who rejoice and the ceaseless voice of pure gladness in Christ Jesus our Lord. To Him be all glory, honor, and worship, with the unoriginate Father and the life-creating Spirit, now and ever, and unto ages of ages. Amen.

Endnotes

[1] Manuscript without number, by its outward appearance resembling the other manuscripts of the collection, containing translations prepared for publication by Saint Theophan; hard binding of blue calico, green spine with gold embossing; dimensions: 21.8 x 32.2 mm. In total the manuscript contains 305 leaves.

Chapter I.
Instructions of the Holy Fathers on
How to Attain Perfection in the Christian Life

1. Someone asked Abba Anthony: what must I observe in order to please God? The elder replied: observe what I command you: wherever you go, always have God before your eyes; whatever you do, have testimony for it from Holy Scripture; and in whatever place you settle, do not leave it quickly. Keep these three rules and you will be saved.

2. Abba Pambo asked Abba Anthony: what should I do? The elder answered him: do not trust in your own righteousness, do not grieve over the past and your renunciation of the world, and be temperate in tongue and stomach.

3. Abba Anthony said: the ancient fathers went into the desert, were healed, and became physicians; then, returning from there, they healed others. But we, barely leaving the world, desire to heal others before healing ourselves. Therefore the sickness festers again in us, and *the last state becomes worse than the first* (Matthew 12:45); and we hear from the Lord: *"Physician, heal yourself first"* (Luke 4:23).

4. Abba Andrew said: the following three virtues are fitting for a monk: voluntary exile, to feel oneself a stranger to all and everything, poverty, and silence with patience.

5. Abba Athanasius, Bishop of Alexandria, said: some of you often say: where is persecution now, that we might undertake martyrdom? But be martyred in conscience, die to sin, mortify your members which are upon the earth, and you will become a martyr by choice. Those of old contended against kings and rulers; you too have an adversary, the devil, prince of sin, and rulers, the demons. To them were sometimes offered an altar, and sacrifice, and the abomination of idol-worship. There is also now a noetic altar in the soul, and sacrifice, and an abominable idol: the altar is the insatiable belly, the sacrifice is sensual pleasures, the idol is the spirit of lust. He who is enslaved to fornication and given over to sensual pleasures has denied Christ and worshipped an idol, for he has within himself the idol of Aphrodite, the foul lust of the flesh. Likewise, one enslaved to anger and rage who does not cut off the frenzy of this passion has denied Christ and has within himself the god Ares,[2] which is the idol of rage. Another, the lover of money and pleasure who closes his heart to his brother and is merciless to his neighbor, has denied Christ and serves idols, for he has within himself

the idol of Hermes[3] and *serves the creature rather than the Creator*, for *the love of money is the root of all evils* (1 Timothy 6:10). So if you abstain and preserve yourself from violent passions, by this you will trample down idols, reject idol-worship, and become a martyr, having confessed the good confession.

6. Abba Bessarion said: when it happens that you are at peace and have no warfare, then humble yourself all the more, lest evil alien joy, self-satisfaction, overtake you, lest we think highly of ourselves and be handed over to warfare; for God often does not allow us to be handed over to it because of our weaknesses, that we not perish.

7. A brother living together with other brothers asked Abba Bessarion: what should I do? The elder answered: keep silence and do not measure yourself (perhaps meaning: do not compare yourself to them, or do not take note of your own measure, or do not measure your labors).

8. Abba Benjamin, as he was dying, said to his children: do this and you will be able to be saved: *Rejoice always. Pray without ceasing. In everything give thanks* (1 Thessalonians 5:16–18).

9. Someone asked Abba Viar: what should I do to be saved? And he answered him: go, make your belly small and your handiwork small, do not be restless in your cell, and you will be saved.

10. Abba Gregory said: God requires the following three virtues of every person who has received baptism: right faith from the soul, truth from the tongue, and chastity from the body.

11. Abba Dioscorus said: if we clothe ourselves in our heavenly garment, we will not appear naked. But if we are not found wearing such a garment, what shall we do, brethren? For we too must hear that voice saying: *"Cast him into outer darkness: there shall be weeping and gnashing of teeth"* (Matthew 22:13). It is shameful for us who have worn the schema for so long to be found at the hour of need without a wedding garment! Oh, what repentance will strike us then! What shame will cover us before our fathers and brothers when they see us being tormented by the angels of punishment! What sorrow will seize Abba Anthony, and Abba Amoun of Nitria, and Abba Paul of Photike, and Abba Amoun of Arabia of Egypt, and Abba Mius of the Thebaid, and Abba Macarius of Alexandria, and Abba Paphnutius the Sidonian, and Abba Ursacius of Fichui, and Abba Ammonius of Chenevri, and all the righteous at that time when they are being received into the kingdom of heaven, while we are cast out into outer darkness.

12. Blessed Epiphanius said: if Melchizedek, the type of Christ, blessed Abraham, the root of the Jews, how much more will the Truth Himself, Christ, bless and sanctify all who believe in Him.

13. He also said that one should acquire Christian books, if one has the means, for the very sight of these books, in itself, makes us slower to sin and disposes us to be more zealous for righteousness.

14. Again he said: reading the Scriptures provides great firmness for not sinning.

15. He also said: ignorance of the Scriptures is a great precipice and a deep abyss.

16. And he said: not to know any of the divine laws is a great betrayal of salvation.

17. He also said: the sins of the righteous are around the lips, that is, on the edges of the constitution, while the sins of the ungodly come from the whole body, that is, the entire constitution is full of sin. Therefore David also sings: *"Set a guard, O Lord, over my mouth; keep watch over the door of my lips"* (Psalm 141:3), and again: *"I said, 'I will guard my ways, lest I sin with my tongue'"* (Psalm 39:1).

18. He also said: to sinners God remits even the present debt, if they repent, as to the harlot and the tax collector, but from the righteous He demands even interest. This means what He said to the Apostles: *"Unless your righteousness exceeds the righteousness of the scribes and Pharisees, you will by no means enter the kingdom of heaven"* (Matthew 5:20).

19. Abba Euprepius said: knowing that God is faithful to Himself and powerful, believe in Him and you will share in His blessings. But if you are faint-hearted, you do not believe. We all believe that God is powerful; we also believe that all things are possible for Him; but you must believe in Him also in your own affairs, that is, that He works signs in you as well.

20. A brother asked the same elder: how does the fear of God come into the soul? And the elder answered: when a person acquires humility and non-acquisitiveness, then the fear of God comes to him.

21. He also said: fear, humility, scarcity of food, and weeping, let these always abide with you.

22. The same Abba Euprepius, still at the beginning of his asceticism, came to a certain elder and said to him: Abba, tell me how to be saved. The elder said: if you desire to be saved, then wherever you go, do not speak first until you are asked. Humbled by this word, Abba Euprepius bowed to the elder and said: truly, I have read many books, but I did not yet know so profitable a rule. And he departed, having received great benefit.

23. Amma Eugenia said: we ought to pray earnestly and remain with Jesus alone, for everyone who remains with Jesus is rich, even though bodily poor. He who prefers the earthly to the spiritual will lose both; but he who seeks the heavenly will certainly be granted earthly goods as well.

24. Abba Irenaeus said to the brothers: let us struggle and stand firm when we are warred against, for we are soldiers of Christ, the heavenly King. Just as soldiers of an earthly king have a bronze helmet, so our army also has its helmet, the good virtues. They have chain-linked armor, and we have spiritual armor, forged by faith. They have a shield, and we have hope in God. They have a spear, and we have prayer. They have a sword, and we have God. In battle they shed blood, but we will offer our will. Our heavenly King has permitted demons to war against us so that we would not forget His benefactions, for in a state of rest many people often do not pray at all, or though they pray, their mind wanders during prayer, they

are the same as those who do not pray, conversing with God with their lips while in their heart discussing worldly matters. How will they be heard? But when we are in tribulation, then we pray soberly; and often, not singing with our lips, we pray with our heart, sending up to God a word of the heart and conversing with Him through sighs. Therefore, brethren, let us also imitate the soldiers of a mortal king and wage war with zeal; even more, let us imitate the three youths of Babylon, let us trample the furnace of passions with purity, let us extinguish the coals of temptations with prayer, and let us put to shame the noetic Nebuchadnezzar, the devil; let us present our bodies as a living sacrifice to God and as a rich whole burnt offering bring to Him a godly mindset.

25. Abba Zeno, a disciple of Blessed Silouan, said: do not settle in a famous place, do not live with a person of great reputation; and never lay a foundation to build yourself a cell.

26. Abba Macarius asked Abba Zacharias: tell me, what does it mean to be a monk? He said to him: you are asking me, father? Abba Macarius answered: I trust you, my son Zacharias, for there is one compelling me to ask you. Zacharias said to him: in my view, father, he is truly a monk who compels himself in all things.

27. They said of Abba Isaiah that once, taking a staff, he went to the threshing floor and said to the landowner: give me wheat. The owner asked him: and did you reap, abba? He answered: no. Then the landowner said to him: how then do you want to receive wheat without having reaped? The elder said: does one who has not reaped not receive a reward? No, answered the farmer, and the abba departed. The brothers who saw this bowed to him and asked him to explain why he had done so. The elder said: I did this as an example of the fact that if anyone does not labor, he w ill not receive a reward from God.

28. Abba Isaiah the Presbyter said: one of the fathers said that a person should above all strive to acquire faith in God, unceasing striving toward God with all desire, guilelessness, non-repayment of evil for evil, endurance of suffering, humble-mindedness, purity, mercy, love toward all, obedience, meekness, magnanimity, patience, holy striving toward God, frequent prayer with pain of heart and true love, asking God not to look back, attention to everything that befalls him, distrust of his own good deeds or service, unceasing invocation of God's help in everything to which he is subjected, in everything that befalls him each day.

29. A brother asked Abba Isaiah for a word of edification, and the elder said to him: if you desire to follow our Lord Jesus, keep His word; if you desire that your old man be crucified with Him, you must cut off from yourself until death those who bring you down from the cross; you must also prepare yourself to endure every humiliation, to put at ease the heart of those who do you evil, to humble yourself before those who wish to rule over you, to maintain silence of the lips, and to condemn no one in your heart.

30. He also said: bodily labor, poverty, voluntary exile, courage, and silence give birth to humble-mindedness; and humble-mindedness removes a multitude of sins. He who does not keep these things, his renunciation of the world is in vain.

31. Again he said: hate all that is in the world, and also bodily rest, for this has made you an enemy of God. Just as a person who has an enemy wages war against him, so we too must wage war against the body, so as not to give it rest.

32. A brother asked Abba Isaiah what the words of the Lord's Prayer mean: *"Hallowed be Thy name"* (Matthew 6:9), and he answered: this is proper to the perfect, for in us who are overcome by passions, the name of God cannot be hallowed.

33. Abba Isaiah told us: once, when I was sitting with Abba Macarius, seven brothers from Alexandria came to him and, testing him, asked: tell us, father, how to be saved? I took a scroll of paper, sat to the side, and wrote down everything that came from his mouth. The elder sighed and, opening his enlightened mouth, said: O brethren! Each of you knows how to be saved, but the trouble is that there is no desire in us to be saved. They said to him: we greatly desire to be saved, but evil thoughts do not leave us. So what should we do? The elder said: if you are monks, why do you associate with laypeople or approach places where there are laypeople? Those who, having renounced the world and clothed themselves in the angelic habit, live among laypeople deceive themselves and lead themselves astray: all their labor is in vain, for what will they gain from laypeople except fleshly consolation? And where there is fleshly consolation, the fear of God cannot dwell, especially in a monk. Why is a monk called a monk? Because he is alone, conversing with God alone day and night. But a monk who spends time among laypeople, sometimes for a day, but usually for two, in order to sell his handiwork and buy necessities, since life without bodily needs is impossible, and then, returning, sincerely repents and grieves over those two days spent in the city for selling his handiwork, such a one will receive no benefit from his monasticism; see what virtues a monk living among laypeople acquires. As soon as he enters monasticism, at first he is usually restrained in tongue, fasting, and humble, until he becomes known and word spreads about him that such-and-such a monk is truly a servant of God. Immediately Satan suggests to the laypeople to bring him all necessities: wine, oil, money, and all kinds of things, saying: holy one! holy one! Hearing "holy one," the humble monk becomes puffed up and, as is usual with vainglory, begins to go sit with them: he eats, drinks, and takes consolation; and when he stands for psalmody, he raises his voice, and the laypeople begin to speak of him with praise, that such-and-such a monk sings psalms and keeps vigils. From this, vainglory overcomes him still more; he becomes still more puffed up and proud; humility completely departs from him, and if someone says an unkind word to him, he answers with something worse. Furthermore, since he sees laypeople day and night, the devil wounds him with the beauty of women and children, and he is in great confusion and great danger, for our Lord Jesus Christ said in the Gospel: *"whoever looks at a woman to lust for her has already committed adultery with her in his heart"* (Matthew 5:28). Let us not count this word as nothing, hearing what else the Lord says: *"Heaven and earth will pass away, but My words will by no means pass away"* (Matthew 24:35). Then worldly cares come to such a monk and he begins to think about bodily needs for a year; having gathered them, he doubles them and finally begins to collect gold and silver, by which the demons cast him down to the very root of love of money. After this, if someone brings him something small, he rejects it, saying: I do not accept this, because I take nothing;

but if someone brings gold or silver or clothing or something else useful to him, he immediately accepts the gift with joy and, setting a table, regales himself with the one who brought it. But the poor man, or rather Christ, knocks outside at the door, and no one heeds, no one hears. To such the Lord our Jesus Christ said: *"It is easier for a camel to go through the eye of a needle than for a rich man to enter the kingdom of God"* (Matthew 19:24). But perhaps he will say that he is not rich, or that being rich he has need of nothing and bothers no one, for what he has, he has from handiwork and from what God sends, and he himself wrongs no one. Tell me, fathers: do the Angels in heaven concern themselves with gathering gold and silver, or with the glory of God? Why did we too, brethren, accept this habit? To gather wealth and corruptible matter, or to be like the Angels? Or do you not know that the fallen angelic order is replenished from monks? Why then, brethren, having renounced the world, do we again in negligence turn aside from the path of humility? Or do you not know that wine, women, gold, fleshly rest, and wandering among laypeople distance us from God? *For the love of money is the root of all evils* (1 Timothy 6:10). As far as heaven is from earth, so far is the money-loving monk from the glory of God. And truly, there is no evil greater than the evil to which the money-loving monk is subject. A monk who loves worldly conversation requires many prayers of the holy fathers. Or do we not hear what Blessed John says: *"Do not love the world or the things in the world. If anyone loves the world, the love of the Father is not in him"* (1 John 2:15). Likewise the Apostle James says: *"Whoever wishes to be a friend of the world makes himself an enemy of God"* (James 4:4). Let us then flee from the world, brethren, as one flees from a serpent. He whom a serpent bites is barely healed. So we too, if we desire to be monks, let us flee from the world. Better, my brethren, to have one battle than many without number. Tell me, where did our fathers acquire virtues, in the world or in the desert? How then do we wish to acquire virtue living in the world? If we do not hunger, if we do not thirst, if we do not bear cold, if we do not dwell with wild beasts and die to the body, how shall we live to the soul? How do we wish to inherit the kingdom of heaven while remaining among laypeople? And how shall we even lift our eyes to it while spinning in vanity? Does not a soldier lose his dignity who, fleeing from war, gives himself over to the trades of life? How much more then shall we, if we only eat and drink, living with laypeople, shall we not forfeit the inheritance of the kingdom of heaven? Let not the devil suggest evil thoughts to you to say: I gather in order to earn a reward through almsgiving as well! For he who does not wish to give alms from a quadrans will not give from a thousand denarii either. No, my brethren! This is the work of laypeople. God does not wish that we monks have gold or silver, clothing and other things. The Lord commanded, saying: *"Look at the birds of the air, for they neither sow nor reap nor gather into barns; yet your heavenly Father feeds them"* (Matthew 6:26). A monk who has gold, silver, and other things does not believe that God can feed him; but if He cannot give us daily bread, then He cannot grant His kingdom either. This I know for certain: if I have necessities and someone else, especially a layperson, of his own accord brings me something, this is by the working of the devil. But if I have nothing and I pray once and twice, then God sends to me, as once to Daniel in the lions' den, knowing that I am in need. But if I not only have need of nothing, but even have gold, silver, and other things, yet do not wish to spend them on my sustenance, but wait for another to bring me what I need, then I become a partner of Judas Iscariot, who, leaving the grace given to him, rushed toward the lust of love of money. Knowing this, the blessed Apostle called love of money not only the root of all evils, but also idolatry (Ephesians 5:5). So you see into what evil this disease draws the monk, casting him even into idolatry, for the money-lover departs from the glory of God and worships a graven human idol, that is, gold. O love of money! You distance the monk from the glory of God! O love of money, bitter and lamentable! You separate the monk from the angelic order! O love of money, root of all evils! You cast the monk into ever greater and greater cares, until you bring him to the point where he leaves the heavenly glory and cleaves to *the rulers of the darkness of this age* (Ephesians 6:12)! O love of money, leader of every evil! You sharpen the monk's tongue for strife, quarrels, and tumult, until you bring him to court, like the laypeople! Woe to the monk who gives free access to himself to the demon of love of money! Woe to the money-loving monk who has abandoned the commandment of the Savior, who said: *"Do not acquire gold or silver"* (Matthew 10:9). Often the devil suggests to him such a thought: rise and keep vigil, and tomorrow invite the brothers and set a table of love. Then the demon goes to the invited brothers and suggests to them: bring your own provisions with you. Such a monk often consoles himself: I do not violate my rule: I fulfill the third, sixth, and ninth hours, not knowing that *"not everyone who says to Me, 'Lord, Lord,' shall enter the kingdom of heaven"* (Matthew 7:21). And how will gold, silver, and other things harm me? Not knowing that where there are gold, silver, and things, there is free access for demons and destruction of soul and body. How will compunction enter the money-loving monk, when he, leaving the will of his Creator who calls him to eternal life, honors and kisses gold? How will compunction enter such a person? However, the devil often arouses tears and sighs in him and makes him beat his breast, saying meanwhile, see, God has given you gold and silver and compunction together, so that the thought of casting out the root of love of money might never come. O my beloved brethren! How is it that we monks have gold and silver, clothing and all kinds of things, never ceasing to gather more and more, while the poor man, or rather Christ, is sick and hungry, endures thirst and cold, and we do not wish to do anything for Him?! What justification shall we present to Christ the Master, that having renounced the world, we seek it again, are restless under the schema, and make this angelic habit worldly, turning it into a trade for gold, from which we either give nothing at all to the needy, or, if we give, we give before others so that we might be praised? No, my beloved brethren! Let us flee from the world. We must be saved in the desert, but truly we shall not be saved among laypeople. For the Lord says that if anyone does not renounce the world and what is in it, and even his own soul, and take up his cross and follow Me, *he is not worthy of Me* (Matthew 10:38–39; 6:24; Mark 8:34–35; Luke 9:23–24; 14:26–27). *"As I live,"* says the Lord (Isaiah 49:18), *"Come out from among them and be separate"* (2 Corinthians 6:17). See, my beloved brethren, how profitable it is to flee from association with worldly people, it is profitable both for them and for us, for all their conversation is about commerce, gatherings, wives, children, cattle. Does not such conversation distance the mind from God? If conversation alone with them distances the mind from God, what harm must there be from eating and drinking with them?

I do not say this because they are unclean, may it not be. But they eat twice a day, eating all kinds of foods and meats, while we abstain from meat and various foods and always eat once a day. But if they see that we eat our fill, they immediately condemn us, saying: see, even monks eat to satiety, not understanding that we too are clothed in flesh just as they are. Again, if they see us abstaining in food, they still condemn us, calling us man-pleasers. Likewise, if they see that we eat with unwashed hands or that we are untidily dressed, they say: see, what crudeness. And again, if they see that we eat with washed hands, they say: see, even monks beautify themselves. And so they destroy themselves on account of us, while we turn out to be partakers and culprits in their destruction. Fleeing therefore, let us flee from their tables and seek their reproach rather than their praise, for it is not their praise that brings crowns. What is the benefit to me if I please men and anger the Lord my God? The Apostle Paul says: *"If I still pleased men, I would not be a bondservant of Christ"* (Galatians 1:10). Do we not pray before the Lord saying: Jesus our God, deliver and save us from their reproach and praise? Let us do nothing to please them. For just as their praise cannot bring us into the kingdom of heaven, so their every reproach cannot exclude us from eternal life. Let us know, my beloved and blessed brethren, that we shall give account to the Lord our God even for every idle word.

34. A brother came to Abba Elijah, the hesychast, in the coenobium of the cave of Abba Sabbas and asked him: Abba, tell me a word of edification. The elder answered him: in the days of our fathers, three virtues were beloved: non-acquisitiveness, meekness, and temperance; but now what rules among monks is: love of possessions, gluttony, and irascibility. Hold to whichever you wish.

35. They said of Abba Theodore of Pherme that he surpassed many in the following three virtues: non-acquisitiveness, asceticism, and fleeing from people.

36. Amma Theodora asked Pope Theophilus about a certain saying of the Apostle, namely what is meant by: *redeeming the time* (Ephesians 5:16). And he answered her: these words indicate profit. Namely: does a time of reproach stand before you? Buy this time of reproach with humble-mindedness and longsuffering and take this profit for yourself. Does a time of dishonor stand before you? Buy it with guilelessness and turn this time into profit for yourself. Thus, if we wish, all adversity will be to our profit.

37. Again Amma Theodora said: *"Enter by the narrow gate"* (Matthew 7:13), for just as trees, if they are not subject to frosts and rains, cannot bring forth fruit, so this present age is winter in relation to us, and if we are not tested by many sorrows and temptations, we cannot become heirs of the kingdom of heaven.

38. She also said that a teacher must be a stranger to love of power, not a partaker of vainglory, and far from pride; he must not be a plaything of flattery, nor blinded by gifts, nor enslaved to the belly, nor carried away by anger, but must be magnanimous, affable, humble-minded with all his strength, discerning, forbearing, attentive, and a lover of souls.

39. Abba John Colobos said: I desire that a person taste a little from all the virtues. And so, each day, rising in the morning, make a beginning of every virtue and commandment of

God, of the greatest patience with fear and longsuffering, of the love of God with all readiness of soul and body and with much humility, of patience in sorrows and guarding of the heart with prayer alone and supplication with sighs, of purity of tongue and guarding of the eyes; of not being angry when dishonored; of being at peace with all, of not repaying evil for evil, of not watching for the falls of others and being below every creature; of renunciation of all things and all that is fleshly, of the cross-bearing of ascetic struggle, of spiritual poverty, of fasting, repentance, and weeping, of spiritual warfare and discernment, of purity of soul, of quiet handiwork, of night vigils, of hunger and thirst, of want, nakedness, and labors. Close your grave as if you have already died, so as to keep in mind that death is near to you every hour.

40. Abba John said: just as it is impossible to remain children all one's life and not grow in experience and knowledge with the increase of years, so too in the monastic life everyone with the passage of time must ascend more and more to the height of virtues.

41. Abba Cassian told of a certain Abba John, a coenobiarch, an elder of lofty life, that when he was dying and with joy and desire departing to God, the brothers surrounded him and asked him to leave them as an inheritance some word, brief but salvific, by the guidance of which they might be able to attain perfection in Christ. And he, sighing, said to them: I never did my own will, and I never taught anyone what I had not first done myself.

42. Blessed John Chrysostom said: sitting down to read the Divine Scripture and other holy books, first call upon God, that He might open the eyes of your heart not only to the precise understanding of what is written, but also to the fulfillment of it, lest knowledge of life and teaching turn to our condemnation.

43. Abba John the Cilician, abbot of Vanor, said to the brothers: children! Just as we fled from the world, so let us flee from the lusts of the flesh.

44. Again he said: let us imitate our fathers, with what deprivations and with what hesychia they lived here!

45. He also said: children! Let us not defile this place, which our fathers cleansed of demons.

46. And he said: this place is a place of ascetics, not of merchants.

47. Once we went up from Gethsemane to the Mount of Olives to the monastery of Abba Abraham. In this monastery there was an abbot, Abba John the Cilician. We once asked him: how can one acquire virtue? And the elder answered us: he who wishes to acquire virtue cannot acquire it otherwise than by hating the evil opposed to it. Therefore, if you desire to have weeping always, hate laughter; if you desire to have humility, hate pride; if you desire to be temperate, hate satiety; if you desire to be chaste, hate sensuality; if you desire to be non-acquisitive, hate love of money. He who desires to dwell in the desert hates cities because of the temptations in them; he who desires to have hesychia hates frequent visits; he who desires to be a stranger to all hates display; he who desires to be restrained in anger hates association

with many; he who desires to be without rancor hates slander; he who desires to be undistracted abides in solitude; he who desires to bridle his tongue, let him stop his ears, so as not to hear much; he who desires always to have the fear of God, let him hate bodily rest and love sorrow and constraint.

48. A brother asked Abba Joseph: when persecution occurs, where is it better to flee, to the desert or to cities and villages? The elder said to him: if you hear that there are Orthodox somewhere, go there, closer to them.

49. He also said: by no means have friendship with a youth and do not live with one; if you can live alone in your cell, this is good; cultivate your own vegetables instead of going to someone to ask.

50. A brother asked him: I want to live with someone on this condition: I would keep hesychia alone in my cell and by handiwork earn what is needed for sustenance, while that one would take care of me. The elder said to him: our fathers did not desire this.

51. They said of Abba Isaac: when he was dying, the elders gathered to him and asked: what should we do after you, father? He answered: you have seen how I walked before you. If you too will follow the commandments of the Lord and keep them, He will send His grace and preserve this place; but if He does not preserve it, you will not remain in this place. For we too, when our fathers were dying, grieved, but keeping the Lord's commandments and their testaments, we stood firm as if they themselves were with us. Do likewise, and you will be saved.

52. A brother asked Abba Hierax: tell me a word on how to be saved. The elder said to him: sit in your cell; if you are hungry, eat; if you are thirsty, drink; only do not slander anyone, and you will be saved.

53. Abba Isidore said: a life without glory usually brings more benefit than glory without life. For life edifies even in silence, while glory without life, despite all its proclamations, only serves as a burden. But if glory and life are joined together, they constitute the beauty of all love of wisdom.

54. He also said: value virtue; do not be concerned about fortune. Virtue is an immortal treasure, but fortune quickly vanishes.

55. Abba Hierax also said: many people strive toward virtue but delay going on the path that leads to it. Others do not even think about what virtue is. Therefore some must be persuaded to abandon their laziness, while others must be taught that virtue is truly virtue.

56. He also said: evil has distanced people from God and divided them from one another; therefore one must flee evil in every way and strive toward virtue, which leads to God and unites one with another. The goal of virtue and chastity is simplicity with wisdom.

57. Abba Joseph of Thebes said: the following three things are honorable before the Lord: first, when someone who is ill has new temptations added to him and he accepts them with thanksgiving; second, when someone performs all his deeds so that they are pure before

the face of God and have nothing human in them; third, when someone lives in perfect obedience to a spiritual father and renounces all his own desires. This last one has one crown more. But I would choose illness.

58. Abba Macarius said: do not spend the night in the cell of a brother who has a bad reputation.

59. A brother asked Abba Macarius the Great about how to attain perfection, and the elder answered: if a person does not acquire great humility in heart and body, and the practice of not measuring himself in any matter, but placing himself in humility below every creature, and also absolutely not condemning anyone except himself alone, bearing reproach, casting away from his heart all malice, and compelling himself to be longsuffering, gentle, brotherly-loving, chaste, temperate, as it is also said: *"the kingdom of heaven suffers violence, and the violent take it by force"* (Matthew 11:12), and also to look rightly with the eyes, to guard the tongue, and to turn the ear away from every vain and soul-destroying hearing; to preserve purity of heart before God and blamelessness of body; to have death before the eyes daily, to extinguish anger and malice, to reject material things and fleshly lusts, to turn away from the devil and all his works and firmly unite with God the King of all and all His commandments, to pray unceasingly, and at every time, in every thing, in every deed to be established in God, then he cannot be perfect.

60. Abba Mark said: the law of freedom teaches all truth, and although many read it, few understand it with regard to the fulfillment of the commandments. Do not seek perfection in human virtues, for there is nothing perfect in them. Its perfection is hidden in the cross of Christ.

61. A brother came to Scetis to Abba Moses and asked him for instruction. The elder said to him: go and shut yourself in your cell, and your cell will teach you everything.

62. Abba Moses said: he who has Jesus near him and converses with Him unceasingly does well not to bring another person into his cell.

63. Again he said: it is impossible to acquire Jesus otherwise than by labor, humility, and unceasing prayer.

64. Abba Matoes recounted: three elders came to Abba Paphnutius, who was called Cephalas, and asked him for instruction. The elder asked them: what do you wish me to tell you, spiritual or fleshly? They answered: spiritual. Then the elder said to them: go, love affliction; prefer sorrow to consolation, dishonor to glory, and giving rather than receiving.

65. A brother asked an elder: what good deed should I do so that I might live through it and be saved? And the elder said: God alone knows what is good. But I have heard that one of the fathers asked Abba Nisterus the Great, a friend of Abba Anthony, about this, and he answered: are not all deeds equal? Scripture says that Abraham was hospitable, and God was with him. Elijah loved hesychia, and God was with him. David was humble-minded, and God

was with him. Therefore, whatever you see your soul disposed toward according to God, do that and guard your heart.

66. Abba Nilus said: a servant who neglects the affairs of his master must be prepared to be subjected to blows.

67. Abba Poemen said of Abba Nisterus: like the bronze serpent given by Moses for the healing of the people, so this elder, having every virtue, healed all in silence. When Abba Poemen asked Abba Nisterus where he had acquired such a virtue, that whatever sorrow befell him in the coenobium, he said nothing and did not murmur, he answered: forgive me, abba. At the very beginning, when I entered this coenobium, I said to my thought: you and a donkey are one and the same. Just as a donkey, when beaten, does not speak, and when reviled, answers nothing, so be you also, as it says in the psalm: *"I was like a beast before You, yet I am continually with You"* (Psalm 73:22–23).

68. The fathers of Sinai told of Abba Orestes that one Sunday he came to church in his garment turned inside out and stood thus among the others. Some of the officials approached and said to him: why, father, have you entered the church with your clothing inside out? Strangers will laugh at us. The elder answered: you have turned Sinai inside out, and no one makes remarks to you, but I have dressed inside out, and this displeases you. Correct what you have turned inside out, and I will correct what I have reversed.

69. Abba Poemen said that three virtues, prudence, attention to oneself, and discernment, are guides of the soul.

70. A brother asked Abba Poemen: how should a person live? The elder said to him: let us look at Daniel: no other accusation was found against him except that he served the Lord his God.

71. Again he said: scarcity, sickliness, affliction, self-constraint, and fasting, these are the working tools of a monk. For it is also said in Scripture: *"Even if these three men, Noah, Daniel, and Job, were in it... as I live,"* says the Lord God... *"they alone would be delivered by their righteousness"* (Ezekiel 14:14, 20). Noah represents non-acquisitiveness, Job represents affliction, Daniel represents discernment. Therefore, if these three virtues are in a person, the Lord dwells in him.

72. He also said: if a monk conquers two things, he can be free from the world. The brother asked: which ones? Indulgence of the flesh and vainglory, answered the elder.

73. A brother asked Abba Poemen: tell me a word of edification. The elder said: our fathers began every work with weeping. The brother said: tell me another word as well. The elder answered: as much as you can, labor at handiwork, so as to give alms from it, for it is written: *"By mercy and faith sins are purged away"* (Proverbs 15:27). The brother asked: what is faith? The elder answered: to believe means to live in humble-mindedness and to give alms.

74. He also said: if your heart does not incline to trust someone, do not pay heed to that person in your heart.

75. A brother asked Abba Poemen: what should I do about my useless friendships? The elder answered: is there anyone who, approaching death, still thinks about the friendships of this world? Do not draw near to them and do not touch them, and they will distance themselves from you on their own.

76. Again he said: when a person intends to build a house, he gathers a large sum of money so as to be able to erect it, and he prepares various kinds of materials. Likewise, let us take a little from all the virtues.

77. He also said: David wrote to Joab: *"Begin the war, and you will capture the city and destroy it"* (2 Samuel 11:25).

78. He also said: Joab said: *"Be of good courage, and let us be strong for our people and for the cities of our God"* (2 Samuel 10:12). This is us.

79. Abba Poemen said: if you see visions and hear voices, do not tell your neighbor about them, for this is the turning of the battle to your side.

80. Again he said: the first time, flee; the second time, flee; but the third time, be a sword (concerning the struggle with thoughts).

81. Abba Poemen said to Abba Isaac: cast off a part of your righteousness, and in a few days you will acquire rest.

82. Abba Bitimius asked Abba Poemen: if someone is displeased with me and I repent before him, but he will not be reconciled because he does not believe my sincerity, what should I do? The elder said: take with you two other brothers and repent before him; if he still will not be reconciled, take five others; if even with them he will not be appeased, take a priest; but if even thus he will not be reconciled and will not believe your sincerity, then pray without disturbance to God, that He Himself may grant him faith, and be at peace.

83. A brother, going off to market, asked Abba Poemen: what do you advise me to do? The elder said to him: be a friend of one who compels himself, and you will sell your goods peacefully.

84. He also said: do not entrust your conscience to a person whom your heart does not incline to trust.

85. He also said: this is the rule of life God gave to the Israelites: to abstain from what is unnatural, that is, anger, rage, envy, hatred, slander against a brother, and the rest that belongs to the old man.

86. He also said: use all possible effort to do no evil whatsoever to anyone, and keep your heart pure in relation to every person.

87. The governor of the region came to Abba Palladius, desiring to see him, for he had heard of his deeds, and taking a scribe, he commanded him: I will go in to the abba, and you write down everything he says to me with complete accuracy. Entering, the governor said to the elder: pray for me, abba, for I have a multitude of sins. The elder answered: sinless is Jesus

Christ alone. The governor asked: shall we give account to God for every sin, abba? The elder answered: it is written: *"who will render to each one according to his deeds"* (Romans 2:6). The visitor asked for an explanation of this word, and the elder answered: it explains itself; however, hear in more detail. Have you wronged your neighbor? You will receive what is due. Have you seized anything from the lowly, beaten the poor, shown partiality in judgment, or dishonored, slandered, defamed, lied, plotted against others' marriages, transgressed an oath, removed the boundaries of the fathers, entered into the possessions of orphans, wronged widows, preferred present pleasure to promised blessings? You will receive worthy recompense for all, for *"whatever a man sows, that he will also reap"* (Galatians 6:7). Likewise, if you have done something good, for that too you will receive manifold recompense, for it is said: *"who will render to each one according to his deeds."* Remember this recompense all your life, and you will avoid a multitude of sins. The governor asked: what then must I do, abba? The elder answered: think about the eternal, endless, and unchanging blessings, where there is no night and no sleep, that image of death; where there are no foods and drinks, those servants of our infirmity; and where there are no sorrows, no sicknesses, no healing, no courts, no commerce, no wealth, that beginning of evils, object of wars, and root of enmity; where is the land of the living, not of those dead in sin, but of those living the true life in Christ Jesus. Then the governor sighed and said: truly, abba, it is as you have said. And having received great edification, he departed to his home, giving thanks to God.

88. They said of Abba Pambo that as he was dying, at the very hour of his departure, he said to the holy men standing by: from the time I came to this desert place and, having built myself a cell, settled in it, I do not remember eating any bread other than that earned by my own hands; I have repented of nothing even to this hour; and I depart to God as if I had not yet begun to worship Him. This is what distinguished Abba Pambo from many! Furthermore, when he was asked about some word of Scripture or about spiritual matters, he did not answer at once but said that he did not know it, and for a month or more he would not give an answer.

89. Abba Pambo said: if you have a heart, you can be saved.

90. They said of the fathers, Abba Pambo, Abba Bessarion, Abba Isaiah, and Abba Paisius, that they were very strong. Once they were conversing together with Abba Aphre, and the presbyter of Mount Nitria asked them how the brothers should conduct themselves. They said: in great asceticism and keeping their conscience from their neighbor.

91. A brother asked Abba Pambo: why do evil spirits prevent me from doing good to my neighbor? The elder answered him: do not speak thus, because by this you call God a liar; rather say: I do not wish to do good deeds. For God said beforehand: *"Behold, I give you authority to trample on serpents and scorpions, and over all the power of the enemy"* (Luke 10:19).

92. Abba Pambo sent his disciple to the city of Alexandria to sell handiwork. During his sixteen-day stay in the city, as this disciple himself told us, he sold the handiwork in the narthex of the church, in the temple of Saint Mark, saw the order of services of the Orthodox church, and learned the troparia. When he returned, the elder asked him: I see, my son, that

you are troubled. Did some temptation befall you in the city? The brother answered: truly, abba, we spend our days in negligence in this desert, for we sing neither canons nor troparia. When I was in Alexandria, I saw how the church orders sing there, and I began to grieve greatly, why do we not sing canons and troparia? The elder said to him: woe to us, my son, that the days have drawn near when monks will abandon the solid food spoken by the Holy Spirit and choose for themselves orders with songs and tones. What compunction, what tears are born from troparia? What compunction has a monk when he stands in church or in his cell and raises his voice like an ox? For when we stand before God, we must stand with great compunction, not with fantasy and distraction. The monks did not go out into this desert in order to, standing before God, exalt themselves with voices, sing songs in rhythm, arrange melodies, wave their hands, and shuffle their feet. We must in great fear and trembling, with tears and sighs, in a reverent, contrite, and quietly humble voice offer prayers to God. I assure you, my son, that days will come when Christians will corrupt the books of the holy Apostles and God-inspired prophets, will erase the sacred writings and write troparia, and in imitation of the Greeks their mind will pour itself out in troparia and Greek rhetoric. For this reason our fathers commanded that the calligraphers in this desert should not write the lives and words of the fathers on parchment, but on paper, for the coming generation will erase the present lives of the holy fathers and write them according to their own will. Then the brother asked him: so what then? Will the customs and traditions of Christians so change, and will there not be priests in the church? The elder answered: in those times *the love of many will grow cold*, and there will be no small tribulation: invasions of peoples, movements of nations, instability among kings, lawlessness among authorities, luxury among priests, negligence among monks; abbots will be careless about the salvation of themselves and their flock; all will be hasty at tables and lazy at prayers, quick to slander and skilled at condemning; they will neither imitate the lives and words of the elders nor even listen to them, idly talking that if they had been in their days, they too would have struggled like them. In those times bishops will be ashamed before the faces of the powerful, judge according to gifts, not defend the poor in judgment, wrong widows, oppress orphans; and among the people will enter unbelief, depravity, hatred, enmity, envy, disputes, thievery, frenzy, drunkenness, fornication, adultery, murder, robbery. The brother said: so what should one do in those times and years? The elder answered: in those days *he who saves his soul will be saved and will be called great in the kingdom of heaven.*

93. Abba Pityrion, a disciple of Abba Anthony, said that he who desires to cast out demons must first conquer the passions, for whatever passion one overcomes, that passion's demon he casts out. Thus, he said, the demon of anger enters following anger; if you tame anger, its demon will also be cast out. The same applies to each passion.

94. Abba Sisoes said: be self-abasing, turn your will backward, be not overly concerned with many things, and you will have rest.

95. He also said: there are people who spend their days in negligence and seek salvation only in word and thought, but are negligent about it in deed; they read the lives of the saints

but do not imitate their humility and non-acquisitiveness, prayer and vigil, temperance and hesychia, sleeping on the ground and genuflections. And they slander the life of the fathers, saying that it is impossible to endure all this, for they do not consider that where God dwells through the grace of divine baptism and the fulfillment of the commandments, there are deeds beyond nature.

96. They said of Abba Thomas that at his death he said to his children: do not live with heretics, have no dealings with authorities, and let your hands not be stretched out for gathering but rather for giving.

97. An elder said: unsheathe your sword, that is, fight, do not yield. The brother answered: the passions do not allow me. Then the elder said: did not the Lord command: *"Call upon Me in the day of trouble; I will deliver you, and you shall glorify Me"* (Psalm 50:15)? Therefore call upon Him, and He will deliver you from every temptation.

98. The elders said that the cowl is a sign of guilelessness, the analavos is a sign of the cross, and the belt is a sign of courage. Therefore let us live in accordance with our garment, doing all things with zeal, lest it appear that we wear a form foreign to us.

99. A brother asked an elder: how does one become a fool for the Lord's sake? The elder answered him: in one coenobium there was a youth who was given to a good elder to watch over him and teach him the fear of God. That elder spoke thus to him: when someone speaks evil of you, bless him; when you sit at table, eat what is unpleasant and leave what is tasty; when you have to choose clothing, leave the good and take the poor. The youth said to him: am I a fool, that you advise me to do thus? The elder answered: I advise you to do thus so that you may be a fool for the Lord's sake and the Lord may grant you wisdom for it. Thus the elder showed us who and by what deeds becomes a fool for the Lord's sake.

100. An elder said: let us stand upon the rock! And let the river rush forth, do not be afraid, and let it not cast you down, but sing in hesychia: *"Those who trust in the Lord are like Mount Zion, which cannot be moved, but abides forever"* (Psalm 125:1).

101. Again he said: for you was Christ born, O man! For your salvation the Son of God came; He was man while being God; He was a reader when in the synagogue, taking the book, He read: *"The Spirit of the Lord is upon Me, because He has anointed Me"* (Luke 4:18); He was a subdeacon when, having made a whip of cords, He *drove out of the temple all... the sheep and oxen... all who sold and bought in it...* and the rest (John 2:15; Matthew 21:12); He was a deacon when, girding Himself with a towel, He washed the feet of His disciples, commanding them to wash the feet of the brethren (John 13:4–5); He was a presbyter when, sitting in the midst of the elders, He taught the people (Luke 2:46–47); He was a bishop when, *taking bread and blessing it, He broke it and gave it to His disciples* (Matthew 26:26); He was beaten with scourges, for your sake, yet you do not bear even one reproach, for His sake; He was buried and rose as God, and He did all things for us, that He might save us. Therefore let us be sober, let us watch, let us abide in prayers, and let us do what is pleasing to Him.

102. This is what one elder said about evil thoughts: I beseech you, brethren, just as we have ceased from evil deeds, so let us also cease from remembrance of them.

103. An elder said: if there was a grievous word between you and another and he denies it, saying: I did not say such a word, do not argue with him, otherwise he, turning around, will say: yes, I said it, so what?

104. An elder said: do not approve every word and do not agree with every word. Be slow to believe, quicker to speak the truth.

105. One of the elders said: at first, when we came together with one another, we spoke about matters of salvation, forming as it were a spiritual chorus, and we ascended to heaven; but now, coming together, we pass into gossip and drag one another down, into a pit of mire.

106. One of the elders said: if our inner man is watchful, he is able to guard the outer man as well; but if not, then with all our strength let us guard the tongue.

107. He also said: it is necessary to have spiritual works, for that is why we came; for great is the labor of teaching with the mouth when we do not do the deeds with the body.

108. An elder said: it is written, at the second and third sin take care, but at the fourth, I will not turn away. The first three sins are: to remember evil, to consent to it in thought, and to utter it with the tongue; but the fourth is to commit the deed. From this last, the wrath of God will not turn away.

109. An elder said: the devil usually attacks the weak side of the monk in the hope that a habit, strengthened by long duration, acquires the force of nature, especially among those who are rather negligent. Do not give yourself rich food, especially when you are healthy, and do not eat what you desire; but in partaking of what God sends you, thank Him at every hour. We have spent temporal goods for the sake of monasticism and yet have not become monks. Be courageous, brother, so as not to wear a foreign form, and guard the seal of Christ, that is, humility.

110. The elders said that a monk must struggle against the demon of despondency and faint-heartedness until death, especially during church assemblies. But when, with God's help, you succeed in this, beware of the thought of self-satisfaction and foolish self-exaltation, and say to this thought: *"Unless the Lord builds the house, they labor in vain who build it"* (Psalm 127:1); I am nothing but earth and ashes (Genesis 18:27). Remember that *God resists the proud, but gives grace to the humble* (Proverbs 3:34).

111. An elder said: whether you sleep or are awake or do anything else, let God be before your eyes, and then the enemy will be able to frighten you with nothing. For if your thought remains in God, the power of God will also remain in you.

112. An elder said: a monk should not be eager to listen to stories about others and condemn, and should not be scandalized.

113. A brother asked an elder: tell me, how can I be saved? And the elder answered: let us try to labor little by little, and we shall be saved.

114. The elders said: God requires of Christians to submit to the Holy Scriptures, to do in deed what they read, and to believe their superiors and spiritual fathers.

115. A brother asked an elder: what should I do about the thoughts that surround me and draw me out of my cell under the pretext of going to the elders? The elder said to him: if you see that thoughts want to draw you out of your cell because of the constraint of the flesh, give yourself a little consolation in your cell, and you will not want to go out. But if the desire to go somewhere comes for the sake of edification of the soul, test your thought and go out. I heard of one elder that when thoughts suggested to him to go visit someone, he would get up, take his melote, and go out; then, having gone around his cell, he would return and give himself consolation, as if to a stranger. Acting thus, he found rest.

116. The elders said that children, even more than women, are a diabolical snare for monks.

117. They also said: where there is wine and children, there is no need of Satan.

118. One zealous brother living alone in his cell, hearing of the virtues of the saints, was inflamed with the desire to imitate them and began to think how he might succeed in them without special labor and ascetic struggle. He went and disclosed this to a great elder. The elder said to him: if you desire to succeed, go and be like a child receiving lessons from a teacher. Just as a child learns one lesson after another, so do you also: give yourself this year as a lesson, to struggle against the belly, and struggle until you learn not to satiate it; further, labor to conquer vainglory until you hate it as an enemy; when you achieve this as well, strive to cast away all material things and entrust the care of yourself to God. Then take courage; for if a person succeeds in these three virtues, he will meet Jesus with joy when He comes.

119. One of the elders said: if you do not first hate, you cannot love: if you hate sin, you will do righteousness, as it is also written: *"Depart from evil and do good"* (Psalm 34:14). However, the main thing required in this is good will. Adam, being in paradise, transgressed the commandment, but Job, sitting on the dunghill, kept temperance. God requires of man only good will and that he fear Him always.

120. A brother who was being tempted came to an elder and revealed to him the temptations he was enduring. To this the elder said: let not the temptations that befall you frighten you, for the enemies, as soon as they see the soul ascending more and more and cleaving to God, become fierce, consumed with envy; but it is impossible that during temptations God should not be present with you along with His Angels, only do not forget to call upon Him with all humility. Therefore, when something like this happens to you, think about the might of our Helper, about our weakness, and about the ferocity of our enemy, and you will receive God's help.

121. An elder said: just as an innkeeper has no authority to bring a stranger into the house without receiving permission from the master of the house, so the enemy will not enter unless he is received.

122. He also said: when you pray, speak thus: how shall I acquire Thee, O Lord? Thou knowest, for I am like a beast and know nothing. Thou hast led me into this salvific order, save me. *I am Thy servant, the son of Thy maidservant* (Psalm 116:16); O Lord, save me as Thou wilt!

123. An elder said: it is impossible to acquire Jesus otherwise than by labor, humility, and unceasing prayer.

124. One of the fathers said that a monk, when among brothers, should always look down at the ground and by no means turn his gaze to a person's face, especially that of a youth; but when he is alone, he should look unceasingly upward, for the demons fear and are greatly vexed when we look upward, toward God.

125. An elder said: God still endures the sins of the world, but the sins of the desert He does not endure. Know, my brother, that he who has withdrawn from the world is not interrogated like a layperson, for the latter has many pretexts for justification, but what can we present to justify ourselves? Truly, fearful fire and the greatest torments await those who, knowing the will of God, despise it and follow their own. Such people, living in pleasures and taking delight in the vain and temporal, often say: I gather money and various things for bodily needs, only to secure my life. Good: this word contains a part of truth, if they truly care only for what is necessary; but having said "I care only for what is necessary for the body," one must not then be carried away when money or good foods are brought to the monk, but calmly limit oneself only to what is needed for the body. Meanwhile, they not only accept money and things but also seek more, and having tasted such foods, they desire even better ones. Either work and no longer accept money, or if you accept, do not work, so as not to become vain; but we desire both. Here we have shown you what is the cause of the passions for which one who appears to be a monk is judged more strictly than laypeople; for while many of the laypeople live honestly, this one does not have mercy on his brother but lives luxuriously and makes the house of God a house of trade, or rather a tavern. At the same time we shall speak in part of what leads into vanity, so that knowing it, we may avoid it and thereby be saved. Many of us think that merely in this, that we have clothed ourselves in the schema, that we say "Lord, Lord," and that we hear "monk, monk," in this alone does this calling consist. Truly, my brethren, if we do not attend to ourselves, it will happen that we fall into a pit still more disastrous than that of laypeople, so that we cannot even cry out to God. Therefore fear and true humility are necessary. Many of our brothers, who appear humble and conduct themselves in a monastic manner, seek the fulfillment of their own will but do not submit to God's will; and being caught by their own desires, in vain cares, distractions, and concerns, they waste the time given them for repentance, which a little later they will greatly desire and seek but will not find.

126. An elder said: take care not to sin, lest you offend God who dwells with you and drive Him out of your soul.

127. An elder said: let us be sober, let us watch, and let us abide in prayers, that we may be saved, doing what is pleasing to God. A soldier, entering battle, cares only about his own soul, as does the hunter, let us imitate them. He who lives according to God, with him God also lives: *"I will dwell in them and walk among them. I will be their God, and they shall be My people"* (2 Corinthians 6:16).

128. A brother living in the Cells came to one of the fathers and told him his thought, namely, a thought of sorrow. The elder said to him: you have cast down a great weapon, the fear of God, and taken for yourself a reed staff, evil thoughts. Rather take for yourself fire, which is the fear of God, and when the enemy approaches you, he will burn from this fire like a reed, for the evil one has no power against one who has the fear of God.

129. An elder said: do not teach before the time, otherwise all your life you will be diminished in understanding.

130. A brother asked an elder: father, tell me what I should do to fulfill the will of God. The elder said: if you desire, my son, to fulfill the will of God, refrain from all unrighteousness, love of possessions, and love of money; do not repay evil for evil, curse for curse, slander for slander, blow for blow. Remember what the Lord said: *"Judge not, that you be not judged"* (Matthew 7:1); *"forgive, and you will be forgiven"* (Luke 6:37); and *"be merciful, that you may obtain mercy"* (Matthew 5:7). Knowing for certain that *the eyes of the Lord are ten thousand times brighter than the sun, beholding all the ways of men* (Sirach 23:19), so that nothing is hidden from Him, neither thoughts, nor reasonings, nor any secrets of the heart, and that we must inevitably stand before the judgment seat of Christ, that each one may receive according to his deeds, let us serve Him with fear and trembling and with all reverence, as He Himself commanded and as the Apostles taught, that we should be sober in prayers and abide in fasts and supplications, asking the all-seeing God *not to lead us into temptation* (Luke 11:4).

131. He also said that one who teaches others salvation must himself first taste the fruit of the teaching, for how can one who has not himself become chaste make another chaste? And one who is gripped by love of money and pursued by its demon, how can he teach others to give alms? Likewise, one who is occupied only with giving and taking, buying and selling, bustling about and spending his days and years in earthly cares, how can he teach others about the blessings to come? For if the teacher himself, leaving the heavenly, gives himself over to the temporal and passing, it is obvious that those who look at him and are taught by him will learn to despise the eternal and turn all their care only to the present life. To such a one God says: *"What right have you to declare My statutes, or take My covenant in your mouth, seeing you hate instruction and cast My words behind you?"* (Psalm 50:16–17). And again: *"Woe... for because of you My name is continually blasphemed among the nations"* (Isaiah 52:5; Romans 2:24). Teaching is a good thing if the teacher also does what he teaches, so that in teaching he also acts and instructs in silence, for blessed is not one who teaches, but *one who does and teaches* (Matthew 5:19).

132. A brother asked an elder: how is it that laypeople, worldly people, do not fall, do not say "we have sinned," and do not exclude themselves from communion, while they despise fasting, neglect prayer, flee from vigils, are tempted by everything, do everything according to their lusts, devour one another in giving and taking, and spend most of the day in oaths and vows? Yet we monks, with all our strict fasting, keeping vigils, sleeping on bare ground, contenting ourselves with dry food, weep and say with tears: we have perished, we have lost the kingdom, we are guilty of Gehenna. The elder sighed and said: you speak well, brother, in saying that laypeople do not fall, for having fallen once with a disastrous and ruinous fall, they cannot rise and have nowhere to fall from. And what concern has the devil to war against those who always lie below and never rise? Monks sometimes conquer and sometimes are conquered; they fall and rise; they wound and are wounded; they are attacked and fall, then resist the devil. But laypeople, because of great folly, remain in their first fall, and not recognizing that they have fallen, they take no care at all to rise from such a fall. Know also, my son, that not only I and you, who appear to be monks yet are far from the monastic life, have need of constant weeping and tears, but even the great fathers, that is, the ascetics and hermits, need tears. Hear me with understanding and comprehend: lies are from the devil (John 8:44), said the Lord; looking at a woman to lust for her He reckoned as adultery (Matthew 5:28); anger at one's neighbor He compared to murder (1 John 3:15); and He declared that we shall give account for every idle word (Matthew 12:36). Who then is such, and where will you find a person who would be free from lies, innocent of lust from looking, never angry at his neighbor in vain, and guiltless of an idle word, so as to have no need of repentance? Know, my son, that one who has not completely lifted himself up onto the cross in humble-mindedness and self-abasement, and has not given himself over to be trampled by all, to non-justification and the following of all this to bear for God's sake with thanksgiving and joy, and to seek absolutely nothing human, that is, neither glory, nor honor, nor praise, nor consolation in food, drink, and clothing, such a one cannot be a true Christian.

133. An elder said: strive to know the good life by experience and do not fear it as impossible.

134. An elder said: if for God's sake you have renounced your relatives, then sitting in your cell do not allow yourself fleshly grief over father, mother, or brother, or tender affection for sons and daughters, or love of a wife, for you have left all these for God's sake. Remember rather the hour of death, when none of them can help you.

135. An elder said: just as a wrestler acts in a single combat, so must a monk act in his struggle with thoughts, stretching out his hands in the form of a cross toward heaven and calling upon God for help. The wrestler stands naked on the field of battle, anointed with oil and instructed by his patron on how to wrestle. From the opposing side comes the adversary, throwing sand or dust so as to more easily seize his opponent. Apply all this to yourself, monk! The patron is God, who gives us victory; the wrestlers are we; the adversary is our enemy; the sand is the things of this world. Do you see the cunning of the enemy? Therefore

stand without possessions and you will conquer, for when the mind is weighed down by matter, it does not receive the immaterial word.

136. An elder said: there was a very wealthy farmer who, wishing to dispose his sons toward farming, said to them: children, do you see how I have become wealthy? You too will be wealthy if you listen to me. They asked him: we beseech you, father, tell us how to do this. Then, in order to turn them away from laziness, he answered them with this stratagem: there is one day in the year, and if anyone works on that day, he will certainly become wealthy, but which day exactly I have forgotten because of old age. So do not leave any day without work, lest you miss this blessed day and make the labors of the whole year futile. So we too, if we labor unceasingly, will find the path of life.

137. A brother asked an elder: why is it that when I go out to work, I neglect my soul? The elder said to him: because you do not wish to fulfill the words of Scripture, which says: *"I will bless the Lord at all times; His praise shall continually be in my mouth"* (Psalm 34:1). Therefore, whether you are in your cell or outside it, or wherever you go, do not cease to bless God not only in word, but in deed and thought glorify your Master. For the Godhead is not circumscribed by place, but being everywhere, embraces all with His divine power.

138. One brother said: I asked an elder about what I should do with my negligence, and the elder answered: if you do not uproot this small grass, that is, negligence, a great stalk will grow from it.

139. An elder said: when you speak instructions to someone about how to live, speak to the listener with compunction and tears. Moreover, desiring to save others, do not speak words foreign to salvation or another's words, lest you remain fruitless until death.

140. An elder said: wherever you go, attend to yourself unceasingly, for it is written: *"The stork's home leads them"* (Psalm 104:17), that is, wherever a monk goes, there is his dwelling. Therefore, everywhere strive to fulfill your rule and hours and evening prayers, and also do not neglect the thoughts, and always have sorrow before your eyes. All this, however, cannot be brought to fulfillment without labor.

141. Again he said: be like a camel, carry your sins and, as if tied, follow the one who knows the way of God.

142. One of the elders said: we fall into greater evil because we neglect the lesser. Pay attention to this word: for example, someone laughs at the wrong time, and another condemns him; the first, forgetting all fear, says: it is nothing, for what does it mean to laugh? From this finally comes buffoonery, and from that come shameful deeds and lawlessness. Thus, through what seems small, the evil one leads into greater sin, and from greater sin it is not far to despair; and despair is contrary to God and ruinous. Sin does not destroy as much as despair, for the one who repents corrects his sin, but the one who despairs perishes. The sin of despair is great. Therefore let us not neglect the small. The enemy suggests it to us with cunning and does not begin battle openly, for the struggle would be easy and victory convenient, especially if we are watchful. It is indeed easy for us, since God has given us full

armor. Wishing us not to neglect the small, hear what He commands: *"whoever says to his brother... 'You fool!' shall be in danger of hell fire"* (Matthew 5:22); he who looks with lustful eyes is the same as an adulterer (Matthew 5:28); to those who laugh He decrees woe (Luke 6:25) and threatens an answer for every idle word (Matthew 12:36). For this reason Job also purified the thoughts of his children with sacrifices (Job 1:5). Knowing this, let us stand firm against the first suggestions and we shall never fall.

143. One of the saints said: it is impossible for a person to taste the sweetness of God while he still finds sweetness in the sweetnesses of this world; likewise, when one tastes the sweetness of God, he will hate all the goods of this age, as is declared in the Gospel: *"No one can serve two masters"* (Matthew 6:24). And as long as we desire connections with people and consolations for the body, we cannot attain to the tasting of God's sweetness. But this I say: if anyone at the present time will sit in his cell, abide in the struggle of silence and prayer, and accomplish his task from the soul, he can be saved.

144. An elder said: do not set the table before the time, when you are alone; do not speak before you are asked, and when asked, say what is proper with discretion.

145. An elder said: see how the devil first struck Job through his possessions and, seeing that he did not depart from God, struck him another blow, on his body. But even so, this courageous fighter did not sin with his lips, for he had the good things of God within him, and always tasting them, he abode in them.

146. Blessed Zosimas, first making the sign of the cross on his lips, spoke thus: such grace has the incarnate Word, God, granted to those who have believed and who believe in Him, that even now it is possible to believe and begin from this day, if we desire, for with firm resolve of the will, with the assistance of grace, anyone who desires can count the whole world as nothing. Then he took a nail that happened to be there and added: who would quarrel or argue or bear a grudge or be offended over this nail, except one who has truly completely lost his mind? But a man of God who is progressing and being perfected, will he not count the whole world as this nail, even if he possessed this whole world? For what harms, I say, is not having, but having with attachment. Who does not know that the body is more honorable than all we have? But if, when time requires it, we are commanded to despise even the body itself, how much more that which is outside it? And just as one must not needlessly, simply by chance, throw away possessions, so one must not cast oneself to death, for this is proper only to one who has completely lost his mind; rather, one must await the time, so that when it comes, one may be ready. Remember that brother who had vegetables! Did he not sow? Did he not labor? Did he not plant and fertilize? He did not pull them out of the ground himself or throw them away, yet he had them as if he did not have them. He was not troubled or alarmed when the elder who came to him, wishing to test him, began to destroy them; he did not even go out to him but hid, and when only one root remained, he said to him: if you wish, father, leave this and let us make a meal from it. Then that saint understood that before him was a true servant of God and not a servant of vegetables, and he said to him: the Spirit of God has rested upon you, my brother. If he had had the vegetables with attachment, this

would have shown itself at once through sorrow and confusion, but he showed that he had them as if he did not have them. The demons, added Saint Zosimas, notice this, and if they see that someone is without attachment to things, that he is not troubled and does not grieve over losses, then they know from this that he walks on the earth but does not have within himself an earthly mindset.

147. He also said: it is bad to be irritated and angry. What is easier than what we hear from the holy and active teacher Abba Amoun, who said: guard yourself carefully so as to keep silent if someone offends you in some matter, and by no means even make a sound until your heart is calmed by unceasing prayer, and then entreat your brother. He who loves the true and straight path, in the hour of confusion strongly reproaches and accuses himself and says: why are you confused, why do you rage, my soul, like one possessed? By this very thing you show that you are sick, for if you were not sick, you would not suffer. Why then, leaving off accusing yourself, do you reproach your brother who has shown you your sickness in deed and truth? Learn the commandments of Christ, *who, when He was reviled, did not revile in return; when He suffered, He did not threaten* (1 Peter 2:23). Have you not heard what He says and shows by deed: *"I gave My back to those who struck Me, and My cheeks to those who plucked out the beard; I did not hide My face from shame and spitting"* (Isaiah 50:6)? But you, wretched one, for one grievous word and dishonor weave innumerable thoughts and plot against yourself like the demons. What can a demon do to such a soul more than what it does to itself? See the cross of Christ and think each day about the sufferings He endured for us, yet we ourselves do not bear a single offense! Truly we have turned away from the right path.

148. He also said: let someone live Methuselah's[4] years, but if he does not walk that straight path which all the saints walked, the path, I say, of enduring dishonor and offenses and courageous patience, he will make no progress at all but will spend the years of his life in vain. And he added: when I was with Blessed Dionysia, a brother asked her for something as a blessing, and she gave him what and as much as she could. But since he was not given as much as he asked, he began to revile her and speak outrageous words about her and me. She was offended and wanted to do him evil. Noticing this, I said to her: what are you doing? By this you are plotting against yourself and destroying all the virtue of your soul. For what you are enduring is worthy of what Christ endured for you. I know, lady, that you have scattered money like refuse, but if you do not acquire meekness, you are like a blacksmith who beats a piece of iron but fashions no vessel. Hear what Saint Ignatius the God-bearer says: "Seek meekness, by which all the power of the prince of this age is destroyed." A sign of renunciation of the world is not to be troubled. It happens that one, having left great treasures, becomes attached to a needle, and this attachment causes him disturbance; then the needle takes the place of treasures for him. So one becomes a slave to a needle, or a cowl, or a mantle, or a book, and is no longer a servant of God. Well did one of the wise say: as many passions as are in the soul, so many masters. And the Apostle says: *"by whom a person is overcome, by him also he is brought into bondage"* (2 Peter 2:19). She listened to me attentively and finally said: may you find the God whom your heart seeks.

149. The blessed one also said: the soul desires to be saved but, being attached to the vain and concerned about it, flees from labors, although, truly, it is not the commandments that are burdensome but evil desires. We have the custom, fearing to drown in the sea or to fall into the hands of robbers, to despise all and hold nothing dear; yet we are not willing to part with anything from our possessions, although we know that in a short time we shall die. But if in danger, in order to live a little longer, we despise all and count it happiness if, losing everything, we ourselves are saved from robbers or from death in the sea (and the one who was raving shortly before over an obol,[5] not sparing it, throws everything away only to preserve this temporal life), then why do we not have the same mind about eternal life? Why is the fear of God not as strong in us as the fear of the sea, as one of the saints said? In confirmation of this he told the following incident: I heard that once a rich merchant named Cavidarius was sailing on a ship with his children for commerce in precious stones and pearls, of which he had many with him. On the ship he took a liking to a certain youth who served him, caressed him, and gave him to taste of what he himself ate. Once this youth heard the sailors conspiring together and deciding to throw Cavidarius into the sea in order to seize his precious stones, and he became sad. With a gloomy face he came to the merchant to carry out his duty as usual. Noticing such unhappiness, the merchant asked him: why are you so gloomy today? The youth did not dare tell the truth and answered: nothing. But the merchant urged him to tell him without fail what was wrong. Then the youth burst into tears and said: the sailors have plotted thus and thus against you. Then the merchant summoned his children and said to them: whatever I command you, do without laziness, and he ordered them to bring the chests of precious stones. Then, spreading out a cloth, he laid out everything from the chests and said: such is our life? For the sake of these things am I in danger of being thrown into the sea, of struggling with the waves, and of dying in a few minutes, taking nothing with me from this world? Throw all this into the sea, he said to his children. They immediately threw everything into the sea. Then the sailors were amazed, and their evil plot was   foiled.

Do you see what wisdom the merchant showed? How suddenly, for the sake of preserving this brief life, he became a philosopher, both in word and deed? And he acted rightly, for he reasoned that if he died, what benefit would these stones be to him? But we do not want to bear even a small injury for the sake of Christ's commandment! If one must grieve, then let it be over the ruin of the one who caused the injury, not over the injury itself, for that one, the wrongdoer, deprives himself of the kingdom of heaven, since *the unrighteous will not inherit the kingdom of God* (1 Corinthians 6:9), while to you, the wronged one, he brings life: "Rejoice and be exceedingly glad," says the Lord, "for great is your reward in heaven" (Matthew 5:12). But we, leaving off grieving over the ruin of a member of Christ, sit and weave thoughts about corruptible, worthless, ruinous, and worthless things. Truly we are worthy of every punishment. God has joined us together like members of one body with one head, Christ our God, as the Apostle also says: *all the members of that one body, being many, are one body* (1 Corinthians 12:12). And *the head of all is Christ* (Ephesians 1:22). Therefore, when your brother offends you, it is the same as a suffering hand or an aching eye causing another member pain. Yet we do not cut off the hand or gouge out the eye, considering the removal of each of these members a greater harm; on the contrary, we place on them the most honorable seal of Christ, the cross, and ask the saints to pray, and we ourselves offer fervent prayers to God, while also preparing collyria[6] and plasters in order to heal the ailing member. And just as we pray for the eye or hand, that they might recover and no longer cause us pain, so pray also for your brother; but we, seeing that the members of Christ suffer such harm, not only do not grieve for them but even persecute them. This truly belongs to those who do not have a merciful heart.

150. He also said: one who has acquired a merciful heart, love, and compassion first brings comfort and benefit to himself, and then to his neighbor; and conversely, malice wounds and injures first the one who has it. And although it seems that he harms his neighbor in regard to possessions, honor, or even the body itself, in reality he deprives himself of life. And he added the following saying: what does not harm the soul does not harm the person either.

151. The blessed one also said: someone said to me: Abba! There are too many commandments, and the mind is darkened when one begins to consider what one keeps and what one does not keep. I answered him: let this not trouble you. Believe that if you are without attachment to things, you will easily fulfill every virtue. Not quarreling over them, you will not bear grudges; and what labor is it to pray for enemies? Is it the same as digging the earth? Therefore, walk the path of patience, bear loss of possessions, give thanks when dishonored, and you will become a disciple of the Apostles, who *departed... rejoicing that they were counted worthy to suffer shame for the name of the Lord Jesus* (Acts 5:41). And they, being pure and holy, bore dishonor for the name of Christ; but we must be dishonored for our sins. We are already dishonored, even if no one dishonors us, and are cursed, for *cursed are those who turn aside from Your commandments* (Psalm 119:21). Dishonor for the name of Christ does not belong to all, not to all, but only to the saints and pure, as I said; but for people like us, it is proper to confess that we are dishonored justly for our evil deeds. Wretched is the soul which, knowing its impure deeds for which it justly suffers what it suffers, sits and in the deception of conscience weaves thoughts, saying: he said such-and-such to me, dishonoring and reviling me. For what happens with craftsmen also happens with the soul. Just as there the master craftsman, having taught the skill to his apprentice, leaves him to work independently and no longer needs to sit by him, but only occasionally checks that he does not become lazy or spoil the work, so also the demons, if they notice that a soul easily accepts evil thoughts and listens to them, hand it over to this satanic craft and no longer need to always be near it, knowing that the soul itself is sufficient to plot against itself; they only come occasionally to see if it has become negligent.

152. Again he said: what is easier than to love all and be loved by all? What consolation do the commandments of Christ not have? But the will does not strive toward them, for if it did, everything by God's grace would be easy for it. A small inclination of our will, as I have

often said, draws God to help. And Blessed Anthony says: virtue requires only our desire. And again: there is no need to wander abroad to obtain the kingdom of heaven, nor to cross the seas to find virtue. What sweet rest does the meek and humble one taste! Truly, *the meek shall inherit the earth and shall delight themselves in the abundance of peace* (Psalm 37:11).

153. The blessed one also said: once I and one brother were walking with laypeople along the road to Neapolis and came to a place where there was a customs post. The laypeople, knowing the custom, paid the toll, but the brother who was with me began to object and say: do you dare demand toll from monks? Hearing this, I said to him: what are you doing, brother? Whether you wish it or not, you are saying nothing other than: honor me as a saint. It would be different if he himself, seeing your good will and humility, were ashamed and said: forgive me. So you are not acting as a disciple of the Meek and Humble One. Give what is due and pass on in peace.

154. He also recounted: another time, when I was in the Holy City, one of the Christ-lovers came and said to me: between me and my brother a small unpleasantness occurred, and he does not want to be reconciled with me; be merciful and speak with him. I gladly agreed and, calling his brother, spoke to him what could incline him to love and peace. He seemed to be persuaded, but then suddenly said to me: no, I cannot be reconciled because I swore by the cross. Then, smiling, I said to him: your oath has this meaning: I swear by Your honorable cross, O Lord, that I will not keep Your commandments but will do the will of Your enemy, the devil. Let it be known to you that we are not only not obliged to stand by our word to do something evil, but we must also repent and be contrite that we resolved to act thus, as the God-bearing Basil also said: if Herod had come to his senses and not fulfilled his oath, he would not have committed the great sin of beheading the Forerunner of Christ. Finally, I presented to him the account from the holy Gospel about how the Lord wanted to wash the feet of the Apostle Peter, but he objected.

155. Again the blessed one said: I was asked how one should bridle anger, and I answered: the beginning of bridling anger is not to speak while the confusion continues. So Abba Moses, when he was abased with words, "why does this Ethiopian come to our assembly?", said: "though I was confused, I did not speak." However, he not only was not confused but even reproached himself, saying to himself: "Black-skinned one! They have treated you rightly! Not being a man, why do you go to an assembly of men?" But we, standing at a very low level and having by great negligence not attained even what belongs to beginners, think that the commandments are lofty and difficult to fulfill. To be confused and not speak does not belong to the perfect, but to beginners; not to be confused at all, according to the word of the holy prophet, *I was ready and was not troubled* (Psalm 119:60), is truly a great virtue. But we do not seek even to make a beginning and do not show even the desire for it, so as thereby to draw God's grace to help us; or if we appear to show desire, it is imperfect and unsteady, unworthy of receiving any good thing from God. What happens with us is the same as with sowing and reaping: we apply the labor of will and receive the gift of grace. Just as a farmer, if God blesses his labor, even having sown little, receives much, as is told of Isaac:

Isaac sowed in that land and reaped in the same year a hundredfold of barley; and the Lord blessed him (Genesis 26:12). So if God blesses the labor of our will, we shall do everything without labor, naturally, with sweetness, and receive benefit from all. Prayer with self-compulsion and patience gives birth to prayer that is easy, pure, and sweet. And the first, with self-compulsion, is a matter of the will, while the second, with sweetness, is a matter of grace. The same is seen in relation to all crafts: when someone takes up some craft with a firm intention to learn it, at first he works with difficulty, the work does not come together, and he often spoils it. However, if the apprentice does not lose heart but again applies himself to the task, and although he spoils it again, does not give up, showing the teacher his good desire, then gradually, having become skilled thanks to patient labor with God's assistance, he begins to do everything with pleasure and ease, providing himself thereby with sustenance. But if the apprentice's courage and patience fail and he abandons this labor, such a one will learn nothing. So also in spiritual matters: one who resolves to practice virtue must not think that he can succeed in it at once, for this is impossible; rather, he must apply effort, and though he does not at first do it properly, let him not give up just because he could not at once fulfill it as he should, but let him again apply effort, like one who wishes to learn a craft. When thus he labors with patience, not losing heart, God will look upon the labor of his will and give him the power to do all things without compulsion. This is what the words of Abba Moses mean: the strength of those who desire to acquire virtues consists in not being fainthearted if they fall, but in again applying the same diligence.

156. He also said that every virtue requires labor, time, and our zealous desire, and above all, God's assistance is needed, for if God does not assist our diligence, our labor will be in vain, just as the labor of a farmer who cultivates and sows his land will be in vain if God does not rain upon his seed. And God's assistance requires our prayers and supplications, for only by them do we draw God's help to our protection. If we neglect prayer, how will God look upon our labor? Likewise, when we pray but pray lazily and distractedly, or quickly become burdened by prayer, we shall be granted nothing, as I always tell you, since God looks upon our diligence and, judging by it, gives His gifts. Was not Abba Moses formerly a chief of robbers? Did he not commit countless crimes, so that he had to hide from his master because of his evil conduct? And yet, since he approached the task zealously and with very warm diligence, we all know what measure he attained, if he is numbered among the chosen servants of God, as the writer of his life says. But we, although we show warmth of diligence at our renunciation of the world, in time, through our negligence, lose it, becoming attached to things that cool us down, empty and worthless things, instead of love for God and neighbor, and we appropriate to ourselves our deeds as if we had done them ourselves and not received them from God. For He says: *"What do you have that you did not receive? Now if you did receive it, why do you boast as if you had not received it?"* (1 Corinthians 4:7).

157. He also said: Jesus is not poor, nor is He powerless to grant us such blessings as He bestowed on the holy patriarchs, if He saw that we receive benefit from what He has given us. But since He sees that, because of our disorder, we are more harmed by the small and few gifts He has given, He does not entrust us with greater ones, lest we perish utterly, for He is

the Lover of mankind. If He saw that we receive benefit from a little, would He not be powerful to give us more, as I said before? God, being good, has given us the possibility to receive benefit from all things, but we, through attachment and misuse, ruin God's gifts and take them away from ourselves, and thus harm ourselves with the very blessings granted to us.

158. He also often said: no one can harm a faithful soul; on the contrary, all that it suffers is turned to its benefit. A laborer also suffers, but in order to receive a reward after labor; but the unfaithful one fruitlessly torments himself with his unbelief. The faithful one, remaining faithful, has great consolation both in his labor itself and in the hope of receiving a reward for his patience; but the unfaithful one, having no assurance of receiving anything from the Lord, what consolation will he have? He sits and rots in his thoughts, having met with some small offense, and talks to himself: he said this to me, and I will say such-and-such to him; he bears grudges and plots deeds that he cannot at all bring to fulfillment. Can people do everything they plot in their malice? No. But only what God permits them, by judgments He alone knows. Often one plots to do evil to another but does not succeed, for God does not permit it; then only human intentions are tested. How many people plotted to harm the holy patriarchs? But since God did not permit it, no one could harm them, as it is written: *He permitted no one to do them wrong; yes, He rebuked kings for their sakes: "Do not touch My anointed ones, and do My prophets no harm"* (Psalm 105:14–15). And when God wishes to show the superabundance of His power, then He moves even the hearts of the merciless to mercy, as is written of Daniel: *and God gave Daniel favor and compassion before the chief of the eunuchs* (Daniel 1:9). Blessed is the soul that through true thirsting for God has prepared itself to receive His gifts. Such a soul He leaves in nothing, but in all things protects it, even in what, through ignorance, it does not ask of Him. Well did the wise man say: *the righteous man is covered by God* (Wisdom 5:16). How many times did Saul attempt to kill Blessed David? What did he not do? How did he not scheme? But since David was covered by the Lord, not only did every scheme of Saul remain futile, but Saul himself was often delivered into the hands of the saint, who nevertheless spared him, not having a hardened and vengeful malice.

159. He also said: I was asked how one can achieve not being angry when others humiliate and slander him, and I answered: one who considers himself worth nothing is not disturbed by humiliation, as Abba Poemen said: if you abase yourself, you will have rest.

160. He also said: one brother, from among those who lived with me and received the schema from me, whom I endeavored to teach every virtue and to whom I sometimes condescended because of his weakness, since he was of delicate constitution, one day he said to me: my abba! I love you greatly. I answered him: I have not yet met a person who loves me as much as I love him. Now you say that you love me, and I believe you, but if some unpleasantness befalls you, you will not remain the same. But me, whatever I may have to endure from you, nothing can turn away from love for you. A little time passed, and he (I do not know what happened to him) began to speak much against me, even to the point of shameful words, and I heard all of it. Then I said to myself: this is a cauterizer of Jesus, and

he has been sent to heal my vainglorious soul, for at that time there was a custom of treating illnesses with cauterization. Through such people, with sobriety and attention, one can regain what we lose through those who flatter us; he is my true benefactor. So I commemorated him as a physician and benefactor, and to those who informed me of his words, I said: he knows only my obvious faults, and even then not all, but only some; those that are hidden are innumerable. After the passage of time he met me in Caesarea, came up to me and, according to custom, embraced and kissed me, and I him, as if nothing had been between us. After such slanders, he no doubt embraced me thus because I had shown no suspicion, not the slightest trace of offense, although I had heard everything. Then he fell at my feet and, embracing them, said to me: forgive me, my father, for the Lord's sake, for I have spoken much evil against you. But I kissed him and gently said: does your love of God remember how once you said that you love me greatly? And I answered that I had not yet found anyone who loved me as much as I love him, and that you would not remain the same if some unpleasantness befell you, but nothing could turn me away from love for you? Let your heart be assured of this: nothing was hidden from me of what you said, but even where and to whom, I heard all, and I never said that it was not so, and no one could incline me to say anything bad about you; on the contrary, I affirmed that all you said was true and that you said it out of love, wishing to draw me to yourself. Never did I also forget to commemorate you in my prayers. I will show you an even more certain sign of love: once my eye became very ill; remembering you, I made the sign of the honorable cross and said: Lord Jesus Christ, heal me for the sake of his prayers, and at once I was healed. This is what he said to the brother!

161. The blessed one also often said: we people do not know how to make ourselves loved and honored, but have lost our reason. If anyone will bear a little with his brother when the latter is angry or grieving on his account, the brother, soon coming to himself and learning how the other bore with him, will lay down his very soul for him. At this the blessed one recalled such an incident: one brother had an abba who was exceedingly meek, whom the whole country honored as an angel of God for his great virtue and the miracles he worked. Once, by the enemy's working, this brother approached the elder and in front of everyone began to slander him extremely. The elder stood and only looked at his mouth, then said: the grace of God is on your lips, my brother! The brother became even more frenzied and said: I know, fool, you say this in order to appear meek. But the elder said to this: truly, my brother, what you say is right. Someone afterward asked him: did you not become troubled, O elder of God? He answered: no, for I felt in my soul that it was as if being covered by Christ. And truly, one must thank such people and honor them: for one who is passionate, to consider them physicians who heal the wounds of his soul; and for one who is dispassionate, benefactors who provide him with the kingdom of heaven.

162. Again the blessed one said: when I was in the Monastery of Tyre, before my departure from there, a certain virtuous elder came to us, and we began to read the memorable sayings of the holy elders, for the blessed one loved to read them and almost breathed them, whereby he also gathered from them the fruit of every virtue. So we came to the account of the elder to whom robbers came and said: we have decided to take everything from your cell.

To which the elder answered: take everything that seems good to you, children. They took everything and left, leaving one bag behind. Discovering the bag, the elder took it and chased after them, crying out: children! Take what you forgot in our cell! Then, amazed at the elder's guilelessness, they returned everything to him and, repenting, said to one another: truly, this is a man of God. When we read this, the elder said to me: do you know, abba, this story has brought me much benefit. I said to him: how, father? He answered: during my time in the places near the Jordan, once I read about this, was amazed at the elder, and said: Lord, grant me also to follow in the footsteps of those whose habit You have deemed me worthy to receive. This feeling of emulation did not leave me; and behold, two days later, robbers attack me. When they knocked at the door, I recognized that it was they and said to myself: thanks be to God! The time has come to show the fruit of emulation. Opening the door, I received them kindly and, lighting a lamp, began showing them the things, saying: do not trouble yourselves, I will hide nothing from you. They asked: do you have gold? Yes, I said, I have three coins, and opened the vessel before them. So they took them and left in peace. And I, said the blessed one with a smile, asked him: did they return, like those who came to that other elder? God forbid, he quickly answered, was that what I desired, for them to return! See what his emulation and readiness for everything brought the elder, concluded the blessed one, for he not only did not grieve but even rejoiced that he was granted such a good thing.

163. In an earlier conversation, said the blessed one, I told you that if we bear a little with our brother who is angry, we will gain his soul. Now I will tell you a story about this that I heard from Blessed Sergius, the abbot of Pediada. Here is what he told me: once we were walking with a certain holy elder and lost our way. Not knowing where to go, we came upon a field of crops and trampled a little of the greenery. Noticing this, the farmer who happened to be working there at that time began to scold us harshly, saying with anger: you are monks! Do you fear God? If you had the fear of God before your eyes, you would not have done this. At that moment the holy elder said to us: for the Lord's sake, say nothing, and to that one he answered with meekness: you speak the truth, child; if we had the fear of God, we would not have done this. The farmer continued to scold us with anger. And the elder again said: you speak the truth, that if we were monks, we would not have done this, but for the Lord's sake forgive us, we have sinned. Then in amazement the farmer fell at the elder's feet and said: forgive me for God's sake, and take me with you. See what, with God's help, said the blessed one at this, the meekness and kindness of this saint could accomplish, to save a soul created in the image of God, which is more desirable to God than tens of thousands of worlds with all their riches.

164. Once, recounted Blessed Zosimas, when I was with Abba Sergius, he asked me to read something from Scripture. I began to read Proverbs and, when I came to the words: *"Where there is much wood, there a fire blazes, but where there is no angry man, strife is quieted"* (Proverbs 26:20), I asked him: what does this saying mean, father? He answered me: just as wood is the cause of the blazing of fire, and if not enough of it is put on, the fire goes out, so there are causes for the passions as well, and if one cuts off these causes, the passions do not act. Namely: the causes of fornication, as Abba Moses said, are eating and drinking to satiety,

sleeping in abundance, idleness, amusements, idle talk, and finery. If one cuts off all this, the passion of fornication will be powerless. Likewise, the causes of anger, as he also said, are giving and receiving, doing one's own will, loving to teach, and considering oneself wise. If one cuts this off, the passion of anger will have no power in him. This also is what the words of Abba Sisoes mean, which he said when a brother asked him: why do the passions not depart from me? Their vessels, that is, their causes, said the abba, are within you; give them their deposit, and they will depart. One who is double-angered, in whom warfare does not cease, is one who is not content with the first irritation but kindles himself to a second anger. Namely: if someone, having flared up in anger, immediately comes to his senses and condemns himself, and even repents before the brother at whom he was angry, such a one is not called double-angered. In him warfare ceases as soon as he has condemned himself and restored peace with his brother. In such a one warfare has no place, as I said before. But one who, having become angry, does not strive to come to his senses but more and more kindles himself to anger, and repents not that he became angry but that he did not say more than he said in his irritation, such a one is called double-angered. In him warfare does not cease, for after anger, rancor, enmity, and malice take hold of him. But may the Lord Jesus Christ deliver us from the portion of such people and grant us the portion of the meek and humble.

165. The blessed one often said: great watchfulness and no small wisdom are needed against the wiles of the devil. For it happens that he brings one into irritation over nothing; it happens that he presents a plausible pretext so that it seems to that one that he is angry justly. But all this is completely improper for one who truly desires to walk the path of the saints, as Saint Macarius says: it is improper for monks to be angry, and it is improper for them to offend their neighbor. At this the blessed one told us the following: once I ordered some books to be written by a skilled scribe. Upon completing the writing, he sent word to me: behold, I have finished the books; send what seems right to you and take them. A certain brother, hearing of this, came from my name to this scribe and, giving a certain payment, took the books. Meanwhile I, not knowing of this, sent our brother with a letter and payment to take them. The scribe, understanding from what happened that he had been mocked, became greatly disturbed and said: I will certainly go and take revenge on him for two reasons, both because he mocked me and because he took what was not his. Hearing of this, I sent word to him: you know, my brother, we acquire books in order to learn from them love, humility, and meekness; but if the acquisition of books from the very start leads to quarrels, I do not want to have them, lest I quarrel, for *a servant of the Lord must not quarrel* (2 Timothy 2:24). Thus, by renouncing the books, I brought it about that the brother was not completely overcome by anger.

166. Once, sitting with us and conversing about things that save the soul, the blessed one began to cite the sayings of the holy elders and, coming to the saying of Abba Poemen, that one who accuses himself finds rest everywhere, and to the word of the abba of Mount Nitria, spoken in answer to the question of what he had found most of all on this path, namely: to accuse and reproach myself always (and the questioner added: there is no other path than this), the blessed one said what power the words of the saints have, for whatever

they said, they said from experience and truth, as the divine Anthony also teaches! That is why their words are powerful, because they were spoken by doers; and as one of the wise said: let your life confirm your words. At this he told us the following incident: during my short stay in the lavra of Abba Gerasimus, we were once sitting with a beloved brother of mine, conversing about soul-beneficial subjects. I recalled these words of Abba Poemen and of that other elder. The brother said to me at this: I have learned by experience the truth of these words and have tasted of the rest provided by fulfilling them. Once in this lavra there was a deacon with whom I lived in sincere friendship. I do not know why, but he came to suspect me in a certain matter, was offended by it, and began to look at me gloomily. Noticing this gloominess, I asked him to explain the reason, and he said: you did such-and-such a thing. Not at all conscious of this in myself, I began to assure him of my innocence, but he said to me: forgive me, I am not convinced. Withdrawing to my cell, I began to examine my heart, had I ever done such a thing?, and did not find it. Then, when I saw him take the chalice and serve, I swore to him on it that I had not done that, but even then he was not assured. Afterward, having entered into myself, I remembered these words of the holy fathers and, in full faith of their truth, turned my thought to myself and said: this sincere deacon of mine loves me and, moved by this love, has revealed to me what his heart holds against me, so that I might be watchful and guard myself from doing this in the future. But, poor soul! Why do you say that you did not do such a thing? A thousand evil deeds have been committed by you, and you have forgotten them. Where is what you did yesterday or ten days ago? Do you remember it? So, did you not also do this, just as you did that and forgot? Thus I resolved in my heart that I had truly done it, but just as I forgot the former, so I forgot this. Then I began to thank God and the deacon, that through him the Lord had deemed me worthy to know my sin and repent of it. Then, with such thoughts, I went to confess before the deacon and thank him. But as soon as I knocked at the door, he opened it and was the first to bow down and say: forgive me, I was deceived by demons in suspecting you, for truly God has assured me that you are innocent, and he did not allow me to persuade him further, saying: there is no need for this now. After this, the blessed one continued: see how sincere humility disposed this brother's heart, not only was he not scandalized at the deacon and not offended, first, that he suspected him, and second, that, being assured by him, he did not accept the assurance, but he even attributed the sin to himself and, moreover, thanked him! Then he added: do you see what this virtue does? To what degrees of advancement it leads those who love it! For if he had wished, he could have had thousands of occasions through the deacon to become a demon; but since he strove toward virtue, he not only was not offended at him but even thanked him, so much did virtue embrace his heart. So if we too will lay beforehand in our heart the seeds of meekness and humility, there will be no place for the enemy to sow evil seeds in it. For he fills us with his evil only when he finds us empty, having no good thought, or rather, when we ourselves incite ourselves to malice and thereby give him occasion for it. On the other hand, when virtue is present and the Lord sees that the soul thirsts for salvation and cultivates good seeds within itself, then for the sake of its good disposition He fills it with His gifts.

167. Once the blessed one recalled the elder who was being robbed by a brother living near him and who, knowing it, never exposed him but labored even more, saying: perhaps the brother is in need? And marveling at the mercy of the saints, he told such an incident: during my stay in Pediada, here is what one of the abbots told me: near our coenobium there lived an elder of a very good soul. In the absence of the elder, a brother living nearby, having been tempted, unlocked his cell, and entering, took his things and books. When the elder returned and, opening the cell, did not find his things, he came to that brother to tell him what had happened. Entering his cell, he saw his things in the middle of the cell, for the brother had not managed to hide them. Not wishing to expose him and put him to shame, the elder pretended that his stomach had seized up and, going out, stayed in the yard for a considerable time, as if for a need, until the brother put away his things. After this, returning, the elder began to speak to him about something else and did not expose the brother. A few days later the elder's things were recognized; they took that brother and put him under guard, while the elder did not know of it. Hearing that the brother was in prison, he came to me, continued the abbot's story, and asked me for some eggs and clean bread, as if for guests who had come to him, and went to the prison to console the brother. As soon as the prisoner saw the elder, he fell at his feet and confessed the theft; the elder consoled him, saying: let your heart be assured, my son, that I did not come here for this, for I did not know at all that you were here because of me; but hearing that you are here, I was grieved and came to console you. Here, look, eggs and clean bread. Now be at peace; I will do everything to get you out of prison. This is what this good elder did, entreating certain influential persons by whom he was known because of his virtue.

168. He also recounted about the same elder that once he went to the market to buy himself clothing. When he had bought it and given one gold coin, he still had to pay some smaller coins. The elder took the clothing and placed it under himself, but meanwhile, as he was counting out the small coins on a board, someone approached and began to pull the clothing out from under him. Feeling this and having an exceedingly merciful heart, the elder began to raise himself little by little, as if bending down for the coins, until the other had pulled out the clothing and gone away. And the elder did not expose him. What was his clothing worth, said the blessed one at this, or the things he lost? But great is the disposition. For he showed that, having them, he was in soul as if he had nothing: he paid no attention when they were stolen and remained unchanged, he did not grieve and was not irritated, for as I always tell you, it is not having that harms, but having with attachment. This one, even if he possessed the whole world, would remain as if he had nothing, for by what he did, he showed himself free from everything.

Endnotes

[2] Ares—the Greek god of war.
[3] Hermes—the Greek god associated with commerce and wealth.
[4] Methuselah—son of Enoch, who lived 969 years (Genesis 5:21–27).
[5] Obol—a small coin of little value (equivalent to approximately 1¾ kopecks at the end of the 19th century).
[6] Collyrium—a medicinal eye salve.

Chapter II.
On the Necessity of
Seeking Stillness with All Diligence

1. Someone said to Abba Arsenius: my thoughts trouble me, saying: you cannot fast nor labor; at least visit the sick, for this too is love. The elder, seeing in this the wiles of demons, answered him: go, eat, drink, sleep, and do not labor, only do not leave your cell, for he knew that patient remaining in the cell brings a monk into his proper order.

2. Holy Abba Anthony, once dwelling in the desert and having fallen into despondency and a deep darkness of thoughts, cried out to God: Lord! I desire to be saved, but thoughts do not allow me. What shall I do in my affliction? How shall I be saved? Then he arose and went out of his cell. And behold, he sees someone resembling himself, who sat and worked; then arose from work and prayed; afterward sat again and plaited rope; then again stood for prayer. This was an Angel of the Lord, sent for the instruction and strengthening of Anthony. And the Angel said aloud to him: do this also, and you shall be saved. Hearing this, Abba Anthony greatly rejoiced and was encouraged. He began to do likewise and was saved.

3. He also said: as fish, remaining long on dry land, die, so also monks, tarrying long outside their cell or dwelling with worldly people, lose their love for stillness. Therefore, as a fish strives toward the sea, so must we abide in our cell, lest remaining outside it we forget about inner watchfulness.

4. He also said: he who lives in the desert and in stillness is free from three temptations: from the temptation of hearing, of the tongue, and of sight; he has only one temptation, the temptation of the heart.

5. Abba Arsenius, while still at the imperial palace, prayed to God thus: Lord! Teach me how to be saved. And a voice came to him: Arsenius! Flee from people and you shall be saved. Having withdrawn to the desert, he again prayed to God with the same words and heard a voice saying to him: Arsenius! Flee, be silent, keep stillness, for in this are the roots of sinlessness.

6. Abba Mark asked Abba Arsenius: why do you flee from us? The elder answered him: God knows that I love you, but I cannot be both with God and with people. In heaven,

thousands and myriads have one will, but among people there are many wills. Therefore, I cannot leave God and be with people.

7. They said of Abba Arsenius that his cell was distant from others by thirty-two miles.[7] He almost never went out of it, for others fulfilled his needs. When Scetis was laid waste, he went out and said: the world has lost Rome, and monks have lost Scetis.

8. Once Abba Arsenius came to a place where reeds grew, which swayed in the wind. The elder asked the brethren: what does this noise mean? The brethren answered him: this is the reeds rustling. Then the elder said to them: truly, if one sitting in stillness hears the voice of a sparrow, his heart cannot preserve its former state; how much more difficult it is for you to preserve it with such noise from these reeds.

9. During the time Abba Arsenius was living in Canopus, a maiden of senatorial rank, exceedingly wealthy and God-fearing, came from Rome to see him. Archbishop Theophilus received her, and she asked him to persuade the elder also to receive her. Coming to the elder, he asked him: such-and-such a maiden of senatorial rank has come from Rome and desires to see you. But the elder would not agree to meet with her. When they told her of this, she ordered animals prepared for the journey, saying: I trust in God that I shall see him, for I did not come to see a man, for there are many men also in my city; I came to see a prophet. When she reached the elder's cell, by God's providence he happened to be outside it. Seeing the elder, she fell at his feet, but he raised her up with indignation and, looking intently at her, said: if you desire to see my face, here it is, look! But she, from shame, did not look upon his face. The elder says to her: have you not heard of my deeds? Upon these you ought to look. And how did you dare undertake such a voyage? Or do you not know that you are a woman and ought not to go out anywhere? Or do you wish, having returned to Rome, to tell other women that you saw Arsenius, and make the sea a road for women coming to me? She said: if it be the Lord's will, I shall not allow anyone to come here, but pray for me and remember me always. The elder said in reply: I shall pray to God that He may blot out the memory of you from my heart. Hearing this, she departed from him in great confusion and, arriving in the city, fell into a fever from sorrow. The blessed Archbishop Theophilus was informed of her illness, and coming to her, he asked her to tell him what was the matter with her. Oh, it would have been better for me never to have come here! I asked the elder: remember me, and he said to me: I shall pray to God that He may blot out the memory of you from my heart. And behold, I am dying from sorrow. The Archbishop said to her: do you not know that you are a woman and that through women the enemy wars against the saints? For this reason the elder spoke thus to you, but for your soul he will pray always. Thus her thought was calmed, and she departed with joy to her homeland.

10. Once Abba Arsenius was living in the lower regions of Egypt and, being troubled by visits, resolved to leave his cell. Taking nothing from it, he went to his disciples Alexander and Zoilus, the Pharanites. To Alexander the elder said: sail up the river, and he did so; and to Zoilus he said: go with me to the river, find me a vessel going down to Alexandria, then you too sail up to your brother. Zoilus, though troubled by this word of the elder, was silent,

and they parted. The elder, having gone down to the regions of Alexandria, fell ill there with a grievous sickness. His disciples meanwhile said to one another: did one of us offend the elder, and for this he departed from us? But they found nothing in themselves. Upon recovering, the elder said: I shall go to my fathers, and sailing up, he arrived at Petra, where his disciples were. When he was near the river, a certain young girl, an Ethiopian, approached and touched him, and when the elder rebuked her, she answered: if you are a monk, go to the mountain. The elder, struck by this word, said to himself: Arsenius, if you are a monk, go to the mountain. At the meeting, Alexander and Zoilus fell at his feet, and the elder also prostrated himself, and they wept, both they and he. Then the elder asked them: have you not heard that I was ill? They answered: we heard. And to his question: why then did you not come to see me?, Abba Alexander said: your departure from us was not well understood and did not serve the benefit of many, for they said that if we had not disobeyed you, you would not have departed from us. The elder said to them: and now people will say: *the dove found no resting place for the sole of her foot and returned to Noah in the ark* (Genesis 8:9). Thus they were reconciled, and the elder remained with them inseparably until his very repose.

11. One of the elders came to Abba Arsenius, and when he knocked at the door, the elder opened, thinking it was his attendant. But seeing that it was another, he fell on his face. The one who came said to him: arise, Abba! Let me embrace you. But the elder answered: I will not arise until you depart, and despite his long entreaties he did not arise until the other departed.

12. They told of a certain brother who came to Scetis to see Abba Arsenius. Having come to the church, he asked the clerics to arrange for him the opportunity to converse with the abba. They said to him: wait a little, brother, and you will see him. But the one who came said: I will not taste anything until I see him. Then the clerics sent one of the brethren to escort him to the elder, for his cell was far away. Having knocked at the door, they entered, greeted the elder, and sat in silence. After some time passed, the brother who was the escort said: I will go, pray for me. The visiting brother, not finding in himself the boldness to remain with the elder, also said: I will go with you. And they went out together. Then the visiting brother asked his escort to take him to Abba Moses, the one from among the robbers. When they came to him, he received them with joy and, having treated them kindly, dismissed them. After this, the brother who had escorted the visitor asked him: behold, I have taken you to the stranger and to the Egyptian; which of these two pleased you more? He answered: the Egyptian pleased me more. Hearing of this, one of the elders prayed thus to God: Lord! Reveal to me this matter, for one for Thy name's sake flees from people, and the other for Thy name's sake receives them with open arms. And behold, two great vessels on the river were shown to him; and he sees that Abba Arsenius and the Spirit of God sailed in stillness on one, while Abba Moses and the Angels of God sailed on the other, and these were feeding him with honeycomb.

13. Once the elders came to Abba Arsenius and earnestly asked him to converse with them. He opened to them, and they asked him to speak a word about those who keep stillness

and have no dealings with anyone. The elder says to them: while a maiden lives in her father's house, many desire to take her in marriage. But when she marries, she no longer pleases everyone: some disparage her, others praise her, and she no longer has such honor as before, when she lived in hiddenness. So it is also with the soul: as soon as she becomes open to all, she cannot please everyone.

14. Abba Bitimius recounted: I was once going to Scetis, and certain people gave me apples to distribute to the elders. Coming, I knocked at the cell of Abba Achilles to give him some, but he said: truly, brother, I would not wish for you to knock now, even if it were manna; do not go to other cells either. Then I went to my cell and brought the apples to the church.

15. Abba Dulas said: if the enemy compels us to abandon stillness, let us not heed him in the struggle against him, for there is nothing equal to stillness and fasting; they provide keen sight to the inner eyes.

16. He also said: cut off associations with others, so that warfare may not so closely beset your mind and disturb the order of your stillness.

17. Abba Eusedrius said: cut off worldly habits, so that your mind may not be disturbed and the rule of your stillness may not be disrupted.

18. Abba Theodore of Pherme said: the man who has come to know the sweetness of the cell flees from people, but not because he despises his neighbor.

19. Again he said: if I do not cut off from myself sentimentality, it will not allow me to be a monk.

20. Abba Joseph once fell ill and sent word to Abba Theodore saying: come, that I may see you before my departure from the body. It was then the middle of the week, and he did not go, but sent word: if you live until Saturday, I will come; but if you depart, we shall see one another in the other world.

21. A brother came to Abba Theodore, that he might teach him to sew mats, and brought cord as well. The elder said to him: go and come here in the morning. When he came, the elder arose, soaked the cord, and sewed the first row for him, saying: do thus and thus, and left him. Having entered his own cell, the elder sat as usual, and at the appointed hour he offered him food and dismissed him. When in the morning the brother came again, the elder said to him: take your cord from here and depart, for you came to cast me into temptation and care. And he did not allow him to remain with him any longer.

22. Amma Theodora said: it is good to keep stillness, for *a man of understanding holds his peace* (Proverbs 11:12). Truly, stillness is a great thing for a virgin or a monk, especially if they are still young. But one should know that as soon as anyone resolves to keep stillness, immediately the evil one comes to him and burdens the soul with despondency, faintheartedness, and thoughts; and burdens the body with illnesses, weakness, and relaxation of the knees and all the limbs. Thus he weakens all the powers of soul and body and implants

the thought: I am ill and have no strength to perform my rule. But if we are vigilant, we shall destroy all such wiles of his. Thus, there was a certain monk whom chills and fever seized when the time came to begin his rule, and a great noise arose in his head. Then he said to himself: behold, I am ill and perhaps will die. Therefore, I will arise and before I die, I will perform my rule. By this thought he overcame himself and performed his rule. When the rule ended, the fever also ended. Again, at the hour of the rule, the fever began, and again the brother overcame himself by the same thought and performed his rule. And thus he conquered the temptation.

23. Abba John said: if a man has in his soul the goods of God, he can remain in his cell, even if he has not the goods of this world. And again, if a man has the goods of this world and has not the goods of God, because of the goods of this world even such a one will remain in his cell. But he who has neither the goods of God nor the goods of this world can in no way remain in his cell.

24. In a certain coenobium there lived a brother who practiced asceticism very strictly. Hearing of him, brethren from Scetis came to see him and went up to the place where he was working. Having given them a greeting, he turned away and continued his work. Those who came, seeing this, said to him: John, he who clothed you in the schema or who made you a monk surely did not teach you to receive kindness from the brethren and to say to them: pray or sit down? He answered them: the sinful John has no time for that.

25. They told of Abba Isidore that whenever any brother came to him, he would flee into his inner cell. The brethren said to him: Abba! What is this you do? He answered: even beasts save themselves by fleeing into their lairs. He said this for the benefit of the brethren.

26. Abba Hierax said: I never spoke nor even wanted to hear worldly talk.

27. There was in Alexandria a scholasticus named Cosmas, a wondrous and virtuous man, humble-minded, merciful, temperate, a virgin, one who kept stillness, a lover of strangers, a lover of the poor. Having great boldness toward him, I once asked him: do me the kindness to tell me how long you have been keeping stillness? Since he was silent and did not answer, I again asked him: for the Lord's sake, tell me. And after a brief silence, he answered: thirty-three years. I again asked him: show me your full love, knowing that I ask for the profit of my soul, and tell me in what you have succeeded in so great a time of stillness? Then, sighing deeply from the depths of his heart, he said: in what can a man succeed, a layman, especially living in his own home? But I again entreated him, saying: for the Lord's sake, tell me and benefit me. And compelled by my persistence, he said: forgive me, in three things I know I have succeeded: in not laughing, in not swearing, and in not lying. Hearing this, I glorified God.

28. Abba Macarius the Great once in Scetis, dismissing the church assembly, said: flee, brethren. One of the elders asked him: Father! Where can we flee beyond this desert? Then Abba Macarius placed his finger on his lips and said: flee from this. Then he entered his cell and, having closed the door, sat in stillness.

29. Abba Moses said to Abba Macarius in Scetis: I desire to keep stillness, but the brethren do not allow me. Abba Macarius says to him: I see that you are by nature soft-hearted and cannot turn away a brother. Therefore, if you desire to keep stillness, go into the desert, into the interior of Petra, and there you will find stillness. Abba Moses did so and found rest.

30. Abba Isaiah asked Abba Macarius to speak a word of edification. The elder said to him: flee from people. Abba Isaiah asked: what does it mean to flee from people? The elder answered: to sit in your cell and bewail your sins.

31. Abba Aio asked Abba Macarius: speak to me a word of edification. Abba Macarius said: sit in your cell, bewail your sins, do not love conversations with people, and you shall be saved.

32. Abba Moses said: a man who flees from people is like a ripe grape, while one who dwells among people is like an unripe grape.

33. Abba Mark said: he who desires to cross the noetic sea must be long-suffering, humble-minded, watchful, and temperate. But whoever casts himself into this sea without these four virtues will only struggle and torment his heart, but will not be able to cross.

34. He also said: one cannot keep stillness with profit already by reason of withdrawing from evil deeds, but if these four mentioned virtues are joined to it together with prayer, there is no swifter path to stillness.

35. Again he said: one cannot keep stillness of mind without stillness of body; nor destroy the middle wall between them without stillness and prayer.

36. Abba Nilus said: the monk who loves stillness is unreachable by the arrows of the enemy, while he who mingles with crowds receives frequent wounds. For in the former, anger gradually becomes briefest, and desire, not being provoked, little by little grows accustomed to strivings more quiet, and every passion in general, not being stirred up, day by day becomes more moderate, and finally ceases altogether, having forgotten with the passing of time its proper activity; only simple remembrances of things remain, while the passionate disposition falls away.

37. He also said: for this reason stillness is good, that in it one does not see what can harm; and what is not seen is not received into the mind; what is not born in the mind does not move the imagination of memory; what does not move memory does not provoke passion; and when passion is not moved, our inner being has deep quiet and great peace.

38. Abba Joseph asked Abba Nisterus: what shall I do with my tongue, for I cannot restrain it? The elder says to him: when you speak, do you have rest? He answered: no. Then the elder said: if you do not have rest, why do you speak? It is better to be silent, and when there happens to be a conversation, listen more than you speak.

39. Abba Poemen said: the beginning of evils is distraction, going here and there and busying oneself.

40. He also said: one must flee from everything carnal. The man who is near carnal temptation is like one standing over a very deep precipice, and the enemy, at whatever hour it seems good to him, easily casts him down. But he who in body stands far from this temptation is like a man standing far from a precipice, and though the enemy drag him to cast him down, while he is dragging and compelling, God sends him help.

41. He also said: if you are silent, you will have rest wherever you happen to dwell.

42. To a certain brother living in the Thebaidan desert, a thought said: what are you sitting here fruitlessly? Arise, go to a coenobium, and there you will bear fruit. The brother went to Abba Paphnutius and revealed his thought to him. The elder said to him: go, sit in your cell, and offer one prayer in the morning, one in the evening, and one at night; when you wish to eat, eat; when you wish to drink, drink; when sleep comes, lie down to sleep; but remain in the desert and do not believe this thought. He also went to Abba John and recounted to him the words of Abba Paphnutius. Abba John says to him: do not offer any prayer at all, only sit in your cell. Then he went to Abba Arsenius and told him of everything. The elder said: keep what the fathers have told you, for I have nothing more to say to you. And he departed.

43. There were in Scetis master craftsmen, Abba Paul and Abba Timothy, who endured troubles from the brethren. Once Abba Timothy says to his brother: what use to us is this craft? They do not allow us to keep stillness the whole day. Abba Paul answered: for us, the stillness of the night is sufficient, if our heart is vigilant.

44. A brother asked Abba Rufus: what is stillness, and what is its profit? The elder answered: to keep stillness means to sit in your cell with discernment and with the fear of God, refraining from malice and high-mindedness. Such stillness, being the parent of all virtues, preserves the monk from the fiery darts of the enemy, not allowing him to be wounded by them. Therefore, brother, acquire such stillness, remembering your departure in death, for you do not know *what hour the thief will come* (Luke 12:39). Therefore watch over your soul.

45. The disciple of Abba Sisoes said to him: Father! You have grown old; let us go and make ourselves a cell closer to a village. The elder said: let us go where there is no woman. His disciple says to him: where is there no woman except in the desert? Therefore, said the elder, lead me into the desert.

46. Abba Amoun of Raithu once came to Cithema to visit Abba Sisoes and, seeing that he was grieving over having left the desert, asked him: why do you grieve, Abba? What could you do in the desert at such an old age? The elder looked at him with a stern expression and answered: what do you say to me, Amoun? Was not the freedom of thought alone in the desert sufficient for me?

47. A brother asked Abba Sisoes: how did you leave Scetis, where you lived with Abba Or, and settle here? The elder answered him: when Scetis began to be populated, I, having heard that Abba Anthony had reposed, came here to the mountain, and finding that here all

was peaceful, settled for a short time. The brother says to him: how many years have you lived here? The elder answered: seventy-two years.

48. They told of Abba Sisoes of Thebes that as soon as the church assembly ended, he would quickly flee to his cell. They said of him that he had demons in him, but he was doing the work of God.

49. A brother said to Abba Sarmatas: my thoughts tell me: go out and visit the brethren. The elder answered him: do not listen to them, but say: I heeded you before, but now in this I cannot heed you.

50. Amma Syncletica said: many, having settled on a solitary mountain, live as if they lived in a crowd, and perish. For it is possible, being among people, to be solitary in mind, and living in solitude, to be mentally always as if in a crowd of people.

51. Abba Tithoes, during his stay in Clysma, being absorbed in contemplation, said to his disciple: pour water on the dates, my son. He answered: we are in Clysma, Abba. The elder said: what am I to do in Clysma? Lead me back to the mountain.

52. An elder said: good sitting in the cell enriches a monk with all good things.

53. He also said: a monk must purchase for himself stillness by disregard for all bodily discomforts.

54. Someone recounted: there were three industrious friends, and one of them chose for himself as his labor to make peace among those who quarrel, according to the word of Scripture: *blessed are the peacemakers* (Matthew 5:9); another, to care for the sick; and the third went to keep stillness in the desert. The first, laboring over the quarrels of people, could not reconcile all and, in despondency, came to the one serving the sick, but found that he too was faint-hearted, not having succeeded in fulfilling his vow. Having agreed, both went to see the one keeping stillness and, telling him of their sorrow, asked him to relate what he had acquired. After being silent for a little while, he poured water into a vessel and said to them: look at the water. And it was turbid. Somewhat later, when the water had settled, he again said to them: look now. When they looked, they saw their faces as in a mirror. Then he says to them: so also he who dwells among people, because of cares and confusions, does not see his sins; but when he keeps stillness, and especially in the desert, then he sees clearly all his faults.

55. A brother came to a certain very experienced elder and says to him: Father! My soul is heavy; I am suffering. The elder said to him: sit in your cell, and God will grant you consolation.

56. An elder said: as on a path trodden through no plant will grow, even though you cast seeds there, because they always trample that place, so it is also with us. But keep stillness from everything, and you will see growing within yourself what before you did not see, because you were walking in it.

57. A brother asked an elder: is it good, Abba, to live in the desert? And the elder answered: when the sons of Israel ceased for a time to wander through the desert and dwelt in tents, then it was given them to know how one must fear God; and ships, while they are tossed about on the sea, remain inactive concerning profit, but when they enter the harbor, then they begin their trade. So also a man will not receive knowledge of the truth if he does not remain patiently in one place. And God Himself chose stillness above all virtues, as is also proclaimed: *On whom shall I look, but on the meek and the silent one and on him who trembles at My words* (Isaiah 66:2). The brother asked again: if by some necessity it happens to speak with a woman, how ought one to answer her? The elder said: such necessity often comes from the devil: the devil has many pretexts as if necessary. But if there arises a true need to speak with a woman, do not allow her to speak at length, and when you yourself begin to speak, compress much into little and dismiss her quickly, for if you remain long, know that the impression from her will disturb your thoughts. The brother asked further: in what way can a man be delivered from the sin of judging? The elder answered: as one who puts fire in his bosom is inevitably burned, so also one who enters into conversation with people will not be pure from the sin of judging. The brother asked: what do the nocturnal imaginings of the devil signify? The elder said: as during the day the devil occupies us with extraneous thoughts so that we might not occupy ourselves with prayer, so also at night he excites our mind with imaginings and, darkening us, turns us from the night prayer. The brother again asked: what must a man do to receive the gift of virtues? The elder answered: whoever desires to learn some craft, leaving aside every other concern, occupies himself with it alone and remains with the teacher, humbling and abasing himself, and thus learns the craft. Likewise the monk, if he does not leave every human care and does not humble himself so as not to think that he is better than such-and-such a one or equal to him, will never acquire virtue; but if he humbles and abases himself, then the virtues and the zeal for them, as for a work, will come of themselves.

58. One of the elders recounted to us: my abba throughout his whole life dearly loved to go away into the more distant desert places and there to keep stillness. Once I asked him: Abba! Why do you flee into the deserts? He who abides near the world, sees it, and despises it for God's sake, has a greater reward. The elder says to me: believe me, my son, until a man comes to the measure of Moses and becomes almost a son of God, until then he cannot receive benefit from the world. But I am a son of Adam and, like my father, as soon as I see the fruit of sin, I immediately desire it, take it, eat it, and die. For this reason our fathers fled into the desert and there mortified gluttony, not finding foods that give birth to passions.

59. An elder said: he who has sinned before God must remove himself from all human love until he is assured that God has become his friend, for human love hedges us off from the love of God.

60. He also said: as a dead man in a city no longer hears the talk or conversations of those living there, nor songs, but for all is dead and is transferred to another place where there is neither noise nor cries of the city, so also the one who takes up the monastic life, as soon as he is clothed in the schema, must go out of his city, leave there his parents, relatives,

and all his acquaintances, and not give himself anymore to the cares and sorrows of this life, nor to the tumults, storms, and waves of this vain and soul-destroying world. For if, having accepted monasticism, he does not go out of his city or village, he is like a dead man lying in a house and decaying, from whom all who smell his stench flee.

61. Again he said: when unsalted meat spoils so that all turn away from it because of its stench, then worms settle in it, live and crawl in it, hide and gnaw at it; yet as soon as salt is put into the meat, immediately the worms living in it perish and disappear, and its stench ceases, for such is the nature of salt. In like manner, the monk who gives himself to earthly affairs and vanities, who does not keep stillness in his cell, who does not arm himself with the fear of God, who abandons prayer, vigil, and fasting, and who does not partake of the power of God, which is prayer, vigil, and fasting, that spiritual salt, spoils and is filled with the stench of evil thoughts, so that God and the Angels turn their faces from him because of the terrible stench of his vain thoughts and the darkness of passions acting in his soul and most impure mind. See how these worms, that is, the spirits of wickedness and the powers of darkness, how they walk in him, live in his impure thoughts, crawl and dive in his soul, devour, corrupt, and destroy it! But as soon as the monk has recourse to God, renounces vanities, and believes that God can heal him, spiritual salt is sent to him, the good and man-loving Spirit, with whose coming all passions flee.

62. He also said: a monk must not care for well-branched and shady trees, nor for goodly flowing springs, nor for meadows of various colors, nor for gardens with all kinds of vegetables, nor for fair houses; he must not live sumptuously, nor think of honors, nor occupy his mind with flocks of sheep and herds of cattle, but must with thanksgiving make use of what is necessary and by a certain strange path lead a life alien to all carnal pleasure. But if a monk, indulging himself, binds himself with such things, he will be able neither to become a friend of God nor to escape the judgment of men, for with this it is necessary for him to quarrel over boundaries and borders, and because of the beauty of houses to receive the notable, because of gardens to be importuned by all, because of flocks of sheep and cattle to deal with slaves and hired workers, because of fields and meadows to come to blows in quarrels, because of vineyards to be entangled in lawsuits, since one will violate the boundary of the vineyard and join something to his own, another will let cattle onto the grass, a third will divert the water flowing into the garden. Therefore, one must not bring himself to the necessity of being tormented thus, of quarreling, of being worse than those who are raging, and of calling upon those in authority for help. What profit is it for a monk, having renounced the worldly, to struggle again over the same things, *for no one engaged in warfare entangles himself with the affairs of this life* (2 Timothy 2:4)? Therefore, let us begin to withdraw from things, let us despise possessions and all that plunges the mind into the waters of this life and brings it down into their depths, let us throw off the cargo so that the ship may rise somewhat and so that the helmsman, the mind, may be saved together with the thoughts sailing on this ship.

63. An elder said: as from a bathhouse, if the doors are opened frequently, all the warmth quickly escapes, so it is with the soul: if a man speaks often and much, then, even though he

sometimes speaks well, he dissipates its warmth through the door of words. Therefore, timely silence is good, for it is the mother of wisest thoughts.

64. A brother asked an elder about how one ought to keep stillness in the cell. And the elder answered: he who keeps stillness in the cell must cast himself down before the face of God and with all his strength resist the evil thoughts sown by the enemy, for this is what it means to flee the world.

65. A brother asked: what is the world? And the elder answered: the world is sinful distraction; the world is laboring beyond one's strength for gain and the satisfaction of carnal desires; the world is thinking that you will remain always in this age; the world is concern for the body above the soul and vainglory in that of which you deprive yourself. I did not say this of myself, but the Apostle John declared it, saying: *do not love the world or the things in the world* (1 John 2:15).

66. He also said: he who keeps stillness, while still in the body, must examine himself every hour: has he passed by those who are to detain him in the air, and has he been freed from them? For as long as he is subject to their slavery, so long is he not yet free from them.

67. A brother asked the same elder: what must one who keeps stillness do? And he said: three things are needed for him: unceasingly to have the fear of God, to pray with patience, and not to withdraw in heart from the remembrance of God.

68. A brother asked an elder: what is stillness, and what is its profit? The elder said to him: to keep stillness means to sit in the cell with discernment and the fear of God, refraining from malice and high-mindedness. Such stillness, being the parent of all virtues, preserves the monk from the fiery darts of the enemy, not allowing him to be wounded by them. O stillness, progress of monastics! O stillness, ladder to heaven! O stillness, way to the Kingdom of Heaven! O stillness, mother of compunction! O stillness, fountain of repentance! O stillness, mirror of sins, revealing to man his transgressions! O stillness, giver of freedom for tears and sighs! O stillness, enlightener of the soul! O stillness, parent of meekness! O stillness, companion of humility! O stillness, guide to a peaceful state! O stillness, converser with the Angels! O stillness, light-bearer of the mind! O stillness, ally of the fear of God, observer of thoughts, and co-worker of discernment! O stillness, parent of every good: support of fasting, bridle of the eyes, of hearing, and of the tongue, barrier against gluttony! O stillness, school of prayer and school of reading! O stillness, calm of thoughts and untroubled haven! O stillness, unceasing prayer to God! O stillness, keeper of unburnt discernment for the young and guardian of untroubled rest for those who sit with willing patience in their cells! O stillness, yoke that is easy and burden that is light, giving rest and bearing those who bear you! O stillness, gladness of the soul and joy of the heart! O stillness, caring only for its own things and hidden converse with Christ, having death before its eyes day and night! O stillness, every day and every night awaiting Christ and keeping its lamp unquenched, unceasingly calling upon Him, saying: *my heart is ready, O God, my heart is ready* (Psalm 56:8). O stillness, destroyer of idle talk and jests, and instead of laughter, giver of weeping to him who has acquired you! O stillness, enemy of shamelessness, hater of boldness, and ever-welcomer of Christ! O stillness, mother of reverence! O stillness, prison of passions! O stillness, field of Christ, bringing forth good fruits! Acquire this, brother, remembering death.

69. One of the elders of the Lavra of Calamon asked a brother living in stillness on the mountain: tell me, brother, what have you acquired in so long a time of your stillness and asceticism? The brother answered him: come in ten days, and I will tell you. The elder came in ten days but found the brother already departed, and he saw a potsherd on which was inscribed: forgive me, Father! While performing my rule, I never left my mind upon the earth.

70. Two brothers lived together in the desert. One of them, every time he remembered the judgment of God, would flee into the deepest desert and walk there alone. The other would follow after him to seek him, and once, after considerable labor, when he found him, he asked: why do you go away? The brother answered him: do you think I do not know that my sins have been forgiven? I know that God has forgiven me my sins, but I undertake this labor so that on the day of judgment I might be a spectator of those being condemned.

71. A brother came to a certain elder at the Lavra of the Eighteenth Mile in Alexandria together with a layman and said to him: give us, Father, instruction on how to live together, for this brother also intends to renounce the world. The elder answered: you do well, my son, to renounce the world, seeking salvation for your soul. Therefore, sit vigilantly in the cell, wherever you decide, only keep stillness, pray unceasingly, and hope in God, children, that He will send you His wisdom for the enlightenment of your mind.

72. He also said: children, if you desire to be saved, flee from people, for we now knock without rest at every door and go about cities and villages, wondering whether we might somewhere buy food for avarice and vainglory and satiate our souls with vanity.

73. Again he said: therefore, let us flee, children, for the Lord is near!

74. They told of a certain elder who kept stillness that he lived in stillness for thirty-five years, fasted every two days, always kept silence, and spoke with absolutely no one; but when there was need to say something, he indicated it by signs. I also saw him in the land of the Heliotes, for he lived there for ten years.

75. An elder said: if you desire to keep stillness, then settle either in a remote desert or in a lavra amidst numerous brethren. If you settle separately, but in a place not so remote, you will meet with great disturbance, for when someone comes there, you will need to receive him, because except at your place, he has nowhere to rest and refresh himself. But if you live in a place where there are many other brethren, then, even if you do not receive the one who comes, your thoughts will not trouble you, for he will be able to find shelter with another; the multitude of brethren will be a cover for you and will give you the opportunity to be at peace.

76. An elder said that prison is to sit in the cell and always remember God. This is what it means: *I was in prison and you came to Me* (Matthew 25:36).

77. An elder said: one person spends a hundred years in a cell and does not learn how one ought to sit in a cell.

Endnotes

[7] One mile is a thousand paces.

Chapter III.
On Compunction of Heart

1. Abba Anthony said: have always before your eyes the fear of God, remember Him Who puts to death and brings to life, Who brings down to Hades and raises up (1 Samuel 2:6). Hate the world and all that is in it; hate all fleshly ease, renounce this life in order to live for God; remember what you have promised to God, for He will require it of you on the day of judgment; hunger, thirst, be naked, keep vigil, weep, wail, sigh in your heart; test yourselves, whether you are worthy of God; despise the flesh, that you may save your souls.

2. It was said of Abba Arsenius that throughout all the time of his life, while sitting at his handwork, he kept a cloth upon his breast on account of the tears falling from his eyes.

3. A brother asked Abba Ammon to give him a word, and the elder replied: go, dispose your thought as it is disposed in criminals who are in prison, who anxiously ask people: "where is the judge? When will he come?" – and they weep in expectation. Likewise the monk must unceasingly attend to his soul and say: "woe is me! How shall I stand before the throne of Christ and how shall I justify myself before Him?" If you will always think thus, you can be saved.

4. He also said: when you sit in your cell, gather your mind and remember the day of death, imagine the deadness of the body at that time, understand that calamity and take up labor, despise the vanity of the world and enkindle zeal, so that your intention to keep stillness may remain always the same and not weaken. Remember also the state in Hades and consider what it is like for the souls there, in what bitter silence and terrible groaning, in what fear, anguish, and expectation, in what torment of soul, in what tears and sufferings. Remember also the day of resurrection and standing before God and think upon that fearful and terrible judgment. Picture to yourself what is appointed for sinners – shame before the face of God and of His Christ, before the face of Angels, Archangels, Principalities, and all people; picture every kind of torment – eternal fire, the undying worm, Tartarus, the darkness over all these things, gnashing of teeth, terrors, and sufferings. Picture also the blessings appointed for the righteous – boldness before God the Father and His Christ, before Angels, Archangels, Principalities, and all the multitude of people, the kingdom and its gifts – joy and consolation. Keep the memory of all this unceasingly in your mind, and at the remembrance of the

condemnation of sinners groan, weep, pour forth tears, fearing in your thought lest you yourself also be among their number, and at the remembrance of the blessings appointed for the righteous, rejoice, be consoled, and be glad and be zealous to be counted worthy of these and to escape from those. See to it that you never forget to remember this, whether you are inside your cell or somewhere outside, never remove your mind from this, so that at least through this you may guard yourself from harmful thoughts.

5. Abba Aio recounted the following about a brother named Apollon, who had previously been a village herdsman and now lived in Scetis: he saw in the field a woman who had a child in her womb, and at the instigation of the devil said within himself: "I want to see how the child lies in her womb," and, ripping open her womb, he saw the child. But immediately his heart was deeply shaken, and coming into great compunction, he went to Scetis and told the fathers what he had done. There he heard them chanting: *The days of our years are seventy years; and if by reason of strength they are eighty years, yet their boast is only labor and sorrow* (Psalm 89:10), and he said to them: "I am forty years old and have not prayed even once; now, if I live another forty years, I will not cease imploring God to forgive me my sins." From that time, not occupying himself with handwork, he prayed unceasingly, saying: "as a man I have sinned, but as God do Thou have mercy on me." And this prayer became his meditation day and night. Another brother lived with him, who often heard him say: "I have grieved Thee, O Lord; *grant me relief, that I may rest a little.*" And an assurance was given him that God had forgiven him all his sins, including the sin of killing the woman, but concerning the child he received no assurance. Yet one of the elders said to him: "God has forgiven you also the sin of killing the child, but He has left you in anguish because this is profitable for your soul."

6. A brother asked Abba Poemen: "thoughts trouble me and compel me, leaving aside my own sins, to notice the faults of my brother." At this the elder related to him the following about Abba Dioscorus: he sat in his cell and wept over himself. His disciple, who lived in another cell, would come to him and, finding him weeping, finally asked him: "Father, why do you weep?" The elder answered: "I weep over my sins." His disciple said to him: "you have no sins, Father." But the elder said: "believe me, my son, if it were permitted me to see my sins, three or four other brothers would not be enough to bewail them."

7. Abba Evagrius said: always remember the eternal judgment, do not forget your departure – and there will be no sin in your soul.

8. Abba Elijah said: I fear three events: when my soul will depart from my body, when I will stand before God, and when the final sentence concerning me will be pronounced.

9. Abba Elijah from among the deacons said: what power does sin have where there is repentance; and what benefit is there from works of love where there is arrogance?

10. Blessed Archbishop Theophilus said: what fear and trembling and what necessity shall we see when the soul is to be separated from the body! For there shall come to us then the hosts of the opposing powers, the princes of darkness, the evil world-rulers, the

principalities and powers – these spirits of wickedness, and in a certain manner rightfully take possession of the soul, presenting all its sins committed knowingly and unknowingly, from youth to the age at which it is overtaken by death; they shall stand and accuse all that it has done. Consider then what trembling the soul will have in that hour – until a sentence is pronounced and its deliverance is accomplished! This is the hour of necessity for it – until it learns what will be determined for it. On the other hand, the divine powers will also stand face to face with the opposing powers and present its good deeds. Consider then in what fear and trembling the soul will abide, standing in the middle, until the judgment over it receives its decision from the Righteous Judge. If it is found worthy, then the demons will be put to shame, and it, being snatched from them, will begin a life without sorrow, as it is written: *the dwelling of all those who rejoice is in You* (Psalm 86:7). Then the words of Scripture will be fulfilled: *sorrow and sighing shall flee away* (Isaiah 35:10); and the freed soul will hasten to ineffable joy and glory, to which it shall be deemed worthy. But if it is found that the soul lived carelessly, then it will hear that most terrible voice: *Let the ungodly be taken away, that he may not see the glory of the Lord* (Isaiah 26:10). Then a day of wrath shall come upon it, a day of tribulation and necessity, a day of darkness and gloom. Delivered over to outer darkness and condemned to eternal fire, the soul shall be tormented there unto endless ages. Where then is worldly glory? Where is vainglory? Where are delights? Where are pleasures? Where is splendor? Where is ease? Where is boasting? Where is wealth? Where is nobility? Where is father? Where is mother? Where are brothers? Which of them will help to deliver it, being burned by fire and seized by bitter torments? But if this is so, then what manner of people ought we to be in our way of life and deeds of piety? What love should we have? What character? What life? What path? What faithfulness? What prayer? What steadfastness? Therefore, beloved, as the Apostle teaches: *looking for these things, be diligent to be found by Him in peace, without spot and blameless* (2 Peter 3:14), that we may be deemed worthy to hear this word of His: *Come, you blessed of My Father, inherit the kingdom prepared for you from the foundation of the world* (Matthew 25:34).

11. The same Abba Theophilus, the Archbishop, as he was dying, said: blessed are you, Abba Arsenius, that you always remembered this hour.

12. The fathers related: that once, when the brethren were eating at an agape meal, one brother laughed at the table. Seeing this, Abba John wept and said: "what is in that brother's heart, that he laughed, when he ought rather to weep, since he is eating alms?"

13. Abba Isaac and Abba Abraham lived together. Once, entering the cell, Abba Abraham found Abba Isaac weeping and asked him: "why do you weep?" The elder answered: "how can we not weep, for our fathers have reposed? And to whom shall we go? Formerly, when we set out to visit the elders, the proceeds from handwork were sufficient to pay for passage. But now we are orphaned, and for this I weep."

14. Abba Jacob said: as a lamp placed in a dark chamber illumines it, so the fear of God, when it enters the heart, enlightens it and teaches all virtues and the commandments of God.

15. Abba John of the Cells related: there lived in Egypt a harlot, beautiful in appearance and very wealthy, whom even persons of rank visited. Once she came near the church and

wanted to enter, but the subdeacon standing at the doors barred her way and said: "you are unworthy to enter the house of God, because you are unclean." When he began to argue with her, the bishop came out at the noise, and the woman complained to him that the subdeacon would not allow her to enter the church. And the bishop said to her: "you cannot enter, because you are unclean." From these words the woman came into compunction and promised to leave her trade, at which the bishop said: "I will believe that you will no longer commit fornication if you bring here all your precious things." She brought them, and they were immediately burned. After this the woman entered the church and said with tears: "if this happened to me here, how must I suffer there?" Having repented, she became a vessel of election.

16. Abba Longinus said: fasting humbles the body, vigil purifies the mind, stillness brings mourning, mourning washes a person as in baptism and makes him sinless.

17. Abba Longinus had great compunction during his prayer and psalmody. Once his disciple asked him: "Abba! Is it a spiritual law for a monk to weep over his rule?" The elder said: "yes, my son, such is the law that God requires. God did not create man for weeping, but for joy and gladness, that they might glorify Him purely and sinlessly, like the angels. Weeping became necessary for man after he fell into sin. Where there is no sin, there is no need for weeping."

18. Some of the fathers asked Abba Macarius of Egypt: "why is it that whether you eat or fast, your body is always dry?" The elder answered them: "the stick with which one turns burning brushwood is inevitably consumed by the fire; in the same manner, if a man purifies his mind in the fear of God, the very fear of God consumes his body."

19. Once the elders who lived on the mountain sent to Abba Macarius in Scetis, asking him to come to them, saying: "Father! That the whole brotherhood may not trouble you, we ask you – come to us, that we may see you before your departure to God." When he came to the mountain, all the brotherhood gathered to him. The elders asked him to speak a word to the brethren. Hearing this, he said: "let us weep, brethren, and let our eyes pour forth tears before we depart to where our tears will burn our bodies." And all wept, fell on their faces, and said: "Father! Pray for us."

20. Abba Paphnutius, the disciple of Abba Macarius, retold the following words of the elder: "when I was a boy, together with other boys I tended young calves. They went to steal figs, and as they ran back, one of them fell; I picked it up and ate it. Whenever I remember this, I sit down and weep."

21. Abba Macarius recounted: "once, walking through the desert, I came upon a skull of a dead man lying on the ground. I moved it with a palm staff, and the skull spoke to me." I said to it: "who are you?" The skull answered me: "I was a priest of idols among the Greeks who lived in this place, and you are Macarius, the Spirit-bearer. Whenever you, taking pity on those in torment, pray for them, they feel some relief." The elder asked it: "what relief is this, and what torments are there?" The skull said: "as far as the heaven is from the earth, so much

fire is beneath us, and we all stand in fire from feet to head. We cannot see anyone's face, for each one's face is turned toward another's back. But when you pray for us, then one partly sees another's face. Such is the relief." The elder wept and said: "woe to the day in which a man was born." Then he asked it again: "is there another torment more grievous?" It answered: "the torment beneath us is more terrible." The elder asked it: "who then is there?" The skull said: "we, who did not know God, have received some mercy; but those who knew God and rejected Him are beneath us." Then the elder took and buried the skull in the ground.

22. A brother asked Abba Moses: "what should a man do when temptation or some hostile thought comes upon him?" The elder answered him: "he must weep before the face of the goodness of God, that He may help him – and he will soon receive peace, if only he asks with understanding, as it is written: *The Lord is my helper; I will not fear. What can man do to me?*" (Psalm 117:6).

23. Abba Moses said: when we are conquered by some fleshly passion, let us not neglect to repent and weep over ourselves, before the weeping of judgment overtakes us.

24. He also said: by tears a man acquires the virtues, and through tears he receives the forgiveness of sins. When you weep, do not raise the sound of your groaning, *lest your left hand know what your right hand does* (Matthew 6:3). The left hand is vainglory.

25. A brother asked Abba Matoes: "give me a word." And he said to him: "cut off from yourself all contention about whatever matter it may be; but weep and wail, for the time is near."

26. When Abba Mark with his abba Silvanus, having left Scetis, came to Mount Sinai and lived there, the mother of Mark visited them and begged the elder with tears to send her son to her that she might see him. Mark put on his sheepskin to go out and came to give a kiss to the elder, but suddenly he began to weep and did not go out.

27. Once Abba Poemen, passing through Egypt, saw a woman who, sitting at a grave, wept bitterly, and he said: "if all the pleasures of this world were to come, they would not turn her soul from weeping. Such weeping the monk too must always have within himself."

28. Once Abba Poemen was walking with Abba Anub through the region of Dioclea and, passing by a cemetery, they saw a woman who was greatly tearing at herself and weeping bitterly. They stopped and looked at her, then went further, and from a man they soon met they learned that her husband, son, and brother had died. Then Abba Poemen, turning to Abba Anub, said: "I assure you, if a man does not mortify all fleshly desires and does not acquire such mourning, he cannot be a monk. All the life of this woman and all her mind is in mourning."

29. He also said: mourning is twofold, that is, it has two effects: it works and it guards.

30. A brother asked Abba Poemen: "what should I do?" The elder answered him: "Abraham, when he came to the land of promise, bought himself a place for burial and

through the grave inherited the land." The brother asked: "what does the grave mean?" The elder said: "a place of mourning and lamentation."

31. A brother asked Abba Poemen: "what should I do with my sins?" The elder answered him: "he who desires to redeem sins redeems them by mourning; and he who desires to acquire virtues acquires them by mourning. Mourning is the way that Scripture and our fathers have handed down to us, saying: weep, for apart from this there is no other way."

32. A brother asked Abba Poemen: "what should I do with the thoughts that so greatly disturb me?" The elder answered him: "let us weep before the face of the goodness of God in all our affliction, until He shows us His mercy."

33. Abba Joseph related that Abba Isaac said: "once, sitting with Abba Poemen, I noticed that the abba was in ecstasy. Having great boldness toward him, I bowed and asked: 'tell me, Father, where were you?'" Being compelled, Abba Poemen said: "my thought was there where the Most Holy Theotokos Mary stood and wept at the Cross of the Savior. And I would desire always to weep thus."

34. A brother asked Abba Poemen: "what should I do?" At this the elder said to him: "when God visits us, what shall we be concerned about then?" The brother answered: "about our sins." The elder said to him: "therefore let us enter our cell and, sitting in it, remember our sins – and the Lord will be with us in all things."

35. Blessed Athanasius, Archbishop of Alexandria, asked Abba Pambo to come from the desert to Alexandria. Coming into the city, the abba saw a woman from the theater and wept. Those who were with him urged him to say why he wept, and Abba Pambo answered: "two things moved me: first – the perdition of this woman, and second – that I do not have such zeal to please God as she has to please worthless people."

36. Abba Paul said: "I am plunged up to my neck in mire and weep before Jesus, crying: have mercy on me!"

37. Abba Silvanus, once sitting with the brethren, came into ecstasy and fell on his face. After a considerable time he rose and wept. The brethren asked him: "what is the matter with you, Father?" But he was silent and wept. When at last they pressed him, he said: "I was caught up to the judgment and saw that many of our order were going away to torment and many of the worldly were going to the kingdom." Thus the elder wept and did not want to leave his cell. If some necessity compelled him to go out, he covered his face with his cowl and said: "why should I look upon this temporal light, from which there is no benefit?"

38. A brother asked Abba Silvanus: "what should I do, Abba, and how shall I acquire compunction, for despondency and sleep greatly overcome me? Rising from sleep, I struggle much with myself, and even though I chant psalms, I cannot overcome sleep." The elder answered: "the fact that you chant psalms is pride and self-exaltation, that is – 'I chant, but my brother does not chant.' Chanting hardens and cools the heart and does not allow the soul to come to compunction. Therefore, if you desire to acquire compunction, leave chanting

and, when you stand at prayer, enter with your mind into the meaning of each verse, remembering at the same time that you stand before the face of God Who searches hearts and reins. When you rise from sleep, first of all let your lips glorify God, but do not begin your rule immediately; instead, go out first from your cell, reciting: 'I believe...' and 'Our Father, Who art in heaven...,' then enter and begin your rule very softly, sighing and remembering your sins and the torment in which you shall be tormented." The brother said: "I, Abba, since I became a monk, have chanted the sequences, the rule, and the hours according to the tones." The elder answered: "that is why compunction and mourning flee from you. Remember the great fathers! How simple they were and knew nothing except a few psalms, knew neither tones nor troparia, and nevertheless they shone like luminaries in the world. Witnesses to my word are Abba Paul the Simple, Abba Pambo, Abba Apollon, and others, who even raised the dead and showed authority over demons not by chanting, nor troparia and tones, but by prayer and fasting; for it is not fine singing that saves a man, but the fear of God and the keeping of the commandments of Christ. Chanting has brought many down to the depths of the earth and has cast down not only laymen but even priests into the pit of fornication and other passions. Moreover, my son, chanting is the work of laypeople, for that is why the people are gathered in church. Consider how many orders there are in heaven, and it is not written of them that they chant by tones, but one order ceaselessly chants: 'Alleluia'; another order: 'Holy is the Lord of Sabaoth'; another order: 'Blessed be the glory of our Lord.' Therefore, my son, love the humility of Christ and attend to yourself, guarding your mind at the hour of prayer; also, wherever you go, do not present yourself as one of great knowledge or as a guide, but be humble-minded, and God will grant you compunction."

39. They said of Abba Serapion that his life was like that of a winged bird. He had absolutely nothing of the things of this age and did not live in a cell, but in a single tunic with a small Gospel in hand, he went about everywhere as if bodiless. Often they would find him outside a village, sitting by the road and weeping bitterly, and when they asked him why he wept so, the elder would answer them: "my Master entrusted His riches to me – but I lost them, and He wants to torment me." Hearing this, they thought that he was speaking to them about gold, and often, giving him a little bread, they would say: "take it, brother, and eat, and the riches that you lost, God is able to send you." The elder would answer them: "amen."

40. Mother Syncletica said: for those who approach to work for God, at first there are many labors and struggles, but afterward comes ineffable joy. As those who wish to kindle a fire are at first smoked and made to weep and thus attain their goal, so we too must enkindle in ourselves the divine fire with tears and labors, for Scripture says: *our God is a consuming fire* (Hebrews 12:29).

41. Abba Hyperechius said: the watchful monk who attends to prayers turns night into day. Piercing his heart, he pours forth tears and draws mercy from heaven.

42. A brother came to Abba Felix with some laymen and asked him to speak a word for edification. The elder was silent. But since the brother strongly entreated him, he said to them:

"do you wish to hear a word?" They answered him: "yes, Abba." And the elder said to them: "there is no more a word. When the brethren asked the elders and fulfilled what they said, God gave the elders a word – what to say and how. But now, since they ask and do not fulfill what they hear, God has taken His grace from the elders, and they find nothing to say, because there is no one who does." Having heard this, they sighed and said: "pray for us, Abba!"

43. They related of Abba Or and Abba Theodore that once, while throwing clay on a cell, they said to each other: "if God should visit us now, what would we do?" Weeping and leaving the clay, each one withdrew to his cell.

44. Near a certain elder lived a brother who was somewhat negligent in the monastic life. When he was dying, some of the fathers were sitting with him, and the elder, seeing that he was departing with gladness and joy, and wishing to provide edification to the brethren, said to him: "we all know, brother, that you were not entirely zealous in asceticism. Why then do you depart with such gladness?" The brother answered: "it is true what you say, Father. But believe me that since I became a monk, I do not know that I ever condemned any man, and if I happened to have displeasure with anyone, I immediately – that same day – made peace with him. And now I wish to say to God: 'Thou hast said, O Master: *Judge not, that you be not judged: forgive, and you will be forgiven*' (Luke 6:37)." Then the elder said: "peace be to you, my son – you have been saved even without labors."

45. An elder related: a certain brother who lived in the Cells spent twenty years exercising himself in reading day and night. Once he arose, sold the books he had and, taking his sheepskin, went into the innermost desert. Meeting him, Abba Isaac asked him: "where are you going, my son?" The brother answered him: "twenty years I have spent, Father, studying the teachings in books; now I wish at last to proceed to fulfill what I learned from the books." The elder made a prayer over him and let him go.

46. Once, having come to Canopus of Alexandria, which is ten miles from the city, we visited Abba Theodore, an ascetic man who possessed the gift of patience. He related to us: "in the Cells there lived a certain brother who had acquired the gift of compunction. It happened once that from the sorrow of heart tears flowed abundantly from his eyes. Noticing this, the brother said to himself: 'this must mean that the day of my death is near.' But no sooner had he thought this than the tears flowed even more abundantly. Seeing that they increased, he thought: 'truly, the time has drawn near' – and each day he wept more and more." Having received great edification from this account of the elder, we asked him about tears: "why do they sometimes come of themselves, and sometimes cannot be found even with effort?" The elder answered: "tears are like snow and rain, and the monk is a farmer. When they come, he must strive so that nothing is wasted, but all enters the garden and waters it. I assure you, children – often one day of rain is more profitable than a whole year and saves all the fruits. Therefore, when we notice that this day has come, let us strive to keep ourselves and, being free from all things, pray attentively to God, for we do not know whether there will be such rain on another day." We asked him again: "how, Father, can a man preserve compunction when it comes?" The elder answered: "let him not go to anyone on that day or

that year; let him keep his stomach and his heart, so that it does not imagine that it weeps like [...];[8] let him exercise himself in prayer and reading. However, when mourning comes to us, it itself will teach us what favors it and what hinders it." At this he related to us the following: "I knew of a certain brother who lived in a solitary cell and wove baskets. When tears came upon him and he stood up for prayer, the tears would immediately stop; but when he sat down again and, taking a strand, gathered his mind, they would immediately return. Likewise, if while reading he came into compunction and stood up for prayer, the compunction would immediately depart, but as soon as he took up the book again, it would return. Then this brother said: 'the fathers spoke well when they said that mourning is a teacher, for it itself teaches a man what is favorable to it.'"

47. An elder related that a certain brother who wished to leave the world was prevented from doing so by his own mother; but he did not abandon his intention and did not cease troubling her, saying: "I want to save my soul." Since with all her effort she could not prevent him, she finally gave her permission. But having left her and become a monk, he spent his life in negligence. It happened that his mother died, and a year later he too fell ill with a grave illness with no hope of recovery and, coming into a trance, was caught up to the judgment, where among those condemned he noticed his mother. Seeing her son there, in amazement she asked him: "my son, what is this? And you are condemned to this place? And where are your words: 'I want to save my soul'?" Put to shame by her words, he stood in grief, having no answer. And then he heard a voice: "take him from here; I sent for another monk of the same name from such-and-such a monastery." When the vision ended and the brother came to himself, he recounted everything to those present, and in confirmation of the truth of what he had seen he asked one of the brethren to go to the aforementioned cenobium and find out whether a brother of the same name had reposed, which was confirmed by the one who was sent. After this, having recovered from the illness and regained strength, this brother shut himself up in a cell and, caring only for his salvation, repented and wept over what he had formerly done in negligence. And such was his compunction that many implored him to relent somewhat, fearing that some harm might not come to him from immoderate weeping. But he did not wish to be comforted and said: "if I could not endure the reproach of my mother, how shall I endure the shame on the day of judgment before Christ and His holy angels?"

48. An elder said: if it were possible for the souls of men to leave their bodies at the resurrection in the second coming of Christ, then the whole world would die from terror and astonishment, for what would it then be possible to behold: the heavens opening and God revealing Himself with wrath and indignation, countless hosts of angels and all mankind. Therefore we must live so that every minute we are ready to give an account to God of our life.

49. A brother asked an elder: "how does the fear of God enter the soul?" And the elder said: "if a man acquires humility, non-acquisitiveness, and non-judgment, then the fear of God will come to him."

50. A brother came to an elder and asked him: "why is my heart hard, and why do I not fear God?" The elder answered him: "I think that if a man will always frighten himself in his heart, he can soon acquire the fear of God." The brother asked again: "what does this frightening consist of?" And the elder said: "in impressing upon the soul in every matter to remember that it must stand before God, and saying to it: 'what help can a man give me?' I think that if a man will constantly exercise himself in this, the fear of God will soon come to him."

51. A certain elder, seeing someone laughing, said to him: "before the face of heaven and earth we must give an account for our whole life, and you laugh!"

52. An elder said: as we carry our sins with us everywhere, so also we must have mourning and compunction with us wherever we may be.

53. A brother asked an elder: "what should I do?" And he answered him: "we must always weep, for here is what happened to one of the fathers: he died, and after several hours returned to life again. We asked him: 'what did you see there, Abba?' He said to us with weeping: 'I heard there the voice of lamentation and unceasing cries: woe is me! woe is me!' Thus we too must always lament."

54. The brother asked again: "Father, why does my soul desire tears, but they do not come? My soul grieves over this." The elder answered him: "the sons of Israel entered the promised land only after forty years of wandering. If you too enter into it, you will no longer fear battle. Therefore it is pleasing to God to keep the soul in grief, so that it may always enkindle within itself the desire to enter that land."

55. A certain zealous brother, coming to Mount Sinai from a foreign land, settled in a small cell. When he entered it for the first time, he found a small tablet on which was written thus: "Moses to Theodore – I am here and I bear witness." Placing this tablet before his eyes, the brother would question the one who wrote it as if he were present: "where then are you now, O man, though you say: 'I am here and I bear witness'? In what world are you at this hour? And where is the hand that wrote this?" Thus he did every day and, unceasingly remembering death, remained in mourning. His handwork was copying books. He took paper from the brethren and indicated what he would write for each one, but he died without writing anything for anyone, only on small columns in each one's notebook he left the following words: "forgive me, my fathers and brethren! I had a small matter with a certain man, and for this reason I did not find time to write for you."

56. Near this brother lived another brother, a native of Elissa. Once, gathering to go to the fortress,[9] he asked the brother who was a scribe: "do me a kindness, watch over the garden until I return." He answered: "good, as much as I can, I will try." When the brother left, the one remaining said to himself: "humble one! Care for the garden while there is time." And standing at evening for prayer, until morning itself he did not cease singing and praying with tears, as also the whole following day, which was Holy Resurrection. The brother, his neighbor, coming toward evening, found his garden destroyed by wild boars and said to him:

"God forgive you, brother, that you did not watch over the garden." He answered: "God sees, Abba – I watched as much as I could; and may God grant us, as He knows, fruit in our small garden." The neighbor said: "believe me, brother – everything is destroyed." "I know," he answered again, "but I believe in God that everything will bloom again." At another time the brother who was a gardener asked the brother who was a scribe: "come, let us water the garden." He answered him: "go water now, and I will water at night." Thus, when there was a drought, the brother who was a gardener grew sad and said to his neighbor the scribe: "ah, brother! If God does not help, this year we will have no water." The other said to him in reply: "woe to us, brother! If the springs of the garden dry up, truly there will be no more salvation for us." This he said about tears. Drawing near to death, this good ascetic asked his neighbor from Elissa: "do me a kindness, tell no one that I am ill, and stay here today, and when I die, take my body and throw it into the desert to be eaten by beasts and birds, for it has sinned much before God and is not worthy of burial." The gardener said to him: "believe me, Abba, my soul hesitates to do such a thing." But the ascetic answered: "let this sin be upon me; and I give you my word that if you listen to me and do thus, I too will help you." When on that same day he died, the brother fulfilled what he had commanded: he threw his naked body into the desert, and they lived twenty miles from the fortress at a place called Metemer. On the third day the one who had departed to the Lord appeared to his neighbor in a dream and said: "may God have mercy on you, brother, as you had mercy on me. Believe me, God has shown me great mercy because my body remained unburied, for He said to me: 'look, for your great humility I have appointed you to be with Anthony.' I also asked about you. Go then, leave your garden and care for another garden. Know that when my soul left my body, I saw how my tears extinguished the fire into which I was to be cast."

57. Two brothers according to the flesh, having renounced the world, came to Mount Nitria and placed themselves under the guidance of one father. God gave them both the gift of compunction and tears. Once the elder saw such a vision: both brothers, standing at prayer, held inscribed scrolls and washed them with their tears. The letters of one of them washed off easily, but those of the other with difficulty, for they appeared as if written with burning ink. The elder entreated God to explain this vision to him, and an angel, appearing to him, said: "the letters on the scrolls are their sins. One of them sinned according to nature, therefore his falls are easily resolved; but the other defiled himself with impure and abominable falls, therefore for repentance he has need of greater labor and greater humility." From that time the elder would say to that brother: "labor, brother, for they are burned and are washed off with difficulty." Speaking thus, the elder did not reveal the whole matter to him until his very death, so as not thereby to cut off his zeal, but only repeated: "labor, brother, for they are washed off with difficulty."

58. A certain one of the fathers lived in Raithu at a place called Chalcan. Another elder came to him and said: "Abba! I grieve when I send my brother away for something." That one said to him in answer: "I, when I send somewhere the brother who serves me, sit near the door and watch. If the thought begins to say within me: 'when will the brother come?' – I answer it: 'but if another brother comes sooner, who is to take you to the Lord, what then?'

And thus, looking at the door, I am contrite each day and weep over my sins, saying: 'which brother will come first – the one below or the one above?'" The elder departed with great profit and afterward himself acted in the same manner.

59. A certain zealous brother during the rule, which he performed together with another brother, was overcome by tears, and he would leave off chanting the verse of the psalm. Once the brother asked him what he pondered during the rule that he wept so bitterly. And he answered him: "always during the rule I see the Judge, Who as if at a trial examines me like a criminal standing before Him and asks why I sinned. Since I do not know what to say in justification, my mouth is stopped, and I leave off chanting the verse of the psalm. But forgive me, brother, that I grieve you, and if it is agreeable, let us each perform our rule separately." The brother objected: "no, Father, although I do not weep, yet looking at you I reproach myself." And God, seeing his humility, granted him also mourning, as He had granted it to his brother.

60. A certain brother came to an elder living on Mount Sinai and asked him: "Father! Tell me a word on how one should pray, for I have greatly angered God." The elder answered: "I, my son, when I pray, speak thus: 'Lord! Grant me to serve Thee as I served Satan, and to love Thee as I loved sin.'"

61. The same elder said: it is good during prayer to raise one's hands to heaven and ask God that the soul, after its departure, may safely pass all those who will try to place obstacles in its path to heaven.

62. On Sinai a certain novice monk was sent by his abba to a brother who had a garden, to ask for a few ripe fruits. Coming to the brother, the novice asked: "Abba, do you have any ripe fruits? My abba asked for a few." He answered: "my son, go and take for your health what is here and what you want." The novice then asked: "and is there the mercy of God here, Abba?" Hearing this, the brother pondered and stood looking at the ground. Then he asked: "what did you say, my son?" He answered: "I said, Abba: is there the mercy of God here?" And he repeated his question a third time. The abba was silent for a good while and, not finding what to answer, said with a sigh: "God is merciful, my son" – and let him go. After this he took his sheepskin and immediately, leaving the garden, went out into the desert, saying to himself: "let us go seek the mercy of God. If this novice asked me and I did not find what answer to give, then what shall I do when God Himself will question me?"

63. A certain brother who lived on Mount Emon came to the holy city and, approaching the governor, confessed his sins to him, after which he asked to be punished according to the laws. The astonished governor, having pondered this within himself, said to him: "listen, man of God, since you yourself have voluntarily repented, I do not dare to judge you, leaving all to the judgment of God, for perhaps God has already forgiven you." But the brother, returning from him, placed chains on his feet and neck and shut himself up in his cell. If any man asked him who had laid these heavy chains upon him, the brother would answer: "the governor." A day before his death these chains broke apart of themselves and fell from him. When his attendant came, amazed at what he saw, he asked: "who broke your chains?" He

answered him: "He Who released my sins, for He appeared to me yesterday and said: 'for your patience I have released all your sins.' Then He touched the chains with His finger, and they immediately fell from me." Having told of this, the brother departed to the Lord.

64. There was in Scythopolis a civil official who committed terrible deeds and defiled his body in every way. Coming to repentance by the action of the grace of God, he renounced the world and, having built himself a cell in a deserted place – in the depth of a ravine – began to struggle for the salvation of his soul. Certain of his acquaintances learned of this and began to send him bread, dates, and everything needful; however, seeing himself at ease – lacking nothing – he said to himself: "truly such an easy life deprives us of peace hereafter; moreover, I am unworthy of this." Therefore, leaving his cell, he departed from there, saying: "let us go, O soul, to affliction, for grass – as food for animals – is the food befitting me who have defiled myself by beastly deeds."

65. When we arrived in Raithu, some of the brethren related to us the following: "there was here a certain elder, hardworking and living above a place called Israel. He also had care for the sobriety of his mind and almost at every step would stop, examine his thought, and ask it: 'what is within you, brother? Where are we?' And if he found his mind chanting and praying, he would say: 'good.' But if he found his thought on something else, he would reproach himself and say: 'go back from there to your work.'" And to himself the elder always said thus: "brother! The hour of departure is near, and I still see nothing within myself." Once Satan appeared to him and said: "why do you labor? Believe me, you will not be saved anyway." The elder answered him: "what is it to you? Let me not be saved, but I will still stand above your head, even if I am below all who are condemned to torment."

66. A certain elder who lived in Raithu had this practice: sitting in his cell, he would gaze pensively at the ground and, continually shaking his head, say with a sigh: "what will be, what will be?" Then, having been silent a little and working on a strand, he would again say, not ceasing to shake his head: "what will be, what will be?" Thus he spent all his days, continually thinking about his departure.

67. An elder said: it befits the penitent to be in solitude, to keep the warmth of zeal, to sorrow in heart, to weep, to have no care for the world, to be a burden to no one, to afflict himself, to accuse and condemn only himself, to live with constraint, to be always watchful, and with sorrow of heart to ask unceasingly of God mercy for himself.

68. An elder said: *for every sin which a man commits is outside the body, but he who commits fornication sins against his own body* (1 Corinthians 6:18), because from it comes defilement; so also every struggle that a man performs is outside the body, but he who sheds tears cleanses both soul and body, for descending from above, they wash the whole body and illumine it.

69. A brother asked an elder: "how, Father, does mourning come to a man?" The elder answered: "mourning is a matter of practice, and he who seeks it must labor for a long time, occupying his mind with thoughts either about the sins he has committed, or about torment, or about death, or about the fathers – how they departed and where they are now – in a word,

about all kinds of subjects that can bring him to compunction." The brother asked: "is it permissible, Father, to remember one's parents?" The elder said: "whatever thought disposes your soul to mourning, with that occupy your mind, and when tears come, then concentrate them on whatever you wish: on the remembrance of your sins or on other good thoughts. Thus I knew of a certain brother, an ascetic, who, when his heart was hard, would beat himself, and from the pain he would begin to weep, and after that he would pass to the remembrance of his sins as well."

70. Again he said: conversation about faith and reading of dogmatic treatises dry up tears and drive away compunction, but the lives and sayings of the elders enlighten the soul.

71. He also said: there is nothing more ruinous than the habit of sin – much labor and time are required to cut it off, and without prolonged labor it is impossible to succeed in this. Meanwhile, though many have been able to labor, time was not given to all, for some were soon visited by death, and God alone knows what will be with them on the day of judgment.

72. A certain brother who lived in solitude in his cell often fell into despondency, for he fell into a grievous sin. At last in tears, not knowing what to do, he said to himself: "what is done is done." But his conscience reproached him, saying: "but what was done was evil." From this he began to weep and wept until his very death.

73. An elder said: he who sits in his cell and chants psalms is like a man striving to see the king; but he who prays with tears is like one who already embraces the king's feet and asks mercy of him, like the harlot.

74. An elder said: accustom your heart little by little to say truthfully about each brother: "this one is higher than I before God"; or: "this one is more zealous than I." Thus you will at last come to place yourself lower than all, and the Spirit of God will dwell in you. But if you demean a brother, the grace of God will depart from you and deliver you to fleshly defilements; your heart will grow hard and no compunction will visit you.

75. An elder said: God requires of an ascetic that he have absolutely no attachment to anything material, not even to a small needle, for even this can hinder his thought from attending to Jesus and mourning.

76. He also said: woe to you, O soul, who have grown accustomed only to ask about the word of God and to hear, but fulfill nothing of what you hear! Woe to you, O body, who, even knowing by what you can be brought to defilement, do not cease desiring it, that is, satiety and delights! Woe to the novice if he fills his belly and believes his own will. For such a one, renunciation of the world is also in vain.

77. A certain brother who lived in Monidia, through diabolical suggestion, often fell into fornication; nevertheless he never allowed himself to fall so far as to leave monasticism, but always, performing his small rule, he implored God with sighing, saying: "Lord! Whether I want it or not, save me. I, being earth, love sins; but Thou, being the mighty God, restrain me. For if Thou have mercy on the righteous, it is nothing great; and if Thou save the pure,

it is nothing wondrous; for they are worthy of Thy mercy. But on me, O Master, make Thy mercies wonderful; in this show Thy love of mankind, *for to Thee the poor is left*" (Psalm 10:14). Thus he prayed every day – whether he fell into sin or did not fall. One night, having fallen into his habitual sin, he immediately arose and began his rule. The demon, struck by his boldness and good shamelessness before God, appeared to him visibly and said: "are you not ashamed to stand before the face of God or even to name His name?" The brother answered him: "this cell is an anvil – you give one blow and receive one. Thus will I struggle with you in patience until my very death, and as for the state in which the last hour finds me, let God's will be done. Only I assure you with an oath: yea, to Him Who came to save sinners by repentance, I will not cease to pray to God against you until you cease to war against me. And we shall see who conquers – you or God!" Hearing this, the demon said to him: "believe me, henceforth I will not fight against you, lest on account of your patience I provide you a crown." And the demon of fornication departed from him from that day. Behold how salutary is patience and not despairing of oneself, even if it should happen that we often fall in battles, sins, and temptations! After this, coming to compunction, the brother sat and bewailed his sins. If his thought said to him: "how well you weep!" he answered it: "anathema to this 'well.' Does God approve that someone should destroy his soul?" Then he would sit and bewail it, not yet knowing whether it would be saved or not.

78. A certain brother lived in solitude in the region of Monidia, and this was always his prayer: "Lord! I do not fear Thee, but send me a fever, some calamity, or sickness, or a demon, that at least in this way my hardened soul may come to fear!" Having said this, he added with compunction: "I know that it is impossible to forgive me, for I have sinned much before Thee, O Master, but for the sake of Thy compassions – forgive me. If this is impossible, punish me here, O Master, but deliver me from punishment there. If even this is impossible, repay me in part here, and there lighten at least a little the weight of my torment, only begin from now to punish me, but not in Thy wrath, O Master." Thus for a whole year, in tears and fasting, he unceasingly importuned God and finally, in great humility of thoughts, said to himself: "but what then does the word spoken by Christ mean: *Blessed are those who mourn, for they shall be comforted?*" (Matthew 5:4). Once, sitting on the ground and weeping as usual, he dozed off from sorrow and saw that Christ appeared to him and with a joyful countenance graciously asked: "what is the matter with you, O man, and why do you weep so?" The brother answered: "I have fallen, O Lord." The One Who appeared said to him: "then arise." The brother answered: "I cannot arise if Thou dost not give me Thy hand." The Lord stretched out His hand and, raising him, graciously said: "why do you still weep, O man, and about what do you grieve?" The brother answered: "how can I not weep, O Lord, and not sorrow, when I have so grieved Thee?" The One Who appeared placed His hand on his head and said: "do not sorrow – God is merciful. Since you yourself torment yourself with such sorrow, henceforth I no longer sorrow over you: if I gave My blood for you, shall I not all the more manifest My love of mankind to every repenting soul?!" Coming to himself after this vision, the brother found his heart filled with great joy and, being assured thereby that God had shown him mercy, in great humility he unceasingly thanked God.

79. A certain brother, having renounced the world, settled on Mount Nitria. Near him was the cell of another brother, who heard how the newly settled brother wept bitterly every day over his sins, and if tears did not come to him, he would say to his soul: "you do not weep, miserable one, and you do not lament? Believe me, if you do not want to weep yourself, I will forcibly make you weep." Then he would get up, take a whip of harsh cord, and beat himself until he began to weep from pain. Marveling at this, the neighboring brother asked God to reveal to him whether he was doing well in tormenting himself thus. And once at night in a dream he saw this brother in a crown, standing in the choir of martyrs, and while he looked at him, he heard a voice: "do you see — this good ascetic, tormenting himself for the sake of Christ, is crowned as a martyr!"

80. A certain elder who lived beyond Clysma once went to Egypt on his affairs and took his disciple with him. Coming to a city called Cynno, they stayed there a whole week and saw how from early morning the men and women of this city went out to the cemetery and wept, each over his own deceased, until the third hour. Seeing this, the elder said to his disciple: "do you see, brother, what they are occupied with? Believe me, if we too do not do likewise, we shall go to eternal torment." Returning to their place, they immediately made graves for themselves at a considerable distance from one another, and each day, sitting from morning, they wept over their souls as over the dead. If ever toward morning the disciple fell asleep, the elder would cry out to him: "arise, brother, arise!" Nevertheless, they had a set hour both for weeping at the graves and for their handwork. Once the brother said to the elder: "Abba! My soul is hard, and I cannot weep." The elder answered: "struggle, my son, a little and labor, and God, seeing your labor, will grant you mourning, which will then come to you without labor. For, I assure you, just as there is no more healing for a heart pierced by an arrow, so also when God wounds the heart with mourning, it remains wounded until death itself, and painful compunction never departs from it; so that wherever such a one goes, mourning in his heart will go with him." Once the elder noticed that his disciple was burdened with food, for that evening they had visitors, and he said to him privately: "do you not know, brother, that mourning is a kindled lamp? If you do not reliably cover it, it will immediately go out; so also much eating extinguishes it; and long sleep hinders it; and condemnation quenches it; and much talking destroys it, and all ease of the flesh annihilates it. He who loves God must give a portion to Christ from everything." The brother asked: "what does this mean, Father?" And the elder answered: "when you happen to have clean bread, leave it for another, and eat unclean bread yourself — for the sake of Christ; if you happen to have good wine, pour a little vinegar into it and drink — for the sake of Christ, Who drank vinegar; also, do not eat to satiety, but leave a little, saying: 'this is Christ's portion'; if you find a soft pillow, leave it and put a stone — for the sake of Christ; if lying down you become cold, endure it, saying to yourself that others do not sleep at all; if you are reviled, be silent, saying: 'for the sake of Christ, for He too was reviled for our sake'; if you are preparing a porridge for yourself, spoil it a little, saying that others — who are worthy — do not even eat bread, but I — unworthy — eat porridge, whereas I ought to eat ashes and dust — and simply mix a little bitterness into everything: into food, into sleep, and into work; live always humbly, remembering how the

saints lived, so that when the last hour comes, it may find us in affliction and constraint, and we may find rest there."

81. An elder said: if a thought suggests to you to prepare various foods for a feast day, do not listen to it – otherwise you will celebrate in the manner of the Jews, for they celebrate thus. But for a monk the best food is mourning and tears.

82. Again he said: if you go out somewhere from your cell and notice that your compunction has somewhat weakened, return quickly and hasten to restore in yourself your former order, that is, mourning.

83. He also said: if you desire to acquire mourning, arrange so that all your vessels and all your things are poor, like those of the brothers sitting in the marketplace (that is, beggars).

84. He also said: if you do not have compunction, know that you have vainglory, for this passion more than all others does not allow the soul to come to compunction.

85. Again he said: when God grants you mourning, do not think that you are doing a great thing, for blessed is he who has no need of mourning. If God sees that a man's heart is puffed up with vainglory over tears, He takes them from him; after this, the heart of such a man again becomes hard – and he perishes.

86. He also said: when God grants you compunction, leave your handwork then, if you see that this is profitable, and give yourself to mourning. Is not the day of your departure near, and God has granted you mourning so that through it you may find at least a little mercy? For just as Satan strives to destroy a man at his death, so God often saves a man at his death, placing good dispositions in his heart.

87. He also said: if there is a cemetery in the place where you live, go there more often and think about those resting there, especially during the battle of the flesh. Also, when you learn that some brother is departing to the Lord, go and be with him, that you may see how the soul is separated from the body.

88. He also said: if, after falling into sin, you turn and begin to sorrow and repent, see to it that you do not cease being contrite and sighing to the Lord until the very day of your death, lest otherwise you quickly fall again into the same pit, for godly sorrow alone is a bridle for the soul, not allowing it to fall.

89. Again he said: as soon as Satan sees that God is showing you His mercy by granting compunction to your soul, he immediately begins to remind you of various matters, as if necessarily needed, saying: "do now this and that, because there is need for it"; or: "go visit so-and-so, because he is sick." He does all this so as not to allow you to be free from everything and not to allow you to taste the sweetness of mourning. But if, having understood Satan's cunning, you take care to preserve mourning, being attentive to humble and contrite prayer, then expect a sorrowful temptation either from people or from demons, for Satan usually wars more fiercely against a man when he resists him more manfully; and anger more than all things destroys the compunction and humility of the soul. If thoughts and demons surround you when you sit quietly in your cell, immediately stand up and pray, and then walk outside, and they will flee from you and be scattered.

90. An elder said: sitting in your cell, keep unceasingly the remembrance of God, and the fear of God will embrace you and will drive out of your soul every sin, every evil, and every iniquity.

91. And he also said: the fear of God saves a man from sin; he who has acquired it has in it a treasury full of blessings.

92. A certain elder who lived in solitude in his cell throughout sixty years of his hermit life never ceased weeping and always said: "God has given us this time for repentance, and therefore we must seek only repentance."

93. About one elder they related that before monasticism he had been a herdsman and tended cattle. Once he came down with them to Jericho, where at an inn one of the cattle stepped on a small child and killed it. Stricken by this, he left everything and withdrew to the Arnon, where he began to live as a hermit and to bewail his sin, saying: "I have committed murder and as a murderer must be condemned at the judgment." Near that place by the river there lived a lion, and the elder began to go every day to the lair of the lion, to beat it and provoke it, so that it might devour him; but the lion did not harm him at all. The elder, seeing his lack of success, said to himself: "I will lie on the path by which the lion goes, and when it goes to the river to drink, it will eat me." He lay down, and after a little while the lion appeared; however, like a person, it calmly jumped over the elder without even touching him. Having been assured by this that God did not impute the sin to him, the elder came to one of the monasteries and spent all the remaining time of his life there, saving instructing all until his very death.

94. A brother asked an elder: "what should I do, Abba, for when I see someone sinning, I condemn him; and if I hear of a negligent brother, I hate him and thus destroy my soul?" The elder answered: "when you hear something of the sort, quickly recoil from this thought and flee to the remembrance of that terrible day and imagine to yourself the fearful throne and the incorruptible Judge; the rivers of fire flowing before that throne and boiling with flame; the unceasing torments and the punishment that has no end; the impenetrable gloom, the outer darkness, the sleepless worm, the unbreakable bonds, the gnashing of teeth, and the inconsolable weeping. This is what you must think about; this is what inescapable calamities you must keep in mind! That Judge will have no need of accusers and witnesses, of proofs and exposures, but as each thing was done, so it will come forth before the eyes of those who sinned. Then no one will come to deliver from torment – neither father, nor son, nor daughter, nor any other relative, nor neighbor, nor friend, nor patron; neither money, nor wealth, nor power will help then, for all this will scatter like dust from under one's feet. The one being judged alone will receive from what was done by him either a verdict justifying him or one condemning him; then no one will be judged for another, but only for that in which he himself sinned. Knowing this, judge no one – and you will be at peace."

Endnotes

⁸ The following word in the manuscript is missing.
⁹ After the massacre of the fathers of Raithu and Sinai, for safety from raids, the main Sinai monastery and church were surrounded by a wall, from which it received the appearance and name – fortress. In case of danger all the fathers who struggled in the various ravines of the Sinai mountains took refuge there.

Chapter IV.
On Self-Control, by Which Should Be Understood Not Only Abstinence in Food, but Generally the Restraint of All Unrighteous Movements of the Soul

1. Once, brethren set out from Scetis to Abba Anthony. Having boarded a ship heading to him, they found in it another elder who was also going there. The brethren did not know him and, sitting on the ship, conversed among themselves about the sayings of the fathers, about the words of Scripture, and about their handiwork; the elder, however, remained silent. When they arrived at the shore, it turned out that this elder was also making his way to Abba Anthony, who, when they came to him, said: "you found a good companion in this elder." Then he said also to the elder: "you found good brethren for yourself, abba." The elder replied: "they are good, but their courtyard has no gate: whoever wishes enters the stall and unties the donkey." He said this because they spoke of whatever came to their lips.

2. Abba Daniel said of Abba Arsenius that he spent his whole life in wakefulness and, when toward morning he had to sleep for nature's sake, he would say to sleep: "come, evil servant." Then, sitting, he would doze off a little and immediately awaken again.

3. Abba Arsenius said: "for a monk, it is sufficient to sleep one hour, if he is an ascetic."

4. Abba Daniel also said of Abba Arsenius: "all the time he lived with us, we prepared for him only one small basket of wheat for the year, from which we ourselves also ate when we came to him."

5. He also related that Abba Arsenius would change the water in which he soaked the palm branches no more than once a year and would only add new water (for he would usually weave cords and sew them until the sixth hour). The elders asked him: "why, abba, do you not change the water for the branches, for it gives off a stench?" And he answered them: "for the incense and myrrh which I enjoyed in the world, I must endure this stench."

6. He also said: "when Abba Arsenius learned that fruits and vegetables of various kinds had ripened, he would ask that some be brought to him, but he would taste of each only once, giving thanks to God."

7. They said of Abba Agathon that for three years he placed a stone in his mouth until he had learned silence.

8. He was once walking with his disciples, and one of them, having found a small green lentil pod on the path, asked the elder: "father! If you bid, I will take it?" The elder looked at him with pleasure and said: "did you put it there?" The brother answered: "no." Then the elder said to him: "how do you wish to take what you did not put there?"

9. They told of Abba Agathon and of Abba Amoun: when they sold some item, they would state the price only once, and then whatever was given, they would take in silence, with a contented manner. And again, when they wished to buy something, they would silently give the asked price and take the purchased item, saying nothing.

10. Abba Agathon once had two disciples who lived as hermits, each by himself. Once he asked one of them: "how do you live, brother, in your cell?" He answered: "I fast until evening and then eat two dry loaves." The elder said to him: "your asceticism is moderate." Then he asked the other as well: "and how do you live?" He answered: "I fast for two days and then eat two dry loaves." The elder said to this: "your asceticism is harder, and you bear a double burden. For it is an ascetic feat if someone eats every day but not to satiety; another, though he fasts for two days, eats to satiety; but you, fasting for two days, do not eat to satiety."

11. Once Abba Achilles came to the cell of Abba Isaiah in Scetis and found him eating. In his bowl he had put salt and water. The elder, seeing how he hid the bowl behind the basket, asked: "tell me, what were you eating?" He answered: "forgive me, abba! I was cutting branches in the heat and put a piece of bread with salt in my mouth; but from the heat my throat became parched, and the bread would not go down, so in order to swallow it, I was compelled to add water. But forgive me!" Then the elder said: "come and see. Isaiah eats broth in Scetis. If you want to eat broth, go to Egypt."

12. One of the elders came to Abba Achilles and, seeing that he was bringing up blood from his mouth, asked: "what is this, father?" And the elder answered: "this is a word of a brother who offended me. I struggled not to reveal it and asked God that it be taken from me, and the word became blood in my mouth. I spat it out and found rest, forgetting the offense."

13. They said of Abba Ammon: being ill, he lay in bed for many years and never permitted his thought to look into his inner cell, so as not to see what was in it, for because of his illness there were many offerings brought to him. When his disciple John would enter or exit, the abba would close his eyes, so as not to see what he was doing, for he knew him to be a faithful monk.

14. Abba Anub said: "from the time the name of Christ was named upon me (James 2:7), no lie has come forth from my mouth."

15. A brother asked Abba Abraham: "if it happens that I eat a lot, what does this mean?" The elder said in answer: "what are you saying, brother? You eat that much?! Or do you think you have come to a threshing floor?"

16. Abba Benjamin said: "when we returned from the harvest to Scetis, they brought us alms from Alexandria, one vessel of pure oil per person, sealed with gypsum. When the time of harvest came again, the brethren would bring what each one had remaining to the church. I did not open my vessel but, having pierced it with a needle, drew off a little oil; and it was on my heart that I had done a great thing. When this time came to give what remained to the church, the brethren brought their vessels sealed with gypsum, but I brought mine pierced, and I was as ashamed as if I had committed fornication."

17. Abba Benjamin, the presbyter of the Cells, related: "we came to a certain elder in Scetis and wanted to give him a little oil, but he said to us: 'that small vessel of oil which you brought three years ago lies just as you then placed it.' Hearing this, we marveled at the life of the elder."

18. He also related: "once we came to another elder, and he detained us to partake of food. The elder set before us radish oil, but we asked him: 'bring us rather a little good oil.' Hearing this, he crossed himself and said: 'whether there is any other oil besides this, I do not know.'"

19. They told of Abba Dioscorus of Nahiat that his bread was only barley and lentil bread, and every year he would appoint for himself some special rule of life, saying: "this year I will not see anyone," or "I will not speak," or "I will not eat cooked food," or "I will not eat fruits," or "vegetables." So he did in every practice, and when he finished one rule, he would begin another, fulfilling it for the entire year.

20. Saint Epiphanius once sent to Abba Hilarion to ask him to come, saying: "come, let us see each other before our departure from the body." When he came, they rejoiced with one another, and then they sat down to eat, and food was brought. The bishop took a portion for himself and gave another to Abba Hilarion. The elder said: "forgive me, but from the time I received the schema, I have not eaten anything slaughtered." The bishop answered: "and I, from the time I received the schema, have not permitted anyone to fall asleep having anything against me, nor have I myself fallen asleep having anything against anyone." The elder said: "forgive me! Your practice is greater than mine."

21. A brother asked Abba Euprepius: "how should I live?" The elder answered: "eat grass, wear grass, and sleep on grass," that is, despise everything and make your heart hard as iron.

22. Abba Evagrius said that one of the fathers said: "a strict ascetic life joined with love quickly leads the monk into the harbor of dispassion."

23. They told of Abba Helladius that he spent twenty years in the Cells and never once raised his eyes to look at the roof of the church.

24. They said of the same Abba Helladius that he ate only bread and salt. When Pascha came, the abba said: "the brethren are now eating bread and salt, and I, for the sake of Pascha, must take upon myself a small labor: since on all days I eat sitting, today for the sake of Pascha I will eat standing."

25. They told of Abba Zeno that once, passing through Palestine and having grown weary, he sat down to eat near a fig garden. A thought said to him: "take one small fig for yourself and eat it; well, what of it?" He answered the thought: "thieves will go to torment. So test yourself here, can you bear the torment?" Having risen, he stood in the heat for five days and, having roasted himself as if on a frying pan, said to himself: "no, you cannot bear the torment." And then to his thought: "if you cannot, do not steal and do not eat."

26. Abba Isaiah said: "love silence more than speaking, for silence gathers treasure, while speaking scatters it."

27. They said that the same Abba Isaiah, having called one of the brethren, washed his feet, then put a handful of lentils in a pot, and when they began to boil, brought them out. The brother said to him: "father! They are not yet cooked." Abba Isaiah answered: "is it not enough for you that you have seen the fire? This too is a great consolation."

28. Abba Isaiah said: "when someone wishes to repay evil for evil, he can offend a brother's conscience even with a single gesture."

29. They asked Abba Isaiah: "what is slander?" And he answered: "slander is ignorance of the glory of God and hatred toward one's neighbor."

30. They also asked: "what is anger?" The abba answered: "anger is quarreling, lying, and ignorance."

31. Abba Theodore said: "you cannot sleep where there are women."

32. Abba Theodotus said: "scarcity of bread emaciates the body of a monk." But another elder said that vigil emaciates the body more.

33. Abba John Colobos said: "if a king wishes to take an enemy city, he first holds back the water and provisions; then the enemies, perishing from hunger, submit to him. So it is also with the carnal passions: if a man lives in fasting and hunger, these enemies of his soul will themselves become weak."

34. He also related: "once, walking along the Scetis road with my weaving, I met a camel driver who by his words stirred me to anger; then, throwing down the baskets, I fled."

35. Again he said: "who is as strong as the lion? Yet because of his belly he falls into snares, and all his strength is humbled."

36. Again he said: "the fathers of Scetis, eating bread and salt, would say: 'let us not press too hard upon bread and salt.' Therefore they were strong in the work of God."

37. A brother asked Abba Isidore: "why do the demons so greatly fear you?" The elder answered him: "because from the time I became a monk, I have struggled not to allow anger to rise to my throat."

38. Of himself Abba Isidore said that it was already forty years since he felt sinful thoughts, yet he never consented either to lust or to anger.

39. Once Abba Isidore went to visit Abba Theophilus, the Archbishop of Alexandria. When he returned to Scetis, the brethren asked him: "how is the city?" He answered: "believe me, brethren, except for the archbishop alone I did not see the face of a man." Hearing this, the brethren were troubled and asked again: "what then, abba, have they turned into chaos?" He said: "no, not that, but the thought to look at anyone did not overcome me." Hearing this, the brethren marveled and were strengthened in the resolve to guard their eyes from distraction.

40. Abba Isaac related: "I knew a brother who, when he was harvesting in the field and wanted to eat an ear of wheat, asked the owner: 'will you permit me to eat one ear of wheat?' Hearing this, the owner marveled and said: 'the field is yours, father, and you ask me?!' See how careful this brother was."

41. They said of Abba Isaac that he would eat the ash from the censer used during the offering along with his bread.

42. Abba Isaac fell ill with a grievous sickness and lay in it for a long time. A brother prepared a little porridge and put plums in it, but the elder did not want to taste it. The brother asked him to eat a little because of his illness, to which the elder said: "believe me, brother, I would wish to lie in this illness for thirty years."

43. One of the elders came to his friend to visit Abba Joseph together with him, and asked him: "tell your disciple to saddle a donkey for us." He answered: "call him, and he will do what pleases you." And to the question, "what is his name," he said: "I do not know." The elder asked: "how long has he been with you, that you do not know his name?" He answered: "two years." Then the one who had come said: "if in two years you have not learned the name of your disciple, what need have I to learn it for one day?"

44. Once brethren visited Abba Joseph. They were sitting and asking him questions. The elder was glad and with love said to them: "today I am a king, for I have become king over the passions."

45. They told of Abba Isidore the presbyter that once a brother came to call him to a meal, but the elder would not agree to go, saying: "Adam was deceived by food and was driven out of Paradise." The brother said to him: "father, are you even afraid to go out of your cell?" He answered him: "I fear, my son, *for your adversary the devil walks about like a roaring lion, seeking whom he may devour* (1 Peter 5:8)." He also often said: "whoever indulges in wine-drinking will not escape the assault of thoughts. Lot, having been persuaded by his daughters

to drink wine, became drunk, and through drunkenness the devil easily drew him into lawlessness."

46. Abba John the Cilician, hegumen of Raithu, said to the brethren: "my children! As we fled from the world, so let us flee from the desires of the flesh."

47. He also said: "let us imitate our fathers, in what strictness and in what stillness they lived here."

48. He further said: "my children! Let us not defile this place which our fathers cleansed of demons."

49. He also said: "this is a place for ascetics, not for merchants."

50. Abba Cassian related that Abba John, the hegumen of the Great Coenobium, once came to Abba Paisius, who had already been living for forty years in the farther desert and, having great love for him and because of that love, boldness, asked him: "what special thing have you done, living for so long as a hermit, not troubled by anyone?" He answered: "since I withdrew into solitude, the sun has never seen me eating." "And me, angry," said Abba John.

51. He also told us, from the words of Abba Moses, that Abba Serapion related about himself: "when I was young and lived with Abba Theonas, upon rising from table, by the devil's instigation I would steal a dry loaf and eat it secretly from my abba. Since I did this for a considerable time, the habit took hold of me, and I could not overcome myself. My conscience tormented me, but I was ashamed to tell the elder about it. It happened, by the dispensation of the man-loving God, that certain fathers came to the abba for counsel and asked him about their thoughts. The elder spoke to them about self-control, and also about how nothing so harms a monk and gladdens the devil as the concealment of thoughts from spiritual fathers. When I heard this, I thought that God had revealed to the elder about me, and coming to compunction, I began to weep; then I took out from my bosom the loaf which by evil custom I had stolen and, falling to the ground, asked forgiveness for past sins and prayer to restrain me from them in the future. Then the elder said: 'my son! Your confession has already delivered you from this captivity of sin: by revealing your sin, you have slain the demon who was destroying you through your silence and to whom you even until now permitted to possess you without contradicting him or exposing him. From now on he will no longer have a place in you, for having been revealed, you have cast him out of your heart.' Before the elder had finished speaking, a demonic power went out from my bosom like a flame and filled the house with stench, as if a great quantity of sulfur were burning. Then the elder said: 'behold, by the miracle of your deliverance that has taken place before us, the Lord has shown us the truth of my words.'"

52. In the coenobium of our holy father the archimandrite Theodosius there lived an elder named Conon, who for thirty-five years kept this rule: he ate once a week, and only bread and water, working unceasingly, and he hardly left the church.

53. Abba Longinus, having grown faint once, said to himself: "though you die of faintness, if you demand food from me before the time, I will not give you even the daily portion."

54. Abba Longinus said to Abba Acacius: "a woman knows that she has conceived when her blood ceases to flow. So also the soul knows that it has received the Holy Spirit when the streams of passionate thoughts cease within it. As long as the soul is possessed by the passions, how can it boast of its dispassion? Give blood and receive the Spirit."

55. Abba Macarius said: "if for you reproach is like praise, and poverty like abundance, you will not die, for it cannot be that one who believes rightly and struggles in godliness should fall into impurity and demonic delusion."

56. They said of Abba Macarius: "when it happened that he was with the brethren, he set for himself this rule: if there is wine, drink for the brethren's sake, but for one cup of wine, do not drink even water for one day." Therefore, when the brethren gave the elder wine for refreshment, he would accept it with joy, in order afterward to torment himself. His disciple, knowing the matter, said to the brethren: "for the Lord's sake, do not give the abba wine, for he will torment himself in his cell." Learning of this, the brethren no longer offered him wine.

57. Abba Macarius said: "if, while making a reproach to someone, you come to anger, you are feeding your passion; one must not, while saving others, destroy oneself."

58. Grapes were brought to Abba Macarius, and he desired to taste them, but for the sake of self-control he sent them to a brother who was sick and who also desired grapes. He, receiving them, rejoiced greatly, but wishing to conceal his self-control, sent them to another brother, as if having no appetite for food. Receiving them, that one also did the same, although he very much wanted to taste them. Thus the grapes passed through the brethren and no one tasted them. Finally, the brother who received the grapes last brought them as some special gift to Abba Macarius, who, having learned and inquired into everything carefully, marveled and gave thanks to God for such self-control among the brethren.

59. Once Abba Macarius of the city went to cut branches. When on the first day the brethren called him to the table, he went and ate, but when on the next day they called him again, he did not go, saying to them: "you need to eat, children, for you are still flesh, but I do not wish to eat today."

60. Abba Menas related: "once a brother from a foreign land came to me and asked me to escort him to Abba Macarius. When we came to him, the elder offered a prayer for us, and we sat down. The brother said to him: 'father! For thirty years now I have not eaten meat, and I am still attacked by the desire for it.' The elder answered: 'do not say, my son, that for thirty years you have not eaten meat, but tell me in all truth how many days it has been since you did not condemn your brother and no idle word came forth from your lips?' Then the brother, bowing to the elder, said: 'pray for me, father, that I may make a beginning.'"

61. They said of Abba Mark the ascetic that for sixty-three years he had this manner of life: he fasted by the week, so that some considered him bodiless, and working day and night, he gave what he earned to the poor; but he himself never took anything from anyone. Hearing of him, lovers of Christ brought him alms, but the elder said: "I do not accept it, for handiwork feeds both me and those who come to me for God's sake."

62. A brother asked Abba Cepha: "if it happens that I am somewhere and I eat three loaves, is it not too much?" The elder said: "have you come to a threshing floor, brother?" He again asked: "if I drink three cups of wine, is it not too much?" The elder answered: "if there is no demon, it is not too much, but if there is, it is too much; moreover, it is not fitting for monks who live according to God to drink wine."

63. Abba Poemen said: "if Nebuzaradan the Archimandrite had not come, then the temple of the Lord would not have been burned (cf. 2 Kings 25:8–11)." This means: if the indulgence of gluttony had not come into the soul, the mind would not have fallen in battle against the enemy.

64. They told of Abba Poemen that once he was called to a meal when he did not want it; the abba went with weeping, but he went, so as not to disobey his brother and not to grieve him.

65. Some were saying to Abba Poemen about a certain monk that he did not drink wine. The abba said to this: "wine is a thing not at all monastic."

66. He also said: "every bodily ease is an abomination before the Lord."

67. Again he said: "if a man will remember the word of Scripture: *for by your words you will be justified, and by your words you will be condemned* (Matthew 12:37), he will choose silence for himself."

68. An elder related: "a brother asked Abba Pambo whether it is good to praise one's neighbor. He answered him: 'it is better to be silent.'"

69. Abba Poemen said: "as smoke drives away bees, and then one takes from them the sweet fruit of their labors, so bodily ease drives away the fear of God from the soul and destroys all its work."

70. One of the fathers related about Abba Poemen and his brethren: "when they lived in Egypt, their mother wished to see them but could not. Noticing that they were going to church, she met them, but they, seeing her, turned back and shut the door before her face. And she, weeping and wailing, cried before the door: 'let me look upon you, my beloved children!' Abba Anub went in to Abba Poemen and said: 'what shall we do with this weeping old woman?' And he, standing inside and hearing her cries and weeping, asked her: 'why do you cry so, old woman?' Hearing his voice, she began to cry even more loudly and with weeping said: 'I want to see you, children! What does it matter if I see you? I am already gray. Hearing your voice, I have become distraught!' The abba asked her: 'do you wish to see us here or in that world?' She in turn asked him: 'if I do not see you here, will I see you in the

other world?' He answered her: 'having forced yourself not to see us here, you will see us there.' And she went away, saying with joy: 'if indeed I shall see you there, then I do not wish to see you here.'"

71. Abba Joseph related that Abba Poemen said: "here is what word is spoken in the Gospel: *he who has a garment, let him sell it and buy a sword* (Luke 22:36)." That is: he who has ease, let him leave it and hold to the narrow way.

72. A brother asked Abba Poemen: "how should those living in a coenobium live?" The elder answered: "he who lives in a coenobium should look upon all as one, guard his lips, and then, without care, he will find rest."

73. Abba Poemen said: "the king-prophet David, when he wrestled with the lion, seized it by the throat and immediately killed it (1 Samuel 17:35); so also we, if we seize our throat and belly, will, with God's help, easily overcome the invisible lion."

74. He also said: "three things I cannot cut off completely: food, clothing, and sleep, but I can cut them off only in part."

75. A brother said to Abba Poemen: "I eat many vegetables!" The elder said: "this is not beneficial for you; rather, eat your bread and a few vegetables and do not go to your father's house for your needs."

76. Abba Poemen said: "the soul is humbled by nothing unless you diminish its bread."

77. They told of Abba Pambo, Abba Bessarion, Abba Isaiah, Abba Paisius, and Abba Aphre that when they conversed together, the presbyter (of Mount Nitria) proudly asked them: "how should the brethren live?" The elders answered: "in great asceticism and careful guarding of the conscience in relation to one's neighbor."

78. Abba Pior ate while walking. When someone asked him: "why do you eat like this?" The abba answered: "I do not wish to take food as a work, but as a side-matter." To another who asked the same, he said: "this is so that even in taking food my soul would not feel bodily pleasure."

79. They said of Abba Peter of Pionitum, who lived in the Cells, that he did not drink wine. When he grew old, the brethren prepared a little wine mixed with water and entreated him to accept it. But the elder said: "believe me, I consider this a seasoning." And he condemned himself even for such a dilution.

80. They told of Abba Paul that he spent the forty days on a small measure of lentils and a jug of water, and with one basket which he wove and unraveled, being in seclusion until the feast.

81. A brother asked Abba Palladius: "father! Tell me what I should do? For three years now I have been fasting every two days and still I cannot get rid of the demon of fornication." The elder said: "child! When the Lord sent the prophet Isaiah to the Israelites, He said to him: *Cry aloud, spare not; lift up your voice like a trumpet; tell My people their transgression, and the house*

of Jacob their sins. They seek Me daily, and delight to know My ways... Yet they say, "Why have we fasted, and You have not seen? Why have we afflicted our souls, and You take no notice?" And He answered them, saying: *In fact, in the day of your fast you find pleasure, and exploit all your laborers. Indeed you fast for strife and debate, and to strike with the fist of wickedness. You will not fast as you do this day, to make your voice heard on high. Is it a fast that I have chosen, a day for a man to afflict his soul? says the Lord. Is it to bow down his head like a bulrush, and to spread out sackcloth and ashes? Would you call this a fast, and an acceptable day to the Lord?* (Isaiah 58:1–5). But you, child, how do you act while fasting?" The brother answered: "from morning I soak branches and work, concentrating on the psalms; when I finish a basket, I pray; at midday I rest a little; having risen, I go out of the cell; then I work again until I make three baskets; when evening comes, I pray and, having made a hundred prostrations, I lie down; afterward I rise again for the rule; on the next day, at the ninth hour, I prepare a cooked dish and eat to satiety." The elder said: "this, child, is not a fast. For if you abstain from foods, but meanwhile slander anyone, or condemn, or bear grudges, or accept evil thoughts, or in thought desire something impure, then your fast is of no use. It is better for you to eat five times a day and refrain from such thoughts than, eating nothing, to be filled with them. What profit is it to abstain from foods and to satiate every other desire? Or do you not know that everyone who fulfills his desire in thought, even without outward foods, is already full and drunk? But if you wish to abstain and fast in such a way that your fast may be pleasing to God, then above all, while fasting, guard yourself from every evil word, from all slander and condemnation, and from hearing anything bad; cleanse your heart from every defilement of flesh and spirit, from every grudge and shameful gain; on the day on which you fast, content yourself with bread, water, and vegetables, giving thanks to God. Also, having calculated how much you would have spent on a full meal if you had one that day, give that amount to a poor brother, or a stranger, or a widow, or an orphan, so that they, receiving it and consoling their souls, may pray for you to the Lord; weary your body with many prostrations and vigils, and hidden meditation; sleep sitting; leave the weaving of soft baskets and take up rough mats, for if youth does not discipline itself with labor and sweat, fasting and vigil, lying on the ground and dry eating, it cannot guard itself from the demon of fornication. Therefore our fathers did not establish that young men should sit in cells or in places of stillness, but set them to live in coenobia, to wear clothing not soft but rough and coarse, and to be held by superiors in all strictness, for idleness and ease, eating twice a day and sleep, are wont to bring upon us not only the demon of fornication, but also of despondency, vainglory, and pride."

82. A brother asked Abba Sisoes: "what should I do? I go to church, but there is often an agape there, and they detain me." The elder answered him: "this is a difficult matter." Abraham, his disciple, asked at this: "if the assembly happens on Saturday or Sunday and a brother drinks three cups of wine, is it not too much?" The elder said: "if there is no Satan, it is not too much."

83. The disciple of Abba Sisoes often said: "abba, get up, let us eat." The elder would ask him: "did we not eat yet, child?" He would answer: "no, father!" And the elder would say: "if we have not eaten, bring it, let us eat."

84. Once Abba Sisoes said with boldness: "believe me, for thirty years now I have not prayed to God about sin, but I pray thus: 'Lord Jesus! Cover me from my tongue.' But even to this day, every day I fall by it and sin."

85. An offering was brought to the mountain of Abba Anthony. Among other things there was also a small cask of wine. One of the elders, having drawn off wine into a small vessel, filled a cup and gave it to Abba Sisoes. He drank it. He gave him a second, and he accepted it too. But when he gave him a third, the abba did not accept it, saying: "stop, brother, or do you not know that there is Satan?"

86. A brother asked Abba Sisoes of Petra about the manner of life, and the elder answered him: "Daniel said: *I ate no pleasant bread* (Daniel 10:3)."

87. A brother asked Abba Sisoes: "if during a journey our guide loses the way, is it necessary to tell him?" The elder said: "no." The brother again asked: "so we should let him lead us here and there?" The elder said: "what then? Should we take a stick and beat him? I know brethren who were traveling and their guide lost the road at night. There were twelve of them, and all knew that they had lost the way, but each struggled not to speak about it. When morning came, the guide realized that they had wandered from the road and said to them: 'forgive me, I lost the way.' They answered: 'we also knew, but we kept silent.' Hearing this, he said with amazement: 'even unto death the brethren refrain from speaking,' and he glorified God. The length of the road on which they wandered was twelve miles."

88. They said of Abba Sisoes of Thebes: "when he was staying in Calamon of Arsinoë, an elder in another lavra fell ill. Hearing of this, he was grieved, for he fasted every two days and that was a day on which he did not eat. Then he said to his thought: 'what then shall I do? If I go, the brethren may force me to eat; but if I wait until tomorrow, the elder may die. But I will do thus: I will go and not eat.' And he went, fasting, and fulfilled the commandment of God without breaking the rule of his life which he kept for God's sake."

89. One of the elders related about Abba Sisoes of Calamon that once, wishing to overcome sleep, he suspended himself over the cliff of the mountain of Petra. But an Angel came and released him, commanding him to do this no more and not to transmit such a practice to others.

90. They said of Abba Sisoes of Thebes that he did not eat bread. On the feast of Pascha the brethren, having made a prostration, asked him to eat with them. The abba said to them: "I will do one thing or the other: either I will eat bread, or the other foods you have prepared." The brethren answered him: "eat only bread." And he did so.

91. Once Abba Silvanus and his disciple Zacharias came to a monastery, and they were persuaded to eat a little food for the road. When they were returning, the disciple saw water along the way and wanted to drink, but the elder said to him: "Zacharias! Today is a fast." He asked: "but did we not eat, father?" The elder answered: "what we ate was a matter of love; but now we must keep our fast, child."

92. They said of Abba Serenus that he worked much but ate always only two dry loaves. Abba Job, of one mind with him and himself a great ascetic, once came to him and said: "in my cell I keep my practice, but when I go out, I condescend to the brethren." Abba Serenus answered: "it is no great virtue if you keep your practice in your cell, but rather when you go out of it."

93. Once brethren from Scetis came to Mother Sarah, and she set before them a basket of fruit. Eating, the brethren left the good fruit and picked out the spoiled ones. Then she said to them: "truly, you are Scetians (ascetics)."

94. Mother Syncletica said: "we who have taken upon ourselves this vow must keep chastity most perfectly. For among laypeople there is also an apparent chastity, but with it there is always also unchastity, because they sin with all their other senses: both when they look immodestly and laugh indecently."

95. She also said: "as poisonous animals are driven away by the sharpest of poisons, so also evil thoughts are driven away by fasting with prayer."

96. Again she said: "let not the luxurious table of wealthy worldly people deceive you, as if it has some advantage in its vain sweetness. They employ the art of cooks, but through fasting and simple food you make your fare more pleasant than their rich table. As it is also said: *the soul that is full loathes the honeycomb* (Proverbs 27:7). Do not fill yourself with bread and you will not desire wine."

97. Abba Tithoes said: "pilgrimage consists in this, that a man has power to restrain his lips."

98. A brother asked Abba Tithoes: "how can I guard my heart?" The elder said: "how can we guard our heart when our tongue and belly are open?"

99. Abba Hyperechius said: "as the lion is terrible to wild donkeys, so is the experienced monk to lustful thoughts."

100. He also said: "fasting for a monk is a bridle against sin. He who abandons fasting is an unbridled horse."

101. He further said: "he who does not restrain his tongue in time of anger will not restrain his passions either."

102. Again he said: "it is good to eat meat and drink wine and not to devour the flesh of brethren with slander."

103. He also said: "the serpent, having whispered to Eve, cast her out of Paradise. Similar to this is also he who slanders his neighbor, for he destroys the soul of the one who hears and does not save his own."

104. The same elder said: "the body of a monk dried by fasting draws his soul out of the deep as with a rope; the fasting of a monk dries up the channels of lusts."

105. He further said: "the chaste monk will be honored on earth and in heaven will be crowned before the Most High."

106. Again he said: "let your lips utter no evil word, for the vine does not bring forth thorns."

107. There was a certain man named Philoromus, a very skilled monk. Having renounced the world in the days of the ill-named Emperor Julian, he spoke to him with boldness, rebuking him and exposing his madness. Julian subjected him to cruel torments, but he endured all with thanksgiving. Upon this valiant fighter the demon brought the warfare of fornication and gluttony, but he alertly entered into combat with him: he put chains on himself, shut himself in seclusion, abstained from various foods, even from wheat bread, and generally from anything cooked with fire. For eighteen years he remained in this ascetic struggle of self-control and conquered the devil. This blessed one related: "for thirty-two years I have not touched any fruit. Once a strong fearfulness attacked me, so that I was afraid of everything, even while working. Then I enclosed myself in a tomb for six years and was delivered from it, having overcome this temptation and conquered the spirit that brought fearfulness upon me."

108. Two brethren lived near each other. One of them would accept everything that came his way, whether money or bread, and secretly place it among the belongings of his neighbor. The latter, not knowing this, marveled at the increase of his possessions, but once he unexpectedly caught his neighbor in this act and said to him with displeasure: "with your fleshly goods you have robbed my spiritual," and he did not forgive him except by extracting from him a promise never to do this again.

109. In the Cells they spoke of a certain elder who lived in seclusion and did not go out even to the church. Once, his brother according to the flesh, who was sitting in another cell, fell ill and sent for him, so as to see him before his departure. But the elder said: "I cannot come, for he is my brother according to the flesh." The other again sent to him with this word: "come at least by night, so that I may see you." But the elder again said: "I cannot, otherwise my heart will not be pure before God." Thus the brother died, and they did not see each other.

110. One of the bishops would go every year to Scetis to the fathers. A certain brother, having met him, invited him to his cell and, having set before him bread and salt, said: "forgive me, master, that I have nothing else to set before you." The bishop answered him: "I wish that, coming next summer, I may not find even salt."

111. A certain brother related that once in a lavra in Egypt they were examining some matter, and all were speaking, both senior and junior; only one kept silent. When all had gone out, one of the brethren asked him: "why did you say nothing?" Compelled by the brother, he answered: "forgive me; I said to my thought: 'if the specter above me does not speak, then you should not speak either.' Therefore I remained silent and said nothing."

112. Once on the feast of Pascha the brethren dined together at the church of the Cells, and giving a cup of wine to one brother, they compelled him to drink. But the brother said to them: "forgive me, fathers; last year you compelled me to drink wine, and afterward I grieved for a long time."

113. Once, a certain elder was setting out for Scetis; another brother was walking with him. When it was time for them to part from each other, the elder said to him: "let us eat together, brother." They ate; it was then morning at the beginning of the week. On Saturday the elder, having completed the morning prayers, came to that brother and asked him: "have you hungered, brother, since we ate together?" He answered: "no, for eating food every day, I do not hunger." The elder said to him: "and I, believe me, my son, have not yet eaten since then." Hearing this, the brother came to compunction and benefited greatly by it.

114. An elder said: "for twenty years I wrestled with a thought that hindered me from learning to see all people as one."

115. Once in Scetis there was a feast. A cup of wine was given to one elder, but he returned it, saying: "take this death away from me." Seeing this, the others who were eating with him also did not accept wine.

116. A certain brother hungered from morning but struggled with his thought so as not to eat at least until the third hour. When the third hour came, he compelled himself not to eat until the sixth. Then, having soaked bread, he sat down to eat, but again rose and said to his thought: "let us endure until the ninth hour." When the ninth hour came, he said a prayer and saw that the demonic temptation was rising like smoke toward heaven from his handiwork, and with that his hunger also ceased.

117. A certain disciple related about his abba that for all twenty years he did not sleep on his side, but slept sitting on his stool on which he also worked; he ate after two days, or after four, or after five, and when this elder ate, one of his hands was extended in prayer. When I asked him: "why do you do this, abba?" He answered: "I place the judgment of God before my eyes and cannot endure otherwise." Once it happened that when we began the rule, I became distracted and lost my place in the words of the psalm. After its completion, the elder said to me: "when I begin the rule, I think that a fire is kindled beneath me, and from this my thought cannot turn aside either to the right or to the left. Where was your thought when we began the rule, that a word of the psalm escaped you? Or do you not know that you were standing before the face of God and conversing with God?"

118. Once at night the elder went out and found me sleeping in the courtyard of the cell. Standing over me, he wept and through tears said: "where is his thought, that he sleeps with such carelessness?"

119. Once in the Cells the firstfruits of wine were brought, to give the brethren a cup each. A certain brother, wishing to flee, went out onto the terrace, then onto the vault, and the vault fell. Those who gathered at the noise began to reproach the brother who had fallen, saying: "it serves you right, you vain one!" But the abba defended him and said: "leave my

son alone; he did a good thing. The man is alive, and this vault will not be repaired for all the time of my life, so that the world may know that in the Cells a vault fell because of one cup of wine."

120. A certain elder came to visit another. The latter said to his disciple: "prepare a little lentils for us," and he prepared them. "Soak some bread for us," and he soaked it, but the elders until the sixth hour of the next day were conversing about spiritual matters, forgetting about food. The elder again said to his disciple: "child, prepare us a little lentils." He answered him: "father, I prepared them yesterday." Then they partook.

121. They also told of an elder who came to one of the fathers. The latter cooked a little lentils and said to the brother: "let us do a small rule." And the one completed the entire Psalter, while the brother recited by heart two of the major prophets. When morning came, the elder who had come went home, not having remembered about food.

122. Once a certain elder fell ill, and since he had not taken any food for many days, the disciple of the elder entreated him to allow him to prepare a little good food for him. Where the disciple was preparing, there were two vessels: one with a small amount of honey, the other with linseed oil which had spoiled and was fit only for the lamp. The brother made a mistake and instead of honey put this oil in the elder's food. The elder tasted it, said nothing, and continued to eat in silence. The disciple compelled him to eat a second bowl; the elder forced himself and ate the second as well. He brought him a third, but the elder did not want to accept it, saying: "I can take no more, my son." The disciple, to encourage him better, said: "it is good, abba! See, I too will eat with you." But having tasted that food and understood his mistake, he fell on his face, saying: "woe is me, abba! I have killed you! And you have left the sin upon me, for you revealed nothing." But the elder said to him: "do not grieve, my son! If God had wanted me to taste honey, then you would have put honey for me."

123. They told of a certain elder that, having once desired a fig, he took it and hung it before his eyes; and though he was not overcome by the desire, he tormented himself, repenting that he had desired it.

124. A certain brother came to a women's monastery to visit his sister when she had fallen ill. His sister was very devout and did not wish to see the face of a man, nor did she wish that her brother should enter among the women because of her. Therefore she sent word to him: "go, brother, pray for me; and by the grace of Christ I shall see you in the Kingdom of Heaven."

125. A certain monk, having met nuns on the road, turned aside from his path. The abbess said to him at this: "if you were a perfect monk, you would not look upon us as women."

126. A brother brought fresh loaves to his cell and called the elders to a meal. Having each tasted two small loaves, they stopped eating. The brother, knowing the labor of their asceticism, bowed to them and said: "for the Lord's sake, eat today until you are satisfied."

And they ate another ten small loaves each. See how much more than necessary the true ascetics ate.

127. A certain elder suffered from a grievous illness: blood flowed profusely from his bowels. A certain brother had dried plums; having prepared porridge and put them in the bottom, the brother brought it to the elder so that he might taste, and asked: "do me the kindness of tasting this; perhaps it will be beneficial for you." The elder looked at him attentively for a long time, and then said: "truly, I would wish that God would leave me in this illness for another thirty years." And the elder would not agree, even in such an illness, to taste even a little porridge. The brother took it and went away to his cell.

128. Another elder lived far away in the desert. A certain brother came to him and, finding him in illness, washed him, prepared a cooked dish from what he had brought, and offered it to the elder to taste. The elder said to him at this: "truly, brother, I had already forgotten that people have such consolation." Then the brother gave him a cup of wine. Seeing the wine, the elder wept and said: "I had not hoped even to death to drink wine."

129. A certain elder took upon himself the struggle of drinking nothing at all for forty days, and if there happened to be great heat, he would rinse out a small jug, fill it with water, and hang it before him. When a certain brother asked him why he did this, the elder answered: "so that by thirst I might weary myself more and receive a greater reward from God."

130. A certain brother was on a journey together with his mother, who was already an old woman. When they came to a river which the old woman could not cross, the son, taking his mantle and wrapping it around his hands so as not to touch his mother's body, lifted her and carried her to the other side. Afterward the mother asked him why he had wrapped his hands, and the son answered: "because the body of a woman is fire; and from this touch comes the memory of other women. This is why I did so."

131. One of the fathers related: "I knew a brother in the Cells who did not break his fast even in the week of Pascha; therefore, when the church assembly ended in the evening, he would flee so as not to eat in the church, and having prepared a little boiled beet, would eat it without bread."

132. Once the fathers came to Alexandria, having been invited by the blessed Archbishop Theophilus to pray and help him destroy the idols. When they were eating with him, meat was also served, and the elders ate, asking no questions. The Archbishop, choosing one piece and offering it to the elder sitting near him, said: "this piece is good; taste it, abba." To this the elders answered: "until now we ate everything as vegetables; but if this is meat, we do not eat it."

133. A certain brother said that he knew an elder who lived on a high mountain and accepted nothing from anyone. Having a little water, he grew his own vegetables and for fifty years kept the rule of never going outside the enclosure. The elder became famous for many healings which he performed over those who came to him daily, and he reposed in peace, leaving five disciples in that place.

134. With a certain great elder lived a very negligent brother, who, seeing that the elder ate once a week, said to him: "abba! Some say that great asceticism leads one to pride." The elder answered to this: "what then, my son, if through negligence comes humility, should we not go and take wives and begin eating meat and drinking wine? Woe to us, my son, how we are mocked and do not see it! Do we not hear what David says: *Consider my affliction and my trouble, and forgive all my sins* (Psalm 25:18). He who has sinned before God must withdraw from all love of men until he is assured that God has become his friend, for the love of men often distances us from the love of God."

135. An elder said: "if you come to someone and after prayer he invites you to sit, ask him: 'father! Tell me a word of life, how do we find God, and pray for me, for I have a multitude of sins.' And only that, say no other word unless you are asked."

136. Again he said: "accustom your eyes not to look upon another's body; if possible, not even upon your own."

137. He further said: "if your soul battles you for various foods, constrain it even in bread, so that it may ask to be satisfied at least with that."

138. Again he said: "if you are still young, flee from wine as from a serpent. Though you drink a cup of love, drink a little and leave it; let those who invited you entreat you and let them swear, but do not heed their oaths. Satan often prompts monks to compel the younger ones to drink wine, for he knows that wine and women distance us from God."

139. An elder said: "it is written of Solomon that he was a lover of women, and the male sex naturally loves the female. But we compel our thoughts to purity and we compel our nature, so as not to fall into such lust."

140. We heard about a certain brother, poor and needy, the following: if someone brought him needed food, he would not accept it if it happened that another had brought something first, and he would say thus: "the Lord my Lord has already fed me, and it is enough for me."

141. The disciple of a certain great elder related about his abba that once at the ninth hour he hungered and wanted to eat. Having set the table, they stood for prayer and sang through two psalms, then the elder began to recite psalms from memory; evening came, morning came, the ninth hour of the next day came, and only then did the elder cease, for his mind was contemplating the mystery on high.

142. An elder said: "overcome the demon of gluttony by saying to him: 'be patient, you will not be hungry.' Eat food as simply as possible, and however much the demon may incite you, eat without haste, for he torments many so that they want to devour everything at once."

143. An elder said: "I knew elders who lived in this desert for seventy years, eating only herbs and dates."

144. An elder said: "nothing so draws a monk near to God as good, honest, and God-pleasing purity, which presents *the body in seemliness and quietness before the Lord* (cf. 1 Corinthians 7:35), as the Holy Spirit testified of it through His luminary Paul."

145. An elder said: "gluttony is the mother of fornication."

146. He further said: "he who bridles the belly can also bridle the tongue."

147. Once the brethren were called together to clean wicker. Among them was one who was sick from asceticism, who, while coughing, was bringing up phlegm, part of which, without his intention, fell upon one of the brethren. A thought began to torment that brother and compel him to say that he should not spit. But the brother immediately bridled his thought and wanted to take it and eat what had been brought up, but then said to himself: "do not eat it, but also do not say anything."

148. An elder said: "self-control is the wealth of the soul. Let us acquire it with humble-mindedness, fleeing vainglory, the mother of evils."

149. Again he said: "fasting is better than sparse eating."

150. He further said: "let us take delight in the Divine words and celebrate in the narratives of the holy fathers, not pleasuring the belly but spiritually rejoicing."

151. They spoke of a certain great elder who lived in the lavra of Abba Peter, that for fifty years he remained sitting in his cave; he drank no wine, nor did he eat clean bread, only bran bread; and he communed three times a week.

152. The fathers told that a certain chaste man was taken to be tortured, and they prepared for him the most grievous torment, determining to violate his chastity, such was their malice! In a certain beautiful garden they set up a bed and bound the saint to it, leaving with him a dissolute woman, so that both by the pleasantness of the place and by the fact that he could not escape the advances of the shameless woman, he was from all sides aroused, unwilling and against his will, to lawless action. But this faithful fighter, feeling the arousal of lust, bit off his tongue and spat it at his violator, thus causing himself terrible pain and torment, but frightening her by drenching her with a stream of blood. Thus the saint achieved victory in the Lord.

153. A certain hermit lived in the innermost desert for thirty years, having for sustenance only a small portion of food. And behold, he began to say to himself: "I am perishing here for nothing, all this time. For so many years I eat nothing else besides this small portion, and I have neither seen a revelation nor performed a sign, such as the monks before me performed; therefore, I shall leave this place and go into the world." Scarcely had he thought this when an Angel of the Lord stood before him and asked: "what were you thinking about?" And he told of his thought. Then the Angel said: "what sign do you wish greater than this? Who gave you the strength to endure for so many years in this place, nourishing yourself on only a small portion? Endure then and ask God to grant you humility." Strengthened by the

Angel and no longer seeking anything else, he remained in that place for all the rest of the time of his life.

154. An elder said: "it is not profitable for a monk to ask: 'how is such-a-one,' or 'how is someone else,' for, distracted from prayer by such a question, he falls into idle talk and condemnation. And there is nothing better than silence."

155. Certain fathers related: "there was here a certain elder, by origin a Pontic, named Peter, who performed many great deeds." About this elder, the brother Theodore, who was later made bishop of Rossa, told us the following: "once he came to me at the holy Jordan in the lavra of Pyrgi, where I lived at that time, and said: 'do me the favor, brother Theodore, go with me to Mount Sinai, for I wish to pray there.' Unable to disobey the elder, I agreed. When we had crossed the Jordan, the elder proposed to me: 'brother Theodore! Let us lay upon ourselves a vow to eat nothing until the holy Mount Sinai.' I answered him: 'truly, father, I cannot do this.' Then the elder alone laid upon himself such a vow and until Sinai itself took nothing into his mouth. There, having communed of the Holy Mysteries, he took food. From Sinai we went to Saint Menas in Alexandria; the elder again ate nothing and only in Alexandria, also after communing of the Holy Mysteries, did he partake of food. From Saint Menas we went back to the Holy City, and again he ate nothing. There, having communed in the Church of the Resurrection of Christ our God, he took food. Thus, on all such a long and difficult journey, the elder ate only once on Mount Sinai, once at Saint Menas, and once in the Holy City."

Endnotes

[10] Archimandrite, chief of the cooks.

Chapter V.
Various Narratives for Strengthening Against the Carnal Warfare That Rises Against Us. On Fornication — That One Must Guard Oneself Against It With All Diligence and Fear

1. Abba Carien said: "A man who dwells with a youth, if he is not strong, goes downward; if he is strong and does not go downward, he does not make progress."

2. Abba Anthony said: "I think that there is a natural movement in the body, inborn to it, but it does not act without the desire of the soul and signifies only a passionate movement. There is also another movement arising from the nourishment and heating of the body by food and drink, by which the heated blood arouses the flesh to action. Therefore the Apostle also says: *Do not be drunk with wine, in which is dissipation* (Ephesians 5:18), and likewise the Lord in the Gospel commanded His disciples: *Take heed to yourselves, lest your hearts be weighed down with carousing and drunkenness* (Luke 21:34). But in those who are struggling there is yet another movement arising from the assault and envy of demons. Thus one must know that there are three kinds of bodily movements: one is natural, another is from undiscerning use of food, and the third is from demons."

3. A brother asked Abba Agathon about fornication, and the elder said to him: "Go, cast your weakness before God, and you will find rest."

4. Abba Gerontius of Petra said: "Many, while being tempted by carnal lusts and not committing sin bodily, fell into fornication mentally, and thus, preserving the virginity of the body, became fornicators in soul. Therefore, beloved, it is good to fulfill the word of Scripture: *Keep your heart with all diligence* (Proverbs 4:23)."

5. A brother asked Abba Daniel: "Give me an instruction, and I will keep it." The abba said: "Never stretch out your hand into the same dish with a woman, and do not eat with her. By this you will escape somewhat from the demon of fornication."

6. Abba Eustonius related concerning Abba Paphnutius, the father of Scetis: "I came there while still young, and the abba did not permit me to remain, saying: 'In my presence in Scetis I will not allow a woman's face to be present, for fear of the warfare of the enemy.'"

7. Abba John Colobos said: "Whoever, having eaten to satiety, speaks with a youth has already committed adultery with him in his thought."

8. Abba Cassian related: "Abba Moses said to us: 'It is good not to conceal thoughts, but to reveal them to spiritual elders, though indeed to discerning ones, and not merely to those grown gray from time. For many, looking to age and revealing their thoughts, instead of healing have fallen into despair through the inexperience of the one who heard them.' Thus a certain brother, one of the very zealous ones, being strongly warred upon by the demon of fornication, came to a certain elder and revealed his thoughts to him. Hearing him, this elder, being inexperienced, grew indignant at the poor man and even called him unworthy of the monastic schema because he received such thoughts. Hearing this, the brother in despair left his cell and went into the world. By God's providence Abba Apollos met him and, seeing that he was exceedingly sorrowful and gloomy, asked him the reason for such gloominess. At first, from faintheartedness, the brother answered him nothing, but afterward, being persuaded by the abba, he told him everything that had happened to him: 'Thoughts of fornication torment me, and I revealed them to the elder; according to his words there is no hope of salvation for me, therefore in despair I am going into the world.' Hearing this, Abba Apollos, like a wise physician, comforted and exhorted him in various ways, saying: 'Do not depart from your place, my son, and do not despair; for I too, at my age and with such gray hairs, am exceedingly tormented by similar thoughts. Do not be fainthearted from this burning, for it is healed not so much by human effort as by the mercy of God. But for this day, listen to me and return to your cell.' The brother did so. And Abba Apollos directed his way to the cell of the elder who had deprived the brother of consolation, and standing outside, he prayed to God with tears, saying: 'O Lord, Who brings temptations for our profit, turn the warfare of the brother upon this elder, that he may learn in his old age, through experience at least, to have compassion on those who are being warred upon, which he did not learn in so long a time.' As soon as he finished his prayer, he saw an Ethiopian who, standing near the cell, was shooting arrows at the elder. Wounded by them, the elder immediately, as if drunken, began to rush to and fro and, unable to endure it, went out of the cell and set off into the world by the same road by which the younger man had gone. Abba Apollos understood what had happened to him, overtook him, and approaching, asked: 'Where are you going in such haste? And what is the cause of the disturbance that overwhelms you?' Sensing that the saint had been given to know what had happened, he from shame said nothing. Then Abba Apollos said to him: 'Return to your cell, henceforth acknowledging your weakness, and consider yourself either as unrecognized by the devil or as despised by him, which is why you were not deemed worthy, like the zealous, to war against him; and what am I saying — to war, when you could not bear even one assault to the end of the day! This happened to you because, having received a younger brother who was being warred upon by the common enemy, instead of inspiring him to struggle, you cast him into despair, not remembering that wise precept which says: *Deliver those who are drawn toward death, and hold back those stumbling to the slaughter* (Proverbs 24:11), nor the parable of our Savior: *A bruised reed He will not break, and smoking flax He will not quench* (Matthew 12:20). For no one would be able either to bear the

assaults of the enemy or to quench the fiery boiling of nature, if the grace of God did not protect human weakness. Therefore, acknowledging in what has happened to us the saving providence concerning us, let us with common prayers beseech God to remove the scourge raised against you: *For He wounds, and then He raises up... He strikes, and His hands heal... He humbles and exalts, He kills and makes alive, He brings down to Hades and brings up* (cf. 1 Kingdoms 2:6-7).' Having said this, Abba Apollos prayed and, having freed the elder from the warfare brought upon him, commanded him to ask God that he be granted a tongue of instruction, that he might know the time when he should speak one word or another."

9. Abba Cyrus of Alexandria, when asked about the thought of fornication, answered thus: "If you do not have thoughts, you have the deed; and this means: he who does not struggle against sin in thought and does not contradict it surely commits it bodily, for he who has the deeds is not troubled by thoughts." At this the elder asked the brother whether he had the habit of conversing with women. And the brother answered: "No. My thoughts are ancient and new painters — memories trouble me and images of women." Then the elder said to him: "Do not fear the dead, but flee from the living, and continue longer in prayer."

10. Someone related about a certain brother who had fallen into sin, that when he came to Abba Lot, he was in such distress that he constantly entered and went out, being unable to sit still. Abba Lot asked him: "What ails you, brother?" And he answered: "I committed a great sin and cannot tell the fathers about it." The elder said: "Confess it to me, and I will bear it." Then the brother revealed to him: "I fell into fornication and desperately strove to accomplish it." The elder said: "Take courage, for there is repentance. Go, sit in a cave and fast two days at a time, and I will bear half of the sin with you." After three weeks had passed, the elder received assurance that God had accepted the brother's repentance; and the brother remained in obedience to the elder until his very death.

11. Abba Matoes said: "A brother came to me and said that slander is worse than fornication. I remarked to him: 'This is a harsh word.' Then he asked me: 'How do you think about this matter?' I answered: 'Slander is bad, but it has a quick remedy, for often the slanderer repents, saying: "I spoke badly"; but fornication is a natural death.'"

12. Abba Olympius of the Cells was being warred upon for fornication, and the thought said to him: "Go, take a wife." He arose, prepared some clay, and making a woman from it, said to himself: "Behold your wife! Now you must work more so that there will be something to feed her," and he worked until he was exhausted. The next day he again prepared clay and made a daughter from it, saying to his thought: "Your wife has given birth; now you must work even more so that there will be something to feed and clothe your child." Doing thus, he exhausted himself to the extreme and said to his thought: "I no longer have the strength to bear such labor." And he added: "If you have no strength to bear this labor, then do not seek a wife either." God, seeing his labor, took the warfare from him, and he found rest.

13. Abba Poemen said: "Just as the armor-bearer of a king always stands ready before the king, so also the soul must always be ready against the demon of fornication."

14. Abba Anuph asked Abba Poemen about impure thoughts which the heart of man begets, and about vain desires. Abba Poemen answered him: *"Shall the axe boast itself against him who chops with it?"* (Isaiah 10:15). "And you — do not give them a hand, and they will remain inactive."

15. A brother came to Abba Poemen and asked him: "What shall I do, father? A thought of fornication torments me. I went to Abba Ivastion, and he said to me: 'Do not allow it to linger in you.'" Abba Poemen answered: "The deeds of Abba Ivastion are above with the Angels, and he forgets that I and you are in fornication. If a monk will restrain his belly and his tongue and will live as a stranger, believe me, he will not die."

16. A brother asked Abba Poemen: "What shall I do? Fornication and anger war against me." The elder answered him: "This is why David said: *'The lion I struck down, and the bear I strangled'* (cf. 1 Kingdoms 17:35). This means: anger I cut off, and fornication I crushed by labors."

17. Abba Poemen said: "As for fornication and slander, a man must absolutely neither utter these two thoughts with his word nor ponder them in his heart. If anyone will utterly condemn them and argue in his heart, he will receive no benefit, but he who angrily turns away from them will have rest."

18. They asked Abba Poemen about defilements, and he answered: "If we order our conduct well and watchfully keep sober, defilement will never happen to us."

19. He also said: "A man who has a youth dwelling with him, being assaulted by some passion of the old man toward him and still keeping him with himself, is like one who has a field being devoured by worms."

20. Someone asked Abba Poemen about fornication, and the elder said: "Great is the help of God that surrounds a man, but we are not permitted to see it with our own eyes."

21. In Scetis there lived a certain brother with Abba Paphnutius who, being warred upon by the warfare of fornication, said: "If I take even ten wives, I will not satisfy my desire." The elder admonished him paternally, saying: "Do not do so, my son, this warfare is from demons." But he did not listen to him, went to Egypt, and took a wife. In time it happened that the elder came to Egypt and met his disciple, who was carrying a basket of potsherds. The elder did not recognize him, but he said: "I am your disciple." Seeing him in such dishonor, the abba wept and asked him: "How did you leave your former honor and come to such dishonor? However, did you take ten wives?" The brother sighed and said: "No, I took only one, and behold, I toil to fill her with bread." The elder called him back, and the brother asked: "But is there repentance, abba?" He answered: "There is." Then the brother, leaving everything, followed him and, entering Scetis, through this trial became a good monk.

22. They related about Mother Sarah that for thirty years she was strongly warred upon by the demon of fornication, but she never prayed that the warfare depart from her, but only said: "O God, grant me strength!"

23. Once this spirit of fornication pressed upon her more strongly, suggesting worldly vanities to her. Not yielding to him, in the fear of God and in ascetic struggle, she once went up to her upper room to pray, and the spirit of fornication appeared to her bodily and said: "You have conquered me, Sarah!" But she answered: "I have not conquered you, but my Master, Christ."

24. Abba Phocas related about Abba Jacob: "When he came over to Scetis, he was strongly warred upon by the demon of fornication. Being close to danger, he came to me and, revealing his condition, said: 'On Monday I will go to such-and-such a cave. I beg you, for the Lord's sake, reveal this to no one, not even to my father, but after forty days have passed, do me the kindness of coming to me and bringing Holy Communion. If you find me dead, bury me, but if alive, give me Communion.' I promised, and after forty days had passed, taking the Holy Communion and some common pure bread with a small quantity of wine, I went to him. Approaching the cave, I smelled a strong stench coming from his body, and I thought that the blessed one had reposed, but entering to him, I found him half-dead. Seeing me, he made as much movement as he could with his right hand and by its gesture reminded me of Holy Communion. I said: 'I have it.' I wanted to open his mouth, but it was firmly clenched. Not knowing what to do, I went out into the wilderness and, tearing a small branch from a bush, was barely able with it and with great difficulty to open his mouth somewhat and give him Communion of the Precious Body and Blood, having broken them into the smallest possible particles. From receiving Holy Communion he received strength. A little later, having moistened some crumbs of ordinary bread, I gave them to him, then more, offering him as much as he could receive. And thus, by the grace of God, within a day he came with me on foot to his cell, having been freed by God's help from the ruinous passion of fornication."

25. A certain elder had a disciple who was warred upon by the demon of fornication. The elder exhorted and entreated him: "Be patient, my son! This warfare is from the enemy." But he said to him: "I can no longer endure, abba, so as not to do the deed." Then the elder, pretending, said to him: "I too am warred upon, my son. Let us go together, do the deed, and return to our cell." The elder had one coin, and he took it with him. When they came to the place, the elder, entering first, gave the coin to the harlot and asked her not to defile the brother. She gave her word to preserve his purity. When he entered, the harlot said to him: "Wait, brother! Although I am a sinner, we have a law, and it must first be fulfilled." Then she told him to stand aside and make fifty prostrations, and she herself stood aside. Having made twenty or thirty prostrations, the brother came to compunction and said to himself: "How can I pray to God, intending to commit such a crime?" He immediately went out, undefiled. God, seeing the elder's labor, took the warfare from his brother; and they returned, glorifying God.

26. A certain brother was sent by his abba for water. Coming to the spring, he met there a woman washing clothes and, being aroused, began to incline her to a fall. But she said to him: "It is easy to listen to you, but I will become for you the cause of great sorrow, for after doing this, your conscience will wound you, and you will either despair or much labor will be

needed for you to return to the rank you now have. Therefore, before you receive a wound, go in peace on your way." Hearing this, the brother was moved to compunction and thanked God and her reasonableness. Returning, he revealed what had happened to the abba, and he marveled at that woman. After this, the brother asked the elder that he never again go out of the monastery. The elder decreed that it be so, and the brother remained in the monastery, not leaving it until his very death.

27. A certain brother went to the river to draw water. There he met a woman who was washing linens and fell with her. Having committed the sin, the brother drew water and set off for his cell. Along the way, demons fell upon him in his thoughts and crushed him, saying: "Where are you going now? There is no salvation for you. Why even cause the world loss?" The brother understood that they wanted to destroy him and answered the thoughts: "From where have you come and are crushing me to bring me to despair? I have not sinned!" And coming to his cell, he continued to keep stillness as before and earlier. The Lord revealed to a certain elder, his neighbor, that this brother had fallen and had conquered. Coming to him, the elder asked: "How do you have yourself?" The brother answered: "Well, abba." The elder asked again: "Did you not suffer anything these days?" He answered: "Not at all." At this the elder said: "God revealed to me that you, having fallen, conquered." Then the brother related everything that had happened to him, and the elder concluded: "Truly, brother, your reasoning crushed the power of the enemy."

28. Someone related that a certain brother who lived in a coenobium was often sent on its business and needs. In a certain village there lived a devout layman who received him with faith every time he came. This layman had a daughter who had recently become widowed, having lived with her husband only two years. The brother was attracted to her, but she, being sensible, was very cautious and tried not to be seen by him. Once, coming as usual, the brother found her alone, for her father had gone away to a nearby city. From this circumstance the warfare rose strongly upon him. Noticing this, she said to him with discernment: "Do not hurry; we are alone here. I know that you monks do nothing without prayer. Therefore, arise and pray to God, and whatever He puts in your heart, that we will do." But being strongly agitated by the warfare, he did not want to do so. Then, knowing that the brother had never known a woman, and wishing to sober him, she said to him: "This is why you are agitated with desire, because you do not know the stench of wretched women." Then, in order to quench his passion, she said: "I have my monthly, and no one can approach me, and this is my stench." Hearing this, the brother came to himself and wept. Then she said to him: "See, if I had entrusted myself to you and we had already committed the sin! With what face would you then have met my father, and how would you have entered your monastery and listened to the chanting of your holy brethren? I beseech you, be sober henceforth and beware of destroying your labor and being deprived of eternal blessings for the sake of a small and vile pleasure." "All this the suffering brother related to me," concluded the narrator, "and I pass it on to you for edification and thank God, Who through the reasonableness and chastity of the woman did not allow the brother to fall completely."

29. A certain monk for a long time was warred upon by the demon of fornication. Once, feeling this warfare in the church assembly, he in great sorrow stripped himself and revealed the action of Satan before the face of the brethren, saying: "Pray for me, for I have been thus warred upon for fourteen years." And for the sake of his humility, the warfare subsided.

30. A certain elder said about the thought of fornication: "We suffer this because of our negligence, for if we believed that God dwells in us, we would not put a foreign vessel into ourselves. Our Master Christ, co-dwelling with us and being present with us, sees our life; therefore we also, guarding ourselves and seeing Him, must not be negligent, but purify ourselves, *just as He is pure* (1 John 3:3)."

31. He also said: "The enemy as it were says to the Savior: 'I send my things into Yours, that I may overthrow Yours; and although I cannot work evil in Your elect, at least I will place fantasies in them at night.' The Savior as it were answers him: 'If a bastard inherits from his father, then these insertions of yours will be imputed as sin to My elect.'"

32. A disciple of a certain great elder, having been carried away by the passion of fornication, went into the world and married. Grieved by this, the elder prayed to God thus: "Lord Jesus Christ, do not permit Your servant to be defiled." And he, lying down with his wife, gave up his spirit undefiled.

33. When asked about evil-doing thoughts, a certain elder said: "I beseech you, brethren, as we have ceased from deeds, so let us cease from memories, for what are we but earth from the earth."

34. A certain brother was agitated by lustful desire. This desire, like fire, burned in his heart day and night, but the brother vigilantly struggled so as not to consent to the thought. After quite a long time, the warfare fled, not having been able to overcome him because of his great endurance; and immediately light came into the brother's heart.

35. Another brother, being warred upon by the passion of fornication, arose at night, came to a certain elder, and revealed his thought to him. The elder comforted him, and the brother, healed, returned to his cell. But the warfare pressed on him again, and he again went to the elder, and he did this several times. The elder did not grieve him but conversed with him about what was profitable for the brother, and said: "Do not yield and come every time the demon wars upon you, in order to expose him, for nothing so torments him as the revealing of his deeds, and nothing so rejoices him as the concealment of thoughts." And this brother came to the elder up to eleven times to expose his thoughts. Once the brother asked the elder: "Do me a kindness, abba, tell me a word." And the elder said: "Believe me, my son, that if God were to permit the thoughts by which my soul is wounded to pass to you, you would not bear them for a minute but would immediately turn back." And because of the great humility by which the elder spoke thus, the warfare of fornication subsided in the brother.

36. A certain brother was being aroused by the demon of fornication, but he struggled, multiplying his ascetic labors and guarding his thought so as not to descend to desire. Finally,

coming to the church, he revealed this to the entire brotherhood, and then a command was given to them to pray for him for a whole week, and the warfare subsided.

37. A certain elder, a desert-dweller, said about the thought of fornication: "Do you want to be saved while resting? No, go and labor; go and sweat; go, seek and you will find; watch and knock, and it will be opened to you. There are in the world wrestlers who are crowned because, despite the multitude of blows they receive, they stand and are courageous. Often one, being struck by two, is aroused to courage by the very wounds and conquers those striking him. See what courage there is in fleshly matters! And you, stand and be courageous, and God will fight for you against the enemy."

38. About the same thought, another elder said: "Be like those passing by taverns and smelling the odors of something cooked or fried. He who wishes to taste enters and eats, but he who does not wish only smells in passing and goes away. So you also repel from yourself the stench of desire; arise and pray, saying: 'Son of God, help me!' Do the same with other thoughts also, for we are not eradicators of evil but those who fight against it."

39. A certain brother, being troubled by lustful desire, came to a great elder and asked him: "Do me a kindness, father, pray for me, for lustful desire troubles me." The elder began to pray for him to God. Another time the brother came again to the elder and said the same thing, although the elder did not neglect to entreat God for him. Then the perplexed elder stood up and prayed thus to the Lord: "O Lord, reveal to me how this brother lives and whence comes such an assault, for I have asked You and he has not received rest." And God revealed to him about him. He saw the brother sitting, and the spirit of fornication beside him, while the Angel of the Lord, sent to help him, stood at a distance and was angry at him because he did not cast himself before God but, taking pleasure in thoughts, had given his whole mind over to the assault. From this the elder learned that the cause of the warfare was in the brother himself, and said to him: "This happens to you because you yourself consent to your thought," and he taught him how one must resist thoughts. He began to be watchful and, with the help of prayer and the instruction of the elders, found rest.

40. A certain great elder had a disciple who was warred upon by the demon of fornication. The elder, seeing his labor and sweat, said to him: "Do you want me to ask God to take the warfare from you?" But the disciple answered: "It is hard for me, abba, but I see fruit for myself from this labor. Therefore, ask God only that He give me patience to bear this." Then the elder said to him: "Now I see that you have advanced and surpass me."

41. They said of a certain elder that he came to Scetis and brought with him a son who was still nursing, who grew up not seeing a woman, but when he came of age, demons began to show him images of women. The son revealed this to his father, who marveled at it. Once they came to Egypt, and the son, seeing women, said to his father: "These are the ones who come to me at night in Scetis." The father answered: "These are village monks; only they have one schema, while desert-dwellers have another." The elder marveled how even in the desert demons show images of women. And they immediately returned to their cell.

42. There was in Scetis a certain brother, a zealous ascetic, into whom the enemy implanted memories of a certain woman, very comely, and sorely tormented him. By God's providence, another brother came from Egypt to Scetis, who among other things in conversation said that such-and-such a woman had died, and it was the woman by memories of whom the ascetic was being warred upon. Hearing this, at night the brother took his tunic, came to the grave of the deceased, and opening the coffin, wiped with his tunic her decomposing remains. Returning and placing it in his cell, he had this stench before him and battled his thought, saying: "Behold the desire you seek! She is before you — satisfy yourself!" Thus he tormented himself with this stench until he had quieted his warfare.

43. They related that once a man came to Scetis with his son and received monasticism there. When his son became a youth, warfare began to war upon him, and he said to his father: "I will go into the world, for I have not the strength to bear the warfare." His father stopped him and persuaded him to be patient, but a little later, the youth again said: "Abba, I have no more strength! Allow me to depart." Then the father said to him: "Listen to me, my son, one more time: take forty pairs of loaves and branches for forty days; go into the innermost desert and remain there forty days; and may God's will be done." He obeyed his father, went into the desert, and remained there in labor, plaiting dry branches and eating dry bread. Having remained in stillness for twenty days and twenty nights, he saw a vision approaching him: it was the image of an Ethiopian woman, so foul-smelling that the youth could not bear her stench — he drove her out and shut himself in. But she said to him at this: "In the hearts of men I seem very pleasant, but because of your obedience and labor, God did not allow me to seduce you and revealed to you my stench." Then the youth thanked God and, returning to his father, said: "Now I no longer wish to go into the world, abba, for I have seen the image of seduction and its stench." The father, having been informed about this, answered: "If you had endured forty days in fasting and fulfilled my command, you would have seen an even greater vision."

44. They said of one of the fathers that while still a layman, he had a wife, and now he was strongly warred upon regarding her. He related this to the elders, and they, knowing that this brother was a laborer and could labor more than others, laid upon him such heavy rules that from them his body grew weak, and he could no longer get up. By God's providence, a certain stranger from among the fathers, having come to Scetis to visit the elders and passing by his cell, saw it unlocked and at first passed it by, wondering that no one had come out to meet him. Then he returned, thinking: "Perhaps the brother is sick," and knocking, entered. Finding him in a severe illness, he asked what was the matter with him. And he told him everything: both about his warfare, and about the rules laid upon him, in fulfilling which he had so weakened, and about the increase of the warfare. Having heard this, the elder was saddened and said to him: "The fathers, being strong, well laid upon you such rules, but listen to my humility — leave all this and take your small food at its time, perform your small rule, and cast your sorrow upon the Lord, for by your own labors you cannot overcome this warfare. Our body is like a garment: if you take care of it, it serves us; but if you neglect it, it

is ruined." The brother listened to the elder, did according to his advice, and the warfare after a few days departed from him.

45. On the mountain, in the regions of Sinai, there lived a hermit who was advanced in piety, and many benefited from his word and were edified by his deeds. Because he was such, the enemy envied him and, under the guise of that same piety, put into him such a thought: "It is not proper for anyone else to work for you or serve you, for you are obliged to serve others and do not serve. At least begin to serve yourself. Therefore, go into the city, sell your baskets, buy what you need, and then return again to your hermitage — and you will be a burden to no one." This the evil one suggested to him, envying his stillness, his occupation with God, and the benefit to many from him, for the enemy from all sides attempts to capture the ascetic. Believing this to be a good word, he left his hermitage — he who was known and glorified by all who saw him, but who was inexperienced in the wiles of the assailant, a hermit — and seeing a woman and speaking with her at length, from inattention he was seduced, went to a deserted place, whither the enemy also followed him, and fell. Understanding that the enemy had rejoiced over his fall, he was ready to come to despair, which exceedingly grieved the Spirit of God, the Angels, and the fathers, many of whom had conquered the enemy in cities and whom he in no way resembled. He grieved greatly and, forgetting that God gives strength to those who sincerely hope in Him and provides remedies for transgression, wanted to throw himself into the river in order to die and thereby give complete joy to the devil. From extreme spiritual anguish his body grew weak, and only the merciful God helped him not to die. Finally, coming to himself, he decided to show greater labor in self-mortification and, returning to his hermitage, shut the door and began to weep as one weeps for the dead, imploring God; he fasted, kept vigil, and wore himself out in contrition of spirit. His body became emaciated, but he still had not received assurance of the acceptance of his repentance. When for their benefit the brethren came to him and knocked at the door, he answered: "I will not open, for I have given my word to spend this year in labors of repentance. Pray for me" — saying nothing more, so as not to scandalize them, because all honored him as a great monk. Thus he spent a whole year in the austerities of repentance. Finally, before the day of Pascha, on the night of the Holy Resurrection, he took a new lamp and, having prepared it, placed it in a new earthen cup, covered it, and stood from evening in prayer, saying: "O merciful and compassionate God, Who desires even barbarians to be saved and to come to the knowledge of the truth! To You I flee, O Savior of souls! Have mercy on me who have greatly provoked You to the joy of the enemy! For behold, I am dead, having listened to him. But You, O Master, Who has mercy on the impious and merciless and teaches neighbors to have mercy, have compassion on my lowliness, for with You nothing is impossible! My soul has drawn near to Hades. Show mercy to me, as You are merciful to Your creation. You Who are able to raise even lifeless bodies on the day of resurrection, hear me, O Lord, for my spirit has failed and my wretched soul and my body have been crushed, which I have defiled by my sin. Revive me who am crushed, and by Your fire command this lamp to be kindled, that having received assurance of mercy, I may keep Your commandments for the remaining time of my life, if You grant it, and not depart from Your

fear, but truly serve You, and more than before!" Thus with tears he prayed on the night of the Resurrection! Then he arose to look whether the lamp had been kindled, and seeing that it had not, he again fell on his face and began to implore the Lord, saying: "I know, O Lord, that a struggle was prepared for me to be crowned, and I did not attend to my steps, being drawn rather by the lust of the flesh to descend into the torment of the impious! Therefore spare me, O Lord! For behold, I again confess my worthlessness to Your mercy before the face of the Angels and the righteous, and if it would not be a scandal to them, I would have confessed to men also. Therefore have compassion on me, that I may also teach others! Yes, O Lord! Revive me!" Having thus prayed three times, he was heard, and arising, he found the lamp kindled. His spirit rejoiced and his heart was glad, and although he was pouring out his soul before the Lord, he marveled at His ineffable mercy and said: "Though I am unworthy even of life, You, O Lord, have had mercy on me and comforted me with this new sign!" In such laudatory and joyful confession he spent all the rest of the night; day dawned, and throughout it he did not cease to rejoice in the Lord, forgetting about bodily food. This wondrous fire he preserved all the days of his remaining life, adding oil and covering it from above so that it would not go out. Thus again the Spirit of God dwelt in him, and he was glorious to all, being humble-minded and rejoicing before the Lord in confession and thanksgiving. And about his death he had a revelation several days beforehand.

46. A certain elder lived in a far-off desert. He had a female relative who for many years had wished to see him. Having learned where he lived, she with fellow travelers from among camel-drivers came to that desert. Being drawn by the devil and having come to the elder's door, she by various proofs assured him that she was his relative and remained with him. The elder, being carried away by desire, fell with her. In the lower regions there lived another hermit, whose water jug, for an unknown reason, tipped over at the hour of taking food. By God's providence he decided: "I will go into the desert and reveal this to the elder," and he went. When evening came, he lay down in a demonic shrine that happened to be on the way, and at night he heard how the demons were saying: "This night we cast the hermit into fornication." Hearing of this, he was grieved. Coming to the elder, he found him sorrowful and asked him: "What shall I do, abba? My water jug at the hour of taking food tips over, I know not why." The elder said to this: "You have come to ask me why your vessel tips over? What am I to do, for this night I fell into fornication?" He answered: "I also learned of this — I spent the night in a shrine and heard how the demons spoke about you." Then the elder said: "I will go into the world." But the one who had come implored him: "No, father! Send the woman away from here, but you yourself remain in your place, for this incident is from the enemy." Listening to him, the hermit remained, increased his ascetic labors, and poured out bitter tears until he came again to his former rank.

47. A certain brother asked an elder: "If through some assault someone happens to fall into fornication, what will happen to those scandalized by it?" And the elder told him the following incident: "There was a renowned deacon in a lavra of Egypt. A certain persecuted citizen came with his whole household to the coenobium, and the deacon, by the assault of the evil one, fell with his wife, which became a shame for all. Then the deacon went to his

beloved elder and revealed his sin. Inside his cell this elder had some small cellars, and the deacon asked him: 'Bury me here alive and tell no one about it.' Thus, having entered into that darkness, he sincerely repented. After some time, the water in the river Nile did not rise, and during a common prayer it was revealed to one of the saints that the water would not rise unless the deacon who was hidden by such-and-such an elder should come. Hearing this and marveling, they brought him out of confinement, and when he prayed, the water rose. Then those who had been scandalized before received great benefit from his repentance and glorified God."

48. Two brothers came to market to sell their handiwork, and when one of them went away, the other fell into fornication. When he returned, the brother called the one who had stayed to go back to their cell, but he answered: "I will not go, because while you were away, I fell into fornication." Then, wishing to gain him, the brother said to him: "The same thing happened to me also when I went away from you; but let us go and repent with contrition, and God will forgive us." Coming to the cell, they revealed themselves to the elders, and they gave them a commandment of repentance; so the brother who had not sinned repented for the brother who had sinned, as if he himself had sinned. God, seeing the labor of his love, after a few days revealed to one of the elders: "For the great love of the brother who did not sin, I have forgiven also the one who sinned." This is what it means: *to lay down one's soul for one's brother.*

49. A certain brother came to an elder and complained to him: "My brother, going here or there, leaves me, and I am grieved." The elder exhorted him: "Be patient with your brother, and God, seeing the work of your patience, will bring him back, for no one can be drawn to oneself by harshness, since a demon does not drive out a demon, but by gentleness you will draw him near, for our God Himself draws people by gentle exhortation." Then the elder told such an incident: "In the Thebaid there were two brothers, and one, being warred upon by the passion of fornication, said to the other: 'I will go into the world.' The brother wept and said to him: 'I will not allow you to depart, brother, so that you may destroy your labor and your virginity.' But he did not want to listen and answered: 'I will not stay — either go with me, and I will return again with you; or let me go, and I will remain in the world.' Then the brother went and revealed this to a certain great elder. The elder said to him: 'Go with him, and God, because of your labor, will not allow him to fall.' And they went together, but as soon as they reached a village, God, seeing the brother's labor, took the warfare from the one being warred upon, who said: 'Let us go, brother, again into the desert; for consider, if I had already sinned, what profit would there be to me from that?' And they returned unharmed to their cell."

50. A certain brother, by demonic suggestion, came to an elder and said: "Such-and-such two brothers are with each other." The elder understood that the demon was mocking them and sent to call them. When evening came, he spread one mat for those two brothers and covered them with one blanket, saying: "They are children of God and are pure." But he

ordered his disciple to confine the other brother separately in a cell and said that he himself has this passion in him.

51. A brother asked an elder: "What shall I do, for an impure thought is killing me?" The elder answered him: "When a mother wishes to wean her child from the breast, she applies aloe to her nipples; the child comes as usual to taste the milk, but sensing the bitterness, runs away. Apply aloe yourself also." The brother said to him: "What is the aloe that I must apply?" The elder said: "The memory of death and of the torments of the age to come."

52. A brother asked another elder about the same thought, and the elder said: "I have never been warred upon by this." The brother, being scandalized by this, went to the first elder and told him what this elder had said and that he was scandalized by it, for he had said something above nature. The elder answered: "The man of God did not say this to you simply. Therefore, go and bow to him, so that he may explain to you the meaning of this word." The brother came to the elder and, bowing to him, said: "Forgive me, abba, that I acted unreasonably in leaving you not as was proper, but I ask you to explain to me how you have never been warred upon for fornication." And the elder said: "Since I became a monk, I have not satisfied myself with bread or water or sleep — and the care for this, which always greatly occupied me, did not allow me to feel the warfare of which you spoke." And the brother went away from him, having received benefit.

53. A brother asked one of the fathers: "Father, what shall I do, for my thought is always in fornication, giving me no rest even for one hour? And my soul is grieved about this." The elder answered: "When demons sow such thoughts, do not converse with them, for it is the work of demons only to propose them, and they are not lazy about this, but they also do not force anyone; it is in your power to accept or not accept them. See what the Midianites did: they adorned their daughters and placed them before the Israelites, but they forced none of them — those who wished fell with them, while others, being indignant, killed them. Likewise also with regard to thoughts." The brother asked again: "What then shall I do? I am weak, and the passion conquers me." The elder said: "Watch for the thoughts, and when they begin to speak to you, do not answer them, but arise, make a prostration, and pray, saying: 'Son of God, have mercy on me!'" The brother asked yet again: "Behold, I read, abba, but there is no compunction in my heart, because I do not understand the meaning of the word." The elder answered: "Just read. I have heard that Abba Poemen and many others of the fathers spoke such words: 'The charmer does not know the meaning of the words he pronounces, but the beast listens, is subdued, and is humbled.' So also you, although you do not know the meaning of the words you read, but the demons, hearing them, depart in fear."

54. The elders said that the thought of fornication is like paper. If it is sown in us, but we, not inclining toward it, reject it from ourselves, it is cut off without labor. If, when it is sown, we are delighted by it and incline toward it, then it, having been transformed, becomes iron and is cut off with labor. Therefore, one must have discernment regarding this thought: for those inclining toward it there is no hope of salvation, but for those not inclining, a crown is prepared.

55. Two brothers, having been carried away by lustful desire, went into the world and took wives. But afterward they said to each other: "What profit have we gained from having left the angelic rank and fallen into such impurity, and in the age to come have to depart into fire and torment? Let us go again into the desert and repent!" Coming and confessing to the elders what they had done, they asked them to give them a commandment of repentance, and the elders confined them for a year. Bread and water were given to them equally, for in appearance they were of equal constitution, and when the time of repentance was fulfilled and they came out, the fathers saw one pale-faced and gloomy, and the other bright-faced and cheerful, and they marveled, because the brothers had received food equally. Therefore they asked the gloomy one: "With what did you occupy your thoughts in the cell?" He answered: "I pondered the evil deeds I had done, and the torment into which I was to depart, and from fear *my bone clung to my flesh* (Psalm 101:6)." They also asked the other what he had pondered in his cell. He answered: "I thanked God that He had delivered me from the impurity of the world and the torment for it and had brought me into this angelic life; and remembering God, I rejoiced." Then the elders said: "The repentance of both is equal before God."

56. A certain elder living in Scetis became seriously ill, and the brethren attended to him. The elder, seeing their labor on his behalf, decided: "I will go to Egypt, so as not to distract them from the monastic rule." Abba Moses warned him: "Do not go — otherwise you will fall into fornication." But he with sorrow answered: "My body is dead, and you say this to me?" And he departed to Egypt. Hearing about him, people began to bring him everything he needed, and a certain virgin, by faith, came to serve the elder. After a little time, the elder, having recovered, fell with her, and she conceived. People asked where this was from, and she named the elder. They did not believe her, but he confirmed it, only he asked that the child be preserved when it was born. When the child was weaned from the breast, on a certain feast day the elder came to Scetis, carrying it on his shoulder, and entered the church while all the brethren were assembled. The brethren, seeing him, began to weep, and he said to them: "Do you see this child? This is a son of disobedience! Therefore, be strengthened, brethren, for I in my old age did this. But pray for me." After this, withdrawing to his cell, the elder made a beginning of his former work.

57. A certain brother was greatly tempted by the demon of fornication, for four demons, having transformed themselves into women who were very beautiful, for forty days disturbed him, that they might draw him into foul union. But since he manfully resisted and did not allow himself to be conquered, God, seeing his good struggle, granted him no longer to have carnal arousal.

58. In the lower regions of Egypt, in a solitary cell, there lived a certain hermit who was renowned. Hearing about him, a certain dishonorable woman, by the devil's suggestion, said to some young men: "What will you give me if I bring down your hermit?" They agreed to give her a certain sum, and she, going out in the evening, came to the cell of the elder as if she had lost her way and knocked. The elder came out, and seeing her, was troubled and

asked: "How did you come here?" She answered with weeping: "I lost my way and came here." Taking pity on her, he brought her into his courtyard, entered his cell, and locked himself in. But that wretched woman began to cry: "Abba! Beasts will devour me here!" Again being troubled, but fearing the judgment of God, he said: "From where has this affliction come upon me?" And opening the door, he brought her inside. Then the devil began to wound him with attraction to her, but the elder understood the warfare of the enemy and said: "The ways of the enemy are darkness, but the Son of God is light." Then he arose, lit a lamp, and since the lust did not cease to inflame him, he added: "Those who do such things will go to torment. Therefore, test yourself here — can you bear the everlasting mortal fire?" Having said this, he placed his finger on the flame of the lamp and burned it; the intense pain from this burning no longer allowed him to feel the burning of the flesh. Doing thus, by morning he had burned all his fingers. That wretched woman, seeing what he was doing, became like stone from fear. In the morning some young men came to the hermit and asked whether a certain woman had not come here the day before. He answered: "She came; she is inside." The young men entered and found her dead. "Abba! She is dead," they said. Then the elder opened his hands, showed them to them, and said: "See what this daughter of the devil has done to me! She has destroyed all my fingers." And having told them everything, he concluded: "It is commanded: *Be... not returning evil for evil* (cf. 1 Peter 3:8-9)." Then he offered a prayer and raised her. The woman arose and, returning to her home, began from then on to live chastely.

59. A certain brother was being warred upon by the demon of fornication. It happened that once, passing through a certain Egyptian village, he saw the daughter of a pagan priest and, having fallen in love with her, said to her father: "Give me your daughter as a wife." The priest answered: "I cannot give her to you until first I learn the will of my god." Coming to the demon, he asked him: "A certain monk wishes to take my daughter as a wife. Shall I give her to him?" The demon said: "Ask him whether he will deny his God, and baptism, and his monastic vow." Returning, the priest asked the monk: "Will you deny your God, and baptism, and your monastic vow?" The brother agreed, but immediately he saw, as it were, a dove fly out of his mouth and fly up to heaven. The priest again went to the demon and said to him: "He has agreed to these three things." But he answered: "Do not give him your daughter as a wife, for his God has not departed from him but still helps him." Returning, the priest said to the brother: "I cannot give you my daughter, for your God still helps you and has not departed from you." Hearing this, the brother said to himself: "What goodness my God shows to me! I, the wretched one, have denied Him, and baptism, and my monastic vow, and He, the All-Good One, still even now helps me." Coming thus to himself, the brother became sober, went into the desert to a certain elder, and revealing his sin, told him everything. The elder answered: "Stay with me in a cave; fast three weeks two days at a time, and I will entreat God for you." And God heard him. After a week had passed, the elder came to the brother and asked him whether he had seen anything. The brother answered: "I saw a dove high under the heavens directly over my head." The elder said to him: "Attend to yourself and implore God diligently!" And after the second week the elder came to the brother and asked whether

he had now seen anything. He answered: "I saw the dove near over my head." The elder commanded him: "Be sober and pray." Again, after the third week had passed, the elder came and asked whether he had seen anything more. "I saw," answered the brother, "that the dove flew down and alighted on my head; I stretched out my hand to catch it, but it rose and flew into my mouth." Then the elder thanked God and said to the brother: "God has accepted your repentance; therefore, attend to yourself." The brother answered him: "From now on I will remain with you, abba, until I die."

60. One of the Theban elders said: "I was the son of a pagan priest; in my childhood I often went with my father to the shrine and saw him enter to offer sacrifice to the idol. Once, entering secretly after him, I saw Satan and his host standing before him. And behold, one of his commanders approached and bowed to him. Satan asked him from where he had come, and he told him: 'I was in such-and-such a country, stirred up a war, produced great bloodshed, and came to report to you.' He asked: 'In how much time did you do this?' The one who had come said: 'In thirty days.' Then Satan commanded him to be beaten with whips, saying: 'In so much time you did only this?!' And behold, another bowed to him, and of this one too he asked from where he had come. The demon answered: 'I was on the sea, raised up winds, sank ships, destroyed a multitude of people, and came to report to you.' He asked in how many days he had done this, and the demon said: 'In twenty days.' And he commanded this one also to be beaten with whips, saying: 'How? In so much time you did only this?' A third approached and bowed to him. And of him also he asked from where he had come. And the demon said: 'In such-and-such a city there was a wedding; I stirred up strife and produced great bloodshed, and they killed the bridegroom and the bride, and I came to report to you.' Satan asked: 'In how many days did you do this?' He answered: 'In ten.' He commanded this one also to be beaten with whips. After these, yet another came and also bowed to him. Satan asked: 'From where have you come?' He answered: 'I was in the desert; for forty years now I have been struggling with one monk, and this night I cast him into fornication.' Hearing this, Satan arose and kissed him; then he took the crown that he wore, placed it on his head, and seated him on his own throne, saying: 'So great a deed you have managed to accomplish!' Seeing this," continued the elder, "I said to myself: 'How great is the monastic rank!' And by God's good pleasure for my salvation, I left the world and became a monk."

61. A certain brother said to an elder: "I think that while a monk who has fallen into temptation will grieve, as one having suffered loss in the work of progress, and labor to arise, one who has come from the world, as making a beginning, will make progress." The elder answered him: "A monk who has fallen into temptation is like a fallen house. If the owner takes care to restore this house, he will find many ready materials: a foundation, stones, much of the woodwork, and he can build the house more quickly than one who has not dug a trench, not laid a foundation, does not have anything he needs, but has only the hope that somehow he will not fail to complete it. Thus, if someone after progress in monastic works falls into temptation and then, becoming sober, comes to himself, he will find in himself many

things needed in readiness, such as habit in reading, psalmody, and handwork, which are the foundation; and while the beginner will still be learning these, he will come to the third rank."

62. A brother asked an elder: "What shall I do, abba, about the thought of fornication?" The elder answered him: "Against this thought strengthen yourself as much as you have strength, for one who is conquered by it most easily comes to despair of salvation. Thus, if a ship on the sea, being fought by waves and storm, loses its rudder, although it is near danger, it still sails; likewise, if the mast breaks or something else is damaged, it is still in good hope while itself remains whole. So also a monk, if through negligence he falls into certain passions, he often escapes from them through repentance; but if once he suffers shipwreck, having fallen into fornication, he comes to despair, for then the ship has gone to the bottom."

63. A certain elder was so virginal that he absolutely did not know what fornication is or whether it exists. Once, going out of his cell, he saw demons in the forms of Ethiopians who surrounded him and aroused desire in him. The elder said: "This member on a man is the same as on a jug — the neck. As the neck on a jug is for passing water through, so this member is for expelling water from a man." Therefore he did not understand what was happening to him. Behold, a stone fell from the roof, and the elder heard a pleasant sound, and following this, a passionate thought came. He went to a certain elder and told him about this. That one said: "Did you see demons? The fallen stone is the devil, and the sound that you heard is the very desire. Therefore attend to yourself and beseech the Lord to help you pass through this warfare." Then, having shown him how one must struggle against demons, the elder offered a prayer and released him. Returning to his cell, he struggled, praying to God, and God granted him to progress to the point that when a brother happened to die, he received information whether his soul was well or ill.

64. A certain elder spoke about lustful thoughts that are in the heart and are not performed in deed as follows: "This is like someone seeing a vineyard, desiring with all his heart to taste of the grapes, but fearing to enter and steal, lest he be caught and lose his life. If such a one is caught outside the fence, he will not lose his life, for he did not enter and did not eat but only desired. Nevertheless, although he does not lose his life, he receives wounds for having desired."

65. A brother told an elder: "Fornication wars against me." The elder said: "If this is good, why do you retreat from it; but if it is shameful, why do you seek it?"

66. They said of a certain elder that once, going along the road, he saw the footprint of a woman and covered it, saying: "Lest a brother see this and receive warfare."

67. A brother asked an elder: "What shall I do, father? My belly torments me, and I cannot refuse it, and meanwhile because of it my body lusts." The elder said to him in answer: "If you do not impose fear and fasting upon your body, it will not walk rightly in God's way." And he presented to him such a parable: "A certain man had a donkey. Once he sat on it to ride, but it carried him along the road here and there. Then he took a rod and began to beat it. The donkey said to him: 'Do not beat me — henceforth I will go straight.' Seeing that it

had improved somewhat, he dismounted from it and placed the rod in the saddlebags on the donkey itself. The donkey did not know that the rod was on it, but noticing that there was none in the hands of its master, it despised its owner and again began to stray here and there through the crops. The master again took the rod and began to beat it until it went straight. It is fitting to act similarly with regard to the body and belly."

68. A certain brother was on the road with his traveling companion, and his thoughts were carried away to fornication. He went to the elders and said to them: "What shall I do, for my heart finds no consolation since I descended to the warfare of the enemy, for I have myself as having committed the sin?" The fathers answered him: "This is not a sin committed — the enemy came to tempt you, but God covered you. You did not submit to him but were cast down by despondency." At this they told him such an incident: "Two brothers, sent from a coenobium to a certain village, were going together, and the demon five times warred upon the elder of them to sin, but he each time resisted him, saying a prayer. When they returned to their father, his face was gloomy, and he, bowing to the father, said: 'Pray for me, father, for I fell into fornication,' and he told how his mind had been warred upon. The elder, being clairvoyant and seeing five crowns upon the brother's head, answered: 'Take courage, my son, for when you came, I saw five crowns upon you. You were not conquered but conquered, since you did not perform the deed of sin; and this is a great struggle when a man, having a convenient occasion for sins, restrains himself from them. He has a great reward, for strong and sharp is this warfare of the enemy, and it is not easy to escape its nets. What do you think about blessed Joseph? Was that a simple matter? No. But what was happening then was as if in a theater — God and the Angels watched him struggle, while the devil and the demons enraged the woman. And when the wrestler conquered, all the Angels glorified God with a great voice, saying: "The wrestler has won a wondrous victory!" It is good not even to commit sin in thought, but if you are tempted, struggle not to be conquered.'"

69. A certain hermit was such a virgin that he did not know what a woman was. Once the demon of fornication began to torment him, and he was being inflamed, but in his inexperience he did not know the object of the desire — so that the servant of God loved, not knowing whose lover he had become. Then the demon showed him a person lying in lewdness with a woman, but God, seeing the extreme deception of the devil, covered the brother and extinguished the warfare.

70. They related about a certain great elder that, coming to a certain coenobium, he saw there a youth and did not want to spend the night in that place. The brethren who were with him asked him: "And you, abba, are afraid?" He answered them: "Believe me, children, I am not afraid, but what is the need for pointless warfare?"

71. They said that once the devil came to a coenobium and knocked. A youth answered to reply; and the demon, hearing him, said: "If you are here, then there is no need for me."

72. The fathers said that it is not God who brings youths into the desert, but Satan, in order to bring down those who wish to live piously.

73. Once a ship was going down the river and put in at a mountain where monks lived. A woman, disembarking from the ship, sat on a hillock and was noticed by a brother who had come to draw water, who, returning, said to the presbyter: "A woman is sitting there by the river, abba, which has never been here before." Hearing of this, the elder took his staff and ran, crying: "Help, brethren, robbers!" And all the brethren ran after him. The boatmen, seeing their haste and understanding the reason, lifted the woman onto the ship and departed from the shore, continuing their journey.

74. A certain pious virgin, living in a city, had a soldier as a neighbor. Once, when her mother was not at home, he broke in to her and, committing violence, took her virginity. After he left, the wretched girl threw off the schema of virginity, sat on a mat, and wept, tearing her clothes. When the mother returned, she told her what had happened and sat and wept inconsolably for many days. Learning of this, clerics and virgins came to her to calm her and said: "It is not from you that this sin came about." But the inconsolable one answered: "God has rejected me. And how can I wear the schema of God, Who does not want me? Could not God have forbidden such audacity? Evidently He sees that I am unworthy of the schema. Therefore I will remain thus." And she remained thus until her death, weeping with salvific weeping in great compunction.

75. A certain brother, living in the desert, when the thought of fornication fell upon him, went, found a hyena's den, and entering it, remained without food for six days. When the hyena came, he became frightened and said: "O Lord! If I can ever defile my body, then let it attack me; but if not, save me from it." And a voice was heard saying: "Castrate him and release him," and immediately the warfare departed from him.

76. A certain brother, being warred upon for fornication, came to an elder and asked him to pray for him, that his warfare might be lightened. The elder promised and entreated God for him for seven days. On the eighth day the elder asked him: "How is your warfare, brother?" He answered: "Badly, for I have not felt any relief." The elder was amazed, but behold, Satan appeared to him at night and said: "Believe me, elder, from the first day that you began to pray for him, I departed from him, but he has his own demon and warfare from himself — from his own throat. But I have no part in this warfare, for he himself wars against himself by eating much, drinking, and sleeping."

77. An elder said: "Evil thoughts are like flies flying into a house. If you destroy them one by one as they fly in, you will meet no difficulty. But if you allow them to fill your house, you will meet great difficulty in destroying them; then either you will be able to accomplish this, or, falling into despondency, you will leave the house to desolation."

78. A certain one of the strict ascetics, living in Ennathos of Alexandria, fell into a great transgression, and the demons, taking advantage of his sorrow, began to cast him into despair. Seeing that despondency was beginning to overcome him, he, like a skillful physician, gave himself over to good hope and said: "I believe in the compassion of God, that He will show me His mercy." When he said this, the demons protested, saying: "Yes! He will show you mercy?!" He answered them: "Who are you? You are all sons of Gehenna and perdition.

Whether He will or will not — what concern is it of yours?" And having been put to shame, they departed.

79. An elder said: "If fornication wars upon your body or your heart, investigate the source from which this warfare has arisen upon you and correct it: whether from food, or from sleep, or from high-mindedness, or from considering yourself better than someone, or from having condemned someone who sinned. For without these causes, a man is not warred upon for fornication."

80. He also said: "If you fall into fornication and the person with whom you fell is nearby, depart from that place, for otherwise you will not repent."

81. He also said: "If you see images of women in a dream, struggle not to remember them during the day, for they are death and destruction of the soul."

82. One of the fathers came to Alexandria with his disciple, and during their stay there, the following incident occurred. A certain abba of the Lavra of the Eighteenth Mile of Alexandria had a son who was a fisherman and had a young wife about eighteen years old. The abba lived with his son, and the enemy of our souls, the devil, aroused in him carnal warfare against his daughter-in-law, and he sought a convenient occasion to be with her but did not find one. The abba often kissed her, and she received this from him as from a father. One night the fishermen came and called the young man to catch fish, and when the son left, the father began to make advances toward his son's wife. She began to say to him: "This is a devilish deed, father! Go, cross yourself!" Despite all his efforts, she did not yield to him. Then, wishing to frighten her, he unsheathed the sword hanging over the bed and said: "If you do not obey me, I will strike you with this sword." She answered him: "If I must be cut even to pieces, I will never do this lawless deed." Then the devil completely possessed the old man, and he, in the fury of his anger, swinging the sword, struck her in the loins and cut her in two. But at the same moment God blinded him, so that he walked here and there, seeking the door, and did not find it. At dawn other fishermen came to call his son; the father answered that his son had gone, and he could not find the door. Opening it and entering, they saw the crime that had been committed, and the old man said: "Seize me and hand me over to judgment, for I committed this murder," which was done according to the laws. Hearing about the incident, the elder suggested to his disciple: "Let us go look at the remains of this maiden." When they came to the Lavra of the Eighteenth Mile of Alexandria, the fathers and monks came out to meet the elder, and he said to them: "Say a prayer, fathers! The remains of this young maiden will not be buried unless with the fathers." Some murmured at this, but the elder explained: "This maiden is my mother and yours, for she died for chastity." After this no one opposed the elder, and she was buried with the fathers, and the elder, bidding farewell to all, together with his disciple returned to Scetis. It happened that in this Scetis a certain brother was strongly warred upon by the demon of fornication. In extreme agitation he came to the elder and revealed this. The abba commanded him: "Go to the Lavra of the Eighteenth Mile of Alexandria, enter the burial place of the fathers, and say: 'O God of Thomais! Help me and deliver me from this temptation of fornication.' And I

hope in God that He will deliver you." The brother, according to the elder's command, went to the Lavra of the Eighteenth Mile and did as he had bidden him. After three days, returning to Scetis, he fell at the elder's feet and said: "By the grace of God and your prayers, father, I have been freed from the warfare of fornication." And to the elder's question of how this happened, the brother related: "I made twelve prostrations, lay down in the burial place, and fell asleep. A certain maiden approached me and said: 'Abba! Take this blessing and go in peace to your cell.' As soon as I took the blessing, I felt that I was freed from my warfare. But what the blessing was, I do not know." The elder said to him: "See what boldness those who manfully struggle for chastity have before God."

83. A brother asked an elder about carnal passions, and he said to him: "They are like those who sang before the image of Nebuchadnezzar: if those who then played on pipes had not enchanted the people, perhaps they would not have worshipped the image. So also the enemy sings to the soul in lustings — will he not beguile it with carnal passions?"

84. An elder said: "A little wormwood spoils a whole vessel of honey. Likewise the sin of the flesh drives out from the Kingdom of Heaven and sends to the Gehenna of fire. Flee, then, humble monk, from the sin of the flesh!"

85. He also said: "Freedom from care, silence, and hidden meditation beget purity."

86. He also said the following: "Even until death keep this and you will be saved: do not eat with a woman; have no friendship with the young; do not sleep, if you are young, on one mat with anyone, except with your brother or your abba, and that with fear and not with contempt; do not give free rein to your eyes; if you must drink wine, take up to three cups and do not break this commandment for the sake of friendship; do not live in that place where you have sinned before God; do not be negligent of your service or rule, lest you fall into the hands of the enemy; compel yourself to meditation in the psalms, for this will deliver you from the captivity of the enemy; love all hardship, and your passions will be humbled; take care not to measure yourself in any deed, and you will receive the disposition to weep over your sins; guard yourself from lying, for it drives away the fear of God; reveal your thoughts to your fathers, and the covering of God will cover you; compel yourself to handwork, and the fear of God will dwell in you."

87. He also said: "Salt is from water, and if it approaches water, it dissolves and vanishes. Likewise also a monk is from a woman, and if he approaches a woman, he grows weak and perishes."

88. Someone said that a certain monk, having been bitten by a snake, came to a city to be treated. A certain pious and God-fearing woman received him for healing; and when he had received some relief, the devil began to sow impure thoughts in him, and he touched her hand. Then she said to him: "Let it not be so, father! I adjure you by Christ. Remember the sorrow and torment of conscience by which, in repenting, you will be torn, sitting in your cell! Remember the groanings and tears which you must pour out after this." When he had heard this and other similar things, the warfare left him, and from shame he wanted to flee,

being unable to look at her face. But she with Christ-like compassion continued: "Do not leave from shame, for you still have need of healing. That thought was not the work of your pure soul but was a counterfeit of the envious one, the devil." And thus, having healed him without scandal, she released him in peace.

89. A certain elder had ten disciples, one of whom, by the devil's temptation, went to a village and there fell into fornication. He went secretly after matins (at two or three o'clock) and returned by dawn, when it was still dark. The brethren finally learned of this deed, and the elder learned, but according to custom he covered the brother, not exposing him. Since the brethren murmured about this to their superior, one morning the abba came to this brother when he had just returned from his expedition. This brother, in order to hide himself more easily, covered himself with a woman's veil, taking on the appearance of a woman. The abba, entering his cell, saw this veil but for the time kept silent, and first asked him: "Where have you been, brother?" He answered: "To the local people, on business." The abba again asked: "So you did not go to the village?" The brother answered: "No, abba." The elder said to this: "And whose is this veil hanging here?" Then the brother fell at the abba's feet and said: "Forgive me; I will not do this anymore." The abba forgave him and entreated him, saying: "Henceforth attend to yourself, my son, for what profit is there to you from this impurity, except shame and reproach from people here and unquenchable fire and the sleepless worm in the age to come?! No, I beseech you, my son! No longer intertwine yourself with deeds with the lewd woman!" Thus, by the love of God for mankind, the patience of the holy elder brought it about that the brother stopped sinning and subsequently became a truly skilled monk. Then all the brethren thanked God for the brother's correction and asked the abba: "Do us a kindness, tell us why you were patient with the brother for so long?" And the elder answered them: "I saw that the devil was pulling him by one hand and dragging him into the world, but I by my patience held him by the other, so that, not enduring exposure in the very deed, he would not go away into the world. And when God was pleased to save His creation, behold, his other hand is with us as well — and all of him is saved. Therefore, when our brother happens to have a temptation, patience with prayer in the expectation that God will somehow correct the sinner is good, for He is entreated about him and has compassion, since severity and exposure, when they are untimely, bring no good."

90. In a certain city a bishop became so seriously ill that everyone despaired of his recovery. In the city there was a women's monastery, the abbess of which came to visit him, bringing with her two sisters. While the bishop was conversing with the abbess, one of her disciples touched his foot, and from this touch the bishop received the warfare of fornication. Then he asked the abbess to leave this sister so that she might serve him, for he had no one to attend to him. Suspecting nothing bad, she left her. When they were left alone, the bishop, being strengthened by the devil, asked her to prepare food — she prepared it. Then he said to her: "Spend the night with me..." and sin was born. Having conceived, she did not want to reveal the guilty one, but the bishop himself acknowledged this sin. Then, having recovered from his illness, he entered the church, laid his omophorion on the altar, and taking his staff, went to a monastery in which he was not known. The abba of that coenobium was clairvoyant

and knew that a bishop would come to his monastery, so he warned the gatekeeper about this, who expected the bishop with a retinue or some other ceremony befitting a bishop, and therefore did not recognize him. But the abba came out to greet him and said: "Good is your coming, master." The bishop, amazed that he was recognized, wanted to flee to another monastery, but the abba stopped him, saying: "Wherever you go, I too will go with you," and he persuaded him to enter the monastery. There the bishop repented in truth, with great warmth of heart, and departed to God in peace; and at the departure of his soul, many signs were performed.

Chapter VI.
On Non-Acquisitiveness and
on Guarding Oneself from Avarice.

1. In the Lavra of Piruia there was an exceedingly non-acquisitive elder who also had the gift of almsgiving. Once a poor man came to him, but the elder had nothing to give him except bread, and so he brought it out. But the poor man said to him: "I do not want bread, but clothing." Then the elder took him by the hand and led him into the cell, where there was nothing except what the elder wore. The poor man was astonished at such virtue in the elder, untied his bag, and poured out all the loaves that were in it, saying: "Take these, abba, and I shall provide for myself in another place."

2. Abba Abraham, abbot of the Monastery of the Most Holy Theotokos of the New, heard that Theodosius, the hesychast, had no clothing to cover his body during winter and sent some to him, but robbers came, stripped the clothing from him, and carried it away. The elder said nothing to them.

3. Certain men asked Abba John of Petra to speak to them a word of salvation, and he said: "Keep non-acquisitiveness and abstinence, for believe me, children, when once in Scetis one of the fathers fell ill and asked for wine or vinegar, they searched for it in all four lavras and did not find any, so non-acquisitive and abstinent were they." And there were at that time about three thousand five hundred fathers there.

4. Two laborers recounted: "We came once to the church to pray and saw there at the gates a certain monk who was selling baskets. Noticing that he did not bargain over the price, we approached him and, wishing to test him, asked: 'Tell us, elder, for how much do you sell these?' The elder answered: 'For ten coins.' We say to him: 'That is much, give them for five.' He agreed: 'Very well, I will give them for that.' We say to him again: 'But even that is much; if you want one coin apiece, we will take them.' The elder said: 'Very well, take them.' We gave him the money and took all the baskets. The elder, taking his staff, went to his cell. We caught up with him and, asking forgiveness for our conduct, asked him: 'Abba, why did you let us have the baskets for one coin apiece? For God's sake, tell us why you acted thus?' The elder answered: 'I always act thus: I set a price but take whatever is given me.' We asked permission to go with him and, coming to his cell and finding a water-skin, a small pot, and a cup, we suggested to him: 'Do you wish us to prepare some porridge, so that we may eat

together?' He answered: 'Prepare it.' When the porridge was ready, he said to us: 'Go to such-and-such a cell and say to the elder living there: your fellow-elder says to you, come and eat porridge with the brethren.' We went and spoke this word to the elder. He asked us: 'Did he not say, "let us eat"?' We answered: 'No.' Then the elder pronounced: 'So, he has reposed.' Hearing this, we were troubled and hastened back together with the elder. And indeed, we found the elder who had sent us reposed and, having prepared him, buried him with tears; and after seven days the other elder also reposed, for they had established between themselves a covenant that the one who reposed first would entreat God to take the other also. And they were not deceived in their blessed agreement, for *the Lord will fulfill the desire of those who fear Him* (Psalm 145:19)."

5. They said of Abba Pambo that he was so non-acquisitive that he had nothing except his clothing. Before his departure, he was weaving a basket and, having finished it, said to his disciple: "Take this basket as a remembrance, for I have nothing else to leave you." And with these words the elder, being seventy years old, surrendered his soul to the Lord. This basket blessed Melania took and kept until her death. She also recounted: "Having come from Rome to Alexandria, I asked Abba Isidore the Hospitable to provide me the opportunity to see Abba Pambo and gave him thirty litrae of gold as alms. The abba did not even look at it but, immediately calling the steward, commanded: 'Take this and distribute it to the poor Libyan monasteries and to the hesychasts who have need.' I expected praise from him for such a large gift of alms, but he only said: 'I have no need to know how much you gave in alms, but He to Whom you gave knows without counting both the amount of money and the disposition with which the alms was given, and He will reward you according to it with eternal blessings.'"

6. A certain brother, having renounced the world and distributed his possessions to the poor, held back a little for himself and came to Abba Anthony. Learning of this, the elder said to him: "If you wish to be a monk, go to such-and-such a village, buy meat, cover your naked body with it, and come here thus." The brother did so, and along the way dogs and birds tore his body. When he returned, the elder asked whether he had done as he had counseled him. Then the brother showed the abba his lacerated body, and Saint Anthony said: "Those who renounce the world and desire to keep something for themselves are thus torn by demons in their battles."

7. Once Abba Arsenius fell ill in Scetis and was in need even of a simple linen shirt. Not having the means to buy one, he accepted alms from a certain man and said: "I thank Thee, O Lord, that Thou hast deemed me worthy to receive alms in Thy name."

8. Abba Mark asked Abba Arsenius: "Is it good to have no consolation at all in one's cell? For I saw a brother who, having a few vegetables, was pulling them up." Abba Arsenius answered: "It is good, but according to the condition of the person, for if he does not have the strength for such a way of life, he will again plant others."

9. Abba Daniel recounted of Abba Arsenius: "A certain official once came to the abba and brought him the testament of a certain senator, his kinsman, who had left him a very

large inheritance. Taking the testament, he wished to tear it up, but the official fell at his feet, saying: 'I beseech you, do not tear it, for otherwise they will take my head.' Then Abba Arsenius said: 'I died before my kinsman, but he has only now died.' And he sent back the testament, accepting nothing."

10. They recounted of Abba Agathon that he labored a considerable time with his disciples on the construction of a cell for himself. After completing the work, they entered it to live, but in the very first week the abba noticed something in that place that was not beneficial to him and said to his disciples: "Arise, let us go from here." The disciples were greatly troubled and asked him: "If you had in mind to move from here, why was it necessary for us to bear such labor in constructing the cell? And people will be scandalized and will say: 'Look, the restless ones have moved again.'" Seeing their faintheartedness, Abba Agathon said to them: "If some are scandalized, others will receive edification and will say: 'Blessed are they, for they moved for God's sake and despised everything.' However, he who wishes to go, let him go; I am leaving now." Then they cast themselves to the ground and implored him until they were permitted to go with him.

11. They also said of Abba Agathon that he frequently moved to another place, having only his knife in his bag.

12. A certain brother came to Abba Agathon and asked him: "Allow me to live with you." But going along the road, he found a little nitre and brought it. The elder asked him where it was from, and the brother answered: "I found it going along the road and took it." Then the elder said to him: "If you were going to live with me, why did you take what you did not put down?" And he sent him to take it back to where he had taken it from.

13. They said of Abba Gelasius that even in his youth he led a non-acquisitive and eremitic life. In those places at that time there were very many other elders who loved such a life, among whom there was a certain elder, exceedingly simple and non-acquisitive in the highest degree, who lived in one cell until his death, though in his old age he had disciples as well. They say that until his very death he kept the commandment with those who were with him not to acquire two tunics and not to be anxious about the morrow. When by divine providence Abba Gelasius founded a coenobium, people even donated many fields to him; he also acquired beasts of burden and oxen for the needs of the coenobium, for He who had helped Abba Pachomius establish a coenobium also assisted Abba Gelasius in the entire organization of the monastery. Seeing him in these occupations, the aforementioned elder, who preserved a sincere love for him, said: "I fear, Abba Gelasius, lest your thought become attached to the fields and other possessions of the coenobium." Abba Gelasius answered him: "Your thought is more attached to the needle with which you work than is the mind of Gelasius to these possessions."

14. Some of the elders said of Abba George the hermit that he spent thirty-five years walking through the desert naked.

15. Abba Euprepius said: "Everything bodily is clay; he who loves the world loves stumbling blocks. Therefore, if something should happen to perish, we ought to accept it with joy and thanksgiving, as those delivered from cares."

16. A brother asked Abba Euprepius about how to live, and the elder answered: "Eat grass, wear grass, sleep on grass; only acquire a heart of iron, despising all things."

17. Abba Theodore of Pherme had three good books. He came to Abba Macarius and asked him: "I have three good books, from which both I myself receive benefit and the brethren, reading them, also receive benefit. So tell me, what must I do: keep them for my benefit and that of the brethren, or sell them and give the proceeds to the poor?" The elder answered: "The deeds are good, but non-acquisitiveness is greater than all." Hearing this, he went, sold them, and gave the proceeds to the poor.

18. Abba Isidore said: "The terrible and all-daring love of possessions, knowing no satiety, drives the soul it has captivated to the edge of evils. Therefore, is it not better for us to expel it at the beginning, for once it has strengthened, it will be unconquerable."

19. Abba Isaac said to the brethren: "Our fathers and Abba Pambo wore old, patched,[11] and palm-leaf garments, but now you wear expensive ones. Go hence, you have ruined the order here." Also, when preparing to go to the harvest, he would say to them: "I give you no more commandments, for you do not keep them."

20. They asked Abba Isaiah: "What is avarice?" And he answered: "Lack of faith in God that He cares for you, lack of hope in the promises of God, and love of ruinous pleasures."

21. One of the fathers recounted that once a certain brother came to the church of the Cells during the time of Abba Isaac in a small cowl. The elder drove him out, saying: "This place is a dwelling of monks, but you, being like a layman, cannot be here."

22. Abba Isaac said that Abba Pambo used to say: "A monk should wear such clothing that, if thrown outside the cell for three days, no one would take it."

23. Abba Isidore said: "If you love the Kingdom of Heaven, despise riches and seek the recompense of God."

24. Again he said: "If you are a lover of pleasure and a lover of money, you cannot live according to God."

25. One of the fathers recounted of Abba John the Persian, who lived in the Arabia of Egypt, that from his great goodness he attained to the deepest innocence. Once he borrowed one gold coin and bought flax for work. A brother came to him and asked: "Give me, abba, a little flax, so that I may make myself a tunic." And he gave it to him with joy. Another brother came to him and also asked: "Give me a little flax, so that I may make a towel." The abba gave to him also with the same disposition. And when others asked, he gave to all with joy. But then the creditor came, demanding his gold coin, and the elder promised to bring it. However, not having the means to repay, he decided to go to Abba James, the giver of alms, and ask him, so as to return it to the brother. On the way he found a gold coin lying on the

ground, but he did not touch it; rather, having said a prayer, he returned to his cell. The brother again came for the debt, and the elder said to him: "I will by all means attend to this." And setting out for the abba, he again saw the same coin on the ground where it was. The elder, having said a prayer, again returned to his cell. A third time the brother came, importuning him, and the elder said: "This time I will certainly bring it." He went to that place and found the coin lying there. Having said a prayer, the elder took it, came to Abba James, and asked him: "Abba, going to you, I found this coin on the road; therefore, do me the kindness of announcing in the vicinity whether anyone has lost it, and if its owner is found, give it to him." The elder announced it for three days, but no one turned out to have lost it. Then the elder said to Abba James: "If no one has lost it, then give the coin to such-and-such a brother, for I owe it to him and, going to you to receive alms and repay the debt, I found it." Abba James marveled that, being in debt and finding a coin, he did not take it immediately and repay. And this too was wondrous in this elder: that if anyone came to borrow something from him, he did not give it himself but would say to the brother: "Go and take what you need." Likewise, when they brought back what had been taken before, he would say: "Put it back in its place." But if the one who had borrowed brought nothing back, he said nothing to him.

26. They said of Abba Julian that he spent seventy years in one small cave, having nothing of the things of this world except a hair shirt and a covering, a wooden cup, and a Gospel.

27. Abba Cassian recounted that a certain senator, having renounced the world and distributed his possessions to the poor, held back something for his own consolation, not wishing to embrace the humility that comes from complete renunciation and the sincere obedience to the coenobitic rule. To him Saint Basil spoke this word: "You have lost the senator in yourself and have not made a monk of yourself."

28. Again he said: "A certain monk lived in the desert in a cave and was informed by his relatives according to the flesh that his father was gravely ill and would soon die and that he should come to receive the inheritance. But he answered them: 'I died to the world before him, and a dead man does not inherit from one living.'"

29. Certain brethren once came to Abba Macarius in Scetis and, finding nothing in the cell except putrid water, said to him: "Abba, go up to the village, and we will give you rest." The elder asked them: "Do you know, brethren, the bakery of so-and-so in the city?" They answered: "We know it." The elder said: "I also know it. And do you also know the garden of so-and-so by the river?" They say to him: "We know it." The elder said to them: "I also know it. Therefore, if I desire anything, I will have no need of you but will obtain it for myself."

30. They recounted of Abba Moses of Scetis: "When, intending to settle in Petra, he was going there, he said to himself: 'How will I gather water for myself here?' And a voice came to him, saying: 'Settle and be anxious about nothing.' And he settled there. Once some fathers came to him, but he had only one jug of water, and that was used up in preparing lentils. The elder was grieved and therefore, going out and coming in, prayed to God. And behold, a rain

cloud came over Petra itself, and water filled all his vessels. The elders asked him later: 'Tell us, why were you going out and coming in?' Abba Moses answered them: 'I was bringing a case against God, saying to Him: Thou hast brought me here, and behold, I have no water, that Thy servants may drink. For this reason I was going out and coming in, imploring God until He sent us water.'"

31. They said of Abba Megethius that if, upon leaving his cell, a thought came to him to depart from that place, he would no longer return to his cell, for he had nothing of the things of this age except one needle with which he split branches. He made three baskets each day, only enough for his sustenance.

32. A brother asked Abba Pistamon: "What shall I do, father? I am troubled and have no peace when selling my handiwork." The elder said to him in answer: "Abba Sisoes and other fathers also sold their handiwork; there is no harm in this. But when you sell, state the price of the item once, a little less; and if you wish to lower the price, it is in your power. And thus you will find peace." The brother again asked him: "If I have all that is needful from wherever it may be, do you advise me to be concerned about handiwork?" The elder answered: "However much you may have, do not abandon your handiwork; do as much as you can, only not with anxiety."

33. They said of Abba Silvanus: "Once his disciple Zacharias went out without him and, gathering the brethren, broke down the fence of the garden and made it more spacious. When the elder learned of this, he took his sheepskin and, going out, said to the brethren: 'Pray for me.' Seeing him, they fell at the elder's feet, saying: 'Tell us what troubles you, father.' And he answered: 'I will not go inside and this sheepskin will not come off me until you move the fence back to its former place.' Then the brethren moved the fence, making it as it had been, and the elder returned to his cell."

34. Abba Silvanus said: "I am a slave, and my master said to me: 'Do my work, and I will feed you. Whether I have anything myself, or whether I steal, or whether I borrow, you need not ask about this, only work, and I will feed you.' Therefore, if I work, I am fed from the wages of my labors, and if I do not work, I am fed by alms."

35. A brother asked Abba Serapion to speak a word to him, and the elder answered: "What shall I say to you? You have taken what belongs to widows and orphans and placed it on this window," for he saw that it was full of books.

36. Blessed Syncletica was asked: "Is non-acquisitiveness a perfect good?" She said in answer: "It is decidedly perfect for those who can bear it, for those who endure it, though they have affliction according to the flesh, have rest in their soul. Just as a stiff garment, when it is washed, is kneaded and wrung out strongly, so also a firm soul is strengthened by poverty, especially voluntary poverty."

37. Abba Hyperechius said: "The treasure for a monk is voluntary non-acquisitiveness. Brother, treasure up in Heaven, for endless are the ages of rest."

38. A certain one of the saints named Philagrius, who lived in the Jerusalem desert and labored diligently so as to have his own bread, was standing once in the marketplace selling his handiwork. At this time someone dropped a purse with a thousand coins, and the elder, finding it, stood in that place, hoping that the one who had lost it would come there. And behold, he comes in tears. The elder drew him aside and gave him the purse. The man held on to him, wishing to give him something from it, but the elder did not want it. Then he began to cry out: "Come, look at the man of God! Learn what he has done!" But the elder hid himself and left the city, so as not to be glorified.

39. Abba Zoicus, the presbyter of Tamiat, recounted that he had heard from his father, Abba Nathaniel, that seven other senators who were monastics in Scetis rivaled Abba Arsenius, and that they, having renounced all that was theirs, used poor clay vessels and said: "May God see and, having mercy, forgive us our sins."

40. A certain man intending to renounce the world came to an elder and said to him: "I desire to become a monk." The elder answered him: "You cannot." He says: "No, I can." The elder said: "If you desire to become a monk, go, renounce everything, and having come here, sit in your cell." He went, distributed what he had, keeping one hundred coins for himself, and came to the elder. The elder says to him: "Now go and sit in your cell." He went and settled in a cell. Then thoughts began to say to him: "The door is old, a new one is required." He went to the elder and revealed to him: "Thoughts say to me that the door is old, a new one is required." The elder answered him: "You have not yet renounced; rather, go, renounce everything, and sit here." He went, distributed ninety coins, and returning, said to the elder: "Behold, I have renounced." And the elder again said to him: "Go and sit in your cell." But thoughts again began to say to him: "The roof is old, it must be changed." And when he revealed this to the elder, the elder said: "Go, renounce." He went, distributed everything, and returning, says to the elder: "Now I have renounced everything." And again, with the elder's permission, he sat in his cell, but thoughts again began to say to him: "Everything here is old and the place is deserted; a lion will come and eat you." He went to the elder and revealed these thoughts of his; but the elder answered: "Say to your thoughts: 'I await everything that may come upon me. Whether the cell falls or a lion comes and eats me, I will the sooner be delivered.' Say thus to your thoughts and sit in your cell without daydreaming, praying often, fearing nothing, and being anxious about nothing." Having done so, the brother found peace.

41. A certain monk was ill. The superior of a coenobium took him in and gave him rest as a poor man who had nothing necessary, and he also said to the brethren who were attending him: "Constrain yourselves a little and give rest to the sick one." Meanwhile, the sick man had a pot full of gold and had hidden it by digging a hole under the bed on which he lay. After a short time the sick man died, having said nothing about the gold, and after his burial the abba gave orders to take away that bed, and at this the hidden gold was discovered. Then the abba said: "If he did not confess about it while still alive, said nothing as he was dying, but placed his hope on the gold, I will not touch it. Go, bury it together with him."

Then fire came down from heaven and held over his grave for many days. And all who saw this marveled and were terrified.

42. A certain young man, desiring to renounce the world, often went out from home for this purpose, but thoughts kept bringing him back, entangling him with possessions, for he was rich. Once, when the young man went out with the same intention, thoughts surrounded him and raised a great clamor to bring him back again, but he, suddenly stripping off his clothing and throwing it down, ran naked to the monastery. At this time God revealed to a certain elder: "Arise and receive My warrior." The elder went out and met the young man, and having learned what had happened, he marveled and clothed him in the schema. From then on, if anyone came to the elder to ask about various thoughts, he would answer himself, but if they inquired about thoughts of renunciation, he would say: "Ask such-and-such a brother."

43. A certain man asked an elder to accept money for his needs, but the elder did not wish to take it, being content with his own handiwork. The man did not cease asking him to accept it, at least for other needy ones. The elder answered: "This would be a double shame: the first, that having no need, I would accept; and the second, that distributing what belongs to another, I would be vainglorious."

44. A certain notable man, having come from a foreign country to Scetis, brought much gold and asked the presbyter to distribute it to the brethren. The presbyter answered: "The brethren have no need." But since this man strongly urged him, the presbyter placed the basket with the gold by the church door and said: "Let the one who has need take." But none of the brethren approached it, and some did not even look at it. Then the presbyter said to him: "God has accepted your love; go and distribute this to the poor." And he departed, having received great benefit.

45. Someone brought money to an elder who had leprosy and said: "Take it for your expenses, for you are already old and infirm." But the elder answered: "You have come to take my sixty-year trophy! For so much time I have been in this sickness and have had need of nothing, for God has provided for and fed me." And he did not agree to accept it.

46. The elders recounted about a certain gardener that he labored diligently and gave everything he earned by his labor to alms, leaving for himself only enough for his sustenance. But then Satan put thoughts in him: "Gather for yourself a small sum, so that when you grow old or become ill, you will have no need for sustenance." Then he gathered a small pot of coins. And indeed, it happened that he fell ill: his leg began to rot, and he spent all the money on physicians, receiving no benefit. Finally, an experienced physician came and concluded: "If the leg is not cut off, your whole body will rot." And he agreed to this, but during the night, having come to his senses and repenting of what he had done, he groaned and wept, saying: "Remember, O Lord, my former deeds, which I did when, working, I gave everything to the brethren." As soon as he said this, an Angel of the Lord appeared to him and asked: "Where is the little pot that you accumulated, and where is the hope that you had in it?" The gardener acknowledged his sin and said: "I have sinned, O Lord, forgive me. Henceforth I

will no longer do this." Then the Angel touched his leg, and it was immediately healed. And rising at dawn, he went to work in the field. The physician came, as they had agreed, with iron instruments to saw off his leg, and learning that he was working in the field, went there in amazement. When he saw the gardener digging the earth, he glorified God, Who had given him healing.

47. A brother asked an elder: "Do you advise me to keep two olokotin (an Egyptian coin) in case of bodily illness?" The elder answered: "It is not good to keep more than is necessary. If you keep two olokotin, you will place your hope in them, and God will no longer care for you; rather, *let us cast all our care upon Him, for He cares for us* (1 Peter 5:7)."

48. Certain Greeks came to Ostracine to give alms and took stewards with them so that they might show them those in extreme need. The stewards brought them to a certain leper, but he refused to accept the offering, saying: "Behold, I have some branches; I weave and, laboring, eat my bread." Then they brought them to the hut of a certain widow with children. When they knocked, her daughter, who was naked, answered, but their mother, a laundress, was at work. The daughter refused to accept clothing and money, saying: "My mother has told me: 'Be bold. If it pleases God and I find work, we will have food for ourselves.'" When the mother came, they also asked her to accept, but she too did not wish to, saying: "I have God as my protector, and you wish to take Him from me!" Discovering such faith in her, they glorified God.

49. An elder said: "If you desire the Kingdom, despise riches, for it is impossible to live according to God for one who is a lover of pleasure and a lover of money."

50. One of the fathers recounted: "There was an elder who had been deemed worthy of great gifts from God and had become very famous because of his virtuous life. The fame of him reached even the emperor, and the emperor sent for him, so as to be deemed worthy of his prayers. Having conversed with the elder and having received much benefit from that conversation, the emperor offered him gold. The elder accepted it, and returning to his place, began to concern himself with improving his field and with other possessions. Once a demoniac came to him as usual, and the elder said to the demon: 'Depart from the creature of God.' But the demon answered him: 'I will not obey you.' The elder asked: 'Why?' And the demon answered: 'Because, having abandoned the care for God and taken up the care for earthly things, you have become like one of us. Therefore, I do not obey you and will not depart.'"

51. A certain brother found on the road a log that had fallen from a camel and brought it to his cell. The abba asked him: "From where did you bring this?" The brother answered: "From the road." And the elder said: "If it was carried there by the wind, bring it inside; but if not, go and put it back in its former place."

52. A certain ascetic was warred against by avarice and from his handiwork acquired first one coin, then another, then a third, then endeavored to bring them to five; and suddenly he became severely ill, for his leg began to rot. He spent on treatment first one, and then all five

coins, but received no relief, and the physician finally said to him that the leg must be cut off, otherwise the whole body would rot. The elder agreed, but during the night, as he wept, an Angel appeared to him, touched his leg, wiped away the sore with his hand, and asked the elder: "Will you still accumulate those five coins? What do you say now?" And having instantly healed him, he became invisible. When the physician came by day, the elder received him and told him what had happened, which so amazed him that he, a Greek, became a Christian.

53. An elder said: "A man who has tasted the sweetness of non-acquisitiveness is burdened by the very clothing he wears and the jug for water, for his mind is occupied with other things."

54. He also said: "How can one who has not hated material things hate his own soul, as the Lord commands?"

55. An elder said: "In your cell do not have clothing that hangs idle, for this is death for you: others more righteous than you are freezing, while you, a sinner, have something superfluous."

56. Again he said: "Do not have any superfluous thing, even the smallest, that lies idle, for you will give an account even for it."

57. He also said: "Do not tolerate gold in your possession your whole life, otherwise God will no longer care for you. But when it comes to you, if you have need of clothing or food, buy it immediately; but if you do not have need, let it not spend the night with you."

58. Again he said: "If you have a cell that barely contains you alone, do not build another out of a desire to find more space in it."

59. He also said: "If you acquire a book, do not adorn its cover; do not keep a costly stand in your chapel either."

60. He also said: "Let your hands never find by touch any silver or gold thing, even a small one, in your cell."

61. Again he said: "Let no new clothing come upon your body, nor a cowl that pleases you."

62. He also said: "Do not hang a towel on your belt, for even this hinders contrition and weeping in you. And in general, let everything, your bed, your vessels, your footwear, your belt, be such that if thieves come, they would not want to take anything that is in your cell."

63. He also said: "If you see a vessel or any tool of your brother, do not desire it, for otherwise you will fall into a greater evil. He who desires a small and poor thing, if he sees something better, will desire that too."

64. He also said: "If you have a vessel, or a knife, or a plough, or anything else, and you see that your thought loves it, cast it away from you, so as to teach your thought to love nothing at all except Christ alone."

65. Again he said: "If you give someone something out of love and your thought begins to grieve, as if you gave much, pay no attention to it, for it is satanic. As much as you are able, live in poverty and humility so as to be yourself more in need of receiving alms. For he who gives rejoices in his heart, thinking that he does a good deed, while he who has nothing and lives in poverty comes to great humility, thinking that he does nothing good and gives nothing. Thus lived our fathers; thus Abba Arsenius found God."

66. An elder said: "Love poverty and do not have beautiful things in your cell, for when the soul seeks some thing and does not find it, it is humbled; and then God consoles it and gives it compunction. As soon as the soul tastes the sweetness of God, it begins to hate even the clothing it wears and its very body. I tell you, my son, that if the soul does not hate its body as its adversary and enemy, allowing it no indulgence, not even in the smallest thing, it will never be able to free itself from the snare of the devil." To a man young in body, Abba Isaiah gives these commandments: "Do not take another by the hand; do not approach another's body, except in great illness, and that with fear; likewise, do not allow another's hand to approach you or to examine you; never tell anyone to remove a speck from your beard, or from your head, or from your clothing; do not sleep near anyone at all your whole life; do not give a kiss even in church to a youth without a beard when he comes from a foreign land, do not laugh with him, lest your soul perish; do not sit down or sit near him, and do not approach each other at all; in the needs of your belly, do not sit with another at all, for the truly reverent one is ashamed even of himself. Many, having despised these things as trifling, have fallen into a pit because of them and perished, for every great evil is at first small and afterward becomes great. May the Lord establish us in His fear."

67. A brother asked an elder: "Tell me, abba, how shall I be saved?" The elder removed his tunic, girded his loins, and, hanging himself up by his hands, said: "Thus must a monk be naked of all the things of the world and crucified in his struggles."

Endnotes

[11] Patched, mended garments.

Chapter VII.
Various Narratives Conducive
to Patience and Courage

1. Brethren came to Abba Anthony and say to him: "speak to us a word, how we may be saved?" The elder answered them: "you have heard the Scripture? That is enough for you." They say: "we wish to hear from you as well, father!" The elder said: "the Gospel says: *if anyone strikes you on your right cheek, turn the other to him also* (Matthew 5:39)." They say to him: "we cannot do this." The elder said to them: "if you cannot turn the other, at least endure the blow on the one." They say: "we cannot do this either." The elder said to that: "if you cannot do even this, at least do not repay what you have received." They say: "we cannot do this either." Then the elder said to his disciple: "prepare a little porridge for them, for they are infirm. If you cannot do this, and you do not wish to do that, then what shall I do for you? Prayer is needed."

2. Abba Anthony also said: "God does not permit such temptations in the present times as there were of old."

3. A brother asked Abba Agathon: "I have been given a commandment, and there is warfare where I must fulfill it. Thus I wish to go for the commandment's sake, yet I fear the warfare." The elder said to him: "if this were a lover of God, he would fulfill the commandment and conquer the warfare."

4. Abba Ammon said: "fourteen years I spent in Scetis, praying to God day and night, that He might grant me to overcome anger."

5. Abba Apollos, disciple of Abba Sisoes, recounted to us concerning himself the following: "at the beginning, when I came to Abba Sisoes, I was warred against by the passions for three years and did not disclose them to the elder; especially I was overcome by lying, slander, and vainglory. Most severe was my warfare concerning the priesthood, and I had dreams as though I were ordained a bishop. Abba Sisoes did not cease to instruct and rebuke me, so that from the multitude of reproofs and rebukes I fled from him and went to Alexandria to my relatives according to the flesh, in order to receive ordination and become a presbyter at the church of the Most Holy Theotokos. When I was going along the road, I met a man of great height, entirely naked, black in color, repulsive in appearance, small-

headed, thin-legged with iron claws, fiery eyes, thick lips, and with skin like that of a donkey. Seeing him, I was filled with terror and sealed myself with the cross. But he drew near to me and, embracing me, kissed me repeatedly and said: 'why do you cross yourself and flee from me? You are my friend, who does my will. Therefore I also have come to accompany you and to help you fulfill your will.' No longer able to bear his stench, I lifted my eyes to heaven and cried out: 'O God! By the prayers of my abba Sisoes, deliver me from this necessity!' And suddenly the apparition became a woman, exceedingly beautiful and comely, who, baring herself, said to me: 'enjoy your lusts, for greatly have you given me rest. I am a rope-weaver, and as many branches as you bring me, so many I weave. But the prayers of Sisoes drive me away from you.' Having said this, she became invisible. Then I immediately returned to my elder and, falling before him, recounted to him and the brethren all that had happened to me. The abba made a prayer over me, and I remained with him forever."

6. Abba Bessarion said: "forty days and forty nights I stood in the midst of thorns, not sleeping."

7. He also said: "for forty years I have not lain on my side, but slept standing or sitting."

8. A disciple of Abba Bessarion recounted: "the life of the abba was like the life of one of the birds, or fish, or one of the wild beasts, without disturbances and cares did he spend all the time of his life. The care of a dwelling did not occupy him, attachment to a place did not possess his soul, nor the desire for satiation with food, nor the acquisition of habitations, nor the collection of books, but he appeared completely free from all bodily passions. Nourished by the hope of future blessings and having secured himself with the rampart of faith, he was firm in spirit as a captive; here and there enduring cold and nakedness and being scorched by the heat, as one forever left without shelter, he wandered, pierced by fear in the desolate precipices or calmly borne, as upon a sea, across the broad uninhabited expanse of sand. If it happened that he came to a more pleasant place, where monks lead a uniform life according to the rule of coenobia, then, sitting at the gates, he wept and was contrite, like one of those cast ashore after a shipwreck. Then, if one of the brethren, coming out, found him sitting like one of the poor petitioners who go about the world, and, approaching, asked him with compassion: 'why do you weep, O man? If you have need of something necessary, you shall receive according to our ability, only come in, partake of our table and be consoled!' He would answer: 'I cannot enter under a roof before I find the possessions of my house, for in various ways I have lost a great fortune: I have fallen prey to sea pirates and suffered shipwreck, I have lost my nobility and from one honored have become dishonored.' If a brother, moved to tears by such words and taking bread, gave it to him with the words: 'take this, father, and the rest God will restore to you, your homeland, kindred, and wealth, of which you have spoken,' he would begin to sob yet more strongly and pour forth tears, crying aloud: 'I cannot say whether I shall be able to find that which, having lost, I seek. For I may lose even more, being daily in danger of death and having no rest from my immeasurable misfortunes, since I must finish this journey amid wanderings.'"

9. Abba Benjamin said: "journey along the royal path, measure the milestones and do not lose heart."

10. A brother came to Abba Victor, the hesychast, in the lavra of Elis and asked him: "what should I do, father? The passion of despondency overcomes me." The elder answered: "just as for those who are sick in their eyes it seems that they see an overly strong light, while for those who are healthy in their eyes it is not strong, so also the fainthearted are distressed by a small sorrow and think it is a great sorrow, but those strong in soul rather rejoice in temptations."

11. Saint Gregory said: "if nothing sorrowful was expected by you when you intended to approach the love of wisdom of the ascetic life, then your beginning is not one of wisdom, revealing in you a dreamer or one quick to change. For if something was expected, then when it is encountered, it is also courageously endured; but if what comes is unexpected, then you easily prove a liar against your vow."

12. Abba Daniel recounted: "there was a certain monk named Dulas, esteemed as great among the fathers. This Dulas at first lived in a coenobium for forty years and said: 'upon due examination I have found that those living in coenobia progress far more and more quickly in the practice of the virtues, if only they remain in their place with a true heart.' And he recounted further: there was in the coenobium a certain brother, humble and lowly in appearance, but great and glorious in mind. All despised him and reviled him, but he was glad and rejoiced and bore it with good cheer when the brethren, at the instigation of the enemy, grieved him in every way: some beat him, others spat upon him, and still others heaped abuse upon him, and this for a span of twenty years. Finally, the enemy could no longer endure his patient endurance and brought upon him such a calamity: he inspired one brother to rob the church, and he, when all the brethren were at rest, entered the church, gathered all the sacred objects and secretly left the coenobium. When the time of the church assembly came, the canonarch entered to light the lamps and prepare the censer and found everything stolen. The brother informs the abba, strikes the semantron, and all the brethren assemble, who, having become agitated, finally decided that no one else could have taken them except that brother, for he had not yet come to the assembly, since if he had not done this, he would have come first now, as always. They sent for him and found him at prayer, entered and forcibly dragged him. He besought them, asking: 'what is it, fathers, what is it?' But they heaped abuse and reproaches upon him and said: 'sacrilege! You who are not worthy even of life! Is it not enough for you that you have disturbed us so long? Now you have even mocked our souls!' He only said: 'I have sinned, forgive me.' They brought him to the abba with the words: 'abba! Here is the one who from the very beginning has been corrupting the coenobium!' And they began one after another to slander him: one said that he had seen him secretly eating vegetables; another, that he stole bread and sold it outside the coenobium; a third, that he had caught him drinking the best wine... And all who lied were believed, but him who spoke the truth they did not heed. The abba removed the schema from him, saying that such deeds are not proper for a Christian. Then they put iron upon his neck and handed him over to the

steward of the lavra, who stripped him and beat him with ox sinews, trying to ascertain whether what they said against him was true. The brother only said with meekness: 'I have sinned, forgive me.' Enraged by his words, he commanded that he be cast into prison, and his feet put in stocks, and wrote to the judge concerning this matter. Soon the judge's servants arrived, placed him with heavy iron upon his neck on an uncovered animal and dragged him to the city. There again they interrogated him: who he was, whence he came, for what reason he had become a monk... but he said nothing more than only: 'I have sinned, forgive me.' Beside himself, the judge commanded that he be laid down and beaten with ox sinews on his back. Stretched out and mercilessly tormented, but with a smiling face, he said to the judge: 'beat, beat; by this you make my gold more brilliant.' The judge answered: 'I shall whiten you more than snow,' and commanded fire to be placed beneath his belly and salt dissolved in vinegar to be poured upon his wounds. Those standing by marveled at such patience and said: 'tell us, where did you put the sacred objects, and you shall be released.' But he answered: 'I am not involved in this matter.' Finally, the judge commanded that the torments cease, that he be taken to prison and guarded without food and without any care for him. Then he sent to the lavra with a command that the abba come with all the brethren. When they came, the judge said to them: 'I have labored much and subjected him to various torments, but could find nothing.' The brethren said to him in reply: 'he has done much other evil, and we for God's sake endured him, awaiting his conversion, but he has come to something even worse.' The judge asked them: 'what then shall I do with him?' They answered: 'what the law commands.' And to the judge's words, 'the law commands that sacrilegious persons be killed,' they said: 'so let him be killed.' Then, dismissing them, the judge commands that the brother be brought and, sitting on the judgment seat, says to him: 'confess, wretch, and you shall be delivered from death.' The brother answered: 'if you command me to say what was not, I will say it, but I have never done anything of what they ask me.' After this, the judge commanded that he be beheaded, and the executioners led the brother to execution. Meanwhile, the one who had taken the objects came to compunction and said to himself: 'now or whenever, the matter will be known, even if here it remains unknown. And what will you do on that day? What will you say in justification of such deeds?' Then he comes to the abba and says to him: 'send quickly, lest the brother die, for the sacred objects have been found.' When the brother was brought to the monastery, all began to ask his forgiveness, but the brother, weeping, said: 'forgive me. I confess great gratitude to you, for through these small afflictions you make me worthy of great blessings. I always rejoiced greatly when I heard that you spoke unseemly things about me, for in return for these small humiliations I hoped to be deemed worthy of great honors on the dreadful day. Especially I rejoiced now and was not offended by what you did to me, foreseeing the recompense of the hoped-for repose in the kingdom of heaven for such temptations.' After this, in three days the brother departed to the Lord: one of the brethren came to him and found him standing on his knees, for he had given up his soul while making prostrations and praying. When this was told to the abba, he commanded that his body be brought into the church and laid before the altar, that the semantron be struck and all the brethren be assembled, so that the brother might be buried in the church with glory. Each of the brethren wished to receive a blessing from the deceased, and seeing this, the abba placed his body in the sacristy and locked it with a key, awaiting the abba of the lavra, so that together with him they might perform the burial. When the father of the lavra came with the clergy, then, having made a prayer, they say to the abba: 'now unlock and let us bury the body, for it is already the ninth hour.' But, entering the sacristy, they found no one, only his clothing and sandals. Then all were amazed and began to glorify God with tears, saying: 'see, brethren, what patience and humility bring us! And as you see now, so also strive yourselves to endure every humiliation and temptation, for by this is acquired the kingdom of heaven by the grace of our Lord Jesus Christ.'"

13. A certain brother lived in a coenobium in obedience and received great benefit, being humbled in all things, but nine things edified him, while one scandalized him; and he moved to another coenobium. Here the number of edifying things decreased by one, for he was edified by eight, but scandalized by two. Then he departed from here also and went to the next coenobium, where seven things edified him and three scandalized him. Proceeding in the same manner, he again left this place, but in the new place five things edified him and five scandalized him. After this, he desired to move one last time to another coenobium, but before he entered it, he took paper and said to himself: "if you will believe your thought, then the whole world will not suffice for your wanderings. Rather lay it down in your heart to endure and write on this paper: you left such-and-such coenobium because you encountered distraction; from such-and-such, for such-and-such reason; and so on, setting down in order all the causes that drove you from this or that coenobium." And at the end he wrote: "if you find all these causes here, will you endure?" And he signed: "in the name of the Lord Jesus Christ, the Son of God, I will endure." After this, he rolled up his writing, placed it in his belt and, having prayed, entered the coenobium. And if he noticed something that troubled him, he would take out his writing in private and, when reading it, he came to the words, "in the name of the Lord Jesus Christ, the Son of God, I will endure," he was calmed, saying to himself: "with God you have made a covenant, from Him also seek help." Not enduring such patience of the brother, the evil one arranged for the brethren to notice how he read his paper and how, having read it, he was healed. Therefore they began to say that he had a spell, for, reading something, he is not troubled, while they are troubled. They went to the abba and said to him: "we cannot be with such-and-such brother, for he is a sorcerer and in his belt is kept his sorcery. If you wish to keep him, then release us." The abba, being spiritual, knew the humility of the brother and, understanding that this was from the envy of the devil, proposed to the brethren: "go, pray, and I will pray, and in three days I will give you an answer." Then, when the brother was asleep, the abba removed his belt and, having read the writing, girded the brother with it again, and after three days, to the brethren's inquiry about what he intended to do, the abba called the brother and asked him: "why do you scandalize the brethren?" He answered: "I have sinned, forgive me and pray for me." Then the abba asked the brethren: "what did you say this brother does?" They repeated: "he is a sorcerer, and his sorcery is kept in his belt!" The abba commanded: "take out his spells!" The brother would not allow his belt to be untied, and the abba ordered it to be cut. When the writing of

the brother was found, the abba gave it to the deacon and commanded him to stand in an elevated place and read it, saying: "let the devil be put to shame in this, who plants sorceries in people!" When all had been read and especially the words, "in the name of Jesus Christ I will endure with the brethren," then the brethren, being ashamed, made a prostration to the abba, saying: "we have sinned!" To which the abba said: "do you make a prostration to me? To God and to this brother make the prostration." Then the abba turned to the brother: "let us pray to God that He may forgive them." And they prayed for them.

14. In the innermost desert of Scetis there lived a eunuch, and his cell was eighteen miles distant from Scetis. Once a week he came to Abba Daniel at night, so that no one knew him except the abba and his disciple. The elder gave his disciple this commandment concerning him: "once a week fill a vessel with water, place it at the door of the cave of the eunuch and, having knocked from outside, withdraw; at the same time say nothing at all to him, but only observe and, if you find a potsherd with writing near the door, bring it with you." And so his disciple did. Once he found a potsherd on which was written: "take the implements and come alone, or also your disciple." The elder, having read what was written, wept with great weeping and, turning to his disciple, said: "woe to you, innermost desert! What pillar is leaving you now! Take these things and follow me. Alas, let us go quickly! Let us hasten to find the elder, lest we be deprived of his prayers, for he is departing to the Lord." And they both went with weeping and found him in a severe fever. The elder threw himself upon his breast, wept much, and then said: "blessed are you, for, caring for this hour, you despised an earthly kingdom and all people." The eunuch answered: "blessed are you, new Abraham and host of Christ! For how many fruits does Christ receive through your hands!" The elder asked: "make a prayer over us, father." The eunuch said: "at this hour I have the greatest need of prayers." The elder answered: "if I had preceded you at this hour, I would have prayed for you." Then the eunuch, raising himself and sitting on the mat, embraced the head of the elder, kissed it and said: "may the God who showed me the way to this place fulfill your old age as the old age of Abraham." The elder took his disciple and, casting him at the knees of the eunuch, asked: "bless my son, father!" He kissed him and said: "O God, Who stands before me at this hour in order to separate me from my body, and Who knows how many steps this brother has walked to my cell for the sake of Your name, grant that the spirit of his fathers may rest upon him, as the spirit of Elijah rested upon Elisha!" Then he asked the elder: "for the Lord's sake, do not remove from me what I wear, but as I am, so send me to the Lord, and let no one else know what concerns me, except you alone. Now let me receive communion" and, having communed, he said: "show love to me in Christ and pray for me." Then he looked to the right side and said: "well have you come, let us go!" Then his face shone like fire. After this, he placed the sign of the cross upon his lips and with the words: "O God! *Into Your hands I commit my spirit,*" gave up his soul to the Lord. The elder and his disciple honored his departure with weeping and began to dig a grave before the cave. Then the elder took off what he wore and commanded his disciple to put this over what was on the deceased, and he wore a faskidion[12] of palm branches on his body and a kentonion[13]. The brother, clothing him, saw that his breast was that of a woman's, like two dried leaves, but he said nothing of

it. When they buried him and made a prayer, the elder says to his disciple: "let us now break the fast and make a commemoration for the elder." They found with him a few dried crusts, soaked them and made a meal. After this, taking the plait that he was making, they went, thanking God, to their cell. Along the way the disciple told the elder: "do you know, father, that this eunuch was a woman, for when I was clothing him, I saw this." The elder said in answer: "I knew also, my son, that she was a woman. Do you wish me to tell you about her? Listen! She was the foremost senatorial lady at court, and the Emperor Justinian desired to bring her into the palace on account of her great wisdom. Theodora learned of this and, becoming indignant, resolved to exile her. Hearing of this, she hired a ship and by night, taking with her some of her possessions, took to flight. Reaching Alexandria, she settled in [...] of Alexandria and established a monastery there, which to this day is called the Monastery of the Patrician (the Senatorial Lady). Upon the death of Theodora, she learned that the emperor intended to bring her back, fled Alexandria by night, came here, to my monastery, and asked me to give her a cell outside of Scetis, having told me all about herself in detail. I gave her this cave, and she, having changed into men's clothing, settled in it. Now it is already twenty-eight years since she has been in Scetis, and no one knew of her except you, me, and one other brother; for, if you and I went away somewhere, I commanded that brother to deliver a jug of water for her, but who she was, no one knew except you alone. How many magistriani the emperor sent to search for her, and not only he, but also the pasha of Alexandria and the whole city searched for her, yet no one learned in what place she was hiding, even to this day. You see how those raised in royal fashion struggle against the devil and crush his body, while we, living in the world, sometimes did not even have bread to be satisfied with, and having received monasticism, we seek consolations, and therefore cannot acquire a single virtue. So let us pray that the Lord may also deem us worthy to attain the same path and together with our holy fathers to find mercy on that day, along with Abba Anastasius the eunuch (for she was called Anastasia), through the prayers and intercession of our Lady the Theotokos, and of all the saints, and of Abba Daniel, before the dread throne of our Lord Jesus Christ."

15. In great Antioch there was a young silversmith named Andronicus, who took as his wife the daughter of another silversmith, John, whose name was Athanasia, which means immortal, for truly she was immortal in deeds and wisdom. Andronicus and Athanasia were very wealthy, but pious and full of good works. Their manner of life was such: the income from their silver work and their property they divided into three parts: one for the poor, another for monks, and the third for their own maintenance and trade; and the whole city loved Andronicus for his meekness. He knew his wife, and she bore him a son, whom he named John. Again Athanasia conceived and bore a daughter, and he named her Mary; and Andronicus resolved henceforth not to approach his wife, yet all his care, together with other Christ-loving men and women, was for the sick and the poor. On Sunday, Monday, Wednesday, and Friday, from evening until morning, Andronicus and Athanasia remained in the church. After twelve years had passed, once Athanasia came home after Matins from the church, went to look at her children and found them moaning. Becoming troubled, Athanasia

took the children, laid them on the bed and pressed them to her breast, and when Andronicus came and called her, supposing she was still asleep, Athanasia said to him: "do not be angry, my lord, our children are sick." Finding a fever upon the children and sighing, he said: "may the Lord's will be done!" Then he went outside the city to pray to the holy martyr Julian, where his parents were buried, remaining there until the sixth hour of the day (noon by our reckoning). But when Andronicus returned, he heard weeping and wailing in his house and saw that nearly the whole city had assembled at his home, for his children had died. Looking at them as they lay together, he went into his prayer room and, falling before the Savior, said: *"naked I came from my mother's womb, and naked shall I return there. The Lord gave, and the Lord has taken away; as it pleased the Lord, so it has come to pass: blessed be the name of the Lord forever"* (Job 1:21). But his wife, from great sorrow, wished to die, saying: "let me also die with my children." The whole city assembled for the burial of the children, the patriarch himself came with his clergy, and they buried the children with Saint Julian together with their forebears. After this, the patriarch took Andronicus to his house, but Athanasia did not wish to depart and remained to spend the night there. At midnight the holy martyr appeared to her in the form of a monk and said: "why do you not give rest to those who repose here?" She answered: "my lord! Do not be grieved at me! I had only two children, and now I have brought both here!" He asked her: "how old were your children?" She answered: "one child was twelve, and the other ten years old." Then he said to her: "why then do you weep for them? Rather weep for your sins! For I tell you, woman, in the same way that human nature requires food and it is impossible not to give it, so also the departed infants shall demand of Christ on that day the blessings to come, saying: 'righteous Judge! You have deprived us of earthly things, do not deprive us of heavenly things.'" Hearing this, she was calmed and changed her weeping to joy, saying: "if my children live in heaven, why should I weep?" Then she began to look for the abba who had spoken with her, but, having gone through the whole temple, she did not find him. She called the gatekeeper and asked him: "where is the abba who entered here?" The gatekeeper answered her: "do you not see that all the gates are locked, and you ask where the abba who entered is?" And he began to philosophize: "know that you have seen an apparition!" Seized with fear, she asked to be let out and, coming home, told her husband everything. Then the blessed Athanasia says to him: "truly, even while our children were alive, I gathered myself more than once to tell you, but I was ashamed; I shall speak now, after their death, if you will listen to me: release me to a monastery to weep for my sins." He answered her: "go and test your thought for one week, and if you remain in this intention, then we shall speak of it." Coming after a week, she spoke the same word. Then the blessed Andronicus summoned his father-in-law, handed over to him all his property and said: "we are going to the holy places to pray, and if on this journey the human lot (death) should befall us, deal with our property according to God, and I ask you, do good for our souls and establish in our house a hospital and a hospice for strangers." Then he freed his servants and, taking two horses and what was needed for the journey, they went out of the city by night. The blessed Athanasia looked back from afar at her house and, looking up to heaven, said: "O God, Who said to Abraham and Sarah: *get out of your country, and from your kindred... and go to a land that I will show you'* (Genesis 12:1), You Yourself guide us in Your fear! Behold, we have left our house open for the sake of Your name, do not close before us the doors of Your kingdom," and, having wept, they went on. Reaching the holy places, they honored the fathers and, having conversed with many of them, set out for Alexandria to Saint Menas, in order to delight in veneration of the martyr. Once, going out at the ninth hour of the day, the blessed Andronicus saw that a monk and a layman, from whom the monk had hired an animal to go to Scetis, were disputing with one another: the layman proposed to set out now and, traveling by night, arrive at Scetis before the heat, but the monk did not agree. Then Andronicus said to the layman: "go, bring one more animal, and let us take them: one for me, another for the abba, so as to set out, for I also intend to go to Scetis." After this, he commanded Athanasia to wait for his return, for women are not permitted to go to Scetis, to which she said with weeping: "you shall answer before Saint Menas if you remain there and do not return to settle me in a monastery," and, having kissed one another, they parted. At the lavra of Scetis, Andronicus venerated the holy fathers and, with difficulty reaching Abba Daniel, disclosed everything to him in conversation. The elder said: "go, bring your wife; I shall give you a letter and you will take her to the Thebaid, to the Tabennisiote monastery." When Andronicus brought his wife, the elder imparted to them a word of salvation and, having written a letter, dismissed them. Upon Andronicus's return, the elder clothed him in the schema and taught him the monastic practices. Having remained with him for twelve years, Andronicus asked the elder to release him to the holy places, and, having made a prayer, the elder released him. Passing through Egypt, Abba Andronicus sat down in the shade to rest from the heat of the sun, and at that time, by the providence of God, his wife, dressed as a man, came up to this place, for she also was going to the holy places; and they greeted one another. The dove recognized her mate, but how could he recognize her, so wasted and blackened as if she were an Ethiopian? And he asked her: "where are you going, abba?" She answered that to the holy places, and when he said: "I also am directing my way there," she proposed: "do you wish, let us go together, but let us go in such silence as though we were not together?" He agreed, and to her question whether he was not a disciple of Abba Daniel, he answered: "yes." To this Athanasia said: "may the prayers of the elder accompany us." Andronicus concluded: "amen." Then together they went and venerated the holy places and returned to Alexandria. Then Abba Athanasius says to Abba Andronicus: "do you wish, let us remain together in one cell?" He answered: "as you command, only first I shall go to receive a blessing from my elder." She said to that: "go, I shall wait for you at the Octodecaton. However, as we traveled in silence, so also in the cell let us remain in silence, and if you cannot bear this, do not come. I, however, shall certainly remain at the Octodecaton." When Andronicus came to the elder and, having kissed him, told him about this, the elder answered: "go, and, loving silence, remain with that brother, for he is a monk such as one ought to be." Having returned, Abba Andronicus found Abba Athanasius, and, protected by the fear of God, they remained together another twelve years; and Abba Andronicus did not know that it was his wife. The elder often came to visit them and say something for their benefit. Once, having visited them, he made a prayer according to custom and departed, but before he had reached Saint Menas, Abba Andronicus caught up with him and reported that Abba Athanasius was departing to the Lord. The elder returned and, seeing Abba Athanasius weeping, says to him: "instead of rejoicing, for you are going to meet the Lord, you weep!" Abba Athanasius answers him: "I weep not for myself, but for Abba Andronicus. But do me this kindness: after my burial, take the letter that lies under my head, read it and give it to Abba Andronicus." After this, having made a prayer and received communion, he reposed in the Lord. When they began to prepare Abba Athanasius for burial, they saw that she was a woman by nature, and, having read the letter, Abba Andronicus learned that this was his wife. And the report of this went throughout the whole lavra, and all glorified God. The elder sent word also to Scetis and to the innermost desert; and all the lavras of Alexandria assembled for the burial, and the whole city, and the Scetians came in white garments, for such was their custom. And they carried out the body of the blessed Athanasia with palms and branches, glorifying God who gave a woman such patience. The elder completed the seven days for the blessed Athanasia and wished to take Andronicus with him, but he did not consent, saying: "I shall die here with my lady." Then, having taken leave, the elder departed, but before he had reached Saint Menas, one brother caught up with him and reported that Abba Andronicus was dying. And the elder again sent to Scetis, that the brethren might return, for Abba Andronicus was following Abba Athanasius. Having returned, they found him still alive, and he, having blessed them, reposed in the Lord. Then a dispute arose between the fathers of the Octodecaton and the Scetians, who said: "he is our brother, and we shall take him to Scetis, that he may help us with his prayers; it is enough for you that we leave you Abba Athanasius." Seeing such commotion, the elder said to the brethren: "truly, if you do not listen to me, then I also shall remain here, and they shall bury me with my son." Then all grew quiet and peacefully buried brother Andronicus. The brethren began to call the elder to Scetis, but he answered them: "allow me to complete the seven days for the brother," but they did not permit him to remain. Thus let us pray that we also may come to the measure of Abba Athanasius and Abba Andronicus, through the prayers of all the saints. Amen.

16. Abba Evagrius said: "were there no temptations, no one would be saved."

17. Abba Isaiah said: "a novice monk, passing from monastery to monastery, is like an animal which, having stopped, dashes this way and that."

18. He also said: "if God wishes to have mercy on a soul, but it is stubborn and does not submit, but does according to its own will, then God permits it to suffer what it does not wish, so that in this way it might itself seek Him."

19. He also said: "nothing is so beneficial for the novice monk as reproach, for what a tree is that is watered daily, that is the novice who is reproached and who endures the reproach."

20. Again he said: "blessed are those whose labors are accomplished with understanding, for they are at rest from every burden and easily escape the snares of the demons and especially enslavement to him who sets obstacles for man in every good work that is

undertaken by him, for he brings sloth upon the mind when it gives itself to attending to God."

21. He also said: "the first of all struggles is exile, especially if you flee to solitude, leaving all your own and carrying with you only perfect faith and hope and a heart strong against your own desires, for they will encircle you with many circles, frightening you in various ways with temptations, harsh poverty, or illnesses, suggesting that if you fall into them, what will you do, having none who know you, who might take care of you? But by this the goodness of God tests you, in order to reveal your zeal and your love for God."

22. Abba Elijah said: "if the mind does not sing together with the body, the labor is vain. He who loves sorrow will find it afterward to be joy and repose."

23. He also recounted: "a certain elder lived in a pagan temple. Demons came and said to him: 'depart from our place.' The elder answered: 'you have no place.' Then they began to scatter his palm branches one after another, but the elder gathered them patiently. Finally, one demon seized him by the hand and dragged him toward the door; when he reached it, the elder grasped with his other hand onto the door and cried out: 'Jesus! Help me!' And immediately the demon fled, and the elder after this began to weep. The Lord asked him: 'why do you weep?' And he answered: 'because demons dare to seize a man and treat him thus.' Then the Lord said to him: 'you yourself allowed this negligence; as soon as you sought Me, you see how quickly I was found by you. I say this because great labor is needed, and without labor no one can have God for his own, for He Himself was crucified for us.'"

24. A certain brother, being in temptation, came to Abba Heraclius, and he, strengthening him, recounted the following incident: "a certain elder had a disciple, very obedient. Once, being in a struggle, he made a prostration to the elder and asked: 'bless me to live in solitude.' The elder answered him: 'look for a place, and we shall make a cell for you.' Going away one milestone, the brother found himself a place; there they also built a cell. The elder says to the brother: 'do whatever I tell you: when you are hungry, eat; when you are thirsty, drink; when sleep draws you, sleep; only do not go out of your cell until Saturday, but on Saturday come to me.' The brother spent two days according to the elder's commandment, but on the third, becoming despondent, he said: 'what is this the elder has done to me?' Then he arose, chanted many psalms and, having eaten after sunset, went to sleep on his mat and saw an Ethiopian lying there, gnashing his teeth at him. In great fear he ran to the elder and knocked at the door, asking: 'abba! Have mercy on me and open!' The elder, knowing that he had not kept his word, did not open to him until morning, and in the morning, opening the door and seeing him pleading, he had compassion and brought him inside. Then the disciple told him: 'I saw a black Ethiopian on my mat when I came to sleep!' The elder answered: 'you suffered this because you did not keep my word.' Then, as far as he was able, he explained to him the rule of the solitary life; and little by little he became a good solitary."

25. A certain brother, living alone in the Cells, had no peace and, coming to Abba Theodore of Pherme, told him of this. The elder said: "go, humble your thought and remain in obedience, living with others." But the brother again returned to the elder and says: "I find

no peace among people either." Then the elder asks him: "if alone you do not find peace, nor living with people, then why did you come to the monastery? Was it not in order to endure sorrows? But tell me, how many years have you been in the schema?" The brother answered: "eight." To this the elder said: "I have been in the schema forty years and have not found peace for a single day, and you in eight years wish to acquire peace!" Hearing this, the brother departed encouraged.

26. Someone asked Abba Theodore: "if something should happen to fall unexpectedly, would you be frightened, abba?" The elder answered: "if heaven and earth collided, Theodore would not be afraid even then." For the elder had prayed to God that fearfulness be taken from him. The brother therefore asked him about this.

27. They said of Abba Theodore and of Abba Lucius of Ennaton that for fifty years they mocked their thoughts, saying: "after this winter we shall move from here." But when summer came, they again said: "after the harvest we shall depart from here." So did these ever-memorable fathers behave all the time of their lives.

28. Amma Theodora said: "once a certain pious man, being reproached by someone, answered him: 'I too could say the like to you, but the law of God closes my mouth.'"

29. On a certain brother, on account of temptation, there bred on his body lice and a great multitude of vermin, but he was one of the wealthy. The demons said to him: "how do you endure such a life, that these insects have bred on you?" But he conquered the demons by his patience.

30. Abba John Colobos recounted: "three philosophers were friends, and one of them, dying, left his son to one of his friends. This foster child, having come to young manhood, went in to his foster father's wife, and the foster father, learning of this, drove him out and, despite his great repentance, did not wish to receive him back, but said: 'go, be a water-carrier for three years, and then I will forgive you.' When after three years he came, the foster father again said to him: 'you have not yet repented, but go and for three years hire people to revile you.' He did this also. After this, the foster father says to him: 'now go to the city of Athens and learn philosophy.' At the gate of this city of philosophers an old man sat and reviled those who entered, and when he began to curse the youth, the latter laughed. The old man asked him: 'what does this mean? For I revile you, and you laugh.' The youth answered him: 'how should I not laugh? For three years I gave money for people to revile me, and now I am reviled for nothing. Therefore I laughed.' Then the old man said to him: 'now enter the city.'" Thus, concluded Abba John, "behold the gates of God, and through these gates our fathers, rejoicing in many reproaches, entered the city of God."

31. He also said: "you see, the first blow that the devil dealt to Job was a blow against his wealth. Then, seeing that he did not despair and did not fall away from God, with a second blow he touched his body. But even at this, this courageous warrior did not sin with the word of his lips, for he had within himself the wealth of God and always remained in it."

32. Abba John the Cilician said: "seventy-six years I have lived in this place, enduring many evils and terrors from demons."

33. Abba Isidore said: "the wisdom of the saints consists in the acknowledgment of the will of God. Man conquers everything by submission to the truth, for then he is the image and likeness of God; but most terrible of all spirits is the following of one's own heart, that is, one's own thought, and not the law of God. And it shall be for him a cause of weeping that he did not know this mystery and did not find the way of God, to labor upon it. Therefore, *now is the time to act for the Lord* (Psalm 118:126), because salvation is in sorrow, as it is also written: *by your patience possess your souls* (Luke 21:19)."

34. Abba Poemen recounted concerning Abba John Colobos that by his prayer to God the passions were taken from him, and he became carefree. He went and said to a certain elder: "I see myself at rest and having no warfare." The elder said to him in reply: "go and ask God that warfare may come, for through warfare the soul advances." Abba John prayed and, when the warfare came, no longer asked that it be taken from him, but said: "grant me, O Lord, patience in the warfare."

35. Abba Poemen said of Abba Copres: "he attained such a measure that, although he was sick and lay bedridden, yet he gave thanks and cut off his own will."

36. Abba Copres said: "blessed is he who bears labor with thanksgiving."

37. They told of Abba Longinus that he was often troubled by the thought of going into the desert, and once he said to his disciple: "do me a kindness, brother, bear with me and, whatever I do this week, say nothing to me." Then he took a palm staff and began to walk around his courtyard; having grown weary, he sat a little and again arose and walked. When evening came, he said to his thought: "those who wander through the desert do not eat bread, but grass; but you, on account of your infirmity, eat a few vegetables." Having done this, he again said to his thought: "those who are in the desert do not sleep under a roof, but in the open air; do the same." And, reclining, he slept in his courtyard. Thus he spent three days, walking around the courtyard, eating a few vegetables toward evening and falling asleep in the open air, and he grew weary. Therefore he forbade his thought that was troubling him and rebuked it, saying: "if you cannot do the works of the desert, then sit in your cell with patience, weeping for your sins, and do not weave fantasies, for everywhere the eye of God beholds our deeds, nothing is hidden from Him, and He assists those who do good."

38. Abba Macarius the Great once came to Abba Anthony on the mountain; when he knocked, Abba Anthony came out and asked him: "who are you?" He answered: "I am Macarius." Then Abba Anthony went into his cell and shut the door, leaving him outside. Then, seeing his patience, he opened the door and, rejoicing with him, said: "for a long time I have desired to see you, having heard of your deeds." He received him as a guest and gave him rest, for he was weary. When evening came, Abba Anthony soaked some palm branches; Abba Macarius asked: "command me also to soak some for myself." He said: "soak them." Abba Macarius made a large bundle and soaked it. Sitting from evening, they conversed about

the salvation of the soul and plaited, and the plaiting was lowered through a window into the cave. In the morning, going in there, Abba Anthony saw how much Abba Macarius had plaited and said: "great power proceeds from these hands."

39. Once Abba Macarius went from Scetis to Terenuthis and along the way went into a pagan temple to spend the night, where there were ancient Greek corpses (mummies). Taking one of them, he placed it under his head in place of a pillow. The demons, seeing his fearlessness, envied him and, wishing to frighten him, began to call out as if to a woman, calling her by name: "such-and-such, come with us to the baths." But another demon answered from beneath Abba Macarius, as if from the dead body: "a stranger is upon me and I cannot go." But the elder was not frightened and began to beat the mummy, saying: "if you can, arise and go into the darkness." Hearing this, the demons cried out: "you have conquered us," and, being thus put to shame, they fled.

40. A brother asked Abba Macarius: "father! What does it mean to endure courageously and to pray?" He answered: "to endure every approaching temptation whether from men or from demons, as it is written: *'I groaned like a woman in labor'* (Isaiah 42:14), that is, I endured. Good is patience and good is patient prayer! Therefore, we must pray to God until He shows His assistance and helps us to correct our ways. It is not proper for monks to be angry at their brother, nor is it proper to offend one's neighbor, but truly, according to the commandment, we must both do and speak. For the Apostle also says: *'we have become as the filth of the world, the offscouring of all things'* (1 Corinthians 4:13); likewise: *'we are fools for Christ's sake'* (1 Corinthians 4:10), and again: *'we are your servants for Jesus' sake'* (2 Corinthians 4:5). Therefore, we must rejoice when we are dishonored and consider a great blessing the sorrows and offenses inflicted upon us for the Lord's sake. The Apostle Peter says: *'if you are reproached for the name of Christ, blessed are you, for the Spirit of glory and of God rests upon you'* (1 Peter 4:14). Therefore, when you are dishonored for the name of God, rejoice, saying: 'blessed are we, for *they were counted worthy to suffer shame for His name'* (Acts 5:41). Do you not know that children must imitate their parents? We ought to know that we are truly children of the holy Apostles, as the Apostle Paul also says: *'for in Christ Jesus I have begotten you through the Gospel'* (1 Corinthians 4:15). Therefore, being children of such men, we must imitate their ways and deeds, for they, being beaten, rejoiced; being slandered, they were not troubled; hearing from Greeks and Jews: *'these who have turned the world upside down'* (Acts 17:6) by their sorceries and enchantments, by all this they were not only not grieved, but even boasting, said: *'being reviled, we bless...'* and so on (1 Corinthians 4:12, 13). Therefore also they wrote these things, so that we might strive to be imitators of them, as the Apostle Paul exhorts: *'imitate me, just as I also imitate Christ'* (1 Corinthians 11:1). Therefore, when we are reviled or slandered and receive wounds, we ought to hold in our heart such a feeling as those have who receive great profit, having become sharers and partakers of the Apostles and holy martyrs, and who await even more, that the profit may be even greater. In this Christians must instruct themselves, so that it may be known to all that they are disciples of those who preached this, and especially monks, who have renounced the world and what is in the world."

41. Abba Matoes said: "I prefer a light practice that is constant to a most toilsome one at the beginning that is soon cut short."

42. When Abba Milesius lived with two of his disciples in the Persian territories, two sons of a prince, brothers according to the flesh, once went out to hunt according to their custom and stretched a cord over a very great space, some forty miles, in order to hunt whatever was found inside this enclosure and to kill it with spears. There they also found the elder with his two disciples and, seeing him, all overgrown with hair like a wild animal, they were amazed and asked: "tell us, are you a man or a spirit?" He answered them: "I am a man, a sinner, and I came here to weep for my sins. But I worship Jesus Christ, the Son of the living God." They said: "there is no other god except the sun, fire, and water" (which they themselves honored), "go and offer sacrifice to them!" He answered them: "you are in error, for these are creatures, but I beg you, be converted and acknowledge God Who created all these things." They say to him: "do you call the Condemned and Crucified One the true God?" The elder said: "yes! The One Who crucified sin and put death to death, Him do I call the true God." Then they began to torment them, trying to force them to offer sacrifice. After many torments they beheaded the brethren, but the elder they tortured for many days. Finally, according to their hunting skill, they set the elder in the middle and began to shoot arrows at him, one from in front and the other from behind. The elder said to them at this: "since you have been of one mind for the shedding of innocent blood, tomorrow at this same hour in a single moment your mother shall be bereft of children and deprived of your love: with your own arrows you shall shed each other's blood." They despised the words of the elder and in the morning went out to hunt; a doe fled from them, and they, mounting their horses, began to chase it and, shooting arrows at it, pierced each other in the heart, according to the word of the elder, which he had spoken to them, foretelling to them their punishment, and they died.

43. Abba Theonas recounted concerning Abba Marcellus that he kept silence near the great city of Antioch in the regions of Lebanon in a certain cave at the foot of the mountain. Abba Marcellus was of a quiet and meek character, reverent, pure, and chaste. The inhabitants of that village had great faith and love for him, and many came and were instructed by him. Having remained in that place for six years, the elder was subjected to many temptations from demons there, as he afterward told me, who wished to drive him out of his cell and prevent his silence, but they did not succeed in this, for he easily bore every temptation that came from them. Finally, a demon, having transformed himself into the elder, began to tempt the women of that city, importuning them, speaking indecent words to them and assuring them that there is no sin in fornicating secretly. He did this not once or twice, but wherever he saw a woman going alone, having transformed himself into the elder, he spoke of this. The women told their husbands about what was happening, and this report spread throughout the whole city. The husbands assembled in the temple of God, and the ruler of the district, having summoned the women, questioned more than twenty of them, who confirmed what their husbands had said. Having heard of this and not understanding that it was the wiles of the devil, this ruler together with the clergy sent young men to drive out the elder in the most

wicked manner, and when they came, they beat the elder with sticks, tore out the hair of his beard, and then, having dragged him out of the cave, beaten and half-dead, streaming with blood, they left him on the road. At that time the inhabitants of Beirut were passing by that way and, finding the elder, began to question him about what had happened, but he only begged them to carry him to his cave. "When the townspeople learned that I was in my cave, they often came to curse and revile me," the elder related to Abba Theonas, "but I endured all this, thanking God. Thus I spent eighteen months in the cave, reviled and reproached by all, sending up prayers to God that the souls of those who offended me might be saved. Finally, it was revealed to the ruler in a dream about the wiles of the devil, and the young men and those women were seized with demonic possession. Then the inhabitants of the city went out with their wives and children to receive a blessing from me, but I withdrew from them and settled on Mount Nitria. So, Abba Theonas," concluded the elder, "if you desire to pass all the days of your life without harm and so that demons may find no pretext to trouble you, do not settle near a city or village and you will have peace."

44. In the lavra of Pyrgion a certain elder named Miroges, who led a very strict life, became sick with dropsy. The elders begged him to accept a remedy, but he said to them: "pray, fathers, that my inner man may not suffer from dropsy. As for this illness, I implore God that I may remain in it forever." The Archbishop of Jerusalem, Eustathius, heard of this Abba Miroges and sent him something for consolation, but the elder in no way consented to receive anything, but only asked: "pray for me, father, that I may be delivered from eternal torment."

45. A brother asked one of the fathers: "father, how does the devil bring temptations upon the saints?" And the elder told him: "on Mount Sinai there lived a certain father named Nikon. Once someone came to the tent of a Pharanite[14] and, finding his daughter alone and falling with her, instructed her to say that Abba Nikon had done this. When her father heard this, he took a sword and went to the elder. However, as soon as he raised the sword to kill the elder, his hand withered. Then the Pharanite told the priests about this, who, having summoned the elder, inflicted many wounds on him and wished to expel him, but the elder begged them: 'for God's sake, leave me here for repentance.' The priests excommunicated him for three years and commanded that no one come to him. For three years on Sundays the elder came to the church, repented, and begged everyone to pray for him. But suddenly, the one who had committed the sin and brought the temptation upon the hermit became possessed and, coming to the church, confessed what he had done, saying: 'it was I who taught them to slander the servant of God.' Then all the people went to the elder and asked forgiveness of him. But the elder said to them: 'forgive? May you be forgiven, but remain here with you? I shall not remain, for in all this time there was not found among you a single one who would have deigned to show me compassion.' And he departed from there." Thus, concluded the elder, "do you see how the devil brings temptations upon the saints?"

46. A brother said to Abba Poemen: "my heart grows weak and faints if even a small sorrow befalls me." And the elder answered him: "is not the wondrous example of patience

in Joseph enough for us, in this one who was nearly still a boy, how he in Egypt, in the land of idolaters, endured such temptation and how God glorified him? We see this example also in Jacob, how he did not leave off holding to God to the end and how they could not turn him from his hope."

47. Abba Poemen said: "the sign of a monk, whether he is a true monk, is revealed in temptations."

48. He also related: "once Abba Isidore, presbyter of Scetis, said to the assembly thus: 'brethren! Is it not for labor that we came to this place? But now here there is no more labor. So I, taking my sheepskin, shall go where there is labor, and there I shall find rest.'"

49. A brother asked Abba Poemen: "father, I see upon myself that wherever I go, everywhere I find help." The elder answered him: "even those who have a sword in their hands have God at that time. Therefore, if we are courageous, He will show us His mercy."

50. They asked Abba Poemen: "to whom does the word of Scripture apply: *do not worry about tomorrow* (Matthew 6:34)?" The elder answered: "this applies to a man who is in temptation and is faint of heart, that he should not be anxious and should not question: 'how long shall I remain in this temptation?' But rather let him hold in mind and say to himself daily: 'only today.'"

51. Abba Paul the Great, the Galatian, said: "a monk who has several necessities in his cell goes out to provide for them and is subjected to the mockery of demons. And I myself suffered on account of this."

52. A certain one of the brethren, a Roman, recounted: "an elder had a very good disciple. Once, in faintheartedness, the elder drove him out the door together with his sheepskin, but the brother endured it and sat outside, not going away. When the elder opened the door and found him sitting, he made a prostration to him and said: 'O father! The humility of your long-suffering has conquered my faintheartedness. Come inside. From now on you are the elder and father, and I am the novice and disciple!'"

53. One of the fathers asked Abba Sisoes: "when I am sitting in the desert and a barbarian comes, wishing to kill me, but I am able to resist him, shall I kill him?" The elder answered: "no, but commit him to God. For whatever temptation may come upon a man, he should say that this has happened to him on account of his sins. But everything good is by the mercy of God."

54. Once Abba Abraham, the disciple of Abba Sisoes, went away on an obedience. And for a considerable time the elder did not wish that anyone else serve him, saying: "I cannot allow any other person to become accustomed to me except my brother," and he allowed no one, bearing all the labor himself, until his disciple came.

55. They said of Amma Sarah that for sixty years she lived above a river and never once bent down to look at it.

56. The blessed Syncletica said: "if you live in a coenobium, do not change your place, for this will harm you very much. As a bird that often rises from her eggs makes them barren and addled, so a monk or virgin grows cold and dies in faith by moving from place to place."

57. She also said: "manifold are the wiles of the devil: if he has not shaken the soul by poverty, he brings the enticement of wealth; if he could not succeed by insults and reproaches, he offers praises and glory; conquered by health, he makes the body sick; not having been able to beguile by pleasures, he tries to overthrow the soul by involuntary labors; by God's permission, he brings on the most grievous illnesses, so that in those who from youth walk through them, he might cut off love for God. But let the body be stricken by the most severe fevers and let it be tormented by unbearable thirst, and you, if, being a sinner, you are subject to this, remember the future punishment, the eternal fire and the appointed torments, and you will not become fainthearted on account of the present. Rejoice that God has looked upon you, and have on your lips this melodious saying: *'the Lord has chastened me severely, but He has not given me over to death'* (Psalm 117:18). Are you iron? By this fire you shall cleanse away your rust. If, moreover, being righteous, you become sick, by this you advance from great to greater. Are you gold? By this fire you shall become more proven. *'A thorn in the flesh was given to you, a messenger of Satan'* (2 Corinthians 12:7)? Rejoice: behold, to whom you have become like! You have been deemed worthy of Paul's portion. You are tried by fever, punished by chills? But the Scripture testifies: *'we went through fire and through water, but You brought us out to rich fulfillment'* (Psalm 65:12). You have received the first; await the second. Practicing virtue, cry out with the word of holy David: *'I am poor and sorrowful'* (Psalm 68:30). Through this duality of sufferings you shall be made perfect, for he also says: *'in trouble You have enlarged me'* (Psalm 4:2). In these gymnastic exercises we shall better train our souls for the contests, for before our eyes we see the adversary."

58. She also said: "if sickness weighs upon us, let us not grieve that because of the infirmity and affliction of the body we cannot sing aloud. All this is sent to us for the destruction of desires. Likewise fasting and sleeping on the ground are prescribed for us against desires. If therefore sickness has weakened the desires, there is no need for words; and this also is great asceticism, to be courageous in illnesses and to send up thankful hymns to God."

59. She also said: "those who fall into transgressions in the world, even against their will, are cast into prison. Let us, on account of our sins, imprison ourselves, so that our voluntary remembrance may avert future punishment."

60. She also said: "when fasting, do not presuppose illness, for those who do not fast often are subject to the same illnesses. Have you begun a good work? Do not slacken from what hinders you as the enemy, for he will be overthrown by your patience. Let those who begin to sail first obtain a favorable wind, but when they have unfurled the sails, and a contrary wind meets them, on account of the wind that has come upon them they do not unload the ship, but, having waited a little or struggled against the storm, they again continue their

voyage. So also let us, when a contrary spirit assails us, spreading the cross like a sail, fearlessly complete our voyage."

61. Abba Hyperechius said: "let spiritual song be in your mouth and hidden meditation lighten the burden of temptations that come upon you! A clear example of this is the traveler who, having grown weary, begins to sing and forgets the toil of the journey."

62. He also said: "we must arm ourselves before temptations, for in this way, when they come, we shall appear skilled."

63. Abba Phort said: "if it is pleasing to God that I live, then He knows how to sustain me; but if it is not pleasing, why should I live?" He also did not accept offerings from everyone, for he said: "if someone brings something for me and not for God, then I have nothing to give him in return, and from God he will not receive a reward, because he did not bring it for Him, and thus an injustice is done to the one who brought it. But those who have entrusted themselves to God and look to Him alone must be so reverently disposed that they do not even think of reproaching anyone, even if they should happen to be wronged a thousand times."

64. They said of Abba Cheremon of Scetis that his cave was forty miles distant from the church, and twelve miles from the marsh where the reeds for his handiwork grew, and from water. From there he brought reeds for himself and two vessels of water, one after another, then sat down and kept silence.

65. Once a demoniac came to Scetis and for a long time was not healed. Finally, one of the elders, having compassion on him, sealed him with the sign of the cross and healed him. Driven out against its will, the demon said to the elder: "since you have cast me out, now I shall enter into you." The elder answered him: "good, by all means come in." The demon entered, and the elder spent twelve years with him, exhausting him by eating twelve dates a day, so that, not able to endure, the wearied demon came out of him. The elder, seeing him come out, asked: "why do you flee?" The demon answered: "may God crush you, for no one is mighty against you except Him."

66. An elder said: "if temptations come upon a man, sorrows are multiplied for him from all sides, so that he might become fainthearted and murmur," and he recounted the following at this: "in the Cells, a temptation came upon one brother: if someone met him, he did not wish to give him a greeting; no one invited him into his cell; if he needed bread, returning from the harvest, no one lent it to him; in church no one called him to the love-feast, as is the custom. Once, coming from the harvest, he did not find even bread in his cell, but despite this he thanked God, and God, seeing his patience, took the warfare of temptations from the brother. And behold, someone came from Egypt and knocked at his door, having brought a camel loaded with bread. But the brother began to weep, saying: 'Lord! Am I then not worthy to suffer a little for Your name's sake?' Thus the temptation passed, and from that time the brethren began to console him both in the church and in their cells."

67. Certain brethren came to a great elder in the desert and asked him: "how do you endure here, abba, bearing such labor?" The elder answered: "all the labor of the life I spend here is nothing in comparison with one day of torment."

68. An elder said: "the ancients did not quickly move from their place, except only for the following three reasons: if there was someone there who had displeasure against him and would not be reconciled despite all efforts to pacify him; if it happened that he was praised by many; or if it happened that he fell under the temptation of fornication."

69. A brother asked an elder: "what shall I do, for a thought troubles me, saying: 'you can neither fast nor work; at least look after the sick, for this also is love.'" The elder, knowing that patient endurance of the cell brings a monk to his proper rank, answered: "go, eat, drink, sleep, only do not leave your cell." When after three days the brother began to be despondent, he took some palm branches and cut them; the next day he began to plait them, and when he grew hungry, he said to himself: "here are a few more branches, I shall plait them and then eat." Having finished them, he again said: "I shall read a little and then eat." Having finished the reading, he again says: "I shall chant a few psalms." And thus, already without anxiety, little by little with God's assistance he made progress, until he came to his proper rank and, having received strength against thoughts, began to conquer them.

70. Someone asked an elder: "why do I become despondent, sitting in my cell?" The elder answered: "because you have not yet beheld either the hoped-for rest or the future punishment, for if you beheld these, even if your cell were filled with worms and you were given over to them up to your neck, you would endure it without despondency."

71. The brethren asked one of the elders to cease from his great labors, but he answered them: "I assure you, children, that Abraham, seeing the great gifts of God, will repent that he did not struggle more."

72. A brother told an elder: "father, my thoughts are scattered, and I am sorrowful." The elder said to him: "you only sit in your cell, and they will come back again, for if a donkey is tied up, her foal, wherever it may go, wandering here and there, comes back to its mother. So also the thoughts of one who patiently remains in his cell for God's sake, although they may scatter somewhat, will afterward return to him again."

73. A certain elder lived in the desert at a distance of twelve miles from water. Once, going to draw water, he became fainthearted and said: "what need is there for such labor? I shall go and live near the water." Having said this, he went back and, seeing someone walking in his footsteps, asked: "who are you?" He answered: "I am an Angel of the Lord and have been sent to count your steps, so that afterward according to their number you may receive your reward." Hearing this, the elder was encouraged and, filled with zeal for labor, moved his dwelling five miles farther into the desert.

74. The fathers said: "if a temptation should happen to you in the place where you live, do not leave that place during the temptation, for otherwise, wherever you go, you will find

before you what you are fleeing. Therefore endure until the temptation passes, so that your departure may be in peace, without scandal, and may not cause sorrow to those living there."

75. A certain brother living in a coenobium loved quiet and tranquility, yet he was often tempted by anger. Finally he said to himself: "I shall go and live as a hermit alone, for if I have no dealings with anyone, my passion will grow quiet." Then he went out and settled alone in a cave. Once he filled a jug with water and placed it on the ground, but the jug accidentally overturned; he filled it a second time, and the same thing happened; he filled it a third time, and it overturned again. Becoming angry, he seized it and smashed it. Coming to himself and seeing that he had been mocked by the demon, the brother said: "behold, I am living as a hermit alone, and yet I am still conquered. I shall go back to the coenobium, for everywhere struggle is needed, and patience, and the help of God." He arose and returned to his former place.

76. A certain brother asked an elder: "what shall I do, father? I bear no monastic practice whatsoever, but I spend my life in negligence: I eat, drink, sleep, fall prey to vile thoughts and no small disturbance, passing from deed to deed and from thought to thought." The elder answered: "sit in your cell, and whatever you can, do without disturbance, for this small amount that you will do now I regard as equal to what Abba Anthony did on the mountain; and I believe that he who sits in his cell for the name of God and guards his conscience will be together with Abba Anthony."

77. They asked an elder: "how might a zealous brother not be scandalized if he sees that some of the brethren return to the world?" And the elder said: "he must imitate dogs that chase a hare. For one of them, seeing the hare, pursues it until he catches it, not being stopped by anything, although the rest, seeing only the pursuer, run along with him for some distance, but then, having changed their minds, turn back. And now only that one, the one who sees, pursues until he catches, not being turned from the object of his pursuit by the fact that the others turned back, paying no attention to precipices, or marshes, or thorns... So also he who seeks the Lord Jesus, gazing unceasingly at the cross, disregards the scandals he encounters until he reaches the Crucified One."

78. An elder said: "as a tree that is often transplanted cannot bear fruit, so neither can a monk who moves from place to place succeed in virtue."

79. Thoughts troubled a certain brother, suggesting that he leave the monastery. He disclosed this to the abba, and the abba said to him: "go, sit in your cell, give your body as a pledge to the walls thereof and do not go out from there. Leave your thought to think what it will, only do not lead your body out of your cell."

80. An elder said: "the cell of a monk is the Babylonian furnace, in which the three youths found the Son of God, and the pillar of cloud from which God spoke to Moses."

81. A certain brother was warred against by thoughts for nine years to leave the coenobium, and every day he prepared his sheepskin to depart, but when evening came, he would say to himself: "tomorrow I shall leave here." But when morning came, he would say

to his thought: "let us compel ourselves to wait through today also for the Lord's sake." When nine years had passed in such activity, the Lord took from him every temptation, and he was at rest.

82. A certain brother, having been subjected to temptation, abandoned the monastic rule out of sorrow, and wishing to begin it again, but being again diverted by sorrow, he would say to himself: "when shall I again become such as I was before?" Yet in his despondency he could not begin it. At last he went to a certain elder and told him of his state, and the elder, hearing of his sorrow, offered him the following example: "a certain man had a field which, through his negligence, became desolate and overgrown with thorns and thistles. Then he decided to cultivate it and sent his son to go and clear the field. The son, coming and seeing the multitude of thorns, became fainthearted and said to himself: 'when shall I manage to remove and clear all that is here?' And he lay down and slept, hardly getting up at all. When the father came to see what he had done and, finding that he had done nothing, asked his son: 'what is the meaning of this, that until now you have done nothing?' The young man answered his father: 'as soon as I came here and saw such a multitude of thorns and thistles, despondency seized me, and from despondency I lay down and began to sleep.' The father said to him: 'cultivate each day a portion of the field equal to the size of your bed, and your work will advance, and you will not be fainthearted.' Having listened to his father, the young man began to do so and in a few days cleared the field. So also you, brother, work little by little and do not become fainthearted; and God by His grace will restore you to your former rank." The brother heeded the elder and, sitting with patience, did as he was taught by him, and by the grace of Christ found rest.

83. A certain elder often fell into various infirmities and was sick. In one year it happened that he was not ill, and therefore he grieved greatly and wept, saying: "now God has forsaken me and has not visited me."

84. An elder said: "a certain brother was tempted by thoughts for nine years, so that he despaired of his salvation. Finally, in piety, he condemned himself and said: 'I have destroyed my soul; therefore I shall go into the world, by which I have been destroyed.' When he was going, a voice came to him on the way: 'the nine years in which you were tempted are your crowns. Return to your cell, and I shall deliver you from thoughts.' You see, it is not good to despair on account of thoughts, for they still bring us crowns if we pass through them well."

85. A certain elder lived in the Thebaid in a cave and had a very capable disciple. It was the elder's custom every evening to instruct him concerning salvation, after which he made a prayer and dismissed the disciple to sleep. It once happened that certain pious laymen, knowing of the elder's great asceticism, came and refreshed them. When they departed, the elder again according to custom sat down to instruct the brother and, conversing with him, fell asleep. The disciple waited for the elder to awake and make a prayer for him, but he kept on sleeping. Then a thought began to trouble the brother to go away to sleep without a blessing, but he constrained himself, resisting it, and remained. The thought again began to stir him up, but he again did not leave; and so he was stirred up seven times and seven times

resisted the thought. At last, when a considerable time had passed, the elder awoke and, finding his disciple sitting, says to him: "have you not left yet?" He answered: "no, for you did not dismiss me, abba." The elder asked: "why then did you not wake me?" The brother said: "I did not dare to touch you, lest I frighten you." Then they arose, performed Matins, and after this prayer the elder dismissed the brother. When the elder was left alone, he came into ecstasy and saw someone showing him a glorious place and a throne in that place, and on the throne seven crowns. The elder asked the one who was showing him: "whose are these?" And he answered: "your disciple's, for God has granted him both this place and throne for his patience, and the seven crowns he received this night." Hearing of this, the elder marveled and, in fear, called the brother and asked him: "what did you do this night?" He answered: "forgive me, abba, but I did nothing." The elder, thinking that he would not disclose it out of humility, said to him: "I shall not release you until you tell me what you did or thought this night." The brother, knowing that nothing had been done by him, was at a loss what to say. At last he says to his father: "I did nothing, abba, except that, being stirred up by a thought seven times to go away without your dismissal, I did not go." Hearing this, the elder knew that as often as the brother resisted the thought, so often was he crowned by God. He said nothing of this to the brother, but for the benefit of others he told this to the fathers, so that we might know that for struggle even with seemingly small thoughts God grants us crowns. Therefore it is good to compel ourselves in all things for God's sake, for *the kingdom of heaven suffers violence, and the violent take it by force* (Matthew 11:12).

86. Once an elder who lived alone in the Cells fell ill and had no one to serve him, therefore he arose and ate whatever was found in his cell. So he remained for a long time, and no one came to visit him. When even after thirty days no one came to the elder, God sent an Angel to serve him. And the Angel was with him for seven days already when the fathers remembered the elder and, becoming worried that he might have died, came and knocked. The Angel withdrew, and the elder cried out from within: "go away from here, brethren." When those who had come removed the door and entered, they asked the elder why he had cried out so. He answered them: "for thirty days I suffered and no one visited me; and behold, for seven days now the Lord has sent an Angel to serve me, but as soon as you came, he withdrew from me." Having said this, the elder reposed, and the brethren, marveling, glorified God, Who does not forsake those who hope in Him.

87. An elder said: "if bodily illness befall you, do not become fainthearted, for if your Master wishes you to suffer in body, who are you to be burdened by it? Is it not He Who cares for you in all things? Is it not by Him that you live? Therefore be of good cheer and ask Him only to reveal what is profitable for you. This is His will: sit with patience and eat what they bring you out of love."

88. A certain monk conquered the devil in all things, and the devil deprived him of his sight. But the monk even after this did not pray that he might see again, but that he might have patience; and for his patience God granted him sight, and he saw.

89. One of the fathers recounted: "when I was in Oxyrhynchus, some poor people came there in the evening to receive alms. When all lay down to sleep, I went out of my cell and saw that one of those who had come had only one mat, half of which was under him and half over him. At that time there was a severe frost, and I heard how, trembling all over, he comforted himself, saying: 'I thank You, O Lord! How many wealthy people are at this hour in prison and bound in chains, and others whose feet are fastened in stocks! But I, like a king, stretch out my legs.' Hearing this, I told it to the brethren, and they received great benefit from it."

90. A brother asked an elder: "father, if sorrow comes upon me, but I have no one to whom I may disclose it, what shall I do then?" The elder answered him: "believe in God, that He will send His grace and help you. I have heard that such an incident occurred in Scetis: there was a certain one in a state of warfare and, having no confidence in anyone, he prepared his sheepskin to leave from there. Then the grace of God appeared to him in the form of a maiden and consoled him, saying: 'do not go anywhere, but remain here with me, for in reality there was nothing of what you heard as evil.' Believing her, he remained, and immediately his heart was healed."

91. A certain elder went to sell baskets, and the demon he encountered made them invisible. The elder stood in prayer and said: "I thank You, O Lord, that You have delivered me from temptation." Then the demon, not able to endure the philosophy of the elder, cried out: "here are your baskets, wicked elder!" The elder took them and sold them.

92. One of the elders spoke thus concerning the poor Lazarus: "we do not see that he practiced any virtue, but we do see that he never murmured against God, that He did not show him mercy, but always bore his burden with thanksgiving and did not condemn the rich man. Therefore God received him."

93. One of the fathers said: "if a tree is not shaken by the wind, it does not put down roots and does not grow; so also a monk, if he is tempted and does not endure, is not strong."

94. An elder said: "we therefore do not advance and do not know our measure, because we do not have patience in the work we begin and wish to acquire virtue without labor; we also move from place to place, thinking to find one where there is no devil."

95. An elder said: "if a monk labors for several days and then grows lazy, then labors again and again begins to be negligent, such a one acquires nothing and will never gain patience."

96. He also said: "if it should happen that you are in a foreign land and no one receives you, do not grieve, but say to yourself thus: 'if I were worthy, God would have given me rest.'"

97. Again he said: "take away temptations, and there will be no saints, for he who flees beneficial temptation flees eternal life."

98. One of the fathers shut himself in his cell for the entire holy forty days of Great Lent. The devil, who always envies those who struggle, filled his cave with bedbugs from bottom

to top, and also his water and bread and everything he had, so that not even a finger's breadth of space was visible not covered by them. But the athlete endured the temptation and said: "even if I must die, I shall not go out until the holy feast." And behold, in the third week of the holy Lent, he saw in the morning an innumerable multitude of large ants creeping into the cave to destroy the bedbugs, how they struck them down as if in battle and dragged them outside. Therefore good is the endurance of temptations, for it always leads to a good end.

99. An elder said: "just as wax that is not heated and softened cannot receive the seal pressed upon it, so also a man, if he is not tested by sufferings and infirmities, cannot contain within himself the seal. Therefore the Lord says to the divine Paul: *'My grace is sufficient for you, for My strength is made perfect in weakness.'* And the Apostle himself boasts, saying: *'therefore most gladly I will rather boast in my infirmities, that the power of Christ may rest upon me'* (2 Corinthians 12:9)."

100. A certain young man, having resolved to renounce the world, went into the desert and, seeing a pillar, said to himself: "whomever I find in this pillar, I shall serve him until death." When he knocked, an elder, a monk, came out and asked him what he needed. He answered: "I have come for prayer." The elder received him and, having given him rest, asked whether he had any special business elsewhere? The young man said: "no, but I desire to remain here." And he left him. However, this elder fell into fornication and had a woman with him, therefore, after some time, he said to the brother: "if you desire to receive benefit, go to a monastery, for I have a wife." The brother answered: "whether you have a wife or a sister, I do not know, but I shall serve you until death." After a year of his service, they said to themselves: "is not the burden we bear enough? But we shall still be required to answer for the soul of this brother as well! So let us depart from here and leave the cell to him." Then, taking what they could, they said to the brother: "we are going on a pilgrimage; but guard our cell." However, as soon as they left, the brother understood their intention and caught up with them. Seeing him and being troubled, they said: "how long will you condemn us? You have the cell; sit and attend to yourself." But the brother answered them: "I did not come for the sake of the cell, but in order to serve you." After this, the woman went to a monastery, and the elder to his place. And thus by the patience of the brother both were saved.

Endnotes

[12] A type of tunic.
[13] An outer garment.
[14] Pharanite: an inhabitant of the city of Pharan.

Chapter VIII.
That Nothing Should Be Done for Show

1. Abba Anthony heard of a young monk who had performed such a miracle: when he saw elders journeying to Anthony and wearied from the way, he commanded the wild asses to come and carry them on their backs until they reached the abba. The elders recounted this to Abba Anthony, and he said concerning it: it seems to me that this monk is a ship laden with goods, but I know not whether he will enter the harbor. A year later, Abba Anthony suddenly began to weep, tear his hair, and lament. His disciples asked him: why do you weep, abba? The elder answered: at this very moment a great pillar of the Church has fallen, — this he spoke of that young monk, and continued: but go and see what has happened. When the disciples arrived, they found him sitting on a mat and bewailing the sin which he had committed. Seeing the disciples of the elder, he entreated them: tell the abba to beseech God to give me ten days, — and I hope to cleanse my sin. But five days had not passed when he departed this life.

2. The brethren praised a certain monk to Abba Anthony, and when he came to the abba, Anthony tested him — whether he could bear dishonor; and finding that he could not bear it, said to him: you are like a village in which the front is beautiful, but the back is plundered by robbers.

3. They said of Abba Arsenius and of Abba Theodore of Pherme that they hated the glory of men more than anything. Therefore Abba Arsenius would not readily receive anyone, while Abba Theodore, though he did receive them, was to them as a sword.

4. In Scetis there was an elder by the name of Daniel who had a disciple. This disciple had lived for some time with an abba named Sergius; and when he reposed, Abba Daniel gave the disciple closest access to himself, loving him. On a great feast the elder with his disciple went to Alexandria to the Pope, for such was the custom, that the abbot of Scetis should visit the Patriarch on this day. When they reached the city, they saw on the street a brother — naked and girded only about the loins with a rag. This brother, feigning foolishness, walked about the city together with other fools-for-Christ, snatching something at the market and giving it to those with him. His name was Mark the Hippian, from a certain coppersmith's workshop where Mark worked, receiving one hundred coins a day, and where he slept on the benches. Of these hundred coins he bought food for himself with twelve, and the rest he

distributed to the other fools-for-Christ. The whole city knew Mark the Hippian because of his foolishness. The elder commanded his disciple to find out where the fool-for-Christ dwelt, and on the following day, having fulfilled what was proper according to custom in regard to the Patriarch, by the dispensation of God, he met Mark in the Great Tetratylos, ran up, seized him, and began to cry out: men of Alexandria, help! The fool-for-Christ Mark meanwhile jested and laughed. A great multitude of people gathered around them, while the disciple of the elders stood at a distance in reverential fear. All said to the elder: do not suffer the offense, he is a fool. The elder answered them: you are fools, for in the whole city I have not found a man except him. And to the church clerics who approached and knew the elder, he commanded them to lead Mark to the Pope. Coming to the Pope, the elder said to him: there is no vessel in Alexandria now such as this one. The Pope, believing that the elder had received assurance of this from God, fell at the feet of the fool-for-Christ and began to adjure him to reveal who he was. And he, as if coming to himself, revealed to them about himself thus: I was a monk, and for fifteen years the demon of fornication possessed me; finally, coming to myself, I said: Mark! For fifteen years you have labored for the enemy; now go and likewise labor for Christ. I went to Pemet and remained there in repentance for eight years. After this I said to myself: enter the city and be a fool-for-Christ for another eight years, — and behold, now eight years of my foolishness are fulfilled. Those who heard this shed tears with one accord. Mark and the elder with his disciple were kept to spend the night in the patriarchate, and when day came, the elder said to his disciple: brother, call Abba Mark to me, that he may offer a prayer for our departure to the cell. The disciple found Abba Mark already having reposed in the Lord and announced this to the elder, the elder to the Pope, the Pope to the strategos, and he commanded that there be no work in the city on this day; while the elder sent his disciple to Scetis with an order to strike the semantron and say to the fathers gathered: go receive a blessing from the elder. And all the Scetians assembled in white garments with palms and branches, as did the Ennatians[15], and those of the Cells from Mount Nitria, and the brethren from all the lavras of Alexandria, so that the body of the blessed Mark, anointed with myrrh, remained unburied for five days. Then all who happened to be in the city, with branches and candles, watering the earth with tears, escorted the body of the blessed Mark the fool-for-Christ, glorifying and praising the man-loving God, Who gives such glory to those who love Him, both now and unto the ages of ages.

5. Once Abba Daniel together with his disciple went from Scetis to the upper Thebaid for the commemoration of Abba Apollos. All the fathers, numbering up to five thousand, like ranks of angels, came out to meet him for seven signs. Prostrating themselves on the sand, they received him as Christ and spread before him, some their garments, others their cowls, shedding rivers of tears. The archimandrite came out and bowed seven times to the elder before he approached him, and kissing one another, they sat down. Then they began to ask the elder to speak a word of edification to them, for he did not readily consent to speak. And when all had seated themselves on the sand outside the coenobium, since the church could not contain them, Abba Daniel commanded his disciple: write, — if you desire to be saved, be zealous for non-acquisitiveness and silence, for upon these two virtues hangs the

whole of monastic life. The disciple gave this writing to one of the brethren, and he translated it into the Egyptian tongue, and when it was read, all wept... and they escorted the elder onward, for they dared not say to him: share our meal. Having entered Hermopolis, the elder sent his disciple to knock at the gates of a monastery and announce that he was there; it was a women's monastery of Saint Jeremiah, in which dwelt up to three hundred sisters. When he knocked, the portress answered him in a gentle voice: save yourself! Welcome is your coming! What do you wish? He asked her: call the mother abbess for me, for I wish to speak with her. The portress answered: she never converses with anyone, but tell me what you wish, and I will convey it to her. He asked her to convey that a certain monk wished to speak with her. After this the deputy abbess came and said to him in a gentle voice: mother has sent me to ask what you wish. The brother answered: I ask that she do us the kindness to allow me to spend the night here with an elder, for it is already evening, and we fear lest we be devoured by wild beasts. She answered him: never does a man enter here, and it is better for you to be devoured by external beasts than by internal ones. The brother said: Abba Daniel of Scetis is here. Hearing this, she opened the gates and ran out with the sisters, spreading their veils from the gates to the place where the elder was, and falling at his feet, they kissed the hem of his garment. When all had entered the monastery, the abbess brought a basin with warm water and herbs and, placing the sisters in two rows, washed the feet of the elder and his disciple, and then, taking a small cup and calling the sisters, she dipped and poured upon their heads, and afterward poured also into her own bosom and upon her head. All the sisters seemed to be like stones, voiceless, and every task was accomplished among them by means of the semantron, while their movements were like those of angels. The abba asked the abbess: is it for our sake that the sisters conduct themselves so reverently, or are they always thus? She answered: they are always thus, your servants, master. But pray for them. The elder asked: tell my disciple to conduct himself likewise, for he is like a Goth — he talks constantly. Meanwhile one of the sisters in torn rags lay in the middle of the courtyard, and the elder asked: who is she — lying there? One of the sisters answered: this is a drunkard, and we know not what to do with her: to expel her from the monastery — we fear sin, but while remaining in the monastery, she troubles the sisters. The elder commanded his disciple to pour the basin upon her, and when he did so, she arose as if from drunkenness. The mother said: master! She is always thus. Then she led him into the refectory, where supper had been prepared for the sisters, and asked: bless your servants to eat before you, master. He blessed them. Only she and the second-ranking sister sat with the guests. The elder was offered soaked rusks, fresh vegetables, dates, and water; to his disciple — a lentil stew, a small loaf, and wine mixed with water; but to the sisters — various dishes, fish, and wine in plenty, and they ate very well. Throughout the meal no one spoke, and when it ended, the elder asked the abbess: what is this you have done? We should have been eating well, yet you were the ones eating well? She answered him: you are a monk, and I offered you the food of a monk; your disciple is a disciple of a monk, and I offered him the food of a disciple; but we are novices, and we ate the food of novices. The elder remarked: may your love be remembered; truly this is edifying for us. When all went to sleep, Abba Daniel said to his disciple: go and see where the drunkard is, she who was lying in the middle of the courtyard. He looked and said that she was in the corner of the granary. Then the elder asked his disciple to remain with him this night, and when all the sisters had retired, they went behind the granary and saw that the "drunken" one had risen and stretched forth her hands toward heaven; her tears flowed like a river; her lips moved; she would rise up and again fall prostrate; and hearing someone from among the sisters come out, she would fall to the ground and snore, — thus she passed her days. Then the elder asked his disciple to call the abbess, and coming together with the second-ranking sister, she watched all night what the "drunken" one did, and began to weep, saying: oh, how much evil have I done to her! When they struck the semantron and word spread among the sisters about the "drunkard," she, having surmised this, hastened to the place where the elder was spending the night, took his staff and his veil, opened the gates of the monastery, and leaving a note: forgive me if I have sinned against you in anything, — she went out and became invisible. When day came, they began to search for her, but found only the note she had left, and there was great lamentation in the monastery. And the elder said: I came here for her sake, for God loves such "drunkards." All the sisters confessed to him what they had done to her, after which the elder, having offered a prayer for them, departed with his disciple to his cell, glorifying and thanking God, Who alone knows how many hidden servants He has.

6. A certain Eulogius, a disciple of the blessed John, Archbishop of Constantinople, a presbyter and great ascetic, who fasted for two days at a time, often continuing his fast for a week, eating only bread and salt, for which he was glorified by people, — this Eulogius came with his disciples to Abba Joseph in Panephos, hoping to see with him greater strictness of life. The elder received him with joy and offered him for refreshment all that he had. The disciples of Eulogius said: the presbyter eats nothing except bread and salt. But Abba Joseph ate in silence. Having spent three days with them, those who came did not hear Abba Joseph and his disciples sing or pray, for hidden was their work, and they departed without receiving benefit. However, by the dispensation of God a fog arose, and Eulogius with his disciples, having lost their way, again returned to the elder, and approaching, they heard them singing. Having waited a considerable time, they knocked, and those within, interrupting their psalmody, received them with joy. Since there was great heat, the disciples of Eulogius drew water into a cup and gave it to him, but river water had been mixed with sea water, and he could not drink. Then, coming to himself, Eulogius fell at the feet of the elder and, wishing to learn their manner of life, asked: what is this, abba? Before, you were not singing, but now, after our departure, you sing; likewise, taking the cup, I found the water salty. The elder said to him: the brother was careless, and by mistake mixed sea water into it. But Eulogius entreated the elder, wishing to learn the truth, and he answered: that small cup of wine was the cup of love, but this is the water which the brethren always drink. He taught Eulogius the discernment of thoughts and cut off from him human glory, so that he became a steward, thereafter ate whatever was set before him, and learned himself also to do things in secret. But now he said to the elder: truly, your work is genuine.

7. Abba Isaiah said: I consider great and pure the victory over vainglory and the advancement in the knowledge of God, for he who falls into the hands of this evil passion of vainglory is a stranger to peace, hardens his heart against the saints, and to crown his evils falls into high-mindedness, which is pride — the mother of all evils. But you, faithful servant of Christ, keep your work hidden, and in the pain of your heart take care lest through man-pleasing you lose the reward for your work, for he who works for show before men has already received his reward, as the Lord also said.

8. He also said: he who loves to be glorified by men cannot be free from envy, and he who envies cannot attain humility of mind; such a one has delivered his soul to his enemies, who draw it into a multitude of evils and destroy it.

9. Again he said: flee vainglory and you will be deemed worthy of the glory of God in the age to come.

10. Once a brother came to Abba Theodore of Pherme and for three days entreated him to speak a word of edification to him, but the elder did not answer, and the brother departed in sorrow. His disciple asked him: abba! Why did you not give the brother instruction? He departed in sorrow. The elder said: truly, I did not speak to him because he is a trader and wishes to glory in the words of others.

11. Another brother asked Abba Theodore: will you advise me, abba, not to eat bread for several days? The elder answered: you will do well, and I have done likewise. The brother then said to him: so then, I shall take my chickpeas to the bakehouse. At this the elder remarked: if you are going to the bakehouse anyway, then prepare bread for yourself there as well, for what is the need of such a display?

12. Yet another brother came to him and began to reason about such things as he had not yet accomplished in deed. The elder said to him: you have not yet found a ship, you have not yet loaded your goods upon it, and not having begun the voyage, you have already arrived in another city. Only when you have accomplished in deed what you now speak of will you arrive at it for the first time.

13. One of the elders recounted the following about Abba Theodore of Pherme: once I came to him in the evening and found him wearing a torn leviton; his breast was bare and his cowl pushed forward. At that time one of the dignitaries came to see him. When he knocked, the elder went out to open and, meeting him, sat at the door to converse with him. I took the end of his maforion and covered his shoulders, but the elder stretched out his hand and threw it off. When the dignitary had departed, I asked him: abba! What is this you did? This man came to you to receive benefit, not to be scandalized. The elder answered: what are you saying to me, abba? Are we still servants of men? We have done what was needful — and that is the end; let him who wishes to be benefited, be benefited, and let him who wishes to be scandalized, be scandalized, and I, as I am, so I meet them. At this he gave a command to his disciple: if anyone comes wishing to see me, do not tell him anything human, but if I am eating, say — he is eating; if I am sleeping, say — he is sleeping.

14. Once one of the magistrates, having heard of Abba Moses, came to Scetis to see him; the elder, learning of this, fled to the marsh. When the magistrate, meeting him, asked: where is the cell of Abba Moses? the elder said: what do you want of him? He is mad. Coming to the church, the magistrate told the clerics: hearing of Abba Moses, I came to see him, but behold, we met an elder going into Egypt, and when asked where the cell of Abba Moses was, he told us that he is mad. Hearing this, the clerics were grieved and asked: what did the elder who spoke thus against the saint look like? He told them: the elder was in worn clothing — tall and black. Then the clerics answered: that is Abba Moses himself, and he spoke thus to you because he met you himself. After this the magistrate departed, having received great benefit.

15. One brother asked Abba Moses: if I go to live in some place, how do you advise me to conduct myself there? The elder said: if you settle in any place, take care not to make a name for yourself, whether by not attending the assemblies, or by not eating at the agape meals, or by something else — this rule will gain you an empty name, and afterward you will encounter no little vexation from it, for people run to where they find such things. The brother asked further: what then should I do? And the elder answered: wherever you live, go along on equal terms with everyone; and what you see done by the reverent people in whom you have faith, do also, and you will be at peace. This is humility, to be equal to others; and people, seeing that you do not make a display of yourself, will accept you equally with everyone, and no one will vex you.

16. Abba Nisterus the Great was once walking through the desert with a brother. Seeing a dragon, they fled. The brother asked the elder: and do you fear, father? The elder answered: I do not fear, child, but it was better to flee, for otherwise I would not have escaped the spirit of vainglory.

17. Once the governor of the region wished to see Abba Poemen, but the elder would not consent to come. Then the governor, under some pretext, seized his sister's son as a criminal and put him in prison, saying: if the elder comes and asks for him, I will release him. The sister came to the door of the elder's cell and wept, but he gave her no answer. Then she began to reproach him: man of brazen bowels! Have compassion on me, for he is my only son. The elder sent word to her: Poemen has not begotten children. Thus she departed. The governor, hearing of this, sent word: even by a single word command, and I will release him. But the elder replied thus: examine the case according to the laws: if he is worthy of death — let him die; if not — do as you will. Having received such a reply, the governor set the prisoner free.

18. Abba Poemen said: teach your heart to keep that which your tongue teaches.

19. He also said: people speak as the perfect, but they act as novices.

20. Again he said: accustom your mouth to speak that which is in your heart.

21. Abba Daniel recounted: once we came to Abba Poemen and ate together. After this the abba said to us: go rest a little, brethren. The brethren went to rest, but I remained, wishing

to speak with him alone, and rising, I went to his cell. The abba, as soon as he saw that I was coming to him, lay down as though he wished to sleep: for such was the work of the elder — to do everything in secret.

22. Abba Poemen said: truly, he who seeks friendship with men departs from friendship with God. It is not good to wish to please everyone, for it is said: *Woe to you when all men speak well of you* (Luke 6:26).

23. Once Abba Adelphius, Bishop of Nicopolis, came to Abba Sisoes on the mountain of Abba Anthony. When the bishop and those with him were preparing to depart, Abba Sisoes persuaded them to partake of food for the journey in the morning; it was, however, a fast day. During the meal, someone from among the brethren knocked, and Abba Sisoes said to his disciple: give them a little porridge, for they are weary. Abba Adelphius remarked: leave this be, lest they say that Abba Sisoes eats in the morning. Looking at him intently, the elder commanded his brother: go and give them. Seeing the porridge, they asked: do you not have guests, and is not the elder eating with you? The brother answered: he is eating. Then they began to grieve, saying: may God forgive you, that you allowed the elder to eat now! Do you not know that for this he will exhaust himself for many days! Hearing of this, the bishop bowed to the elder and said: forgive me, abba! I thought in a human way, but you acted in a godly way. Abba Sisoes answered him: if God does not glorify a man, the glory of men is nothing.

24. Abba Amoun of Raithu asked Abba Sisoes: when I read the Scriptures, my thought wishes to compose beautiful words, that I might have them ready in case of a question. The elder answered to this: there is no need for this, but rather from purity of mind acquire for yourself both freedom from care and the word.

25. Once a certain magistrate came to see Abba Simon. Hearing of this, the abba girded himself and climbed a date palm to clean it. Those who came cried out to him: elder! Where is the hermit? He answered: there is no hermit here. Receiving such an answer, they departed.

26. At another time another magistrate came to see the elder. Those nearby informed the abba beforehand, saying: abba, prepare yourself! A magistrate, hearing of you, is coming to receive a blessing from you. Abba Simon said: very well, I shall prepare myself. Putting on his rough tunic, the elder took bread and cheese and, sitting at the gates, began to eat. When the magistrate came with his retinue and saw this, he was repelled by it, saying: is this the hermit of whom we have heard? And they immediately departed.

27. One brother came to Abba Serapion, and the elder, according to custom, proposed to offer a prayer for him, but he, calling himself a sinner and unworthy even of the monastic habit itself, did not consent. The elder wished to wash his feet, but he uttered the same words and did not accept this either. The elder, offering him food, himself began to eat with him and instruct him, saying: if you wish to benefit yourself, then with patience sit in your own cell, attend to yourself and your handwork, for visiting the elders will not bring you as much benefit as such sitting will. Hearing this, the brother was offended and so changed in

countenance that this could not be hidden from the elder, and Abba Serapion said to him: until now you were saying that you are a sinner, and you accused yourself as if unworthy even of life, but when I reminded you with love of what is profitable, you became so angry! If you wish to be humble, manfully endure what is inflicted upon you by others, and do not apply idle words to yourself. Hearing this, the brother repented before the elder and departed with great benefit.

28. The holy Syncletica said: as a treasure, when opened, is quickly spent, so also a virtue, when displayed and made known to all, is corrupted and perishes; and as wax melts before the fire, so the soul melts away from praise and renounces its labor.

29. Again she said: as it is impossible at the same time to be both plant and seed, so it is impossible for us to bear heavenly fruit when worldly glory surrounds us.

30. Once Abba Tithoes was sitting, and a brother was near him. Not knowing of this, Abba Tithoes sighed; he did not notice the brother because he was in ecstasy. But afterward, making a prostration, the abba said: forgive me, brother! I have not yet become a monk, for I sighed in your presence.

31. They said that a certain elder dwelt in stillness in the lower regions of Egypt, and a certain faithful layman attended to him. It happened that the layman's son fell ill, and he long entreated the elder to come and offer a prayer over his child, until finally the elder went with him. However, the layman ran ahead and, entering the house, called out: come and meet the hermit! The elder, seeing from afar that they were coming out to meet him with lamps and understanding the purpose of this, threw off his garment, cast it into the river, and began to wash it, standing naked. Seeing this, his attendant was ashamed and began to ask the people, saying: go back, for the elder is deranged. Then, approaching him, he asked: abba! What is this you have done? Everyone was saying that the elder is possessed. And I wished to hear this, — answered the elder.

32. Once in the Cells, on the occasion of a feast, all the brethren were partaking of the meal in the church. One brother said to the one serving: I do not eat cooked food, but only salt. The server called out to another brother in the hearing of all: such-and-such a brother does not eat cooked food, bring him salt. Then one of the elders rose and said to the one eating only salt: it would have been better for you today to eat meat in your cell than to hear this voice in the presence of all.

33. One brother, a good ascetic who did not eat bread, came to a certain elder. At that time other strangers also happened to be there, and the elder prepared a little cooked food for them. When they sat down to the meal, the brother-ascetic took only soaked chickpeas for himself and ate them. After the meal the elder took him aside and said: brother! When you come somewhere, do not display your way of life. If you wish always to keep your rule, sit in your cell and do not go out anywhere. Instructed by the word of the elder, this brother henceforth never displayed himself in his meetings with the brethren.

34. One of the fathers recounted that in Palestine, by a river near a village where the blessed Silouan dwelt, there lived a brother who pretended to be mad, and if any of the brethren visited him, he would immediately begin to laugh, so that those who came, leaving him, would go away. Once three of the fathers came to Abba Silouan and, having offered prayer, asked him to send someone with them to visit the brethren in their cells, adding: do us the kindness to command a brother to lead us to all. The elder in their presence commanded a brother to lead them to all, but privately he whispered: see that you do not lead them to that madman, lest they be scandalized. When they were going about the cells, those who had come asked their guide: do us the kindness to take us to all. He said: very well, — however, according to the word of the elder, he still did not lead them to the cell of the madman. Upon their return the elder asked them: did you see the brethren? They answered: we did, and we thank you, only we grieve that we were not with all. The elder asked the brother who had led them: did I not tell you to take them to all? The brother answered: I did so, father. But privately he said to him: only to the mad brother I did not lead them. As they were departing, the fathers repeated to the elder: truly we thank you that we saw the brethren, but we grieve that we did not see all. Then the elder, having considered what had happened, went to that fool-for-Christ brother, and without knocking, quietly and unexpectedly entered and found him sitting on his stool, and before him two baskets — one on his right hand, the other on his left. Seeing the elder, he, according to his custom, began to laugh. But the elder said: leave this now and tell me about your sitting. But he continued to laugh. At this Abba Silouan says to him: you know — except on Saturday and Sunday I do not leave my cell, but I came in the middle of the week, for God has sent me to you. Frightened by this, the brother made a prostration to the elder and said: forgive me, father; from morning I sit and place these pebbles before me, and if a good thought comes to me, I throw a pebble into the right basket, but if a bad one — into the left. In the evening I count them, and if there are more in the right — I eat, but if in the left — I do not eat. When in the morning a bad thought comes to me again, I say: see what you are doing? Again you will not eat. Hearing this, Abba Silouan was amazed and said: truly, the fathers who came to me were angels who wished to make known the virtue of the brother; moreover, great joy and spiritual gladness were in me in their presence.

35. An elder said: when you come somewhere, do not display your way of life: for example, that you do not eat oil, or cooked food, or fish... — only do not permit yourself wine if you fear warfare, and though they may reproach you for this, pay no attention to it.

36. He also said: if a brother comes to you, take the weeping off your face and hide it in your heart until you have sent the brother away. Then again put the weeping on your face, and the demons will flee when they see it with you.

37. About the Scetians they said: if anyone came to know of their spiritual work, they no longer considered that work a virtue, but as it were a sin.

38. An elder said: man-pleasing destroys all the quality of a man and leaves him dry.

39. Again he said: he who displays and makes known his good deeds is like one sowing on the surface of the earth: the birds of the air fly down and destroy what was sown; but he who hides his way of life is like one who sows only a single furrow, but inside the earth — and he reaps very much.

40. An elder said: either, fleeing, flee from men, or mock flattery and men, presenting yourself as a fool.

41. A certain cenobiarch had great glory among men and was father of two hundred monks. To him, in the guise of a poor old man, Christ came and asked the gatekeeper to inform the abba that such-and-such a brother had come. With great difficulty the gatekeeper went in to report to him about the newcomer, but found him conversing with another. Standing for a while, he tried to inform him about the poor man, not knowing that it was Christ, but the abba shouted at him: do you not see — I am conversing with others? Wait. But the long-suffering Lord remained at the gates, awaiting his coming. Around the fifth (eleventh) hour a certain rich man arrived, and the cenobiarch hastily ran out to meet him. Seeing him with the rich man, the Lord, rich in mercy and friend of the humble, asked and entreated: I wish to speak with you, abba. But he, paying no attention to him, entered the coenobium with the rich man, caring for his hospitality as a stranger, and after the hospitality escorted him to the gates and returned, burdened with cares, forgetting the poor and meek elder. When evening came, the cenobiarch still did not deign to receive the blessed and true Stranger, and He departed, having revealed Himself thus: tell the abba: if you desire the glory of men, then for your former labor and many struggles I will send you visitors from all four directions, for you love to be anointed and to anoint; but the blessings of My kingdom you shall not taste. Thus the Almighty was recognized in the poor man.

Endnotes

[15] Ennatians — inhabitants of the city of Ennat.

Chapter IX.
On How One Must Guard Oneself from Judging

1. Once, in the coenobium of Abba Elijah, a temptation befell a certain brother, and having been expelled from there, he went to Abba Anthony on the mountain. After the brother had stayed with him for a year, the abba sent him back to the coenobium from which he had come. But the brethren, seeing him, expelled him again. Returning to Abba Anthony, he said to him: "they did not wish to receive me, father!" Then the elder sent him back with these words: "a ship suffered shipwreck at sea and lost its cargo; only a little was with difficulty saved to shore; yet you wish to sink even that which was saved." When the brethren heard that he was sent by Abba Anthony, they immediately received him.

2. Abba Agathon, whenever he noticed something and his thought wished to judge it, would say to himself: "Agathon, do not do the same thing yourself!" And thus he would quiet his thought.

3. Once Abba Agathon fell ill, as did one of the elders. While they lay in the cell and the elder was reading the Book of Genesis, when he came to that place where Jacob says: *"Joseph is no more, Simeon is no more, and you would take Benjamin ... you would bring down my gray hair with sorrow to Sheol"* (Genesis 42:36, 38), he remarked: "are not the other ten enough for you, Abba Jacob?" But Abba Agathon said to him: "cease, elder! *It is God who justifies. Who is he who condemns?*" (Romans 8:33–34)

4. Abba Anthony foretold to Abba Ammon: "you are to advance in the fear of God." Then he led him out of the cell and, pointing to a stone, said: "revile this stone and strike it." He did so. Abba Anthony says to him: "did the stone say anything to you?" He answered: "no." Abba Anthony said: "so also you are to attain this measure," — which indeed came to pass, for Abba Ammon advanced so greatly that from the abundance of his goodness he no longer saw evil. Thus, when he became a bishop, a maiden who was with child was once brought to him, and they asked him to give her a penance, but he, having signed her womb with the cross, commanded that six pairs of burial shrouds be given to her, saying: "lest she or her child die when the time comes to give birth, and nothing be found for burial." Then her accusers said to him: "why have you done this? Give her a penance!" He answered them:

"you see, brethren, how close she is to death. What then am I to do?" And he released her. The elder never dared to condemn anyone.

5. Once Abba Ammon came to a certain place for a meal. There was a certain one there who had a bad reputation, and it happened that at that time a woman came and entered the cell of the maligned brother. The brethren, learning of this, became so agitated that they wished to expel the brother immediately, but hearing that Bishop Ammon was there, they came to the abba and asked him to go with them. As soon as the brother learned of this, he hid the woman under a large vat, and Abba Ammon, understanding this and wishing to conceal the matter for God's sake, sat down upon the vat and told the brethren to search the cell. When the woman was not found, Abba Ammon said: "what is this? May God forgive you!" Then, having prayed, he told everyone to withdraw and, taking the brother by the hand, said to him: "attend to yourself, brother!" And having said this, he departed.

6. They related that a certain brother who had sinned was being expelled by the presbyter of the church. Then Abba Bessarion rose and went out together with him, saying: "I too am a sinner."

7. Abba Elijah related: "it seemed to me as though a certain brother took a gourd of wine under his arm. Wishing to put the demons to shame, for it was a vision, I said to the brother: 'do me a kindness, lift this up for me.' When he lifted up his garment, it turned out that he had nothing. I have recounted this so that you — whether you see something with your own eyes or hear it — would not believe it. Especially guard your thoughts, recollections, and reasonings, knowing that often demons implant them in order to defile the soul with thinking on unprofitable things and by them to nullify the remembrance of one's own sins before God."

8. Abba Isaiah said: "if a thought comes to you to judge your neighbor for some sin, think first that you are even more sinful than he. Do not believe that what you think you do well is pleasing to God, and you will not dare to judge your neighbor."

9. He also said: "not to judge one's neighbor and to humble oneself — this is a place of peace for the conscience."

10. They related that once a boy came to Abba Isaiah for healing from a demon; brethren from an Egyptian coenobium also came. Going out, the elder saw that a brother was sinning with the boy, and he did not expose him, saying: "if God, who created them, does not consume them with fire, then who am I to expose them?"

11. Abba Poemen asked Abba Joseph: "tell me, how may I become a monk?" Abba Joseph answered: "if you wish to find rest both here and there, then at every deed say to yourself: 'who am I?' — and judge no one."

12. Abba Isaac came to a coenobium and, seeing a brother sinning, judged him. When afterward he returned to the desert, an Angel of the Lord appeared and, standing before the doors of his cell, said: "I will not allow you to enter." The elder, entreating the Angel, asked

what this meant, and the Angel answered: "God sent me with these words: ask him, where does he command me to cast the sinning brother whom he judged?" The elder at once repented, and the Angel said: "God has forgiven you, but henceforth beware of judging anyone before God has judged him."

13. Abba Paphnutius, the disciple of Abba Macarius, said: "I once asked my father to tell me a word, and he said: 'do evil to no one and judge no one; keep this and you shall be saved.'"

14. They said of Abba Macarius the Great that he was like an earthly god. For as God covers the world, so Abba Macarius would cover sins, which, seeing, he would as if not see, and hearing, he would as if not hear.

15. Once in Scetis a brother sinned. When a gathering was convened, they sent for Abba Moses, but he did not wish to come. The presbyter again sent to him, saying: "come, for everyone awaits you." He rose, took a worn-out basket and, having filled it with sand, carried it on his back. The brethren, coming out to meet him, asked: "what does this mean, father?" The elder answered: "these are my sins pouring out behind me; yet I do not look at them, but have come now to judge the errors of others." Hearing this, they said nothing to the brother and forgave him.

16. Abba Moses said: "a man must die to every other person, so as not to judge him in anything."

17. He also said: "the end of all things is not to judge one's neighbor, for when the hand of the Lord slew every firstborn in the land of Egypt, there was not a house where there was not one dead." A brother asked him what this saying meant. The elder answered him: "if it is granted to us to see our own sins, we will not see the sins of our neighbor, for it is senseless for a man who has his own dead one to go weep over the dead one of his neighbor. But to die to one's neighbor means to bear the burden of one's own sins, not troubling oneself about another — whether he is good or bad. Do no evil to any man and do not even think evil in your heart against anyone; do not despise one who does evil, do not associate with one who does evil to his neighbor, and do not rejoice with one who does evil to his neighbor. This is what it means to die to one's neighbor. Do not disparage anyone, but say: 'God knows each one.' Do not be of one mind with the one who disparages, do not rejoice in his disparagement, and do not hate the one who disparages his neighbor — this is what it means not to judge! Have enmity with no one, do not hold enmity in your heart, and do not hate one who has enmity with his neighbor — this is what peace means! In all this, comfort yourself thus: for a short time there is labor, but by God's grace — rest unto the ages. Glory. Amen."

18. They said of Abba Mark of Egypt that for thirty years he did not go out of his cell. A certain presbyter had the custom of coming and performing the Holy Offering for him. The devil, seeing the patience of the virtuous man, devised to tempt him through judging and suggested to a certain demoniac to come to the elder under the pretext of prayer. When this one possessed by the spirit came, before any other word he cried out to the elder: "your presbyter has the stench of sin upon him; do not allow him to enter unto you any more." But

the God-inspired man said to him: "everyone casts filth outward, but you have brought it in to me. It is written: *'Judge not, that you be not judged'* (Matthew 7:1). Besides, even if he is a sinner, may the Lord save him, for it is said: *'Pray for one another, that you may be healed'* (James 5:16)." With this word, having made prayer, the abba cast the demon out of that man and released him in health. When the presbyter came according to his custom, the elder received him with joy; and the good God, seeing the elder's guilelessness, showed him such a sign: when the presbyter stood before the Holy Table, "I saw," the elder recounted, "that an Angel of the Lord descended, laid his hand upon the presbyter, and he became like a pillar of fire. When I marveled at such a vision, I heard a voice saying to me: 'O man! Why do you marvel at this? If an earthly king does not permit his nobles to appear before him unclean but only with great glory, how much more will the Divine power purify the ministers of the ineffable mystery who stand before the face of heavenly glory.'" Thus the courageous warrior of Christ, Mark of Egypt, having become great, was counted worthy of this gift because he did not judge the presbyter.

19. A brother asked Abba Poemen: "tell me, how may I become a monk?" The elder said: "if you desire to find rest here and in the age to come, then at every deed say: 'who am I?' And judge no one."

20. Once the presbyter of Pelusium heard about certain brethren that they frequently went to the city to bathe and were negligent about themselves. Coming to the church gathering, he removed the schema from them; however, afterward his conscience began to torment him and, repenting, he came to Abba Poemen, overcome by thoughts and carrying the brethren's tunics. When he disclosed to the elder what had happened, the elder asked him: "do you not also have something of the old man? Have you stripped him off?" The presbyter answered: "I am a partaker of the old man." The elder said thereupon: "therefore, you are also like the brethren, for if you are even a little partaker of the old nature, you are altogether subject to sin." Then the presbyter, having summoned all eleven brethren and having repented before them, clothed them in the monastic schema and released them.

21. The same elder said: "it happens that a man seems to be silent, yet his heart judges others; such a one speaks unceasingly. And it happens that a man speaks from morning until evening, yet keeps silence — that is, he says nothing without benefit."

22. A certain brother asked Abba Poemen: "father, if I see the fall of a brother, is it good to cover it?" The elder answered: "at whatever hour we cover the fall of our brother, at that hour God also covers ours; and at whatever hour we expose the fall of a brother, at that hour God also exposes ours."

23. A brother said to Abba Poemen: "when I see a brother about whose fall I have heard, I do not wish to bring him into my cell; but when I see a good one, I rejoice with him." The elder answered thereto: "if you do a little good for the good brother, then do double for the other, for he is infirm." Thus, in a certain coenobium there was one named Timothy. The hegumen, having heard a bad report about a temptation of a certain brother, asked Timothy about it, and he advised that the offender be expelled. When he was expelled, the brother's

temptation fell upon Timothy to such a degree that he was in danger. Then Timothy wept before the face of God, saying: "I have sinned, forgive me." And a voice came to him: "do not think that I have done this to you for anything other than that you despised your brother in the time of his temptation."

24. On Mount Athlibis there lived a great hesychast, and when robbers attacked him, the elder cried out. His neighbors heard this, seized the robbers, and sent them to the governor, and he put them in prison; but afterward the brethren began to grieve, saying: "they were handed over because of us." Then they went to Abba Poemen and told him about this matter. Abba Poemen wrote to that elder: "rejoice concerning the first betrayal — whence it came; and then you will understand the second. For if you had not first been betrayed from within, you would not have committed the second betrayal." Having heard the word of Abba Poemen — for he was renowned in all that land — the hesychast, even though he had never gone out of his cell, went to the city, led the robbers out of prison, and before all set them free.

25. Abba Poemen said: "it is written: *'What your eyes have seen, declare'* (Proverbs 25:8); but I say to you: even if you touch with your own hands, do not testify of it with certainty." And he recounted how a certain brother was mocked in this manner: it seemed to him that his brother was sinning with a woman; and he, being strongly warred against, approached and, thinking that it was they, kicked them with his foot, saying: "stop at last! How long?" But it turned out that they were sheaves of wheat. "Therefore I told you: even if you touch with your own hands, do not expose."

26. Certain of the fathers asked Abba Poemen: "how did Abba Nisterus so greatly endure his disciple?" Abba Poemen answered them: "if it were I, I would even put a pillow under his head." Then Abba Anub asked: "and what would you say to God?" Abba Poemen answered that he would say: "You said: *'First remove the plank from your own eye, and then you will see clearly to remove the speck from your brother's eye'* (Matthew 7:5)."

27. In a certain coenobium a brother once fell. In those parts lived a hermit who for a long time had gone out nowhere, and the abba of the coenobium came to this elder and related to him about the fallen one. The elder said: "expel him." Having left the coenobium, the expelled brother came to a certain pit and wept. It happened that at that time certain brethren were passing there on their way to Abba Poemen. Hearing the weeping and entering, they found him in great sorrow and urged him to go to the elder, but he did not wish to and said: "here I will die." Having come to Abba Poemen, they told him about this, and he, releasing them, asked them to tell the brother that Abba Poemen calls him. The brother came, and the elder, seeing how he was slain by sorrow, rose, gave him a kiss, and rejoicing with him, asked him to eat; meanwhile, he sent to that hermit with the words: "for many years I have desired to see you, having heard about you, but through the laziness of both of us we have not yet seen one another. Now, since there is God's will for this and a good occasion, take the trouble to come here, and let us see each other." That hermit, though he never went out of his cell, hearing this, said: "if God had not prompted the elder, he would not have sent for me," — therefore he rose and came to him. Having kissed each other with joy, they sat

down, and Abba Poemen said to him: "in a certain place lived two men, and both had dead ones. One of them left his own dead one and went to weep over the dead one of his brother." Hearing this word, the elder was brought to compunction by it, for he remembered what he had done, and said: "Poemen is high-high — in the heavens; but I am low-low — on the earth."

28. Certain of the fathers asked Abba Poemen: "if we see any brother sinning, do you command us to expose him?" The elder answered them: "as for me, if there is need to pass through that place, I will pass by and not expose him."

29. A certain brother asked Abba Poemen: "what am I to do, for I am bored sitting in my cell?" The elder answered: "despise no one, judge no one, slander no one — and God will give you rest, and your sitting shall be untroubled."

30. A brother asked Abba Poemen: "father, what am I to do?" And the elder said: "it is written: *I will declare my iniquity, and I will take care concerning my sin'* (Psalm 37:19)."

31. Once Abba Poemen came to the regions of Egypt. It happened that a brother who had a woman was living near him, but the elder never exposed him, and the brethren knew nothing of the matter. When that woman gave birth, the elder, learning of it, told his younger brother: "take these vegetables and give them to the neighbor, for now he has need of them." The brother did as the elder commanded, and this was so edifying for the sinning brother that he was brought to compunction and after a few days sent the woman away, giving her what he had. Then he said to the elder: "from now on I begin repentance." Afterward he arranged a cell for himself nearby and through it would enter to the elder, who guided him on the path of God and gained him.

32. Once in Scetis there was a gathering on account of the fall of a brother. The fathers spoke, but Abba Pior kept silent; then he rose and went out; taking a sack, he filled it with sand and carried it on his shoulders; he also took a small basket with sand and carried it before him. When the fathers asked him what this might mean, he answered: "this sack in which there is much sand represents my sins, for they are many, but I have left them behind so as not to grieve over them and weep; and these few sins of my brother are before me, and I occupy myself with them, judging him. But this must not be done; rather, I ought to bring my own sins before me and be concerned about them, asking God for mercy." Then the fathers, rising, said: "truly, this is the way of salvation."

33. Abba Paphnutius recounted the following: "once, while traveling, I lost my way because of fog and found myself near a village. Seeing there people conversing indecently with one another, I began to pray about my sins. And behold, an Angel of the Lord came with a sword and says to me: 'all who judge their brethren shall perish by this sword, but since you did not judge but humbled yourself before the face of God as if you yourself had committed the sin, for this your name has been inscribed in the book of the living.'"

34. An elder said: "why do you judge the fornicator, if you are chaste? — by this you equally transgress the law, for He who said: *'You shall not commit adultery'* (Matthew 5:27), also said: *'Judge not'* (Matthew 7:1)."

35. They related about a certain elder who lived in Egypt in a solitary cell. A certain brother and a certain virgin had the custom of coming to him. Once they came to the elder together, and when evening came, the elder spread out a mat and lay down in the middle of them. The brother, being warred against, rose up against the virgin, and they committed sin. The elder sensed this but said nothing, and when morning came, he saw them off, showing them no severity or gloom. Along the way they said to one another: "did the elder understand or not?" And returning to him, they repented and asked: "Abba! Did you understand how Satan mocked us?" The elder answered them: "I understood." They say to him: "where then was your thought at that hour?" He said: "my thought was there where Christ was crucified; there it stood and wept." Then they asked the elder for a rule of repentance, departed, and became chosen vessels.

36. A certain elder used to eat only three dry biscuits each day. Once a brother came to him, and when they sat down to eat, the elder offered him also three biscuits; but afterward, seeing that the brother still needed more, he offered three more. When they had eaten their fill and risen, the elder judged the brother and said to him: "one must not, brother, work for the flesh." The brother repented before the elder and departed. On the following day, when it came time for the elder to eat, he set out three biscuits for himself according to his custom, but having eaten them, he was still hungry; nevertheless, he denied himself. On the next day the same thing happened. Later, beginning to grow weak, the elder understood that this was abandonment by God, and therefore, having fallen down before the face of God, he prayed concerning the abandonment that had befallen him. And he sees an Angel who said to him: "this has happened to you because you judged your brother. Know therefore that he who is able to practice abstinence or to do any other good thing does so not by his own power but by the grace of God, which strengthens every man."

37. A certain presbyter from the clergy used to come to a certain hermit and perform the Offering of the Holy Mysteries for him. Once someone came to this hermit and disparaged the presbyter, and when, according to his custom, the presbyter came to perform the Offering, the scandalized hermit did not open his cell to him, and the presbyter returned. And behold, the hermit hears a voice: "men have taken My judgment." And then, as if in a rapture, he sees a golden lake with very good water in it and someone dark drawing and pouring it out. The hermit wanted to drink, but he would not, since the one drawing was dark. And again a voice came to him: "why do you not drink of this water, and what does the dark one drawing it mean here? He only draws and pours out." Having come to himself and having understood the power of the vision, the hermit summoned the presbyter and allowed him to perform the Offering for him as before.

38. In a coenobium there were two great brethren, each of whom was counted worthy of the gift of seeing the grace of God upon his brother. It happened once that one of them

went out of the coenobium on a Friday, and seeing outside someone eating in the morning, he said to him: "at this hour are you eating, on a Friday?" On the following day, during the customary rule, his brother saw that the grace of God had departed from him and began to grieve. Entering afterward into the cell, he asked him: "what have you done, brother, for today I did not see the grace of God upon you as before?" The other said: "I am conscious of nothing evil in either my word or my deed." His brother asked him: "have you not spoken a word to someone?" Then the brother recalled what he had said and answered: "yesterday morning I saw a certain one eating outside the coenobium and said to him: 'at this hour are you eating, on a Friday?' In this consists my sin. But labor together with me for two weeks, and let us entreat God that He may forgive me." They did so, and after two weeks the brother saw that the grace had again come upon his brother. They were comforted and gave thanks to God.

39. A certain one of the fathers said: "there is under the sun no people like the Christian people; and in this people there is no rank like the rank of monks. However, much harm comes to them because the devil leads them into remembering wrongs against their brethren, and they often say: 'he said this to me, and I said that to him'; their own impurities are before them, yet they do not see them, but occupy themselves with the affairs of their neighbor. From this they suffer much harm."

40. A certain holy man, seeing one who was sinning, wept and said: "he — today, but I, surely — tomorrow." Thus, even if someone should sin in your presence, do not judge him, but consider yourself more sinful than he, even if he be a layman.

41. A brother asked one of the elders to explain to him by an experienced word: "if I see someone doing some deed and I relate it to another, yet I see that I do not judge him but only speak — is this not disparagement?" The elder said: "if you speak out of passion, having something against him, it is disparagement; but if you are free from passion, what you have said will not be disparagement — but so that evil may not be multiplied."

42. Likewise another brother asked an elder: "if I come to some elder and say to him that I wish to live together with such-and-such a one, and he knows that this is not beneficial for me, how should he answer me? If he says: 'do not go' — has he not judged him by his thought?" The elder answered: "not many possess such subtlety. Therefore, if there is in him a movement of passion and he speaks thus, he will thereby harm himself, and his word will have no power. What then is it better for him to say? Better: 'I do not know' — for by this he will free himself from judgment. But if he is free from passion, he will not judge anyone but will blame himself, saying: 'I am not disposed aright,' and therefore — it is implied — 'it is not beneficial for you.' If the questioner is discerning, he will not go, for the elder said this not out of malice but so that evil may not be multiplied."

43. A certain one of the saints, hearing that a certain brother had fallen into fornication, said: "oh! How badly he has acted." Some days later that brother reposed, and an Angel of God came with his soul to the elder and asked him: "look, the one whom you judged has reposed; so, where do you command me to place him — in the kingdom or in hell?" And

afterward the elder until his very death begged God for forgiveness in this, weeping and greatly grieving.

44. A certain one of the saints said: "there is no better commandment than not to judge any of the brethren. Yet it is also commanded: *'You shall surely rebuke your neighbor, and not bear sin because of him'* (Leviticus 19:17). Therefore, if you see a brother sinning and do not say to him with love: 'how long am I to see the same sin in you?' — his blood shall be required at your hands; but if, having been lovingly rebuked, he persists in the same thing, he shall die in his sin. Thus it is good to rebuke with love but not to revile and despise as an enemy."

45. An elder said: "if you see someone laughing or eating much, do not judge him; rather say: 'blessed is he, for he has no sins, and therefore his soul rejoices.'"

46. A certain great elder lived in Syria, in the regions of Antioch, and had a disciple who was quick to judge if he saw anyone falling. The elder often admonished him about this, saying: "truly, my son, you are deceived and only destroying your soul, for *'what man knows the things of a man except the spirit of the man which is in him?'* (1 Corinthians 2:11). Besides, many often do considerable evil before men yet secretly repent before God. Also, we see the sin, but the good deeds he has done are known to God alone. Moreover, many who have spent their whole life badly have often at their end been found in repentance and have been saved; it also happens that because of the prayers of the saints sinners are accepted. Therefore, even if a man sees something with his own eyes, he must in no way judge another person. The Son of God alone is the Judge, and a man who judges another is liable to judgment as an adversary of Christ, because he seizes judgment, the authority and power that the Father gave to Him."

47. An elder said: "if you see with your own eyes your brother falling, immediately say: 'anathema to you, Satan — my brother is not guilty of this.' And strengthen your heart not to judge your brother, because otherwise the Spirit of God will depart from you."

48. An elder said: "why do you judge the murderer, or the fornicator, or the grave-robber, or any other of the lawless? They have their judge. Do not examine the deeds of others from only one side, but be curious also about your own falls, which are often worse than those. You also have often looked with unchaste eyes, which, as you yourself know, is already fornication. You also have often reviled your brother; it is not unknown to you that concerning this too the Lord said: *'whoever says to his brother, "You fool!" shall be in danger of hell fire'* (Matthew 5:22). But most terrible of all is that perhaps you approach the Holy Mysteries unworthily and become guilty of the Body and Blood of Christ (1 Corinthians 11:27). And it is revealed that he whom you judge killed a common man, but you kill Christ Himself, becoming guilty of slaying Him, for *'he who eats and drinks in an unworthy manner eats and drinks judgment to himself'* (1 Corinthians 11:29), that is, just as those Jews crucified Christ, so also those who partake unworthily of His Body and Blood do the same thing. And this judgment upon them is entirely just, for one who has torn the royal purple or stained it undergoes one and the same punishment; so that both those who then cut His body and those who now defile Him by partaking of Him with an impure soul shall undergo equal judgment, according to the word of the Apostle."

49. Someone asked an elder: "why am I unable to live with the brethren?" The elder answered: "because you do not fear God, for if you remembered that Lot was saved even in Sodom by not judging anyone, you could get along even if you were placed among wild beasts."

50. An elder said: "if you see that a brother has sinned, do not lay the cause of it upon him, but upon the one who wars against him, and say: 'as he has been conquered, so have I.' Weep, seek help from God, and suffer with him who has suffered unwillingly, for none of us wishes to sin before God, but we are all led astray."

51. A certain elder recounted: "when I lived in the innermost desert, a certain brother came to me from a monastery to visit, and I asked him how the fathers were living. He said: 'well, by your prayers.' I also asked him about a certain brother who had a bad reputation. The brother answered: 'he has not yet changed this bad reputation.' Hearing this, I uttered: 'alas!' — and together with this word I sank into sleep. In a rapture I saw myself standing on holy Golgotha and our Lord Jesus Christ crucified between the thieves. When I rushed to approach and venerate Him, He, seeing me, loudly commanded the Angels standing before Him: 'cast him out, for he is My adversary in that before My judgment he has judged his brother.' When I was being cast out and was going out, my mantle was caught by the closed door and I left it there. Immediately waking, I said to the one who had come to me: 'this day is evil for me.' He asked: 'why, father?' Then I recounted what had been seen by me in the dream and added: 'my mantle signifies the covering of God that was upon me and of which I am now deprived.' From that day — I speak as before the Lord of glory — I spent seven years wandering through the deserts, not eating bread, not entering under a roof, and not seeing a single person, until again, in a similar manner, I beheld my Lord commanding that my mantle be returned to me." Hearing this about such a wondrous elder, we said: *"If the righteous one is scarcely saved, where will the ungodly and the sinner appear?"* (Proverbs 11:31)

52. An elder said: "nothing so angers God, nothing so strips a man bare and places him in a state of abandonment, as disparagement, judgment, and contempt of one's neighbor. That judgment is more grievous than any sin, the Lord Himself also says: *'Hypocrite! First remove the plank from your own eye, and then you will see clearly to remove the speck from your brother's eye'* (Matthew 7:5), that is, the Lord likened the sins of one's neighbor to a speck, but judgment to a plank — so ruinous is judgment! It exceeds every sin! Thus, brethren, there is nothing more grievous, nothing more destructive than judging one's neighbor. Why do we not rather judge ourselves and our evil deeds, which we know precisely and for which we must give account to God? Why do we seize God's judgment? What concern of ours is His creature? What concern of ours is our neighbor? What concern of ours is another's burden? Each of us, brethren, has something to be concerned about! Let everyone attend to himself and to his own evil deeds! To justify or condemn belongs to God alone, who knows both the state of each one, and the strength, and the conversion, and the gifts, and the disposition, and the readiness — and therefore judges as He alone knows."

53. He also said: "let us acquire love toward our neighbor, let us acquire mercy toward him, so as to preserve ourselves from the terrible disparagement, judgment, and contempt that threaten us; let us help one another as our own members, for we are one in relation to another — the same as the members of a body, as the Apostle also says: *'we, being many, are one body in Christ, and individually members of one another'* (Romans 12:5), and *'if one member suffers, all the members suffer with it'* (1 Corinthians 12:26)."

Chapter X.
On Discernment

1. Abba Anthony said: some have worn out their bodies with asceticism, but because they lacked discernment, they were far from God.

2. Certain brethren went to Abba Anthony to tell him about visions they had been having, and to learn from him whether they were true or from demons. They had a donkey that died along the way, and as soon as they came to the elder, he, anticipating them, asked: how did the little donkey die on the road? The brethren said to him: how do you know this, Abba? He answered: the demons showed me. They say to him: we came precisely to ask you about this: the visions we often have, are they true, and are we not being deceived? The elder, by the example of the donkey, convinced them that they were from demons.

3. A certain man, hunting wild beasts in the desert, saw Abba Anthony jesting with his brethren. The elder, wishing to convince him that it is sometimes necessary to condescend to the brethren, commanded him: put an arrow in your bow and draw it. He did so. The elder commanded him to draw it more, and he drew it more. The elder again said: draw. The hunter answered: if I draw it beyond measure, the bow will break. Then Abba Anthony says to him: so it is also in the work of God: if we strain the brethren beyond measure, they will soon be crushed. Therefore, it is necessary sometimes to condescend to them. Hearing this, the hunter was moved to compunction and, having received great edification from the elder, departed. The brethren likewise, having been encouraged, returned to their place.

4. A brother said to Abba Anthony: pray for me. The elder answered him: neither will I have mercy on you, nor will God, if you yourself do not take care and do not entreat God.

5. Abba Anthony said: God does not permit temptations upon this generation as upon the ancients, for He knows that it is weak and cannot bear them.

6. He also said: the time will come when men will go mad, and if they see anyone not going mad, they will rise up against him, saying: you are mad, because he is not like them.

7. In a certain coenobium a brother was slandered for fornication. He came to Abba Anthony, and brethren from the coenobium also came after him to heal him and take him back, accusing him of having done such a thing; but he defended himself, saying that he had

done nothing of the sort. At that time Abba Paphnutius Cephalas happened to be there and told the following parable: I saw a man on the bank of a river who had sunk into the mire up to his knees; some came to give him a hand and sank him up to his neck. Then Abba Anthony said to them concerning Abba Paphnutius: behold a man who is able to heal and save souls. Brought to compunction by the word of the elders, they made a prostration to the brother and, persuaded by the fathers, took him back to the coenobium.

8. Once Abba Anthony received a letter from Emperor Constantius asking him to come to Constantinople, and, being uncertain what to do, he asked Abba Paul, his disciple: should I go? He answered: if you go, you will be called Anthony; but if you do not go, Abba Anthony.

9. Once Abba Anthony came to Abba Amoun on Mount Nitria, and when they saw each other, Abba Amoun said: since by your prayers the brotherhood has multiplied and some wish to build cells at a distance in order to live in stillness, at what distance from here do you command them to build? He answered: let us eat at the ninth hour and go walk through the desert and look at the place. They walked through the desert until the sun began to set, and then Abba Anthony said: let us make a prayer and set up a cross: let those wishing to build, build here, so that those there, intending to come to those here, may come after eating their morsel at the ninth hour, and those here may set out having done the same, and thus both groups will be undistracted in their mutual visitation. That distance was twelve miles.

10. Abba Mark asked Abba Arsenius: why are some good people, at the time when they are dying, struck with severe torment in their bodies? The elder answered: so that, being salted as with salt, they may depart there pure.

11. Abba Daniel, the disciple of Abba Arsenius, recounted: once Abba Alexander was struck with illness and for this reason lay on the ground face upward. It happened that at this time Abba Arsenius came to speak with him and saw him lying thus. After they had conversed, Abba Arsenius asked: who was that layman whom I saw here? Abba Alexander says to him: where did you see him? Abba Arsenius answered: when I was coming down from the mountain and looked in this direction, I saw someone lying in the cave on the ground face upward. The other, making a prostration to him, said: forgive me, it was I, for illness struck me. The elder says: and I thought it was a layman, therefore I asked you.

12. Abba Daniel recounted that certain brethren, intending to go to the Thebaid for flax, said: on this occasion let us also see Abba Arsenius. When they came, Abba Alexander went in and says to the elder: brethren who have come from Alexandria wish to see you. The elder commanded him to find out from them for what reason they had come. Having learned that they were going to the Thebaid for flax, Abba Alexander reported this to the elder, and he said: truly, they will not see the face of Arsenius, for they did not come for my sake, but on account of their own business. Give them rest and send them away in peace, telling them that the elder cannot receive them.

13. Abba Peter, the disciple of Abba Lot, recounted: I was once in the cell of Abba Agathon when a brother came to him and asked: I want to live with the brethren. Tell me

how I should live with them? The elder answered: as on the first day when you entered into their midst, so also all the days of your life keep yourself as a stranger, so as not to be presumptuous with them. Abba Macarius asked: what does presumption produce? The elder said: presumption is like a great heat, from the face of which, when it comes, all flee, and it destroys every fruit of the trees. Abba Macarius says to him: is presumption so destructive? And Abba Agathon answered: there is no passion more destructive than presumption, for it is the mother of all passions. Therefore a worker should not be presumptuous, even if he is alone in his cell. I know of one brother who, having lived a year in a cell in which there was a ledge for reclining, said: I would have left the cell and not known of this ledge, had another not pointed it out to me. Such a one is a true worker and combatant.

14. They recounted of Abba Agathon: some came to him, having heard of his great discernment and, wishing to test whether he would get angry, say to him: are you Agathon? We hear that you are a fornicator and proud. He answered: indeed, it is so. Again they say to him: are you Agathon the slanderer and idle-talker? He said: I am. Again they say: are you Agathon the heretic? He answered: no, I am not a heretic. Then they asked him: tell us, why did you accept the former charges, but this word you could not bear? And he explained: the former I attribute to myself, because there is benefit in that for my soul, but heresy is separation from God. Hearing this, they marveled at his discernment and departed with edification.

15. They asked the same Abba Agathon: what is greater, bodily labor or guarding of the heart? The elder answered: man is like a tree: bodily labor is the leaves, and guarding of the heart is the fruit. But since according to Scripture: *every tree which does not bear good fruit is cut down and thrown into the fire* (Matthew 3:10), it is evident that all our diligence should be about the fruit, that is, about guarding the mind. Nevertheless, the covering and adornment of leaves, which is bodily labor, is also needed.

16. Abba Agathon was wise in noetic work, not lazy in bodily work, and moderate in all things: in handwork, in food, and in clothing.

17. He, having come to Scetis when there was an assembly there concerning some matter and a decision had already been determined, said: you have not resolved the matter well. They asked him: who are you that you speak thus? The Abba answered: a son of man, for it is said: *If you truly speak righteousness, judge uprightly, O sons of men* (Psalm 58:2).

18. He also said: if an angry man raises even a dead man, still he will not be pleasing to God.

19. He also said: if someone is dear to me above others, and I perceive that he is leading me into diminishment, I will cut him off from myself.

20. Abba Daniel said that before Abba Arsenius came to our fathers, they lived with Abba Agathon. Abba Agathon loved Abba Alexander, for he was ascetic and meek. It happened that when all his disciples were washing palm branches in the river, Abba Alexander was washing unhurriedly, and the brethren, coming to the elder, said: brother Alexander did

nothing. The elder, wishing to heal them, said to him: brother Alexander! Wash well, for this is laziness. Hearing this, he was grieved, but afterward the elder comforted him, saying: did I not know that you do well? But I said this to you in their presence in order to heal their thought by your obedience, brother.

21. One of the fathers recounted that in The Cells there was a certain hardworking elder who wore a mat. When he came to Abba Ammon, the latter, seeing him in the mat, said: this will not benefit you at all. The elder asked him: three thoughts trouble me: either to wander through the deserts, or to go away to a foreign land where no one would know me, or to shut myself up in a cell without seeing anyone and eating every other day. Abba Ammon answered him: it is not profitable for you to do any of these three things, but rather sit in your cell, eat a little each day, always have the word of the publican in your heart, and you can be saved.

22. Once three elders came to Abba Achilles, one of whom had a bad reputation. One of the elders asked: Abba! Make me a fishing net. He said: I will not make it. And another asked: do us a kindness, make us one net, so that we may have a memento of you in the monastery. He also refused him for lack of time. Finally, the one with the bad reputation says: make me one net, so that I may have something from your hands, Abba! And he immediately answered: for you I will make it. Afterward the two elders said to him privately: why, when we asked you, did you refuse us, but to him you said, for you I will make it? The elder says to them: to you I said, I will not make it, and you were not offended, attributing the refusal to my lack of time; but if I do not make a net for him, he will think: surely the elder heard about my sin and did not want to make it, and thereby I would immediately have cut the cord. Thus I encouraged his soul, lest such a one be swallowed up by sorrow.

23. Abba Ammoï said: once we came, I and Abba Bitimius, to Abba Achilles and heard him repeating the words: *"Jacob, Jacob... do not be afraid to go down to Egypt"* (Genesis 46:2-3); and for a long time he repeated this saying. When we knocked and he opened to us, he asked where we were from. Fearing to say that we were from The Cells, we answered: from Mount Nitria. The Abba says: what can I do for you, since you have come to me from such a distance? And he led us in. We asked him to say a word of edification to us, and in the cell we saw a long rope. The elder said: from evening until now I have plaited twenty cubits of this rope, and truly I have no need of it, but fearing lest God be angry with me and reproach me, saying: why, having strength to work, did you not work? I labor and do a little according to my strength. Having received edification, we departed.

24. They said of Abba Ammoï that once he prepared fifty measures of wheat for his use and spread it out in the sun. However, before it dried, he saw something there that was not profitable for him and said to his disciples: let us leave this place. They were greatly grieved, and the elder, seeing their grief, said to them: is it because of the bread that you are grieving? Truly, I know of such ones who fled, leaving painted cupboards with parchment books, and did not even close the doors, but went away leaving them open.

25. They recounted of one elder that for fifty years he did not eat bread and drank water infrequently and said: I have put to death in myself fornication, avarice, and vainglory. Abba

Abraham, hearing of this, came to him and says: did you say this? The elder confirmed it. Then Abba Abraham asked him: suppose you enter your cell and find a woman on your mat. Can you think that she is not a woman? He answered: no, but I will fight with the thought so as not to touch her. Abba Abraham said to this: you have not put the passion to death—it lives, only it is bound. Again, suppose you are walking and you see stones and potsherds, and in the midst of them gold. Can your mind consider the latter equal to the former? The elder answered: no, but I will fight the thought so as not to take it. The Abba said: the passion lives, only it is bound. Again Abba Abraham asks: suppose you hear of two brothers, that one loves you while the other hates and slanders you. If they come to you, will they be equal to you? He answered: no, but I will fight the thought so as to do good to both the one who loves me and the one who hates me. Abba Abraham says to him: therefore the passions live, only they are bound by the saints.

26. Abba Abraham recounted of one of the fathers who was a scribe and who did not eat bread. Once a brother came to him and asked him to copy a book for him. The elder always had his mind in contemplation and copied the book with omissions and without placing punctuation marks. The brother, receiving it and wishing to add the punctuation marks, found the omissions and said to the elder: there are omissions, Abba! The elder answered: go and first fulfill what is written, then come, and I will write what is lacking.

27. Once Abba Agathon asked Abba Alonius: how can I keep my tongue from speaking lies? Abba Alonius answered him: if you do not lie, you will commit many sins. He said: how is this? The elder answered him: for example, two men committed murder before you, and one of them fled to your cell. Now those searching for him ask you: was the murder committed before you? If you do not lie, you will hand the man over to death; but it is better to leave him before God without bonds, for God knows all.

28. They said of Abba Antianos, an elder of the Thebaid, that in his youth he accomplished many ascetic labors, but in old age he fell ill and became blind. Because of his weakness, the brethren provided him with many comforts and themselves placed food in his mouth. They asked Abba Aio about this: what will become of the elder as a result of such great comfort? And the Abba answered them: I assure you that if his heart desires and willingly accepts this, then even if he eats but one date, God will deduct it from his labor; but if he does not desire it and accepts it unwillingly, God will preserve his labor whole, for they compelled the elder against his will; but they will receive their reward.

29. A certain elder left his cell with the field belonging to it near Nicopolis to Abba Gelasius. A certain farmer, a relative of the deceased elder, came to Bacatas, who was then the leader in Nicopolis of Palestine, and requested that field, claiming it should pass to him by law. This Bacatas, being a powerful man, attempted to take the field from Abba Gelasius by force, but the Abba would not yield, not wishing to give the cell to a layman. Once Bacatas, seeing Abba Gelasius's animals transporting olives from the field that had come to the Abba, forcibly seized them and took the olives to his own house; but afterward he barely, with great disgrace, released the animals with their harnesses. The blessed elder did not argue at all about

the fruit, but he would not yield possession of the field for the aforementioned reason. Angered, Bacatas, prompted also by other matters, for he loved litigation, set out for Constantinople, going on foot. Having arrived in the region of Antioch and hearing of Saint Symeon, who at that time was shining like a great luminary, for he was above a man, Bacatas, being a Christian, wished to see him. But Saint Symeon beheld him from the pillar and, as soon as he entered the monastery, asked: where are you from, where are you going, and why? He answered: I am from Palestine and I am going to Constantinople on many needs, hoping by your holy prayers to return and fall at your feet. Saint Symeon says to him: do you not wish to say, most hopeless of men, that you are going against a man of God? You will have no good journey, and you will not see your home again. Therefore, if you will listen to my counsel, hasten from here to him and repent before him, if only you reach your place alive. At that very hour, seized by a fever and placed on a litter by those with him, he was sent to his own country to repent before Abba Gelasius; but according to the prophecy of the saint, he died without reaching home. About this his son, also named Bacatas, recounted after his father's death to many men worthy of credence.

30. They said the following about Abba Daniel: when barbarians came to Scetis, the fathers fled; but the elder, saying: if God does not take care of me, then why do I even sit here? passed through the midst of the barbarians, and they did not see him. Afterward he says to himself: behold, God has shown His care for me, and I did not die; do now the human thing also and flee as the fathers. He arose and fled.

31. Abba Daniel said: to the measure that the body grows fat, the soul wastes away; and to the measure that the body wastes away, the soul grows fat.

32. Abba Daniel recounted that when Abba Arsenius was living in Scetis, there was a monk there who was stealing things from the elders. Abba Arsenius took him into his cell, wishing to win him over and give the elders rest, and said to him: whatever you want, I will provide for you, only do not steal. And he gave him gold and small coins, and clothing, and everything needful, but he would go away and steal again. Then the elders, seeing that he did not cease stealing, expelled him, saying: if a brother has some sin of weakness, one must bear with him; but if he steals, expel him, for he both destroys his own soul and disturbs all who live in that place.

33. They asked Blessed Epiphanius: why are the commandments of the law ten, but the beatitudes nine? He answered: the decalogue is equal in number to the plagues of Egypt, and the number of the beatitudes is a threefold image of the Trinity.

34. They also asked him: is one righteous man sufficient to propitiate God? He answered: certainly, for He Himself said: *"If you find a man who does justice and seeks the truth, I will be merciful to him"* (Jeremiah 5:1).

35. Once Blessed Ephraim was walking, and at someone's instigation a certain harlot approached him to incline him to shameful intercourse, or at least to move him to anger, for no one had ever seen him angry. He said to her: follow me. And when they came to a crowded

place, he proposed: in this place let us do as you wished. Seeing the multitude of people, she asked him: how can we do this with such a crowd and not be ashamed? Then he said to her: if we are ashamed before men, how much more should we be ashamed before God, *who brings to light the hidden things of darkness* (1 Corinthians 4:5). Thus shamed, she departed.

36. They said of Abba Zeno that at first he did not want to accept anything from anyone. Therefore, those who brought things departed in sorrow because he did not accept them, and those who came wishing to receive something from the great elder went away without consolation, for he had nothing to give. At last the elder said: what am I to do, for those who bring things grieve, and those who wish to receive are not consoled? Here is what I must do: if anyone brings something, I will accept it, and if anyone asks, I will give it to him. Having done so, he himself was at peace and satisfied everyone.

37. Brethren came to Abba Zeno and asked: father, what does it mean, what is written in the Book of Job: *"The heavens are not pure in His sight"* (Job 15:15)? The elder answered: the brethren have left aside their sins and investigate the heavens. The interpretation of this saying is as follows: since God alone is pure, therefore he said: *"The heavens are not pure."*

38. They said of Abba Zeno that he was small in stature, thin in body, but very inward-looking and full of desire and fervor for God. He also had great compassion for people, and from everywhere laymen and monks came to him, opened their thoughts, and received healing.

39. We came to one of the fathers who had once dwelt near holy Zeno, and when he extended to us a word of edification, we asked him about a certain thought, speaking thus: if someone has a thought and is overcome by it, but at the same time strives to be edified by a word about purity read from the fathers, wishing to correct the deed according to their word and cannot, is it good to open this to one of the fathers, or should he strive to fulfill only what he has read, contenting himself with his own conscience? The elder answered us: he should open it to another who can benefit him and not rely on himself, for no one can help himself, especially if he has reached the point of becoming sick with the passions. Then he continued: something similar happened to me in my youth. I had a sickness of soul and was overcome by it. Hearing that Abba Zeno had healed many, I also resolved to go and open myself to him, but the devil hindered me, saying: you already know what you should do—use what you have read. Why should you go and scandalize the elder? And it was thus: when I was ready to go to him, the warfare would recede from me so that I would not go; but when I agreed not to go, the passion would flood me again. When I was again about to go, the enemy would set up the same snares against me, not allowing me to open myself to the elder. If sometimes I did come to the elder to open myself, the enemy would not permit it, troubling my heart with shame and saying: you already know how you should heal yourself! What need is there to communicate this to another? You are not negligent about yourself and know what the fathers have said. All this the enemy instilled in me so that I would not open my sickness to the physician and receive healing. The elder noticed that I had thoughts but did not expose me, waiting until I myself would open them to him; therefore he instructed me in the right

path and let me go. Finally, being contrite and weeping, I said to my soul: how long, wretched soul, will you not want to receive healing? People come to the elder from afar and are healed, but you, having a physician so close, are ashamed and remain unhealed? And, being kindled in heart, I arose and said to myself: if, coming to the elder, I find no one with him, I will understand that this is God's will for me to open my thought to him. I came and found no one. The elder as usual instructed me about the salvation of the soul and how one can cleanse oneself from impure thoughts, but I was again ashamed to open myself to him and asked him to let me go. The elder, having made a prayer, went to see me off to the outer gates, walking ahead; but I, tormented by thoughts whether to tell the elder or not, was walking slowly behind him. He did not look at me and had already taken hold of the door to open it for me, but seeing how greatly my thoughts were tormenting me, he turned to me and, striking my chest, asked: what is the matter with you? I too am a man. As soon as the elder said this word to me, I felt as if he had opened my heart—I fell on my face at his feet, entreating: have mercy on me. He says to me: what is the matter with you? I answered: you know what need I have. He said to me: you yourself must reveal what is the matter with you. When with shame I opened my passion to him, he says to me: why then were you ashamed to tell me this? Am I not also a man? Do you want me to tell you about myself? Is it not three years now that you have been coming here with such thoughts and have not revealed them? Since I remained as before prostrate before him and entreated: have mercy on me for God's sake, he said: go, do not neglect your prayer, and do not condemn anyone. I returned to my cell, did not neglect prayer, and by the grace of God and the prayers of the elder was no longer tormented by that passion. However, after a year, such a thought attacked me: perhaps God in His mercy did this for you, and not because of the elder? I go to him, wishing to test him, and, leading him aside, I make a prostration and say: I entreat your godly love, father, pray for me about that thought which I once opened to you. Having left me lying at his feet and having been silent a little, he says: arise and know the meaning. Hearing this, I wished from shame that the earth would swallow me; having risen, I could not look at the face of the elder and departed to my cell in amazement.

40. That same elder, in confirmation of the virtues of the law and for our edification, recounted to us the following: two brothers, living in the same lavra each in his own cell, visited each other. Once one of them said to the other: I want to go to Abba Zeno and open a certain thought to him. At this the other also said: I too wish to open my thought to him. And they went together. Each, privately, told the elder about his thought, but one fell at the elder's feet, entreating him with tears, and he said to him: go, do not betray yourself, do not condemn anyone, and do not neglect your prayer. And this brother returned healed. But the other brother, having opened his thought, did not ask the elder with great earnestness, but only said: pray for me. After some time the brothers met, and one asked the other: when we went to the elder, did you open the thought you wished to tell him about? He answered: I opened it. The brother asked again: did you receive benefit from opening it? He said: I did; by the prayers of the elder God healed me. But I, though I also opened it, confessed the other, felt no relief. Then the one who was healed says: how did you ask the elder? And the brother

told him that he had asked him to pray for him, since he had such-and-such a thought. To this the healed brother said: but I, opening myself to him, wetted his feet with my tears, entreating him to pray for me, and by his prayers God healed me. Therefore, concluded the elder, one who asks someone among the fathers concerning thoughts must ask with anguish and from the whole heart, as if asking God, and then he will receive help; but one who opens them negligently or even as a test will not only not receive benefit but will even be condemned.

41. Abba Isaiah said: simplicity and not measuring oneself purify the heart from evils.

42. He also said: whoever walks with his brother in craftiness will not escape heartfelt sorrow.

43. Again he said: vain is the service of one who says one thing but in his heart craftily holds another. Do not cling to such a one, lest he infect you with his infectious poison.

44. He also said: gain, honor, and pleasures fight against man until his very end, but one must not yield to them.

45. Abba Theodore of Pherme said: if you have friendship with someone, and it happens that he falls into the temptation of fornication, then if you can, give him a hand and pull him up. But if he falls into heresy and does not accept your persuasions to turn back, quickly cut him off from yourself, lest you yourself be dragged into the same pit if you tarry with him.

46. One of the fathers recounted that in the time of Abba Isaac a brother came to the church at The Cells in a small cowl. The elder drove him out, saying: you cannot be in the church, for here are monks, but you are a layman.

47. One of the elders came to Abba Theodore and said to him: behold, such-and-such a brother has returned to the world. The elder answered to this: do you marvel at this? Do not marvel. But marvel rather if you hear that anyone was able to escape the jaws of the enemy.

48. He once came to Abba John, a eunuch from birth, and in the course of conversation said: when I was living in Scetis, the works of the soul were our work, and handwork we considered as a supplement; but now the work of the soul has become a supplement. A brother asked him: what work is the work of the soul, which we now consider a supplement, and what is the supplement, which we now consider the work? The elder answered: everything done according to the commandment of God is the work of the soul, but to work for oneself and to accumulate—this we should consider a supplement. The brother asked: explain this subject to me. And the elder said: suppose you hear about me that I have fallen ill, and you should visit me, but you say to yourself: shall I leave my work and go now? I shall rather finish my work and then go. Then another occasion will arise, and you will not go at all. Again: another brother says to you: help me! And you think: shall I leave my work and go work with him? Thus, if you do not go, you abandon the commandment of God, which is the work of the soul, and you will do the supplement, that is, the work of your hands.

49. He also said: there is no other such virtue as not despising one's neighbor.

50. One brother said to Abba Theodore: I want to fulfill the commandments. The elder told him about Abba Theonas, that he too once said: I want with God's help to fulfill my intention. Then he took wheat, prepared bread, and sat in his cell.

51. Abba Abraham the Iberian asked Abba Theodore of Eleutheropolis: what is better, father, for me to acquire glory or dishonor? The elder answered: as for me, I prefer to acquire glory rather than dishonor, for if I do a good deed and am glorified, I can condemn my thought as unworthy of this glory; but dishonor comes from vicious deeds. With what can I console my heart when people will be scandalized by me? Therefore it is better to do good and be glorified. Abba Abraham said: you have spoken well, father!

52. They asked Mother Theodora: how is it possible, hearing with the ear various speeches, whatever they may be, to remain with the one God? She answered: as, sitting at a table where there are many good foods, you do partake of them, but without relish, so also when worldly speech reaches your ear, keep your heart turned to God. With such a disposition, hearing without relish, you will not suffer any harm.

53. It happened that certain elders in Scetis were eating together. Abba John Colobos was with them. A certain presbyter stood up to offer a cup of water, but no one dared to accept it from him except Abba John. The elders were amazed and said to him: how did you, being the least of all, dare to accept service from the presbyter? He answered them: when I stand up to offer the cup, I rejoice if all accept it, so that I may have a reward. So I myself accepted it now so that the one offering may have a reward and so that he may not be grieved that no one accepted it from him. When he said this, they were amazed and were edified by his discernment.

54. A brother asked Abba John: how is it that my soul, having its own wounds, is not ashamed to condemn its neighbor? The elder told him this parable concerning condemnation: a poor man had a wife, but seeing another woman who pleased him, he took her also. Both of them were naked. In a certain place there was a great feast, and they asked him to take them with him. He put them in a barrel and, getting on a ship, arrived at that place. When it became hot and the people dispersed, one of them, looking out and seeing no one, jumped out and in the midst of the refuse found some rags, made herself a girdle, and walked about boldly. But the other, being naked and sitting inside, said: behold, this harlot is not ashamed to walk about naked. Her husband grieved at this and said: that one at least covered her shame, but you are entirely naked and are not ashamed to speak thus. Such also is the matter of finding fault.

55. The elder also spoke of the soul desiring repentance: in a city there was a beautiful harlot who had many lovers. A certain magistrate, coming to her, said: promise me to live chastely, and I will take you as my wife. She promised, and he took her into his house. The lovers, wishing to have her, decided thus: if we enter the house of the magistrate who took her and he finds out, he will torment us; but let us go around the house and behind it whistle to her—she, recognizing the tone of the whistle, will come out to us; and then we will no longer be guilty. But she, hearing the whistle, plugged her ears, ran into the innermost

chamber, and shut the doors. The harlot, explained the elder, is the soul; her lovers are the passions and men; the magistrate is Christ; the innermost chamber is the eternal dwelling; the whistlers are the evil demons, but the soul desiring repentance always flees from them to the Lord.

56. One of the fathers asked Abba John: who is a monk? The elder said: a laborer, for he labors himself in every work. Such is a monk.

57. Once the fathers came to Abba Isaac to make him a presbyter. Hearing of this, he fled to Egypt and, reaching a certain field, hid in the grass. The fathers chased after him, arrived at the same field, and decided to rest there, for it was night, and let the donkey graze. The donkey came upon the elder and stood over him. In the morning, looking for the donkey, they found Abba Isaac also and, amazed, wanted to bind him, but he did not allow it, saying: I will no longer flee, for in your intention there is the will of God, and wherever I flee, I will come upon the same.

58. Abba Isaac said: do not bring young boys here, for in Scetis four churches have become deserted because of them.

59. Abba Poemen asked Abba Joseph: what should I do when the passions approach me, resist them or allow them to enter? The elder answered him: let them enter and then fight with them. And Abba Poemen returned to Scetis. Later a certain one from Thebes, coming to Scetis, told the brethren that when he asked Abba Joseph about an approaching passion, whether to resist it or allow it to enter, the Abba said: by no means allow the passions to enter, but cut them off at once. Hearing this, Abba Poemen came to Abba Joseph and said to him: Abba, I entrusted my thoughts to you; and behold, you said something different to the Theban. The elder answered him: do you not know that I love you? And did you not say to me, tell me as if to yourself? He said: so it was. Then the elder continued: if the passions enter and you allow it yourself and accept blows from them, that is, struggle with them, they will make you more skilled. This I said to you as to myself. But there are others for whom it is more profitable that the passions not approach them at all, and such should cut them off at once.

60. One brother asked Abba Joseph: Abba! What should I do, for I can neither lead a strict life nor work and give alms? The elder said to him: if you cannot do any of this, at least keep your conscience clean from all evil toward your neighbor and you will be saved.

61. One of the brethren recounted: I once came to lower Heraclea, to Abba Joseph. In the monastery he had a beautiful fig tree, and in the morning he says to me: go and eat. It was then Friday, and I did not go because of the fast, but afterward, entreating the elder, I asked: for God's sake tell me this thought: behold, you said to me, go and eat, but I did not go because of the fast, yet I was troubled on account of your commandment, thinking with what thought you commanded this and what I should have done. The elder said: the fathers at first do not speak to the brethren directly, but more obliquely, and when they see that they fulfill

the oblique commands, then they speak to them truly, knowing that they are obedient in all things.

62. A brother asked Abba Joseph: I want to leave the coenobium and dwell in solitude. The elder said: where you see that your soul finds rest and is not harmed, there sit. The brother asked again: what then do you advise me to do, for I find rest both in the coenobium and alone? The elder answered: if you find rest both in the coenobium and alone, then place both these thoughts of yours as if on scales and, where you see more benefit for yourself and which thought outweighs, do that.

63. One recounted: once we came, I and the wise Sophronius, to Abba Joseph in Ennat, and the elder began to converse with us with joy and eagerness. He was adorned with every virtue and was experienced in secular learning. When we were sitting and conversing about soul-saving subjects, a certain Christ-lover from Aila came and gave the elder three gold coins, saying: accept them, honorable father, and pray for my ship, which I have loaded and sent to Ethiopia. But the elder paid no attention to him at all. The lord Sophronius said to him: accept them, father, and give to one in need. The elder answered to this: a double shame, my son, to take what one has no need of and with one's own hands be obliged to reap thorns belonging to another. Oh, if only I could reap the thorns of my own soul! Besides, my son, it is written: if you sow, sow your own, for another's is more bitter than thistles. Especially, my son, I do not accept because his request is not a request for the soul. The other asks him: so what then? If a man does something as alms, does God not reckon it to him? The elder answered: there is a great difference in almsgiving according to the purpose of the alms: one gives them for the blessing of his house, and God blesses his house; another gives alms for the sake of his ship, and God has mercy on his ship; another gives them for the sake of his children, and God guards his children; and another gives them for glory, and God glorifies him. God does not despise anyone, but gives each what he wants, if it does not harm his soul; however, all these already receive their reward, for they have earned nothing before God, since the purpose of their alms was not the benefit of the soul. You gave alms for the blessing of your house— God blessed your house; you gave for your ship—God saved your ship; you gave for your children—God preserved your children; you gave for glory—God glorified you; so what does He owe you? Therefore give for your soul, and your soul will be saved, for it is written: *"The Lord will give you according to your heart"* (Psalm 20:4), and there are many rich people who, thinking they are giving alms, anger God. We asked him: explain this word to us, father! The elder said: God commanded that first-fruits of wheat, barley, vegetables, wine, oil, flax, and fruits should be set apart for Him, as well as the firstborn of men and of clean animals, and that these latter should have no blemish, that is, that their ears should not be cut off or their tail severed, and that the fruits should be choice, if they are brought to God for the remission of sins. But the rich do the opposite: they eat the good things themselves and distribute the worthless to the poor; they drink the choice wine themselves and give the sour to widows and orphans; they also throw to the poor ragged and patched garments and spoiled and rotten fruits, imitating Cain—therefore what they bring to God is not accepted. If some rich person has a son or daughter who is well-formed and beautiful, he concerns himself with a dowry

and marriage and seeks out handsome youths; but if someone has a son or daughter lacking a limb or deformed and emaciated, the male child is placed in a men's monastery and the female in a women's. Such people ought to consider and reflect: if we, wishing to honor mortal and corruptible men, offer them the first and choicest things and strive to present what seems most honorable to them, should we not all the more bring to God the most honorable and choicest!? It is known that God, in requiring that we express our thanksgiving to Him in words or make some vow, requires this not as one needing words, but to teach us to be grateful and not to be negligent about what has come forth from our mouths, that is, that what we have composed and determined to give to God, we should give with great diligence and eagerness, fear and love. For as Noah's sacrifice, giving off smoke and fumes, was borne before the face of the Lord as *"a sweet aroma,"* as it is written: *"And the Lord smelled a soothing aroma"* (Genesis 8:21), so, on the contrary, the offerings, sacrifices, and gifts of wicked people are reckoned an abomination before the Lord. Listen to what the prophet says to the Jews, who were then still the people of God: *"Incense is an abomination to Me"* (Isaiah 1:13). Thus the wickedness of those offering made the fragrant incense an abomination. Therefore, one who wishes to be saved must not only perform prayers and almsgiving in simplicity and with all eagerness, but also, intending to bring something to God, bring the most honorable and glorious, so that our prayer may not return to our bosom with shame, and our sacrifice, being found impure, may not remain unaccepted, and our fruits, rotten and worthless, may not be reckoned as Cain's sacrifice. We also asked the elder: does consent to a thought harm the soul? He answered: if impure and unclean thoughts did not harm it, then it would not receive benefit from pure, pious, good, and God-loving thoughts either. But in reality, as the latter benefit it, so the former harm it, for if outwardly we enjoy countless worldly comforts and ease, but inwardly a storm and tumult from the confusion of thoughts is breeding, there is no benefit to us from the outward peace, just as countless walls and fortifications do not help a city when it is being betrayed by those living within it. Therefore, if we guard ourselves from consent to impure thoughts, the Lord has promised us a great and lofty attainment of the Kingdom that surpasses our understanding, enjoyment of ineffable blessings, communion with angels, and deliverance from Gehenna—all this and the like, which has no limit, no end, and knows no change, being firm and immovable. But seeing that we doubted what we heard from him, the elder stood before us and, lifting his eyes to heaven, said for us to hear: Jesus, our God, who made heaven and earth and sea, Deliverer of our souls! If what I have said to the brethren is false, let this stone remain whole; but if it is true, let it split apart. And with this word the stone split into five parts—and this stone was a fragment of a column four cubits high. Marveling and having received benefit, we went on our way, and the elder, seeing us off, said: children! Come to me next Saturday, for I have need of you. Coming on Saturday at the third hour, we found the elder at rest and buried him, and departed thanking God that He had deemed us worthy to prepare and commit to the earth such a saint.

64. Abba Jacob said: to be a stranger is greater than to receive strangers.

65. He also said: it is not words only that are needed, for in the present time there are many words among people, but what is needed is deed—this is required, not words, which bear no fruit.

66. Abba John, a eunuch, being still young, asked an elder: how were you able to accomplish the work of God without toil, while we cannot accomplish it even with toil? The elder answered: we were able because we had the work of God as our main work, and the needs of the body as the last; but you have the needs of the body as the main work, and the work of God as not so necessary—that is why you toil much. Therefore the Savior said to His disciples: *"O you of little faith... But seek first the kingdom of God and His righteousness, and all these things shall be added to you"* (Matthew 6:30, 33).

67. Abba Isidore said: if you lawfully engage in fasting, do not be puffed up; but if you are puffed up, then it is better to eat meat. For if while fasting you are proud-minded, what is the use of fasting? It is better for a man to eat meat than to be puffed up and boastful.

68. He also said: those learning should love true teachers as fathers and fear them as rulers; and at the same time they should not dissolve fear on account of love or darken love on account of fear.

69. He also said: if you love salvation, do everything that leads you to it.

70. Someone asked Abba John the Persian: we have taken such toil upon ourselves for the sake of the Kingdom of Heaven! But shall we inherit it? The elder answered: I believe the promise to inherit the heavenly Jerusalem revealed in the heavens, *for He who promised is faithful* (Hebrews 10:23). And why should I not believe? I have become hospitable like Abraham; meek like Moses; holy like Aaron; patient like Job; humble-minded like David; a lover of the desert like John; tearful like Jeremiah; a teacher like Paul; faithful like Peter; wise like Solomon; and like the thief I believe that He who has granted me these things by His goodness will grant the Kingdom as well.

71. Once Abba Longinus asked Abba Lucius about the following three thoughts: I want to go on pilgrimage. The elder answered him: if you do not restrain your tongue, you will not be a pilgrim wherever you go. Even here, restrain your tongue and you will be a pilgrim. The other again said to him: I want to fast. The elder answered: the prophet Isaiah said: *"If you bow down your head like a bulrush... will you call this a fast acceptable?"* (Isaiah 58:5), but rather cut off evil thoughts. Abba Longinus says a third time: I want to flee from men. The elder answered to this: if you do not first live as you should with men, you will not be able to live as you should even alone.

72. They said that in Scetis two brothers were living, and Abba Macarius, the city one, excommunicated them. Some went and told Abba Macarius the Great, the Egyptian, about this. The elder said: it is not the brothers who are excommunicated, but Macarius is excommunicated (and he loved him). Hearing that he was excommunicated by the elder, Abba Macarius fled to the lake. When Abba Macarius the Great came out to him and saw that he was bitten by mosquitoes, he said to him: you excommunicated the brothers, and they

would have gone to the village; but I excommunicated you, and you fled here, like a good maiden to her bridal chamber. But I summoned the brothers, questioned them, and they said that nothing of the sort had happened. See to it also, brother, that you are not mocked by demons, for you saw nothing, but accept repentance for your sin. The other said: give me whatever penance you wish. The elder, seeing his humility, said: go and fast three weeks, taking food once a week—for such was his practice: always to fast a week at a time.

73. A brother came to Abba Macarius and asked him: Abba, tell me a word, how can I be saved? The elder said: go to the cemetery and revile the dead. The brother went, reviled them, threw stones at the graves, and coming back told the elder about it. The elder asked him: did they not say anything to you? He answered: nothing. The elder said: go again tomorrow and praise them. The brother went and praised them: Apostles! Saints! Righteous ones! Then he came to the elder and reported that he had praised them. The elder asked him: did they not answer you? He answered: nothing. Then the elder said to him: you see how much you dishonored them, and they answered you nothing; how much you glorified them, and they said nothing to you. So also you, if you wish to be saved, be dead, think neither of the insults of men nor of their glory, like the dead, and you will be saved.

74. Abba Macarius, once passing through Egypt with the brethren, heard a boy say to his mother: Mama! One rich man loves me, and I hate him; and one poor man hates me, and I love him. Hearing this, Abba Macarius was amazed. The brethren asked him: what do his words mean, father, that you are amazed? The elder answered them: truly, our Lord is rich and loves us, and we do not want to listen to Him; but our enemy, the devil, is poor and hates us, and we love his impurity.

75. Abba Macarius said: if we remember the evil done to us by men, we take away the power of remembrance of God; but if we remember the evil from demons, we will be safe from their arrows.

76. Abba Matoes said: Satan does not know by which passion the soul will be conquered, and therefore he sows, not knowing whether he will reap, now thoughts of fornication, now thoughts of fault-finding, now other passions; and to whichever passion he sees the soul inclining, that one he teaches it.

77. A brother asked Abba Matoes: father, what should I do if a brother comes to me on a fast day or in the morning? I am troubled. The elder answered him: if you eat with your brother without being conquered by hunger, you do well; but if you are not expecting anyone and eat, this means indulging your own will.

78. Some of the fathers asked an elder: if porridge is left over for another day, do you want the brethren to eat it? The elder answered: if it has spoiled, it is not good to force the brethren to eat it, lest they fall ill afterward; and in such a case let them throw it out. But if it is good and they throw it out from caprice and cook another, this is bad.

79. He also said: formerly, when we gathered together and spoke about salvation, we strengthened one another thereby and ascended on high, rising to the heavens. But now, when we come together, we come to fault-finding of one another and we fall down below.

80. A certain soldier asked Abba Mios: does God accept repentance? The elder instructed him at length about this and then says to him: tell me, beloved, if your cloak is torn, will you throw it away? He answered: no, I will mend it and use it again. The elder said to him: if then you spare your garment, will not God spare His own creation?

81. Once Abba Macarius came to Abba Pachomius of Tabennisi, and Abba Pachomius asked him: there are brethren who do not conform to the rule; should I punish them? Abba Macarius answered him: punish and judge righteously those who are under you, but outside— judge no one, for it is said: *"Do you not judge those who are inside? But those who are outside God judges"* (1 Corinthians 5:12-13).

82. They recounted of Abba Netras, the disciple of Abba Silvanus: when he lived in his cell on Mount Sinai, he had a moderate rule regarding the needs of the body. But when he was made bishop in Pharan, he restricted himself strictly. His disciple said to him: Abba! When we were in the desert, you did not labor thus. The elder answered: there was the desert, stillness, and poverty, and I wanted to govern the body in such a way as not to fall ill and not to seek what I did not have. But here is the world and temptations: if I fall ill, here there is someone to support me. Therefore I fear lest I destroy the monk in myself.

83. Once village presbyters came to the monastery where Abba Poemen was. Abba Anub went in and asked him: shall we invite the presbyters in now? For a long time he stood, but Abba Poemen did not give him an answer, and he went out in sorrow. Those sitting near the elder say to him: why did you not give him an answer? Abba Poemen said: this is not my concern, for I am dead, and a dead man does not speak.

84. Once a brother from the region of Abba Poemen went to another country and, visiting a hermit there who was loved by all and to whom many came, told him about Abba Poemen. Hearing of the virtues of Abba Poemen, the hermit wished to see him and, upon the brother's return, soon came to him, saying: do me the kindness of taking me to Abba Poemen. When they came to the elder, the brother said to him: this is a great man, loved and highly respected in his country; I told him about you, and he came, wishing to see you. The elder received him with joy, and having kissed each other, they sat down. The stranger began to speak from Scripture about spiritual and heavenly subjects, but Abba Poemen turned his face away and gave no answer. The other, seeing that the Abba would not speak with him, was grieved and, going out, said to the brother: in vain did I make such a journey! For I came to the elder, and he does not even want to speak with me. The brother went in to Abba Poemen and asked him: Abba! This great man who has such fame in his country came for your sake; why then did you not speak with him? The elder answered: he is from above and speaks of heavenly things, but I am from below and speak of earthly things. If he had spoken to me about the passions of the soul, I might have answered him, but he spoke of spiritual things, and I know not of these. Going out, the brother said to the stranger: the elder does

not readily speak from Scripture, but if someone speaks to him about the passions of the soul, he answers him. Coming to compunction from this, the stranger went in to the elder and asked: what should I do, Abba, for the passions of the soul have mastery over me? The elder looked at him joyfully and answered: now your coming is good; now I open my mouth and fill it with good things. The hermit received great benefit and said: truly, this is the true path, and he returned to his country, thanking God that he was deemed worthy to visit such a saint.

85. Some recounted that once Abba Poemen and his brothers had no success in their work (they were engaged in plaiting cords), for there was nothing with which to buy flax, and Abba Poemen did not want to accept anything from anyone, fearing disturbance. A certain well-wisher of theirs told a devout merchant about this, and he, wishing to do the elder a service and making it appear that he had need of the cords, brought a camel and took them away. After this, a brother who had heard what the merchant had done came to the Abba, and wishing to praise him, said: truly, Abba, he took the cords without having need of them, but only to do you a service. Abba Poemen, hearing that he had taken the cords without having need of them, commanded his brother: go hire a camel and bring them back, otherwise Poemen will no longer live here with you; for I do not want to do injustice to a man who has no need, so that he should suffer loss through it and take away the value of my labor. The brother went with great effort and brought them back, otherwise the elder would have departed from them. Seeing the cords, the Abba rejoiced as one finding a great treasure.

86. A brother said to Abba Poemen: I have committed a great sin and want to repent for three years. The elder says to him: that is much. Or at least one year, continued the brother. The elder answered: that is also much. Those present asked: then forty days? And he again said: much. And he added: I assure you, if a man repents from his whole heart and determines not to commit the sin again, then in three days God will accept him.

87. Abba Isaiah asked Abba Poemen about impure thoughts. Abba Poemen answered him: behold, a chest is full of clothing! If it is left so, the clothing will spoil in time; so also with thoughts: if we do not fulfill them bodily, they will vanish in time or, as it were, rot away.

88. Abba Joseph asked him about the same, and Abba Poemen answered him: if a snake and a scorpion are placed in a vessel and sealed, in time they will die; so also evil thoughts, implanted by demons, are worn out by patience.

89. A brother came to Abba Poemen and said to him: I sow my field and from what I gather I make an agape. The elder says to him: you do well. The brother departed from him with joy and with even greater zeal applied himself to love. Hearing of this saying, Abba Anub says to Abba Poemen: do you not fear God, that you spoke thus to the brother? The elder was silent, and after two days he sent for that brother and says to him in the hearing of Abba Anub: what did you say to me that other time? My mind was on something else. The brother repeated. Then Abba Poemen said to him: I thought you were speaking about your brother, a layman; but if you yourself are doing such a thing, it is not monastic. Hearing this, the brother was grieved and said: I know no other work besides this, and I cannot but sow my field. When he had departed, Abba Anub made a prostration to the elder, saying: forgive me.

Abba Poemen said: I too knew before that this is not monastic work, but I spoke to him according to his thought and gave him zeal for progress in love. But now he departed in sorrow and will do the same anyway.

90. Abba Poemen said: if a man sins and denies it, saying he has not sinned, do not reprove him, for otherwise you will cut off all his zeal. But if you say to him: do not despair, brother, but be on your guard from now on, you will arouse his soul to repentance.

91. He also said: experience is good, for it makes a man skilled.

92. He also said: a man who teaches and does not do what he teaches is like a spring that gives drink and cleansing to all but cannot cleanse itself; in it remains mud and all manner of impurity.

93. A certain brother came to Abba Poemen and said to him: I have many thoughts, and I am in danger from them. The elder led him outside and says: spread open your bosom and do not let the wind in. The brother said: I cannot do this. If you cannot do this, concluded the elder, then you cannot prevent thoughts from coming either; but your task is to resist them.

94. Abba Poemen said: if three live together, and one of them keeps stillness well, another is sick and gives thanks, and the third serves them with a pure mind, the work of all three is the same.

95. Abba Joseph asked Abba Poemen: father, how should one fast? Abba Poemen answered him: I approve of one who eats every day, but eats a little, so as not to be satiated. Abba Joseph says to him: when you were young, did you not fast every other day, Abba? The elder said: indeed, and every three days, and every four, and for a week. But all this the fathers tested as men of strength and found that it is good to eat every day, but a little; they handed down to us this royal path because it is easier.

96. A brother asked Abba Poemen: an inheritance has been left to me. What should I do with it? The elder says to him: go and in three days come back; then I will tell you. When he came as he had determined, the elder answered: what can I say to you, brother? If I say, give it to the church, they will hold banquets there; if I say, give it to your relatives, there will be no reward for you; and if I say to you, give it to the poor, you will not take care of that. Therefore arrange it as you wish; it is no concern of mine.

97. Abba Poemen said: if a thought about needful bodily necessities comes to you and you fulfill it once; if it comes a second time and again you fulfill it, then if it comes a third time, do not attend to it at all, for it is empty.

98. A brother asked Abba Poemen: if I see something, do you want me to speak of it? The elder answered: it is written: *"He who answers a matter before he hears it, it is folly and shame to him"* (Proverbs 18:13). Therefore, if you are asked, speak; if not, be silent.

99. One brother asked Abba Poemen: can a man rely on one single practice? The elder answered him: Abba John Colobos said: I desire that a man partake, even if only a little, of all the virtues.

100. Abba Poemen related: Abba Ammon said: one spends his whole life carrying an axe and does not understand how to fell a tree, while another, having learned this, fells it in a short time. This axe, he said, is discernment.

101. Abba Poemen said: the will of man is a bronze wall between him and God and a repelling stone. Therefore, if a man abandons it, he too says: *"By my God I can leap over a wall"* (Psalm 18:29); but if his righteousness is founded on his will, the man grows faint.

102. Once some heretics came to Abba Poemen and began to find fault with the Archbishop of Alexandria, claiming that he had received ordination from presbyters. The elder was silent and, calling his brother, said: set a table before them and send them away in peace.

103. He also said: Abba Sisoes used to say that there is a shame that is passionlessness, having sin.

104. One brother asked Abba Poemen: if a man falls into some transgression and turns back, will he be forgiven by God? The elder answered: God, who commanded men to do this, will He not Himself do much more? And He commanded the Apostle Peter to forgive *"up to seventy times seven"* (Matthew 18:22).

105. A brother asked Abba Poemen: can a man take all his thoughts for himself and give none of them to the enemy? The elder answered: there is such a one who takes ten for himself and gives one away.

106. Abba Poemen said: not a monk is he who murmurs; not a monk is he who takes revenge; not a monk is he who is wrathful.

107. Some elders came to Abba Poemen and asked him: do you advise us to nudge any of the brethren who doze during the church assembly, so that he may be watchful at the vigil? He answered them: as for me, if I see a brother dozing, I place his head on my knees and give him rest.

108. They said of a certain brother that he was warred upon by blasphemous thoughts but was ashamed to tell of it. Wherever he heard of a great elder, he would go to him to open himself, but as soon as he came to him, he was ashamed to confess. He often came to Abba Poemen. The elder saw that he had thoughts and grieved at his concealment. Once, seeing him off, he said to him: how long have you been coming here intending to reveal your thoughts to me, but when you come you do not want to express them and each time go away heavily troubled by them. So, tell me, my son, what do you have? The brother answered him: a demon wars on me with blasphemous thoughts, and I was ashamed to say it. Then he told the matter and immediately felt relief. The elder said to him: do not grieve, my son, but when such a thought comes, say: I have no part in this; your blasphemy is upon you, Satan, for my

soul does not want such a thing. And every thing that the soul does not want, continued the elder, is short-lived. And thus the brother departed from the elder healed.

109. A brother asked Abba Poemen: why do demons drag my soul into fellowship with one who is greater than I and cause me to despise one who is lesser than I? The elder answered him: therefore the Apostle said that *"in a great house there are not only vessels of gold and silver, but also of wood and clay... Therefore if anyone cleanses himself from these, he will be a vessel for honor, sanctified and useful for the Master, prepared for every good work"* (2 Timothy 2:20-21).

110. Abba Poemen said: one living in a coenobium needs to have three things: humility, obedience, and readiness for communal work.

111. A brother told Abba Poemen the following: during my extreme need I asked one of the saints for a thing for my use, and he gave it to me as alms. So, if God establishes me, should I give it as alms to others or rather to the one who gave it? The elder said: it is righteous before God to return it to him, for it is his property. The brother asked: if I bring it to him and he says that I should give it as alms as I wish, what should I do? The elder answered: nevertheless, the thing remains his property. If someone gives you something of his own accord, without your asking, it is yours; but if you obtain it from a monk or layman by asking, and he does not want to take it back, then the reasoning is this: you should distribute it as alms for him before his eyes.

112. A brother asked Abba Poemen: what does it mean to *be angry with his brother without cause* (Matthew 5:22)? He said: to be angry without cause is to be angry over every injury with which your brother injures you. Even if he gouges out your right eye and cuts off your right hand, and you become angry with him, you are angry without cause. But if he separates you from God, then be angry.

113. One brother asked Abba Poemen: what does it mean to repent of sin? The elder answered: not to do it in the future, for the righteous are called blameless because they left their sins and became righteous.

114. A brother asked Abba Poemen: can a man be dead? He answered: when a man falls into sin, then he becomes dead, but when he turns to good, then he will live and do good.

115. Abba Poemen said: to teach one's neighbor is fitting for one who is sound and dispassionate, for what need is there for someone to build another's house and destroy his own?

116. He also said: what is the use of approaching a craft and not learning it?

117. He also said: everything excessive is from demons.

118. Again he said: hunger and drowsiness do not allow us to see even small things.

119. One of the elders asked Abba Poemen: who is it that says: *"I am a companion of all who fear You"* (Psalm 119:63)? The Abba answered: this is said by the Holy Spirit.

120. One brother came to Abba Poemen and in the presence of some who were sitting there praised a certain brother, saying that he hates wickedness. Abba Poemen asked him: what does it mean to hate wickedness? The brother was confused and, not finding what to answer, bowed to the elder and asked: tell me, father, what does it mean to hate wickedness? The elder said: he hates wickedness who hates his own sins and considers his neighbor righteous.

121. A brother said to Abba Poemen: what should I do with the heaviness that comes upon me? The elder answered: both on small boats and on large ones there are belts with ropes, so that when there is no favorable wind, they can put them on and tow the boat little by little, until God sends a favorable wind. Again, if they notice that a storm is rising, they put in to shore and drive in a stake so that the boat will not be tossed.

122. A brother asked Abba Poemen about the attack of thoughts. The elder answered him: this matter is like a man having fire on his left side and a vessel of water on his right; when the fire flares up, he takes water from the vessel and extinguishes it. This fire is the seed of the enemy, and the water is casting oneself before God.

123. A brother asked Abba Poemen: what is better, to speak or to be silent? The elder said: whoever speaks for God's sake does well, and whoever is silent for God's sake also does well.

124. The brother asked Abba Poemen again: how can a man avoid speaking ill of his neighbor? The elder answered: we and our brethren are two pictures: at the hour when a man attends to himself and accuses himself, his brother is honorable before him; but when he himself seems good to himself, he finds his brother bad before his face.

125. Someone asked Abba Poemen about despondency, and the elder answered: despondency stands at every beginning, and there is no passion worse than it. But as soon as a man recognizes what it is, he is at peace.

126. A brother asked Abba Poemen: I want to go live in a coenobium. The elder said: if you enter a coenobium and do not have freedom from care about every event and every thing, you will not be able to live in coenobitic fashion, for there you will not have authority even over a jug.

127. The brethren of Abba Poemen said to him: let us leave this place, for the monasteries here disturb us, and we are destroying our souls. Behold, even children are crying and do not let us keep stillness. Abba Poemen said to them: is it for the sake of angelic voices that you wish to leave here?

128. A brother said to Abba Poemen: my body has grown feeble, but the passions have not grown feeble. The elder says to him: the passions are thorny prickles.

129. A brother asked Abba Poemen: how should I sit in my cell? The elder answered: from the visible side, to sit in the cell means to engage in handwork, to take food once a day, to be silent, and to read with reflection; but from the invisible side, to make progress in the

cell means to bear self-condemnation in every place, wherever you may go, not to neglect the hours of the rule and the hidden work, and when it is time to rest from handwork, to stand for the rule, performing it without disturbance. The end of all this is to have good companionship and to avoid bad companionship.

130. They recounted: it happened that some of the fathers, among whom was Abba Poemen, entered the house of a certain Christ-lover. When they were eating, meat was set before them, and all ate it except Abba Poemen. Knowing his discernment, the fathers marveled at this and, when they arose, said to him: you are Poemen and you acted thus! The elder answered them: forgive me, fathers! You ate, and no one was scandalized, but if I had eaten, then many brethren coming to me would have been scandalized and begun to say: Poemen ate meat, and are we not to eat!? And all marveled at his discernment.

131. Once Paisius got into a fight with his brother, so that blood was flowing. Abba Poemen was there but said nothing to them. When Abba Anub came in and saw this, he asked Abba Poemen: why did you allow the brothers to fight and say nothing to them? Abba Poemen answered: they are brothers and will make up again. Abba Anub remarked to him: you see what they have done, and you say they will make up again? Abba Poemen said: place in your heart that I was not here inside.

132. A brother asked Abba Poemen: what should I do, for sorrow comes upon me, and I waver? The elder answered: violence makes both small and great waver.

133. The superior of a coenobium asked Abba Poemen: how can I acquire the fear of God? Abba Poemen answered him: how can we acquire the fear of God when our belly is like a vessel filled with cheese and a barrel of salted fish?

134. A brother asked the same: Abba! There were two men, one a monk and the other a layman. One evening the monk decided to cast off the schema, and the layman decided to become a monk, but that same night both died. So, what is accounted to them? The elder answered: the monk died a monk, and the layman died a layman, for in whatever state they were found, in that they departed.

135. Abba Isaac came to Abba Poemen and saw him pouring a little water on his feet. Having boldness toward him, he said: how is it that some lived more strictly and afflicted their bodies in every way? Abba Poemen answered: we have been taught to be not body-killers but passion-killers.

136. A brother said to Abba Poemen: I am harming my soul by staying with my Abba. Should I still remain with him? The elder saw that there was indeed harm, but marveling how he still asked whether to remain with him, says: if you wish, remain. After some time the brother came again and said that he was harming his soul, and the elder again did not command him to leave. When the brother came a third time, saying: truly, I will no longer stay with him, Abba Poemen said: now you have become wise! Go and do not stay with him any longer. And he added: is there a man who, seeing harm to his soul, still has need to ask!?

Experienced elders are questioned about hidden thoughts, but concerning manifest sin there is no need to ask; rather one should immediately cut it off.

137. Abraham, the disciple of Abba Agathon, asked Abba Poemen: why do demons war against me? Abba Poemen said to him: do demons war against you? Demons do not war against us when we fulfill our own desires, for then our desires become our demons: they torment us so that we fulfill them. Do you wish to know with whom demons warred? It was with Moses and those like him.

138. A brother said to Abba Poemen: I am troubled and want to leave my place. The elder asked him: because of what matter? The brother answered: because I hear something about a certain brother, and it does not benefit me. The elder said: what you heard is not true! The brother disagreed, saying: it is true, father, for the brother who said it is a trustworthy man. The elder answered to this: no, he is not trustworthy—if he were trustworthy, he would not have told you this. Since God, having heard the cry of Sodom, did not believe until He saw with His own eyes, neither should we believe what people say. The brother said: I too saw with my own eyes. Hearing this, the elder looked at the ground and, picking up a small twig, asked: what is this? The brother answered him: it is a speck. Then the elder looked at the roof beam of the cell and again asked: and what is that? The brother said: a beam. Then the elder continued: place in your heart that your sins are this beam, and the sins of your brother are like this speck. Hearing the word of the elder, Abba Tithoes was amazed and said: how shall we bless Abba Poemen? His words are precious stones—they are full of joy.

139. Once Abba Sirem came with his disciple Isaac to Abba Poemen and says to him: what should I do with this Isaac? He does not listen to my word. Abba Poemen said: if you wish to benefit him, show him virtue by deed, because while he attends to your word, he still remains idle; but if you show him by deed, that will remain in him.

140. Again he said: the power of God does not dwell in a man who serves the passions.

141. He also said: when we pursue rest, it flees from us; but when we do not pursue it, it pursues us.

142. Abba Poemen recounted: one brother asked Abba Moses: in what way does a man make himself dead to his neighbor? He answered him: unless a man places in his heart that he has already been three years in the grave, he will not attain to this measure.

143. There was a certain one called Abba Pambo, and they said of him that for three years he prayed to God thus: do not glorify me on earth. But God so glorified him that no one could look at him because of the glory that his face had.

144. Once two brothers came to Abba Pambo, and one of them asked him: Abba! I fast every other day and eat two loaves; am I being saved or am I going astray? And the other said: Abba! By my handwork I earn two coins a day, keep some for food, and give the rest as alms; am I being saved or am I going astray? Abba Pambo did not give them an answer, though they earnestly entreated him. After four days, when they intended to leave, the clerics

consoled them, saying: do not grieve, brethren, God will not leave you without reward: such is the elder's custom—not to speak until God Himself suggests it to him. The brothers came to the elder and asked him: Abba! Pray for us. He asked: do you wish to go? They confirmed it. Then the elder, calling to mind their deeds, began to write on the ground, saying: Pambo fasts every other day and eats two loaves; is he a monk because of this?—No. Pambo earns two coins and gives alms from them; is he a monk because of this?—Not at all. Then he continued: these deeds are good, but if you keep your conscience clean toward your neighbor, by that you will be saved. And the brothers, satisfied with this, departed with joy.

145. They said of Abba Pambo that there was never a smile on his face. Once the demons, wishing to make him laugh, tied a feather to a piece of wood and were carrying it, making noise and shouting: come on! come on! pull! pull! Seeing them, Abba Pambo laughed. The demons began to circle and shout: ha! ha! Pambo laughed! The Abba said to them in reply: I did not laugh, but I mocked your weakness, that so many of you are carrying one feather.

146. A brother asked Abba Pambo: why do demons hinder me from doing good to my neighbor? The elder said in answer: do not say this, for by this you make God a liar; but rather say that you do not at all want to give alms. For anticipating that, God testified: *"Behold, I give you the authority to trample on serpents and scorpions, and over all the power of the enemy"* (Luke 10:19).

147. Abba Palladius said: a soul laboring not according to God must either learn faithfully what it does not know, or teach clearly what it has learned. But if it does not want either, then it is sick with foolishness, for an ignorant word and no hunger for the word, which a God-loving soul always hungers for, is the beginning of apostasy.

148. Mother Sarra sent word to Abba Paphnutius with this saying: did you do God's work by allowing the brother to be dishonored? Abba Paphnutius said: as one doing the work of God, I have no dealings with anyone.

149. One recounted: Abba Paphnutius was bishop in a certain city of the Thebaid. He was God-loving, lived ascetically, and wondrous signs came through him. During the persecutions his eye was gouged out, and Emperor Constantine, highly esteeming this man, often summoned him to the imperial palace and kissed him on his gouged-out eye—such was the reverence Constantine had for him! But I shall recount one deed of Paphnutius, which by his counsel was accomplished to the perfection and good of the Church. The bishops who had gathered in those times at Nicaea thought it good to introduce a new law, by which sacred persons, such as bishops, presbyters, deacons, and subdeacons, should not cohabit with wives whom they had taken while still laymen. Then Paphnutius, standing in the midst of the assembly of bishops, exclaimed: this heavy yoke should not be laid upon the consecrated men, lest by excess of strictness we harm the Church even more, for, as it is said, *marriage is honorable.* Again, not all can bear the struggle of dispassion; perhaps they will not remain in chastity, whereas cohabitation with a lawful wife should be called chastity. By the ancient tradition of the Church it is sufficient for them not to marry again afterward and not to divorce the one who was taken when he was still a layman. Thus spoke Abba Paphnutius, he

himself having no part in marriage and having known no woman, for from youth he had been raised in a monastery and was adorned with chastity. Convinced by the words of Paphnutius, the bishops ceased their investigation of this matter, leaving it to the will of those who wished to abstain from marriage.

150. The elders recounted that Paisius, the younger brother of Abba Poemen, once found a small vessel with a thousand coins and said to his elder brother, Abba Anub: you know that the word of Abba Poemen is very strict; let us go somewhere and build ourselves a monastery and live without care. Abba Anub asked: with what shall we build? The other showed him the coins. Abba Anub was extremely grieved, thinking that they would harm his soul, and said: good, let us go and build a cell across the river. Abba Anub placed the vessel in his cowl, and when, crossing the river, they reached the middle, Abba Anub deliberately turned so that the cowl with the coins fell into the river, and he himself began to grieve as if in sorrow. Abba Paisius comforted his brother, saying: do not grieve, Abba! Since the coins have gone from us, let us return to our brother. Having returned, they lived with Abba Poemen in peace.

151. A certain monk, a Roman by birth, settled in Scetis near the church and kept a servant who attended him. The presbyter, seeing his weakness and knowing in what comfort he had lived before, sent to him whatever by God's providence came to the church. Having lived twenty-five years in Scetis, this monk became clairvoyant and was renowned. One of the great Egyptian elders, hearing of him, came to see him, hoping to find in him a strict bodily life befitting this place; however, he saw that he wore fine clothing, that under his mat was laid leather and there was a small pillow, that his feet were clean and in sandals, and he was scandalized. The elder, by his gift of clairvoyance, knew of his scandal and said to his attendant: let us make a feast today for the sake of the Abba! The other found some vegetables and cooked them. At the appointed time they rose and ate, and the elder offered a little wine, which he had because of his weakness, and they drank. With the coming of evening they read twelve psalms, and likewise at night. When later the elder stood alone at vigil, he heard them saying to one another: hermits in the deserts have more rest than we who live in coenobia. Therefore in the morning, when they were leaving to visit another elder, his neighbor, he asked them: bow to him from me and say: do not water the vegetables. The neighbor, hearing this word, understood what it meant and for this reason worked until evening fasting, and in the evening performed a great rule and afterward said: for your sake, since you are weary, let us break the fast today and eat a little, for we do not have the custom of eating every day. He set dry bread and salt before them and, saying: for your sake we must make a feast today, poured a little vinegar into the salt. Rising from the table, they stood for prayers and continued until morning. Then the elder said to them: for your sake we will not perform the full rule today, so as to give you a little rest, for you are from far away. In the morning they prepared to leave, but the elder began to entreat them: stay with us awhile; and if you cannot stay long, at least three days for the commandment's sake and according to our hermit custom. And they, seeing that he would not let them go, fled secretly.

152. A brother asked Abba Sisoes: why do the passions not depart from me? The elder answered: because their vessels are inside you; give them their pledge, and they will depart.

153. Some asked Abba Sisoes: if a brother falls, should he repent for a year? The Abba answered: that word is harsh. They asked again: six months? He said: that is much. At least forty days? they continued. He answered: that is also much. Then they said: so what then, if a brother falls and there suddenly is an agape, should he too enter the agape? The elder answered them: no, but he must repent for a few days, for I believe God that if such a one repents with his whole soul, in three days God will accept him.

154. Abba Joseph asked Abba Sisoes: in how much time can a man cut off his passions? The elder says to him: do you want to know the time? Abba Joseph answered: yes. Then the elder said: at the very hour when a passion comes, cut it off.

155. A brother asked Abba Sisoes: what should I do, Abba? I fell. The elder answered him: arise. The brother said: I arose and fell again. The elder says: arise again. The brother asked: until when? And the elder answered: until you are taken either in good or in falling, for in whatever state a man is found, in that he departs.

156. A brother asked Abba Sisoes: what should I do with the passions? The elder answered: *each one is tempted when he is drawn away by his own desires* (James 1:14).

157. Once Abba Sisoes came from the mountain of Abba Anthony to the outer mountain of the Thebaid and settled there. In those places were Meletians living in Calamon of the Arsinoite region. Certain brethren, hearing that the Abba had come to the outer mountain, wished to see him, but said: what shall we do? On the mountain there are Meletians—the elder will not suffer harm from them, but we, wishing to converse with the elder, might fall into temptation from the heretics. And they did not go to see the elder, lest they encounter them.

158. Abba Sisoes of Thebes asked his disciple: tell me what you see in me, and I will tell you what I see in you. The disciple answered: you are good in mind but somewhat strict. The elder said to this: you are good, but your mind is light.

159. One of the elders said: I asked Abba Sisoes to tell me a word, and he said: if a man can avoid something and does not keep it, he is satisfying a sinful need.

160. One brother came to Abba Silvanus on Mount Sinai and, seeing the brethren working, said to the elder: *"Do not labor for the food which perishes"* (John 6:27); and *"Mary has chosen the good part"* (Luke 10:42). Then the elder says to his disciple: Zacharias! Give the brother a book and put him in a cell where there is nothing. When the ninth hour came, the one who had come began to look toward the door, wondering if they would send someone to call him to the table, but since no one came, he went to the elder and asked: did not the brethren eat today, Abba? The elder answered: they did. He says: why then did they not call me? The elder said to him: because you are a spiritual man and have no need of this food, but we, being carnal, want to eat and therefore work. You, reading all day, have chosen the good

part and do not want to eat carnal food. Hearing this, the brother made a prostration, saying: forgive me, Abba! The elder said: Mary also has need of Martha, for through Martha is Mary also praised.

161. An elder recounted: once a brother who had fallen into grievous sins came to contrite repentance and decided to open himself to an elder, but he did not tell him the deed itself, only thus: if such thoughts come to someone, is there salvation for him? That one, being inexperienced in the discernment of thoughts, answered him: you have destroyed your soul. Hearing this, the brother said: if I have destroyed my soul, then I will go back into the world. As he was going, the thought came to him to open his thoughts to Abba Silvanus, for the Abba was very discerning. Coming to him, the brother likewise did not tell him the deed itself, but again in the same manner as to the first elder. Abba Silvanus, opening his mouth, began to speak to him from Scripture, that there is no condemnation for those who only have thoughts. Encouraged by what he heard, with good hope the brother also revealed to him the deed itself. The elder again, like a good physician, bound his soul with the plaster of the divine Scriptures, assuring him that there is repentance for those who turn to God with understanding. Afterward my Abba went to that first father and told him about this, adding: that despairing one who wanted to go back to the world now shines like a star in the midst of the brethren. I have related this in confirmation of how dangerous it is to open one's thoughts or deeds to those who have no discernment.

162. A brother asked Abba Sarmatas: my thoughts tell me: do not work, but eat, drink, and sleep. The elder answered: when you hunger, eat; when you thirst, drink; when you want to sleep, sleep. Then another elder came to that brother, and the brother told him of the words of Abba Sarmatas. The elder said: this is what he means: when you greatly hunger and thirst to the point that you can no longer endure, then eat and drink; and when you have stayed awake a very long time and want to sleep, then sleep. This is what the elder said to you.

163. Two elders, great hermits from the region of Pelusium, going to Mother Sarra, said to one another: let us humble this old woman. Then they say to her: see that you do not become proud in your thought and say: behold, hermits come to me, a woman. Mother Sarra answered them: I am a woman by nature, but not by thought.

164. Mother Sarra said: if I pray to God that all people be at peace with me, I will have to be at the door of each one with repentance. But I would rather pray that my heart be blameless toward all.

165. She also said to the brethren: I am a man, and you are women.

166. Holy Syncletica said: those who gather sensible wealth amid toils and worldly misfortunes always seek more, counting as nothing what they have and striving for what they do not have. But we, having nothing and even of what is necessary for us desiring to acquire nothing, do so for fear of God.

167. Again she said: there is a sorrow that is salvific and there is a sorrow that is destructive. The work of salvific sorrow consists in sighing either over one's own sins, or over

the infirmities of one's neighbors, or lest one fall from one's intention, or so as to be deemed worthy of perfect mercy. There is also an enemy's sorrow, full of foolishness, which some also call despondency. This spirit must be driven away by prayer, and especially by psalmody.

168. She also said: it is dangerous to teach for one who has not been raised to this by the active life. For as one who has a dilapidated house, receiving strangers, destroys them in the event of its collapse, so also these, not having first built themselves up, destroyed even those who came to them: by words they summoned them to salvation, but by the badness of their character they rather injured the combatants.

169. Again she said: it is good not to be angry; but when this happens, know that He who said: *"Do not let the sun go down on your wrath"* (Ephesians 4:26) did not give you even one day for this passion, while you wait until all the time of your life sets. Why do you so hate the one who has offended you? It is not he who offended you, but the devil. Hate the disease, not the sick one.

170. Mother Syncletica also said: there is an asceticism that is instituted by the enemy, for his disciples do the same things. How then do we distinguish divine and royal asceticism from tyrannical and demonic? Clearly, by moderation. Let there always be one rule of fasting for you: do not fast four or five days and then break the fast with a multitude of foods, for immoderation everywhere is destructive. Fast while you are young and healthy, for old age will come with infirmities. Therefore, store up food for yourself while you have strength, so that when you have no strength, you may find rest.

171. Again she said: the more combatants advance, the stronger adversaries they grapple with.

172. She also said: it is said to us: *"Be wise as serpents and harmless as doves"* (Matthew 10:16). We are commanded to be as serpents so that the attacks and wiles of the devil may not be hidden from us, for like is more quickly recognized by like; and the harmlessness of the dove indicates purity of deeds.

173. Abba Hyperechius said: truly wise is not he who instructs by word, but he who teaches by deed.

174. Once Paul, the disciple of Abba Or, went to buy branches and found that others had preceded him and given a deposit. Abba Or never gave a deposit, but at the proper time sent money and bought. Then his disciple went to another place for branches. The gardener said to him: once someone gave me a deposit and has not come back again. So, take these branches yourself. The disciple took them and, coming to the elder, told him about this. As soon as the elder heard of this, he clapped his hands and exclaimed: Or is not working this year!—and would not allow the branches to be brought inside, commanding that they be taken back to their place.

175. Near the dwelling where Abba Or lived there was a certain prince named Longinus who gave much alms. Coming to one of the fathers, he asked to be taken to Abba Or, and

when he visited the Abba, the father praised the prince, saying he is good and gives much alms. The Abba understood and said: yes, he is good. Then the visitor began to ask him: allow him, Abba, to come and see you? Abba Or answered to this: truly, he will not cross this valley and will not see me.

176. An elder said: this voice—turn now—cries out to man until his last breath.

177. An elder said: Joseph of Arimathea took the body of Jesus and *wrapped it in a clean linen cloth* and laid it *in his new tomb* (Matthew 27:59-60), that is, in a new man. Thus everyone who carefully does not sin should take care not to offend the God who dwells with him and not to drive Him from his soul. The ancient Israel was given to eat manna in the wilderness; but to the true Israel is given the Body of Christ.

178. One brother lived in a solitary cell in Egypt, keeping himself in great humility. In the city he had a sister who was a harlot, destroying many souls. The elders often importuned him about her and at last persuaded him to go to her, hoping that somehow by his counsel he might stop the sin committed through her. When he was approaching the place where his sister lived, one of her acquaintances saw him and warned her: your brother is coming, and he is already at your door. Alarmed, she left her lovers, whom she was entertaining, ran out to him with her head uncovered, and wanted to embrace him, but he said: my own sister! Spare your soul! How many people are perishing through you! And how will you bear the eternal and bitter torments? Coming to trembling from these words, she asked: but now is there salvation for me? He answered: if you want it, there is salvation. Then she fell at her brother's feet and asked him to take her with him into the desert. He says to her: put a covering on your head and follow me. But she said: let us go; it is better for me to bear the shame of an uncovered head than to enter that workshop of lawlessness. On the way he spoke to her about repentance, and when he saw that someone was coming toward them, he asked her: since not everyone knows that you are my sister, step aside from the road a little until they pass. When those they met had passed, he turned to her: now let us go on our way, my sister. But she gave no answer, and when he approached, he found her dead and saw that her feet were covered with blood, for she was unshod. When he told this to the fathers, they disagreed in their opinions, but to one of the elders God revealed that because she had resolutely cut off all care for the flesh and scorned her very body, without groaning enduring grievous wounds, He accepted her repentance.

179. A brother from abroad said to an elder: I want to go to my homeland. The elder said to him: know, brother, that going here from the place of your homeland, you had the Lord as your companion, but when you go back, you will no longer have Him.

180. A brother said to a certain elder: I do not see any warfare in my heart. The elder answered to this: you have four gates, and anyone who wishes enters and exits through you, and you do not notice it. But when you set up a door and, having closed it, do not allow evil thoughts to enter through it, then you will see them standing outside waging war against you.

181. They recounted of a certain elder who lived in a temple at Clysma that for his handwork he always worked on what was needed at the time: when it was the season for catching fish, he wove nets, and when cords were needed, he spun flax, but he never undertook to work to order so that his mind would not be disturbed by business.

182. A certain cenobiarch asked our holy father Cyril, Pope of Alexandria: who is higher in activity: we who have brethren under us and guide each in various ways to salvation, or hermits who save themselves alone? The Pope answered: between Elijah and Moses there is no difference, for they equally pleased God.

183. One monk was working on the day of a martyr. Seeing this, another monk said to him: is it permissible to work today? He answered: today a servant of God was being torn and tortured in torments. Should I not also labor myself a little today at work?

184. A certain sinner, having repented, entered into stillness. It happened that soon after, stumbling on a stone, he injured his foot, so that much blood flowed, and he grew faint and gave up his soul. Then demons came, wishing to take his soul, but the angels said to them: look at this stone and see his blood, which he shed for the Lord's sake! When the angels said this, his soul was freed.

185. They asked an elder: what should a monk be like? He answered: in my opinion, like one alone with the One alone.

186. Someone asked an elder: why, when I walk through the desert, am I afraid? He answered: because you are still alive.

187. Someone else asked an elder: what should those wishing to be saved do? The elder was weaving a plait and, without interrupting his handwork, answered: behold—you see?

188. Again he asked the elder: why do I often become faint-hearted? He answered: because you have no discernment.

189. Someone asked an elder: why do I often have temptation to fornication? He answered: because you eat and sleep too much.

190. They asked an elder: what should a monk do? And he answered: do every good and distance yourself from every evil.

191. The elders said: one should never give a pledge to thoughts.

192. The elders also said: of every thought that attacks you, ask: are you ours or from the enemy? And it will certainly confess.

193. The elders said that the soul is like a spring: if you clear away the overgrowth, it is cleansed; but if you allow debris to accumulate, it becomes choked and perishes.

194. One elder said: I believe that there is no such injustice in God as to take one from prison and cast him into prison.

195. An elder said: to constrain oneself in everything is the path of God.

196. He also said: do not do anything, but having first tested your heart—whether what you intend to do is according to God.

197. Again he said: if a certain monk only prays when he stands for prayer, such a one does not pray at all.

198. He also said: discernment is above all virtues.

199. He also said: it is a shame for a monk if, having left his own things and become a stranger for God's sake, he then departs into torment.

200. The elders said: if you see a young man ascending to heaven by his own will, grab him by the foot and cast him down, for this is profitable for him.

201. An elder said: this generation does not seek what is now but what is tomorrow.

202. He also said: our work is to burn firewood.

203. Again he said: do not wish to be not despised.

204. He also said: woe to the man when his ill fame is greater than his deeds.

205. An elder said: presumption and laughter are like fire consuming reeds.

206. Again he said: one who constrains himself for God's sake is equal to a confessor.

207. He also said: whoever becomes foolish for the Lord's sake, him the Lord will make wise.

208. He also said: behold what God requires of man: mind, word, and deed.

209. Again he said: behold what man needs: to fear God's judgment, to hate sin, to love virtue, and always to pray to God.

210. He also said: if you see that you have a thought against someone, know that he also has a thought against you.

211. A brother asked an elder: is it good to have brief fellowship with one's neighbor? The elder answered him: such fellowships have no power to break the bridle, for you have fellowship with your brother. If you wish to have fellowship, have it with God.

212. A brother asked an elder for a prayer, hastening to the city. The elder said to him: do not hasten to the city, but hasten to flee from the city, and you will be saved.

213. One brother asked the fathers: is one defiled by having had an impure thought? There was an investigation among the fathers about this, and some said: yes, he is defiled; others said: no, otherwise it would be impossible for us simple ones even to be saved; what is required is only not to carry them out bodily. Then the brother went to a more skilled elder and asked him about this. The elder answered: each one is required to be pure according to the measure of his perfection. The brother asked the elder: for the Lord's sake, explain to me how this is. The elder said: suppose some enticing object is lying here, and two brothers come in: one having a great measure of perfection, the other a lesser. If the thought of the perfect

one says: I would like to have this object, and he does not dwell on it but immediately cuts it off, he is not defiled. But one who has not yet attained to a great measure is not defiled if he desires and even dwells with the thought, so long as he does not take the object.

214. An elder said: once a certain brother fell into grievous transgressions but came to contrition and repented to God.

215. He also said: not that thoughts enter us serves for our condemnation, but that we make bad use of them, for through thoughts one can suffer shipwreck, and through thoughts one can be crowned.

216. A brother asked an elder: what should I do? A multitude of thoughts overcome me, and I do not know how to fight with them. The elder answered: do not fight with all of them, but with one, for all thoughts have one head. Therefore, you must notice which head it is and fight with it. Then the other thoughts will themselves be humbled.

217. An elder said: one who wishes to live in the desert should be able to teach and not need to be taught, lest he suffer harm.

218. A brother asked an elder: Abba! I ask the elders, and they speak to me about the salvation of the soul, but I do not retain anything from their words. What is the point of my asking them, since I do nothing, and I am all impurity? The elder had two empty vessels and said to the brother: go bring one vessel, pour oil in it, swirl it out, and put it back in its place. He did so twice. Afterward the elder says to him: now bring both vessels together and see which of them is cleaner. The brother says to him: the one in which I poured oil. Then the elder said: so it is also with the soul; though it retains nothing of what it asks about, it becomes more pure than that of one who does not ask at all.

219. One brother was keeping stillness, and demons, under the guise of angels, wanted to deceive him: they would wake him for the performance of the rule and show him lights. The brother came to a certain elder and reported: Abba! Angels come to me with light and wake me for the rule. The elder said: do not listen to them, my son! They are demons, and when they come to wake you, say to them: when I want, I will get up myself, and I have no need of you. The brother, having received a commandment from the elder, returned to his cell. That same night the demons came as usual and woke him, and the brother answered them: when I want, I will get up myself, and I have no need of you. They say to him: that evil elder is a liar; he deceived you, for once a brother came to him to borrow some small coins, and he, having them, lied, saying he did not have them, and did not give them. From this recognize that he is a liar. When morning came, the brother came to the elder and told him about this. The elder says: I admit that I had coins and that a brother came asking, but I did not give them to him, for I saw harm in that for our souls. Then I judged it better to transgress one commandment in order not to transgress ten and not to fall into trouble. But you do not listen to the demons who want to deceive you. And the brother, strengthened by the elder, returned to his cell.

220. Some of the fathers recounted about one great elder: when anyone came to him asking for instruction, he customarily spoke thus: behold, I take the place of God and sit on the throne of judgment; so, what do you wish that I do for you? If you say: have mercy on me! then God says to you: have mercy on your brother also. If you want Me to forgive you, forgive your neighbor also. Is there then unrighteousness with God? Let it not be! Therefore it is in our power to be saved, if you so desire.

221. They said of one elder, a great laborer, that once when he was performing his rule, another elder, also great, happened to come to him and heard from outside that he was reproaching his own thoughts, saying: how long then? And on account of one word, all that vanished!? The one who came, thinking he was reproaching someone else, knocked to enter and reconcile them, but entering and seeing no one there, by his boldness toward the elder he asked him: Abba! With whom were you reproaching? He answered: with my own thought, for I know by heart fourteen books, but I heard one word outside the cell, and when I came to perform my rule, all that I knew was made void, and only that one word came into my memory. Therefore I was reproaching my thought.

222. Some brethren from a coenobium came to a certain hermit. He received them with joy, and according to the custom of hermits, seeing that they were wearied from the journey, prepared a table for them before the usual time and set before them whatever was at hand. With the coming of evening they read twelve psalms, and likewise at night. When later the elder stood alone at vigil, he heard them saying to one another: hermits in the deserts have more rest than we who live in coenobia. Therefore in the morning, when they were leaving to visit another elder, his neighbor, he asked them: bow to him from me and say: do not water the vegetables. The neighbor, hearing this word, understood what it meant and for this reason labored them until evening without food, and in the evening performed a great rule and afterward said: for your sake, because you are wearied, let us break the fast today and eat a little, for we do not have the custom of eating every day. He set dry bread and salt before them and, saying: for your sake we must make a feast today, poured a little vinegar into the salt. Rising from the table, they stood for prayers and continued until morning. Then the elder said to them: for your sake we will not perform the full rule today, so as to give you a little rest, for you are from far away. In the morning they prepared to leave, but the elder began to entreat them: stay with us awhile; and if you cannot stay long, at least three days for the commandment's sake and according to our hermit custom. And they, seeing that he would not let them go, fled secretly.

223. An elder said: the prophets composed books; our fathers came and put them into practice; those who came after them learned them by heart; but this generation has come— they copied them and put them in cupboards idle.

224. A brother said to one of the fathers: if it happens that I oversleep and miss the hour of the rule, then my soul from shame no longer wants to perform it. The elder answered to this: if you wake before morning, rise, close the door and windows, and perform your rule, for it is written: *Yours is the day, Yours also is the night,* for at every time one can glorify God.

225. An elder said: one eats much and still remains hungry, while another eats little but is satisfied. Thus the one who eats much and remains hungry has greater value than the one who eats little but is satisfied.

226. An elder said: even though the holy fathers labored here, they also received a certain portion of rest. He said this because they were free from worldly cares.

227. He also said: if a brother knows of a place conducive to progress but does not go there because of the burden of bodily needs, such a one does not believe that God exists.

228. A certain brother asked a young monk: what is better, to be silent or to speak? The youth said to him: if the words are idle, leave them; if they are good, give place to the good and speak. However, even if they are good, do not delay but quickly cut them off, and you will find rest.

229. One of the fathers said: a man should always have an inner work, for when he is occupied with the work of God, then the enemy, coming once and again, will find no place to remain. And conversely, when one is in captivity to the enemy and the Holy Spirit comes, He departs from us because of our wickedness, since we do not give Him place in ourselves.

230. One brother, having just received the schema, thought to become a hermit and immediately shut himself up, saying: I am a hermit. The elders, hearing of this, came, pulled him out, and made him go around all the cells of the monks, making a prostration at each one and saying: forgive me, I am not a hermit but a novice.

231. Two brothers by blood were practicing the hermit life, but the first in the schema was the younger in age. One of the fathers came to visit them; they set out a basin, and the younger in the schema came forward to wash the elder's feet. But the elder, taking him by the hand, led him aside and placed the older brother there. The elders standing by remarked to him: the younger one, Abba, is first in the schema. The elder said to them: I take the priority of the younger and add it to the age of the older.

232. Once some Egyptian monks came to Scetis to visit the elders and, seeing that they were eating with some haste because of hunger from long fasting, were scandalized. The presbyter, learning of this and wishing to heal them, announced in the church to the brotherhood: fast, brethren, and continue your usual rule of asceticism. The Egyptian visitors wanted to leave, but the presbyter detained them. Having fasted one day, they grew gloomy, though he gave them only two fast days, whereas the monks of Scetis fasted the whole week. When Saturday came and they sat down to the table, the Egyptians hastened to eat, but one of the elders, taking one of them by the hand, said: eat more skillfully, like monks. But he pushed his hand away, saying: let me go, for I am dying of hunger, not having eaten anything cooked the whole week. Then the elder said to them: if you, having fasted two days, were so exhausted, how were you scandalized at the brethren who always keep the practice of eating once a week? The visiting monks repented of their sin and, having received great benefit, departed with joy.

233. An elder said: if anyone, remaining in some place, does not produce the fruit proper to that place, then the place expels him as one who does not do the works of the place.

234. He also said: if anyone does some work following his own will, and this work is not according to God, but he does not know it, such a one must afterward certainly come to the path of God. But if someone clings to his own wish, which is not according to God, and does not want to listen to others, considering himself knowledgeable in his matter, such a one comes to the path of God with difficulty.

235. An elder said: as the order of monks is more honorable than laymen, so also a monk who is a stranger should be a mirror of every good thing for local monks.

236. One of the fathers said: if a worker lives in a place where there are no workers, he cannot make progress but can only strive not to descend below. But a non-worker, if he does not live with workers, will make progress if he is vigilant, and if he is not vigilant, at least he will not descend below.

237. An elder said: if the soul has the word but has no fruit, it is like a tree that has leaves but no fruit. As with a tree, when it is full of fruit, the leaves are also more beautiful; so also the word is more becoming to a soul that has good practice.

238. Once three brothers came to Scetis to a certain elder, and one of them said to him: Abba! I have learned the Old and New Testament by heart. The elder says to him: you have filled the air with words. The second said: I have copied the Old and New Testament for myself. The elder answered the second: and you have filled cupboards with notebooks. The third said: moss has grown on my hearth. The elder answered him: and you have driven hospitality from yourself.

239. A brother asked an elder: why do I perform my small rule with weariness? The elder answered: love of God is known from one performing the work of God with all earnestness, compunction, and an undistracted thought.

240. Once brethren came to a great elder, and he asked the first: what do you work? He answered: I weave plaits, Abba. The elder said: may God weave you a crown, child! He asked the second: what do you work? He answered: mats. He said: may God strengthen you, child! He asked the third: what do you work? He answered: sieves. The elder said: may God preserve you, child! He asked the fourth: what do you work? He answered: I am a calligrapher. He said: you know for yourself. He asked the fifth: what do you work? He answered: linen cloth. The elder said: this is not my concern. For one who weaves plaits, if he is vigilant with God's help, weaves himself a crown; mats require strength, for they are hard to work; sieves require watchfulness, for they are sold in villages; a calligrapher needs to humble his heart, for this work tends to proud-mindedness; but linen cloth is a tradesman's business. Thus, if anyone sees from afar that someone is carrying baskets, or mats, or sieves, he says: that is a monk—for grass goes into our handwork. But if he sees someone selling cloth, he says: look, merchants have come—for this work is worldly, and it is profitable for few.

241. One of the fathers recounted that a certain brother, very devout, had a poor mother. When a great famine came, he took loaves and hastened to bring them to his mother. And behold, a voice came to him: will you take care of your mother, or shall I take care of her? The brother, reflecting on the power of this word, fell face down on the ground and asked God: You, Lord, take care of us!—arose and returned to his cell. On the third day his mother came to him and said: such-and-such a monk gave me much wheat; take it and make loaves, so that we may eat from it. Hearing this, the brother glorified God and, filled with good hope, progressed by the grace of God in every virtue.

242. A brother reported to an elder: suppose I come to some place with brethren, and a basket of fruit is set before us, but the brethren often do not want to eat, either from self-restraint or because they have already eaten, while I am hungry. So what should I do? The elder answered: if you are hungry, then look at how many are sitting and how much has been set out and eat as much as you think is your portion. Let this not be a stumbling block for you, for you are satisfying a natural need. But if you are overcome and eat more, this will be harmful to you.

243. A brother asked an elder: what is fault-finding and what is condemnation? The elder answered: fault-finding refers generally to a person's whole character, and condemnation refers to manifest deeds. Thus, every word that you cannot say to your brother's face, that is, you cannot point to his deeds but speak behind his back, is fault-finding. For example, if someone says that such-and-such a brother is good and kind, but disorderly and has no discernment, that is fault-finding. But if someone says that such-and-such a brother is a merchant and lover of money, this is condemnation, for you have condemned his deeds. And this is worse than fault-finding.

244. One elder, coming to the river and finding that the bank, undisturbed and peaceful, was overgrown with reeds, sat down there and, cutting branches, wove a plait, throwing what he made into the river. He did this until people came and saw him. Then he arose and departed, for he worked not out of need but for labor and stillness.

245. One brother was warred upon by a thought—to go visit a well-known elder, but he kept putting it off from day to day, saying: I will go tomorrow. Thus he struggled with the thought for three years. Finally he said to the thought: imagine that you have come to the elder and said to him: good health to you, good elder! For so long I have desired to see your holiness. Then he set out a basin, washed himself, and spoke as if from the mouth of the elder: welcome, brother! Forgive me that you have labored so much for my sake! May the Lord repay you! Then he prepared food, ate and drank his fill. And immediately the warfare departed from him.

246. An elder said: I sit here in solitude in weaknesses and afflictions not for any good or benefit, but because only the strong are able to live among brethren.

247. He also said: if anyone attempts to do good in the place where he lives and cannot, let him not think that he can do it in another place.

248. They asked an elder about those who go here and there and ask for prayers but themselves live in negligence, and the elder answered: *the effective, fervent prayer of a righteous man avails much* (James 5:16), that is, when the one who asks for prayer also cooperates and strives and with all diligence and heartfelt anguish guards himself from evil thoughts and deeds. But if he lives in disorder, there will be no benefit for him, even if saints pray for him, for it is said: *one who builds and one who tears down* (Sirach 34:23), what profit do they have—only toil? And at this he recounted the following incident: one hermit, very discerning, wanted to settle in The Cells but did not find one ready. One elder had a separate cell on the side and offered it to the newcomer, saying: live there until you find another for yourself. When he settled there, people began coming to him for edification, as to a stranger, and bringing what was needed, and he received this and entertained them. The elder who had given him the cell envied this and began to slander him, saying: so many years I have lived here in great asceticism, and no one comes to me, but to this flatterer, who has been here only a few days, so many come! And once he says to his disciple: go and tell him to leave, for I need the cell myself. The disciple went and asked the newcomer: my Abba wishes to know how your health is. He answered: ask his prayers, for I feel a little heavy in my stomach. The disciple returned and told the elder that he would look for a cell and move. After two days the elder again says to his disciple: go and tell him that if he does not leave, I will come and drive him out with a stick. Coming, the disciple said to the newcomer: my Abba, having learned that you are unwell, was greatly grieved and sent me to look in on you. The newcomer says: tell him: by your prayers I am feeling better. Returning, the disciple told the elder that with God's help he would vacate by Sunday. Since Sunday came and he did not vacate, the elder, taking a stick, went to beat him and drive him out. The disciple says to the elder: let me run ahead to see if there is anyone with him, so that they may not be scandalized. And coming, he says: my Abba is coming to invite you to his cell. The other, hearing of such love from the elder, came out to meet him, bowed to him from afar, and said: I myself am coming to your holiness; do not trouble yourself, father! Then God, seeing the disciple's work, softened the elder's heart, and he, throwing down the stick, ran to embrace the visiting elder and led him to his cell as one who had heard nothing. Afterward he asked his disciple: did you not tell him anything of what I said? He answered: no. The elder greatly rejoiced at this and, understanding that there was envy in him sent by the enemy, gave rest to the visiting elder. And to his disciple he fell at his feet and said: you are my father, and I am your disciple, for by your work the souls of both of us have been saved.

249. One holy Abba, the father of a coenobium, adorned with every virtue, but especially with humility and meekness, merciful, compassionate, and surpassing many in love, prayed to God thus: Lord! I know that I myself am a sinner, but trusting in Your compassions, I hope to be saved by Your mercy! I pray, therefore, Master, to Your goodness, that my companions not be separated from me in the age to come either, but deem them worthy also of Your Kingdom together with me by Your goodness. He offered such a prayer every day, and the man-loving God deemed him worthy of such an assurance: the commemoration of a saint was to take place in another monastery, not far from theirs; when they asked him to

come, he heard in a dream: go there, but send your disciples ahead, and afterward go yourself alone. Meanwhile the Lord, who for our sake became poor and became all things to all that He might save all, taking the form of a sick beggar, lay in the middle of the road. The disciples, approaching and finding Him suffering, asked the reason, and He answered them: I am sick, my animal threw me and ran away, and I have no one to help Me. They said to Him: what can we do for You, Father? We are on foot. And leaving Him, they departed. A little later their Abba comes, finds Him lying and groaning, and learning the reason, asks: did not some monks pass by here shortly before? He answered: they did, but learning the reason, they passed by, saying: we are on foot—what can we do for You? The Abba asked Him: can You walk little by little? Let us go together. He said: I cannot. Then the Abba says to Him: come then, I will carry You; God will help, and we will reach the place. He said: how can this be for you? And such a distance! But go and pray for Me! But the Abba answered: I will by no means leave You! Here is a stone; I will place You on it, then lift You and carry You. Having done this, at first he felt on himself the weight of a man, then it became lighter and lighter, and finally there was no weight at all. The Abba was amazed at this, and He whom he carried became invisible and said to him in a voice: you always pray for your disciples that they too may be deemed worthy of the Kingdom of Heaven together with you; but your measure is one and that of your disciples another. Make them also come to your measure, and leave off your request, for I am just and will render to each according to his deeds.

250. They said of one saint that, being a confessor during the persecutions, he endured many torments and was even placed on a red-hot bronze seat. When later Blessed Constantine became emperor and all Christians were freed from bonds and this saint, having recovered, was returning to his cell, as soon as he saw it from afar, he said: woe is me! Again I go to afflictions! He said this because of the attacks of demons there and the warfare with them.

251. An elder said: if you see someone fall into water and you want to help him, give him your staff and pull him by it; and know this, that if you cannot pull him out, he will pull you down, and both will drown. He said this about those who undertake to help someone beyond their measure.

252. A brother came to an elder, not having visited him for quite a long time, and the elder asked him: where have you been, child, for such a long time? He answered him: in Constantinople, father, on some unavoidable business. The elder again asked him: what then did you hear or see there that was edifying? The brother answered: there was almost nothing edifying; much that was noisy comes to mind, but all of that is mostly earthly, and only one thing especially struck me: I saw laymen so despising wealth as could not be said of those dwelling in the desert. The elder asked: explain to me, how is this? And the brother recounted: I saw two rich men, one of whom was suing the other, saying that the latter owed him two thousand coins, presenting the promissory note of his father, while the other maintained that the debt had been paid by his father, and the note remained because of their sincere friendship. Since they could not agree between themselves, the matter came to an oath, and the one who was in debt says: if I swear that the debt was paid by my father, I will be

considered a shameful profiteer; let us rather do this: either I will swear that the debt was paid by my father and pay them to you a second time, or you swear that he remained in debt to you, do not take them from me, and return the note. And all marveled, hearing such reasoning from the man. The elder said: and you, child, being young, rightly marveled, but if you look more deeply into the matter, you will find nothing great here, but only an excess of vainglory and man-pleasing. The brother asked: how is this, father, when he despised such a sum only on account of one suspicion? The elder answered: one who despises wealth should, as far as possible, also take thought for the good of his neighbor, for the commandment of our Lord and God commands both. If he knew for certain that his father had paid the debt and offered to swear and also pay it a second time, what else did he do but present his brother before God and men as unjust and a manifest shameful profiteer, while proclaiming himself both very wealthy and non-acquisitive, which is not so much the virtue of non-covetousness as a stamp of vainglory, or more precisely, of envy and anger. The brother asked again: so, what then should he have done when an oath was proposed to him about the debt? The elder answered: if he were perfect, he would neither swear nor propose an oath in return, especially when he is rich and knows for certain that the debt was paid; and how much better it would have been for him to suffer loss for the sake of avoiding an oath and preserving love, expecting recompense from God! He said this out of vainglory, to show people that the one bringing him to oath is unjust, and this is a matter of envy and mutual hatred. So attend, child: only that which is done with a good purpose and a God-loving thought is acceptable to God. And the brother, having received benefit, departed.

253. An elder said: he who praises a monk delivers him to Satan.

254. Again he said: all that a man thinks of—from heaven and below, if he thinks it—but he who perseveres in the remembrance of Jesus stands in the truth.

255. The son of a monk living in Scetis was taken by a magistrate into service. Informing him of this, the boy's mother asked the father to write to the magistrate to release him. The monk asked the messenger: if this one is released, will they not take another? He answered: they will. The elder said: what profit is it to me, then, if releasing him, I transfer the joy from the heart of his mother and put that sorrow into the heart of another woman?

256. The same elder earned much by his handiwork and, leaving as much as was needed for his own necessities, distributed the rest to the poor. When a famine came upon those lands, his mother sent his son to him and asked him to give them some bread. Hearing of this, the elder asked his son: are there also others in that place who are in need, as you are? He answered: there are many. Then, shutting the door before his face, he said with tears: depart, my child! He who cares for those will also care for you. A brother asked him afterward: did your heart not ache when you sent your son away thus? The elder answered: if a man does not compel himself to every deed, he will have no reward.

257. An elder said: every evil not accomplished in deed is not evil, and every righteousness not accomplished in deed is not righteousness, for he who has neither evil nor

good thoughts is like the land of Sodom and Gomorrah, which is full of salt and produces neither fruit nor plants. But good earth produces both wheat and tares.

258. An elder recounted: when I was with a certain elder, a virgin came to him and said: I have fasted two hundred weeks at six days each and have read the Old and New Testament. What yet do I lack, and what further labor should I take upon myself? The elder asked her: has dishonor become to you as honor? She answered: no. Or loss, as gain; or strangers, as your own according to the flesh; poverty, as abundance? She answered: no. Then the elder said to her: so then, you have fasted six days in vain and have read the Old and New Testament in vain. You deceive yourself. Go and labor! You have nothing.

259. An elder said: if a man voluntarily gives himself over to sorrow, then truly God will number him among the martyrs, for instead of blood, tears are reckoned to him.

260. Again he said: a little child who interferes in our conversation is like a man casting fire into his brother's bosom.

261. The elders said: discipline, brethren, little children, lest otherwise they discipline you.

262. A certain brother came to Mount Pherme to a great elder and said to him: Abba! What should I do? My soul is perishing! The elder asked him: why, child? The brother said: when I was in the world, truly, I fasted much and kept vigil, and great compunction and warmth were within me; but now, Abba, I see absolutely no good in myself. The elder answered him thus: believe me, child, all that you did when you were in the world, you did zealously out of vainglory and human praise, and that was not pleasing before the face of God. Therefore Satan did not war against you, for he had no need to cut off your zeal. But now, seeing that you have enrolled yourself for Christ and have gone out against him, he also has armed himself against you. Yet one psalm read by you now with compunction is more pleasing to God than the thousands you read in the world; and He receives your small fasting more than the weeks with which you fasted in the world. The brother said to him: now I do not fast at all, but all the good I had in the world has been taken from me. The elder said: brother! What you have is enough for you, only endure, and all will be well. But since the brother persisted, saying: truly, Abba, my soul is perishing, the elder continued: believe me, brother, I did not wish to tell you this, lest your thought be harmed; but seeing that you have fallen into despondency from Satan, I will tell you: the way you think, that when living in the world you were doing good and going well, is pride, and thus the Pharisee destroyed all the good he had done. But that you now see yourself as doing absolutely no good, this alone is enough for you, brother, unto salvation, for this is humility: thus was the publican justified, who had done nothing good. God is more pleased with a sinner and a negligent one with a contrite heart and humility, than with one who does much good and thinks within himself that he is doing good. And the brother, receiving great benefit, made a prostration to the elder and said: now, Abba, my soul is saved through you.

263. They asked an elder: what does it mean to give an answer for every idle word? He said: every word about bodily things is idle talk, and only speaking about the salvation of the soul is not idle talk. However, to guard against everything and to keep silence is better, for when you begin to speak of the good, evil will come in to its harm.

264. Once Satan appeared to an elder and said: you are not a Christian. The elder answered him: whoever I may be, I am still higher than you. Satan said thereupon: I tell you, you will go to torment. The elder answered: you are not my judge and not my God.

265. A brother asked an elder: Father, why is our generation unable to maintain the asceticism of the fathers? The elder answered: because it does not love God, does not flee from people, and does not hate the things of the world. When a man flees from people and things, compunction and asceticism come to him of themselves. For just as one who wishes to extinguish a fire that has broken out in a field, if he does not run ahead and cut off the material that is before the fire, will not extinguish it, so also a man, if he does not go away to such a place where he would find even his bread itself with difficulty, cannot acquire asceticism, for what the soul does not see, it does not quickly desire.

266. He also said: he who steals, lies, or commits any other sin often immediately after committing the sin sighs, reproaches himself, and comes to repentance; but he who holds rancor in his soul, whether he eats, drinks, sits, or walks, is always consumed as if by rust, and sin is inseparable from him. Therefore his prayer becomes a curse to him, and no labor of his, even if he were to shed his blood for Christ, will be accepted.

267. An elder said: if anyone comes and you see that they are from afar, stand in prayer and say: Lord Jesus Christ, deliver us from accusation and slander, and return them in peace from this place.

268. Again he said: if your body is weak, then satisfy its needs accordingly, lest it fall into illness and you begin to seek rich foods and burden the one who serves you.

269. An elder was asked about nocturnal defilement, whether in the form of union with a woman or by itself. He answered: one should not attribute this to oneself at all, but think that it is as if you had merely blown your nose. Likewise, if you happen to walk through the marketplace and, passing by a tavern, smell the odor of meats, did you taste them or not? You will certainly say no. So also that does not defile you; but if the enemy sees that you are fearful, he will attack you all the more. However, beware that upon awakening, having come to yourself, you do not descend to it in thought.

270. The Scetian elders were asked concerning fornication: when a man sees a face and is struck by it, does this serve as a reproach to him? They answered: this matter is like a table full of foods: if someone, seeing them, desires to taste of them, but does not stretch out his hand to take anything, he does not partake of them.

271. A brother asked an elder: is it good to visit elders, or is it better to keep stillness? He answered: to visit elders was the rule of the ancient fathers.

272. One elder said: I have hated the vainglory of the younger novices, because they labor, yet have no reward, attending to the praises of men. Another elder, more discerning, answered him: I altogether permit this, for it is better for the younger ones to be vainglorious, only let them not be negligent. Let one of them now, out of vainglory, compel himself to practice abstinence, keep vigil, suffer want, acquire love, and bear sorrows for the sake of praise. But after such a life, the grace of God will come to him and say to him: why do you not labor for My sake, but labor for people? Then he will resolve to pay no heed to human glory, but only to God. Those who heard this said: truly it is so.

273. A certain brother, overcome by sorrow, importuned an elder: what should I do, for thoughts press upon me and say: you have renounced the world in vain, you cannot be saved? The elder answered him: even if we could enter the promised land, it is still better for us to let our bones fall in the wilderness than to return to Egypt.

274. They asked an elder: is it good to mediate in disputes between brethren? He answered: flee from this, for it is said: *His ears are heavy, that he cannot hear a matter of blood, and his eyes are closed, that he cannot see injustice* (Isaiah 33:15).

275. Again they asked the elder: how can a man live alone? And he answered: a wrestler, if he does not first fight in the ranks with others, cannot learn the art of conquering, so that afterward he may fight one on one against an opponent. So also a monk, if he is not first trained by life among the brethren and does not learn the art of discernment of thoughts, will not be able, living alone, to withstand them.

276. They asked an elder: is it good to study the divine Scriptures? He answered: a sheep receives from the shepherd good grass for food, but also eats the plants of the wilderness. So when wormwood begins to burn it, it brings up the good grass, and its mouth is sweetened, and the taste of the wormwood ceases. So also for a man, meditation on the sacred Scriptures is good against the assault of demons. Whoever happens to be in church with many or with few, and shuts his mouth and ceases to cry out to God, does the work of demons, for the demons, unable to bear hearing the hymns of praise to Christ, cause the singers to be silent.

277. An elder said: argument delivers a man over to anger, anger delivers him to blindness, and blindness causes him to do every evil.

278. In the Thebaid there was a monk who led an extremely ascetic life: in long vigils, abiding in prayers and supplications, having great non-possessiveness, wearing down his body with fasting and labors. At first he ate every evening moistened vegetables, as much as one could grasp with one hand; then, after some time, he was content with the same measure every other day; keeping this rule regarding food for a long time, he finally reached the point where he took food only once a week, on Sunday toward evening, eating whatever vegetables happened to be available and wild plants, observing such weekly fasting for a long time. But the inventor of evil, the devil, envying him, attempted to draw him into the same fall by which he himself had fallen, through pride. So a thought of self-conceit came to him: since you are keeping such a strict life and fasting as no one among men keeps, you ought also to show

signs, so that you yourself may become more zealous in asceticism, and people may receive edification, and seeing the works of God, may marvel and glorify *our Father in heaven*. So let us also ask for signs, for the Savior Himself said: *Ask, and it will be given to you* (Matthew 7:7). And the monk began to send up prayer to God for this with most earnest petition. But the man-loving God, *who desires all men to be saved* (1 Timothy 2:4), seeing his very deception and remembering his labor and struggles, did not allow the enemy to completely tempt him and cast him into the most dangerous fall of pride, wherefore the word of the psalm is fitting for him: *Though he fall, he shall not be utterly cast down; for the Lord upholds him with His hand* (Psalm 36:24). Then there came to his mind the word spoken by the Apostle: *Not that we are sufficient of ourselves to think of anything as being from ourselves* (2 Corinthians 3:5). If even such a one is not sufficient, he thought, how much more do I have need of instruction! Let me go to such-and-such a hermit, and whatever he says to me and advises, I will accept as from God, for the guidance of my salvation. The abba to whom he wanted to go was great and renowned, had advanced in contemplation, was able to benefit those who came to him, and knew how to properly instruct those who asked. When he came to him, the elder saw two apes on his shoulders, which, having encircled his neck with a chain, were each straining to pull him toward itself. Seeing this and, as a God-taught man, knowing the cause, he sighed and wept secretly. After prayer and the customary greeting, they sat in silence for about an hour, for such was the custom among the fathers there. After this, the monk who had come said: Father! Have mercy on me and give me instruction concerning the path of salvation. The elder said: I, child, am insufficient for this and myself require guidance. He said again: do not refuse, Abba, to benefit me, for I am heartily disposed to believe you and have given my word to accept your counsel. But the elder refused, saying: you will not listen to me, therefore I refuse. The monk gave his word again that he would listen to him, like an angel, whatever he might command him. Then the elder said to him: take this bag with small coins, go to the city, buy ten loaves of bread, ten measures of wine, ten pounds of meat, and bring them. He began to grieve, but nevertheless he went. Along the way a multitude of thoughts arose in him: what did the elder have in mind, and how am I going to buy such things, and the worldly people will be scandalized when I take them... And so, with weeping and tears, he came to the city, and being ashamed, through one person he bought the bread, and through another the wine, and he grieved: woe to me, wretched one! How am I to buy meat: myself or through another? Yet although with shame, he secretly found a layman, gave him money, and he bought it and gave it to him. When he brought all this to the elder, the elder reminded him: do not forget that you gave me your word to obey in everything I tell you! So take this, go to your cell, and after prayer partake each day of one loaf, one measure of wine, and one measure of meat, and in ten days come here. Hearing this and not daring to contradict, he took everything and went, weeping and grieving over this matter: from what fasting to what have I come! Should I do this or not? But if I do not, I will offend God, because I gave my word that whatever the elder tells me, I will accept as from God. And now, Lord, look upon my sorrow, have mercy on me, and forgive me my transgressions, for I am compelled to do this against the rule of fasting I have established. In tears he came to his cell and did as the elder had commanded him, but he applied himself more to prayer and, approaching food, seasoned his bread with tears, saying: *Lord, why have You forsaken me?* And God looked upon his repentance and humility and granted consolation to his heart, and he understood the reason why it happened that he had become so negligent, as he supposed, and giving thanks to God, he confessed this prophetic word: *All our righteousness is like a filthy rag* (Isaiah 64:6), and *Unless the Lord builds the house, they labor in vain who build it; unless the Lord guards the city, the watchman stays awake in vain* (Psalm 126:1). Then he came again to the elder, his body wearied and exhausted more than when he spent weeks without food. The elder immediately saw that he had humbled himself and received him with a joyful countenance. Having made a prayer, they sat in silence, then the elder began to speak: the man-loving God has visited you and has not allowed the enemy to gain mastery over you, who is always accustomed to deceive those advancing in virtue by bringing them to self-conceit, compelling and disposing them to undertake excessive labors, so as thus to cast them down. For no sinful passion is as abhorrent to God as pride, and no virtue is as honorable as humility. We see an example of both in the Pharisee and the publican. Extremes on either side are blameworthy, for as one elder says: everything that is beyond measure is from demons. Therefore walk the royal path, according to Scripture, and turn neither to the right nor to the left, but keep to the middle. As regards the taking of food, eat with measure every evening; but if need arises, without deliberation break the time, whether you need to break it because of illness or some other reason before the appointed hour; and again, if it happens that you eat every other day, do not deliberate, for *we are not under law but under grace* (Romans 6:15). But when eating, do not be filled to satiety, but keep yourself in temperance; especially abstain from fine foods, but always embrace the plain ones. Guard your heart, striving in every way to be humble-minded, for *the sacrifice to God is a broken spirit; a broken and a humbled heart, God will not despise* (Psalm 50:19). And again the same holy David testifies: *I was brought low, and the Lord saved me* (Psalm 114:5). Also through the Prophet Isaiah the Lord says: *But on this one will I look: on him who is humble and contrite and trembles at My word* (Isaiah 66:2). Therefore, child, casting all your hope upon the Lord, go in peace on your path, and *He shall bring forth your righteousness as the light, and your judgment as the noonday* (Psalm 36:6). With such instructions the elder strengthened the brother and, having partaken with him of what was at hand, dismissed him rejoicing in the Lord. Returning, he said: *Let those who fear You turn to me, those who know Your testimonies* (Psalm 118:79); and *The Lord has chastened me severely, but He has not given me over to death* (Psalm 117:18), and *Let the righteous strike me; it shall be a kindness. And let him rebuke me* (Psalm 140:5). And to himself he said: *Return to your rest, O my soul, for the Lord has dealt bountifully with you,* and the rest (Psalm 114:6, 7). And having come to his cell, he began to live according to the commandment of the elder, spending all the time of his life in humility and compunction, until he attained *to a perfect man, to the measure of the stature of the fullness of Christ* (Ephesians 4:13).

279. They asked an elder: what is the monastic life? And he answered: a truthful mouth, a blameless body, a pure heart.

280. An elder said that our fathers entered within by cutting off the thoughts of the desires of the will; but we, if we are able, will enter through meekness.

281. An elder said of Moses: when he wished to strike the Egyptian, he looked this way and that way and saw no one, that is, he examined his thoughts and was persuaded that his intention had nothing evil in it, but that what he was doing, he was doing for God. And then he struck the Egyptian.

282. An elder spoke concerning the following verse of the psalm: *And I will set His hand over the sea, and His right hand over the rivers* (Psalm 88:26). This refers to the Savior: His left hand is on the sea, which is the world, and His right hand is on the rivers, that is, on the Apostles, who watered the world with faith.

283. One of the fathers said: Scripture says that a clean animal chews the cud and is cloven-hoofed. Such also is a man who truly believes and receives the two Testaments, which are found in all their fullness in the holy Church, but among heretics with various deficiencies. A man must bring up good food, but not bad. Good food consists of good thoughts, the traditions of the holy fathers, and the like, while bad food consists of evil thoughts about various sins and transgressions of men.

284. An elder said: if a brother sitting in his cell has some saying come upon his heart, and he runs after this saying, not having attained to the measure and not being led by God, then demons appear and interpret that saying for him as he wishes.

285. A certain brother asked an elder: in what does the cultivation of the soul consist, so that it may bear fruit? The elder answered: the cultivation of the soul consists of stillness of the body, much bodily prayer, and paying no attention to the falls of others, but only to one's own. If a man abides in this, his soul will not delay in bearing fruit.

286. A brother asked one of the fathers about the thought of blasphemy, saying: Father, the demon of blasphemy does violence to my soul; do me a kindness, tell me, why has this befallen me and what should I do? The elder said to him in answer: the thought of blasphemy attacks us because of accusing, belittling, and judging others, and especially because of pride, when someone does his own will, is negligent in prayer, becomes angry and wrathful. All these are signs of pride, which disposes us to the passions shown: accusing, belittling, and judging; and from them is born also the thought of blasphemy. If this thought tarries long in the soul, then the demon of blasphemy will hand the man over to the demon of fornication and derangement of mind; and if the man does not sober up, he perishes.

287. A brother asked an elder: Father! What does the prophet mean when he says: *There is no salvation for him in his God* (Psalm 3:3)? The elder answered: he means unclean thoughts, which suggest to the soul apostasy from God, when it is in sorrow because of the temptations that befall it.

288. An elder said: one must flee from all who do lawlessness, even if they are friends and relatives, even if they have the rank of a priest or even a king, for departing from those who do lawlessness grants us friendship with God and boldness before Him.

289. Again he said: it is better to live with three who fear God than with myriads who do not fear the Lord. For in the last days in coenobia, among a hundred living there, you will still find those being saved, but in fifty you will count them very few. All will become corrupt, loving feasts and gluttony; all will love the desire for power and love of money, for *many are called, but few are chosen* (Matthew 20:16).

290. He also said: it is not profitable to cleave to lawlessness: neither in church, nor in the marketplace, nor in council, nor in court, never and nowhere. Therefore one must utterly depart from communion with a lawless one, for every lawless one is worthy of abhorrence and subject to eternal torment.

291. An elder said: there is nothing more pitiable than a mind which philosophizes about divine things without God. He who teaches in church or in his cell must first fulfill himself what he speaks of and teaches, as it is said: *The hardworking farmer must be first to partake of the crops* (2 Timothy 2:6).

292. A brother asked an elder: Father! How is it that some see revelations and visions of angels? The elder answered: blessed, child, is he who always sees his own lawless deeds, for such a one is constantly vigilant. The brother continued: I, Father, a few days ago saw how one brother cast out a demon from another brother. The elder said to him: I do not wish to cast out demons and heal diseases, but I wish and entreat God that a demon not enter into me and that I may cleanse myself of unclean thoughts; then I would become great. For if anyone purifies his heart of unclean thoughts and without laziness performs the hours and the order of his rule, he will undoubtedly, together with the wonder-working fathers, be counted worthy of the kingdom of God.

293. One of the fathers recounted: there was in Thessalonica a convent of virgins. One of the virgins, through the action of our common enemy, left the convent and fell into fornication. After this fall she remained for a considerable time in fornication, but then repented, and with the help of the All-Good One, who assisted her to repentance, she came to her coenobium and at the gates reposed. Concerning her death, one of the saints received such a revelation: he saw how the holy Angels came to take her soul, and demons followed them; they disputed among themselves: the holy Angels said that she had come to repentance, but the demons asserted that since she had served them for so long a time, she was theirs, and how did she repent, if she did not even reach the coenobium? The Angels said: from the time when God saw that her intention inclined to this, He already accepted her repentance, and she was mistress of her repentance by reason of the purpose she had formed, and the Master of life is the Lord of all. Shamed by this word, the demons departed. The holy elder who saw the revelation, and the bishop, related this to the others, which we also heard and have passed on to you. Therefore, brethren, knowing this, with the help of God let us be strengthened not to yield to thoughts in any sin, but let us contradict them and resist, and especially let us guard ourselves from leaving our monastery, for we know whence we depart, but where we shall end up after departing, we do not know.

294. An elder said: the saints, having Christ within themselves, inherit both the present through dispassion and the future, for both the present and the future belong to Christ. Therefore, he who has Him, has both Him and what is His. But he who has passions, even if he possessed the whole world, has nothing except the passions that possess him.

295. Again he said: do not marvel that, being a man, you can become an angel, for equal-to-the-angels glory is set before you, and the Giver of Contests has promised it to those who contend.

296. Again he said: a man will never be good, even if he desired to be good, unless God dwells in him, for *No one is good but One, that is, God* (Mark 10:18).

297. He also said: he who is wronged and willingly forgives his neighbor is by nature like Jesus; he who does not wrong and is not wronged is by nature like Adam; but he who wrongs, or exacts usury, or acts maliciously is by nature like the devil.

298. A brother came to a certain elder and said to him: Abba! Tell me a word, how to be saved? The elder said to him: if you come to anyone, do not begin to speak before he asks you. The brother, coming to compunction from this word, made a prostration to the elder and said: truly, I have read many books, but nowhere have I found such instruction. And having received great benefit, he departed.

299. An elder said: a wandering mind is steadied by reading, vigil, and prayer; burning desire is extinguished by hunger, labor, and withdrawal from others; raging anger is calmed by psalm-singing, patience, and almsgiving. However, all this should be done at its proper time and in its proper measure, for everything untimely and unmeasured is short-lived, and what is short-lived is more harmful than beneficial.

300. The brethren asked an elder: why does the soul not strive toward the promises that have been announced by God through Scripture, but readily inclines to what is impure? The elder answered: because, I think, it has not yet tasted of the things above, and therefore it desires what is impure.

301. An elder said: if you live in some place and see such as have consolation, do not heed them; but if there is one so poor there that he hardly has bread, heed him, and you will find rest.

302. An elder said: falsehood is the old man, and truth is the new man.

303. Again he said: the root of good deeds is truth, and falsehood is death.

304. An elder said: believe, children, in what I shall say: as great is the praise and how great is the glory when kings renounce the world and become monks, for the intelligible is more honorable than the sensible, so great is the shame for a monk who abandons the monastic habit and becomes a king.

305. Again he said: brethren, if nature arouses desires, the increase of asceticism extinguishes them.

306. One elder asked another: why am I not permitted to be open with the elders concerning my thoughts? The elder answered him: the enemy rejoices over no one so much as over those who do not reveal their thoughts.

307. An elder said: do not live in that place where you see that some envy you; otherwise you will not make progress.

308. An elder said: if dishonor has become to you as praise, poverty as wealth, and want as plenty, then you will not die, for it is impossible for one who believes rightly and labors in godliness and righteousness to fall into the impurity of passions and the deception of demons.

Chapter XI.
On the Necessity of Always Being Watchful

1. Abba Anthony said: I have known monks who, after many labors, fell and came to derangement of mind because they trusted in their own work and disregarded the commandment of Him who said: *"Ask your father, and he will show you; your elders, and they will tell you"* (Deuteronomy 32:7).

2. He also said: if possible, a monk should reveal to the elders how many steps he takes in his cell and how many drops he drinks, lest he err in some way even in this. Thus a certain brother found a secluded and quiet place in the desert and asked his father: allow me to live in it, and I trust in God and in your prayers that I shall labor there well. But his abba did not permit this, saying: I know truly that you will labor much, but because you will have no elder, you will trust in your own work as though it were pleasing to God, and because you will believe in yourself as though you fully fulfill the work of a monk, you will lose both your labor and your understanding.

3. Abba Anthony said: when a blacksmith takes a piece of iron, he first considers what he ought to make—a scythe, a knife, or an axe. So also must we first consider which virtue to pursue, lest we labor in vain.

4. A brother asked Abba Arsenius to tell him a word, and the elder said to him: with all the strength you have, strive that your inner work may be according to God, and you will conquer the outward passions.

5. He also said: if we seek God, He will appear to us; and if we hold fast to Him, He will remain with us.

6. Abba Daniel recounted: Abba Arsenius once called me and said: give rest to your father, so that when he departs to the Lord, he may pray for you, *"that it may be well with you"* (Exodus 20:12).

7. Abba Agathon said: a monk should not allow his conscience to accuse him of any deed.

8. He also said: without keeping the commandments of God, a man will not succeed in any virtue.

9. He also said: every man should wisely behold the judgment seat of God.

10. Once Abba Ammon came to cross a river and, finding there a boat that was being cleaned, sat down beside it. When another boat came, carrying persons of rank, they offered to take him across with them, but the abba replied: I do not board any boat except a public one. Meanwhile, as they were preparing the boat, he sat holding a bundle of branches, plaited a cord, and then unraveled it again; afterward he crossed over. The brethren then made a prostration before him and asked: Father, why did you do this? The elder replied: as an example, that one should not always walk according to the thought of zeal.

11. They said of Abba Ammoes that when he went to church, he would not allow his disciple to walk close beside him, but at a distance; and if the disciple approached to ask him about a thought, he would answer what was needful and immediately send him away from himself, saying: I do not allow you near me so that when we speak of soul-beneficial things, some idle conversation may not intrude.

12. Abba Ammoes asked Abba Isaiah at the beginning: how do you regard me now? He replied: as an angel, Father. Later, in his final years, he asked him again: how do you regard me now? He said: as Satan, for even though you speak a good word to me, it is like a sword to me.

13. They said of Abba Ammoun, who lived for two months on a small measure of barley, that once he came to Abba Poemen and said to him: when I go to a neighbor's cell or he comes to me for some need, we are afraid to speak with one another, lest some idle conversation intrude. The elder said to him: you do well, for youth has need of guarding itself. Abba Ammoun asked him: what then did the elders do? Abba Poemen replied: the elders who had made progress had nothing foreign within them to speak of with their lips. He asked again: therefore, if there is need to speak with a neighbor, do you bid me speak from Scripture or from the words of the elders? The abba said: if you cannot be silent, it is better to speak from the words of the elders than from Scripture, for in this there is no small danger.

14. Abba Alonius said: if a man does not say in his heart that he alone and God are in this world, he will not have rest.

15. He also said: if a man wills it, then from morning until evening he can come to the measure of God.

16. Abba Bessarion, at his departure, said: a monk ought to be all eye, like the Cherubim and Seraphim.

17. Once Abba Ammoes and Abba Daniel were traveling together. Abba Ammoes asked: when shall we too, Father, settle in a cell? Abba Daniel replied: who then takes God away from us even now? God is in the cell, and outside He is also.

18. Abba Isaiah said: faintheartedness and the fact that a man's mind reproaches him do not allow us to see the light of God.

19. He also said: let us ask of God that He grant us mourning for our sins, and let us make an effort on our part to flee from human company, not to be familiar with worldly people, and not to speak vain words, lest the vision of God become darkened in our mind, for it is impossible for one who hears or speaks worldly words to have boldness of heart before God. But he who says, "I suffer no harm from hearing or speaking about worldly matters," is like a blind man who does not see the light of a lamp held up to him. This is evident also from the example of the sun, which illumines the whole world, yet when a small cloud comes over it, it covers both its brightness and its warmth. Those who have the vision know this.

20. He also said: strive to flee from these three passions that subvert the soul: avarice, love of honor, and ease, for when they master the soul, they do not allow it to make progress.

21. Abba Isaiah said: people turn their mind either to sins, or to Jesus, or to men.

22. Abba Peter said: once I asked my Abba Isaiah: who is a servant of God? And he answered me: if anyone is enslaved to any passion, he is not considered a servant of God, but is a slave of that which masters him. And while he is in this captivity, he cannot teach another who is mastered by the same passion, for it is absurd to teach him or to entreat God for him before freeing oneself from that same passion. Indeed, how will he entreat for another while he himself is afflicted by the same ailment? He is neither a servant of God, nor a friend, nor a son, so as to entreat for another, but rather he must often pray to be freed himself, and if he is not freed from that to which he himself is enslaved, his face is filled with shame before God. Therefore, since he is subject to passions, he must weep that he has not been granted boldness toward God, for this boldness is true purity, which God requires of every man.

23. Abba Isaiah said: whoever seeks the Lord with heartfelt pain, him the Lord will hear; and if he asks Him for something with understanding, zeal, and labor of heart, binding himself to nothing worldly, but caring only for his soul, that He may present it uncondemned before His throne, then He will grant it to him.

24. Abba Theodore of Enaton said: if God reckons against us our negligence in prayers and our sloth in psalmody, we cannot be saved.

25. Abba Theodore of Scetis said: a thought comes and disturbs me and occupies me; it has no power to produce a deed, but it only hinders me in virtue. But a watchful man, having cast it out, rises to prayer.

26. Abba Theonas said: through the distraction of our mind from contemplation of God, we are taken captive by the passions of the flesh.

27. Amma Theodora said: there was a monk who, because of the multitude of temptations, said to himself: go away from here. But as soon as he took up his sandal, he saw someone else who, putting on his own sandals, said to him: is it because of me that you are leaving? But I will go ahead of you, wherever you may go.

28. Once some of the brethren came to test Abba John Colobos, for he would not allow his thought to be occupied with the affairs of this age or to speak of them, and they said: we thank God! This year there has been much rain; the date palms have drunk their fill and are putting forth shoots; the brethren will find handwork for themselves. Abba John answered them: so also the Holy Spirit—when He descends into the hearts of the saints, they put forth shoots in the fear of God.

29. They recounted of him that he plaited a cord for two baskets and sewed it all into one basket, not noticing this until he drew near to the very wall, for his thought was occupied with contemplation.

30. Abba John said: I am like a man sitting under a great tree who, seeing many beasts and serpents coming against him, when he cannot stand against them, runs up onto the tree and is saved. So also I: I sit in my cell and watch as evil thoughts rise up against me, and when I have no strength against them, I flee to God in prayer and am saved from the enemy.

31. In Scetis there was an elder, diligent in bodily work, but not firm in memory. He came to Abba John to ask about forgetfulness, but having heard a word from him, he returned to his cell and forgot what Abba John had told him. Again he went to him and, having heard a word from him, returned, but when he reached his cell, he forgot it. Many times he came to him, but upon returning, forgetfulness always overcame him. Afterward, once meeting the elder, he said to him: you know, Abba, I have again forgotten what you told me, but so as not to trouble you, I have not come. Then Abba John said to him: go light a lamp. And he lit it. He also said to him: bring other lamps and light them from it. He did so. Then Abba John asked the elder: has this lamp suffered any harm from your lighting other lamps from it? He answered: no. The abba said: so also John—if the whole of Scetis should come to me, it would not distance me from the grace of God. Therefore, whenever you wish, come, having no second thoughts. And through the patience of both, God took forgetfulness from the elder. Such was the work of the Scetians: to give zeal to those who are warred against and who force themselves, that they might bring profit to one another in good.

32. A brother asked Abba John: what should I do, for a brother often comes to take me to work, and I, poor one, am weak and grow weary at the work? What then should I do according to the commandment? The elder answered: Caleb said to Joshua the son of Nun: *"I was forty years old when Moses the servant of the Lord sent me... to spy out the land... and now, here I am this day, eighty-five years old... As yet I am as strong this day as on the day that Moses sent me; just as my strength was then, so now is my strength for war, both to go out and to come in"* (Joshua 14:7, 10–11). So also you: if you can, going out the same as you came in, go; but if you cannot, sit in your cell, weeping for your sins. When they find you weeping, they will not force you to go out.

33. He also said to his disciple: let us honor the One, and all will honor us. But if we despise the One, who is God, then all will despise us, and we shall go to perdition.

34. They said of Abba John that once he came to the church in Scetis, and hearing certain brethren quarreling, he returned to his cell, walked around it three times, and only then

entered it. Some brethren, seeing this, were amazed and came and asked him why he did so. He answered them: my ears were full of disputing. So I walked around in order to cleanse them and to enter the cell in quietness of mind.

35. Once a brother came to the cell of Abba John in the evening and was hurrying to leave. But while they were conversing about virtues, morning came, and they did not notice it. The abba went out to see the brother off, and they continued their conversation until the sixth hour. Then the abba brought the brother back into the cell, and only after eating did he depart from him.

36. Abba John said: prison is sitting in the cell and always remembering God. And this is what is meant by the words: *"I was in prison and you came to Me"* (Matthew 25:36).

37. A brother came to get baskets from Abba John Colobos. The abba came out to him and asked: what do you want, brother? He answered: baskets, Abba. Going into the cell to bring them out, he forgot about them and sat down to sew. The brother knocked again, and when the abba came out, he requested: bring the baskets, Abba. He went in and again sat down to sew. When the brother knocked yet again, he came out and asked him: what do you want, brother? He answered: baskets, Abba. Then Abba John took him by the hand, led him into the cell, and said: if you want baskets, take them and go, for I am not at leisure.

38. Once a camel driver came to Abba John to take his handwork and go elsewhere. But the abba, entering to bring out the weaving for him, forgot about it, having his mind stretched toward God. The camel driver pestered him, knocking at the door, and again Abba John, entering the cell, forgot about it. When the man knocked a third time, the abba, entering the cell, kept repeating: weaving—camel; weaving—camel...

39. They said of Abba John that when he returned from the harvest or from visiting elders, he would occupy himself in prayer, reading with meditation, and psalmody, until his thought was established in its former order.

40. Abba Isidore said: when I was younger and sat in my cell, I had no measure for the prayer rule; night and day were my prayer rule.

41. He also said: once I went to market to sell a little handwork, and seeing that anger was approaching me, I left the goods and fled.

42. Abba Joseph said to Abba Lot: you cannot be a monk unless you become entirely like a burning fire.

43. They said of Abba Apollos that he had a disciple named Isaac, taught in every good work. He acquired stillness during the holy Offering, and when he left the church, he would not allow anyone to enter into conversation with him. His word was this: *"To everything there is a season, a time for every purpose"* (Ecclesiastes 3:1). Therefore, when the service was finished, he hastened to reach his cell as though driven by fire. Often after the service, a small dried loaf and a cup of wine were given to the brethren, but he would not take it, not because he rejected the blessing of the brethren, but in order to keep the stillness of the service. It happened that

he fell ill. The brethren, hearing of this, came to visit him and, sitting beside him, asked: Abba Isaac, why do you flee from the brethren after the service? He answered: I do not flee from the brethren, but from the evil cunning of demons. For if someone lights a lamp and delays standing in the wind, the lamp is extinguished by the wind; so also we, being enlightened by the holy Offering, if we delay outside the cell, our mind becomes darkened. Such was the life of the venerable Abba Isaac!

44. Abba Cassian recounted about an elder living in the desert that he prayed to God that He would grant him never to drowse during spiritual conversation, but in case of words of slander and idle talk, to fall asleep immediately, so that his ears would not receive this poison. He used to say that the devil is a zealot for idle talk and an enemy of all spiritual teaching, and pointed to the following example: when I was conversing with some brethren about soul-beneficial matters, they were overcome by such deep sleep that they could not move their eyelids. Wishing to show the demonic influence, I introduced an idle word into the conversation, and they immediately perked up with joy—they woke up. Then I groaned bitterly and said: as long as we were discussing heavenly matters, the eyes of all of you were closed in sleep, but as soon as an idle word poured forth, you all immediately became alert. Therefore, brethren, I beg you—recognize the influence of the evil demon and pay attention to yourselves, guarding against drowsiness when you do or hear something spiritual.

45. Abba Poemen, with many tears, besought Abba Macarius, saying: tell me a word— how to be saved? The elder replied: the thing that you seek has departed from monks.

46. Abba Macarius the Great said: the soul, during psalmody, ought with contrition to gather its thoughts and think of nothing else except the expectation of the Lord, and to preserve its innermost love for Him alone. As a mother gathers her children into her house for instruction in teaching, so also the soul must gather its thoughts from everywhere, as its own children, even though they have been scattered by sin, in order that He, coming to it, for its possible unceasing gathering of thoughts and expectation of the Lord in firm faith, may teach it true prayer and undistracted entreaty to Him alone.

47. Abba Moses said: a man cannot enter into the army of Christ unless he becomes entirely like fire, unless he despises honor and ease, cuts off fleshly desires, and keeps all the commandments of God.

48. He also said: let us seek reverence, virtue, meekness, and respectfulness toward every man, that we may flee from impudence—the mother of evils.

49. They said of Abba Nisterus, dwelling in Raithu, that every year he would take three weeks of fasting and in each week would sew six baskets.

50. Abba Nisterus said: a monk ought every evening and every morning to give an account of what he has not done of that which God wills, and what he has done of that which He does not will; and to observe such a practice all his life. So lived Abba Arsenius. Strive each day to stand before God without sin, and so pray to God as one who is present before Him who is present, for He is truly present to you. Do not legislate, do not judge anyone. It

is alien to a monk to swear, to break oaths, to lie, to curse, to revile, to laugh, and one must remember that he who is honored and praised above his worth loses much.

51. Abba Xanthias said: the robber was on the cross and by one word was justified, while Judas was numbered among the Apostles and in one night lost all his labor and descended from heaven to hell. Therefore, no one should boast while doing good, for all who trusted in themselves have perished.

52. Abba Olympius recounted: once a pagan priest came to Scetis, entered my cell, and spent the night. Seeing the life of the monks, he asked me: living thus, do you see nothing from your God? I answered him: nothing. The priest said: when we serve our god, he hides nothing from us, but reveals his mysteries to us. But you, undertaking such labors—vigil, stillness, asceticism—you say you see nothing. Therefore, if you see nothing, surely you have evil thoughts in your hearts that separate you from your God. That is why He does not reveal His mysteries to you. I went and recounted to the elders the words of the priest. They were amazed and said: it is truly so, for impure thoughts distance a man from God.

53. Abba Orsisius said: I think that if a man does not properly guard his heart, he will forget everything he has heard and grow negligent; then the enemy, finding a place for himself in him, will cast him down. Similarly, if oil is not added through negligence to a lamp that is prepared and burning, it gradually goes out, and finally darkness completely overcomes it; moreover, a mouse walks around it and seeks to eat what is in the lamp, but before it goes out, it cannot steal the oil; but as soon as it notices that there is neither light in it nor warmth of fire, it overturns the lamp itself, and if it is clay, it is shattered, but if it is bronze, it can be restored again by the master. So, to the degree that the soul grows negligent, to that degree the Holy Spirit withdraws from it, until the burning within it is completely extinguished, and finally the enemy, consuming the zeal of the soul, defiles the body also with evil. But if a man is of good disposition toward God and has merely been drawn into negligence, then God, being merciful, implanting in him His fear and the remembrance of torments, prepares him to be vigilant and to conduct himself henceforth with great steadfastness until the time of His visitation.

54. Abba Poemen, while still young, went to an elder to ask him about three thoughts, but when he came to the elder, he forgot one of them. Returning to his cell, as soon as he took hold of the key to unlock it, he remembered the word he had forgotten, and leaving the key, he returned to the elder; and the length of the journey was very great. The elder said to him: you came quickly, brother. He recounted to him that as soon as he took hold of the key, he remembered the word he had forgotten, and without opening the cell, he returned here. The elder said to him: you are a shepherd of angels! And your name shall be known throughout all the land of Egypt.

55. They said of Abba Poemen that when he wished to go to the service, he would sit apart, examine his thoughts for about an hour, and then go out.

56. Abba Poemen said: if a man makes a new heaven and a new earth, even then he should not give himself over to carelessness.

57. He also said: someone asked Abba Paisius: what should I do with my soul? It is insensible and does not fear God. Abba Paisius answered: go attach yourself to a man who fears God, and when you draw near to him, he will also teach you to fear God.

58. He also said about Abba Pior that he made a beginning every day.

59. When Abba Isaac was sitting with Abba Poemen, the crow of a rooster was heard, and he asked the elder: is there such a thing here, Abba? He answered: Isaac! Why do you compel me to speak? You have not forgotten how to hear this, but one who is watchful pays no attention to such things.

60. A brother asked Abba Poemen: tell me a word. And the elder said to him: when a pot is heated from below by fire, neither a fly nor any other crawling thing can touch it; but when it grows cold, then it is accessible to them. Likewise, as long as a monk abides in spiritual work, the enemy finds no way to bring him down.

61. He also said: the malice of men is hidden behind them.

62. Abba Poemen often used to say: we have no need of anything except a watchful heart.

63. Abba Poemen related that a brother said to Abba Simon: if I go out of my cell and find a brother idly distracted, I too become distracted with him; if I find him laughing, I too laugh with him; but when I return to my cell, I cannot have rest. The elder said to him: do you want to go out of your cell and, seeing those who laugh, to laugh yourself, and seeing those who talk, to talk yourself, and then entering your cell, to find yourself such as you were?! The brother asked: but what then should one do? The elder answered: keep guard inside the cell, and keep guard outside the cell.

64. He also said: this voice cries out to man until his last breath: *"Today be converted!"*

65. He also said: these three things are most necessary: to fear the Lord, to pray, and to do good to one's neighbor.

66. He also said: a man cannot see the outward enemies, but when they rise up within, then if anyone struggles, he casts them out.

67. He also said: the fact that we do not foresee a matter does not allow us to advance toward the better.

68. He also said to Abba Anuv: *"Turn away my eyes, that they may not look upon vanity"* (Psalm 119:37), for license destroys souls.

69. He also said: if the soul withdraws from all contentiousness during conversation, as well as from human commotions and disturbances, then the Holy Spirit will come to it, and then it will be able to give birth, being itself barren.

70. He also said: the beginning and the end is the fear of God, for it is written: *"The fear of the Lord is the beginning of wisdom"* (Proverbs 1:7). Again, when Abraham prepared the altar, the Lord said to him: *"Now I know that you fear God"* (Genesis 22:12).

71. Abba Pambo said: with the help of God, since I renounced the world, I have not repented of any word that I have spoken.

72. Someone asked Abba Peter, the disciple of Abba Lot: when I am alone in my cell, my soul is at peace, but when a brother comes to me and speaks to me a word about anything external, my soul becomes disturbed. Abba Peter said that Abba Lot used to say to him: your key unlocks my door. The brother said: what does this word mean? He answered: if someone comes to you and you ask: how are you? Where have you come from? How are the brethren? Do they love you or not?—then you open your door to the brother and hear what you do not wish to hear. He said to him: it is so. What then should a man do when a brother comes to him? The elder answered him: mourning teaches all things, but where there is no mourning, it is impossible to guard oneself. The brother said: when I am alone in my cell, mourning is with me, but when someone comes to me, or I myself go out of my cell, I no longer find it. The elder said to him: it has not yet submitted to you, but is with you only as if on loan for a time. For in the law also it is written: *"If you buy a Hebrew servant, he shall serve you six years; and in the seventh year he shall go out free for nothing. But if the servant says, 'I love my master... and will not go out free,' then his master shall bring him before the judges. He shall also bring him to the door, and his master shall pierce his ear with an awl; and he shall serve him forever"* (Exodus 21:2, 5–6). The brother asked: what does this word mean? The elder answered: if a man labors in any work according to his strength, then whenever he seeks it for his use, he will find it. He said to him: do me the kindness of explaining what this means. The elder said: an adopted son does not remain with anyone forever in service, but a natural son never leaves his father.

73. Once Abba Sisoes was sitting in his cell. When his disciple knocked, the elder cried out to him: flee, Abraham, do not enter—I am not at leisure now.

74. A brother earnestly asked Abba Sisoes to tell him something, and the elder said: sit in your cell with watchfulness, cast yourself upon God with many tears, and you will find rest.

75. A brother said to Abba Sisoes: I wish to guard my heart, and I cannot. The elder answered: how can we guard our heart when the door of our tongue stands open?

76. Once during Abba Silvanus's stay on Mount Sinai, his disciple, departing for a task, said to him: Father, let out the water and irrigate the garden. Going out for this, the elder covered his face with his cowl and looked only at his feet. At that time a brother came to him and saw from a distance what he was doing. Afterward, when they had gone in, the brother asked: tell me, Abba, why did you cover your face with your cowl and thus irrigate the garden? The elder answered: so that, my son, my eyes would not see the trees and my mind would not be occupied with them, leaving its own work.

77. Once they asked Abba Silvanus: what work did you pursue, Abba, that you received such understanding? He answered: I never allowed into my heart a thought that angers God.

78. Abba Moses asked Abba Silvanus: can a man lay a new beginning every day? The elder said: if he is a doer, he can lay a new beginning even every hour.

79. Abba Serapion said: the soldiers of the king, standing before him, cannot look either to the right or to the left; so also a man, if he stands before God and attends to Him with fear every hour, nothing of the enemy can frighten him.

80. Blessed Syncletica said: let us be watchful, for through our senses, against our will, thieves enter. And how can a house not become sooty when its windows are open and smoke rushes in from outside?

81. She also said: we must arm ourselves in every way against the demons, for they both approach from without and produce movements from within. The soul is like a ship: as a ship is sometimes sunk by external waves and sometimes goes down because water has entered inside, so also we: sometimes we perish from outward sins, and sometimes we perish through inner thoughts. Therefore, one must watch the outward assaults and drain off the inner floods of thoughts.

82. She also said: children! We all know how to be saved, but through our own negligence we lose salvation.

83. She also said: here we cannot live without anxieties, for Scripture says: *"Let him who thinks he stands take heed lest he fall"* (1 Corinthians 10:12). We sail in uncertainty. Our life is called a sea by the sacred singer David; but on the sea there are places with underwater rocks, there are stormy places, and there are also calm places. We, it seems, sail in the calm part of the sea, while those in the world sail in the stormy part. We sail by day, guided by the Sun of righteousness, but it often happens that a worldling, caught in storm and darkness, saves his ship through vigilance, while we, being in calm, are sunk to the bottom through negligence, when we abandon the helm of righteousness.

84. Abba Hyperechius said: let your memory always be in the kingdom of heaven, and you will easily inherit it.

85. He also said: let the life of a monk be, in imitation of the angels, one that burns up sin.

86. Abba Or said to Abba Sisoes: I think that if a man does not carefully guard his heart, he will forget all that he has heard and grow negligent; and then the enemy, finding a place in him, will cast him down.

87. In the region of the Jordan there was a hermit who had been struggling for a considerable time. He was granted the gift of not being subject to the assaults of the enemy, so that before all who came to him for benefit, he reviled the devil, saying that he is nothing and has no power against ascetics, but destroys only those whom he finds defiled like himself and always enslaved to sin. He did not sense that he was being covered by the help of God and therefore was not subject to the battles of the adversary. Once, by God's permission, the devil appeared to him face to face and said: what have I done to you, Abba? Why do you

revile me? I have caused you no vexation. The elder spat upon him and again uttered those same words: get behind me, Satan, for you can do nothing against the servants of Christ. Then Satan spoke these words: so-so; henceforth you are to live another forty years, and in so many years I shall not find even one hour not to assail you. And having cast this snare, he became invisible. The elder was immediately surrounded by thoughts and began to reason: so many years already I have been here, yet God wills that I live another forty years! I shall leave here and go into the world, look for people to serve me, stay with them several years, and then return and take up my asceticism again. Having thus thought, he fulfilled it also in deed: he rushed out of his cell and began his journey. He had not gone far when an Angel of the Lord was sent to help him, and he asked him: where are you hastening, Abba? He said: to the city. The angel said to him: return to your cell, and there is nothing between you and Satan; henceforth consider yourself mocked by him. Then, coming to himself, the elder returned to his cell, and after three days he reposed.

88. Someone saw a young monk laughing and said to him: do not laugh, brother, for by this you drive away from yourself the fear of God.

89. They said of an elder that when he was sitting in his cell, a brother came to visit him and heard the elder inside his cell arguing and saying: oh! How very good! For how long? Go away from here! Come to me, friend! Then, entering, the brother asked him: Abba, with whom were you speaking? He answered: I was driving out my evil thoughts and calling forth the good ones.

90. An elder said: I lower the spindle and place death before my eyes before I draw it up.

91. He also said: what I was able to understand in reading, I did not repeat.

92. He also said: a man who has death before his eyes every hour conquers faintheartedness.

93. An elder said: a monk ought every evening and every morning to address a word to himself and say: what have we done of that which God wills, and what have we not done of that which God does not will? And in this manner to repent. So a monk ought to do! So lived Abba Arsenius.

94. An elder said: if someone loses gold or silver, he can find other in its place; but he who has lost time cannot find another.

95. One of the elders came to another elder, and during their conversation, one of them said: I have died to the world. But the other elder said to him: do not trust in yourself until you have departed from the body, for even though you, as you say, have died, Satan has not died.

96. An elder said: as a soldier and a hunter, going into battle, do not concern themselves whether another is wounded or saved, but each concerns himself only with himself, so also a monk should act.

97. An elder said: just as no one can harm one who stands close to the king, so also Satan can do nothing to us if our soul is close to God, as it is also said: *"Draw near to God and He will draw near to you"* (James 4:8). But since we are often distracted by thoughts, the enemy easily draws our wretched soul into shameful passions.

98. An elder said: rising in the morning, say to yourself: body, work so as to be fed; soul, be watchful so as to inherit the kingdom.

99. They recounted of an elder that when thoughts said to him: leave off today and repent tomorrow, he would contradict them, saying: no! But today I will repent, and tomorrow God's will be done.

100.   The elders said: there are three powers of Satan that precede every sin: forgetfulness, negligence, and desire. For when forgetfulness comes, it begets negligence; from negligence is born desire; and from desire a man falls. If the mind is watchful against forgetfulness, then it does not come to negligence; if it does not grow negligent, it will not come to desire; if it does not come to desire, by the grace of Christ it will never fall.

101.   An elder said: strive to be silent, care for nothing, attend to your secret meditation, lie down and rise up with the fear of God, and you will not fear the assault of the ungodly.

102.   An elder said to a brother: the devil is an enemy, and you are a house. The enemy unceasingly casts into your house every impurity that comes to hand, and it is your task not to be lazy in casting it out. But if you grow negligent, the house will be filled with so much filth that you will no longer be able to enter it. Therefore, the first thing he casts in, cast out immediately, and your house will always be clean for the grace of Christ.

103.   One of the elders said: when they blindfold an ox, it walks around the machine for drawing water; but if they do not blindfold it, it will not go. So also the devil: if he succeeds in closing the eyes of the mind of a man, he humbles him in every sin; but if the eyes of a man are enlightened, he can easily flee from him.

104.   They recounted that on the mountain of Saint Anthony lived seven brothers who took turns guarding the dates during the harvest in order to drive away the birds. One of them was an elder who, having stood his day's watch, cried out: away with you, inward evil thoughts, and outward birds!

105.   They said of an elder from Scetis that when he was dying, the brethren surrounded his bed and, clothing him in the schema, began to weep. The elder opened his eyes and laughed; then again he laughed; and he laughed a third time. The brethren besought him: tell us, Abba, why do we weep while you laugh? He answered: I laughed the first time because you all fear death; I laughed the second time because you are not prepared; I laughed the third time because I go from labor to rest. And immediately the elder fell asleep.

106.   The brethren recounted: we came to the elders and, after the customary prayer, kissed one another, sat down, conversed, and intending to leave, asked for a prayer.

Then one of the elders asked us: what, did you not pray then? We answered: when we came in, Abba, there was a prayer; then we have conversed until now. The elder said: forgive me, brethren! One brother who sat with you and conversed made one hundred and three prayers. After these words, the elders prayed and dismissed us.

107.   One of the fathers said: a certain diligent monk at first attended to himself, but then it happened that he grew somewhat negligent. Coming to himself in this negligence, he said: O soul! How long will you be negligent of your salvation, not fearing the judgment of God? May you not be dissolved in this negligence and be delivered over to eternal torments. Speaking thus to himself, he aroused himself to the work of God. Once, when he was performing his rule, demons came and disturbed him. He said to them: how long will you disturb me? Are you not satisfied with my negligence in the past time? The demons answered him: when you were in negligence, then we too were negligent about you; but when you rose up against us, we also rose up against you. Hearing this, he aroused himself still more to the work of God and made progress by the grace of Christ.

108.   An elder said: a man must guard his work lest he lose it. He who labors much but does not guard has no benefit, while he who labors but little yet guards—his work stands. Then he recounted such an incident: an inheritance came to a brother; when he wanted to prepare a love feast for the departed, it happened that a stranger brother came to him. Waking him in the night, he asked him: get up and help me. But the brother begged him, saying: I am weary and cannot. Then he said to him: if you will not go to help, get up and leave here. The stranger got up and left. On the following night he saw in a dream that he had given wheat to a baker, but the baker did not give him even one loaf. Rising, he went to a great elder and recounted this to him. The elder said: you did a good deed, but the enemy did not allow you to receive a reward. Therefore, a man must be vigilant and guard his work.

109.   An elder said: never did I take a step forward with my foot without knowing where to place it; but even knowing this, I did not give myself over completely to it until I noticed the guidance of God.

110.   To a certain holy man, at the very hour of his death, Satan appeared and said to him: you have escaped from me. The elder answered: I do not yet know. You see to what degree the fathers were watchful, so as not to boast of any work.

111.   An elder recounted: in Scetis there was a brother who diligently performed his prayer rule but was negligent in everything else. Once Satan appeared to one of the elders and said to him: O wonder! Such-and-such a monk, doing my will, holds me tightly under his arm so that I do not depart from him, meanwhile saying every hour: "Lord, deliver me from the evil one!"

112.   An elder said: in every matter, at every hour, say to yourself: what will happen if God visits me?—and see what your thought answers you. If it condemns you, immediately leave, drop the work you are holding, and take up another in which you would have boldness to be found, for a worker must be ready at every hour to depart on his way. Therefore,

whether you sit at handwork, or walk the road, or take food, always say this to yourself: what will happen if God calls me? And see what your conscience answers you, and hasten to do what it says. If you wish to know whether mercy will be with you, ask your conscience and do not cease doing this until your heart is assured, and your conscience tells you: we believe in the compassions of God, that He will assuredly show us His mercy. But attend strictly to your heart—lest it speak this word with doubt. And if there is doubt even by a single hair, the mercy of God is still far from you.

113.   An abba and a brother withdrew into the innermost desert, where they spent six days apart from one another, and on the seventh they came together: they performed prayers, ate, saying nothing to each other, and parted. To one of them demons began to come and deceive him, showing him beforehand in images the future deeds of the brethren and what was to happen in other places. Hearing afterward that this and that indeed occurred, he believed them, thinking that these were holy powers. Meanwhile, they turned him away even from going on the appointed days to his brother. Fortunately, he went to visit a sick brother and proposed to some in the monastery, as if about another, the question: is it possible for anyone to know what is to happen in the world? Hearing this and understanding that the brother was in delusion, they reproached him, saying: if you occupy yourself with this, then from now on do not come to us. He immediately repented and rejected all of it. When he returned and the demons again came to deceive him, the brother called them liars; then their faces changed into animals, and they departed with threats.

114.   Someone recounted about a monk who asked God that he might be granted to be like Isaac, one of the patriarchs. After many petitions, a voice came to him from God: you cannot be like Isaac. The monk said: if not like Isaac, then like Job. The divine voice said: if you struggle with the devil as he did, then you can be. The monk agreed, and again he heard the voice of God: go now to your cell. After several days, the devil, having transformed himself into a soldier, came to the monk and said: I beg your reverence, have mercy on me, who am being pursued by the king! Take these two hundred pounds of gold, this maiden, and this servant boy, and hide them with you in a hidden place, and I will go to another land. The monk, not recognizing the snare of the devil, said to him: my son, I cannot take this upon myself: I am a man of no account and cannot keep them. The one transformed into a soldier urged the monk more strongly, and he said to him: go, my son, and hide them in the nearby cave. But finally, being persuaded, he took both the gold and the maiden and the servant boy, and after several days a battle arose in him over the maiden, and he, mocked by the demon, corrupted her; then, repenting of what had happened, he killed her. Further, his thought said to him: kill the boy also, so that he does not betray the deed—and he killed the boy also. Then his thought said to him: take the money left with you and flee to another place, so that trouble does not come to you from the one who deposited it. So he departed to another village and on this money built a chapel. When he had finished this work, the devil appeared again in the guise of a soldier and began to cry out: help! Woe! This monk has built this building with the money I left with him! However, the local inhabitants, rising up against him, drove him away with dishonor, and he departed with bold threats, but the monk after that

found no peace for himself day or night, being warred against by thoughts. Finally, overcome by the thought to leave that place, he said to himself: it is already coming to the point where my deeds may be discovered. So I will take part of the money remaining with me and go to a distant city where that soldier cannot come. And he went to a city, met there a maiden—the daughter of the executioner, and having spoken with her father, took her as his wife. After some time a newly appointed governor of that region came and asked the officials who should be the executioner, since the former executioner had died. They answered him that from of old they had the custom—whoever took the wife or daughter of the deceased executioner as his wife also took his position, even if unwilling. Then they brought this man—once a monk—to the governor, and against his will he was bound to serve at the tribunal. Later, when certain criminals were caught, the governor commanded the present executioner to prepare pitch and other instruments of torture for them, and at this time Satan appeared in his former guise and began to cry out and demand judgment as one wronged, and by order of the governor he recounted: this executioner was once a monk. Being pursued by enemies, I left with him much gold, also a servant boy and a maiden. Therefore, command him to return my deposit to me. To the governor's questions, the present executioner, once a monk, at first denied it, but then confessed to the killing of the boy and the maiden and to the spending of the money. As a result, the governor commanded that the wretched executioner be put to death, and when they were leading him to the place of execution, his accuser approached him and asked: do you know, Abba, who I am? He answered: I think an angel who left with me the boy, the maiden, and the money, and whom I came to know to my misfortune. Then he said to him: I am Satan, who deceived the first-formed Adam, who wars against men and does not permit, insofar as it is in my power, anyone to be saved or to be like Isaac or Job, but am zealous by all means to make everyone like that Ahithophel, Judas Iscariot, Cain, the elders of Babylon, and others like them. Know then that you too have fallen into my snares, not knowing how to fight in the invisible battle. Do not undertake through pride a battle that is beyond your strength! Having said this, he became invisible. Thus the wretched monk, mocked by the demon for his high-mindedness, was put to death. Let us also beware of asking God for what is beyond us and of undertaking works that we have not the strength to accomplish. It is better to go by the royal road, so that, turning aside neither to the right nor to the left, we may be saved from the present evil age, keeping in all things humility of mind.

115. The disciple of a great elder recounted: once we were walking along the road, and the elder paused a little. I said to him: Abba, go slowly. He asked me: do you not hear?—and added: the angels are singing in the heavens. We too must be watchful. And Abba Anthony said that a monk ought to care for nothing except the salvation of his soul.

116. An elder said: in everything that I do, from small to great, I look at the fruit—that is, what will come of it, whether in thoughts or in deeds.

117. Two philosophers came to an elder and asked him to tell them a word for their benefit. The elder was silent. The philosophers asked: do you answer us nothing, Father?

Then the elder said to them: that you are lovers of words, I know; and that you are not lovers of the wisdom of truth, I testify. How long will you learn without knowing how to speak? Therefore, let your philosophy be the constant remembrance of death; and by silence—by stillness—you will preserve yourselves.

118.   An elder said: a monk, after renouncing the world yet giving himself over to the turmoil and cares of this wretched life, is like a poor beggar deprived of all life's necessities, who, from great despondency, vainly reasoning about how to be fed and clothed, falls asleep and sees himself in a dream as a rich man, throwing off his rags and clothing himself in bright garments, but, waking from joy, finds the same poverty. So also a monk, if he is not watchful but spends his days in cares over which his thoughts laugh and by which demons exhaust him, mocking him as though his cares and troubles were for God—at the hour of the separation of soul from body, he will find himself destitute, poor, and naked, bereft of every virtue. And then he will know what blessings watchfulness and attention to oneself bestow, and what torments the cares of life bring.

119.   An elder said: always remember the good, that you may also do it, for the thought of a man is not hidden from God. Let your mind be pure from every evil.

120.   He also said: let us be watchful, brethren, in the hour of battle; let us not grow slack and entangle ourselves in thoughts about evil deeds—let no evil thought find an entrance into our souls.

121.   He also said: let us struggle for the sake of future blessings; let us prepare ourselves for our departure and not spend our time in vain.

122.   An elder said: it is written: *"The righteous shall flourish like a palm tree"* (Psalm 92:12). This word signifies the good, right, and sweet that comes from lofty deeds. The palm tree has one heart—white, in which is all its strength. Something similar can be found also in the righteous, for they have a single and simple heart, looking to God alone, and it is white, being illumined by faith; and all the work of the saints is in their heart. But the sharpness of the branches signifies their resistance to the devil.

123.   An elder said: the Shunammite woman received Elisha when she had communion with no man. They say that the Shunammite woman represents the person of the soul, and Elisha represents the person of the Spirit of God. So in whatever hour the soul departs from fleshly mingling, in that hour the Spirit of God comes to it; and it can give birth, being itself incorporeal.

124.   An elder said: it is written: *"For two or three transgressions I will be on guard, but at the fourth I will not turn away."* The first is to think evil; the second is to consent to the thought; the third is to speak of it; and the fourth is to do it in deed. At this, the wrath of God will not turn away.

125.   One of the fathers said: the eyes of a pig are so naturally fashioned that it necessarily looks at the ground and can never look up at the sky. So also a soul that delights in desires cannot look up at the sky, having sunk into the mire of sensuality.

Chapter XII.
On the Necessity of Praying Unceasingly and Soberly

1. Brethren came to Abba Anthony and proposed to him a certain passage from the book of Leviticus. The elder went out into the desert, and Abba Ammon secretly followed him, knowing his custom. The elder, having gone a considerable distance, stood at prayer and cried out: O God, send Moses, and he will explain these words to me! And a voice came to him speaking with him. Abba Ammon said that he heard the voice, but did not understand the meaning of the words.

2. They said of Abba Arsenius that on Saturday evening, before the beginning of Sunday (according to the church order), he would raise his hands toward heaven, leaving the sun behind him, and pray until it again shone upon his face; and then he would sit down.

3. The brethren asked Abba Agathon: which virtue, father, in the ascetic life has more labor? He answered them: forgive me, I think there is no greater labor than to pray to God, for whenever a man intends to pray, the enemies want to cut him off from this, knowing that nothing so impedes them as prayer to God. Moreover, in every ascetic endeavor which a man undertakes, if he will pass through it with patience, he finally acquires rest, but prayer requires struggle until the last breath.

4. Abba Dulas, a disciple of Abba Bessarion, recounted: I came once to the abba in his cell and found him standing at prayer. His hands were stretched out toward heaven, and he remained in this struggle for fourteen days. Afterward he called me and said: follow me, and we went into the desert. Having become thirsty, I say to him: Abba! I thirst! Then the elder took my sheepskin cloak, went a stone's throw away, and having made a prayer, brought it back to me full of water. Continuing on our way, we came to a certain cave, and entering it, found a brother who was sitting and working a plaited rope: he did not look at us, did not greet us, and did not at all want to enter into conversation with us. The elder said to me: let us leave here. Perhaps this elder has not received an intimation to speak with us. We set out for Lyco and came to Abba John. After greeting him, we made a prayer, and they sat down to converse about a vision which he had seen during prayer, wherein Abba Bessarion said that a command had gone forth to destroy the temples, but this had already been done, and they were destroyed. On our return we again approached the cave in which we had seen the

brother, and the elder said to me: let us go in to him, perhaps God has put it in his heart to speak with us. But upon entering, we found him dead. Then the elder says to me: come, brother, let us prepare his body, for it was for this that God sent us here. When we were preparing his body for burial, we discovered that by nature it was a woman, and the elder said: behold, even women conquer Satan, while we disgrace ourselves in the cities. And glorifying God, the protector of those who love Him, we departed.

5. The abba of a certain monastery in Palestine informed Blessed Epiphanius, Bishop of Cyprus: by your prayers we have not been negligent of our rule, but have carefully observed the third, sixth, and ninth hours. In reply to this, Blessed Epiphanius reproved them, saying: you are manifest idlers, passing all the other hours of the day without prayer, for the true monk ought to have prayer and psalmody unceasingly in his heart.

6. He also said: the Prophet David did not pray by hours: *at midnight I rose* (Psalm 119:62), *before dawn I cried* (Psalm 119:147), *early in the morning I stood before You* (Psalm 88:13), *at dawn I made my prayer* (Psalm 5:3), *during the day and at noon I implored* (Psalm 55:17). Therefore he also said: *Seven times a day I praise You* (Psalm 119:164).

7. Abba Evagrius said: it is a great thing to pray without distraction, but an even greater thing to chant the psalms without distraction.

8. He also said: when you are faint of heart, pray, as it is written, but pray with fear and trembling, soberly and vigilantly, for so ought one to pray, especially when the wicked and cunning invisible enemies of ours wish to tempt us by this very thing.

9. Again he said: when an enemy thought rises up in the heart, do not seek this or that in prayer, but against the hostility, sharpen the sword of your tears.

10. Once Abba Moses came to draw water and found Abba Zacharias praying at the cistern, and the Spirit of God sitting upon him in the form of a dove.

11. Abba Isaiah, the presbyter of Pelusium, said in reproof to the brethren who were eating at the agape meal in the church and conversing with one another: be silent, brethren! I know a brother who sits together with you and drinks cups as you do, yet his prayer ascends to God like fire.

12. Abba Lot once came to Abba Joseph and says to him: Abba! According to my strength I fulfill my small rule and my small fast, prayer, secret meditation, stillness, and according to my strength I guard my thoughts. What else must I do? The elder stood up, stretched out his hands toward heaven, and his fingers became like lamps of fire. Then he says to him: if you wish, become wholly fire.

13. Abba Jacob said that a certain elder recounted: when I was younger and dwelt in the desert, I had near me a youth who lived in solitude. Once, coming to visit him, I heard that while praying he was asking God that he might live in peace with the wild beasts. Then, after prayer, he went up to a hyena that was nearby nursing her young, lay down beside them, and began to nurse alongside them.

14. The elder also recounted that at another time he heard him praying and asking God: grant me the gift of befriending fire. Then, kindling a flame, he knelt in the midst of it and thus prayed to the Lord.

15. Once there came to Abba Lucius in Enaton certain monks, the so-called Euchites (that is, pray-ers), and the elder asked them: what is your handiwork? They answered: we do not touch handiwork, but as the Apostle commanded, we pray without ceasing. The elder asked again: do you not eat? They said: we eat. He says: do you not sleep? They answered: we sleep. Then the elder asked: who then prays for you when you sleep? They found no answer to give him to this. And he said to them: forgive me, you do not do as you say. But I will show you that even while being occupied with my handiwork, I pray unceasingly. Having soaked a few palm branches, I sit down with God, and working from them a plaited rope, I say: *Have mercy on me, O God, according to Your great mercy; and according to the multitude of Your compassions, blot out my transgression* (Psalm 51:1). Is this not prayer? They said: it is prayer. The elder continued: passing the whole day in work with prayer, I earn more or less sixteen coins, of which I give two at the door (to those who ask), and with the rest I acquire food; and when I eat or sleep, he who received the two coins prays for me, and thus by the grace of God the commandment to pray unceasingly is fulfilled in me.

16. Once Abba Macarius, over the course of four whole months, visited a certain brother daily and always found him at prayer. Marveling at this, the elder said: behold, an earthly angel.

17. Certain ones asked Abba Macarius: how ought we to pray? The elder answered them: there is no need for many words, but one ought, raising the hands, to say: Lord! As You will and as You know! And when warfare presses upon you, say: Lord, help! He knows what is profitable for us and will show us mercy.

18. Abba Moses said: if the deed does not accord with the prayer, then you labor in vain. Someone asked him: what does it mean for the deed to accord with the prayer? The elder answered: it means not to do any longer that concerning which you prayed, for when a man abandons his own will, then God is reconciled to him and accepts his prayer.

19. Abba Nilus said: whatever you do in revenge against a brother who has offended you, all that will become a stumbling block to you during prayer.

20. Again he said: prayer is an offshoot of meekness and the absence of anger.

21. He also said: prayer is a remedy for sorrow and despondency.

22. He also said: *go, sell what you have and give to the poor* (Matthew 19:21); then *take up your cross* (Matthew 16:24) and deny yourself, that you may be able to pray without distraction.

23. Again he said: whatever we endure with patient wisdom, we shall find the fruit of it at the time of prayer.

24. He also said: wishing to pray as one ought, do not grieve your soul, otherwise you run in vain.

25. He also said: do not desire that things be with you as it seems to you they ought to be, but as it is pleasing to God, and you shall be undisturbed and thankful in your prayer.

26. A brother asked Abba Poemen: father, is it good to pray? The elder answered him: Abba Anthony said that from the face of God there goes forth a voice saying: *"Comfort, yes, comfort My people!" says your God* (Isaiah 40:1).

27. When Julian the Apostate was going against the Persians, he sent a demon to the west to bring him certain information from there. Having reached the place where a certain monk was living, the demon became motionless and remained in that place for ten days, being unable to move forward, for the monk did not cease praying either by day or by night. Therefore the demon returned to the one who had sent him without success. He asked: why did you delay? The demon answered: I delayed and came back without success because I spent ten days waiting for the monk Publius to stop praying so that I might pass him by, but he did not cease, and I could not cross that place, and so I returned. Having grown angry, the impious Julian said that upon his return he would deal with him; however, by the will of providence, he was slain a few days later. Then one of those who had been with him, departing, sold all that he had and gave it to the poor; then he came to the elder, received monasticism, and having become a great ascetic, reposed in the Lord.

28. A brother asked Abba Sisoes: father, what shall I do? How shall I be saved? How shall I please God? The elder answered: if you wish to please God, depart from the world, withdraw from the earth, leave creation, pass over to the Creator, unite yourself to God in prayer and in weeping, and you shall find rest in this present age and in the age to come.

29. They said of Abba Tithoes that if, while standing at prayer, he did not quickly lower his hands, his mind would be caught up on high. Therefore, when it happened that he prayed together with the brethren, he endeavored to lower his hands quickly and not to delay, lest his mind be caught up.

30. A certain elder recounted that for four months he went daily to a certain brother in Scetis and never once found him idle. Coming once and standing outside at the door, he heard him saying with weeping: Lord! If my cry to You does not reach Your ears—have mercy on me in my sins!—even so I shall not weary of entreating You.

31. A certain hermit saw a demon who was urging another demon to go and wake a sleeping monk, and heard him say to him: I cannot do this, for once I woke him, and he, rising up, burned me with psalmody and prayer.

32. The elders said that prayer is the mirror of the monk.

33. A certain elder said: just as one cannot see one's face in murky water, so too the soul, unless it be cleansed from all that is foreign, cannot pray.

34. The elders said of a certain brother that he never left off his handiwork, and his prayer ascended unceasingly to God. He was also very humble and well-ordered.

35. An elder said: when a man keeps himself from offending his neighbor, then let him be bold in thought that his prayer is accepted by God; but whoever offends his neighbor, his prayer is abominable and unacceptable, for the groaning of the offended one does not permit the prayer of the offender to ascend before the face of God.

36. An elder said: if you are occupied with handiwork in your cell, and the hour of your prayer comes, do not say: I will finish this small quantity of branches or this small basket and then I will get up; but rise each hour and render to God the debt of prayer, otherwise, little by little, you will grow accustomed to being negligent of your prayer and service, and your soul will become empty of every work, both bodily and spiritual.

37. Again he said: if you hear of someone that he has spoken ill of you, then when he comes to you, do not show him the appearance that you have learned of it, but be cordial with him and let your face be gracious toward him, that you may have boldness in prayer.

38. A certain elder recounted: once a certain brother living in Egypt was traveling on the road, and since evening overtook him, on account of the cold he entered a tomb to spend the night. Passing by, demons said one to another: look what boldness this monk has, that he spends the night in a tomb! Let us go and drag him out! Another answered him: why should we drag him out? He is ours, for he does our will: he eats, drinks, speaks ill of his neighbor, and is negligent of prayer recitation. Instead of lingering over him, let us rather go and trouble those who vex us and fight against us day and night with their prayer.

Chapter XIII.
On How One Must Be Hospitable
and Give Alms with a Good Heart

1. Abba Apollos said concerning the reception of brethren: one must bow down to the brethren who come, for we bow down not to them, but to God. When you see your brother, you see the Lord your God, and this we have received from Abraham (Genesis 18:2). And that one should receive brethren at one's place and urge them to refreshment, this we have learned from Lot, who compelled the Angels to enter his house (Genesis 19:3).

2. Blessed Epiphanius said that God grants justification for the very smallest thing to those who seek to purchase it for a small piece of bread, for poor clothing, for a cup of water, for a single obol. He also added the following: when a man, on account of poverty or for trading needs, borrows from another man, then, when repaying, although he expresses gratitude, out of shame he repays secretly. But the Master God, on the contrary, borrows secretly and repays before the face of Angels, Archangels, and the righteous.

3. Abba Daniel once came to Alexandria with his disciple and saw a naked man from Ommata, who was sitting on the street and saying: give alms, have mercy! The elder said to his disciple: do you see this man from Ommata? I tell you that he is of great measure. Do you want me to show you who he is? Stay here. The elder approached and said to that man: do me a kindness, brother! I have nothing with which to buy palm leaves, so as to work and feed myself. The man from Ommata answered him: what do you see in me, abba? I am naked, like a beggar, and you, despite this, say: give me something, so that I may buy palm leaves for work! Nevertheless, wait! The elder gave a sign to his disciple to follow them. They went outside the city to Saint Mark, for there that man had a cell, and the man from Ommata said to the elder: wait for me, abba! Then he brought to the elder a basket with grapes, apples, and figs, three keratia (a sixth part of a scruple) of small coins, then took out of his mouth one trimission (a coin) and gave it to the elder, saying: pray for me, abba! Coming to his disciple, the elder wept and said: how many hidden servants God has! As the Lord lives! I will reject nothing from his blessing, for this is a gift of love. Several days after their departure from there, they heard that the steward had fallen gravely ill and lay at the church of Saint Mark, and that the holy Apostle and Evangelist Mark appeared to him and said: summon such-and-such a man from Ommata; he will lay his hand on the place of illness, and you will be healed.

When this was carried out, and he prayed and laid his hand, the illness immediately passed. This became known throughout the whole city; and the Pope himself, hearing of it, went out to see him, but found that he had already reposed in the Lord. Then the report of this spread throughout the whole city and in Scetis, and that elder came from there with his disciple and with many fathers, and together with the townspeople all received a blessing from the blessed one, and they carried out his body with great thanksgiving and glorification, and laid him above Abba Mark the Fool-for-Christ. His life was such: with what he received in alms, he bought apples, grapes, and dates, and through the agency of another distributed them to strangers and the sick on Sundays; and for forty-eight years he performed such a virtue of service to others to the glory of God.

4. Once Abba Daniel, the presbyter of Scetis, was in the Thebaid with one of his disciples. Sailing from there down the river, at the direction of the elder, they put in at a certain village, and the elder said: today we will stay here. The disciple began to murmur: how long will we wander about? Let us go to Scetis. But the elder said: no; today we will stay here. And they sat in the middle of the village, like strangers. The brother asked the elder: is it pleasing to God that we sit here, like laymen? Let us go, at least, to the church of the martyr! But the elder insisted: no; we will sit here until late evening. The brother began to argue with the elder and said: because of you I am to die wretchedly. While they were speaking, an old layman approached, tall in stature and entirely gray-haired. Seeing Abba Daniel, he began to kiss his feet with tears, and also kissed his disciple, and said to them: command that I enter my house. He was carrying a lantern and going around the streets of the village, seeking strangers. Taking the elder and his disciple, as well as whatever strangers he found, he went to his house. There he poured water into a basin and washed their feet. He had no relatives either in his house or in any other place, except God alone. He also set a table before them, and after eating, he threw the remaining scraps to the village dogs, for it was his custom not to leave a single crumb from evening until morning. The elder led him aside to a private place and until nearly dawn conversed with him about salvation with many tears. In the morning, having kissed one another, all departed. On the way the disciple, making a prostration to the elder, asked: do me a kindness, father, tell me who that old man is? And why do you know him? But the elder did not wish to speak of it to his disciple. Bowing down to him, the brother again asked him: much else have you entrusted to me, but concerning this elder you do not wish to speak? (The elder had revealed to him the virtues of many saints.) And since the elder did not reveal it, the brother became angry and did not speak with him all the way to Scetis, and upon arriving at his cell, the brother did not bring the elder his small meal (the elder, by custom, ate at the eleventh hour all the days of his life). When evening came, the elder came to the brother's cell and asked him: why, child, have you left your father to die of hunger? The brother answered him: I have no father, for if I had a father, he would love his own child. The elder said to him: do you really have no father? — and rushed to the door to leave. The brother could not bear to see the elder grieved, for he loved him greatly, ran after him, held him, and, kissing him, said: as the Lord lives! — I will not let you go until you tell me who that old man was. The elder said to him: first prepare for me a little to eat, and then I will tell

you. After eating, he said to the brother: do not be stiff-necked, for because of your gainsaying and murmuring in the village I revealed nothing to you about that elder. But see that you tell no one what you will now hear. This elder is named Eulogius, a stonecutter by trade. Every day he earns one keration by his handiwork, tastes nothing until evening, and in the evening, returning to the village, gathers all the strangers he finds into his house and feeds them, and throws the remaining scraps to the dogs, as you yourself saw. He has had the trade of a stonecutter from his youth, and now he is about a hundred years old. The Lord gives him strength, and to this day every day he earns the same keration. When I was younger — some forty years ago — I came to sell my handiwork in that village. In the evening he took me and other brethren according to his custom of hospitality. Coming there and seeing the virtue of this man, I began to fast for weeks at a time and to ask God that He might grant him greater means, so that he might have the opportunity to do even more good. Having fasted for three weeks and being half-dead from the ascetic labors, I fell asleep and saw that someone in priestly form came to me and asked: Daniel! What is the matter with you? I answered: I have given my word, my Master, to Christ not to taste bread until He hears my request for Eulogius the stonecutter, that He grant him a blessing to do even more good. He said to me: no; it is better for him as it is. But I said: rather, Lord, grant him this, so that through him all may glorify Thy holy name. He answered me: I tell you — it is better for him as it is. But if you wish Me to grant him greater means, become surety for his soul, that it will be saved with him, and I will give him this. I pledged, saying: from my hands require his soul. And I saw, as if we were standing in the holy Church of the Resurrection; a young Child was sitting on the holy stone, and Eulogius was standing at His right hand. He sent one of those standing before Him and said to me: has this one become surety for Eulogius? All said: yes, Master! He said again: tell him that I will certainly require the surety from him. I answered: yes, Master! It is upon me, only give it to him. And I saw — they began to pour a multitude of gold into the bosom of Eulogius, and however much they poured, his bosom held it all. Waking up, I understood that I had been heard, and glorified God. Eulogius, having gone out to his work, when he struck the stone, heard a certain sound, and striking again, discovered a cave full of money. Astonished at this, he thought: this is the money of the Israelites. What then shall I do? If I take it home, the ruler will hear, will come and take it, and I may even have trouble. It is better that I go to another land, where no one knows me. Then he hired pack animals, as if for transporting stones, loaded the money by night and transported it to the river, leaving that good work which he had done every day. Taking a ship, he reached Byzantium, where at that time the elder Justin was reigning, and donated much money to him, gave gifts to the nobles, and became prefect of the praetorium, also buying himself a large house, which to this day is called the house of the Egyptian. Two years later, I saw again in a dream the same young Child in the Church of the Resurrection and wondered: where then is Eulogius? But shortly afterward I saw how Eulogius was dragged from the face of the Child by an Ethiopian. Waking up, I said to myself: woe is me, a sinner! I have destroyed my soul! Then, taking my bag, I went to that village, as if to sell my handiwork. Long did I wait, thinking Eulogius might come, but evening came, and no one invited me. Finally I asked an old woman: God bless you, old woman! Bring me a little bread, that I might eat, for I have not yet eaten today. She brought a little stew, and setting it before me, sat some distance away and began to say the following soul-saving words: master abba! Do you not know that you are young and ought not to go about in villages? Do you not know that the monastic habit requires stillness? — and other things of the kind. I answered her: what then do you command me to do? I have come to sell my handiwork. She continued: though you may sell your handiwork, you ought not to tarry in the village. If you desire to be a monk, go to Scetis. I said to her at that: leave off such words for now and tell me, is there really not among you a God-fearing man who would receive strangers? She said to me: oh! What have you said, father abba! We had here a stonecutter who did much good for strangers. Seeing his good works, the Lord granted him grace; and he, as we hear, is now a patrician. Hearing this, I said to myself: you have committed this murder. Then I hired a ship and arrived at Byzantium. Having inquired about the house of Eulogius the Egyptian, I came and sat at his gates, waiting until he should come out. At last he appeared with great pomp. I cried out to him: show me a small mercy; I wish to speak with you in private. But he paid no attention to me and only struck me with his staff in contempt. I ran ahead and again cried out, and again received a blow. Thus I suffered for four weeks, not having the occasion to speak with him. Falling into despondency, I went, with weeping, and prostrated myself before the icon of the Most Holy Theotokos and addressed the Savior: Lord, release me from the surety for this man, or I too will go into the world! Having accepted this in my mind, I fell asleep and heard a great noise and a voice: the Empress is passing. I saw that thousands and myriads of ranks were going before Her, and I cried out: my Lady! Have mercy on me! She stopped and asked: what is the matter with you? What do you need? I said: I have become surety for Eulogius, who is now a patrician; command that I be released from the surety for him. But She said: this is no concern of Mine! As you wish, so fulfill the surety! Waking up, I resolved: even if I must die, I will not depart from his gates until I find the occasion to speak with him. I came again to the gates, and when he came out, I cried out to him, but the gatekeeper ran up and struck me so many blows that my whole body was covered with wounds. After this, having become even more despondent, I said to myself: I will go to Scetis, and if God wills, He will save both me and Eulogius. Finding an Alexandrian ship and boarding it, I lay down from grief and fell asleep. And behold, I saw myself again in the Church of the Holy Resurrection, and that Child sitting on the stone and looking at me so sternly that from fear I trembled like a leaf and could not open my mouth, for my heart had turned to stone. He said to me: you shall not avoid fulfilling your surety! — and commanded two of those standing by to bind my hands and hang me, saying: do not become surety beyond your strength and do not contradict God! But I still could not open my mouth. Everything was already prepared for my hanging, when a rumor passed: the Empress is coming. Seeing Her and gaining boldness, I fell before Her and said in a quiet voice: Lady of the world! Have mercy on me! She asked: what do you want again? I answered: they wish to hang me for my surety for Eulogius! She promised: I will pray for you! And I saw — She approached and kissed the feet of the Child. Then He asked me: will you no longer do such a thing?! I answered: I will not, Master! I prayed for him, supposing that he would be even more useful. But I have sinned, Master! Forgive me! Then He commanded that I be released and said: go to your cell and do not inquire how I will bring Eulogius back to his former rank. Waking up, I rejoiced with great joy at the cancellation of my surety and sailed, giving thanks to God, and three months later I heard that Emperor Justin had died and Justinian had become emperor, before whom Hypatius, Densiocrates, Pompeius, and this Eulogius were accused. Those he beheaded and took all their property, but Eulogius, who had fled from Constantinople by night, he ordered to be killed wherever he might be found, and that one, having exchanged his bright garments for the clothing of a villager, returned to his home. The whole village gathered to see Eulogius, and they said to him: blessed is your coming! We have heard that you have become a patrician. He answered: is that so! If I had become a patrician, would I see your faces?! No, that was some other Eulogius, and I went to venerate the holy places. Then, coming to himself, he said: poor Eulogius! Get up, take up your stonecutting and go labor. Here there are no palaces. Lest you lose your head! Thus, taking the tools of his trade, he went to that stone where he had found the money, supposing he would find more, and struck until the sixth hour and found nothing. He recalled his past fortune, glory, and abundance, but, coming to himself, said: poor Eulogius, labor! Here is Egypt! Thus, little by little, the Holy Child and our Lady the Theotokos restored him to his former rank, for God is not unjust so as to forget his former labors. Some time later, I came to that village to sell my handiwork, and behold, toward evening, according to his former custom, he came and took me to his house. Seeing him, all covered in dust, I groaned and, shedding tears, said: *how great are Your works, O Lord! In wisdom You have made them all. Who is so great a God as our God? You are the God who does wonders, You alone! He raises the poor out of the dust, and lifts the needy out of the ash heap. The Lord makes poor and makes rich; He brings low and lifts up. Your wonders and Your judgments — who shall fathom them? I, a sinner, attempted something that was not my concern, and my soul nearly dwelt in Hades* (see Psalm 103:24; Psalm 76:14; Psalm 112:7; 1 Kingdoms 2:7; Psalm 93:17). At the house he poured water, washed my feet and those of the other strangers, and set a table before us. After eating, I asked him: how are you, Abba Eulogius? He answered: pray for me, father abba! I am poor and have nothing in my hands. I said: oh, if only you had not at all had what you had! He asked me: why then, abba? Have I offended you in something? How have you not offended? — I said, and told him all that had happened. We both wept, and he said: pray for me, father abba, that God may grant me what is needful. From now on I will amend. But I said: truly, child, do not expect from the Lord anything of the things of this world, except a keration from your labors! And behold, for so many years now God has given him strength to earn a keration by the labors of his hands. Now I have told you, child, how and why I know him, but do not tell anyone of this. This did Abba Daniel entrust to his disciple upon their return from the Thebaid. Wondrous is God's love for mankind! How quickly it raised up Eulogius and then again humbled him, because this was saving for him. Let us also pray that we may be humble, that at the dread judgment seat of our Lord Jesus Christ we may find mercy before the face of His glory.

5. The disciple of Abba Theodore recounted: once a seller of onions came to us and filled a whole bowl for me. The elder said: fill it with wheat and give it to him. We had two heaps of wheat: one of clean wheat, and another of unclean. I filled his bowl with the unclean. The elder looked at me intently and with sorrow, so that from fear I fell and broke the bowl. Getting up, I made a prostration to the elder, asking forgiveness. The elder said: get up, you are not to blame, but I have erred in that I commanded you. Then he went in himself, filled a sack with clean wheat, and gave it to the seller together with his onions.

6. They said of Abba Theodore that when Scetis was laid waste, the elder came to live on a farm and grew weak, being already old. Some would bring him food, but what the first one brought, the elder gave to the second, and so in order — what he received from one, he gave to another. He himself, at the hour of taking food, ate what the one who came at that time brought.

7. They said of Abba John Colobos: all that he earned by his labor during harvest, he took and brought to Scetis, saying: my widows and my orphans are in Scetis.

8. Some of the fathers came to Abba Joseph in Panephos to ask about the reception of brethren-strangers: ought one to relax oneself and freely eat with them? But before they asked him, the elder said to his disciple: attend to what I will now do, and be patient. Then he took two reed stools, placing one on his right side and the other on his left, invited them to sit, and went into his innermost cell; there, having put on beggar's rags, he came out, passed through the midst of the brethren, and went in again; having changed into his ordinary clothes, he came out and sat among them. The brethren were amazed at the elder's actions, and he asked them: did you notice what I was doing? They answered: we noticed. Was I changed by the poor rags? They said: no. Then the elder said to them: if I am the same in both garments, so that neither one changed me nor the other harmed me, so also ought we to act in receiving strangers, according to the holy Gospel, which says: *Render therefore to Caesar the things that are Caesar's, and to God the things that are God's* (Matthew 22:21). So then, when brethren come to us, let us receive them freely, but when we remain alone, then it is needful that mourning remain with us constantly. Hearing this, the fathers marveled that he had revealed what was in their hearts before they had asked him about it, and they glorified God.

9. Abba John Cassian recounted: we came from Palestine to Egypt, to one of the fathers, and when he had entertained us as strangers, we asked him: why, in receiving brethren-strangers, do you not keep the rule of fasting, as is the custom in Palestine? He answered us: fasting is always with me, but you I cannot keep with me always. Of course, fasting is a useful and necessary thing, but it depends on our own will, while the fulfillment of the commandment of love is necessarily required of us by the law of God. Receiving you, and in you Christ, I must with all diligence refresh you. But when I see you off, I can again resume the rule of fasting, for *can the sons of the bridechamber fast while the bridegroom is with them?... But the days will come when the bridegroom will be taken away from them, and then they will fast* (Matthew 9:15; Mark 2:19–20).

10. He also recounted: we came to a certain elder, and he set food before us. When we were already satisfied, he asked us to eat more. I refused, saying that we could eat no more. The elder said: six times have I set a table before brethren who came, and, asking each of them to eat, I ate with them myself, and I still want to eat, but you, having eaten this once, are so satisfied that you can eat no more.

11. Once in Scetis a command was given to fast the following week. At that time, as it happened, brethren came to Abba Moses from Egypt, and he prepared a little stew for them. The neighboring monks, seeing the smoke, said to the clerics: Moses has broken the command and has prepared stew for himself. They answered: when he comes, we will speak to him. When Saturday came, the clerics, knowing the lofty life of Abba Moses, said to him before the whole assembly: Abba Moses! You have broken the commandment of men and have kept the commandment of God.

12. A brother, seeing that Abba Nisterus wore two garments, asked him: abba, if a poor man comes and asks you for clothing, which will you give him? He answered: the better one. The brother asked further: and if another asks you, what will you give him? The elder said: half of the other. The brother again asked: and if yet another asks you, what will you give? He answered: I will tear what remains and give him half, and with the rest gird myself. The brother said: and if even this someone asks of you, what will you do? The elder said: I will give him what remains, then sit in some place until God sends something and covers me, for I will ask of no one else.

13. A brother said to Abba Poemen: if I give my brother a little bread or something else, the demons defile it as done by me for man-pleasing. The elder said to him: even if it is done for man-pleasing, let us still give to the brother what is needful. And he told him such a parable: two farmers lived in one place. One of them sowed and gathered a little unclean grain, but the other, being lazy, did not sow and gathered nothing. So if there should be a famine, which of these two will find something to live on? The brother answered: the one who gathered a little grain, even though it was unclean. The elder said: so let us also sow a little, even if unclean, so as not to die of hunger.

14. A brother came to Abba Poemen in the second week of Great Lent and, having opened his thoughts to him and received consolation, said to him: I hesitated a little whether to come here today. The elder asked: why? The brother answered: I said to myself: perhaps on account of Great Lent he will not open to me? Abba Poemen said: we have not learned to close the wooden door, but rather the door of the tongue.

15. Abba Theodore of Pherme asked Abba Pambo: tell me a word. And he said to him with great effort: have mercy on all, for mercy finds boldness before God.

16. Mother Sarrah said: it is useful for people to give alms, for even though at first it may be from man-pleasing, it afterward passes over to the pleasing of God.

17. They recounted of Abba Serapion that, meeting a poor man in Alexandria who was trembling from the cold, he stopped and began to reason with himself: how is it that I, who

suppose myself to be an ascetic, wear a tunic, while this poor man, or rather Christ, is dying of cold? Truly, if I leave him to die, on the day of judgment I shall be condemned as a murderer. Then, stripping himself like a good wrestler, he gave his garment to the poor man and sat holding under his arm the small Gospel which he always carried with him. A keeper of order passing by asked him: Abba Serapion! Who has stripped you? Taking out the small Gospel, the abba said to him: this is what has stripped me. Getting up and going further, he met someone being tortured for a debt, and, having nothing to give him, the immortal Serapion sold his small Gospel, gave the money for the debt of the tortured man, and returned to his cell naked. Seeing him naked, his disciple asked him: abba! Where is your garment? The elder answered: I have sent it on ahead, child, to where we shall need it more. The disciple asked again: and where is the small Gospel? The elder said: truly, child, Him Who said to me each day: *go, sell what you have and give to the poor* (Matthew 19:21; Mark 10:21; Luke 18:22), Him Himself I have sold and given to Him, that on the day of judgment we may find boldness before Him.

18. Abba Timothy, the presbyter, said to Abba Poemen: there is in Egypt a certain woman who commits fornication and gives the payment for it in alms. Abba Poemen said: she will not remain forever in fornication, for in her is seen the fruit of faith. It happened afterward that the mother of the presbyter Timothy came to him, and he asked her: is that woman still committing fornication? She answered: yes, and she has even added lovers to herself; however, she has also added to her almsgiving. Abba Timothy told this to Abba Poemen, but he repeated: she will not remain in fornication. When the mother of Abba Timothy came again, she said: do you know? That harlot wished to come with me, so that you might pray for her. Hearing this, he told it to Abba Poemen, and he said to him: rather, you go and speak with her. Seeing him and hearing from him the word of God, she was smitten with compunction, wept, and said: from now on I will cleave to God and will no longer commit fornication. And, entering a monastery, she pleased God.

19. An elder recounted that a certain man had a wife and a daughter who was still only a catechumen in Christianity, and, desiring to renounce the world, he divided his property into three parts. However, his daughter died during the period of catechesis, and the father, for the sake of her soul's salvation, distributed her portion of the property to the poor, and also the portion of his wife and his own, while not ceasing to pray for her to God. During his prayer, a voice came to him: your daughter has been baptized, do not grieve! But he did not believe this, and the invisible one spoke to him again: open the tomb. Will you find her? Coming to the tomb, he dug it open, but did not find her there, for she had been transferred to the faithful.

20. One of the fathers recounted: a certain magistrianus, sent by the emperor on business, discovered on the way a poor man who had died and who was naked. Having compassion on him, he sent his servant ahead, and he himself took off one of his garments and covered the dead man with it. Several days later, he was again sent on business and, riding out of the city, fell from his horse, injuring his leg. The physicians tried in vain to heal him, and after five

days the leg turned black. Then the physicians decided to cut off the leg, lest the whole body be ruined and the man die. The sick man signaled to his servant to go out to the physicians and learn of their intention, and they said: if the leg is not cut off, the man will perish. Tomorrow we will come, and what is pleasing to God, that we will do. The servant went in to his master and with tears told him of this. In great grief from the great sorrow, the master could not fall asleep and saw at midnight — a lamp was burning beside him — that a certain man entered, approached him, and asked: why are you weeping? What is your sorrow? And he told him what had happened. The one who appeared said to him: show me your leg. Then, having anointed it, he said: now get up and walk. Leaning on the visitor, the sick man stepped, limping. Then the one who appeared said to him: are you still limping? Lie down again, — and again anointed his legs, saying: now get up and walk! He got up and began to walk soundly. Then the visitor said to him: now lie down and rest, — and added the words of the Lord concerning almsgiving: *Blessed are the merciful, for they shall obtain mercy* (Matthew 5:7). And: *For judgment is without mercy to the one who has shown no mercy* (James 2:13), and other similar things, then said: farewell. The magistrianus asked him: for God's sake, Who sent you, tell me — who are you? The visitor said to him: look at me. Do you recognize your garment? He answered: I recognize it, lord! It is mine! Then the one who appeared said to him: I am the one whom you, seeing dead on the way, covered with your garment, and God has sent me to heal you. So, always give thanks to God, — and went out, and the healed man glorified God, the source of every good.

21. Another magistrianus, returning from Palestine to Constantinople, in the region of Tyre met a man who, looking about at the road, walked alone, not having a guide. Hearing the sound of a horse's hooves, he lay down by the road, stretching out his hands, and, according to the custom of the poor, spoke certain supplicating words, asking for alms. At first the magistrianus passed him by with negligence, but, having ridden a little, he repented and, returning to the one asking, gave him a coin. The man, receiving it, prayed for him, saying: I believe in God that this commandment will deliver you from temptation. The magistrianus received this prayer with faith and arrived in a city where there were certain soldiers asking the governor of the city to put them on a ship, but he, day after day, put them off, not resolving the matter. Seeing the magistrianus, they asked him to dispose the governor, that they might depart, and he, having told him what was needful concerning his own affairs, also reminded him about the soldiers. The governor agreed to send the soldiers if the magistrianus would take them with him on the ship, and, when he agreed, they set sail, having caught a favorable wind. It happened that at night, while at the edge of the ship, the magistrianus was thrown into the sea by a blow from the sail, and although the sailors heard his fall and tried to rescue him, because it was night and the wind was strong, they could not do so. Carried by the waves, the magistrianus already considered himself the inevitable victim of death, yet by God's will, on the following day he was noticed from another passing ship and pulled up. When both ships came to the city, the sailors went into an inn, and some, with sighs, told of the magistrianus's fall, while others, to general joy, told of his rescue, and he later told them that the poor man to whom he had given a coin on the way had carried him,

walking on the water. Hearing this, they glorified our Savior God. From what has been recounted, let us learn that alms from the heart do not perish, but in time of need God repays the almsgiver. So, according to the divine Scripture, let us not refuse to do good to the needy when our hand is not lacking.

22. One of the lovers of Christ, who had the gift of almsgiving, said that he who gives alms ought to give as if he himself were receiving. Such alms draw one near to God.

23. Someone recounted: in Alexandria a certain rich man fell ill and, fearing death, distributed thirty litrai of gold to the poor. Then, having recovered, he began to regret what he had done, and disclosed this to his most pious friend, who said: rather, you ought to rejoice that you have brought this to Christ. But he was not consoled by this. Then his friend, who was also wealthy, said to him: here are your thirty litrai! Only go to Saint Menas and say: it was not I who fulfilled the commandment of love, but this man, — and take them. When they came to the saint, he spoke thus and took the gold, but on going out, at the doors, he died. They offered the gold to its owner: take what is yours. But he answered: may this not be mine before the Lord, for from the time I gave it to Christ, it is His. Distribute it to the poor. Hearing of what had happened, all were seized with fear and glorified God for the good disposition of this man.

24. A certain elder lived with a brother, having all things in common. The elder was merciful, and when a famine came, many came to his door to receive alms, which he gave to all who came. Seeing this, the brother said to the elder: give me my portion of the bread, and with your portion do what you will. The elder divided the bread and gave alms from his own portion, so that very many came to him, hearing that he gave to all. God, seeing that he gave to all, blessed his bread. Meanwhile, the brother used up his own and asked the elder: I still have a few other loaves, abba; take me back into community. The elder answered him: I will do as you wish. And they began to live as before. Although afterward there was a harvest, those in need still came to them for alms. Once, going into the bread-store, the brother saw that there was no more bread, but a poor man came, and the elder commanded to give him alms. When the brother said that there was no more bread, the elder said: go and look! Entering, he found the bread-store completely full of bread. Seeing this, he was seized with fear and, learning from this the faith and virtue of the elder, glorified God.

25. An elder said: it happens that someone does much good, but the evil one suggests to him to pay attention to petty things, in order to destroy the reward of all his good deeds. Thus I once sat in Oxyrhynchus with a presbyter who gave alms. A widow came and asked him for a little wheat. He said to her: bring a sack, and I will fill it for you. She brought it. Unfolding it, he said to her: it is large, and put the widow to shame. I asked him: abba! Did you sell the wheat? He answered: no, but I gave it to her as alms. Then I said: if you gave it to her as alms, why did you speak of the measure and thus put the widow to shame?

26. A brother came to a certain hermit and, going out, said to him: forgive me, abba, that I have hindered you from fulfilling your rule. He said to him in answer: my rule is to refresh you and send you away in peace.

27. A certain hermit lived near a coenobium and performed many ascetic labors. Brethren who had come to the coenobium compelled him to eat before the appointed hour, and afterward they asked him: are you not grieved at this, abba? He answered: my grief is when I do my own will.

28. They said of a certain elder who lived in Syria by a desert road that his work was such: at whatever hour any of the monks was going from the desert, he would with all hospitality provide him refreshment. Once a hermit came to him, and he offered him refreshment, but the hermit would not accept it, saying: I am fasting. The elder was grieved and said to him: do not despise your son, I beseech you, and do not pass me by. Come, let us pray! Here is a tree: with whomever it bends when that one bows the knee and prays, him let us follow. The hermit bowed the knee in prayer — and nothing happened. The host bowed the knee — and immediately the tree bowed with him. Assured by this, they glorified God.

29. A certain monk had a poor brother, a layman, and whatever he earned by his labors, he gave to him. However, however much he gave him, the brother kept becoming poorer. The brother told an elder about this, and the elder said to him: if you will listen to me, give him nothing more, but say: brother, when I had, I gave to you, but now you, from what you earn by your labors, bring to me. And when he brings you something, take it from him and give it to a stranger or to a poor elder whom you know, and ask him to offer a prayer for him. The brother, returning, did so: when his brother the layman came, he said to him as the elder had commanded. The layman went away with sorrow, and the first day after this he took some vegetables from his labors and brought them to him. Receiving them, the brother gave them to the elders and asked them to pray for him, and the layman returned home with a blessing. Another time he brought him vegetables and three loaves. Taking them, the brother did as before, and the layman again returned with a blessing. Coming the third time, he brought a multitude of food, and wine, and fish. Seeing this, the brother was amazed, gathered the poor, and refreshed them. Then he asked his brother: do you no longer have need of bread? The layman answered: no, my lord. When I took something from you, it was as if fire entered my house and devoured everything. But from the time I have not taken from you, God blesses me. The brother went and told the elder all that had happened, and the elder said to him: do you not know that the work of a monk is fire and, wherever it enters, it burns? It is better for your brother to give alms from his own labors, for thus he receives the prayers of the saints and is blessed.

30. A certain Theban monk had from God the gift of service — to give what was needful to everyone who came. It happened that in a certain village he was distributing alms. And behold, a certain woman approached him for alms, dressed in rags. Seeing her in rags, he opened wide his hand to give her more, but his hand closed and he drew out a little. Then another woman came, well dressed. Looking at her garments, he wished to give her less, but his hand opened wide, and he drew out much. When he afterward asked about the one and the other, he was told that the well-dressed woman was of noble birth, but had become poor

and for the sake of reputation wore good clothing, while the other had purposely dressed in rags so as to receive more.

31. Once two brothers came to a certain elder. This elder's custom was not to eat every day, but, seeing the brethren, he rejoiced and said: fasting has its reward, but he who eats for love's sake performs two virtues: he leaves his own will and fulfills the commandment of love. And so he refreshed the brethren.

32. One of the Egyptian saints lived in a desert place; some distance from him was another man, a Manichaean by faith, a senior among those whom they call seniors, who was going to one of his co-religionists, and once evening overtook him in that place where the Orthodox saint lived. The Manichaean struggled with himself and feared to ask for lodging, supposing that the other, knowing of his Manichaeism, might perhaps not receive him, yet extremity compelled him to knock. The elder opened and, recognizing him, received him with joy: offered prayer, refreshed him, and prepared a bed. At night, coming to himself, the Manichaean reflected: how is it that he showed no suspicion? Truly, he is a man of God! Then he came to him, fell at his feet, and said: from now on I am Orthodox! And thus he remained with him forever.

33. There was a certain well-to-do man who had grown rich by bribes, extortions, and injustices. At last, coming to himself and fearing the judgment of God, he went to a teacher and said: I beseech you — my mind is captive to the cares of this life, heal me, lest I perish. The teacher gave him a book of King Solomon. Reading it, he found: *He who has pity on the poor lends to the Lord* (Proverbs 19:17), closed the book, and gave it to the teacher, saying: who is more trustworthy than God? He gives me both the principal sum and the interest on it, if I am merciful to the poor. Then he went, sold all his property, and distributed it to the poor, keeping nothing for himself except four dinars for the support of his body. Thus he himself became poor, and no one wished to show him mercy. After a time, he said to himself: I will go to Jerusalem, to the Lord my God, to contend with Him, for He has deceived me into distributing all my property. Going to Jerusalem, he saw two men quarreling with each other, for they had found a stone lost from the vestments of Aaron the high priest, but did not know this. He asked them: why are you quarreling? They answered: we have found a stone, but we do not know what it is. He said to them: give it to me and take four dinars. They gladly gave him the stone. Coming to Jerusalem, he showed it to a goldsmith, and the goldsmith, recognizing the stone, asked him: where did you find this stone? For three years now all Jerusalem has been in distress over this stone. Go, give it to the high priest, and he will enrich you. Meanwhile, as he was going to the sanctuary, an Angel of the Lord appeared to the high priest and said: a man will come to you with the lost stone, — give him gold, silver, and precious stones, as many as he wishes, and then say to him: do not be faint-hearted in your heart and do not disbelieve God, that *he who has pity on the poor lends to the Lord.* Behold, you have been repaid sevenfold in this age, and in the age to come you shall be given eternal life.

Chapter XIV.
On Obedience

1. Abba Anthony said: obedience with abstinence subdues beasts.

2. Abba Arsenius said to Abba Alexander: when you have trimmed your branches, come partake of food with me; but if strangers come, partake with them. Abba Alexander worked little by little and without haste, and when the time came to partake of food, he still had a certain number of branches left to trim. Wishing to keep the word of the elder, he remained to finish his handiwork, while Abba Arsenius, seeing that he was delayed, partook of food alone, supposing that he had strangers. Abba Alexander came to the elder when evening had already fallen, and the elder asked him: did you have strangers? He said: no. The elder asked again: why then did you not come? He answered: you said to me, when you have trimmed your branches, then come. I did not come, keeping your word, for only now have I trimmed them. The elder marveled at his exactness and said: break your fast quickly, so that you may be able to complete your rule, and drink water, otherwise your body will become faint.

3. Abba Abraham came to Abba Arius. When they were sitting, a brother came to the elder and asked him: Father, tell me, what must I do to be saved? The abba said to him: go, and this year partake of bread and salt in the evening; afterward come, and I shall tell you. He went and did so. At the end of the year, the brother again came to Abba Arius; it happened that Abba Abraham was there as well. The elder said to the brother: go, and this year fast for two days at a time. When the brother had gone, Abba Abraham asked Abba Arius: why do you give other brethren an easy yoke, but lay heavy burdens upon this brother? The elder answered him: the brethren come with questions and depart the same, but this one comes for the sake of God to hear a word, for he is a doer, and whatever I tell him he will do diligently. Therefore I also speak to him the word of God.

4. A certain elder recounted that Saint Basil, having arrived at a certain coenobium, after a fitting instruction asked the hegumen: do you have here a brother possessing obedience? He answered him: they are all your servants and diligently strive for salvation, Master! He asked him again: do you have one who truly possesses obedience? Then he brought to him a certain brother, and Saint Basil commanded him to serve him during the meal. After the food was received, the brother gave him water for washing, after which Saint Basil said to him: go, and I will give you water to wash, and the brother permitted him to pour the water. Afterward

he said to him: when I enter the sanctuary, come, and I will make you a deacon. After this was accomplished, he also made him a presbyter and took him with him to the episcopate because of his obedience.

5. Abba Isaiah spoke to novices and those under obedience to the holy fathers: as the first dye does not fade, as for example the purple on porphyry garments, and as young shoots are easily turned and bent, so are novices who are under obedience.

6. They recounted of Abba John Colobos that, having withdrawn to a certain Theban elder in Scetis, he dwelt in the desert. The elder took a dry stick of wood and, having planted it, said to Abba John: water it every day with a pitcher of water until it bears fruit, and the water was so far from them that one would go in the evening and return only by morning. After three years, the tree came to life and bore fruit. The elder took its fruit, brought it into the church, and said to the brethren: receive, partake of the fruit of obedience.

7. They said of John, the disciple of Abba Paul, that he had great obedience. In a certain place there was a cemetery in which a hyena lived. The elder, seeing dung there, said to John: go and bring it. He asked the elder: and what shall I do, abba, about the hyena? He, jesting, said: if it attacks you, bind it and bring it here. The brother went there in the evening, and behold, the hyena came out against him. According to the word of the elder, he rushed to seize it, but it fled, and chasing after it, he kept saying: my abba said that I should bind you, and finally, having caught it, he bound it. Meanwhile the elder was troubled, waiting for him, and behold, John came with the bound hyena. Marveling at this, but wishing to humble the disciple, the elder struck him, saying: foolish one! You have brought a mad dog here to me? The elder immediately untied it and set it free.

8. They said that Abba Silouan had a disciple named Mark, who possessed great obedience, who by craft was a calligrapher, and whom the elder loved because of his obedience. Abba Silouan had eleven other disciples, who grieved that he loved Mark more than them. Hearing of this, the other elders were saddened, and once, having come to him, they reproached him. Then, calling them, he went out and began knocking at the cell of each in turn, calling: brother so-and-so, come here, I have need of you! But not one of them came out to him at once. When he came to the cell of Mark and, knocking, said: Mark!, the latter, hearing his voice, immediately leapt out to him. He sent him on an obedience and asked the elders: where then are the rest of the brethren, fathers? Then, entering the cell of Mark and taking his handiwork, he saw that he had begun to write a letter, "Ω," but hearing the voice of the elder, had thrown down his pen without finishing the letter. Then the elders said: truly, he whom you love, abba, we also love, for God also loves him.

9. They said of Abba Silouan that once, walking through Scetis with the elders, he desired to show them the obedience of his disciple and why he loved him. Seeing a small wild boar, he asked him: do you see, child, that small buffalo? He answered him: I see it, abba! How fine its horns are! He replied: indeed, abba! The elders marveled at his answer and received edification from his obedience.

10. Once the mother of Abba Mark came with great pomp to see him. The elder went out to her, and she said to him: abba! Tell my son to come out, that I may see him. Going in, the elder said to him: go out, that your mother may see you! He was dressed in patched clothing and was begrimed from the kitchen. Going out because of obedience, he closed his eyes and said: farewell!, but saw no one. The mother, not recognizing him, again sent word to the elder, saying: send my son to me, that I may see him! He asked Mark: did I not tell you to go out, that your mother may see you? He answered: I went out according to your word, abba! But I beseech you, do not tell me to go out again, lest I disobey you. The elder went out to the mother and said to her: he is the very one who came out to you and said: farewell! And having consoled her, he dismissed her.

11. They said of Abba Megethius that he was exceedingly humble, having been taught by the Egyptians, and visited many elders, including Abba Sisoes and Abba Poemen. Once, as he himself recounted, one of the saints came to him and asked him: how do you live, brother, in this desert? He answered: I fast for two days and eat one loaf of bread. The abba said to him: if you will listen to me, eat half a loaf every day. Having done so, he found repose.

12. Abba Mius the Cilician said: obedience for obedience: whoever listens to God, him God will also hear.

13. Abba Moses said to a certain brother: acquire obedience, from which are born: humility, patience, magnanimity, compunction, and brotherly love, for these are our weapons of warfare.

14. He also said: go, brother, into the obedience of truth, in which is humility, in which is strength, in which is joy, in which is patience, in which is magnanimity, in which is brotherly love, in which is compunction, in which is love, for the one who possesses obedience is filled with all the virtues.

15. Again he said: a monk who fasts and is under a spiritual father, but does not possess obedience and humility, will acquire no virtue and does not even know what a monk is.

16. A certain layman of exceedingly devout life came to Abba Poemen, where there were also other brethren wishing to hear a word from the elder. The elder said to the faithful layman: speak a word to the brethren. He excused himself, declining: forgive me, abba! I have come to learn. But, persuaded by the elder, he said: I am a layman, a vegetable seller, and in trading, I make small bundles out of large ones; I buy for a small sum and sell for a larger. However, I am not able to speak from Scripture, but I shall tell a parable. A certain man asked his friend: I have a desire to see the king; go with me. The friend answered him: I will go with you to the middle of the road. He said to another friend: accompany me to the king. That one said to him: I will accompany you to the royal palace. He said to a third: come with me to the king. The friend said to him: I will go, I will enter the chamber, and I will stand before the king; then I will call you and bring you in to the king. The brethren asked him: what is the meaning of this parable? He answered: the first friend is asceticism, which guides to the middle of the way; the second is purity, which reaches to the heavens; and the third is

almsgiving, which with boldness brings one to the King Himself, God. And the brethren, having received edification, departed.

17. Once four Scetians came to the great Pambo, dressed in skins, and each revealed to him the virtue of the other: one fasted much; another was non-acquisitive; the third had great love; and of the fourth they said that he had been twenty-two years in obedience to an elder. Abba Pambo answered them: I say to you that the virtue of this last one is greater than all, for each of you holds to his own will in acquiring this or that virtue, but this one does the will of another, having cut off his own will. Such ones are confessors, if they preserve the same practice to the end.

18. Abba Rufus said that one living in obedience to his spiritual father will receive a greater reward than one living as a hermit in the desert by himself. To this he added that one of the fathers recounted: I saw four ranks in heaven: the first rank, a man sick and thanking God; the second rank, one zealous in hospitality, standing in it and serving; the third rank, one praying in the desert and not seeing people; the fourth rank, one living in obedience to a father and submitting to him for the Lord's sake; and this last one, ranked there for obedience, wore a golden chain and shield and had greater glory than the others. I, he said, asked my guide: why does this lesser one have greater glory than the others? He answered: the one who loves hospitality does so by his own will; the one in the desert withdrew there by his own will; but this one, who has obedience, having abandoned the fulfillment of his own will, hangs, as it were, upon God and his father, and therefore has greater glory than the others. Therefore, children, obedience that is for the Lord's sake is good! Hear some small indication of the fruits it brings. O obedience, salvation of all the faithful! O obedience, mother of all the virtues! O obedience, discoverer of the Kingdom! O obedience, opener of the heavens and one who leads people there from the earth! O obedience, nourisher of all the saints, from whose breasts they were nourished and reached perfection! O obedience, cohabitant of the angels!

19. A certain man from the Thebaid came to Abba Sisoes, wishing to become a monk. The elder asked him whether he had anyone in the world. He answered: I have one son. The elder said to him: go, throw him into the river, and then you shall be a monk. As he was departing, the elder sent a brother to prevent him from doing so; and when he was about to throw his son, the brother said to him: stop! What are you doing? He answered: the abba told me to throw him. The brother said: the elder afterward said that you should not throw him. Then, leaving his son, he came to the elder and became an accomplished monk because of his obedience.

20. A certain man asked Abba Sopatrus: give me a commandment, abba, and I will keep it. He said to him: let no woman enter your cell, do not read apocrypha, and never argue about anything, for from this come stubbornness and division on both sides. These things cannot be beneficial to a monk.

21. They said of Abba Saius and Abba Moius that they lived together. Abba Saius had great obedience, but was very severe. The elder would say to him, testing him: go, steal! He

would go and steal from the brethren because of obedience, giving thanks to God for everything, and the elder, receiving it, would secretly give it back to the brethren. Once it happened that they were on a journey, and Saius grew weak. The abba left him in his weakness, and coming, said to the brethren: go bring Saius, for he lies as if slain. They went and brought him.

22. Abba Seridus, the head of a coenobium near Gaza on the river Thaph, had a certain friend, an Egyptian living in Ascalon, who had a disciple. Once he sent his disciple in wintertime with a letter to Abba Seridus, that he might give him a roll of paper. When this young man came from Ascalon, there was exceedingly heavy rain, so that the river Thaph became threatening. Having delivered the letter to Abba Seridus, this young man said to him, despite the rain: give me, abba, the paper, and I will go. He said to him: it is raining. Where will you go now? The young man answered him: I have a commandment and cannot remain. And since he insisted, the abba gave him the paper, and he set out. The abba said to those with him, among whom was Abba Dorotheus: let us go and see what he will do at the river! And at that time heavy rain was falling. Reaching the river, the young man went far from them, took off his garments, and wrapping the paper in them, fastened them on his head; then, saying to them: pray for me, he threw himself into the river. Abba Seridus affirmed that there was nothing to expect but to send someone to the sea to find his body. Meanwhile, straining and struggling against the force of the water, although he was carried far, he nevertheless reached the other bank of the river. Marveling at his obedience even unto death, they glorified God. Such is obedience, which the fathers call obedience without reasoning, and which gives great boldness before God to those who have been deemed worthy of it. May He also deem us worthy of the same grace, so that, having passed the days of our life without anxiety and in peace, we may find mercy before the face of God.

23. Mother Syncletica said: being in a coenobium, let us prefer obedience to asceticism, for the latter teaches arrogance, but the former teaches humility.

24. Again she said: we must govern the soul wisely, and when we are in a coenobium, not seek our own and not serve our own opinion, but sincerely obey the father in faith in all things. We have given ourselves over to exile, that is, we have placed ourselves outside all worldly cares. Therefore let us not seek what belongs to the place from which we were cast out. There we had glory, here we have reproach; there we had abundance of food, here we lack even bread.

25. Abba Hyperechius said: obedience is a precious thing for a monk. He who has acquired it will be heard by God and will stand with boldness before the Crucified One, for the Lord Who was crucified *became obedient to the point of death* (Philippians 2:8).

26. One of the fathers recounted: a certain scholasticus from Theopolis (Antioch) came to a certain recluse, asking him to receive him and make him a monk. The elder said to him: if you wish me to receive you, go, sell your possessions, give to the poor, according to the commandment of the Lord, and then I will receive you. He went and did so. After this, he again said to him: you must keep another commandment, namely, not to speak at all. He

agreed and spent five years in silence. Many began to glorify him, and then the abba said to him: it is not beneficial for you to remain here; I will send you to a coenobium in Egypt. And he sent him to Egypt, but did not say, as he sent him, whether he should speak or not; and he, keeping the commandment, continued to be silent. The abba who received him, wishing to test whether he spoke or not, sent him on an errand during a flood, so as to make him say that he could not cross over. He also sent a brother after him to see what he would do. Coming to the river and having no way to cross, he knelt down, and behold, a crocodile appeared, received him upon itself, and carried him to the other bank. The brother who saw this returned and announced it to the abba and the brethren, and they were amazed. A year later, he reposed, and the abba sent word to the one who had sent him: although you sent us a mute, you sent an angel of God. The recluse sent answer: he was not mute, but, keeping the commandment which I gave him in the beginning, he remained without speaking. All marveled and glorified God.

27. A certain elder had a disciple who had been handed over to him by another, and wishing to retain him, he disposed him to have perfect obedience, so that when the elder said to him: when the furnace is blazing strongly, go take the book that is read in the assembly and throw it into the fire, he went and did so without reasoning. But when the book was thrown in, the fire went out, that they might know how good obedience is, for it is a ladder to the Kingdom of Heaven.

28. There was in a coenobium a certain man from the world who had his son with him. Wishing to test him, the abba said to him: do not speak with your son, but regard him as a stranger. He answered: I will do according to your word, and he spent many years without speaking with him. When the hour of his son's calling came and he drew near to death, the abba said to the father: go now and speak with your son. He answered him: if you command it, let us keep the commandment to the end. The son reposed, and he did not speak with him. All marveled at how joyfully he accepted the commandment of the abba and kept it.

29. The elders said: if someone has faith in another and gives himself over in obedience to him, that one has no need to attend to the commandments of God, but to entrust his desires to his father; and there is no sin for him before God, for God requires nothing so much from a novice as self-constraint through obedience.

30. A certain brother from Scetis, going off to the harvest, came to a certain great elder and asked him: tell me, what should I do, for I am going off to the harvest? The elder said to him: if I tell you, will you believe me? The brother answered: truly, I will obey you. Then the elder said: if you believe me, then refuse this harvest, come, and I will tell you what to do. The brother, having refused the harvest, returned to the elder, and he said to him: enter your cell and for fifty days eat once a day with dry salt, and afterward I will tell you another thing. He went, did so, and again came to the elder. He, seeing that he was a doer, taught him how he should sit in his cell. The brother came to his cell, fell on his face to the ground, and for three days wept before God. After this, when his thoughts said to him: you have been exalted, you have become great, he placed his sins before himself and said: but what about these sins

of mine? If his thoughts said to him: you have committed many sins, he answered: I will perform my small services to God and trust that He will show me mercy. The spirits, defeated by him, finally appeared to him perceptibly and said: we are crushed by you. He asked: why? And they answered: if we exalt you, you have recourse to humility; and if we humble you, you rise to the heights.

31. A certain elder had a servant in a village. Once it happened that he delayed in bringing what the elder needed, and his supplies of food were exhausted and his handiwork, which he had in his cell, came to a halt, so that he grieved, having neither handiwork nor food. Then he asked his disciple: do you wish to go to the village? He answered: as you wish, so I will do. Because of the temptations, the brother was afraid to approach the village, but so as not to disobey his father, he agreed to go. The elder said to him: go, and I trust in the God of my fathers that He will protect you from every temptation. Thus, having prayed, he sent him off. Coming to the village and inquiring where their servant lived, he found his house, but it happened that he and all his household were outside the village at a commemoration, except for the daughter, who, hearing the knock, opened the door and, learning that he was asking about her father, asked him to enter and even drew him in, but he did not agree. Finally, after much urging, she brought him into the house. Noticing impure movements within himself and troubled by his thoughts, the brother, sighing, cried out: Lord! By the prayers of my father, save me in this hour. Having said this, he immediately found himself at the river, on the road to the monastery, and returned unharmed to his father.

32. Two brothers according to the flesh came to a monastery. One of them was an ascetic, and the other had great obedience. The father said to this one: do this, and he did it; do that, and he did it; he said: eat early in the morning, and he ate; and all in the monastery glorified him because of his obedience. Provoked by envy, his brother, the ascetic, resolved: I will test him to see whether he has obedience. And coming to the father, he said: send my brother with me to go to such-and-such a place. The abba let him go. Coming to a river in which there were many crocodiles, he said to him: go down into the river and cross it. He went down; the crocodiles came, rubbed against his body, but did not harm him. Seeing this, the brother said to him: come out of the river now. Going further, they saw a body lying on the road, and the ascetic said: if we had some rag, we would place it upon him. But the one having obedience said: let us rather pray, perhaps he will rise. They stood in prayer, and while they prayed, the dead man rose. The ascetic boasted that this had happened because of his asceticism, but God revealed to the father of the monastery both how he had tempted his brother with the crocodiles and how the dead man had risen. When they came to the monastery, the abba said to the ascetic: why did you treat your brother so? For it was because of his obedience that the dead man rose.

33. A certain brother who had three sons in the world came to a monastery, leaving them in the city, but did not reveal to the abba about the children. After three years of dwelling in the monastery, thoughts began to bring his children to his memory, and he grieved greatly over them. The abba, seeing him in sorrow, asked him: what is the matter with you? Why are you so sad? Then he told him: I have three sons in the city, and I wish to bring them to the monastery. The abba agreed. Coming to the city, he found two of his sons had reposed, and with the third he came to the monastery. Seeking the abba, he found him in the bakery. The abba, seeing him,

kissed him, then, taking the child, stroked him, embraced him, and also kissed him. Then he asked the father: do you love him? He answered: I love him. Again he asked: do you love him very much? He answered: very much. Hearing the answer, the abba said: take him and throw him into the furnace, that he may be burned. The father took his child and threw him into the furnace, but the flame immediately became dew. And this brother was glorified like the patriarch Abraham.

34. An elder said: brethren! The Lord established as the beginning for His disciples affliction and narrowness, but the one who flees from the beginning removes himself from the knowledge of God. Just as letters constitute the beginning of learning for children, guiding them to the knowledge of the sciences, so too the monk only in labors and afflictions, having obedience, becomes a co-heir with God and a son of God.

35. An elder said: God requires of Christians that everyone should listen to the divine Scriptures and should fulfill by deed what he reads, obeying the superiors and the Orthodox fathers.

36. A brother, having been offended by someone, came to a certain elder in his cell and said to him: Father! I am grieving. The elder asked him: why? He answered: a certain brother offended me, and the demon disturbs me, prompting me to take revenge on him. The elder said to him: listen to me, my son, and God will deliver you from this passion. Go to your cell and, being still, pray diligently to God for the brother who offended you. He did as the elder told him, and in one week God took away the anger from him because of the force he did to himself and because of his obedience to the elder.

37. A certain brother who was in obedience for God's sake to a spiritual and holy elder said to him: Father! Scripture says that *we must through many tribulations enter the kingdom of God*, yet I see that I have no tribulation whatsoever. What should I do? Lest I lose my soul? When he said this, the elder answered him: do not grieve over this; it is not your concern. Everyone who gives himself over in obedience to the fathers should be without care and at rest.

38. A certain elder had a disciple who possessed great obedience: whatever the elder told him, he accepted with joy and faith and obeyed him diligently in all things. When he needed clothing, the elder gave him material, and he sewed from it a handsome garment with great adornment. Upon completion of the work, the elder called him to himself and asked: child! Have you sewn that garment? He answered: I have sewn it, father, and adorned it well. He said to him: go, give it to such-and-such a brother or to such-and-such a sick person. He went and gave it with readiness. Then the elder gave him other material, and similarly, after the garment was sewn and adorned, he said to him: give it, child, to such-and-such a brother. He immediately gave it with readiness, never grieved and never murmured, saying: here I labor, I sew and adorn, and he takes it and gives it to another, but every good work, as soon as he heard it, he performed with readiness. And if ever he asked the elder about some thought, he accepted what he heard from him with such conviction and faith and kept it so faithfully that he never asked the elder a second time about the same thought.

Chapter XV. On Humility

1. Abba Anthony, once peering into the depth of the judgments of God, prayed thus: Lord! Why do some die without living long, while others grow old? Why are some poor, while others are rich? Why are the unrighteous rich, while the righteous are poor? And a voice came to him, saying: Anthony! Attend to yourself, for those are the judgments of God, and it is not profitable for you to know them.

2. Abba Anthony said to Abba Poemen: this is the great work of a man, to lay his sin upon himself before the face of God and to expect temptation until his last breath.

3. He also said: no one can enter into the kingdom of heaven without temptation, for without temptations, no one would be saved.

4. He also said: I saw all the snares of the enemy, spread out upon the earth, and, sighing, I said: who then can pass through them? And I heard a voice saying to me: humility.

5. Once the elders came to Abba Anthony, and Abba Joseph was with them. The elder, wishing to test them, proposed a saying from Scripture and began asking, starting with the youngest: what does this saying mean? Each one spoke according to his ability, and to each one the elder said: no, you have not hit upon it. After all, he asked Abba Joseph: what do you say about this word? He answered: I do not know. Abba Anthony said: truly, Abba Joseph has found the way, because he said: I do not know.

6. Certain three of the fathers had the custom of coming to Abba Anthony every year. Two of them would ask him about their thoughts and the salvation of the soul, but one was always silent, asking nothing. After quite a long time, Abba Anthony said to him: behold, for so long you have been coming here and you ask me nothing? He said in reply: for me it is enough to see you, father.

7. Once demons came upon Abba Arsenius and troubled him. Those who attended him, coming to him and standing outside the cell, heard him crying out to God, saying: O God! Do not forsake me! I have done nothing good before Thee, but grant me, according to Thy grace, to make a beginning!

8. They said of him that, just as no one at court wore clothing better than his, so in the church no one dressed worse than he.

9. Someone said to blessed Arsenius: how is it that we, with such wisdom and such learning, have nothing, while these wild simpletons and Egyptians have acquired such virtues? Abba Arsenius said to him: we from worldly learning have nothing, while these simpletons and Egyptians have acquired virtues through their labors.

10. Once Abba Arsenius was asking an Egyptian elder about his thoughts. Another, seeing this, asked: Abba Arsenius, how is it that you, being versed in Roman and Hellenic learning, are asking this simpleton about your thoughts? He answered him: the Roman and Hellenic learning I know, but the alphabet of this simpleton I have not yet learned.

11. Abba Arsenius said: a monk is a stranger, therefore, as in a foreign land, let him not meddle in anything and he will find rest.

12. The elders used to say that once in Scetis some small figs were distributed, and, as they were of no value, they did not send any to Abba Arsenius, lest he be offended. The elder, hearing of it, did not go to the assembly, saying: you have excommunicated me by not giving me the blessing that God sent to the brethren, which I was not deemed worthy to receive. Hearing of this, all benefited from the elder's humility, and the presbyter brought him figs and led him to the assembly with joy.

13. Abba Daniel used to say: once certain fathers came from Alexandria to see Abba Arsenius. One of them was the uncle of the elder Timothy, Archbishop of Alexandria, who was called the non-acquisitive, and he had with him one of his brother's sons. The elder was then ill and did not wish to meet with them, lest others also come and begin to trouble him. And they returned in sorrow. At that time he was dwelling at Petra of Upper Troy, but when there happened to be an attack by barbarians, Abba Arsenius departed and was dwelling in the lower regions. Hearing of this, they again came to see him, and he received them with joy. One of the brethren who was with them said to him: do you know, abba, that we came to visit you in Troy, and you did not receive us? The elder said: you ate bread and drank water, but I, truly, child, chastising myself, did not taste either bread or water until I learned that you had reached your place, for on my account you had taken up the labor. But forgive me, brethren. And, being comforted, they departed.

14. They used to say of Abba Arsenius that once in Scetis, when he was ill, the presbyter went and, bringing him to the church, laid him on a bed with a small pillow under his head. And behold, one of the elders, coming to visit him and seeing him on the bed and the pillow under him, was scandalized, saying: is this Abba Arsenius? And on such a thing does he lie? The presbyter, taking him aside, asked: what occupation did you have in your village? He answered: I was a shepherd. How, he said, did you spend your life? He said: I spent it in great need. And how do you now live in your cell? He answered: now I have more rest. Then the presbyter said to him: do you see this Abba Arsenius? When he was in the world, he was the father of emperors, and thousands of servants with golden belts and necklaces, all in silk, attended him. He had costly beds. You, being a shepherd, did not have in the world such comfort as you have now, but he does not have here the consolation that he had in the world. And so now you have rest, while he endures need. Hearing this, the other came to

compunction and, making a prostration, said: forgive me, abba! I have sinned. Truly, this is the true way, for he came to humility, but I to comfort! Thus, having received benefit, the elder departed.

15. Abba Daniel said that Abba Arsenius, drawing near to his end, gave us this command: do not be concerned to make a love-feast over me, for if I have prepared such a feast for myself, I shall find it.

16. When Abba Arsenius drew near to his end, his disciples became troubled. He said to them: the hour has not yet come; but when the hour comes, I will tell you. I will be judged with you before the dread judgment seat if you give my remains to anyone. They asked: what then shall we do, for we do not know how to bury you? The elder answered them: do you not know how? Tie a rope to my foot and drag me to the mountain. The elder's usual saying was this: Arsenius! For what purpose did you come forth from the world? If you speak, you will often repent; but if you are silent, never. When he drew near to his end, the brethren, seeing that he was weeping, asked him: surely even you are afraid, father? He answered them: truly, the fear that is with me at this hour has always been with me from the time I became a monk. And the elder reposed. Abba Poemen, hearing that he had reposed, shed tears and said: blessed are you, Abba Arsenius, that you wept over yourself in this world, for he who does not weep over himself here will weep eternally there. Therefore, whether here voluntarily, or there from torments, it is impossible not to weep.

17. Abba Daniel used to say that Abba Arsenius never wished to speak when asked anything from Scripture, though he could have if he had wished; likewise, he never wrote letters. When from time to time he came to church, he would sit behind a pillar, so that no one would see his face and he would not see the face of another. His appearance was angelic, like Jacob: he was all gray-haired, well-built in body, but thin; his beard was long, reaching to his waist; his eyelashes had fallen out from tears; he was tall, but bent from old age, and was ninety years of age. At the court of Theodosius the Great of blessed memory, he spent forty years and was the father of the most divine Arcadius and Honorius; he also spent forty years in Scetis; ten in Troy of upper Babylon, opposite Memphis; three years in Alexandrian Canopus, and for the last two years he came again to Canopus and there reposed, having completed his course in peace and the fear of God, *for he was a good man, full of the Holy Spirit and of faith* (Acts 11:24). To me he left his leather tunic, his white hairshirt, and his palm sandals, and I, unworthy, wore them for a blessing.

18. Abba Daniel also related of Abba Arsenius: once he called my fathers, Abba Alexander and Abba Zoilus, and, humbling himself, said to them: demons are warring against me, and I do not know whether they may have robbed me during sleep. Labor with me this night and watch over me, lest I doze during the vigil. They sat down, one on his right hand and one on his left, from evening, in silence. Afterward my fathers said: we fell asleep and, waking, did not know whether he had dozed. Toward morning, however (God knows whether he did it deliberately, so that we would think he had slept, or whether nature actually

inclined him to sleep), he sighed three times and, rising, said: I slept, did I not? We said in reply: we do not know.

19. Abba Agathon, drawing near to his end, remained three days with his eyes open and unmoving. The brethren, touching him, asked: Abba Agathon, where are you? He answered them: I stand before the judgment seat of God. They said to him: and are you afraid, father? He said to them: according to my strength I strove to keep the commandments of God, but I am a man, and do I know whether my work is pleasing to God? The brethren said to him: are you not confident that your work was according to God? The elder answered: I dare not think this until I stand before God, for the judgment of God is one thing and that of men another. When they wished to ask him another word, he said to them: do me a kindness, do not speak with me now, for I am not at leisure. And he reposed in joy, for they saw him depart with such an expression as one who is greeting his friends and beloved.

20. They used to say of Abba Ammon that certain ones came to be judged by him, but the elder pretended to be foolish. And behold, a woman was standing near him and said: this elder is a fool. Hearing this, the elder called her to him and said: how many labors have I expended in the deserts to acquire this foolishness, and am I to lose it today because of you!

21. They asked Abba Ammon: what path is the narrow and sorrowful path? He answered: the narrow and sorrowful path is to force one's thoughts and to cut off one's desires for the sake of God. This is what it means: *"See, we have left all and followed You"* (Matthew 19:27).

22. Abba Poemen used to say: a brother came to Abba Ammon and said to him: abba, tell me a word! He stayed with him seven days, and the elder did not answer him. Then, seeing him off, he said to him: go, attend to yourself, for my sins have become a dark wall between me and God.

23. Abba John related that Abba Anub, Abba Poemen, and the rest of their brethren, being brothers by birth and monks in Scetis, when the Mazices came and laid it waste, first withdrew from there to a place called Terenuthis, until they might find where to dwell, and stayed there several days in an ancient temple. Abba Anub said to Abba Poemen: do me a kindness, you and your brethren: let each one this week keep silence separately, not seeing one another. Abba Poemen answered: let us do as you wish. And they did so. In that temple there was a stone statue. The elder, Abba Anub, rising in the morning, would throw stones at the face of the statue, and in the evening would say to it: forgive me. Thus he did all week. On Saturday, when they came together, Abba Poemen said to Abba Anub: I saw, abba, that all week you threw stones at the face of the statue and then made a prostration to it. Does a faithful man do this? The elder answered: this deed I did for your sake. When you saw me throwing stones at the face of the statue, did it speak or become angry? Abba Poemen said: no. And again, when I made a prostration, was it irritated or did it speak? Abba Poemen said: no. Let us then do likewise. We are seven brethren. If you wish to remain all together, let us be like this statue, which, whether it is reviled or praised, is never disturbed. But if you do not wish to be thus, behold, there are four gates in this temple: let each of you go wherever he wishes. They all fell to the ground and said to Abba Anub: let us do, father, as you wish, and

let us listen as you tell us. And Abba Poemen used to say: we remained together during the time of our life, acting according to the word of the elder that he spoke to us. He appointed one of us as steward, and whatever he set before us, we ate, and no one of us could say: bring me something else, or: we want to eat such-and-such. Thus we spent all the time of our life in quietness and peace.

24. Abba Alonius said: if I had not destroyed everything, I could not have built myself up.

25. They related of the bishop of Oxyrhynchus, named Aphthus: when he was a monk, he performed many strict ascetic labors; but when he became a bishop, he wished to use the same strictness even in the world, but was not able to do so. Then he cast himself down before God, saying: has grace departed from me because of the episcopacy? And it was revealed to him: no, but there was the desert, and since there was no man, God helped you; but here is the world, and men help you.

26. Blessed Gregory the Theologian said: in what manner can we plunge into saving humility, having forsaken the disastrous puffing-up of pride? When we strive for it in every way and neglect nothing, as if not fearing any harm to ourselves thereby. For the soul becomes like its occupations, and is imprinted and transformed by what it does. Therefore let your appearance, and clothing, and gait, and sitting, and food, and standing, and bed, all be marked by poverty; likewise your psalm-singing, and song, and piety before your neighbor, let these also be directed toward poverty, and not toward arrogance. Do not thunder with sophistic words, nor with overly sweet-voiced songs, nor with proud and lofty discourses, but in everything cast off grandeur. Be quiet with friends, kind to petitioners, loving toward the poor, comforting to those who suffer misfortune, caring for those in sorrow, completely disdaining no one, gentle in admonition, gracious in reply, ready for everything, accessible in everything.

27. Abba Daniel used to say that in Babylon the daughter of one of the leading men was possessed by a demon. Her father had a beloved monk who said to him: no one can heal your daughter except certain hermits whom I know. But if you ask them directly, they will not agree because of humility. Let us rather do this: when they come to the market, pretend that you wish to buy their handiwork from them, and when they come to receive the price for it, we will ask them to make a prayer, and I believe that she will be healed. So they went out to the market, found a disciple of those elders sitting there to sell their wares, took him with the baskets, and brought him to their house to receive the price for them. When the monk entered the house, the demoniac came up and struck him on the cheek, but he turned to her the other, according to the commandment of the Lord. The demon, tormented by this, cried out: O compulsion and violence! The commandment of the Lord is driving me out. And the maiden was cleansed at once. When the elders came, they were told what had happened, and they glorified God and said: it is customary for the pride of the devil to fall before the humility of the commandment of Christ.

28. Abba Epiphanius said: the Canaanite woman cries out and is heard (Matthew 15:22); the woman with the issue of blood is silent and is blessed (Matthew 9:22); the Pharisee cries out and is condemned; the publican does not open his mouth and is heard (Luke 18:10–14).

29. Abba Evagrius said: the beginning of salvation is self-condemnation.

30. There was once an assembly in The Cells on some matter. Abba Evagrius began to speak, but the presbyter said to him: we know, abba, that if you were in your own country, you would long ago have been a bishop and head of many, but now you sit here as a stranger. He apologized but was not troubled and, shaking his head, said to him: truly so, father, but *once I have spoken, I will not speak again* (Job 40:5).

31. Abba Carion said: the labor of my ascetic struggles is much greater than that of my son Zacharias, but I have not attained to his measure in humility and silence.

32. A certain brother, an Egyptian, came to Abba Zeno in Syria and complained to the elder about his thoughts. The elder said in amazement: the Egyptians conceal the virtues they have, but always accuse themselves of sins they do not have. But the Syrians and Greeks claim for themselves virtues they do not have, and conceal the sins they do have.

33. They used to say that in a certain village someone fasted so much that he was nicknamed "the Faster." Having heard of him, Abba Zeno called him to himself, and he came to him with joy. After they had prayed, they sat down. The elder began to work in silence, but the faster, finding nothing to talk about, began to feel greatly oppressed and finally said to the elder: pray for me, abba! I want to go home. Why? asked the elder. He answered: my heart is as if on fire, and I do not know what is happening to it. When I was in the village, I fasted until evening, and nothing like this ever happened to me. The elder said to him: in the village you were fed through the ears, but now go, and from this time take food at the ninth hour, and whatever you do, do it in secret. When the faster began to do so, he would wait for the ninth hour with difficulty. Those who knew his rule said: truly, he is possessed by a demon. When he came to the elder and told him everything, he answered: such a path is pleasing to God.

34. Abba Moses once said to Brother Zacharias: tell me what to do. Hearing this, he fell down to his feet and said: are you asking me, father? The elder answered him: believe me, child Zacharias, I saw the Holy Spirit descending upon you, and this compels me to ask you. Then Zacharias, taking the cowl from his head, placed it under his feet and, trampling on it, said: if a man is not thus crushed, he cannot be a monk.

35. Once Abba Zacharias, living in Scetis, came into a state of contemplation. He revealed it to his elder, Abba Carion. The elder, though a doer, was not skilled in this regard and, rising, struck him, saying: this is from demons. Meanwhile the thought remained with him, and coming by night to Abba Poemen, he revealed to him about this matter and about how his inner being burned. The elder, seeing that this was from God, said to him: go to such-and-such an elder and do whatever he tells you. When he came to that elder, the elder,

before the other asked him anything, told him everything and that his vision was from God, but then added: go and submit to your father.

36. Abba Poemen used to say that Abba Moses asked Abba Zacharias, when he was drawing near to his end: what do you see? He said to him: is it not better to be silent, father? The other said: indeed, child, be silent. At the very hour of his death, Abba Isidore, sitting beside him, looked up to heaven and said: rejoice, my child Zacharias, for the gates of the kingdom of heaven have been opened to you.

37. Abba Isaiah said: love of human glory gives birth to falsehood, but turning away from it strengthens the fear of God in the heart. Do not be a friend of the glorious of the world, lest the glory of God be taken from you.

38. He also said: when performing your rule, if you perform it in humility, as one unworthy, it is accepted by God; but if something of pride rises in your heart and you consent to it, or you remember someone else who is sleeping or negligent and condemn anyone, know that your labor is fruitless.

39. He also said of the humble man that he has no tongue to speak of anyone as negligent, or to contradict anyone burdening or oppressing him; nor does he have eyes to notice the sins of another or to look at him with contempt; nor does he have ears to hear what is unprofitable for his soul; nor does he have a mouth to reveal the sins of another or to censure anyone; nor does he have any concern with anything except his own sins. But he is at peace with all according to the commandment of the Lord, and not from any other attachment, for even if someone fasts for six days at a time and gives himself to great labors, but apart from the path of humility, all his labors are in vain.

40. He also said: he who has acquired humility knows his sins. And if weeping also accompanies humility, and both remain with someone, they will cast out from his soul every demonic thought and will nourish his soul from their own value and from the holy virtues. He who has weeping and humility does not care about human reproach, for they constitute his full armor, preserve him from anger and vengeance, and teach him to bear everything that befalls him. What insult or anger can approach one who weeps over his sins before God?!

41. He also said: casting oneself down before God with understanding and submission to the commandments in humility give birth to love, and love gives birth to dispassion.

42. They asked Abba Isaiah what humility is, and he said: humility is to consider oneself the most sinful of all men and to abase oneself before God, knowing that one has done nothing good for Him. And the works of humility are these: to be silent, not to measure oneself in anything, not to argue, to obey, to keep one's eyes downcast, to have death before one's eyes, not to lie, not to speak idly, not to contradict an elder, not to insist on one's own will, to bear reproach, to hate comfort, to compel oneself to every work, to be sober, to cut off one's own will, to offend no one, to envy no one.

43. He also said: use your strength to be unlearned, so that you may be occupied with weeping, and take care with all your strength not to argue about the faith and not to dogmatize, but follow the universal Church, for no one can comprehend the Godhead.

44. He also said: he who has acquired humility ascribes the reproach of his brother to himself, saying: I have erred; but he who despises his brother thinks that he is wise and has not wounded anyone. He who has the fear of God takes care concerning the virtues, whether even one has escaped him somewhere.

45. He also said: let your tongue not speak, but let your deed be your word. Humility is above deed; do not speak otherwise than according to conscience, and do not teach without humility, that the earth may receive your seed.

46. He also said: it is not wisdom to speak, but it is wisdom to know the time when one should speak and answer what is due. Be unknowing though having knowledge, that you may escape many labors, for he draws labors upon himself who declares himself to be knowledgeable. Do not boast of your knowledge, for no one knows anything. The end of all things is to reproach oneself and to place oneself below one's neighbor in cleaving to the Godhead.

47. Abba Isaiah said of humility: let us remember Him Who had nowhere to lay His head. Consider, O man, what your Master became for your sake: a Stranger, having no dwelling place, and do not be high-minded. O Thine ineffable love for mankind, Lord, that for me, a creature, Thou didst so humble Thyself! He Who made all things by a word has nowhere to lay His head! So why do you, a lowly man, fret about buildings? Why are you blind in insatiability? Why do you put on airs? Why do you not gather and treasure up the wealth laid up there? *Test all things; hold fast what is good* (1 Thessalonians 5:21).

48. It once happened that Abba Theodore was with the brethren. When they were eating, they took the cups in silence out of reverence and did not say: forgive. Abba Theodore said: the monks have lost their piety, to say: forgive.

49. A brother asked Abba Theodore: I want to fulfill the commandments. The elder answered him: Abba Theona also once said: I want to fulfill my thought with God's help. Then, taking flour, he went to the bakery and prepared loaves. The poor asked, and he gave them the loaves; others asked, and he gave them the basket and the garment he was wearing, and he came to the cell girded only with his cloak. In spite of all this, he reproached himself, saying: I have not fulfilled the commandment of God.

50. A brother said to Abba Theodore: tell me a word, for I am perishing. With difficulty he said to him: I too am in danger. What then am I to say to you?

51. They used to say of Abba Theodore that, when he was ordained a deacon in Scetis, he did not wish to take up the diaconate and fled to various places. The elders brought him back and said: do not abandon your diaconate! Abba Theodore said to them: leave me. I will pray to God, whether He will assure me that I must stand in my place of service. Praying to

God, he said: if it is Thy will that I stand in my place, then assure me. And a pillar of fire was shown to him from earth to heaven, and a voice was heard saying: if you can be like this pillar, go and serve as a deacon. Hearing this, he resolved in no way to consent. When he came to the church, the brethren, making a prostration to him, said: if you do not wish to serve as a deacon, at least hold the chalice. But he did not consent even to this, saying: if you do not leave me, I will depart from this place. And they left him.

52. The blessed Archbishop Theophilus once visited Mount Nitria. The abba of that mountain came to him, and the archbishop asked him: what have you found on this path, father? The elder answered: to always accuse and condemn myself. Abba Theophilus said to him: there is no other path than this.

53. The same Archbishop Theophilus once visited Scetis. The brethren who had gathered asked Abba Pambo: say a word to the Pope for his benefit. The elder said to them: if he is not benefited by my silence, neither will he be benefited by my word.

54. Mother Theodora used to say that it is not asceticism, nor vigil, nor any other labor that saves us, but only sincere humility. For a certain hermit who drove out demons once asked them: by what are you driven out? By fasting? They said: we neither eat nor drink. By vigil? They said: we do not sleep. By living in the desert? They answered: we live in the deserts. So then, by what are you driven out? They said: nothing conquers us except humility. You see, humility is the conqueror of demons.

55. They used to say of Abba John Colobos that once he said to his elder brother: I would wish to be without care, as the angels are without care, doing no work, but serving God unceasingly. Having taken off his garment, he went into the desert, but after spending a week there, he returned to his brother. When he knocked at the door, his brother responded and, without opening the door, asked: who are you? He answered: I am John, your brother. The other said: John has become an angel, and he is no longer among men. He begged him, saying: it is I, but the other did not open to him and left him to grieve until morning. Finally, opening to him, he said: you are a man and have need to work in order to feed yourself. Then, making a prostration, the brother said: forgive me.

56. Abba John, hearing at the harvest that a brother was speaking to his neighbor with anger: hey, you!, left the harvest and ran away.

57. Abba John said that humility is the door of heaven, and our fathers, through much reproach, rejoicing, entered through it into the city of God.

58. He also said: humility and the fear of God are above all virtues.

59. He also said: who sold Joseph? One brother answered: his brothers. The elder said to him: no, but his humility sold him. For he could have said: I am your brother; he could have contradicted, but in silence, by humility, he sold himself. And humility made him a ruler in Egypt.

60. Abba John said: having left the light burden, that is, to condemn oneself, we have taken upon ourselves the heavy one, that is, to justify oneself.

61. He, sitting once in the church, sighed, not knowing that someone was behind him. But learning of it, he made a prostration, saying: forgive me, abba! For I am not yet catechized.

62. He also said to his brother: though we may be utterly despised before the face of men, let us yet rejoice that we may be honored before the face of God.

63. He was fervent in spirit (Romans 12:11). Someone, coming to him, praised his work, and he was working at plaiting, but Abba John was silent. The other again said the same word to him, but he still was silent. But the third time he said to the brother who had come: as soon as you came in here, you drove God away from me.

64. He was once sitting in Scetis, and the brethren surrounded him, asking about their thoughts. One of the elders said to him: John! You are like a harlot who adorns herself and multiplies her lovers. Abba John, interrupting him, said: you speak the truth, father! After this, one of his disciples asked him: were you not inwardly troubled, abba? He answered: no, for as I am outwardly, so I am inwardly.

65. One of the fathers said of him: who is John? By his humility he has hung the whole of Scetis on his little finger.

66. Abba John Colobos used to say that a certain spiritual elder, a recluse, was renowned in the city and had great fame. It was revealed to him that a certain one of the saints was about to be released from the body and that he needed to go and give him a kiss before he reposed. He thought to himself: if I go by day, people will run after me, and there will be great glory for me, but I take no delight in this. So I will go in the evening in the dark and hide from everyone. Thus he went out of his cell in the evening, wishing to hide; but behold, from God two angels are sent with lamps to light his way, and the whole city came running, seeing his glory. Thus, the more he thought to flee glory, the more he was glorified. By this was fulfilled what is written: *everyone who exalts himself will be humbled, and he who humbles himself will be exalted* (Luke 14:11).

67. Abba John of Thebes said: a monk before all virtues must acquire humility, for it is the first commandment of the Savior, Who says: *"Blessed are the poor in spirit, for theirs is the kingdom of heaven"* (Matthew 5:3).

68. Abba Poemen said of Abba Isidore that he would plait a bundle of palm leaves every night. The brethren asked him: relax a little, for you have already grown old. He said to them: if they burn Isidore and scatter his ashes to the wind, even then I will not have deserved any mercy, because the Son of God came here for our sake.

69. He also used to say of Abba Isidore that his thoughts would say to him: you are a great man! But he would answer them: am I then equal to Abba Anthony, or have I become altogether like Abba Pambo and the other fathers who were pleasing to God? Bringing this to his remembrance, he would find rest. But when the enemies would lead him to

despondency, saying: because of this you are to be cast into torment, he would answer them: even if I am cast into torment, I will find all of you beneath me.

70. He also said: since the height of humility is great and the depth of pride's fall is deep, I counsel you to embrace the one lovingly and not to fall into the other.

71. Abba Isaac used to say: when I was younger, I lived with Abba Cronius, and he never ordered me to do anything, although he was old and already trembled, but he himself would rise and hand the cup of water to me and to everyone else. I also lived with Abba Theodore of Pherme, and he likewise never ordered me to do anything, but he himself would set the table and say: brother, if you wish, come and eat. I would say to him: abba, abba! I came to receive benefit, so why do you not tell me to do something? But he kept silent. I went and told the elders. The elders came to him and said: abba! The brother came to your holiness to receive benefit. Why then do you not tell him to do something? The elder answered them: am I a cenobiarch, that I should command him? I tell him nothing, but what he sees me doing, let him do also. From then on I would anticipate the elder and do it myself, if I saw that the elder wished to do something. And he, whatever he did, did in silence. This also taught me to do things in silence.

72. Abba Isaac said: I never brought into my cell a thought against a brother who had offended me, and I myself tried not to leave a brother in his cell having a thought against me.

73. Abba James said that one who is praised should think of his sins and consider that he is unworthy of what they say about him.

74. A brother asked Abba Cronius: by what means does a man come to humility? The elder answered: by the fear of God. The brother said to him: and how does he come to the fear of God? The elder said: in my opinion, he needs to renounce everything, give himself over to bodily labor, and, as much as he is able, remember the departure from the body and the judgment of God.

75. Abba John of Thebes said: a monk before all else must acquire humility, for this is the first commandment of the Savior. *"Blessed are the poor in spirit,"* He says, *"for theirs is the kingdom of heaven"* (Matthew 5:3).

76. Abba Cronius said that Abba Joseph of Pelusium told them: when I was living on Sinai, there was a certain brother there, good and living ascetically, but also comely in body. He would go to church for the services wearing only a patched and worn small cloak. Once, seeing him going thus to the assembly, I said to him: brother! Do you not see that the brethren are like angels in church at the services? How is it that you always come here dressed like this? He said: forgive me, abba! I have no other garment. I took him to my cell and gave him a tunic and everything he needed. Then he began to dress like the rest of the brethren and was in appearance like an angel. Once it was necessary to send ten brethren to the emperor on some matter, and among those departing they appointed him as well. Hearing of this, he made a prostration to the fathers and said: for the Lord's sake, forgive me. I am a slave of a certain great man there, and if he recognizes me, he will strip me of the schema and make me serve

him again. The fathers believed him and left him behind. But later, from a man who knew him well, they heard that in the world he had been a prefect of the praetorium and had invented such a pretext so as not to be recognized and not to find trouble from men. Such was the zeal of the fathers to flee the glory and comforts of this world.

77. In Scetis there was a monk named Abba Carion, who had two children whom he left with his wife and withdrew. After some time, a famine came upon Egypt, and his wife, pressed by need, came to Scetis, bringing with her also the two children, a son named Zacharias and a daughter, and she sat at a distance from the elder by the lake, for a lake adjoined Scetis, where churches were built and there were springs of water. It was the custom in Scetis: if a woman came to speak with her brother or with someone else of whom she had need, they would converse sitting far from one another. The wife said to Abba Carion: behold, you have become a monk, yet there is famine among us. Who then will feed your children? Abba Carion said to her: send them here to me. The wife said to the children: go to your father! They went, but the girl returned again to her mother, while the boy came to his father. Then he said to her: see, it has turned out well. You take the girl and go, and I will take the boy. Thus he raised him in Scetis, and everyone knew that this was his son, but when he grew up, murmuring arose in the brotherhood because of him. Hearing of this, Abba Carion said to his son: let us leave here, because the fathers are murmuring. The boy said to him: abba! Everyone here knows that I am your son, but if we move to another place, they will not call me your son there. He said to him: let us go to the Thebaid, and they went there, but as soon as they had taken a cell there and lived several days, the same murmuring arose there because of the youth. The father said to him: Zacharias! Let us go to Scetis. But here too, after a few days, they began again to murmur because of him. Then Zacharias, the youth, went to the Nitrian natron lake, undressed, entered it, and submerged himself up to his very nose. Having remained in it for quite a long time, as long as he could, he ruined his body and became like a leper. Coming out of it and putting on his clothes, he came to his father, who barely recognized him. When afterward, as usual, he came to Holy Communion, the holy Isidore, the presbyter of Scetis, to whom it had been revealed what he had done, seeing him, marveled and said: Zacharias, the youth, last Sunday came and communed as a man, but now he has become an angel.

78. Once the fathers of Scetis, having gathered, were discussing Melchizedek, having forgotten to invite Abba Copres, but afterward they invited him also and asked about this. He, striking himself on the mouth three times, said: woe to you, Copres; woe to you, Copres; woe to you, Copres! Why have you left that which God commanded you to do and are investigating that which He does not require of you? Hearing this, the brethren fled to their cells.

79. They asked Abba Longinus: what virtue is higher, father? The elder said: I think that just as pride is worse than all, so that it even cast one down from the very heavens, so also humility is able to raise a man up from the very abysses, even if he were sinful as a demon. For this reason the Lord also blesses the poor in spirit (Matthew 5:3).

80. He also said: just as a dead man does not eat, so a humble man cannot condemn a person, even if he were to see him worshiping idols.

81. Abba Macarius related about himself: when I was young and living in a cell in Egypt, they took me and wanted to make me a cleric in the village. Not wishing to accept this upon myself, I fled to another place. A certain pious layman used to come to me, take my handiwork, and provide for my needs. It happened through temptation that a certain maiden in the village fell and conceived in her womb. They asked her who had done this to her, and she said: the hermit. Then they came and took me to the village, hung sooty pots and handles of jugs around my neck, and led me around the village with noise, beating me on both sides, saying: this monk has defiled our maiden; take him, take him! And they beat me almost to death. One of the elders, approaching, said: how much are you going to beat this stranger monk?! And he who provided for my needs followed behind in shame, for they also greatly reviled him, saying: look what the monk has done, about whom you testified! Then her parents said: we will not let him go until he gives a surety that he will feed her. I asked my attendant, and he stood surety for me. Coming to my cell, I gave him all the baskets I had, saying: sell these and give them to my wife for her sustenance. Then I said to my thought: Macarius! Behold, you have found yourself a wife; you need to work a little more to feed her. Thus I worked day and night and sent to her. When the time came for that wretched one to give birth, she labored many days and could not deliver. And when they asked her what this meant, she said: it is because I slandered the hermit and falsely accused him. He is not guilty, but such-and-such a young man is guilty. Then he who served me came and told me with joy: that maiden could not give birth until she confessed that she had slandered you, and you are not guilty. And behold, the whole village wants to come here with honor and ask your forgiveness. Hearing of this, lest people trouble me, I fled to Scetis. And this is the first reason why I came here.

82. Abba Peter said: since Abba Macarius treated all the brethren with guilelessness, some of them asked him: why do you conduct yourself this way? He said: for twelve years I labored for my Lord, that He might grant me this grace, and all of you advise me to abandon it!

83. Once Abba Macarius was walking from the lake to his cell, carrying palm leaves. On the way the devil met him with a great curved knife and wanted to strike him, but could not. Then he said: great is the violence I suffer from you, Macarius! I am not able to prevail against you! Everything that you do, I do also: you fast, and I do too; you keep vigil, and I do not sleep at all. There is only one thing by which you overcome me. Abba Macarius asked: what is that? He answered: your humility, and therefore I am not able to prevail against you.

84. Once Abba Macarius went to Abba Anthony and, having conversed with him, was returning to Scetis. The fathers came out to meet him, and, while they were talking, the elder said to them: I said to Abba Anthony that we do not have the Offering in our place. The fathers began to speak about something else and did not ask about the elder's answer, and Abba Macarius did not tell them. Concerning this one of the fathers said: when the fathers see that the brethren forget to ask about a matter profitable to them, the elders compel

themselves to say the beginning of the word, but if they are not further pressed by the brethren, they do not continue the word further, lest they appear to be speaking when not asked, and lest it be as idle talk.

85. They used to say of Abba Macarius: if a brother came to him as to a holy and great elder with fear, he would say nothing to him; but if one of the brethren spoke to him as if disdaining him: abba! When you were a camel driver and stole natron and sold it, did not the guards beat you?, to such a one the abba would answer with joy, about whatever he might ask him.

86. Once a demon appeared before Abba Macarius with a knife, intending to cut off his foot, but because of the elder's humility he had no power to do so. Then he said to him: what you have, we also have; in humility alone do you differ from us and overcome us.[16]

87. They used to say of Abba Macarius the Egyptian that once, ascending from Scetis to Mount Nitria, when he was already approaching that place, he said to his disciple: go a little ahead. When the other had gone ahead, he met a certain Hellenic priest and shouted at him: hey, hey, demon, where are you running? Then that one, turning around, beat him and left him half dead. Taking his staff and running a little further, he met Abba Macarius, who said to him: be saved, be saved, laborer! He approached him and asked: what good have you found in me, that you greeted me so? I see, said the elder, that you labor and do not know that you labor in vain. The other said to him: I came to compunction from your greeting and recognized that you are from the portion of God. But another evil monk, meeting me, reviled me, and I inflicted mortal wounds on him. The elder understood that it was his disciple, and the priest, having seized his feet, said: I will not let you go until you make me a monk. They went up to where the monk was, lifted him and brought him to the church of the mountain. The brethren, seeing the priest with him, were amazed, but, learning what had happened, made him a monk. Afterward many of the Hellenes became Christians through him. After this Abba Macarius said: a bad word makes even a good person bad, but a good word makes even a bad person good.

88. Abba Macarius said: when I was younger, I became despondent in my cell and went out into the desert, saying to my thought: whomever you meet, ask him for benefit. I met a youth pasturing oxen and said to him: what am I to do? I am hungry! He said to me: eat. I said: I have eaten, and I am still hungry. He said to me: eat again. I said again: I have eaten many times, and I am still hungry. Then he said: are you a donkey, abba, that you always want to eat? And having received benefit from that, I withdrew.

89. They used to say of Abba Moses that when they made him a cleric and put the ephod upon him,[17] the archbishop said to him: behold, you have become all white, Abba Moses! The elder answered him: only outwardly, lord pope, but do you also see within? The archbishop, wishing to test him, said to his clerics: when Abba Moses enters the sanctuary, drive him out and follow him, so that you may hear what he says. When the elder entered,

they began to revile him: go out, Ethiopian! Going out, he said to himself: they have treated you well, charcoal-skinned, black one, not a man... Why do you enter among men?

90. Abba Poemen related that a brother asked Abba Moses: how must a man die to himself for his neighbor? The elder answered him: unless a man places in his heart that he has already been three days in the grave, he will not attain to this word.

91. Abba Moses said: unless a man holds in his heart that he is a sinner, God will not hear him. A brother asked: what does it mean to hold in one's heart that he is a sinner? The elder answered: he who bears his own sins upon himself does not see the sins of his neighbor.

92. A brother asked Abba Moses: what helps a man in all his labor? The elder answered: God is the helper, for it is written: *"God is our refuge and strength, a very present help in trouble"* (Psalm 46:1). The brother asked further: the fasts and vigils that a man performs, what do they serve? The elder said: they bring the soul to humility, for it is written: *"Consider my affliction and my trouble, and forgive all my sins"* (Psalm 25:18). If the soul produces these fruits, then because of them God, Who is over it, will have mercy.

93. The brother asked again: behold, a man beats his slave for a sin that he has committed. What should the slave say? The elder answered: if the slave is good, he will say: have mercy on me, I have sinned. The brother said: and should he say nothing else? The elder answered: nothing, for as soon as he lays the guilt upon himself and says: I have sinned, his master will immediately have mercy on him.

94. Abba Matoes said: the closer a man draws to God, the more he sees himself as a sinner, for even Isaiah the prophet, seeing God, called himself wretched and unclean (Isaiah 6:5).

95. He also said: when I was younger, I used to say to myself: I too do something good. But now that I have grown old, I see that I have not a single good deed in myself.

96. A brother came to Abba Matoes and said to him: how did the Scetians do more than what is written, loving enemies more than themselves? Abba Matoes answered: but I do not even love him who loves me as much as I love myself.

97. Abba James related: I used to go to Abba Matoes, and leaving him, I told him that I wanted to visit The Cells. He asked: give my greeting to Abba John. Coming to Abba John, I said to him: Abba Matoes gives you his greeting. The elder said to me: behold, Abba Matoes is truly an Israelite, *in whom is no deceit* (John 1:47). After a year had passed, I again came to Abba Matoes and conveyed to him the greeting from Abba John. The elder said: I am unworthy of the elder's word. However, if you hear that some elder praises his neighbor as himself, know that he has attained a great measure, for it is perfection to praise one's neighbor more than oneself.

98. Once Abba Matoes came from Raithu to the region of the Magdaloi, and his brother was with him. The bishop detained the elder and ordained him a presbyter. Then, when they were together at the table, the bishop said: I know, abba, that you did not want this, but I

dared to do it so as to be blessed by you. The elder answered him with humility: my thought did somewhat desire this, but this is burdensome for me, that I must be separated from the brother who is with me, because I cannot perform all the prayers alone. The bishop said to him: if you know that he is worthy, I will ordain him too. Abba Matoes said: whether he is worthy, I do not know; I only know that he is better than I. The bishop ordained him also, but both of them reposed without approaching the altar to perform the Offering. And the elder used to say: I trust in God that there is no sin upon me for the ordination, since I do not perform the Offering, for ordination is the portion of the pure.

99. A brother asked Abba Matoes: tell me a word. And he said: go and entreat God to give weeping to your heart and humility; always attend to your own sins, do not judge others, be lower than all; also do not have friendship with a youth or acquaintance with a woman; do not have a heretic for a friend, cut off boldness from yourself; restrain your tongue and your stomach, likewise drink little wine; if someone begins to speak about something, do not argue with him, but if he speaks well, say: it is so, and if badly, say: you know what you are saying, and do not argue with him about what he says. In this consists humility.

100.   A brother asked Abba Matoes: what am I to do, for my tongue troubles me: when I come among people, I cannot restrain it, but I condemn them in every good deed and reprove them. So what am I to do? The elder answered: if you cannot restrain yourself, then flee to solitude, for this is a weakness. He who lives with brethren must be not four-cornered but round, so that he can roll toward all. Then he said: I too live in solitude not by virtue but by weakness, for strong are those who enter among people.

101.   Abba Mius used to tell of an elder who lived in Scetis, that he had been one of the slaves and became very discerning. Every year he would go to Alexandria and bring tribute to his masters. They would meet him and bow to him, but the elder would pour water into a basin and wash their feet. They would say to him: no, father, do not burden us! But he would answer them: I confess that I am your slave, and I thank you that you have allowed me to serve God freely. And I will wash your feet, and you receive this tribute of mine. They would refuse and not accept, so he said to them: if you do not wish to accept, then I will remain here and serve you. Fearing this, they would let him do what he wished and would see him off with many provisions and great honor, that he might hold love-feasts for their sake. From this he became renowned and beloved in Scetis.

102.   Abba Nilus said: blessed is the monk who considers himself the refuse compared to all others.

103.   Abba Poemen, hearing about Abba Nisterus, who lived in a coenobium, wished to see him and sent word to his abba to send Abba Nisterus to him. Not wishing to send him alone, the abba did not dispatch him, but after some time, the steward of the coenobium, having a thought, asked his abba to let him go to Abba Poemen, to reveal his thoughts to him. The abba said to him: take the brother with you, because the elder had asked that he be sent. Coming to the elder, the steward revealed his thoughts to him and was healed, and after this the elder asked Abba Nisterus: how did you acquire such a virtue, that whatever

sorrow befalls you in the coenobium, you say nothing and do not meddle in anything? Constrained by the elder's request, the brother said: forgive me, abba! When I entered this monastery, I said to my thought: you and the donkey are one and the same. Therefore, as a donkey is beaten and does not speak, as it is reviled and answers nothing, so be you also, as the Psalmist also says: *"I was like a beast before You. Nevertheless I am continually with You"* (Psalm 73:22–23).

104.   Abba Xanthias used to say: a dog is better than I, because it also has love and will not come into judgment.

105.   Abba Orsisius said: an unbaked brick placed in a foundation near a river will not last even one day, but a baked one will be like stone. So also a man who has carnal thinking and is not baked, as Joseph was, with the fear of God, crumbles as it were when he receives authority, for such have many temptations, since they are among men. Therefore it is good for one who knows his measure to flee from the burden of authority, though those firm in faith remain unshaken. And concerning the most holy Joseph himself, if anyone wished to speak, he would say that he was not of this earth. To how many temptations was he subjected? And in what land? There, where there was then not even a trace of reverence for God. But the God of his fathers was with him and delivered him from every sorrow, and now he is with his fathers in the kingdom of heaven. Likewise, let us also, knowing our measures, strive that we may escape the judgment of God.

106.   Once the local governor took someone from the village of Abba Poemen into custody. All came and asked the elder to go and free him. He said to them: leave me for three days, and then I will come. During those days Abba Poemen prayed to the Lord, saying: Lord! Do not grant me this favor, otherwise they will not let me live in this place. Then the elder came and asked the governor, but he said to him: does the abba plead for a robber?! And the elder rejoiced that he did not receive this favor from him.

107.   Abba Poemen said: a brother asked Abba Alonius, what is self-abasement, and the elder said: it is to place oneself lower than the irrational beasts, knowing that they are not subject to condemnation.

108.   Abba Joseph related: when we were sitting with Abba Poemen, he called Agathon "abba." We said to him: he is still young. Why do you call him abba? The elder answered: his mouth has made it so that he should be called abba.

109.   Abba Poemen said: we remain in many temptations because we do not keep our rank and name, as Scripture also says. Do you not see, because the Canaanite woman accepted the name given her, the Savior comforted her (Matthew 15:27). Also because Abigail said to David: *"On me, my lord, on me let this iniquity be"* (1 Samuel 25:24), he listened to her and loved her. Abigail represents the person of the soul, and David represents the Godhead. Therefore, if the soul humbles itself before the Lord, the Lord will love it.

110.   Abba Poemen said: do not measure yourself, but cleave to a man who conducts himself well.

111.	A brother asked Abba Poemen: what is the lofty? The elder answered him: a righteous deed.

112.	Abba Poemen said that Abba Paphnutius was great but fled the lesser services (the prayer rule).

113.	He also said: a brother living with brethren asked Abba Bessarion: what am I to do? The elder answered: be silent and do not measure yourself.

114.	He also said: if you abase yourself, you will have rest, wherever you may live.

115.	Abba Poemen said that if a man will accuse himself, he will stand firm everywhere.

116.	Abba Poemen said that if a man attains to the measure of this apostolic word: *"To the pure all things are pure"* (Titus 1:15), he will see himself as worse than every creature. A brother asked: how can I consider myself worse than a murderer? The elder said: if a man attains to the measure of that word and sees a man committing murder, he will say: he did this sin only once, but I murder every day.

117.	A brother asked Abba Anub about the same word, saying: what is it that Abba Poemen said? Abba Anub said to him: if a man attains to the measure of this word, then, seeing the sins of his brother, he will make his righteousness swallow them up. The brother asked: what is his righteousness? The elder answered: to always accuse oneself.

118.	A brother said to Abba Poemen: if I fall into a wretched fall, my thought devours me and reproaches me: why did you fall? The elder said to him: at whatever hour a man falls into a transgression, let him only say: I have sinned, and immediately he will find rest.

119.	They used to say of Abba Poemen that he never wished to give a word above the word of another elder, but always praised him.

120.	They used to say that when certain brethren came to Abba Poemen, he would first send them to Abba Anub, because he was older in years, but Abba Anub would say to them: go to Abba Poemen, because he has the gift of the word. But if Abba Anub sat with Abba Poemen, Abba Poemen would not speak at all in his presence.

121.	A certain brother, living outside his village and not entering it for many years, used to say to the brethren: look how many years have passed since I went to the village, yet you go there all the time. They told this to Abba Poemen, and the elder answered: I would have gone there by night and walked around the whole village, so that my thought would not boast that I had not gone to it.

122.	Abba Poemen said: for a man, humility and the fear of God are always as necessary as the breath that comes from his nostrils.

123. A brother asked Abba Poemen: how must I conduct myself in the place where I live? The elder answered him: have the mind of a stranger wherever you live; do not wish that your word have precedence, and you will find rest.

124. He also said: to cast oneself down before God, not to measure oneself, and to throw one's will behind one's back are the tools of the soul.

125. A brother asked him: what must I attend to while sitting in my cell? The elder answered him: I am a man plunged into the deep mire up to the neck, bearing a burden upon my neck and crying out to God: have mercy on me!

126. Abba Poemen said that blessed Abba Anthony said: the great dominion of man is to cast his sin upon himself before the face of the Lord and to expect temptation until his last breath.

127. He also said: with groanings all the virtues have entered this house, except for one virtue, without which it is difficult for a man to stand. They asked him: what is it? He said: to condemn oneself.

128. A brother, coming to Abba Poemen, asked him: what am I to do? The elder answered him: go and draw close to one who says: what do I desire? And you will have rest.

129. He also said that Abba Theona said: even if someone acquires a virtue by himself, God does not grant him grace, for He knows that he was not faithful, laboring by himself. But if that one goes to another for service and obedience, then He will abide with him.

130. He also said: do not fulfill your own will, for it is necessary to humble yourself before your brother instead.

131. He also said: if a man keeps his rank, he will not be disturbed.

132. He also said: if a man has seen something and has not kept it, how can he teach his neighbor?

133. He also said: a man living together with his neighbor must be like a stone pillar: when reviled, not to be angered, and when praised, not to be exalted.

134. Abba Poemen said: I say that I will be cast into that place where Satan will be cast.

135. A brother asked Abba Poemen: brethren live with me; is it good that I command them? The elder answered: no, but do the work yourself first, and if they wish to live, they will see to themselves. The brother said to him: they themselves wish that I command them. The elder answered: no, but be an example for them, not a lawgiver.

136. Abba Poemen said: if a brother comes to you and you see that there is no benefit for you from his coming, search within your mind and find out what thought you had before his coming, and you will see what the cause of the lack of benefit is. However, if you do this with humility and attention, you will be blameless before your neighbor, bearing upon

yourself the burden of your sins. If a man sits with someone in shame, that is, in sincerity, he will not fall, for God is always before his face. And as I see it, from such sitting a man acquires the fear of God.

137.   He also said: we find ourselves in such labors because we do not take part in our brother as Scripture commanded us to take part. Or do we not see how the Canaanite woman, following the Savior, cried out and entreated for the healing of her daughter, and the Savior accepted her and comforted her.

138.   Abba Poemen related: once the elders were sitting and eating, and Abba Alonius was serving them. The elders began to praise him, but he answered nothing to this. Someone asked him privately: why did you not answer the elders when they praised you? Abba Alonius said to him: if I had answered them, it would have meant that I accepted the praise.

139.   He also said: the earth upon which the Lord commanded to offer sacrifice is humility.

140.   Abba Peter related: we, seven hermits, came to Abba Sisoes when he was living in Clysma and asked him to tell us a word. He said: forgive me, I am a simple man. But I went to Abba Or, who had been ill for eighteen years, and to Abba Aphre, and made a prostration to them, that they might tell me a word. Abba Or said: what shall I say to you? Go and do what you see. God is the God of him who seeks more and more or who compels himself to everything. Abba Or and Abba Aphre were from the same country, but the peace between them was great until their very departure from the body. Abba Aphre had great obedience, and Abba Or had humility. I stayed with them for several days, observing them, and I saw a great wonder that Abba Aphre performed. Someone brought them a small fish, and Abba Aphre wanted to prepare it for the elder. He had a knife in his hand and was cutting the fish when Abba Or called him; then he left the knife in the fish without finishing cutting it. I marveled at his great obedience, that he did not say: wait until I cut the fish. I asked Abba Aphre: where did you find such obedience? He answered me: it is not mine, but the elder's. Then he said to me: go and see his obedience. Then he cooked the fish, deliberately spoiled it, and set it before the elder. He ate and said nothing. The abba asked: is it good, father? He answered: it is good. Afterward he brought him some very well-prepared fish and said: I spoiled it, father. The other answered: indeed, you spoiled it a little. Later Abba Aphre said to me: do you see what the elder's obedience is?! Thus I withdrew from them and strove with all my might to keep everything I had seen with them. This is what Abba Sisoes said. One of us asked him: do us a kindness, tell us also a word yourself! He said: he who holds to having no portion with understanding fulfills all Scripture. Another of us asked him: what is pilgrimage, father? He said: be silent and say to yourself: I have no concern with that, in every place wherever you come. And this is pilgrimage.

141.   They used to say of Abba Peter and Abba Epimachus that they lived very harmoniously in Raithu. Once, when there was a meal at the church, they were urged to go to the table of the elders, and with great difficulty only Abba Peter went there. Later, Abba

Epimachus said to him: how did you dare to go to the table of the elders? He answered: if I had sat with you, the brethren would have asked me, as an elder, to bless first, and I would have been among you as the senior. But now, having gone to the elders, I was the least of all and humbler in thought.

142.   Abba Peter said: one should not be exalted when the Lord does something through us, but rather give thanks that we were deemed worthy to be called by Him. And this, he said, is profitable to think concerning every virtue.

143.   Abba Poemen related that Abba Paphnutius said: all the days of the life of the elders, twice a month I would go to them, being twelve miles distant from them, and I would tell them every thought, but they would say nothing other to me than this: wherever you go, do not measure yourself and you will be at rest.

144.   Peter, the presbyter of Dios, when we were walking with someone, despite the fact that because of his priesthood they urged him to go ahead, would stand behind, confessing his sins, as it is written in the life of Abba Anthony. And this he did, offending no one.

145.   One of the brethren came to Abba Sisoes on the mountain of Abba Anthony and, while they were talking, asked Abba Sisoes: have you not yet attained to the measure of Abba Anthony? The elder said: if I had one of the thoughts of Abba Anthony, I would become entirely like fire. However, I know a man who with difficulty can bear his thought.

146.   A brother said to Abba Sisoes: I see that the remembrance of God always abides with me. The elder said to him: it is no great thing that your thought is always with God; what is great is to see yourself lower than every creature, for this and bodily labor lead to humility.

147.   Certain ones came to Abba Sisoes to hear a word from him, but he said nothing to them, only repeating to everything: forgive me. Seeing his baskets, they asked his disciple Abraham: what do you do with these baskets? He answered: we use them here and there. Hearing this, the elder said: Sisoes also eats from here and from there. And the brethren were greatly benefited, hearing this, and departed with joy, being edified by his humility.

148.   Three elders came to Abba Sisoes, having heard of his deeds, and the first asked him: father! How can I be delivered from the river of fire? But he did not answer him. The second said: father! How can I be delivered from the gnashing of teeth and the worm that does not sleep? The third asked: father! What am I to do, for the remembrance of the outer darkness kills me? The elder said to them in answer: I do not remember any of these things. God is merciful, and I hope that He will show me mercy. The elders, hearing his word, departed in sorrow, but the elder, not wishing to allow them to depart in sorrow, called them back and said: blessed are you, brethren! I envied you! The first of you spoke of the river of fire, the second of Tartarus, the third of darkness. If your mind possesses such remembrance, it is impossible for you to sin. What then shall I do, being hard of heart, to whom it is not

given to see even that there is torment for men, and because of this I sin every hour. Then, having repented before him, they said: as we have heard, so we see.

149.   When once Abba Sisoes came to Clysma, certain laymen came to see him. They spoke much, but the elder said not a word to them. Finally one of them said: why do you trouble the elder? He does not eat, and therefore he cannot speak. The elder answered: I eat when there is need.

150.   Once Arians came to Abba Sisoes on the mountain of Abba Anthony and began to disparage the Orthodox. The elder did not answer them anything, but, calling his disciple, said: Abraham! Bring me the book of Saint Athanasius and read it. They fell silent, and it was made manifest that they were in heresy. Then he dismissed them in peace.

151.   A brother asked Abba Sisoes of Thebes: tell me a word. He said to him: what have I to say to you? I read in the New Testament and turn aside to the Old.

152.   The same brother asked Abba Sisoes of Petra about the word that Abba Sisoes of Thebes had said. The elder answered: I lie down in sin and rise up in sin.

153.   Abba Sisoes said: seek God, but do not seek where He dwells.

154.   A brother asked Abba Sisoes: what am I to do? He answered: the work you must seek is steadfast silence and humility, for it is written: *"Blessed are all those who wait for Him"* (Isaiah 30:18). Thus you can be saved.

155.   Abba Sisoes asked a certain brother: how are you? He answered: I spend my days in vain, father. The elder said: if I also spent my days in vain, I would be grateful.

156.   A brother asked Abba Sisoes: tell me a word. He said: why do you make me speak in vain? Behold, what you see, that do.

157.   They used to say of Abba Sisoes that once, sitting, he cried out in a loud voice: O woe! His disciple asked him: what is the matter with you, father? The elder said: I seek one man to talk to and do not find him.

158.   They used to say of Abba Sisoes that when he fell ill, the elders were sitting with him, and he was speaking with someone. The elders asked him: what do you see, abba? He answered: I see that they have come for me, and I am entreating them to leave me a little to repent. One of the elders said to him: if they leave you now, can you be fit for repentance, that is, for labors? The elder said: even if I cannot labor, I will groan a little over my soul, and that is enough for me.

159.   A brother asked Abba Sisoes: what path leads to humility? The elder said to him: the path leading to humility is this: abstinence, prayer to God, and the struggle to be lower than every man.

160.   One of the fathers said: I asked Abba Sisoes: what is meant by what is said about idols in the psalm? The elder answered: concerning idols it is written: *"They have mouths, but they do not speak; eyes they have, but they do not see; they have ears, but they do not hear"* (Psalm

135:16–17). Such also must the monk be. Likewise, idols are an abomination, and he must consider himself an abomination.

161.	Abba Sarmatas said: for me, a man who has sinned, if he has known that he sinned and repented, is better than one who has not sinned and considers himself righteous.

162.	Abba Serenus said: all my time I have spent in labors: I reaped, sewed, plaited, but with all this, if the hand of God had not fed me, I could not have been fed.

163.	Mother Syncletica said: just as it is impossible to build a ship without nails, so it is impossible to be saved without humility.

164.	She also said: imitate the publican, lest you be condemned with the Pharisee, and choose the meekness of Moses, so that, having circumcised your heart, you may turn it into fountains of waters.

165.	A brother asked Abba Tithoes: tell me a word! He asked: do you have faith in me? He answered: I do. So, he said to him, go and what you see me doing, do also. The other said: what then do I see in you, father? The elder said: that my thought is lower than all men.

166.	Abba Hyperechius said: the tree of life, growing high, is humility.

167.	An elder said: he who has humility humbles the demons, but he who does not have humility is mocked by the demons.

168.	In a certain city there was a bishop who, by the action of the devil, fell into fornication. Although no one knew of his sin, once, when there was a full assembly in the church, he himself confessed his sin before all, saying: I have fallen into fornication. Then he took off his omophorion and, laying it on the altar, said: I can no longer be your bishop. Then all with weeping cried out: let your sin be upon us, only remain in the episcopate. He said to them: then make it so that I am guilty. Then he ordered the great church doors closed, fell down at the small exit from it, and said: let him have no part with God who, going out, does not trample me with his feet. At his word all did so, and when the last one was going out, there was a voice from heaven: for the sake of his great humility, I have forgiven him his sin.

169.	An elder said: not only speak humbly, but also be humble in mind, for it is impossible for you to be exalted in the works of God without humility.

170.	A certain great hermit asked: why do you so war against me, Satan? Hearing that, Satan said: because you also war fiercely against me.

171.	Two brothers according to the flesh lived together, and the devil came to separate them from one another. Once the younger brother was lighting the lamp and, turning it, by the action of the devil, overturned it. The other brother in anger beat him, but he, bowing down, said: be patient with me, brother, I will light it again. And behold, the power of God came and tormented the demon until morning. The demon went and told his chief what had happened, and as he was telling, a Hellenic priest heard it, went and, having become a monk, from the very beginning held to humility and said that humility destroys all the power of the enemy, as he had heard from the demon himself: when I disturb the monks, and one of them makes a prostration, all my power is destroyed.

172.   The elders said: the crown of the monk is humility.

173.   They asked an elder: how does the soul acquire humility? And the elder answered: if it concerns itself only with its own sins.

174.   An elder said: just as the earth never falls downward, so neither does he who humbles himself.

175.   An elder said: humility does not become angry and does not anger anyone.

176.   One of the desert elders was struck on the cheek by a demoniac who was foaming terribly. The elder turned to him the other, and the demon, not being able to bear the burning of humility, immediately came out.

177.   An elder said: when a thought of high-mindedness or pride rises within you, examine your conscience: have you kept all the commandments, do you love your enemies and grieve over their wounds, do you consider yourself an unprofitable servant and more sinful than all? And then do not think highly of yourself, as if you were correct in everything, knowing that this thought destroys everything.

178.   An elder said: he who is honored or praised more than his worth suffers great harm, but he who is not honored at all by men will be glorified from above.

179.   A brother asked an elder: is it good to make many prostrations? The elder answered: we see that when Joshua fell on his face, then God appeared to him.

180.   They asked an elder: why are we so warred against by demons? And he said: because we throw away our weapons, that is, the not-seeking of honor, humility, non-acquisitiveness, and patience.

181.   A brother asked an elder: if a brother brings words to me from outside, do you wish, abba, that I tell him: do not bring them? The elder said: no. The brother asked: why? The elder answered: because, having told our neighbor not to do this, we might ourselves be found doing the same, if we cannot keep to that. The brother said: so what is to be done? The elder answered: if you wish, be silent. This example is enough for your neighbor.

182.   They asked an elder: what is humility? And he answered: humility is to forgive your brother who sins against you before he repents before you.[18]

183.   An elder said: in no temptation accuse other people, but yourself alone, saying: this has happened to me because of my sins.[19]

184.   A brother asked an elder: what is humility? The elder answered: to do good to those who do evil to you. The brother said: if someone has not attained to this measure, what is he to do? The elder said: let him flee, having taken hold of silence.

185.	A brother asked an elder: in what does pilgrimage consist? The elder said: I knew a stranger-brother who, being in a church where there happened to be a love-feast, sat down together with the brethren at the table. Some asked: who invited this one too? And they said to him: get up and leave here! He got up and left, but others, taking pity on him, went and called him back. Afterward they asked him: what was in your heart when you were sent out and when you were brought back in again? He answered: I placed in my heart that I am the same as a dog: when they drive it away, it runs off; when they call it, it comes again.

186.	Once certain ones came to the Thebaid to a certain elder and brought with them a demoniac, that he might heal him. The elder, after fervent prayers for him, said to the demon: come out of the creature of God! The demon said to the elder: I will come out, only tell me: who are goats and who are lambs? The elder answered: I am a goat, but the lambs God knows. Hearing this, the demon cried out loudly: behold, I come out because of your humility, and came out that very hour.

187.	A certain Egyptian monk lived in the outskirts of Constantinople in the time of the Emperor Theodosius the Younger. Once the emperor, passing that way and leaving everyone behind, came alone and knocked at the monk's door. He opened to him and, although he recognized who he was, received him as one of the officials. When the emperor entered, the elder made a prayer, and they sat down. The emperor began to ask him: how do the fathers who are in Egypt live? He said: all are praying for your salvation. Then he said to him: eat a little, soaked some dried bread for him, poured in a little oil, and put out some salt. The emperor ate. The elder gave him water, and he drank. Then the emperor asked him: do you know who I am? The elder answered: God knows you. Then the emperor said to him: I am the Emperor Theodosius! And the elder immediately bowed to him. The emperor said to him: blessed are you, for you have no worldly cares. Truly, born to the throne, I have never eaten bread or drunk water with such pleasure as now. From then on the emperor began to honor the elder, but the elder fled and came back to Egypt.

188.	A certain elder-hermit, wandering through the desert, thought to himself that he had fulfilled all the virtues and began to pray to God, saying: show me what I lack, and I will do it! God, wishing to humble his thought, said to him: go to such-and-such an archimandrite, and whatever he tells you, do it. And God revealed to the archimandrite: a certain hermit will come to you; tell him: take a whip and pasture the swine. When the elder came to the archimandrite, they kissed one another, and they sat down, and the hermit said: tell me what to do, that I may be saved. The other said to him: will you do whatever I tell you? He said: I will do it. The other said: take a whip and go pasture the swine. The hermit went and pastured the swine. Those who knew him and had heard of him, learning that he was pasturing swine, said: look at that hermit about whom we have heard! He must have gone out of his mind or has a demon in him, since he is pasturing swine. But God, seeing his humility, with which he bore such reproach from men, returned him to his former place.

189.	An elder said: do not say in your heart against your brother: I am more sober than he and live more ascetically, but submit to the grace of Christ in the spirit of poverty and love unfeigned, lest you fall into the spirit of boasting and lose your labor, for it is written: *"Let him who thinks he stands take heed lest he fall"* (1 Corinthians 10:12), but be seasoned with salt in the Lord.

190.   An elder said: I have never overstepped my rank to go higher, and I have never, being brought down in humiliation, been disturbed, for all my care is to pray to God until He leads me out of the old man.

191.   A brother asked an elder: tell us about salvation, abba! However, even if you tell us, we will not keep it, because our land is salty and bitter.

192.   The elders said: when we are not warred against, then we must humble ourselves all the more, for God, seeing our weakness, covers us, but if we become proud of ourselves, He will take away His covering from us, and we will perish.

193.   To one of the brethren the devil appeared, having transformed himself into an angel of light, and said to him: I am Gabriel and have been sent to you. But the brother said: see whether you have not been sent to another, for I am not worthy of this. And the devil immediately disappeared.

194.   The elders said: even if an angel should visibly appear to you, do not receive him, but humble yourself, saying: I am not worthy to see an angel, because I live in sins.

195.   They used to say of a certain elder that, sitting in his cell and laboring, he saw demons openly and disdained them. The devil, seeing himself overcome by the elder, appeared to him and said: I am Christ. Seeing him, the elder closed his eyes. The devil asked: why do you close your eyes? I am Christ. The elder answered him: I do not wish to see Christ here. And the devil, hearing this, disappeared.

196.   To another elder the demons said: do you wish to see Christ? But he said to them: anathema to you and to that of which you speak! For I believe in my Christ, Who said: *"If anyone says to you, 'Look, here is the Christ!' or 'There!' do not believe it"* (Matthew 24:23). And they immediately disappeared.

197.   They related of an elder that for seventy weeks he would take food only once each week and prayed about one saying of Scripture, but God did not reveal it to him. Finally he said to himself: I have undertaken so many labors and have achieved nothing. I will go to my brother and ask him. But as soon as he had closed the door to go, an Angel of the Lord was sent to him, who said: the seventy weeks that you fasted did not ascend before God, but when you humbled yourself and went to your brother, I was sent to reveal that word to you. And having explained to him the word about which he had asked, he departed from him.

198.   An elder said: if someone with the fear of God and humility commands a brother to do some work, then the word, having gone forth from his mouth for God's sake, disposes the brother to submit and do what was commanded. But if someone commands a brother not according to the fear of God, but in lordship, wishing to rule over him, then God, Who sees what is hidden in the heart, does not move the brother to obey and do it, for the

work done for God is manifest, and the work of lordship is manifest. What is of God is humble and consoling, while that which is with lordship is full of anger and disturbance, because it is from the evil one.

199.   An elder said: in my opinion, defeat with humility is better than victory with pride.

200.   An elder said: do not despise him who is with you, for you do not know whether the Spirit of God is in you or in him. I say, him who is with you, that is, the one who serves you.

201.   A brother asked an elder: if, living with brethren, I see something improper, do you advise me to tell them? The elder answered: if there are those older than you or your peers, you will have more rest if you are silent. You yourself will diminish yourself and will be without care. The brother said to him: so what am I to do, for the spirits disturb me? The elder answered: if that burdens you, then remind them once with humility and, if they do not listen to you, leave your labor, cutting off your will before God. But see that you do not show yourself off, so that your care may be according to God. However, as I think, it is better to be silent, for in this there is humility.

202.   A certain brother was offended at another brother. The latter, hearing of this, came to repent before him, but the brother did not open the door to him. He went to a certain elder and told him about this. The elder said in answer: see whether you do not have self-justification in your heart, condemning the brother as guilty and justifying yourself? For this reason he was not moved to open to you. However, here is what I will tell you: although he sinned against you, go and place in your heart that you sinned against him, and justify your brother. Then God will move him to come into concord with you. The brother believed and did so. When afterward he came to the brother and knocked, the other, as soon as he heard the knock, opened, was the first to repent before him, and from the heart kissed him, and they were afterward in great peace with one another.

203.   They used to say of one of the fathers that for seven years he prayed to God for a certain gift, and it was given to him. Then he went to a certain great elder and revealed the gift to him. That elder, hearing this, grieved and said: great labor! Go and pray to God another seven years, that this gift be taken from you, for it is not profitable for you. He went and did so, and the gift was taken from him.

204.   A brother asked an elder: in what does a man's progress according to God consist? The elder answered: the progress of man is humility, for to the degree that one descends into humility, to that degree one ascends to progress.

205.   An elder said: either, fleeing, flee from men, or mock the world and men, making yourself one who is warred against in many things.

206.   An elder said: if, humbling yourself, you say to someone: forgive me, you will burn the demons.

207.	An elder said: if you acquire silence, do not consider yourself as practicing a virtue, but say: I am not worthy even to speak.

208.	An elder said: if the baker did not put a covering over the eyes of the grinding animal, it would turn around and eat up its labors. Thus we too receive, by the dispensation of God, coverings, so that we may not see the good that we do, and, blessing ourselves, lose our reward. Therefore we are sometimes left in shameful thoughts and see them alone, so that we may condemn ourselves. And these shameful thoughts serve us as a covering for our small good, for when a man condemns himself, he does not lose his reward.

209.	They asked an elder: what is humility? And he answered: humility is a great and divine thing. And the path to humility is bodily labors and to consider oneself a sinner and lower than all. A brother asked: what does it mean to be lower than all? The elder said: it means not to pay attention to the sins of others, but always only to one's own, and to pray to God about them unceasingly.

210.	A brother asked an elder: tell me, what work should I keep in order to be saved? The elder answered: if you can bear to be humiliated, this will be above all virtues.

211.	An elder said: he who bears humiliation, reproach, and loss can be saved.

212.	An elder said: do not have acquaintance with the abbot and do not visit him often, for through this you will acquire boldness and will finally yourself wish to be an abbot.

213.	A certain holy man, seeing one sinning, wept bitterly and said: this one today, but I tomorrow. Thus, however someone may sin before your face, do not condemn him, but consider yourself more sinful than he.

214.	In a coenobium there was a certain brother who would take upon himself all the sins laid against him by the brethren, and he would even accuse himself of fornication, saying: I did it. Some of the brethren, not knowing his practice, began to murmur and said: how many sins has this one committed, yet he does not work at all! But the abba, knowing his practice, said to them: for me, one mat of his with humility is better than all of yours with pride. And do you wish to receive assurance from God? Then he brought three of their mats each and one mat of that brother and, having kindled a fire, threw them in. They all burned except the mat of the brother. Seeing this, the brethren in fear made a prostration to him and afterward had him as a father.

215.	A certain monk, having received a wound, not only bore it but also made a prostration to the one who had inflicted it, and the wound was immediately healed.

216.	An elder said: do not put into your heart condemnation of your brother for any deed whatsoever.

217.	They asked an elder: how is it that some say they see visions of angels? The elder answered: blessed is he who always sees his sins.

218.   A certain elder, living by the Jordan, entered a cave at the time of the heat and found a lion there, which began to gnash its teeth and roar. The elder said to it: why do you grieve? There is room; both I and you can fit. And the lion, not being able to bear this word, went out.

219.   A brother asked an elder: why is it that when I make a prostration to one who has something against me, I see that he is not sincere with me? The elder said: tell me the truth: do you not have self-justification in your heart when you make a prostration to the one who has sinned against you, thinking that he has sinned against you, and only according to the commandment do you make a prostration to him? The brother answered: I do indeed have it. The elder said: for this reason God does not lay it on his heart to be sincere with you, because you do not make a prostration to him with the conviction that you have sinned against him, but on the contrary, you consider him to have sinned against you. But even if he has sinned against you, place in your heart that you are the sinner against your brother, and justify him; then God will lay it on his heart to be sincere with you. And at this he told him the following case as an example: there were two pious laymen who, having agreed together, left the world and became monks. Through misguided zeal, not having understood the Gospel word rightly, they made themselves eunuchs for the sake of the kingdom of God. The archbishop, hearing of this, excommunicated them. But they, thinking that they had done well, became indignant at him, saying: we made ourselves eunuchs for the sake of the kingdom of God, and they have excommunicated us; but let us go and tell this to the Archbishop of Jerusalem! They went and told him everything. The archbishop said to them: I too excommunicate you. Grieved by this, they went to Antioch to the archbishop and told him about their matter, but he also excommunicated them. They said to one another: let us go to Rome to the Pope, and he will vindicate us. Coming to the great Archbishop of Rome, they told him what the archbishops had done to them and added: now we have come to you, because you are first among all. But he also said to them: I too excommunicate you, and be you excommunicated. In perplexity they said one to the other: they connive with one another, because they gather together at councils. But let us go to the holy man of God, Epiphanius, Bishop of Cyprus, for he is a prophet and does not accept the person of man. When they were approaching his city, it was revealed to him about them, and he sent to meet them, saying: do not even enter this city. Therefore, coming to themselves, they said: truly, we have sinned. Let those have excommunicated us unjustly, but surely this prophet too? Behold, God has also revealed to him about us. And they condemned themselves for the deed they had done. Then God, Who knows hearts, seeing that they had condemned themselves in truth, gave an assurance about this to Epiphanius, Bishop of Cyprus, and of his own accord he sent to bring them and comforted them, received them into communion, and afterward wrote to the Archbishop of Alexandria: receive your children, for they have repented in truth. So, said the elder, this is the healing of man, and this is what God wants: that man place his sin upon himself before His face!

220.   An elder said: I prefer to be taught rather than to teach.

221.   An elder said: modesty with humility is good everywhere, for one may be cordial and show himself loving, but if he does this beyond measure, he is condemned, while the modest one, having fenced himself with humility, always has honor.

222.   He also said: humility is more powerful than all power, and one of the fathers related: near one another there were two bishops who had a quarrel with each other, of whom one was rich and powerful, and the other was humble. The powerful one sought to do harm to the humble one, and the latter, hearing of it, said to his clergy: we will overcome him by the grace of God. They said to him: master! Who can overcome him? He answered: wait, children, and you will see the mercy of God. So, having waited until the other was to celebrate the feast of the martyrs, he said to his clergy: follow me, and what you see me doing, do also, and we will overcome him. They wondered within themselves: what will he do?! They came to that bishop, and as the procession was passing before the whole city gathered, the humble bishop fell at his feet with all his clergy and said: forgive us, master! We are your servants. The other, struck by such an action and coming to compunction, because God changed his heart, seized the bishop's feet and said: you are my master and father! From then on perfect love was established between them. Then the humble bishop said to his clergy: did I not tell you, children, that we would overcome him by the grace of Christ! And if you too are at enmity with anyone, do the same by the grace of our Lord Jesus Christ.

223.   An elder said: if we were zealous for humility, we would have no need of chastisement, for all troubles come upon us because of pride. If an angel of Satan was given to the Apostle, *to buffet him, lest he be exalted above measure* (2 Corinthians 12:7), how much more shall Satan himself be given to trample upon us who are puffed up, until we humble ourselves.

224.   A brother asked an elder: in what does a monk's success consist? The elder answered: humility leads a monk to progress.

225.   An elder said: the crown of a monk is humility. If a monk condemns himself in every deed with great humility and love for God, then wherever he lives, he will have rest by the grace of Christ.

226.   To a certain elder, because of his great humility, God sent down the gift of foresight. But the elder, having for the first time foreknown that people were coming to visit him, began to pray to God that this gift be taken from him. Then he went to another great elder and asked him, saying: suffer with me, that this thing be taken from me. Thus, each sitting in his own cell, they prayed to God about this, and a voice came to the elder: behold, I take it from you, but whenever you wish, you will have it.

227.   There was a certain lover of the brethren, full of love and never thinking evil. Another brother stole some things and placed them with him, and he did not know of it. After several days, the things were recognized, and the elder, brought to the assembly, making a prostration, said: forgive me, I repent! Later the brother who had stolen the things came and, talking with the elder, asked him: did you steal the things? The elder made a prostration to the brother and said: forgive me. Likewise, if any of the brethren fell and denied it, he

would make a prostration and say: I committed this sin, forgive me. So full of love and humility was this venerable one that he never offended anyone even by a word.

228. A certain hermit was made a bishop and, out of modesty and love of stillness, punished no one, long-sufferingly bearing the falls of each. Thus, his steward did not look after the church's things as he should, and some said to him: why do you not punish the steward, who is so negligent? But the bishop put off the punishment. The next day those who had grieved him because of the steward came again, and the bishop, learning of it, hid himself from them. They, coming and not seeing the bishop, began to look for him and, finding him, asked: why did you hide from us? He answered: because that which I have acquired over sixty years, praying to God, you want to steal from me in two days.

229. An elder said: if there is a grievous word between you and a friend, and he denies having said it, do not press him, saying: you did say it. Because he will turn and say: I did indeed say it, so what? And there will arise between you an even greater unpleasantness. At this he related: two elders in The Cells were conversing about a word of Scripture. One erred in a word, and the other told the presbyter about it. The presbyter rose, went to that elder, and asked him: did you say this word? He answered: I said it. He said to him: when you come to the church, deny having said this word. When he came to the church, the presbyter asked him: did you say such-and-such a word? He answered: no. He asked the other elder: did you hear such a word? He also denied it and made a prostration. And there was great peace.

230. Once in Scetis a brother called another brother, saying: come to me in my cell and I will wash your feet. But he did not go. The other a second time and a third said the same to him; he did not go. Finally the brother came to his cell and, making a prostration, asked him: come to my cell! He rose and went with him. The brother asked him: why did you not come before, though I often asked you? He answered: when you spoke only with words, I was not moved to go. But when I saw the monastic deed, that is, the prostration, I went with you with joy.

231. A brother asked an elder: what am I to do? Vainglory disturbs me. The elder answered: you do well, for you created heaven and earth! Brought to compunction by this, the brother, making a prostration, said: forgive me, for I have done nothing of the kind! The elder said to him: if He Who created them came to us in humility, then you, a clay vessel, why are you vainglorious? And what have you done, poor man?

232. They used to say of two brethren that, when they were sitting together and conversing, a small unpleasantness arose between them. One of them, returning to his cell, could not sit still and, coming to his brother, made a prostration to him. The other said to him: forgive me, it did not even come to my mind that there was any unpleasantness between us. Abba Abraham went and told Abba Poemen about this matter, and the elder said: one of them has found the way, for he showed humility by deed.

233.   An elder said: he is not humble who abases himself, but he who accepts reproach and dishonor from his neighbor with joy.

234.   In The Cells there was a certain brother who came to such humility that he always prayed thus: Lord! Send me a fever, for being healthy I disobey Thee.

235.   A certain brother renounced the world together with his father according to the flesh, and both remained in one monastery. After some time, the brother heard about his father that he had healed a sick man from a demon, and he went and told a great elder about this, saying with sorrow: abba! My father has made progress and driven out a demon from a brother, but I remain in negligence, and no progress is seen in me. The elder said to him: truly, my son, progress is not to drive out demons or heal the sick, for this is not done by man, but by the power of God and the faith of the one who comes, and many, not understanding this, have fallen into pride from healings and perished. But I say that if a man comes into true humility, there is no greater progress than this, because it never falls, for he who has humbled his soul—where can he fall when he has cast himself down to the ground? A sign of this is when someone, being dishonored, rejoices.

236.   A certain skilled brother came from Scetis to the Thebaid and entered a coenobium in which almost all the brethren were holy men from those called Tabennesiots. Having stayed there several days, he said to the archimandrite: make a prayer, abba, and let me go, for I cannot remain here! The abba asked: why, my son? The brother answered: because here there is no labor, and therefore no reward. All the fathers here are ascetics, but I am a sinful man and will go where I can meet with reproach and humiliation, for these save a sinful man. Marveling at this and knowing that he was a doer, the abba dismissed him, saying: go, my son, be of good courage, and let your heart be strengthened, and *wait on the Lord* (Psalm 27:14).

237.   An elder said: humility has often saved many even without labors, as the publican and the prodigal son testify about this, who, having spoken only a few words, were saved. The labors of a man, if there is no humility with them, destroy him, for many have fallen into pride from the great labors they undertake, as the Pharisee did.

238.   A brother came to an elder and asked him: how are you, father? The elder answered: badly. The brother said to him: why, abba? The elder said: behold, for eighteen years I have stood before God, cursing myself and saying: *"Cursed are those who stray from Your commandments"* (Psalm 119:21). Hearing this, the brother departed, having received great benefit from the elder's humility.

239.   Once a rich man from a foreign land came to Raithu and gave the brethren a coin each in alms, and also sent one to a hesychast sitting there in his cell. That night the elder saw a field full of thorns and someone saying to him: go and reap in the field of him who gave you the coin. In the morning the hesychast sent for the Christ-loving man who had sent him the coin and returned it to him, saying: receive, brother, the coin. Where am I to go and reap another's thorns! Oh, if only I could clear my own!

240.	An elder said: if you sit in the desert in stillness, do not hold in your mind that you are doing something great, but rather consider yourself a dog that has been driven out from among men and tied up because it attacks people and bites them.

241.	An elder said: if a man labors always to accuse, reproach, and humble his soul secretly, he will convince it that it is more dishonorable than dogs and beasts, for they have never angered their Creator and will not come to judgment. It is far better not to arise at the judgment than, having arisen, to be eternally tormented.

242.	A brother, tormented by impure thoughts, grieved and from great humility said: if I have thought such things, there is no part for me in salvation. He went to a great elder and asked him to pray for him, that the Lord might relieve him of the thoughts. The elder said to him: this is not profitable for you, my son. But the brother did not cease persuading the elder. The elder prayed to God, and the warfare was taken from the brother, but soon he fell into high-mindedness and pride, so he went to ask the elder that the thoughts and humility that he had before might return.

243.	A brother came to one of the fathers in the lavra of Abba Dulas, which is above Jericho, and asked him: father! How are you? The elder answered: behold, for thirty years, standing at prayer, I have been lying before God in my prayer, for I bear ill-will against my brother, but to God I say: *"Forgive us... as we forgive"* (Matthew 6:12); all my care is only about eating, but I say: *"I forgot to eat my bread"* (Psalm 102:4); I sleep until morning, but I sing: *"At midnight I will rise to give thanks to You"* (Psalm 119:62); I have no compunction at all and say: *"I am weary with my groaning"* (Psalm 6:6) and *"my tears have been my food day and night"* (Psalm 42:3); I think evil in my heart and say: *"the meditation of my heart shall be acceptable in Your sight"* (Psalm 19:14); I do not fast, but I say: *"My knees are weak from fasting"* (Psalm 109:24); full of pride, comforting my flesh in every way, I say, as if mocking myself: *"Consider my affliction and my trouble, and forgive all my sins"* (Psalm 25:18); I am not ready, but I say: *"My heart is steadfast, O God"* (Psalm 57:7; 108:1), and in general all my service and prayer serve for my conviction and shame. The brother said to the elder: I think, father, that David spoke all this about himself. The elder sighed and answered: what are you saying, brother! Believe me, if all that we sing before the face of God is not kept, we will go to perdition.

244.	An elder said: if you condemn your brother and your conscience torments you, go make a prostration to him and say: I condemned you, and strengthen yourself, lest you be mocked, for condemnation is the death of the soul.

245.	He also said: if you hear of the great ascetic labors of the holy fathers, resolve to do the same yourself, calling upon the name of the Lord, that He may strengthen you for the work you have undertaken. Then, if you accomplish it, give thanks to God; but if you do not accomplish it, reproach your weakness, know your powerlessness, humble your thought until the day of death, as one incapable, poor, and impatient, and accuse your soul always that it began and did not finish.

246.   He also said: if you live in the desert and see that God cares for you, do not be exalted in your heart, for otherwise God will take His help from you, but say rather: because of my fainthearted-ness and weakness, God shows His mercy to me, that I may endure and not despair.

247.   An elder said: if you take up asceticism and then relax, begin it again and do not cease to do so until your very death, for in whatever state a man is found, in that he will depart, whether in negligence or in self-control. Every day, year, and week examine yourself: have you progressed in prayer, fasting, stillness, and above all in humility? For this is true progress of the soul, that it humble itself more and more from day to day, saying: every man is better than I, for without this thought, even if a man works signs, even if he raises the dead, he is far from God.

248.   He also said: if a man praises you to your face, immediately remember your sins and ask him: for the Lord's sake do not praise me, brother, for I am unstable and cannot bear it. But if it is a great man, pray to God, saying: Lord! Cover me from the praise and blame of men.

249.   He also said: if a brother condemns a brother before you, take care not to condemn him yourself and not to say: yes, it is so. But either be silent or say to him: I, brother, am condemned myself and cannot condemn another, and thus you will save both yourself and him.

250.   An elder said: if you, having fallen ill, ask something from someone for your need and he does not give it to you, do not be offended at him, but rather say: if I were worthy to receive, God would have laid it on the brother's heart to give me this alms. But know that there is reason for receiving alms. The perfect never receive anything from anyone; the middling do not say that something be given to them, but when someone gives of his own accord, they accept it as sent from God; but if we are weak and cannot work out our needs, let us ask with great humility, always condemning ourselves.

251.   He also said: if you do not have spiritual humility or spiritual prayer, keep at least bodily ones, and for the sake of the bodily ones, the spiritual will come; otherwise you labor in vain.

252.   He also said: if impure thoughts disturb you, do not hide them, but immediately tell them to your spiritual father and expose them, for the more a man hides his thoughts, the more they multiply and gain strength. But just as a serpent, if it only comes out of its hole, immediately flees away, so does an evil thought, when exposed, immediately vanish, and just as a worm spoils wood, so an evil thought spoils the heart. He who reveals his thoughts is quickly healed, but he who hides them is sick with pride, for if he has faith in no one to reveal his battles to him, this is a sign that he has no humility, since the humble sees everyone as holy and good, and himself alone as a sinner. However, if a man calls upon God with all his heart and goes to ask some man about his thoughts, then that man, or rather God Himself, Who opened the mouth of Balaam's donkey, will always give him a profitable answer through that man, even if the one questioned is unworthy and sinful.

253.   He also said: if they keep you at a love-feast and seat you in the last place, do not murmur in your thought, but rather say: I am unworthy even to sit here. For I tell you, sorrow

does not come upon a man unless from above, from God, either for his testing or for his sins, and he who does not hold this in his mind does not believe that God is a righteous Judge.

254. He also said: if a thought of pride disturbs you, say to the demon: God says that *everyone who exalts himself will be humbled* (Luke 18:14), and if you do not cease telling me that I am good, I will be convinced that I am estranged from God, for *God resists the proud* (Proverbs 3:34; James 4:6; 1 Peter 5:5).

255. One of the elders said: in our land the elders once gathered for benefit, and one of them, rising, took a small shoulder-cloth lying on his seat, placed it on his shoulders, holding it with both hands, stood in the midst of all, looking east, and prayed, saying: O God! Have mercy on me! And he answered himself: if you want Me to have mercy on you, put down what you carry on your shoulders, and I will have mercy on you! Then again he said: O God! Have mercy on me! And he answered himself: I told you, put down what you carry on your shoulders, and I will have mercy on you. Having repeated this several times, he sat down. The fathers asked him: tell us, what did that mean, what you did? He answered: the shoulder-cloth that I carry on my shoulders is my will. I asked God to have mercy on me with it, and He told me: put down what you carry on your shoulders, and I will have mercy on you. Thus we too, if we wish to be shown mercy by God, let us leave our own will and obtain mercy.[20]

256. They asked an elder: what is humility? And he answered: humility is when your brother sins against you, you forgive him before he repents before you.

257. An elder said: in no temptation accuse another man, but yourself, saying: this happened to me because of my sins.[21]

258. They asked an elder: in what does a man's progress consist? He answered: in humility, and there is no other progress, for to the degree that one descends into humility, to that degree one ascends to the heights.

259. They asked an elder: how can the soul acquire humility? He answered: if it concerns itself only with its own sins.

260. One of the fathers told this parable concerning humility: the cedars said to the reeds: how is it that you, being weak and powerless, are not broken by the storm, while we, being so great, are crushed by it? The reeds answered: we, when the storm comes and the winds blow, sway with the wind this way and that, and therefore we do not break, but you, resisting the winds, are put in danger. Then the elder said: one should turn aside when a word of reproach occurs and not give place to anger, rather than resist, lest one fall into improper thoughts and deeds.

Endnotes

[16] A retelling of apophthegm 83.
[17] Ephod: a liturgical vestment of white color.
[18] See also apophthegm 255.
[19] See also apophthegm 257.
[20] See also apophthegm 182.
[21] See also apophthegm 183.

Chapter XVI.
On Guilelessness

1. They said of Abba Gelasius that he had a book bound in leather, in which the entire Old and New Testament was written, and which was worth eighteen gold coins. It lay in the church so that any brother who wished could read it. A certain wandering brother, having come to visit the elder and seeing it, was tempted, stole it, and departed. The elder did not pursue him to take it back, though he knew of it. This brother went to the city and, having found someone who wished to buy it, asked sixteen gold coins. The one who wished to buy said to him: first give it to me, I will inquire about it and then pay you the price. The brother gave him the book, and the other, taking it, brought it to Abba Gelasius to show him and told him the price the seller had named. The elder said to him: buy it, it is good and worth the price quoted to you. This man, returning, spoke differently: behold, he said, I showed it to Abba Gelasius, and he said to me: it is expensive, it is not worth the price you quoted. Hearing this, the brother asked him: and the elder said nothing else to you? He answered: nothing. Then the brother said: now I no longer wish to sell it. And coming to compunction, he went to the elder, repented before him, and asked him to accept the book, but the elder did not wish to accept it, to which the brother said: if you do not take it, I will have no peace. The elder answered him: if you will have no peace, then I will take it. And the brother was edified by the elder's conduct until his very death.

2. They recounted that Abba Euprepius, when he was once being robbed, himself carried out his belongings and gave them. The thieves carried out everything that was inside, but forgot their staff. Seeing it, Abba Euprepius was grieved, took it, and ran to catch up with them to return it. They did not take it, fearing lest something might happen, but the abba, meeting some who were going the same way, entreated them to give them their staff.

3. Abba Zeno said: he who desires that God quickly hear his prayer, as soon as he rises and stretches out his hands, before all else, before prayer for himself, must pray from the soul for his enemies. For such a deed, whatever he asks of God, he will be heard by Him.

4. Once robbers attacked Abba Theodore. Two held him, while the third carried out his belongings. When the thief, having carried out the books, wished to take his levitōn, the abba said to them: leave this. But they did not wish to. Then the abba, shaking his arms forcefully,

cast down the two, and they, seeing this, were frightened. The elder said to them: fear nothing, but divide all this into four parts: take three for yourselves and leave one for me. They did so, that the elder's portion would include the levitōn in which he went to the assembly.

5. Once Abba John Colobos was sitting before the church, and the brethren, surrounding him, confessed their thoughts to him. One of the elders, seeing this and being warred upon by envy, said to him: your vessel, John, is full of poison. Abba John answered him: so it is, abba, and you said this only because you see the exterior; if you were to see the interior as well, what would you say?

6. They said of Abba Isidore, the priest of Scetis: if anyone had a brother who was weak, or fainthearted, or quarrelsome and wished to drive him out, the abba would say: bring him to me. He would receive him and by his longsuffering would save him.

7. Abba Poemen recounted about Abba Isidore: if he spoke to the brethren in the church, this one word alone he would say to them: brethren, *forgive, and you will be forgiven* (Luke 6:37).

8. The elder said about Abba John the Persian: when evildoers came to him, he brought out a basin and asked to wash their feet. They were ashamed and began to bring forth repentance.

9. They said of John of Thebes, the younger disciple of Abba Ammoy, that for twelve years he served the elder while he was sick and was always beside him, sitting on a reed mat. The elder seemed to disregard this and, despite the fact that he labored much around him, never said to him: may you be saved. But drawing near to death, when the elders were sitting with him, he took him by the hand and said: may you be saved, may you be saved, may you be saved! And he entrusted him to the elders, saying: this is an angel, not a man.

10. They said of Abba Longinus that once one of his disciples was slandered with the purpose of having him cast out. For this purpose, those who were with Abba Theodore came to him and said: abba, we have heard certain things about this brother, and if you command, we will take him away from you and bring you another good brother. The elder answered them: I will not drive him away, for he gives me rest. But when the elder heard the reason for this, he said: woe to me! We come here to become angels, and we become unclean irrational beasts.

11. Abba Macarius the Egyptian, finding a man with a pack animal stealing his necessities, approached the thief as though he were a stranger, helped him load the animal, and with great tranquility sent him off, saying: *For we brought nothing into this world, and it is certain we can carry nothing out* (1 Timothy 6:7). *The Lord gave, and the Lord has taken away; as it pleased the Lord, so it has come to pass* (Job 1:21). Blessed be the Lord in all things!

12. They said of Abba Macarius that in his absence a robber entered his cell. Coming to the cell and finding the robber loading his things onto a camel, he himself took some of the things and loaded them onto the camel together with him. When they finished, the robber

began to push the camel to make it rise, but it would not get up. Abba Macarius, seeing that it would not rise, went into the cell, found a small hoe, and bringing it out, placed it on the camel, saying: brother, this is what the camel was waiting for. The elder struck it with his foot and said: get up. For the sake of the word, it immediately rose, but having gone a little way, lay down again and would not rise until they took all the things off it. Then it went.

13. Once there was an assembly in Scetis, and the fathers, wishing to test Abba Moses, humiliated him, saying: why does this Ethiopian come into our midst? Hearing this, the abba kept silent. When the brethren dispersed, they asked him: were you not troubled? He answered: *I was troubled and did not speak* (Psalm 76:5 LXX).

14. About Abba Motius, his disciple Abba Isaac recounted (both of them later became bishops) that at first the elder established a monastery in Heraclea. Having departed from there, he came to another place and there built another. Through the working of the devil, a certain brother was found who was hostile to the elder and insulted him. He arose and went to his village, built himself a cell, and enclosed himself in it. Some time later, the elders of that place from which he had departed went to him to entreat him to return to his monastery, and they took with them the brother who had insulted him. Approaching the place where Abba Sorius was, they left with him their mantles and the brother who had grieved the elder. When they approached and knocked, the elder let down the ladder, looked out, recognized them, and asked: where are your mantles? They answered: over there with the brother who insulted you. The elder, out of joy, taking an axe, broke down the door and, going out, ran to the brother; he was the first to make prostration before him and gave him a kiss; he brought them into his cell, entertained them for three days, feasting himself as well, which he was not in the habit of doing, then arose and went with them. After this, he was made a bishop. And his disciple, Abba Isaac, was also made a bishop by blessed Cyril.

15. Paisius, the brother of Abba Poemen, had an acquaintance with someone outside his cell. Abba Poemen did not want this and, running to Abba Ammon, said to him: Paisius, my brother, has such-and-such an acquaintance, and I have no peace. Abba Ammon said to him: Poemen! Are you still alive? Go, sit in your cell, and place in your heart that you have been in the grave for a year already.

16. Abba Poemen said: whatever difficulty comes upon you, victory over it lies in silence.

17. Again he said: evil in no way destroys evil, but if someone does evil to you, do good to him, so that by goodness and benefaction you may destroy evil.

18. Abba Poemen heard of someone who fasted for six days at a time, yet had not learned to cast out anger.

19. Blessed Pior, working for someone at the harvest, reminded him of payment, but the other put it off until another time, and the elder returned to the monastery. Another time, when the season came, he harvested for him again and worked diligently, but again the other gave him nothing, and the elder returned to the monastery. Upon the completion of the third year, the elder, having finished the customary work, returned, having taken nothing himself.

When the Lord blessed that man's house, he took the wages and went through the monasteries seeking the saint, and barely finding him and giving him the wages, fell at his feet, saying: the Lord has had mercy on me. But the elder returned the wages so that the other might give them to the priest in the church.

20. Abba Paul Cosmit and Timothy, his brother, lived in Scetis, and there were frequent disputes between them. Finally Abba Paul said: how long shall we live thus? Abba Timothy said to him: do me the favor: when I attack you, you bear it, and when you attack me, I will bear it. Acting thus, they had peace for the rest of their days.

21. A brother, offended by another brother, came to Abba Sisoes and said to him: offended by a certain brother, I want to avenge myself. The elder admonished him: no, my son, it is better to leave the matter of vengeance to God. But he said: I will not cease until I avenge myself. Then the elder, rising, said: let us pray, brother! And he continued: O God! We no longer have need of Your care for us. We ourselves take vengeance for ourselves. Hearing this, the brother fell at the feet of the elder and said: I will no longer contend with the brother. Forgive me, abba!

22. Spyridon, a shepherd of sheep, had such holiness that he was deemed worthy to become a shepherd of people as well, and in one of the cities of Cyprus, namely Trimythous, was made a bishop. Because of his great freedom from love of display, having received the episcopate, he continued to tend sheep. Once at midnight, thieves, having secretly approached the sheepfold, attempted to steal the sheep, but God, Who guards the shepherd, preserved the sheep as well: the thieves were bound by an invisible power at the sheepfold. Morning came, and the shepherd came to the sheep. Seeing the thieves with their arms twisted behind them, he understood what had happened and, having prayed, released them. Then, having instructed them sufficiently and exhorted them to live better by their own labors rather than by dishonesty, he gave them one ram and let them go, saying to them with a good-natured smile: so that your vigil may not have been in vain.

23. Once a Libyan brother came to Abba Silvanus on the mountain at Panephos and said to him: I have an enemy who has done me much evil: he took away my field when I was still in the world, he has often made accusations against me, and behold, now he has hired poisoners to destroy me. I wish to hand him over to the magistrate. The elder said to him: do as your heart lies, my child. The brother said: so, abba! Truly, if he is punished, there will be much benefit for his soul. The elder said: as it seems to you, my child, so do. The brother said to the elder: rise, father, make a prayer, and I will go to the magistrate. The elder rose and began to read: Our Father..., but when it was time to say: *and forgive us our debts, as we forgive our debtors*, the elder said: and do not forgive us our debts, as we do not forgive our debtors (Matthew 6:12). The brother said to him: not so, father! The elder said: how then, my child? Truly, if you wish to go to the magistrate so that he may exact vengeance for you, then Silvanus will make no other prayer for you. Then the brother, making a prostration to the elder, forgave his enemy.

24. A certain brother made a counterfeit key and, unlocking the cell of an elder with it, would take his small coins. The elder wrote on a piece of paper: beloved brother, whoever you may be, do me the favor of leaving me half for my needs, and dividing the money into two parts, he placed the paper there. The other, entering, tore up the paper and again took everything. Then, when after two days he was dying, his soul would not leave him. Then, calling the elder, he confessed: pray for me, father! I stole your money. The elder said: why did you not say this sooner? He prayed, and the other gave up his soul.

25. Another man, handed over to torture by his slave woman, as he was going to his death and seeing this slave woman who had betrayed him, took off the gold ring that he wore and gave it to her, saying: I thank you, for you have brought me so many blessings.

26. A certain laborer, seeing a man carrying a dead person on a bier, said to him: you carry the dead? Go carry the living.

27. They said of a certain monk: the more someone reviled or insulted him, the more he turned to that person, saying: such people are the cause of improvement for the diligent, while those who praise us deceive and trouble the soul, for it is written: *those who bless you deceive you* (cf. Isaiah 3:12 LXX).

28. Once robbers came to the monastery (cell) of an elder and said to him: we have resolved to take everything that is in your cell. He answered them: take, children, everything you please. And so they took everything they found in his cell and departed, but they forgot a bag that was hanging there. The elder took it and, pursuing them, called out: children! Take what you forgot in our cell. Amazed by the guilelessness of the elder, they returned everything to his cell and repented, saying to one another: truly, this is a man of God.

29. The brethren were going to a holy elder who lived in a desert place, and near his monastery they met children tending cattle and speaking indecent words. Having opened their thoughts to the elder and received benefit from seeing him, they asked him: how, abba, do you tolerate these children and not command them to cease their indecency? The elder answered them: truly, brethren, for several days I have wanted to say something to them, and I forbid myself, saying: if I cannot bear this small thing, how will I bear it when a great temptation comes upon me. And therefore I say nothing, so that I might become accustomed to endure everything that befalls me.

30. They said of a certain brother who lived near a great elder that he would enter his cell and steal. The elder saw this but did not expose him; rather, he worked even more, saying: perhaps the brother has need, though he himself endured great sorrow, barely finding his bread. When the elder drew near to death, the brethren surrounded him, and he, seeing among them the one who had robbed him, called out: come near to me, and kissing his hands, said: I thank these hands, for through them I will enter the kingdom of heaven. The brother came from this to compunction, repented, and himself became a skilled monk from the deeds he had seen in the great elder.

31. One of the elders said: I have heard from certain saints that there are younger ones who guide elders into life, and he recounted the following: there was a certain drunken elder who would make one mat each day, sell it in the village, and drink up the price. Then a certain brother came to him and, remaining with him, also made one mat. The elder would take this one too and, having sold them, would drink up the price of both, and to the brother he would bring a little bread each evening. Thus three years passed, and the brother said nothing to him. Finally the brother said to himself: behold, I am naked and eat my bread with scarcity; I will gather myself and depart from here. But again he reconsidered, saying: where am I to go? I will continue living here, for I live with him in common for God's sake. And immediately an Angel appeared to him and said: do not go anywhere from here, for tomorrow I will come for you. On the next day, the brother asked the elder: do not go anywhere, for today my own will come to take me. When the hour came for the elder to depart, he said to the brother: they are not coming today, child; they are late. The brother said to him: no, abba, they will certainly come, and saying this, he reposed. Then the elder said with weeping: woe to me, child! For many years I have lived in negligence, while you in a short time have saved your soul by patience. From then on, the elder became sober and became skilled.

32. They recounted of another elder: he had a youth living with him, and seeing that he was doing something not beneficial to him, he said: do not do this. But the youth did not listen to the elder, and the elder left the youth to his own will, condemning himself. Once this youth, having locked the cell in which the bread was kept, went away and left the elder without food for thirteen days, and the elder did not ask him: where were you? Or: where did you go? The elder had a neighbor who, noticing that the youth was delayed, would prepare a little cooked food for the elder and, passing it to him over the wall, would ask him to eat. And if he asked: why has the brother delayed so?, the elder would answer: when he finds time, he will come.

33. Some recounted: once philosophers wished to test the monks. A certain monk, well-dressed, was passing by, and they said to him: hey you, come here! He became angry and reviled them. Another monk passed by, a Libyan, and they said to him: hey you, monk, wicked elder, come here! He approached with haste. They struck him on the cheek, and he turned the other to them. Then they immediately rose and bowed down to him, saying: behold, a true monk! Then they seated him with themselves and asked: what more than we do you do in the desert? You fast, and we fast; you keep vigil, and we keep vigil; and whatever you do, we do also. So what more than we do you do, living in the desert? The elder answered them: we hope in the grace of God and guard the mind. Then they said: this we cannot keep. And having received benefit, they dismissed him.

34. In a certain place lived two monks. A certain great elder came to them and, wishing to test them, took a staff and began to destroy the vegetables of one of them. The brother, seeing this, hid himself, and when the last root remained, he said to the elder: if you wish, abba, leave this. I will make a dish of it, and we will eat together. Then the elder made a

prostration to the brother, saying: because of your guilelessness, brother, the Spirit of God has rested upon you.

35. A certain brother in Scetis found robbers plundering his cell and said to them: hurry, before the brethren come and prevent me from fulfilling the commandment of Christ, Who said: *from him who takes away your goods do not ask them back* (Luke 6:30).

36. The elder said: if you hear that someone hates or reviles you, send or give him a small blessing according to your ability, so that in the hour of judgment you may have boldness to say: forgive us, O Master, our debts, as we too have forgiven our debtors.

37. A brother, traveling, lost his way and asked some people to learn it, and they were evildoers. They directed him into empty places, and one of them followed him to rob him. They had to cross a small canal, and when they began to descend into it, a crocodile rushed at the robber. But the servant of God did not despise him and cried out to the evildoer, pointing to the intention of the beast, and the other, out of gratitude for his rescue, did nothing to the elder.

38. One of the Egyptian fathers recounted: once I decided to travel and, boarding a ship, arrived in Athens. When I was entering the city, I saw a certain elder-monk, well-dressed with a closed Babylonian bag (satchel), who was running, and others were running after him. When he entered the city, a great multitude of people gathered to him, and they led him to the theater. I asked one of them who this was, and he answered: he is one of the Hellenes, the best of the philosophers; he became a Christian, built himself a monastery (cell), and became a monk. Now, after fifteen years, he has entered the city, and we are running so that we might hear what he will say. I too went with them. The archons came and asked him: tell us, if you have something to say. He said: there is no people under heaven like the Christian people, and there is no order like the order of monks, but this alone harms them: that the devil leads them into remembrance of wrongs against one another, so that they say: he said such-and-such to me, and I said such-and-such to him, while meanwhile his own impurities are before him, and he does not see them. Hearing this, all greatly glorified him, and he departed.

39. One of the fathers said: if someone reviles you, bless him; if he accepts the blessing, good for you both; if he does not accept it, then he will receive reviling from God, and you will receive blessing.

40. The elder said: if anyone comes to mind who has insulted, or dishonored, or reviled, or caused harm to someone, that person should remember him as a physician sent from Christ and should regard him as a benefactor, for the very fact that you grieve over what was done to you is a sign of a sick soul, because if you were not sick, you would not suffer. Therefore you should rejoice over your brother, that through him you learn of your sickness, and you should pray for him and accept what he causes you as healing medicine sent from Jesus. But if you grieve, it is as if you say to Jesus: I do not wish to accept Your medicines; I wish to rot in my wounds.

41. Again he said: he who desires to be healed of dreadful wounds of the soul and to be delivered from sickness must patiently endure what is given to him by the physician, for even one suffering from bodily sickness not only reluctantly agrees to amputation or taking a purgative, but even remembers it with displeasure. Nevertheless, being convinced that without this it is impossible to be delivered from the sickness, he endures everything given to him by the physician,

knowing that through a small unpleasantness he will be delivered from a long-lasting sickness. The cauterizer of Jesus is he who dishonors and reviles you, yet delivers you from vainglory; the purgative of Jesus is he who causes you harm, yet delivers you from covetousness. He who flees healing temptation flees eternal life. Who would have given Saint Stephen such glory as he obtained through those who stoned him?

42. Again he said: those who condemn me I do not condemn, but I call them benefactors, and I do not reject the physician of souls who gives the medicine of dishonor to a vainglorious soul.

43. Again he said: we see the Cross of Christ, we read of His sufferings, yet we ourselves do not endure even a small insult.

44. The elder said that with Isidore the Great, the priest of Scetis, there was a brother who served as deacon, whom, on account of his virtue, he wished to make a priest so that after his death he would be his successor, but the other, out of reverent fear, did not submit to ordination and remained a deacon. One of the elders, through the enmity of the devil, became envious of this brother and, when all were in church for the service, went and placed his own book in his cell, then came and said to Abba Isidore: one of the brothers has stolen my book. Abba Isidore was amazed, saying: this has never yet happened in Scetis. The elder who had placed the book said to him: send two fathers with me to search the cells. They went; the elder led them through all the cells of the brethren and finally brought them to the cell of that brother, found the book there, and brought it to the priest. That brother, making a prostration before Abba Isidore in the presence of all the brethren, said: I have sinned, give me a penance. The other imposed a penance on him: not to commune for three weeks. The brother would come to every service before the church and prostrate himself before all the brethren, saying: forgive me, for I have sinned. After three weeks he was received into communion, but immediately the one who had slandered him became possessed and began confessing to all: I slandered the servant of God. The whole church began to pray for him, but he did not receive healing. Then Abba Isidore said to the brother before all: pray for him, for you were slandered; therefore only through you can he receive healing. The brother prayed, and the elder was immediately healed.

45. There was in the city of Theopolis[22] a certain patriarch, very merciful, compassionate toward sinners, tender-hearted, and loving toward mankind. Once one of his servants stole gold from him and out of fear fled to the Thebaid of Egypt. While he was wandering there, Egyptian barbarians, more savage than the very beasts, seized him and led him to the farthest borders of that land. The blessed Bishop Alexander, learning of this, ransomed him as a captive for eighty-five gold coins and, when he returned, received him so tender-heartedly, lovingly, and graciously that someone living at that time in that city said: there is nothing better than to sin before the patriarch of this city.

Endnotes

[22] In Antioch.

Chapter XVII.
On Love

1. Abba Anthony said: I no longer fear God, but I love Him, for *perfect love casts out fear* (1 John 4:18).

2. Again he said: from our neighbor come life and death. For if we gain our brother, we gain God, but if we cause our brother to stumble, we sin against Christ.

3. They said that one of the elders asked God to show him the fathers, and he saw them all, except Abba Anthony. Then he says to the one who was showing him: where then is Abba Anthony? He answered: in the place where God is, there he is.

4. Abba Agathon said: I never fell asleep having anything against anyone, and as far as I was able, I never allowed anyone to sleep having anything against me.

5. He also said: I never gave a love-feast, but giving and receiving counsel was for me a love-feast, considering that gaining my brother is for me an offering of fruit.

6. When the brethren were speaking about love, Abba Joseph said: we have seen what love is, and he told the following about Abba Agathon: he had a knife; a brother who came to him praised it, and he did not permit him to leave otherwise than by taking the knife.

7. Abba Agathon said: if it were possible for me to find a leper and give him my body and take his, I would gladly do so. For this is perfect love.

8. They also said of him that once, having come to a city to sell his wares, he found a sick stranger, abandoned in the marketplace, for whom there was no one to care, and, having rented a small room, he remained with him; from his handwork he paid the rent, and the rest he used for the needs of the sick man. Thus he lived there four months, until the sick man recovered, and then he returned to his cell in peace.

9. They told of Abba Agathon that he carefully fulfilled every commandment: if he got into a boat, he was the first to take hold of the oar; when brethren came to him, immediately after the prayer his own hand would set the table, for he was filled with the love of God.

10. Once Abba Agathon was going to the city to sell his wares and on the way found a leper. The leper says to him: where are you going? Abba Agathon answered: to the city to sell

wares. He said to him: do me a kindness, take me there. He lifted him up and carried him to the city. The leper says: where you will be selling wares, lay me down there also. He did so. When he sold one item, the leper asked: for how much did you sell it? He answered: for such-and-such. He said: buy me some kind of pastry! He bought it. Again he sells another item. The leper asks: for how much? He answers: for such-and-such. He says: buy me such-and-such. And he bought it. When in this manner he had sold all his wares and wanted to go, the leper says to him: are you going? He answers him: I am going. He said: do me a kindness, carry me back to where you found me. He lifted him up and carried him to the former place. The leper says to him: blessed are you, Abba Agathon, by the Lord in heaven and on earth. But, raising his eyes, the elder saw no one, for it was an Angel of the Lord, come to test him.

11. Abba Amoun of Nitria came to Abba Anthony and says to him: I undertake greater labor than you, yet why is your name magnified among men more than mine? Abba Anthony answered him: because I love God more than you.

12. There was an elder in the Cells named Apollon, who, when someone came to ask him for some work, would go with joy, saying: with Christ I shall work today for the sake of my soul, for He is its reward.

13. Abba Isaiah said: love is sitting beside God with unceasing thanksgiving; and in thanksgiving God rejoices, and it is a sign of rest.

14. Abba Theodore of Ennaton related: when I was younger and lived in the desert, I went to the bakery to bake two loaves for myself and found there a brother who also wanted to bake loaves but had no one to help him. I left my own and helped him, but just when I was finished, another brother came, and I helped him too and prepared his loaves; then a third came, and I did the same for him. Thus I did for every one who came and prepared six loaves. Finally, when they ceased to come, I baked my own two loaves.

15. Once Abba John was going with other brethren from Scetis, and the one guiding them lost the way, for it was night. The brethren said to Abba John: what shall we do, abba? The brother has lost the way; shall we not perish, having gone astray? The elder says to them: if we tell him, he will be grieved and ashamed, but I will pretend to be exhausted and will say: I cannot walk, I will remain here until morning. And he did so. And the rest said: neither will we go, but we will sit with you. Thus they sat until morning, without troubling the brother.

16. Abba John Colobos said: one cannot build a house from the top down, but from the foundation to the top. They say to him: what does this word mean? He answered: the foundation is the neighbor, whom you must first gain, because on him hang all the commandments of Christ (Matthew 22:39, 40).

17. They told of Abba John: a certain maiden's parents died, and she was left an orphan. Her name was Paisia. She decided to make her house a hospice for the fathers of Scetis, and thus she spent a considerable time, receiving strangers and giving rest to the fathers. But her property was exhausted and she began to be in want. Dissolute people attached themselves to her and turned her from her good purpose, so that she began to live wickedly, falling even

into fornication. The fathers, hearing of this, were greatly grieved and, summoning Abba John Colobos, said to him: we have heard that this sister is living wickedly, but she, when she was able, showed us her love, and now we must show our love to her and help her. Therefore, take the trouble to go to her and, according to the wisdom given you by God, set her affairs in order. Abba John came to her and says to the old woman doorkeeper: tell your mistress about me. But she sent him away, saying: you first ate up her substance, and now she is poor. Abba John says: tell her that I can help her greatly. All who were there, smiling, asked: what can you give her, seeking so insistently to see her? He answered them: how do you know what I can provide for her? The old woman went and told her about him. The maiden says to her: these monks are always going about the Red Sea and finding pearls. Then, having adorned herself, she says: bring him here. When he entered, she, anticipating him, sat down on the bed; Abba John, approaching, sat down beside her and, looking into her face, said: why have you despised Jesus, that you have come to this? Hearing this, she was as if drenched with frost, and Abba John, bowing his head, began to weep intensely. She asked him: abba, why are you weeping? He raised his head a little, but then lowered it again with weeping and answered: I see that Satan is playing with your face, and how shall I not weep? Hearing this, she says to him: is there repentance for me, abba? He said: there is. Then she says to him: take me wherever you wish. He said: let us go. She rose and followed him. Abba John noticed that she did not arrange anything at all and said nothing about her house, and he marveled. When they came to the desert, it was already late. He made a small pillow of sand for her, and at a short distance one for himself, crossed it and said: sleep here. Then he fulfilled his prayers and himself reclined. Waking around midnight, he saw a luminous path extending from heaven down to her, and the Angels of God bearing up her soul. He rose, went to her, pushed her with his foot and, seeing that she had died, fell on his face, praying to God, and heard that one hour of her repentance was accepted more than the repentance of many who repent for a long time but do not show such fervor in repentance.

18. Abba John said that our father Anthony used to say: I never preferred what was profitable to me over the profit of my brother.

19. Abba Hilarion came from Palestine to the mountain to Abba Anthony. Abba Anthony says to him: well have you come, daystar, rising at dawn! And Abba Hilarion said: peace to you, pillar of light, illumining the universe!

20. One of the elders came to Abba Lot at a small lake of Arsinoites, asked him for a cell, and he gave him one. The elder was unwell, and Abba Lot gave him rest. If anyone came to Abba Lot, he would send them to visit the sick elder as well. But the elder was proposing to them the teaching of Origen, and Abba Lot was grieved by this, lest the fathers should think that they too were of the same mind, yet he was afraid to send him away from that place because of the commandment. Once Abba Lot went to Abba Arsenius and told him about the elder. Abba Arsenius says to him: do not cast him out, but say to him: behold, whatever God has given, eat, drink as much as you wish, only do not speak such words. If he wishes, he will correct himself, and if he does not wish to correct himself, he will of his own accord

ask to leave from there, and the occasion for it will no longer be from you. Abba Lot, having returned, did so. The elder, having listened to him, did not wish to correct himself, but began to ask: for God's sake send me away from here, because I can no longer endure the desert. And so he departed, and Abba Lot accompanied him with love.

21. Abba Peter told of Abba Macarius that, having once come to a certain hermit and finding him sick, he inquired whether he would like to eat something, because in his cell he had nothing. When he said he wanted a pastille (a fragrant cake), the good man was not too lazy to go to Alexandria and bring it to the sick man. And this wondrous deed was known to no one.

22. Before the arrival of Abba Poemen with his brothers in Egypt, there was a certain elder there who had fame and great honor, but when Abba Poemen came there from Scetis, people left him and began to come to Abba Poemen, so that the other became offended. Abba Poemen said to his brothers: what shall we do with this great elder, for people have drawn us into causing offense, having left the elder and turned to us, who know nothing? How shall we bring rest to the elder? Then he says to them: prepare some food, take a vessel of wine, and let us go to him, that we may partake together. Perhaps by this we shall bring rest to him. So they took the food and went. When they knocked at the door, his disciple responded and asked: who are you? They answered: tell the abba that Poemen desires to receive a blessing from him. When the disciple said this, he answered: go away, I have no time. But they, standing in the heat, said: we will not leave until we are deemed worthy to see the elder. The elder, moved by their humility and patience, opened to them. They entered and, when they were partaking, he said to them: truly, not only what I have heard about you, but a hundred times more have I now seen in your deed. And he became their friend from that day.

23. Abba Poemen related that if a brother came to Abba John Colobos, he would bestow upon him the love of which the Apostle speaks: *Love suffers long and is kind* (1 Corinthians 13:4).

24. Again he said: no one can find greater love than this, *to lay down one's life for his neighbor* (John 15:13), for if anyone hears a word of insult and, being able himself to say the same, strives not to say it, or if, being wronged, he bears it and does not repay in kind, such a one lays down his soul for his neighbor.

25. A brother asked Abba Poemen: I have found a place in which there is every consolation for the brethren. Do you wish me to settle there? The elder answered: remain where you will not be harmful to your brother.

26. A brother asked Abba Poemen: if a brother has some of my money, do you wish me to ask him for it? The elder answered: ask him once. The brother said: what then shall I do, for I cannot overcome my thought? The elder says to him: leave your thought to be troubled, only do not offend your brother.

27. They said of Abba Poemen: when he lived in Scetis with two of his brothers and the younger was causing them grief, he said to the other brother: the younger brother is disturbing us; let us depart from here. And, having gone out, they left him. He, noticing that they were long absent, came out and, seeing them already at a great distance, began to run after them, crying out. Abba Poemen said: let us wait for the brother, for he will become exhausted. Having caught up with them, the brother made a prostration, saying: where are you going and leaving me alone? The elder said to him: you trouble us, therefore we are departing. He answered: true, true, but wherever you wish, let us go together! The elder, seeing his guilelessness, says to the other brother: let us return, brother, for he does not do this intentionally, but the devil does it to him. And, having returned, they came to their place.

28. It once happened that Abba Pambo was going with the brethren in the regions of Egypt. Seeing some laymen sitting, he said to them: stand up, greet the monks, that you may be blessed, for they often converse with God and their mouths are holy.

29. They said of Abba Paphnutius that he did not drink wine. Once, going along the way, he came upon a band of robbers. They were drinking wine. Their chieftain knew him and knew that he did not drink wine, but seeing that he was greatly exhausted, he filled a cup with wine and, with sword in hand, said to him: if you do not drink, I will kill you. The elder, seeing that he wished to fulfill the commandment of God, and desiring to gain him, took it and drank. Then the chieftain bowed to him and said: forgive me, abba, that I offended you. The elder answered: I believe in God that for this cup He will show you mercy both in this age and in the age to come. The chieftain said: I too believe in God that from now on I will do no evil to anyone. Thus the elder gained the whole band, having abandoned his own will for the Lord's sake.

30. Once Saracens came and robbed Abba Sisoes and his brother. They went out into the desert to seek something for themselves to eat. The elder came upon the remains of camel fodder and, having dug it out, found two beans. He ate one and held the other in his hand. The brother, coming at that moment, found him eating and said: is this love? You found food and are eating alone, without calling me?! Abba Sisoes says to him: I have not deprived you, brother! Behold, I have kept your portion in my hand.

31. They said of Abba Silvanus that he sat in a hidden cell, where he made one hundred baskets, having a little dried peas and eating them. Once a man came from Egypt with a donkey loaded with bread and, having knocked at his cell, left them beside it. The elder took the baskets, placed them on the donkey, and sent him off.

32. Abba Hyperechius said: absolve your brother from his sins without heavy reproach, for God does not reject those who turn to Him. But let no word of malice and guile dwell in your heart against your brother, that you may be strong to say: *Forgive us our debts, as we also forgive our debtors* (Matthew 6:12).

33. Someone related that a certain magistrianus-agent, young and of handsome appearance, served in the emperor's economic affairs. In one city he had a friend, one of the

notables, who had a young wife, and when the magistrianus happened to be in that city, his friend would receive him, lodge him in his house, and dine with him in the presence of his wife, out of friendly love for him. Since the magistrianus visited him frequently, the friend's wife developed thoughts toward him, while he knew nothing of it. She, however, out of chastity, did not reveal this to him, but endured, suffering, and when the magistrianus happened to be away on a journey for a long time, she fell ill from her thoughts and took to bed. Her husband summoned physicians, and, having examined her, they said to him: does she not have some suffering of the soul, because there is no bodily illness? Her husband, sitting constantly beside her, implored her, saying: tell me, what is the matter with you? She at first did not reveal it out of fear and shame, but then she revealed it, saying: do you know what, my lord? Whether from love or from simplicity, you bring youthful faces here, and I, as a woman, have become attached to the magistrianus. Hearing this, her husband was reassured and, when a few days later the magistrianus came, went out to meet him and said: you know, my brother, how I love you; out of love I have received you and you have been at table together with my wife? And behold, my wife has developed thoughts toward you. Hearing this, the magistrianus not only did not develop thoughts toward her, but was greatly grieved out of love for her husband and said to him: do not sorrow! God is our Helper! Then he went, took off his fine clothing and, taking a candle, burned his head and face, thereby destroying all his former beauty, becoming like an ancient leper. Then he put on plain clothing and came to the house of his friend. His wife was lying down, and her husband sat beside her. The magistrianus uncovered his head and face and, showing them, said: thus has the Lord done to me! She, seeing him after such beauty in such disfigurement, was amazed, and God, for the sake of his deed, took the warfare from her. She immediately rose, having rejected all her former thoughts. And the magistrianus took her husband aside to a private place and said: behold, by God's help, your wife has no evil, and from now on she shall not see my face again. This is what it means to lay down one's soul for love's sake and to repay good for good!

34. Two brothers were taken to be tortured and after the first torments were cast into prison. They had a disagreement between themselves, and one of them, making a prostration, said to his brother: tomorrow we must finish our lives; therefore let us cast away our enmity and restore love. But the brother would not agree to reconciliation. When on the next day they were brought to the place of torture, the one who had not accepted reconciliation immediately denied Christ, and the archon asked him: why did you not deny yesterday, under such torments? He answered: I bear malice toward my brother and did not wish to be reconciled with him; therefore I was deprived of God's help.

35. In one city there was a money-changer. One of the citizens brought him a note for five hundred gold coins and said: take this note and, if I have need, pay out in parts. When he gave him the note, no one was there, but one of the notables, passing by the money-changing shop, heard and saw how the note was given to the money-changer, while he himself remained unnoticed. After several days, the one who had given the note came and says to the money-changer: give me part of the money, for I have need. The other, relying on the fact

that there was no witness, denied it, saying: you gave me nothing, and he went out in great distress. The notable met him and asked: what is the matter with you? And he learned of what had happened. He says to him: did you truly give it to him? He answers: truly. Then the notable says to him: say to the money-changer: go, confirm to me before Saint Andrew, and that is enough for you. (And there was a church at the place of the martyrdom of Saint Andrew.) When the money-changer was to come to swear, the notable took his servant, saying to him: do not be troubled by what I am now going to do, but bear with it, and he went to the church, threw off his garment, and began to act as if possessed, crying out and making senseless sounds. When those others also entered, he spoke: behold, this madman took five hundred gold coins from this man and now wishes to swear that he did not take them. Then he seized him and began to choke him, crying out: Saint Andrew says to you: return the five hundred gold coins to this man. The other became frightened and in fear confessed, promising: I will bring them. He says to him: bring them at once. He went and immediately brought them. Then the one who had feigned possession said to the owner of the gold coins: Saint Andrew says: lay six gold coins upon the table. He laid them down with joy. When they had departed, he dressed properly and went out, making his way to the money-changer, who, seeing him, began to look him over from top to bottom. He said to him: why do you look at me so? Believe me, by the grace of Christ, I have no demon, but when that man gave you the note, I, passing by, heard and saw it clearly. If I had simply told you, you would have said: one witness is not sufficient. Therefore I staged this drama, so that you would not destroy your soul and that man would not lose his money.

36. A certain exceedingly Christ-loving and pious monk had a beloved hermit. When the hermit died, the brother, entering his cell, found fifty gold coins, was astonished, and began to weep, fearing lest the hermit had offended God by these coins. After long prayer for him, he saw an Angel of God, who said to him: why do you grieve so over the hermit? That for which you pray, leave to the love of God for mankind, for if all were perfect, upon what would God's love for mankind be made manifest? The brother, being assured by this that the hermit was forgiven, became of good cheer and glorified God with all his heart.

37. An elder sent his disciple to Egypt for a camel,[23] to transport baskets there. When the disciple was leading the camel to Scetis, another elder met him and said: if I had known you were going to Egypt, I would have asked you to bring a camel for me too. The brother went and told his father about this. The elder says to him: take the camel and give it to the elder, saying: we have not yet made ready; take the camel and fulfill your need. And go yourself with him to Egypt and bring the camel back again, to transport our baskets. The brother went to that elder and said as his abba commanded him. The elder took the camel and loaded it. Having reached Egypt, they unloaded the baskets and the brother, taking the camel, said to the elder: pray for me. He asked: where are you going? The brother answered: to Scetis, to bring our baskets too. The elder was moved and, making a prostration, said with tears: forgive me, your great love has taken my fruit.

38. An elder said: if someone asks something of you and you immediately give it to him, let your thought also be favorably disposed toward the giving, as it is written: *whoever compels you to go one mile, go with him two* (Matthew 5:41). This means: if someone asks something of you, give it to him from soul and body.

39. In the Cells there were two brothers, and the elder of them asked the younger: let us live together, brother. He says to him: I am a sinner and cannot live with you, abba! But the other said to him: no, you can. The elder was so pure and chaste that he did not even wish to hear that a monk has thoughts of fornication. The brother says: leave me for this week, and then we will speak again. After a week the elder came to him, and the younger, wishing to test him, said: I fell into great temptation this week: I went to a village on an errand and fell with a woman. The elder asked: is there repentance? The brother answered: there is. The elder said: I will bear half of your sin for you. The brother says to him: now we can live together. And he remained with him until his very death.

40. They said of a certain brother that, having finished his baskets and attached handles to them, he heard his neighbor saying: what shall I do? The market is near, and I have no handles for my baskets. Then the brother, detaching the handles from his own baskets, brought them to the brother and said: these are extra for me, take them for your baskets, and thereby made it so that the brother's baskets were sold while his own remained.

41. They told of a certain elder in Scetis that he was sick and desired to eat fresh bread. Hearing of this, one of the ascetic brethren took his cloak, put dry bread in it, went to Egypt, and, having exchanged it for fresh bread, brought it to the elder. The brethren, seeing that it was still warm, were amazed, and the elder did not wish to taste it, saying: this is the blood of my brother. But the elders implored him: for the Lord's sake, eat, lest the brother's sacrifice be in vain. Then he yielded to their request and ate.

42. A brother asked an elder: why do many labor in ascetic struggles even now, yet do not receive such grace as the ancients? The elder answered him: then there was love and each drew his neighbor upward, but now there is a cooling of love and each draws his neighbor downward. Therefore we do not receive grace.

43. Once three brothers went for the harvest and took sixty arourae (a measure of land) for themselves. One of them fell ill on the very first day and returned to his cell. After this, one of the remaining said to the other: you see, our brother has fallen ill; let us compel our thought a little and let us believe that by his prayers we can reap his portion too. When the work was finished and they were going to receive their wages, they called the brother as well, saying: come, take your wages, brother! But he said: what wages shall I receive, not having reaped? They said: by your prayers your portion of the harvest was also finished; therefore come, take your wages. After a long dispute among themselves, when one said: I will not take, and the others would not agree to let him not take, they all went for judgment to a great elder. The brother said to him: father, we three went to reap. When we came to the field, on the very first day I fell ill and returned to my cell, not having reaped even one day, and the brethren compel me to take wages, which I have not at all reaped. The other two said: father,

the three of us took sixty arourae to reap. If we had all worked, we would scarcely have finished them, but by the prayers of our brother we very quickly finished the harvest. Therefore we say to him: take your wages, but he does not wish to. Hearing this, the elder was amazed and said to his brother: strike the semantron, that all the brethren may assemble. When all had come, he said to them: come, brethren, hear today a righteous judgment! And the elder told them everything. All judged that the brother should take the wages and do with them what he wished. The brother took them and went with weeping and sorrow.

44. An elder said: our fathers had the custom of coming to newly-beginning brethren who had resolved to struggle in solitude and watching over them, lest anyone be harmed in thought by a temptation from demons, and, if any of them was found to be harmed, they would bring him to the church, set out a basin, and after prayer over the sick one, all the brethren would wash, and then pour the water upon him. And he was immediately cleansed.

45. Two elders lived together for many years and never had any quarrel between them. Then one of them said to the other: let us have one quarrel too, as people do. The other answered: I do not know how a quarrel happens. The first said to him: behold, I will place a brick in the middle and will say: this is mine, and you say: no, this is mine, and thus a beginning will be made. They placed a brick in the middle and one says: this is mine, and the other said: no, this is mine. Then the first said: if it is yours, then take it and go. And so they parted, having been unable to quarrel with each other.

46. An elder said: I never desired a deed profitable to me but causing loss to my brother, having that hope that the profit of my brother is for me also a deed that bears fruit.

47. A certain ascetic, having found a demoniac who could not fast, out of the love of God, as it is written: *look not only to his own interests, but also to the interests of his neighbor* (Philippians 2:4), prayed that the demon might pass into him and that the other be freed from it. God heard his prayer, and the ascetic, burdened by the demon, endured, persevering in fasting, prayer, and struggle. For this, and even more for his love, in a few days God delivered him from the demon.

48. A brother asked an elder: there are two brothers: one of them practices stillness, fasting six days and undertaking great labor, while the other serves those who are suffering. Whose deed will God accept more favorably? The elder says to him: if the brother who fasts six days were even to hang himself by the ribs, he still could not be equal to the one who serves those who are suffering.

49. A brother served a certain sick father, whose body had begun to rot and emit foul-smelling discharge. Then his thought said to the brother: flee from here, for you cannot bear this stench. The brother took a potsherd and collected the discharge from the sick man into it. His thought again began to say to him: flee, but he said to the thought: if I wish to leave, then I will drink this. Then his thought said to him: do not flee and do not drink such stench. Thus the brother labored and endured, serving the elder, and God, seeing the labor of the brother, healed him.

50. One of the fathers went to the city to sell his handwork and, seeing a naked beggar, had compassion on him and gave him his garment. The beggar went and sold it. The elder, learning of what he had done, became sorrowful and regretted that he had given him the garment. That night Christ appeared to the elder in a dream in his garment and says: do not sorrow, for behold I am wearing what you gave Me.

51. The elders said: everyone must appropriate to himself everything concerning his neighbor and sympathize with him in all things: rejoice and grieve together with him, and in general be so disposed as if he bears his body, and grieve as if about himself when some sorrow befalls the other, concerning which it is also written: *so we, being many, are one body in Christ* (Romans 12:5) and *now the multitude of those who believed were of one heart and one soul* (Acts 4:32).

52. An elder said: hear what our Lord Jesus Christ says: *By this all will know that you are My disciples*, and, showing by what, He did not say: by miracles, but by what? *if you have love for one another* (John 13:35). And again, He said to His Father: *by this they will know that You sent Me, if all may be one* (John 17:21). And He says to the disciples: *A new commandment I give to you, that you love one another* (John 13:34). Such a one is more honorable and radiant than one who raises the dead, for that is a work of God's grace, but this is also of your labor and zeal; this is the work that is properly Christian; this shows the disciples of the crucified Christ; without this, even martyrdom itself cannot be profitable.

53. One monk had over him another monk, who lived in a cell ten miles distant from him. His thought said to him: call the brother, that he may come and take bread. Then he thought again: for the sake of bread do I wish to trouble the brother for ten miles? I will rather carry half a loaf to him myself. He took it and went to the brother's cell. While going, he stumbled, injured the toe of his foot, blood flowed, and he began to weep from pain. Then an Angel of the Lord came and asks him: why are you weeping? He answers: I injured my toe, and it hurts. The Angel said to him: do you weep because of this? Do not weep, for the steps you have made for the Lord are numbered and are of great price before the face of God. And doubt not this. Behold, before you I will take a portion of your blood and bear it up before God. Then with thanksgiving he went to that monk and, having given him the bread, told him of God's love for mankind and returned to his cell. After one day, he took the other half of the bread and again went to the monk, but the other was coming to him, and they met on the road. The one who had done the good deed began to say to him: I have found a treasure, and you wish to steal it. The other said to him: do you alone fit through the narrow gates? Leave room for us to enter together with you. While they were still speaking, an Angel of the Lord appeared to them and said: your dispute has ascended to God as fragrant incense.

54. Two brothers lived together. It happened that the one of them who attended to their needs began to bring less than usual. The one remaining in the cell began to think that he either was spending it on something bad or was cheating him. And so, desiring to know the cause, he followed after him and saw how he entered an immoral place. Then he imagined to himself that he himself had gone to the immoral place and, falling down before his brother, asked for repentance. After the brother, by frequently asking the sinful one for prayers for himself as a sinner, had turned him to repentance, the hour of his calling came, and he, drawing near to death, confessed to his brother: I am pure of this sin, but I took it upon myself for your sake, that you

might repent. When the brother reposed, the one who had sinned increased his ascetic struggle of repentance even more.

55. Another, having learned of a similar sin of his brother with a maiden, did not expose him, but sighed in silence and multiplied his prayers, also asking the brother who lived with him to pray for him, adding that he had sinned greatly and wished to repent before death. The amazed sinner, struck by his brother's repentance, himself repented and began to do the same. When the brother who had not sinned was called, in the hour of his death he revealed this to the brother.

56. Another, when his brother, having left monasticism, returned to the world, imagined to himself that he had the same intention and began to repent. Through this, finally, the other also repented and returned, and they began to struggle even more strictly.

57. Certain brothers came to Mount Diocius and learned to make paper. They worked for hire, but since they were unskilled, no one ordered from them. An elder came to them and asked: why are you not working? They, being honest, answered: because we work poorly. The elder, knowing a certain doer of God's will, says to them: go to such-and-such an elder, and he will give you work. They came to him, and the elder gladly agreed to give them work. The brothers say to him: we work poorly, father. The elder answered them: I believe in God that by your diligence you will advance to better. Thus the elder, rich in love, kindled in them a zeal for work, and soon the work went well. Truly, *the violent take it by force* (Matthew 11:12).

58. A brother asked an elder: why is it that, performing my small service, I see that sometimes I have no warmth in my heart, and sometimes no zeal? The elder says to him: how else would it be shown that a man loves God!? And he said further: as for me, my body has never been able to fully fulfill my heart's desire.

59. A certain brother went to buy linen from a widow. Having sold it to him, she sighed. The brother asked her: what is the matter with you? The widow answered: God has sent you today to provide for your brethren and my orphans. The brother, hearing this, was grieved and, taking the linen, threw it back into the widow's lap, and thereby showed her mercy.

60. An elder said: do not demand love from your neighbor and, loving someone, do not be troubled if you do not meet a response, but rather show love to your neighbor yourself and be at peace, for thereby you will also bring your neighbor to love.

61. He also said: that you are weak in love for your brethren happens to you because you accept thoughts of suspicion, believe your own heart, and do not wish to endure anything that is not according to your will. Therefore you must, with God's help, above all not at all believe your own suspicions, with all care and all strength humble yourself before the brethren, and cut off your own will for their sake.

62. Again he said that love according to God is stronger than natural love.

Endnotes

[23] Camel.

Chapter XVIII.
On Those with the Gift of Foresight

1. Once it was revealed to Abba Anthony in the desert: in the city there is one like unto you, a physician by trade, who gives his surplus to those in need and every day sings the Trisagion with the Angels of God.

2. They said of Abba Anthony that he was a bearer of the Spirit, but for the sake of men he spoke of nothing, though he foresaw both what is and what is to come.

3. A brother came to Scetis, to the cell of Abba Arsenius, and, peering through the door, saw that the elder was all like fire. The brother was worthy to see this. When he knocked, the elder came out and, seeing the brother amazed, asked: did you knock long and did you see anything? He said: no. And, having conversed with him, the elder dismissed him.

4. Abba Daniel said: Abba Arsenius told us, as if about some other person, but likely it was he himself, that a certain elder was sitting in his cell and a voice came to him, saying: come, I will show you the deeds of men. He rose and went out. The speaker led him to a certain place and showed him an Ethiopian cutting wood. He cut a great bundle, tried to lift it, and could not. Instead of removing some from it, he began again to cut wood and add to the bundle. And he did this many times. Going on a little further, he showed him another man who was standing by a lake. Drawing water from it, he poured it into a vessel full of holes, and the water flowed out again into the lake. Then he says to him: come, I will show you something else! And he sees a temple and two men sitting on horses and holding a beam by its ends, one opposite the other. They wished to pass through the door and could not, because the beam lay crosswise to it, and neither of them humbled himself to carry the beam behind the other so that it might pass lengthwise, and therefore both remained outside the door. These, said the guide, are those who bear the yoke of righteousness with pride and do not humble themselves to correct themselves and go on the humble path of Christ, and therefore remain outside the Kingdom of God. And the one cutting wood is a man burdened with many sins, who, instead of repenting, adds new iniquities to his sins. And the one drawing water is a man who does good deeds, but, having an admixture of wickedness in them, by that ruins even his good. Thus a man must always be sober in his deeds, lest he labor in vain.

5. Some brothers had a sorrow in the place of their dwelling, and, wishing to leave it, they went to Abba Ammon. The elder at that time was sailing on the river and, seeing the brothers walking along the shore, asked the boatmen to put him ashore. Calling the brothers, he said to them: I am Ammon, to whom you are going. And he comforted them and disposed them to return to the place from which they had come, for the matter was not one of harm to the soul, but only of human sorrow.

6. Our Father Daniel of Pharan said: Blessed Arsenius told us, as if about some other person, but likely it was he himself, that one Scetiot was a great worker, but simple in faith, and through simplicity he erred, saying that the Bread which we receive is not essentially the Body of Christ, but only an image of it. Two elders, hearing of this and knowing that he was great in life, considered that he spoke thus in innocence and simplicity, and therefore came to him and said: Abba! We have heard about someone who speaks words contrary to the faith, that the Bread with which we commune is not essentially the Body of Christ, but only an image of it. The elder confessed: it is I who say this. Then they began to persuade him: do not hold thus, Abba, but as the Universal Church has handed down, for we believe that this Bread is truly the Body of Christ, and not only an image of it. Just as in the beginning God, taking dust from the earth, created man in His own image, and no one can say that this image of God does not exist, though it is not visible, so also concerning the Bread, of which He said: *"This is My body"* (Matthew 26:26; Mark 14:22; Luke 22:19), we believe that it is truly the Body of Christ. The elder answered: unless I am assured by the deed itself, I cannot be fully persuaded. They said to him: let us pray to God this week concerning this mystery, and we believe that God will reveal it to us. The elder received this word with joy and prayed to God, saying: Lord! You know that not out of malice do I not believe, but lest I wander in ignorance. Reveal to me, O Lord Jesus Christ! Likewise the elders, returning to their cells, besought God: O Lord Jesus Christ! Reveal to the elder this mystery, that he may believe and not lose his labor! God heard them. When the week had passed, they came on Sunday to church and stood, the three of them, apart in one row; the elder was in the middle. Their eyes were opened, and when the Bread was placed on the holy altar, it appeared to all three of them, yet to them alone, as an Infant. When the priest stretched forth his hand to break the Bread, an Angel of the Lord descended from heaven with a knife, slew the Infant, and poured out His blood into the chalice. When the priest was dividing the Bread into small parts, the Angel also was cutting small parts from the Infant. But when they approached to receive the Holy Mysteries, to the elder alone was given bloody flesh. Seeing this, he cried out: I believe, O Lord, that this Bread is Your Body and this chalice is Your Blood. And immediately the flesh in his hand became bread according to the mystery, and he communed, giving thanks to God. Then the elders said to him: God knows human nature, that it cannot eat raw flesh, and therefore He conceals His Body in bread and His Blood in wine, when the faithful receive them. Thanking God for the elder, that He did not allow him to lose his labors, all three returned to their cells with joy.

7. The same Abba Daniel told of another great elder, who lived in the lower regions of Egypt, that through simplicity he said that Melchizedek is the Son of God. Blessed Cyril,

Archbishop of Alexandria, was informed of this, and he sent for him. The Archbishop, knowing that the elder was a wonder-worker and that whatever he asked of God, He revealed to him, and that he spoke this word through simplicity, employed this wise measure: when the elder arrived, he said to him: Abba! I entreat you, since one thought tells me that Melchizedek is the Son of God, and another that he is not, but a man, a high priest of God, and since I am in doubt about this, I have sent for you, that you might pray to God, and He would reveal this to you. The elder, emboldened by his virtues, said with boldness: give me three days, I will ask God and tell you who Melchizedek was. He went and began to pray to God concerning this. After three days he came to Blessed Cyril and said: Melchizedek is a man. The Archbishop asked him: how did you learn this, Abba? The elder answered: God showed me all the Patriarchs: they all, one after another, passed before me, from Adam to Melchizedek, and the Angel said to me: this is Melchizedek, and believe that he is truly such. Then the elder, returning, himself began to proclaim that Melchizedek is a man, and Blessed Cyril was greatly gladdened by this.

8. Holy Bishop Epiphanius related that in the time of Blessed Athanasius the Great, crows flying around the temple of Serapis incessantly cried: cras, cras... The Hellenes, approaching Blessed Athanasius, demanded: wicked old man! Tell us, what do the crows cry? He answered them: the crows cry cras, cras..., and in the Ausonian[24] tongue "cras" means "tomorrow." Tomorrow you shall see the glory of God. And on the following day came the news of the death of Julian the emperor. On this occasion the pagans gathered and cried out against Serapis: if you did not want him, why did you accept his gifts?

9. He also related that in Alexandria there was a charioteer whose mother was named Mary. During the horse races he fell, but rose, overtook the one who had pushed him, and prevailed. Then the crowd cried out: the son of Mary fell, but rose and conquered. While this cry still resounded, a rumor passed through the crowd concerning the temple of Serapis, that Theophilus the Great had come, overthrown the idol of Serapis, and taken possession of the temple.

10. Abba Ephraim, being yet a youth, saw a dream or vision, as though upon his tongue a vine had sprouted, grew, and filled all the earth beneath the sky. It was exceedingly fruitful, and the birds of heaven came and ate its grapes, and the more they ate, the more its fruits multiplied.

11. One of the holy elders once saw in a vision a host of Angels descending from heaven by the command of God with a scroll in their hands, that is, with a book written within and without. They asked one another: who should receive it? And some said one person, and others another. They were told: truly, those too are holy and righteous, but this book no one can receive except Ephraim. And the elder saw that they gave the scroll to Ephraim. Rising in the morning, he heard Ephraim, and as though a fountain flowed from his mouth when he composed discourses. Then the elder understood that what proceeded from the mouth of Ephraim was from the Holy Spirit.

12. The disciple of Abba Eulogius related to us: the elder sent us to Alexandria to sell handiwork and gave us a commandment not to remain there more than three days. If, he said, you remain longer, I am free from your sin. We asked him: how then do other monks, conversing day and night with laymen in cities and villages, not suffer harm? Then, opening his truthful lips, the elder said to us: believe me, children! After I became a monk, I spent thirty-eight years in Scetis without going out. After the thirty-eight years had passed, I went with Abba Daniel to Pope Eusebius in Alexandria on a certain matter. Entering the city, we saw a multitude of monks, and I beheld that some were being beaten in the face by crows, others were embraced by naked women who whispered in their ears, others were struck by boys, also naked, who smeared them with human dung, and still others, I saw, came with knives, cut off human flesh, and gave it to the monks to eat. From this I understood that, whichever passion a monk falls into, such demons hover near him and converse with him in thought. Therefore, brethren, I do not want you to tarry long in the city, lest thoughts, or rather demons, disturb you.

13. They said of Abba Zeno that while living in Scetis, he went out of his cell one night toward the lake and, losing his way, wandered three days and three nights. Worn out and fainting, he fell and awaited death. But behold, a youth stood before him, holding bread and a vessel of water in his hands, and said to him: rise, eat. But the elder, rising, began to pray, thinking it was a phantom. The youth said to him: you have done well. And he prayed a second and a third time. Again the youth said: you have done well. Then the elder took and ate. After this the youth said to him: as far as you have wandered, so far are you from your cell, but rise and follow me. And immediately he found himself at his cell. The elder said to him: enter, make a prayer for us! But when the elder entered, the youth became invisible.

14. Abba John related that one of the elders in ecstasy saw such a vision: three monks stood on the shore of the sea, and a voice came to them from the other shore: take fiery wings and fly to me. Two of them took such wings and flew to the other side, but the third remained, weeping bitterly and crying out. Then wings were given to him also, only not fiery, but weak and powerless, and he, with difficulty and much sorrow, sinking and rising, reached the other shore. So also this generation, if it receives wings, receives not fiery ones, but weak and powerless, barely sustaining them.

15. One elder, entering the cell of Abba John, found him sleeping, and an Angel of God standing before him and weaving above him. Seeing this, he withdrew. When the elder arose, he asked his disciple: did anyone come here while I slept? The disciple said: such-and-such an elder came. Abba John knew that the elder was of equal measure with himself and had seen the Angel.

16. In the lavra of Epistimius, at a distance of fifteen stadia from the lavra of our holy father Sabbas, there was a wondrous hermit named John, who lived together with his disciple. His disciple, seeing the tumults and calamities caused by the Saracens, daily inflicted upon the Holy City of Christ our God, asked his father: since I am certain, father, that God conceals nothing from you of what He intends to do, I entreat you, tell me, will the city be taken? The

elder said to him: how can I know about this, being a sinful man? But the disciple did not cease asking him, wishing to learn of this. Then the elder, with tears, told him: since I see, child, that you painfully wish to learn of this, I will tell you what God has shown me. Five days before this, I was sitting at prayer concerning this and saw, as though I were caught up before Holy Golgotha. All the people with the clergy cried out: Lord, have mercy! Raising my eyes, I saw our Lord Jesus Christ nailed to the cross, and the Most Holy Theotokos, the Lady of the world, fervently praying to Him for the people. But He was turning His face away from the people, saying: I will not hear them, for they have defiled My altar. Crying out long with tears and groaning, Lord, have mercy, we passed into the church of Holy Constantine and there also cried out: Lord, have mercy! I went into the church together with the clergy. When I descended to venerate the place where the honorable wood of the Life-giving Cross was found, I saw that stinking dung was coming forth from there into the church. Two elders of priestly appearance stood there, and I said to them: do you not fear God, that we cannot even pray because of this filth?! Whence is this stench lying here? They said: from the iniquities of the clergy of this place. I asked: can you not clean it, so that we may have access to pray? They answered: believe, brother, that which you see here will not be cleansed except by fire. Having told this, the elder wept and said to his disciple: here is what I will tell you, child! A decree has been issued that I am to be beheaded. I greatly entreated God to forgive me, and it was revealed to me that this will certainly come to pass, but He alone knows that I have never shed human blood upon the earth. While they were speaking, barbarians attacked them. The disciple fled from fear, but they seized the elder and killed him, then quickly departed. Returning and seeing the elder dead, the disciple wept bitterly and buried him with the fathers.

17. The holy fathers prophesied thus concerning the last generation: what, they said, have we done? The great Abba Ischyrion replied: we have fulfilled the commandments of God. Others asked: and those who will come after us, what will they do? He answered: they will come to half of our work. They said: and what of those who will come after them? And the answer was: the men of that generation will do nothing at all, but temptation will come upon them, and those who prove worthy in that time will be shown to be better than us and our fathers.

18. They said of Abba Longinus that once a shipowner[25] brought him gold from the profit of his ships, but he did not wish to accept it and said to him: there is no need of this here, but do me the kindness, sit upon your beast and hasten to the bridge of Saint Peter, where you will find a young man, dressed in such-and-such clothes. Give him all the gold, asking what is the matter with him. The shipowner hastened there, came, and found the young man, as the elder had told him, and asked him: where are you going, brother? I was at Abba Longinus, and he sent me to you to give you this gold. The young man, hearing of Abba Longinus, told him of his grief: I have fallen into great debts and, having nothing with which to pay, I am going outside the city to hang myself. And that you may believe, here is the rope with me. And, taking the rope from his bosom, he showed it to him. The shipowner gave him the gold and returned him to the city, then, returning to Abba Longinus, told him

everything. Then the elder said to him: believe me, brother, if you had not hastened and found him, both I and you would have been judged for his soul.

19. At another time, when the fathers were sitting in the cell of Abba Longinus and asking him about various things, he suddenly rose and, saying nothing to anyone, went out of the cell and hastened to the lake. When he reached the lake, a ship was putting in to shore, having come from the regions of Egypt, on which was a holy elder who was going to visit the Abba. They kissed one another in the Holy Spirit and stood for prayer. The Egyptian was saying to God: Lord! Did I not entreat You that nothing be revealed about me to the elder and that he not undertake labor for my sake! They came to the cell of Abba Longinus, and on the morrow the Egyptian reposed.

20. Abba Macarius lived in the deep desert and was a hermit there alone, and somewhat lower was another desert, in which many brethren lived. Once the elder looked upon the road and saw Satan coming in the form of a man and passing by him. He appeared clothed in a linen garment resembling a sticharion, which was full of holes, and on each hole hung a gourd. The elder asked him: where are you going, great one? He answered: I am going to visit the brethren. The elder said: and why do you have these gourds? He said: I am carrying dishes for the brethren. The elder asked: and all these with dishes? He answered: yes, if someone does not like one, I will offer another, but certainly, at least one of them, will please him. Having said this, he went on. The elder continued to watch the road until he returned, and, seeing him, said: be saved! He answered: where shall I find salvation?! The elder asked: why so? Because, he said, they have all become like wild beasts to me and no one accepts me. The elder asked again: what, do you not have even one friend there? He answered: only one monk there is my friend, and it is well that at least he believes me and, when he sees me, spins around like the wind. The elder asked the brother's name, and he answered: Theopemptus. And having said this, he departed. Then Abba Macarius rose and went to the lower desert. The brethren, hearing of it, took palm branches and went out to meet him. Each of them prepared himself, thinking that perhaps the elder would stop with him, but he asked for Theopemptus and, finding him, entered his cell. Theopemptus received him with joy. When they were left alone, the elder asked: how are things with you, brother? He said: by your prayers, well. The elder asked again: do not thoughts war against you? Ashamed to speak the truth, he answered: it seems I am well. The elder said to him: behold, how many years I have struggled, and everyone honors me, but even me, an old man, the spirit of fornication troubles. Then Theopemptus also said: believe me, Abba, me too. The elder confessed concerning himself that other thoughts also war against him, so as thereby to dispose the brother to confession. Then he said to him: how do you fast? He said, until the ninth hour. The elder said: fast until evening and struggle, read also from the Gospel and from the psalms; when a thought comes, do not attend to what is below, but always to what is above, and the Lord will quickly help you. Having thus instructed the brother, the elder departed to his own desert. Looking upon the road, he again saw that demon and asked him: where are you going now? He answered: to visit the brethren, and went on. When he was returning, the saint said to him: how are the brethren? He answered: badly. The elder asked: why? And he said: they

are all savage, and what is worse, even the friend who listened to me, he too, I do not know how, has become corrupted and no longer loves me, but has become the most savage of all. I have sworn not to go there anymore, except after some time. Having said this, he departed, leaving the elder, who entered his cell.

21. Abba Macarius said to the brethren concerning the desolation of Scetis: when you see a cell being built near the lake, know that the desolation is near; when you see trees, it is at the doors; but when you see youths, take up your sheepskins and depart.

22. Abba Macarius related, wishing to encourage the brethren: a demon-possessed youth came here with his mother, and he said to her: rise, old woman, let us go from here! She said: we cannot go on foot. The youth said: I will carry you. And I marveled at the cunning of the demon, how he wished to drive them away from here.

23. They said of Abba Macarius that, once going to church for the service, he saw near the cell of one of the brethren a multitude of demons, of whom some had transformed themselves into women and spoke shameful words, others into boys and also spoke obscenities, and others leaped about and transformed themselves into various forms. The clairvoyant elder, seeing this, sighed and said: surely this brother lives in negligence, and therefore the evil spirits so shamelessly surround his cell. When the service ended, returning, he entered the brother's cell and said to him: I am grieved, brother, and I have faith that if you pray for me, God will lighten my grief. The brother, repenting before the elder, said to him: Father! I am unworthy to pray for you. But the elder did not cease asking the brother: I will not leave here until you give me your word to make one prayer each night for me. And the brother submitted to the elder's command, which he made to give him occasion to begin praying at night. The brother rose at night and made a prayer for the elder. When the prayer was finished, coming to compunction, he said to himself: wretched soul! You pray for such an elder, and will you not pray for yourself? And he made a fervent prayer also for himself. Thus he spent the whole week, making each night two prayers, one for the elder and another for himself. On Sunday, going to church, Abba Macarius again saw the demons standing around the brother's cell, but very gloomy, and he understood that the demons were gloomy because the brother had begun to pray. Rejoicing, he entered the brother's cell and said to him: do me the kindness, add one more prayer for me! The brother made two prayers for the elder, again came to compunction, and said to himself: O wretched soul! Add also another prayer for yourself. Thus all week he made four prayers each night. The elder, passing by again, saw the demons gloomy and silent and, entering the brother's cell, asked him to add yet another prayer for him. The brother began to make six prayers each night, adding also one prayer for himself. When the elder came again to the brother, the demons raged against him and reviled him, indignant at the brother's salvation. But Abba Macarius, glorifying God for the brother's advancement, entered his cell and persuaded him not to be negligent but to pray unceasingly, and departed from him. And the demons, seeing the great diligence the brother had taken up for prayer, by the grace of God withdrew from him.

24. If the King of ages richly grants His blessings to the worthy in praise and glory of His name and unto the salvation of those who hope in Him, then it is right, for the sake of benefit, to tell of the deeds accomplished by the venerable Macarius, for he, having attained the perfection of virtue according to God and having risen above all the passions, was vouchsafed the contemplation of the bodiless powers and heavenly mysteries, being equal to the angels, as some of his disciples said, who had heard from him himself about the revelations which God had blessed him to know. They said that, when the Abba entered the temple of Jannes and Jambres, a terrible demon, the inventor of evil, the devil, waged fierce war against him, but since he had no success in this battle, the defeated all-cunning one appeared himself to the saint and showed him the varied wiles of his deception, for God compelled him to confess them, even against his will. Thus, wandering in the deepest desert, the good warrior of Christ, Macarius, saw an old man who was coming toward him and carrying something very heavy. His whole body was hung with vessels, in each of which was seen a feather, and this served him as an outer garment. Planting his staff and gazing at the righteous one, he stood face to face with him and asked: what are you doing, wandering in this desert? Holy Macarius answered: desiring to find God, I flee from deception. But who are you, old man? Tell me, for your appearance is foreign to human salvation. Say to me, what is that with which you are hung? Unwillingly, he told him of it, saying: he whom you call Satan and the devil, that is I, and these vessels contain that with which I variously attract people to myself and strive to incline them to do evil, suitable to each member, overturning by the feathers of lusts those who listen to me, and I rejoice at the fall of those conquered by me. Hearing this, Abba Macarius said to him with boldness: since Christ has delivered you up to be mocked by His saints, explain to me each kind of poison that you have, for you have appeared so that we might know the manifold wiles of your cunning, and, knowing them, the all-wicked arrows of your deception, we might not consent to your suggestions. He said: I will tell you, even unwillingly, my craft, for I cannot conceal what you see. So learn the power of each vessel! If I find someone constantly studying the law of God, I hinder him, bringing upon him a headache, anointing from the vessel that is on my head; if someone wishes to keep vigil in prayers and psalmody, I take from the vessel that is on my eyelids and draw him to sleep, bringing drowsiness; what you see on my ears is directed toward suggesting disobedience, so that those wishing to be saved do not hear the word of truth; with what I have at my nose, I arouse young men to fornication with fragrant odors; with the enchantments at my mouth, I accustom those who listen to me to foods, through which I accomplish all that I wish, every form of slander and foul speech and all the seeds of my deeds, from which my lovers cultivate a multitude of fruits worthy of me; to arouse pride, I enchant the high-minded one with seasonings that are at my neck, and from there also I draw out for those who love my deeds in this life the bait of glory and riches and of everything that seems good to those who have departed from God; what you see on my breast disposes to the reception of my suggestions, and from that I intoxicate hearts with the drunkenness of impiety, darkening the pious thoughts of those wishing to remember the future and taking away their memory by forgetfulness. The vessels on my belly are full of insensibility; with them I dispose the

unreasonable to live irrationally and like cattle, after the likeness of beasts; those beneath the belly draw the corrupt to mingling and to foul fornication; what you see on my hands is prepared for the service of the envious and murderers, that they may more quickly succeed in my deeds; what I have behind, on my back and shoulders, is the darkness of my ambushes, from which I fiercely war against those who attempt to rise against me, I lay snares and cast down those who trust in their own strength; those vessels which, as you see, are arranged on my thighs and hips are full of nets and snares, with which I corrupt the feet of those walking on the path of piety, turning them to my path, for, sitting in the midst of the paths of life and death, I attack those wishing to go to life and drive them onto the path of death, assisting them in every way to walk on it, and I sow it with thorns and thistles, so that they reject the path of truth. But you never once wish to listen to me, so that I might have at least a little comfort, but you always burn me, having powerful armor. Therefore I wish to flee to my servants, for you have a good Master Who speaks gently with His servants and guards you as His own child. Hearing this, the skillful warrior of Christ sealed himself with the sign of the Cross and said: blessed be God, Who has delivered you up to shame before those who hope in Him and has preserved me from your deception, that, having conquered you, I may receive a crown from my Master! Flee far from here, O Belial, smitten by Christ; do not touch the small number of those walking on the narrow and sorrowful path of salvation! Be content with your own and spare those living in the desert! When the saint said this, Satan vanished, leaving behind a foul-smelling smoke. Then the saint, bending his knees, began to pray, saying: glory to You, O Christ, refuge of the storm-tossed and salvation of those who flee to You. Amen.

25. Once (in Petra) Abba Moses was fiercely warred upon concerning fornication and, no longer having strength to sit in his cell, went and revealed this to Abba Isidore. The elder urged him to return to his cell, but he did not consent, saying: I no longer have strength, Abba! Then the elder, taking him with him, led him up onto the roof and said: look to the west! He looked and saw a multitude of demons, who were in confusion and in violent readiness for battle. Abba Isidore said to him again: look also to the east! He looked and saw an innumerable multitude of holy Angels, clothed in glory. Then Abba Isidore said: behold, these are they who are sent by the Lord to help the saints, and those in the west are they who war against them. Therefore, those who are with us are far more! Then Abba Moses gave thanks to God, took courage, and returned to his cell.

26. Abba Moses, while in Scetis, said: if we keep the commandments of our fathers, then I pledge to you before God, the barbarians will not come here; but if we do not keep them, this place will be laid waste.

27. Once the brethren were sitting with Abba Moses, and he said to them: today barbarians will come to Scetis; rise and flee. They asked him: and you, Abba, will you not flee? He answered: I have been waiting for this day for many years, that the word of the Lord might be fulfilled, Who says: *"For all who take the sword will perish by the sword"* (Matthew 26:52). They said to him: and we will not flee, but will die with you. There were seven brethren, and

he answered them: that is none of my concern; let each one look to himself how to act. But behold, the barbarians are already approaching the door. The barbarians indeed entered and slew them, and only one of them escaped death by hiding behind the wicker, and he saw seven crowns descend from heaven and crown them.

28. Some of the fathers related concerning Abba Marcellus of the Thebaid that his disciple said to them: going on Sunday to the church assembly, the Abba prepared himself for this by reading from memory some part of Scripture, and when he read with meditation, his lips did not move, so that no one might hear him, and when he stood in church, his breast was wet with tears, for he said: throughout the entire service, I see the whole assembly as though in fire, which after the dismissal of church again departs.

29. They said of Abba Silvanus: when he wished to go to Syria, his disciple Mark said to him: Father! I do not wish to leave here, and I will not allow you to depart, but wait here, Abba, three days. And on the third day he reposed.

30. They said of Abba Pachomius: they were carrying the body of one who had died. Meeting him on the way, Abba Pachomius saw that two Angels were following after the bier. Pondering this, he asked God to reveal to him what this might mean. Then two Angels approached him, and he asked them: why do you, being Angels, follow after the dead man? The Angels answered: one of us is the Angel of Wednesday, the other the Angel of Friday. Since this man, while he lived, did not cease to fast on Wednesday and Friday, we also follow after his body, and as he kept the fast on our days until his very death, so we also glorify him who struggled in the Lord.

31. Blessed Paul the Simple, the disciple of Abba Anthony, related to the fathers that once he came to a monastery to visit the brethren and profit them. After the customary conversation, they went to the holy church of God to perform the usual service. Blessed Paul looked attentively into the face of each one entering the church, to know what the soul of each was like in health, for he had this grace given him by God, to see what each one is like in soul, as we see one another's faces. Meanwhile, as all entered with a radiant gaze and cheerful countenance, and the Angel of each walked beside him rejoicing, he saw one who was gloomy, whose whole body was black, and demons held him on both sides and drew him each to himself, attaching a rope to his nostrils and placing a muzzle on his face, while his Angel walked far behind with a sad and downcast gaze. Then Paul wept and, striking himself on the breast with his hand, sat before the church, bitterly lamenting the one whom he had seen in such a state. The brethren, noticing this wondrous thing in the man and his sudden change to tears and weeping, were stirred and asked and entreated him to reveal what he had seen, each one fearing lest he had done something, and they asked him to go with them to the service. But he, declining their questions and refusing the latter request, sat outside the church in silence, torn in his heart for the brother he had seen. When the service ended and all were coming out, Paul again looked attentively at each one, to know, having seen how they had entered, how they were coming out. And he saw that the brother, previously black and gloomy, was coming out of the church radiant of face and white of body, the demons were

walking very far behind him, and the holy Angel was near him, bright, joyful, and rejoicing. Then Paul, springing up from joy and blessing God, cried out: O, the ineffable love of mankind and goodness of God! O, the compassion and ineffable mercy of God! Then, hastily running up to a high staircase, he exclaimed: *"Come and see the works of God"* (cf. Psalm 46:8; 66:5), how they are fearful and wondrous (cf. Psalm 119:129; 139:14)! *"Come and see"* Him *"who desires all men to be saved and to come to the knowledge of the truth"* (1 Timothy 2:4)! *"Come, let us worship and fall down before Him"* (Psalm 95:6), and let us say that You alone can forgive sins! All ran together with haste, wishing to hear what would be spoken. When all had gathered, Paul related what he had seen before all entered the church and what he had seen after, and he asked that brother to tell the reason for which God had granted him such a change. The brother, exposed by Paul before all, openly confessed the following concerning himself: I am a sinner and until this day have long lived in fornication, but now, entering the holy church of God, I heard the word of the holy Prophet Isaiah, or rather of God Himself speaking through him: *"Wash yourselves, make yourselves clean; put away the evil of your doings from before My eyes. Cease to do evil, learn to do good... Though your sins are like scarlet, they shall be as white as snow... If you are willing and obedient, you shall eat the good of the land"* (Isaiah 1:16–19). I am a fornicator, and being moved to compunction of soul at this word, I groaned deeply in my heart, saying: O God! *"Who came into the world to save sinners"* (1 Timothy 1:15)! What You have now promised through the prophet, fulfill in deed upon me, a sinner unworthy! For behold, from now on I give You my word, I promise and confess to You from my whole heart, that I will no longer do these evil deeds and will reject all iniquity and will serve You henceforth with a pure conscience. Now, O Master, from this hour, receive me who repent and fall down before You and have already rejected all iniquity! With such vows I came out of the church, having resolved in my soul to do nothing evil anymore before God. All who heard this cried out with one voice to God: *"O Lord, how great are Your works! In wisdom You have made them all"* (Psalm 104:24). Therefore, O Christian, knowing from the Divine Scriptures and Divine revelations how great a goodness God has toward those who sincerely flee to Him and by repentance correct their former falls, so that He returns to them again the promised blessings, not exacting payment for their former sins, let us not despair of our salvation, for just as through the Prophet Isaiah He promised to wash those mired in sins, to make them white as wool and snow, and to vouchsafe them the blessings of the heavenly Jerusalem, so also through the Prophet Ezekiel He assures us with an oath that He does not desire the destruction of the sinner: *"As I live,"* says the Lord God, *"I have no pleasure in the death of the wicked, but that the wicked turn from his way and live"* (Ezekiel 33:11).

32. Blessed Paul the Simple related: I had a disciple who fell into various sins, but I did not know of it. When he died, I prayed fervently to God and entreated the Most Holy Theotokos to show me where he was after his departure. After I had sat at prayer for many days, I came into ecstasy and saw two persons carrying my disciple, who from head to feet was entirely like a hardened potsherd, having no movement, neither bodily nor of soul, and who said nothing. Struck to the depths of my soul by this, I remembered the word of the Lord, spoken concerning the one not clothed in a wedding garment: *"Bind him hand and foot,*

take him away, and cast him into outer darkness; there will be weeping and gnashing of teeth" (Matthew 22:13), for the binding of hands and feet means nothing other than the extinction and inaction of every thought and desire of evil which were not directed according to God's will in this age. Coming to myself from the ecstasy, I began to grieve and lament deeply for him to the point of exhaustion, to give alms and offerings for him, to entreat the Most Holy Theotokos to have mercy on him and to beseech the man-loving God on his behalf; I also began to afflict myself with ascetic struggles and dry fasting, having already reached such old age. After several days, I saw the Most Holy Theotokos, Who asked me: why do you grieve and so exhaust yourself, O elder? I answered: I grieve for my brother, my Lady, for I saw him in an evil state. She said to me: did you not yourself ask to see him? And behold, you have been satisfied! But I answered: truly so, I asked, but I did not wish to see him in such a state, for what profit is it to me to see him and to weep and be torn apart? The Most Holy Theotokos said to me: go, for the sake of your humility and labor and love, I will show him to you, that you may not grieve. And on the morrow I saw the brother coming toward me joyfully and gladly; he walked of his own accord and, smiling, said to me: your prayers, Father, have entreated the Most Holy Theotokos, Who loves you greatly, and She has entreated the Savior to release me from bonds, for I was tightly bound by the bonds of my sins. When the brother said this, I was filled with joy and suddenly saw the Most Holy Theotokos, Who asked me: are you satisfied now, O elder? I answered: yes, my Lady! And I greatly rejoiced that I saw him at rest. Then She said to me: therefore, do not cease to commemorate your brother in prayers, alms, and offerings, for almsgiving and offering for the departed greatly propitiate God.

33. Once Zacharias, the disciple of Abba Silvanus, entering the Abba's cell, found him in ecstasy with his hands stretched out to heaven, and, closing the door, went out; then he came again around the sixth and ninth hours and found him in the same position. Finally, knocking at the tenth hour, he entered and, finding him resting, asked: what has happened to you today, Father? He answered: I was a little ill, child! But the disciple embraced his feet and said: I will not leave you until you tell me what you saw. Then the elder said to him: I was caught up to heaven and saw the glory of God; I stood there until now and have now been released.

34. Abba Phocas, of the coenobium of Abba Theognius of Jerusalem, related: when I was living in Scetis, in the Cells there was a certain Abba Jacob the Younger, whose father according to the flesh was also his father in the spirit. In the Cells there are two churches: one Orthodox, with which he was in communion, and another of the Aposchists (schismatics), and since Abba Jacob had the grace of humility, he was loved by all, both Orthodox and Aposchists. The Orthodox said to him: Abba Jacob, let not the Aposchists deceive you and draw you into communion with themselves! Likewise the Aposchists said to him: know, Abba Jacob, that by communing with the Dyophysites (those acknowledging two natures in Jesus Christ), you are destroying your soul, for they are Nestorians and slander the truth. Abba Jacob, being simple and distressed by what was said to him from both sides, resolved within himself to turn to God in prayer and enclosed himself in a silent cell outside the lavra, having put on burial garments, as before death, for the Egyptian fathers had the custom of preserving

the tunic and cowl in which they received the holy schema until death and being buried in them, putting them on only on Sundays for Holy Communion and then immediately putting them away again. So Abba Jacob, having withdrawn to that cell, prayed to God, and, having fasted greatly, he fell to the floor and lay there, having suffered much in those days, as he later said, from the demons, especially in mind. But after forty days had passed, he saw a Youth entering him joyfully and saying to him: Abba Jacob! What are you doing here? And he, immediately enlightened and receiving strength from seeing Him, said: Master! You know what is with me, for some tell me not to leave the Church, and others say that the Dyophysites are deceiving you. And I, being at a loss and not knowing how to run, resolved upon this deed. The Lord answered him: where you are, there it is good. And with this word he found himself at the doors of the holy Orthodox and Catholic Church.

35. They said of a certain elder that once he was walking through the desert, and two Angels were walking with him, one on his right hand and the other on his left. They saw a dead man lying on the way, and the elder held his nose from the stench. The Angels did the same. When they had gone on a little, the elder asked them: and do you smell this? They answered: no, but for your sake we also held our noses. We do not smell the impurities of this world, and they do not approach us, but souls living in sins we do smell.

36. Someone related that in Scetis, when the clergy were performing the Offering, something like an eagle descended upon the Offering, but no one saw it except the clergy. Once someone asked the deacon for something, and he said to him: I have no time now. When he came with the priest to perform the Offering, the likeness of an eagle did not descend, as was customary. The priest asked the deacon: what does it mean that the eagle did not descend as usual? Either in me or in you there is some offense. Therefore, step away from me, and if he descends, it will be clear that he did not descend because of you. As soon as the deacon stepped away, the eagle immediately descended. At the end of the service the priest asked the deacon: tell me, what have you done? He assured him, saying: I do not know of any sin in myself, except that when a brother came to me and asked for something, I answered him: I have no time. Then the priest said to him: was it not for your sake that he did not descend, since the brother had grief against you?! The deacon went and repented before the brother.

37. One elder related about a bishop who, having arrived on a Sunday in a certain village, commanded the deacons to call the village priest for the celebration of the Holy and Divine Mysteries. Finding a priest from among the villagers, who was exceedingly simple, they brought him to the bishop, and he ordered him to serve the Liturgy. When the priest entered the altar and, having vested, approached the altar, the bishop saw that he was all on fire, but was not consumed. At the end of the Liturgy the bishop took him aside to the diaconicon and said: bless me, true servant of God! The priest answered: how can a priest bless a bishop, having received ordination from him? But do you bless me, Master! The bishop said: I cannot bless one who, offering the Holy Gifts, stood all on fire, for *"beyond all contradiction the lesser is blessed by the better"* (cf. Hebrews 7:7). The priest asked: and does it happen, honorable Master,

that a bishop or priest, standing before the Holy Mysteries, is not all on fire? The bishop was exceedingly amazed at the purity and simplicity of this man and, having received great benefit, departed.

38. One elder related: someone lived for a long time in the innermost desert and acquired the gift of foresight, so that he conversed with Angels, and here is what happened: two brothers, monks, hearing of him, wished to see him and profit from him. They went out of their cell and set off on foot to seek the servant of God. After several days they were approaching the elder's cave and saw from afar someone resembling a man, clothed in bright garments and standing on one of the hills at a distance of three signs from the elder, who called out to them: brethren, brethren! They responded and asked: who are you and what do you wish? He said to them: tell the Abba to whom you are going to speak: remember about consolation. Coming to the elder, they kissed him as was customary and, falling at his feet, asked him to speak a word of salvation to them. Having received great profit from his instructions, they told him about the man whom they had seen while coming to him, and what he had commanded them to say to him. Hearing this, the elder knew who it was, but pretended not to know and said: no man lives here. But they urged him to tell them who the one they had seen was, often bowing to him and embracing his feet. The elder raised them up and said: give me your word that you will not spread word about me as about some saint until my very death, and I will tell you about him. The brethren promised, and the elder said to them: he whom you saw in the bright garment is an Angel of God, and he comes here to comfort me and strengthen my infirmity. Having said this, the blessed elder reposed, and the brethren buried him with hymns and prayers. Let us also strive to be imitators of his virtues by the grace of our Lord Jesus Christ, *"who desires all men to be saved and to come to the knowledge of the truth"* (1 Timothy 2:4).

39. Two brothers, having agreed between themselves, became monks. Having accepted monasticism, they built for themselves two cells at some distance from one another, and each lived as a hermit separately for the sake of silence. The brethren did not see one another for many years, because they never came out of their cells. It happened that one of them fell ill, and the fathers came to visit him. In their presence he sank as though into sleep, and when he came to himself again, the fathers asked him: what did you see, brother? He answered them: I saw that Angels of God came and took me and my brother and carried us to heaven. The opposing powers met us, but they had no power against us, and only when we had already passed through their region did they say: great is the boldness of innocence. Having said this, the brother reposed. The fathers sent word of the departed to his brother, but the messenger found him also already departed. And all, in amazement, glorified God.

40. An elder said: we have heard how some of the saints, having Christ within themselves, related about the mutual agreement of four elders, who gave one another their right hands to live in one mind and one spirit in this age, so that afterward they might be together also in heaven, believing the Master's voice, saying: *"If two of you agree on earth concerning anything that they ask, it will be done for them by My Father in heaven"* (Matthew 18:19). Three of them, sitting at

asceticism, lived in silence in the desert, while the fourth served them in their needs. It happened that two of them died in the Lord and passed to the place of rest, and two remained, the attendant and the silent one. By the suggestion of the wicked demon, the attendant fell into fornication, and it was revealed to one of the holy clairvoyant elders that the two who had reposed were beseeching God for the attendant, saying: deliver the attendant to be devoured by a lion or some other beast for the cleansing of his sin, so that he too may come to the place in which we are, and so that our union may not be broken. And behold, when the attendant was walking, as usual, to his work and returning from there, a lion met him and wished to kill him. The silent one learned of this by revelation, stood at prayer, and asked God for the brother, and the lion immediately stopped. So, while the two fathers who had already reposed were asking God, saying: we pray You, Master, let him be devoured, that he too may enter into blessedness with us, and do not hear the one praying for him on earth, the elder in his cell with all earnestness and with tears entreated God to have mercy on the brother and deliver him from the lion. God heard the cry of this elder and said to the fathers who were in heaven: it is right to hear that elder, for you are already at rest, having escaped from the labors and fasts of life, but he is still bound by the bonds of the flesh and is subject to the battles of the spirits of wickedness. Therefore, it is right to give grace to him rather than to you. The lion immediately withdrew from the brother, and he, coming to his cell, found the elder all in tears for him, told him everything that had happened, and confessed his sin, and seeing that God had spared him, he repented and in a short time came to his former measure. Then both of them reposed in the Lord, and it was revealed to that clairvoyant elder that all four, according to the unfailing promise of our Lord Jesus Christ, are in one place.

41. They related: another brother, who went about on the affairs of a large coenobium, also fell into the pit of the impurity of fornication, and they saw that when he died, his face became black, like soot on a pot. Then the father of the monastery, a spiritual man, gathered the whole brotherhood and said: this brother left the world, but you know how wholeheartedly he labored for our peace and silence on various affairs. Being a man, he slipped by the suggestion of the evil one, and since he fell into sin because of us, come, let us labor earnestly for him and pray to the man-loving God, Whose *"tender mercies are over all His works"* (Psalm 145:9). So they began to fast and entreat God with tears to show His mercy upon the departed brother. Three days and three nights, in fasting, without any food, they wept and mourned over the brother's perdition. And it came to pass that their abba came into ecstasy and saw that the Savior had compassion on the brethren's labor, while the devil was reviling and shouting: Master! This one is mine, I beg You. He is from my deeds, and I assisted him to sin. Being righteous, Lord, judge righteously. The Savior said to him in answer: I am righteous, but also merciful. The limit of My righteousness is mercy and love of mankind. Therefore it is not proper for Me, the merciful and man-loving One, to despise the prayer of so many holy men for one who was wounded because of those very ones who are praying for his sin. He could have remained peacefully in the monastery and, like everyone else, escaped the arrows of the enemy, but, going about on the affairs of the brethren, he, being a man, fell. Do you not see how all have given themselves over to death for his sake and all are dying for

the sake of one? Persuade them to cease praying for him, and take him. But when so many souls, in danger of perishing from hunger, with tears pray and entreat Me for him, not departing for three days and three nights from prayers, sighs, and genuflections, with heads covered in ashes, when such a multitude asks for a brother who fell into sin not with intention and not with deliberation, but through being carried away, as a man, is it not proper for them to receive their petition?! If even with earthly kings it happens that the petition of a whole city for someone already condemned to death changes the royal decree and snatches the guilty one from the hands of the executioner, shall not I all the more, the King who is in truth righteous and man-loving, grant My soldiers their petition, offered for one from their midst?! When the Savior said this, the devil vanished. The abba, coming to himself from the ecstasy, told everything to the brethren, and they rejoiced with great joy. After this the brother's face began little by little to be cleansed of blackness and finally became completely clean. Convinced thereby that God had numbered his soul among the inheritance of life, they took up his remains and buried him, rejoicing at the brother's wondrous salvation, for *"the Lord is near to all who call upon Him in truth"* (Psalm 145:18).

42. One elder related about a certain bishop, that we too might be stirred to zeal for the salvation of the soul: they reported to this bishop, as he himself said, about two worldly women, that they were living unchastely. The bishop, suspecting the informers, had recourse to God with prayer, to learn the truth, and received what he desired, for God granted him the ability to know from the appearance of those approaching for communion with the Holy Mysteries the disposition of the soul and what sins each was subject to. And the bishop saw that the faces of sinners were black, like soot or like a burned log, and their eyes fiery and fierce, while the faces of others were bright and clean of gaze. And when they approached the mystery, the Body of Christ seemed to burn some, while it illumined others and, entering through the mouth, made their whole body luminous. Among both the former and the latter were those who had accepted monasticism as well as those living in marriage. After the men, the bishop went to the women, to give them also the mystery and see what they were like in their souls. And among them some were gloomy, fiery-eyed, and fierce, while others were bright and pure. The two women about whom the bishop had been told also approached, and he saw that their faces were pure and their gazes bright, and after receiving the Holy Mysteries their bodies shone with heavenly light. After this the bishop again began to entreat God to show him the meaning of the revelations he had seen. And an Angel of the Lord appeared to him and commanded him to ask about each one. The holy bishop first of all asked about those women: is the report about them true or false? The Angel answered: all that was said about them is true. The bishop asked the Angel: how then, at the time of receiving the Holy Mysteries, were their faces bright and their gazes pure, and after receiving the Mysteries did not a small light illumine their bodies? The Angel answered to him: they came to a sense of their sins and propitiated God with tears and sighs, alms and confession, having firmly resolved not to fall into such sins anymore, if God forgives them their sins. God has forgiven all their sins, and henceforth they will live chastely, piously, and righteously. The bishop marveled not so much at the women's conversion as at the mercy of God, Who

not only did not subject them to punishment but even vouchsafed them such a great gift. The Angel said: does this amaze you?! There is no sin capable of conquering the mercy of God, for the good and man-loving God restores those who fall down before Him with a contrite heart, confessing their sins, and not only frees them from torments but also ceases His wrath against them and vouchsafes them honor. God so loved the world that He gave His only-begotten Son for it. Will He not forgive and bless His own when they, after falling, turn again to Him with repentance? The man-loving God knows our weakness, the strength of the passions, and the malice of the devil, and therefore He is long-suffering toward the fallen, awaiting their conversion, and mercifully receives the penitent, immediately surrounding them with all the gifts of His grace. Then the bishop asked the Angel: show me now, I pray you, the meaning of the difference in the other faces. The Angel of the Lord answered him: the bright of face and the pure of gaze are those who live chastely, are compassionate and merciful; the gloomy are fornicators and in general slaves to every lust and pleasure; the fiery-eyed are those who bear malice in their heart, the wrathful, quarrelsome, and envious. So, continued the Angel, take care of them, for you were vouchsafed this revelation so that, turning them to repentance, you might save their souls and receive a great reward for it in the Kingdom of our Lord.

43. They said about a certain brother that once on Sunday he rose to go, as usual, to the church assembly, but suddenly the devil began to suggest to him, speaking in his thoughts: where are you going? To church?! To commune of bread and wine? And people say that this is the Blood of the Lord? Do not allow yourself to be deceived! The brother believed the thought and did not go to church. Meanwhile the brethren were waiting for him in church, for such was the custom: not to begin the Sunday service until all had gathered. Having waited a while and seeing that he did not come, they went to him, thinking, had he fallen ill or had he died? Entering his cell, they asked him: why do you not come, brother? The brother was ashamed to tell them the truth, but they, guessing that there was some cunning of the devil here, bowed down before him and asked him to reveal to them the evil counsel and wile of the devil. The brother confessed and said: forgive me, fathers! I had already risen, as usual, to go to church, but a thought said to me that what I am going to commune of is not the Body and Blood, but simple bread and wine, and I did not go. So if you wish me to go with you to church, heal my thought concerning the Holy Offering. The brethren said to him: let us go, and we will beseech God to show you the divine power of the Holy Mystery. The brother rose and went with them to church. After long and earnest prayer for the brother, they finally began to celebrate the Divine Liturgy, placing him in the middle of the church, and he did not cease wetting his face with tears until the very dismissal of the church. At the end of the service the brethren asked him: if God revealed something to you, tell us, that we too may profit thereby. And he, with tears, rejoicing and trembling at the same time, began to speak: when, after the reading of the Apostle, the deacon came out to read the holy Gospel, the roof of the church opened and heaven appeared. At the proclamation of the holy Gospel, the deacon standing at the lectern became all like fire. And I saw also that the earth opened in the holy altar and the priests serving the Holy Mysteries stood in fear; I saw also that heaven

opened and from there fire descended, and after the fire a multitude of Angels, and among them were two majestic persons, of unspeakable beauty, from whom came a radiance like lightning. The Angels stood around the Holy Table and a Child in the midst. When the priests approached to break the Bread of Oblation, I saw those two persons at the Holy Table take the Child by the hands and feet, slay Him with a knife, and pour out the blood into the holy chalice standing on the Holy Table, then cut up the body into pieces and laid them out on the portions of the bread, and the bread became Body. When the brethren approached for communion of the Holy Mysteries, Body was distributed to them, but with the word "Amen," pronounced by them, it became bread in their hands. When I also approached, Body was distributed to me, and I could not commune. And there was a voice saying in my ears: man! Why do you not commune? Is this not what you demanded? Then I cried out: be merciful to me, O Lord! I cannot eat Body. And it was said to me: if a man could eat body, he would always receive the Body of God, as you do now. But since a man cannot eat body, therefore the Lord our God has willed to distribute it in the form of bread. So if you have believed, commune. I said: I believe, Lord! And immediately the Body which I held became bread in my hand, and I, thanking God, communed of the Holy Mysteries. When the Divine service was ended, I saw that the roof of the church again opened, and the heavenly hosts ascended to heaven. Hearing this, the brethren were moved to compunction and, with contrite hearts, each went to his cell, thanking God.

44. One elder related: a certain virgin, advanced in years and having progressed in the fear of God, I asked about the cause of her departure from the world, and she, sighing, began to speak to me thus: my father was meek and quiet, but weak in body, so that he spent almost his whole life bedridden. When he was well, he worked humbly in the field and patiently gathered what was needed for the household. He led such a solitary life that he rarely entered into conversation with anyone in our village, and he so loved silence that to those who did not know him he seemed mute. But my mother was of a completely opposite character: she was curious about everything, even beyond the boundaries of our dwelling; when she spoke, it seemed that her whole body was a tongue; she argued and quarreled with almost everyone; she loved to drink wine, associated with dissolute people, and ruined the household, but meanwhile knew no illness and was healthy all her life. When my father, worn out by illnesses, died, the air immediately became disturbed, there were terrible thunders and lightnings, storms and rains, so that for three days his body could not be committed to the earth. Then everyone in the village, shaking their heads, said: what evil was secretly hidden among us! Surely this is an enemy of God, when creation itself does not allow us to commit him to the earth. But lest his body rot and cause harm, though with difficulty, in rain and storm, they resolved to bury him. After that my mother, having received freedom, gave herself over to even greater dissolution, but when she died, the weather was clear and everything, it seemed, contributed to the brightness of her funeral. I was left a small child, but when afterward I came out of childhood and the passions began to awaken and tickle my inexperienced heart, one evening I sat down and began to reflect on what path of life to choose: should I go on my father's path, in meekness, piety, and purity, or choose my mother's path? But, I thought,

what profit was there for my father from such a life? Always illnesses and sorrows, and even after death the earth, as it were, did not receive his body. If his life had been pleasing to God, he would not have suffered so many evils. My mother's life seemed more certain: she lived according to all the desires of her heart, was always healthy, and was vouchsafed a bright burial. So my mother's life is better, for it is more certain to believe one's own eyes and follow what is surely known. Meanwhile night came, and sleep overcame me. And behold, in a dream there appeared to me one tall of stature, terrible of appearance, who sternly asked: tell me, such-and-such, what thoughts do you have in your heart? Trembling from fear, I could not even look at him, but he, in an even more terrible voice, demanded that I tell him what I had been thinking. Confused by fear, I forgot what I had been thinking and said: I remember nothing. He reminded me of everything. Being exposed, I confessed it and asked forgiveness, offering in excuse the reason that had prompted me to think thus. Then he said to me: go and see the lot of your father and the lot of your mother, and then choose for yourself what you wish. And taking me by the hand, he led me into a garden filled with every kind of tree with fruits, filled with beauty surpassing all description. When we came to the middle, my father met us and embraced me, calling me his beloved child. I asked to remain with him, but he said: now this is impossible, but if you go in my footsteps, you will come here in a short time. I again began to entreat my father, but the Angel who had led me there said: go now and see where your mother is. And we entered a dwelling filled with darkness and stench, where he showed me a furnace burning with fire and boiling pitch. Some terrible beings stood around the furnace; I looked down and saw my mother in the fire up to her very neck; she gnashed her teeth, being burned by fire and consumed by worms. Seeing me, she cried out: woe is me, my child! Woe is me from my deeds! Honesty and chastity seemed laughable to me, and for fornication and drunkenness I did not believe there would be punishment, and see what I suffer for brief pleasure. But help me, my child, remember the travails of birth, the cares of upbringing, and help your mother! In pity I stretched out my hand to her, but the fire burned it. From the unbearable pain I cried out loudly and awoke. Those who were with me in the house also awoke and ran to me, asking the cause of my fright. I told them what I had seen and, thanking the love of mankind of the Lord, chose the path of life of my father. This is what the honorable virgin related to me. So, knowing what terrible torments await sinners and how comforting are the dwellings of those who go on the path of God's commandments, let us resolve in our hearts to depart from evil and do good, that by the grace of the Lord we may inherit eternal life.

45. Some of the fathers said that when holy Peter, Archbishop of Alexandria, was dying, a certain virgin had a vision, and she heard a voice saying: Peter is the beginning of the Apostles, and Peter is the end of the martyrs.

46. One of the fathers said that for monks three things are of great value, to which they should attend with fear, trembling, and spiritual joy: communion of the Holy Mysteries, the meal of the brethren, and the washing of their feet. Then he related the following example concerning this: there was a certain elder, great and clairvoyant, and it happened that he was eating with a multitude of brethren. Sitting at the table, the elder attended in spirit and saw

that some were eating honey, others bread, and still others dung. He marveled within himself and asked God, saying: Lord, reveal to me this mystery, for, while the same food is set before all at the table for eating, they appear so changed that some are eating honey, others bread, and still others dung. And there was a voice to him from above: those eating honey are they who sit at the table with fear, trembling, and spiritual joy, who pray unceasingly, and their prayer, like incense, ascends to God; those eating bread are they who give thanks for eating what God has given; and those eating dung are they who murmur and say: this is good, but that is rotten. But one ought not to think thus, but to glorify God and send up praises to Him, that the word of Scripture may be fulfilled: *"Therefore, whether you eat or drink, or whatever you do, do all to the glory of God"* (1 Corinthians 10:31).

47. An elder said: often, when the deacon said, "Greet one another," I saw the Holy Spirit upon the lips of the brethren.

48. One of the fathers said that once, when the elders were sitting and conversing about the profit of the soul, there was among them one with the gift of foresight, and he saw Angels walking among them and filling them with fragrance. But when another conversation arose, the Angels withdrew and pigs came, filled with stench. Then, when they again began to speak about the profit of the soul, again the Angels came and filled them with fragrance.

49. They said of a great elder in Scetis: when the brethren were building any cell, he went out with joy and, laying the foundation, did not leave until they had finished it. Once, going out to build a cell, he was very gloomy. The brethren asked him: why are you so gloomy and sad, Abba? He answered: this place will be laid waste, children, for I saw that in Scetis a fire was kindled, and the brethren, taking palm branches, began to beat it and put it out; it was kindled again, and they again put it out, but when it was kindled a third time, it engulfed all of Scetis, and the brethren could no longer put it out. This is why I am gloomy and sad.

50. One elder was exceedingly clairvoyant. He affirmed, saying: the same power which I saw at Illumination (that is, Baptism), I saw also upon the garment of a monk when he receives the schema.

51. One elder, who had received the gift of seeing what happens, said: I saw a brother secretly studying in his cell. Behold, the devil came and stood outside his cell. While the brother was studying, he could not enter him, but when he ceased studying, then the demon entered his cell and warred against him.

52. One of the fathers related that near him lived two brothers: one was a stranger, and the other was a local. The stranger was somewhat negligent, while the local was very zealous. It happened that the stranger reposed, and the elder, being clairvoyant, saw a multitude of Angels accompanying his soul. When they reached heaven and were about to enter, there was an inquiry about him, but a voice came from above, saying: true, he was somewhat negligent, but for the sake of his being a stranger, open to him. Afterward the local also reposed, and all his relatives came to him. The elder, seeing that there was no Angel with him, was amazed and, falling on his face before God, said: why did the stranger, being negligent, attain such

glory, while this zealous one was vouchsafed nothing of the sort? And there was a voice to him: this zealous one, when he was drawing near to death, opened his eyes and, seeing his relatives weeping, was comforted in his soul, but the stranger, though he was negligent, seeing none of his own, groaned and wept, and God comforted him.

53. One of the fathers related: in the desert of Heliopolis lived a hermit, whose needs were fulfilled by a faithful layman. In the city there was a man, rich but impious, and when he died, the whole city accompanied him, and the bishop, with candles and censers. The one who fulfilled the elder's needs brought him bread, but, finding him eaten by a hyena, fell on his face before God, saying: I will not rise, Lord, until You reveal to me the meaning of the fact that that impious man had such glory, while this one, who served You day and night, died in this manner. Then an Angel of the Lord came and said to him: that impious man had a few good deeds and received a reward for them here, so that there he might find no consolation, but this hermit, though he was adorned with every virtue, yet, being a man, he too had some weaknesses, for which he was recompensed here, so that there he might be found pure before the face of God. Satisfied by what he had heard, he went back, glorifying God for His judgments.

54. They said of one elder: he prayed to God to see demons, and it was revealed to him: you have no need to see them. But the elder did not cease praying for this, saying: Lord! You are able to cover me with Your hand! Then God opened his eyes, and he saw the demons: like bees they surrounded a man, gnashing their teeth at him, but the Angel of the Lord drove them away.

55. A brother, moved to anger against his brother, stood at prayer and asked God to show him long-suffering toward his brother, that the temptation might pass harmlessly. And immediately he saw smoke coming forth from his mouth.

56. A certain elder spoke about a holy man, that, not having learned either the psalms or the prayers of communion, when for his great love of God he was vouchsafed the priesthood, he read all of it as if he had learned it. He was exceedingly virtuous and performed healings. Also this was great in him, that for sixty years of his ascetic life he did not see a woman, but three days before his death he did see one and, calling his disciples, revealed this to them, and after three days he reposed.

57. There was a certain hermit who did not work but only prayed unceasingly, yet each evening, entering his cell, he found bread there and ate. Once another brother came to him with palm branches and taught him to weave them. When evening came, the elder went as usual to eat and found nothing, and therefore lay down with grief, and it was revealed to him: when you were occupied with Me all the time, I fed you; but when you began to work, then by your handiwork earn food for yourself.

58. A brother asked an elder: is it the name that saves a man, or the deed? The elder answered: I know a brother who once, while praying, came to such a thought: how does the soul of a righteous man and the soul of a sinner leave the body? Not wishing to grieve him,

God satisfied his desire in this way: once he was sitting in his cell, and a wolf came in to him, took him by his clothing, and dragged him out. The brother rose and followed him. Having led him to a certain city, the wolf left him and went away. The brother entered a monastery outside the city, in which dwelt an elder who bore the name of a great hermit. He was ill and was awaiting his final hour. The brother saw that great preparations were being made of candles and lamps, and the whole city was saying: God, through his prayers, gave us bread and water and saved our city for his sake, and if something happens to him, we will all perish. But behold, the hour of his death drew near, and the brother saw a hellish apparition with a fiery trident and heard a voice descending from above: since his soul never gave Me rest for a single hour, be merciless in expelling his soul, for he shall never see rest. That one, having thrust the fiery trident into his heart, tormented him long before expelling his soul. After this the brother entered the city and, sitting down, wept. Then he saw a stranger, cast out on the street, who was ill and had no one to care for him. The brother remained with him for the day. The hour of his death drew near, and the brother saw that the Archangel Michael and the Archangel Gabriel came for his soul and, sitting down one on the right hand and the other on the left, comforted his soul and asked it to come out, but since it did not wish to come out, the Archangel Michael, leaving the body, said to the Archangel Gabriel: release it and let us go. But he said to him: we have been commanded by the Lord to bring it forth without pain, therefore we cannot do violence to it. Then the Archangel Michael cried out with a loud voice: Lord! What is pleasing to Your holy will concerning this soul, for it does not wish to come out? And there was a voice to him, saying: behold, I am sending David with his psaltery and all the singers, that, hearing the sweetness of their singing, it may come out with joy, but do not do violence to it. All descended and surrounded it, and when they sang hymns, it came out and, giving itself into the hands of the Archangel Michael and the Archangel Gabriel, ascended to heaven with joy.

59. He also related about one elder that once he came to the city to sell things and sat at the gate of a certain brother who was drawing near to death. Sitting in this place, he looked into the distance and saw two black horses, and upon them riders, also black and terrible in appearance, holding fiery rods in their hands. Having reached the gate, they set their horses there and entered the house. The sick man, seeing them, cried out with a loud voice: Lord! Have mercy on me and help me. Those who had been sent said to him: now, when the sun is setting, do you seek the help of God? Why did you not seek it in broad daylight? Now there is no hope for you and no consolation. And thus they took his wretched soul and departed.

Endnotes

[24] The Ausonian language is the Latin language.
[25] Shipowner: an owner or master of ships.

Chapter XIX.
Concerning Wonderworkers

1. Do not live with the proud, lest the action of the Holy Spirit be taken from your soul, and you thereby become a dwelling place of every evil passion. If you observe, O man, such precautions and, having become free from all things, always remember God in truth, then soon your soul will behold within itself the light of Christ, and you will never be darkened. To Him be glory and dominion unto the ages of ages. Amen.

2. They told of an elder who lived in the Thebaid and was by origin from the lower regions of Egypt, that he would take cerastes (horned serpents), venomous vipers, scorpions, and other snakes in his hands and tear them in two. The brethren, making a prostration to him, asked him: tell us, for what manner of life did you receive such grace? He said: forgive me, fathers, but if anyone acquires purity, then all things will be subject to him, as they were to Adam when he was in paradise before the transgression of the commandment.

3. Abraham, the disciple of Abba Sisoes, was once tempted by a demon. The elder, learning of his fall, stood up and, stretching out his hands to heaven, said: O God! Whether Thou wilt or whether Thou wilt not, I will not depart from Thee until Thou heal him. And he was immediately healed.

4. A layman once came with his son to Abba Sisoes on the mountain of Abba Anthony, but on the way his son died. The father was not troubled but, with faith, brought him to the elder and fell down before him with his son, as though bowing to receive a blessing from the elder. However, upon rising, the father left his son at the feet of the elder and went out. The elder, thinking that he lay there for the purpose of veneration, for he did not know of his death, says to him: arise and go out. He arose and went out. The father, seeing him, was astonished and, entering, bowed to the elder and told him of the matter. The elder, hearing of this, was grieved, for he did not wish this to happen, and his disciple commanded the layman to tell no one until the elder's repose.

5. They told of Saint Spyridon that he had a virgin daughter named Irene, as devout as her father. One of their acquaintances deposited a certain precious ornament with her for safekeeping. To preserve more securely what had been entrusted to her, she hid it in the ground. A short time later, she died, and after some time the one who had entrusted the item to her came and, not finding the maiden alive, began to demand it from her father, now

threatening him, now beseeching him. The elder, considering it a sin to lose the entrusted item, came to the grave of his daughter and asked God to show him before the time the promised resurrection, and he was not disappointed in his hope: the maiden at once appeared to her father alive and, pointing out the place where the ornament lay, departed. The elder took what had been hidden and returned it to its owner.

6. Two brothers, sincere men, lived in Scetis. It happened that one of them fell ill, and the other brother came to the church and asked the presbyter to make the offering for him. The presbyter, hearing of this, said to the brethren: let us go and visit the brother! They came, prayed over him, and departed. On another Sunday, the presbyter asked the brother: how is the brother? He answered: pray for him. And the presbyter again took the brethren and went with them to the sick man. When they arrived and sat near him, he began to expire. Meanwhile, the brethren began to dispute among themselves: some said that he was deemed worthy of the Comforter, while others doubted this. Hearing this, his brother said to them: do you wish to know who has power? Then, turning to the brother, he asked: are you departing, my brother? He answered: I am departing, but pray for me. But he said to him: truly, my brother, I will not allow you to depart before me. Then, turning to the brethren who had come, he said: give me a mat! He took the mat, bowed his head, and was the first to give up his soul, and after him the sick man also died. Then the fathers, having prepared both of them, carried them out and buried them, rejoicing that they had received the noetic light.

7. A brother had an elder, and, seeing that he prepared the dead well, he asked him: will you prepare me thus when I die? The elder answered: I will prepare you so well that you will say: enough. After a short time, the brother died, and the word of the elder was fulfilled, for, having prepared him reverently, he asked him before all: did I prepare you well, child, or is something still lacking? And the brother uttered a voice: well, father, you fulfilled your promise.

8. The fathers related: there was a certain abba of a coenobium, and it happened that a brother who was serving him, having been offended by something, left the monastery and withdrew to another place. The elder continually went to him and asked him to return, but he would not agree. The elder did this for the course of three years, and the brother, finally persuaded, returned. The elder commanded him to go and gather something into piles, and the servant, carrying out the command, through a diabolical action injured his eye. The elder, grieving over this, consoled him in his suffering, but the servant said to him: I am to blame myself—I was subjected to this for the labors I caused you. After a short time, the illness of the eye passed, but the impairment of vision remained. Once the elder commanded him to go cut palm branches, and while he was performing this work, through a diabolical action a branch snapped back and struck his other eye. Then he came to the monastery and fell silent, doing nothing more. And the elder again grieved over him. Finally, the time of the elder's calling came, and, knowing it beforehand, he sent for the brethren and said: my calling is near; therefore, look after yourselves. Then each one, approaching him, asked: upon whom are you leaving us, abba? But the elder was silent. Then he sent for the blind man and told him of his

calling. He wept and asked: upon whom are you leaving me, a blind man? The elder said to him: pray that I may have boldness before God, and I hope that on Sunday you will be serving the liturgy. Several days after his repose, the blind man received his sight and became the abba of the coenobium.

9. One of the elders sent his disciple to bring water. The well was far from their cell, and the brother forgot to take the rope and learned of it only when he had already arrived at the well. Then, having made a prayer, he called out: well, my abba said to fill the vessels with water! The water at once rose up, and when the brother had drawn water, the water went down again to its place.

10. One Scetian elder dwelt on Mount Paisius. A certain demoniac from the court was brought to him, and he healed him. The healed man brought him a bag full of gold, but the elder did not wish to accept it and, seeing that he was grieved by this, took an empty bag and commanded the gold to be distributed to the poor as alms. From the bag, which was of hair and rough, the elder made himself a tunic[26] and wore it for a long time, mortifying his flesh.

11. They said of a certain elder who lived in Scetis that a demon came to him, wishing to enter, but he bound him outside the cell. Then another demon came, and he bound him also. Finally, a third came and, finding two bound, asks them: why have you stopped here outside? They answered him: the one sitting inside does not allow us to enter. Growing furious, he attempted to enter, but the elder bound him also. Then, fearing the prayers of the elder, they began to ask him: release us! He said to them: go! And they departed in shame.

12. They said of a certain elder that his cell was always as bright as day, and just as by day he read and worked, so also by night.

13. Once an elder went with a brother to draw water. The brother, arriving at the lake before him, saw a dragon and returned to the elder. The elder says to him: go and trample his head with your foot. But he was afraid and did not go. When the elder came, the serpent, seeing him, was ashamed and crawled away into the desert.

14. Another time, having need to cross the river Chrysorrhoe, he made a prayer and crossed it to the other bank on foot. In amazement, the brother bowed to him and asked: how did your feet feel while you were walking on the water? The elder answered: to the heel I felt water, but beyond that it was solid.

15. A brother related: another time we were going to a certain elder; the sun began to set, and the elder, having prayed, said: I pray Thee, O Lord! Let the sun stand still until I reach Thy servant. And it was so.

16. A demoniac came to Scetis. Prayer was made for him in the church, but the demon did not come out, for he was fierce. The clerics said: what shall we do with this demon? No one can cast him out except Abba Bessarion, but if we ask him, he will not even come to church. Here is what we shall do! He comes to church before everyone. Let us arrange for the sick man to sleep in his place, and when the elder comes, we will stand for prayer and say

to him: awaken the brother also, abba! And they did so. When the elder came in the morning, they stood for prayer and say to him: awaken the brother also. The elder said to him: arise and go out. At once the demon went out of him, and he was healed.

17. The disciples of Abba Gelasius related that once fish was brought to them, and the cook, having fried it, took it to the cellarer. The cellarer, due to some need, went out of the storeroom, leaving the fish in a vessel on the floor and commanding a boy—a foster child of the blessed Gelasius—to guard it until he returned, but the boy was tempted and began to eat the fish. When the cellarer entered and saw that he was eating, sitting on the floor, he grew angry and carelessly struck him with his foot. The boy began to cough and died. The cellarer, seized with fear, placed him on his bed and, covering him, went and fell at the feet of Abba Gelasius and told him what had happened. The elder forbade him to tell anyone else about this and commanded him in the evening, when all had settled, to carry the boy to the diaconicon, place him before the altar, and depart, which the cellarer did. Then the elder himself came and began to pray, and when the hour of the midnight psalmody arrived and the brethren had assembled, the elder came out from the diaconicon and the boy followed behind him. Of this matter, until the very repose of the elder, no one knew except the elder himself and the cellarer.

18. One of the fathers related concerning Abba Xois of Thebes: once he was going to Mount Sinai and, when he was returning from there, he met a brother who said to him with a sigh: abba, we are suffering from drought. The elder asked him: why then do you not pray and ask God? The brother answered: we both pray and ask, but there is no rain. The elder says to him: surely you do not pray earnestly?! Do you wish to know that this is so? And, stretching out his hands to heaven, he began to pray. At once rain began to fall. Seeing this, the brother, terrified, fell on his face and bowed to the elder, but the elder fled. The brother told everyone what had happened, and all who heard glorified God.

19. Abba Xanthias once came from Scetis to Terenuth. There, where he stopped, because of his fatigue they brought a little wine. Some, hearing of his arrival, brought a demoniac to him. The demon began to revile the elder: have you brought me to this wine-drinker? The elder did not wish to cast him out, but because of the reproach he said: I believe in Christ that before I finish this cup, you will come out. When the elder began to drink, the demon cried out: you burn me, you burn me! And before the elder finished the cup, he came out by the grace of Christ.

20. A certain woman, having an ailment on her breast called cancer, heard of Abba Longinus and sought to see him. The abba lived in Enaton of Alexandria and, while the woman was seeking him, the blessed one happened to be gathering wood there on the shore of the sea. Seeing the elder and not knowing that it was he himself, she asked him: abba, where does Abba Longinus, the servant of God, live? He answered: what do you want from this hypocrite? Do not go to him—he is a hypocrite. But what is the matter with you? The woman showed him her ailment. He made the sign of the cross over that place and dismissed her, saying: go, and God will heal you, for Longinus cannot help you in any way. The woman

went, believing his word, and was immediately healed. After this, telling some people about this matter and describing the features of the elder, she learned that it was Abba Longinus himself.

21. Another time they brought a demoniac to Abba Longinus, but he said to them: what can I do for you? Better go to Abba Zeno. When Abba Zeno began to press upon the demon, casting him out, he began to cry out: do you think, Abba Zeno, that I am coming out because of you? Behold, Abba Longinus over there is praying against me and pressing me, and I am coming out fearing his prayers, but to you I would not have given an answer.

22. Another time a woman came to him, having an incurable ailment on her hands, with another woman, and stood outside his cell by the north window, fearing to enter. He said to her: go away from here, woman! But she did not leave and did not cease looking at him through the window, saying nothing. The elder perceived her ailment in spirit, arose and, shutting the window, said: go, now you have nothing. And she was healed from that hour.

23. Yet another time someone, coming to him, took his cowl and brought it to one who was suffering. As soon as he approached the door, the sufferer cried out: why have you brought Longinus here to cast me out? And immediately the demon went out of him, and he became well.

24. Abba Sisoes said: when I was in Scetis with Abba Macarius, seven of us went to reap together with him. While we were reaping, behind us a widow was gathering ears of grain and weeping without ceasing. The elder called the owner of the field and asked him: what is the matter with this old woman, that she weeps without ceasing? He answered: her husband took goods for safekeeping and suddenly died, not having said where he put them. The owner of those goods wishes to take her and her children as his slaves. The elder says to him: tell her to come to us when we rest during the heat. The woman approached, and the elder asked her: why do you always weep so? She answered: my husband took goods for safekeeping and died, not having said where he put them. The elder says to her: go and show me where you buried him. Then he took the brethren with him and went with her. Arriving at the place, the elder said to her: go now to your house. Then, having prayed with the brethren, the elder called out to the dead man: such-and-such! Where did you put the goods entrusted to you? He answered: they are hidden in my house, at the foot of the bed. The elder says to him: sleep again until the day of resurrection. The brethren, having seen this, fell at the feet of the elder in fear, and he said to them: this was not done for my sake, for I am nothing, but God did this deed for the sake of the widow and orphans. But this is great, that God wills the soul to be without sin, and then, whatever it asks—it will receive. Then he went to that widow and told her where the entrusted goods lay. She took them, returned them to the owner, and freed her children. And all who heard of this glorified God.

25. They said of Abba Macarius that once, going from Scetis with a load of baskets, he sat down exhausted and began to pray, saying: O God! Thou knowest that I have no more strength. And at once he found himself at the river.

26. A certain man in Egypt had a paralytic son. He brought him to the cell of Abba Macarius and, leaving him weeping at the door, himself went far away. The elder saw the weeping child and asked him: who brought you here? The boy answered: my father threw me here and left. The elder said to him: arise and catch up with him. The boy was immediately made well, arose, and caught up with his father, and they went to their home.

27. Once Abba Milesius, passing through a certain place, saw that someone was holding a monk, accusing him of committing murder. The elder, having questioned the brother, learned that he had been slandered, and asked those holding him: where is the slain man? They showed him. Having approached the slain man, he commanded everyone to pray, and when the elder himself stretched out his hands to God, the dead man arose. The elder asked him before all: tell us, who killed you? He said: having come to church, I gave money to the presbyter, and he killed me, then carried me to the monastery of this abba and threw me there. But I ask you, take the money from him and give it to my children. Then the elder says to him: go, sleep until the Lord comes and raises you! He departed and fell asleep.

28. Once a great many elders came to Abba Poemen. Then one of the relatives of Abba Poemen, whose son's face had been turned backward through a diabolical action, took his son and, sitting outside the monastery, wept. It happened that one of the elders came out and, seeing him, asked: why do you weep, O man? He answered: I am a relative of Abba Poemen, and behold, such a calamity has befallen my son! We wanted to bring him to the elder, but we were afraid, for he does not wish to see us. And now, seeing your arrival here, I dared to come. Therefore, abba, have compassion on me—take my son and pray for him! The elder took him and, entering, out of prudent caution did not bring him directly to Abba Poemen but, beginning with the lesser brethren, said: make the sign of the cross over this child. When all had made the sign of the cross over him in order, he finally brought him also to Abba Poemen, but the abba did not wish to allow him near. All began to entreat him, saying: as all have done, so do you also, father. He sighed and, rising, began to pray: O God! Heal Thy creature, that the enemy may not have dominion over him. Then he made the sign of the cross over him. He was immediately healed and was returned to his father in health.

29. A certain Saracen, a pagan by faith, related to those living in Clysma and to us: I went to the mountain of Abba Anthony to hunt. Having arrived there, I saw a monk on the mountain who was sitting, holding a book and reading it. Approaching, I wanted to take aim so as to frighten him or even kill him, but as soon as I came near, he stretched out his right hand to me and said: halt! And I stood thus day and night, unable to move even a little from the place where I stood. Then I say to him: for the sake of the God whom you worship, release me. He said: go in peace. Then I was able to leave the place where I stood, and I marveled at the boldness of that man.

30. Near the Dead Sea there is a mountain called Ommardim, very high. On this mountain lived hermits who had their own garden, which was six signs distant from them. The hermits there had a gardener, one of their own. When they needed to send to the garden for vegetables, they would prepare their donkey and say to him: go to the garden to the

gardener and bring vegetables. The donkey would go to the gardener alone and, arriving at the door, would knock on it with his head. The gardener would immediately load him with vegetables and release him. And everyone could see how the donkey ascended the mountain alone and served only the elders, but would not let anyone else near.

31. In the region of Asia there was a certain stylite, very virtuous and renowned. Below him he had a monastery. A certain need arose, and the brethren persuaded him to go to Constantinople to petition the emperor. Having arrived there, he stayed at a guesthouse attached to an orphanage. Since it was winter, some were sitting around burning coals and warming themselves. They were heretics. When he also sat down with them, they began to tempt him with their heresy. He said to them: I believe rightly, but if you believe better, do what I will do. Then he stood without shoes upon the fire, stood for a rather long time, and was not burned. Seeing this, they were ashamed, struck by this wondrous miracle; and all who heard glorified God.

Endnotes

[26] Tunic—an undergarment.

Chapter XX.
Concerning the Sign-Bearers[27]

1. Abba Ammon told of how he put a basilisk to death: once he went into the desert to draw water from a well and saw a basilisk. Then he fell on his face and said: Lord! Either I must die or it must. And by the working of the power of Christ, the basilisk was immediately rent asunder.

2. A certain brother from Scetis came to Abba Ammon and says to him: my father sends me on an obedience, but I fear fornication. The elder said to him: at the very time when temptation comes upon you, say: O God of hosts, through the prayers of my father, deliver me! Thus once a maiden locked the door behind him, but he cried out loudly: O God of my father, deliver me! And he immediately found himself on the road to Scetis.

3. Once a certain governor came to Pelusium and wished to demand from the monks a poll-tax such as was required from laymen. On this account all the brethren gathered together to Abba Ammonotha and decided that some of the elders should go to the emperor. Abba Ammonotha says to them: there is no need for such labor, but rather keep stillness in your cells and fast for two weeks, and by the grace of Christ I alone will accomplish this matter. The brethren dispersed to their cells, while the elder kept stillness in his. When fourteen days had passed, the brethren were troubled concerning the elder, for they had not seen him go anywhere. They said: the elder has neglected our matter. On the fifteenth day the brethren gathered together, as they had agreed beforehand, and the elder came to them, holding in his hands a document with the imperial seal. Seeing this, the brethren were astonished and asked the elder: when did you bring it, Abba? The elder answered: believe me, brethren, that this very night I went to the emperor, and he wrote this document for me. From him I went to Alexandria and registered it with the officials and then returned to you. Hearing this, the brethren, seized with fear, made prostration to him. Thus their matter was accomplished, and the governor troubled them no more.

4. Abba Dulas, the disciple of Abba Bessarion, said: we were walking once along the seashore. I was thirsty and said to Abba Bessarion: I am exceedingly thirsty. The elder offered a prayer and says to me: drink from the sea. The water became sweet, and I drank. Then I filled a vessel with the water, lest I should want to drink later, but the elder said: here is God, and everywhere is God.

5. One of the fathers was sitting in his cell. A demon came and, entering into the elder's bedroom, began reading the Book of Numbers. Then, having grown bored, he transformed himself into a poor man and went out, limping, to the elder with a staff and a basket. The elder says to him: do you know how to read? He answered: we know the Old Testament. The elder asked: but do you not know the New? And the demon, as soon as he heard of the New Testament, immediately vanished.

Endotes

[27] One who bears upon himself the sign, the mark of consecration to the schema; a schema-monk.

Chapter XXI.
On the Manner of Life of Holy Men

1. Once when Abba Anthony was praying in his cell, a voice came to him, saying: Anthony! You have not yet reached the measure of a certain Scetian living in Alexandria. In the morning Abba Anthony arose, took a palm staff, and went to him, and having reached the place, entered his dwelling. The man, seeing the elder, was confused, but he said to him: tell me of your deeds. The man answered: I do not know that I have done anything good, except for one thing only, that rising in the morning and sitting down to my handwork, I say: this whole city, from small to great, will enter the kingdom for their righteous deeds, and I alone will inherit torment for my sins; and in the evening, before falling asleep, I say the same word. Hearing this, Abba Anthony said: truly, you, like a good goldsmith, sitting in your house with tranquility, have inherited the kingdom, while I, lacking discernment, though having lived in the desert, have during my lifetime not reached this measure.

2. Once blessed Archbishop Theophilus came to Abba Arsenius with a certain official and asked the elder, wishing to hear a word from him. The elder, having remained silent for a while, asked them: will you fulfill what I tell you? They answered: we will fulfill it. Then the elder said to them: if anywhere you hear of Arsenius, do not go to him.

3. Another time the archbishop, wishing to come to the elder, first sent to inquire whether he would open the door for him. The elder answered him thus: if you come, I will open the door for you, but if I open it for you, I will also open it for everyone, and then I will no longer remain here. The archbishop, hearing this, said: if by my coming I drive him away, then it is better for me not to go to him.

4. Two of the fathers asked God to reveal to them what measure they had reached, and a voice came to them: in a certain Egyptian village there is a layman named Eucharistus with a wife named Maria. You have not yet reached their measure. Both elders went to that village, inquired, and found his cell, and in it only his wife, and asked her: where is your husband? She answered: he is a shepherd, he tends sheep, and led them into the cell. When evening came, Eucharistus came with the sheep and, seeing the elders, prepared a table for them, brought water, and washed their feet. The elders said to him: we will not taste anything until you reveal to us your practice. Eucharistus with humility said to them: I am a shepherd, and this is my wife. The elders continued to ask him, but he did not want to reveal it to them.

Then the elders say: God sent us to you. Hearing this word, he became afraid and said to them: we received these sheep from our parents. When God grants us increase and we acquire something from them, we divide it into three parts: one for the poor, another for hospitality, and the third for our own needs. Since I took a wife, we have not known the marriage bed, neither she nor I, and each of us sleeps separately; at night we wear hair shirts, and during the day we wear ordinary clothing. Until now no one has known about this. Hearing this, the elders marveled and returned, glorifying God.

5. Abba Theodore the Byzantine told us: while still a youth, being in Constantinople, I received monasticism, in my twentieth year. Three years after that a thought came to me to go to Jerusalem, and I, finding a ship sailing to Ionia, boarded it. We sailed successfully for six days, then a storm arose, and after four days of distress, we were cast upon the shore of Alexandria. That was the month of January, and I resolved to spend the winter in the desert of Scetis. I came to Abba Nilus, and he gave me a small cell near himself. When Lent came, I said to him: Abba! Give me a commandment for these holy days. The elder says to me: what? You have been here so many days already and did not ask for a commandment, and now you ask for one? I say to him: now it is Lent, and I wish to labor in these holy days. The elder answered me: but are the other days of the year evil, unprofitable, and unclean? Or do the sun, moon, and stars shine only on these days, and not on the others? I, my son, hear what Divine Scripture says: *Yours is the day, Yours also is the night* (Psalm 74:16), and *I will bless the Lord at all times* (Psalm 34:1); also: *His praise shall continually be in my mouth* (Psalm 34:1); and again: *Every day I will bless You* (Psalm 145:2), and the Apostle says: *Pray without ceasing. In everything give thanks* (1 Thessalonians 5:17–18). Thus, if for you only these days are holy and are days of ascetic labor and toil, while the other days are for rest and comfort, then blessed are you! I, child, know in Christians three ranks: slaves, hirelings, and sons. A slave must always serve his master with fear and diligence; a hireling also, if he wants to receive his wages, must always work without sloth, without deceit, and without murmuring, giving himself no rest either in winter or in summer, or in spring, or in autumn. Thus, my child, if you are a slave, then for 365 days of the year you are obliged to work with all diligence and love; if you are a hireling, again you must work without sloth the whole year, so as to be enriched with virtues; but if you are a son, then even with this you must always honor your father, so as to inherit his estate, and not so that you sometimes honor your father and at other times offend him. Truly I tell you, child, God requires of monks that they always labor, pray unceasingly, read and meditate with attention and sobriety, both on special feasts and during Pentecost, and on Sunday, and on Saturday. A lazy slave is not deemed worthy of freedom; a bad hireling is deprived of his wages; and a son disobedient to his father loses the inheritance. I said to him: Abba, if you do not close the doors, I will always come to converse with you. He said to me: it is not a wooden door that bars the entrance to the demon and to sins, and it is not conversation with men of like passions that repels him. When you wish, come, and when you wish, depart. Thus the elder did not give me a commandment. Returning to my cell, I kept silence until the day of the Forty Martyrs. On that day I came to him, and when after prayers we sat down, I say to him: in my monastery, Abba, there is a great celebration today and on

the Annunciation of the Most Holy Theotokos, and we permit wine, oil, and fish. The elder asked: for what reason do you do this? I answered him: in honor of the saints, of the Most Holy Theotokos, and of the Forerunner. The elder said: you celebrate many bright Sundays: the Forerunner, the holy martyrs, the day of the Theotokos, the week of Palm Sunday, Great Thursday, fourteen Saturdays and Sundays in the seven weeks of the fast, and also the bright Resurrection of the Savior Jesus! Thus, if you permit wine, fish, and oil on these twenty Paschas, how do you fast on the other days? I answered: in our monastery, father, we do not eat bread, wine, or oil for three days; on Saturday and Sunday there is cooked food with oil, and on Tuesday and Thursday we eat fruits and vegetables. The elder said: it is not bread that gives birth to sin and not vegetables that give birth to righteousness, but I will tell you, child, it happens that those who fast for two days eat for three and sleep for four, and that those who eat vegetables and abstain from bread are armed in soul and body against each other and devour one another, darken the mind, weigh down the heart with much sleep, and wound the conscience; thinking they are fasting, they practice gluttony; thinking they are keeping vigil, they sleep even more; wishing to honor the martyrs, they provide the body with laurels through much eating and much sleeping. The martyrs endured every kind of torment: beating with sinews, hanging, burning, gouging out of eyes, cutting off of fingers, scraping of ribs, pressing of the head, boiling in pitch, wasting through hunger and cold, and they instead of all this give themselves over to comforts, permitting fish, wine, oil, sikera, and honey. Thus, child, if you wish to honor the martyrs, the Most Holy Theotokos, and John the Forerunner, honor them with abstinence and vigil, not with gluttony; with prayer, fasting, and patience, not with much drinking; with purity, chastity, and virginity, not with pleasure and luxury. Let us present to God in the hour of prayer a sober mind, a heart not darkened by foul thoughts, a bright conscience that repels evil thoughts, an awakened thought free from consent to evil memories, and we will rejoice God, attract the help of the angels, acquire the protection of the Most Holy Theotokos and John the Forerunner, and make friends and protectors of the holy martyrs! But when, fasting for two days, we then eat threefold and sleep fivefold, while the mind remains in fantasies, evil thoughts spring up as from a fountain, the heart is defiled, the conscience is darkened, the tongue sings hastily, and the eyes wander here and there, then the devil is comforted, the demons rejoice, while we boast in vainglory, not noticing our own ruin.

6. A certain man named Paul, a nobleman, who had a wife worthy of himself and great wealth, conceived the intention of becoming a monk and, calling his wife and children, said to them: I wish to sell you. They said: do what you wish and what you consider best. He took his wife and half of his property and, coming to a women's monastery, says to the sisters: I wish to sell you this woman here. Understanding his good intention, they gladly agreed to it, and when the agreement was concluded, he gave over both his wife and half of his property to the abbess. In like manner he also took his children to another monastery, doing the same. Finally, in yet another monastery, he did the same also with himself, and then said to the abba: if you will command, I would like to enter alone into the house of prayer. The abba agreed. Entering and closing the doors, he stretched out his hands to heaven and cried out to God:

O God! You know that I have surrendered myself to You from all my heart. And a voice came to him: I know and have received you with all compassion. Thus he lived in the coenobium as a slave, performing all tasks and being lower than all, and for such humility he was exalted by God, for after his death myrrh flowed forth and many other signs were wrought.

7. Brother! Without labor one cannot live and without struggle one cannot be crowned. Labor, struggling for salvation, and pray unceasingly, and God will help you, *who desires all men to be saved and to come to the knowledge of the truth* (1 Timothy 2:4).

8. Once Abba Macarius came from Scetis to Mount Nitria for the commemoration of Abba Pambo, and the elders asked him: say a word to the brethren, father! He said: I have not yet become a monk, but I have seen monks, for when I was sitting in my cell in Scetis, a thought attacked me and said: go into the desert and see what you will see there. I struggled with this thought for five years, saying to myself: is it not from demons? But since the thought did not depart, I went into the desert. There I found a lake and an island in the midst of it. Beasts of the desert came to drink from the lake, and I saw among them two naked men. My body trembled with fear, for I thought they were spirits. They, seeing that I was afraid, turned to me: do not fear, we too are men. I asked them: from where are you and how did you come into this desert? They answered: we are from a coenobium, we agreed between ourselves and came out here. One of us is an Egyptian, and the other is a Libyan. Then they also asked me: how is the world? Does the water come in its season? And is there abundance in the world? I said: yes. And again I asked them: how can I become a monk? They say to me: if one does not renounce all that is in the world, he cannot be a monk. I said to them: I am weak and cannot do as you do. They said: if you cannot do as we do, sit in your cell and weep for your sins. I also asked them: when it is winter, do you not become cold? And when there is scorching heat, is your body not burned? They answered: God has so disposed us that neither in winter do we become cold, nor in summer does the burning of the sun harm us. That is why I said that I have not yet become a monk, but I have seen monks! Forgive me, brethren.

9. Abba Bitimius recounted that Abba Macarius said: when I was living in Scetis, two young strangers came there, and one of them had a beard. They came to me and asked: where is the cell of Abba Macarius? I said: why do you seek him? They say: we heard of him and of Scetis and came to see him. I say to them: I am Macarius. They made a prostration and said: we wish to remain here. Seeing that they were tender and from wealthy families, I say to them: you cannot live here. The older one says: if we cannot live here, then we will go to another place. Then I said to my thought: why do I drive them away? Perhaps they will even be scandalized. Labor will make them run away of themselves. And I say to them: come and make yourselves a cell, if you can. They said: show us a place, and we will make one. I gave them an axe, a sack full of bread, salt, and showing them a hard rock, said: cut through here, then bring wood from the lake, cover it, and live. I thought that because of the labor they would go away, but they asked me: what do they work at here? I answered: plaiting. Then I took palm leaves from the lake, showed them the beginning of the plaiting and how to sew

them together, then said: make baskets and give them to the guards, and they will bring you bread. After this I withdrew. They patiently did all that I told them and did not come to me for three years. Thoughts fought against me: what is their practice, if they have not once come to me to ask about a thought? Those far away come, but these are nearby and have not asked, and they do not go to others, except silently coming to church to receive the Gifts. Fasting for a whole week, I prayed to God that He might reveal their practice to me. After the week passed, I went to them to see how they lived. When I knocked, they opened and kissed me in silence. Having said a prayer, I sat down. The older one gave a sign to the younger to go out, and he himself sat down to plait, not saying a word. At the ninth hour he knocked, the younger one entered, prepared a little cooked food, set the table at a sign from the older one, and placed on it three dry loaves in silence. I said: arise, let us eat. And rising, we ate; he brought a jug of water, and we drank. When evening came, they asked: are you leaving? I said: no, I will stay here. They spread out a mat for me on one side and, taking off their belts and analavoi, lay down together on one mat, opposite me. When they had lain down, I again prayed to God that He might reveal their practice to me. Then the roof opened, and it became light as day, but they did not see the light. Supposing that I had already fallen asleep, the older one nudged the younger one in the side, they arose, girded themselves, and lifted up their hands to heaven. I watched them, but they did not notice. Then I saw demons like flies attacking the younger one, and some wanted to sit on his lips, others on his eyes, and I saw an Angel of God with a fiery sword who protected him and drove the demons away from him, but they could not come near the older one. When around morning they lay down to sleep, I pretended that I had awakened, and they did the same. The older one said only this: do you want us to sing the twelve psalms? I said: very well. Then the younger one sang five psalms by six verses, with one alleluia each, and at each verse a fiery lamp went forth from his mouth and ascended to heaven. In like manner, when the older one opened his mouth to sing, something like a fiery cord went forth from his mouth, reaching to the very heaven. And I also recited a little from memory and, departing from them, said to them: pray for me. They made a prostration in silence. From this I learned that the older one was already perfect, but the enemy still fought against the younger one. After several days the older one fell asleep, and after three days the younger one also. After this, whenever any fathers came to Abba Macarius, he would lead them to their cell, saying: come see the martyrdom of the young strangers.

10. Once Abba Macarius was praying in his cell, and a voice came to him: you have not yet reached the measure of two such women living in a certain city. Rising in the morning, the elder took a palm staff and went to that city. Having reached the place of their dwelling, he knocked at the door, and one of them came out and received him into the house, then the other came also. He called them, and they came and sat down with him. The elder said to them: for your sake I came from the desert and undertook such labor; tell me of your practice, what it is and of what sort. They say to him: tell us, father, what practice you expect to find in us, when each of us was with her husband this very day? Then the elder made a prostration before them and implored them, saying: reveal your virtue to me! They said to him: we are by

worldly standards strangers to each other, but it happened that we were married to two brothers according to the flesh, and behold, now fifteen years have we lived in this house and do not know whether we ever quarreled with each other or spoke a bad word to one another. It came to our minds to leave our husbands and enter the rank of virgins, and we strongly implored our husbands about this, but they did not agree to release us. Not having succeeded, then, in this intention of ours, we made a covenant between ourselves and God: until death itself not to utter with our lips any worldly word. Hearing this, Abba Macarius said: truly, *there is neither virgin nor married woman, neither monk nor layperson*, for God seeks the disposition of the heart and grants the Holy Spirit to all.

11. Abba Poemen said that Abba Anthony said of Abba Pambo: by fearing God he brought it about that the Holy Spirit dwelt in him.

12. Abba Poemen said: many of our fathers were strong in asceticism, but in subtlety of discernment, only one here and one there.

13. Abba Poemen said: we saw three bodily labors in Abba Pambo: not eating until evening every day, silence, and handwork.

14. They used to tell of Abba Poemen: when any elders were sitting with him and, discoursing about the elders, mentioned Abba Sisoes, he would say: leave Abba Sisoes alone, for his deeds are beyond telling.

15. They said of Abba Pambo: as Moses received the image of the glory of Adam when his face was glorified (Exodus 34:29), so also the face of Abba Pambo shone like lightning, and he was like a king sitting upon his throne. Such also were Abba Silouan and Abba Sisoes.

16. When Abba Romanus was approaching his end, his disciples gathered around him and asked him: how must we govern ourselves? The elder answered: I do not remember ever having told any one of you to do something without first preparing my thought not to be angry should they not do what I tell them to do. In this way we lived all our time in peace.

17. When Abba Sisoes was living on the mountain of Abba Anthony, his attendant was slow to come to him, and for about ten months the abba saw no one. Walking on the mountain, he met a Pharanite who was hunting wild beasts. The elder asked him: from where have you come, and how long have you been here? He answered: truly, Abba, I have been here eleven months and have not seen a single person except you. Hearing this, the elder entered his cell and struck himself, saying: behold, Sisoes! You thought you had done something, but you have not even done what this layman has done!

18. They said of Abba Sisoes that when he was approaching his end and the fathers were sitting with him, his face shone like the sun, and he said to them: behold, Abba Anthony has come! After a short while, he says again: behold, the company of prophets has come! And his face shone even more. Then he said again: behold, the choir of Apostles has come! The light of his face doubled, and he seemed to be speaking with someone. The elders asked him: with whom are you conversing, father? He said: behold, Angels have come to take me, and I am

asking them to leave me a little while to repent. The elders say to him: you have no need to bear repentance, father. But he said to them: truly I do not know whether I have even made a beginning. Then all perceived that he was perfect. Then again his face became like the sun, and fear fell upon all of them, and he said to them: see, the Lord has come and says: bring to Me the vessel of the desert! And immediately he gave up his spirit, becoming like lightning, and the dwelling was filled with fragrance.

19. The same Abba Sisoes, sitting in his cell, always kept the doors closed.

20. Someone asked Abba Sisoes about Abba Pambo, and he said: Pambo was great in his deeds.

21. One of the fathers said: a certain one, once conversing with Abba Silouan, saw that his face and body shone like an angel's, and he fell on his face. The abba himself said that others also have this gift.

22. They said of Abba Sarmatas that often, with the counsel of Abba Poemen, he would spend forty days in fasting, and these days passed before him as nothing. Abba Poemen, coming to him, asked: tell me, what have you seen, undertaking such labor? He answered him: nothing. Abba Poemen says to him: I will not leave you until you tell me. Then he said: I have seen one thing only, that when I say to sleep, "go," it departs, and when I say, "come," it comes.

23. Abba Matoes said of Abba Tithoes that no one can open his mouth against him for anything, but like pure gold standing evenly on the scales, so also is Abba Tithoes.

24. Abba Philoromus said: from the time I was reborn by water and Spirit until now, I have not eaten black bread for nothing, but from my labors, from the work of my hands, I gave two hundred gold coins to lepers. He was a very quick calligrapher and did not cease writing even in the eightieth year of his age, while in mind he never departed from God.

25. Abba Psenthaisius, Abba Surus, and Abba Psoius said: listening to the word of our father Pachomius, we were greatly edified, being stirred by him to zeal for good deeds. Seeing also that even when he was silent his deeds served as a word, we marveled and said to one another: we thought that all the saints from their mothers' wombs were made by God holy and unchangeable, and not free, and that sinners cannot live piously, having been created such. But now we see clearly the grace of God upon this our father, that though descending from Hellenic parents, he has become so godly and so adorned with all virtues. Can we all not also follow him, as he follows the saints? And is it not written: *Come to Me, all you who labor and are heavy laden, and I will give you rest* (Matthew 11:28)? So let us live with this man and die with him, for he leads us by the right path to God.

26. They said of Abba Or that he not only never lied, never swore an oath, and never cursed anyone, but he never even spoke without necessity.

27. Abba Or said to his disciple: see that you never bring a foreign word into this cell.

28. They said of Abba Or and Abba Theodore that they always made good beginnings and unceasingly gave thanks to God.

29. There was a certain hermit who grazed together with buffaloes. He prayed to God, saying: Lord! Teach me what I lack? And a voice came to him: go to such-and-such a coenobium and do what they tell you. He went and remained there. He did not know how to perform the obediences that lay upon the brethren, and the younger ones began to teach him, saying: do this, simpleton; do that, foolish elder. In sorrow he again began to pray to God: Lord! I do not know how to serve men; send me again to the buffaloes. And released by God, he went again into the field to graze with the buffaloes.

30. An elder recounted that a certain elder, living in the desert and having served God for many years, prayed thus: Lord! Assure me whether I have pleased You? And he saw an Angel who said to him: you have not yet become such as a certain gardener living in such-and-such a place. Marveling at this, the elder said to himself: I will go to the city to see him and learn what practice he follows that has surpassed the practice and labor of so many years of mine. So the elder went to the place of which he had heard from the Angel. Finding the man sitting and selling vegetables, he sat with him for the rest of the day. When he finished selling, the elder asked him: can you, brother, receive me into your cell for this night? With great joy he received him, and when they came to the cell and the gardener did everything for the elder's comfort, the elder said to him: do me a kindness, brother, tell me about your manner of life. He did not want to reveal it, but the elder did not cease asking him. Finally, persuaded by his persistence, he said: I always eat in the evening, keeping for myself from the sale only enough for food, and I give the rest to the poor, and if I receive any of the servants of God, I spend it on them. Rising in the morning and sitting down to my handwork, I say: this whole city, from small to great, will enter the kingdom for their righteous deeds; I alone will inherit torment for my sins; and also in the evening I again say the same word. Hearing this, the elder said to him: this practice is good, yet it is not powerful enough to surpass my labors of so many years. When they sat down to eat, the elder heard singing on the street, for his cell was in a good location, and asked him: desiring so much to live according to God, how do you remain in this place? Are you not disturbed by hearing these songs? He answered him: I assure you, Abba, that I have never been disturbed or scandalized by this. Hearing this, the elder says to him: what then do you think in your heart when you hear them? He said: that they will all go to the kingdom. Hearing this, the elder marveled and said: this is the practice that surpasses the labor of so many years of mine. Then, making a prostration, he said: forgive me, brother, I have not yet reached this measure, and without eating anything, he departed again into the desert.

31. One of the fathers recounted that two friends, merchants from Apamea, traded abroad, one of whom was rich and the other of moderate means. The rich one had a wife, very beautiful and chaste, as her deeds showed. When her husband died and his friend desired to take her for his own wife, but was ashamed to speak of it, fearing he would not receive consent, she, being sensible, understood this and said to him: Lord Samson (for such was his

name), I see that you have some thoughts, but tell me what is on your mind, and perhaps I will satisfy you. At first he was ashamed to speak, but then he opened himself to her and asked her to agree to be his wife. She says to him: if you do what I tell you, then I agree. He answered: I will do whatever you command. She said: go to your shop and fast until I call you, and I also will eat nothing until I call you. He agreed. She did not specify when she would call him, and he thought it would be that same day, but meanwhile a day passed, then a second, and a third, and she did not call him; however, he endured, whether from passion for her or because God so arranged it and gave him patience, knowing where He intended to call him, for he afterward became His chosen vessel. On the fourth day she sent for him, but he was so exhausted that he could no longer walk on foot and was carried to her. She prepared a table and, spreading a bed, says to him: here is the table and here is the bed! Which do you command, and to that will we turn? He answered her: I implore you, have mercy on me and let me eat a little, because I am dying of hunger, and from extreme exhaustion I do not even know what a wife is. Then she says to him: you see, when you became hungry, you preferred food to me and to any other wife and to pleasure. So when you have such thoughts, use this remedy and you will be freed from every improper thought, for believe me, after my husband I will not be joined to you or to anyone else, but under the protection of Christ I hope to remain a widow forever. Then, moved to compunction and marveling at her wisdom and chastity, he said to her: since the Lord has been pleased to look upon me and save me through your prudence, then what do you advise me to do? She, not trusting in youth and beauty and fearing lest she herself might sometime suffer from the same thing, says to him: I think that for God's sake you love no one more than me. He said: truly so. She continued: and I truly in God love you, but since there is a word of the Master saying: *If anyone comes to Me and does not hate his father and mother, wife and children, brothers and sisters, yes, and his own life also, he cannot be My disciple* (Luke 14:26), let us distance ourselves from each other, so that the Lord may reckon to you that you have renounced a wife for His sake, and to me that I have renounced a husband for His sake. Behold, in our country, in Apamea, there is a monastery of recluses, and if you sincerely desire to be saved, renounce the world there and you will truly please God. He at once, leaving all his property, hastened to that monastery, lived there until his very death, and became skilled, having a pure mind and spiritually contemplating saving things. All this Abba Samson himself told to the one who recounted it.

32. One of the hermits told the brethren living in Raithu, where there were seventy palm trees, by which Moses made camp with his people when they came out of Egypt: I once thought to go into the innermost desert, hoping to find someone living there even more as a desert dweller than I and serving God. Having walked four days and four nights, I found a cave and saw a man sitting in it. I knocked according to monastic custom, but he did not move, for he was dead. Without thinking at all, I entered, took him by the shoulder, and he immediately crumbled and turned to dust. Looking around and seeing a monastic tunic, I touched it, and it too crumbled and became nothing. Amazed by this, I went out and found another cave and the footprints of a man. Taking courage, I approached the cave and knocked, but again no one answered me. I entered and found no one. Standing outside the

cave, I said to myself: certainly a servant of God must come here, wherever he may be. And when day came, I saw buffaloes coming, and a servant of God, naked, whose private parts were covered by his hair. As he approached me, thinking that I was a spirit, he stood for prayer, for, as he told me later, he had been greatly tempted by spirits. Understanding this, I said to him: I am a man, a servant of God! Look at my footprints, feel me, for I am flesh and blood. When after the amen he looked at me, he was greatly comforted and, leading me into the cave, asked: how did you come here? I answered: I came into this desert to seek out servants of God, and the Lord has not deprived me of what I desired. Then I also asked him: and how did you come here? How many years have you been here? How are you nourished? Being naked, how do you not have need of clothing? He said: I was in a Theban coenobium, and my work was to prepare linen cloth. A thought came to me saying: leave here and live alone. There you will be able to keep stillness and receive strangers, and thereby acquire a greater reward. Having agreed with this thought, I tested it in deed: I established a monastery and gathered subordinates. I earned much and gave all that I acquired to the poor and to strangers. But our enemy the devil, envying, as always, the future recompense due me because I turned my labors to the glory of God, induced a certain virgin who had ordered work from me to order more when I had finished and delivered the work. From this arose habit and excessive familiarity, then the grasping of hands, laughter, and embraces, and finally we, wretched ones, begat lawlessness. Having spent six months in this fall with her, I thought that today or tomorrow I must certainly die and be subject to eternal torment, for if he who corrupts the wife of a husband is subject to punishment and torment, what torments does he deserve who has corrupted a handmaid of God! So, leaving everything to the woman, I secretly fled to this desert. Here I found a cave, a spring, and a palm tree, which gives me twelve branches with fruit a year, one branch each month, the fruit of which is enough for me for thirty days. Then, after a considerable time, my hair grew long, and when my clothes wore out, I began to cover with them as much as necessary and proper of my body. I asked him again: was it hard for you here at first? He answered: at first I suffered greatly from my liver, so that I could not stand for the rule and lay crying out to the Most High. When I was in extreme weakness and could not even move, a man entered the cave, stood by me, and asked: what ails you? Somewhat strengthened by him, I said that I suffered from my liver and showed him the place. He folded his fingers together and, cutting that place as if with a sword, took out my liver and showed me the wounds on it. Then he cleaned it with his hand, and placing it in its former place, closed the wound and said: now you have become healthy, so serve the Master Christ as you ought. From then on I became healthy and spend my days here without labor. I asked him for a long time to allow me to live in the cell I had seen before, but he said that I would not be able to endure the fury of the demons here. Reasoning the same myself, I asked him to pray and let me go. He prayed and let me go. I recounted this to you for your benefit.

33. Something similar was also told by another elder, who was afterward made bishop in the city of Oxyrhynchus, as if it were the word of someone else who had recounted such an incident to him, but it was he himself: I once took a notion to go into the innermost desert,

where dwells the race of Mazices, to see whether I might find some humble man there serving God, and taking some dry bread and water for about four days, I began the journey. When four days had passed, my food was exhausted and I was at a loss as to what to do, but taking courage, I surrendered myself to the will of God and walked another four days without food. Finally, from lack of food and the toil of the journey, my strength was exhausted, and I lay on the ground as if half dead. Then someone came and touched his finger to my lips, and I was at once so strengthened as if I had not traveled and had not been exhausted by hunger, and so I arose and went further into the desert. After four days I again grew weak and began to pray, stretching out my hands to heaven. And behold, the same man again touched my lips with his finger and again strengthened me. Seventeen days after that I finally found a cell, water by it, a palm tree, and an elder standing there whose hair served as clothing. He was all gray and fearsome in appearance. Seeing me, he stood for prayer, and upon finishing it, having said amen, he recognized that I was a man. Then, taking me by the hand, he asked: how did you come here? I answered: by the help of you who truly serve God, I have traversed this desert, and as for persecutions, they have ceased by the grace of Christ. Tell me then, how did you come here? He sighed bitterly and began to speak: I was a bishop. Persecution arose, and I, fearing the torments before me, offered sacrifice, but then, coming to myself, I recognized my lawlessness and condemned myself to death in this desert. And behold, it is already forty-nine years that I have lived here, repenting and praying that my sin might be forgiven. The Lord has been pleased to sustain my life with this palm tree, but I received no assurance of the forgiveness of my sin until the forty-eighth year and was comforted only this present year. Having said this, he quickly arose and ran outside, stood for prayer, and prayed for quite a long time. Having finished the prayer, he came back to me, and I gazed at his face with amazement and fear, for it was like fire. He said to me: do not be afraid, the Lord has sent you to bury my body, and with this word he gave up his spirit. I tore my exomis and left half for myself, and with the other half I wrapped his holy body and committed it to the earth. At once the palm tree dried up and the cell fell. I prayed for a long time with tears to God that He might restore the palm tree for me and thereby bless me to spend the rest of my days in that place, but since this did not happen, I said to myself: this is not the will of God, and having prayed, I hastened to an inhabited place. And behold, the same man who had touched my lips before came again and strengthened me. Having come to the brethren, I recounted this to them and urged them not to despair, but to seek God with patience.

34. One of the fathers recounted: in a certain village a bishop died. The villagers came to the archbishop and asked him to ordain a new bishop for them, and he said to them: give me one whom you consider worthy to shepherd the flock of Christ, and I will ordain him as your bishop. They answered: we do not know such a one, but we will accept the one whom your angel will give us. The archbishop asked: are you all here? They answered: no. He said to them: go, gather everyone and come to me, so that your bishop may be chosen with the consent of all. They all gathered and came to him, asking him to ordain a bishop for them. The archbishop said to them: give me the one whom you desire, and I will ordain him. But they repeated: we will not accept another, but only the one whom your angel will give us. He

asked: are you all here? They answered: we are all here. He asked again: none of you has remained behind? They said: no one, except the one who is holding our lead donkey. Then the archbishop asked: will you agree to the one I appoint? They all said: we will agree and ask your holiness to give us the very one about whom God will inform you. The archbishop ordered them to bring in the one who was outside holding the lead donkey and asked them: will you agree if I ordain this one as your bishop? They answered: we will agree, we will agree. He ordained him for them, and they returned with great joy with him to their village. In that village there occurred a drought. The newly ordained bishop implored God to send them rain, and God said to him: go in the morning to such-and-such gates and whoever enters first, detain him. He will pray, and there will be rain. The bishop did so. He went with his clergy to those gates and stood by them. An elder came with a load of firewood for sale. The bishop rose and stopped him. The elder put down the bundle of firewood, and the bishop began asking him: pray, Abba, that rain may come. The elder prayed, and rain immediately came as if from the floodgates of heaven and would not have stopped had the elder not prayed again. After this the bishop said to him: do me a kindness, Abba! For our benefit tell us about your life, so as to move us also to zeal for virtue. The elder said: forgive me, master! As you see, I go out and chop myself a small bundle of firewood. Having sold it, I do not keep for myself more than enough for two loaves of bread, which I eat, and I give the rest to the poor. I spend the night in the church, and the next day I go out again and do the same. If winter comes, I remain two or three days without food until good weather comes again and I can go out and chop firewood for myself. The bishop and his clergy received great benefit and glorified God. And to the elder the bishop said: you have truly fulfilled the word of Scripture: *I am a stranger on the earth* (Psalm 119:19).

35. One of the fathers asked God to reveal to him what measure he had reached. And God revealed to him: in such-and-such a coenobium there is a brother who is better than you. The elder went to that coenobium, where he was received with joy by all, including the abbot himself. The elder said: I want to see and greet all the brethren. The abbot ordered all to gather, and all came except the one about whom the elder had received the revelation. He asked them: is there any other brother? They say to him: there is, but he is a fool and works in the garden. The elder asked them to call him, and they called him. Seeing him, the elder arose and kissed him, and leading him aside, asked: reveal to us what practice you have. The brother answered: I am a foolish man. But after the elder's insistent requests, he finally said: I do not know what my abba does with me and what trial he employs for me, but every day he cuts the rope of the mat I plait, and behold, for thirty years I have endured this, never allowing my thought to hold anything against the abba, but always with patience I plait the ropes again, giving thanks to God. Hearing this, the elder marveled, for this showed also his other practice.

36. Two of the fathers, great elders, while passing through the desert of Scetis, heard a groan from beneath the earth, and finding an entrance to a cave, entered and saw there a holy virgin, an elderly woman, lying on the ground, and they asked: when did you come here, mother, and who attends to you?, for there was no one in the cave except her alone, lying in

illness. She answered: for thirty-eight years I have spent in this cave, serving Christ and being nourished by plants. I have never seen a single person here except you. God sent you to bury my body. Having said this, she fell asleep. The elders glorified God and, having buried her body, departed.

37. They recounted of a certain hermit: he once went out into the desert in one exomis and walked for three days, then climbing onto a rock, he saw below grass and a man grazing like the beasts; he came down quietly and seized him. The elder was naked, and since he could not bear the scent of a human being, he broke free and ran. The brother chased after him and cried out: I am chasing you for God's sake, wait for me! The elder turned and said: and I am running from you for God's sake. Then the brother threw off his exomis and again chased after him. Seeing that he had thrown off his garment, the elder received him and said: when you cast off all the matter of this world, I gladly waited for you. The brother asked him: father! Tell me a word, how to be saved? He said to him: flee from people, and you will be saved.

38. In one place two like-minded brothers were monastics. They led a life of extreme asceticism and in all virtues. It happened that one of them became a cenobiarch, while the other remained a hermit. The latter, having reached perfection in asceticism, began to work great miracles, healed the demon-possessed, and foretold the future. The one who from being an ascetic had become a cenobiarch, hearing that his like-minded companion had been granted such gifts, secluded himself from people for three weeks and diligently implored God to reveal to him why that one worked miracles and had become famous among all, while he was not deemed worthy of any such thing. And an Angel of the Lord appeared to him, saying: that one lives for God alone, sighs and weeps before Him day and night, endures hunger and thirst for the Lord's sake, while you, with your labors, have the company of brethren, and human consolation is sufficient for you.

39. They said of the Scetians that they did not exalt themselves when one surpassed another in virtues. They were all ascetics, and one ate every two days, another every four, and another every week; there were also those who did not eat bread, and those who did not drink. And in short, they were adorned with all virtues.

40. An elder said: one must not be concerned about anything except the fear of God. I, he said, though I am sometimes compelled to be concerned with the needs of the flesh, never think of it before the time.

41. An elder said: as vessels that have become blackened are cleaned again, so also believers, though they are blackened when they sin, are brightened again through repentance. For this reason, faith is rightly likened to a tinsmith.[28]

42. An elder said: immediately after monastic renunciation of the world, neither the devil nor his demons are permitted to tempt a person strongly, so that having fallen, he might not be extremely struck by it and might not immediately turn back to the world. But when the monk has progressed somewhat, both by time and deed, then the battles of fleshly desires and passions are permitted against him. And then the man troubled by them needs to humble

himself, weep, condemn and reproach himself alone, and thus, through temptations, he is taught patience, experience, and discernment, always fleeing to God with tears. Others, however, not having discernment, were struck by temptations to excess and, losing their minds, cut themselves with a knife or threw themselves into chasms from extreme sorrow and despair. Some of those troubled by demons of fornication or blasphemy did something similar: some of those burning with lust cut off their members, while others took wives, having been carried away by Satan through the strong movement of the passion of fornication. Therefore, let us accustom ourselves not to despair or be faint of heart, but rather to endure, be of good cheer, and give thanks to God in every temptation, tribulation, and violence from the devil, for thanksgiving to God destroys all the wiles of the enemy. As hands that are soiled with pitch are not cleansed except by oil, so also we spiritually hunger for the mercy and loving-kindness of our Savior Jesus Christ and are cleansed of the sins that defile us, approach with boldness His compassion, and are saved.

43. Brother![29] Without labor one cannot live and without struggle one cannot be crowned. Labor, struggling for salvation, and pray unceasingly, and God will help you, *who desires all men to be saved and to come to the knowledge of the truth* (1 Timothy 2:4).

44. A certain brother came to a physician and asked: is there such a medicine that could heal the multitude of my sins? The physician said: there is, and listen: go, take the root of spiritual poverty, flowers of humility, leaves of patience, and branches of prayer, mix all this and grind it in the mortar of endurance and obedience, sift it in the sieve of good thoughts, pour it into the vessel of a pure conscience, and pour over it streams of pure tears, then kindle beneath it the flame of divine love, and when it boils, pour it into the vessel of discernment and stir it with thanksgiving. Finally, draw it out with the spoon of heartfelt contrition and wipe yourself with the cloth of confession. In this way you will cleanse the multitude of your sins.

45. The elders said: as fire consumes wood, so must the work of a monk consume the passions.

46. The brethren of one coenobium said of a brother of that monastery that he had the following three virtues above all the monks: great fasting, long vigils, and much handwork.

47. They said of one elder that he grazed by the Dead Sea and spent seventy years naked, being nourished by grass alone.

48. They said of one elder who lived in Scetis that he had this rule: at night he slept four hours, stood for the rule four hours, and worked four hours, and during the day he worked until the sixth hour, from the sixth until the ninth hour he read and cut himself branches, then prepared food and took care of other things needed in the cell. Thus he spent all the days of his life.

49. An elder said: shame and fearlessness often lead to sin.

50. Again he said: if you, O man, will wish to live according to the law of God, then in the Lawgiver you will find the Rewarder.

51. Again he said: if you will wish willingly to transgress the commandments of God, then you will find the devil as your helper in the fall.

52. An elder said: freedom from care, silence, and hidden meditation give birth to purity.

53. An elder said: wherever a bee flies, it makes honey; so also a monk, wherever he goes, does the work of God.

54. Again he said: Satan is a rope-maker; as much as you give him hemp, so much does he plait. This he said concerning thoughts.

55. An elder also said: when a brother wishes to go to another brother, the demon of slander either arrives there before him or comes to that brother after him.

56. He also said: God does not want the lazy and idle one.

57. An elder said: give up your will, and you will receive strength.

58. An elder said: thanksgiving before God intercedes for weakness.

Endnotes

[28] A tinsmith.
[29] See also apophthegm 7.

Chapter XXII.
A Conversation of the Holy Elders,
Questions and Answers, Most Profitable for the Soul

1. Question. How should a monk remain in his cell? Answer. He should withdraw from acquaintance with many people, so that when his thought is free from all things, the knowledge of the Lord may dwell in him.

2. Question. Who is a monk? Answer. A monk is a dove. As a dove, flying up into the air in its time and spreading its wings, if it delays long outside its nest, is beaten by bloodthirsty birds and loses its comeliness, so also a monk, going out to the church assembly and spreading abroad his thoughts, if he delays long outside his cell, is beaten by demons and becomes subject to the darkening of his thoughts and loses their brightness.

3. Question. By what thought does the devil drive a monk from his cell? Answer. The devil is a charmer. As a charmer draws a beast from its burrow with beguiling words, and having caught it, leads it through the streets of the city and delivers it to the mockery of the people, and then, when it grows old, burns or drowns it, so also thoughts draw a monk to leave his cell and subject him to the same fate.

4. Question. If a monk goes out on obedience and meets a woman on the road, how can he escape the warfare of fornication? Answer. He cannot escape the warfare, but he can escape the deed, if he remains silent at the hour of the meeting, for as from the striking of a flint against steel a spark is kindled, so from the conversation of a woman with a man, sin is kindled.

5. Question. By what thought does fornication descend into a person? Answer. Not one, nor two, nor five, nor ten thoughts are appointed for fornication, for all the thoughts of the devil have fornication hidden within them.

6. Question. Is it good to have two tunics? Answer. To have two tunics and not to have ruinous malice is good. The body has need of covering, and having what is necessary and sufficient, with these let us be content.

7. Question. How should the service of psalm-singing be performed, and what is the measure of fasting? Answer. Nothing more should be done than what has been commanded, for many, desiring more, afterward could not perform even the little.

8. Question. If a brother asks me to come to him to drink a cup of wine, is it good to go to him? Answer. Flee from wine-drinking as a deer from snares, for many have fallen through this into a pit of thoughts.

9. Question. If a brother disturbs me, do you want me to make a prostration to him? Answer. Make a prostration to him and cut yourself off from him, for we have Abba Arsenius, who said: have love for all, and withdraw from all.

10. Question. What does it mean for a person to bring a sacrifice of thanksgiving to the church? Answer. This deed is a treasure laid before the face of God. And what you cast down here flows out above.

11. Question. I wish to be a martyr for God's sake. Answer. If in time of need someone intercedes for his neighbor, this is equal to the furnace of the three youths.

12. Question. Why does fornication so attract a person? Answer. Because the devil knows how fornication estranges us from the Holy Spirit, for he hears what the Lord says: *"My Spirit shall not strive with man forever, for he is indeed flesh"* (Genesis 6:3).

13. Question. How should one keep stillness in the cell? Answer. Sitting in the cell, one should have absolutely no remembrance of any person.

14. Question. What, then, is the practice one should have, that the heart might be unceasingly occupied by it? Answer. This is the perfect practice of a monk: to attend always to God without distraction.

15. Question. How should the mind drive away evil thoughts? Answer. It cannot do this in any way by itself and has no such power, but as soon as the soul falls under the power of thoughts, it should immediately flee to Him Who made it, and He will melt them like wax, for *our God is a consuming fire* (Hebrews 12:29).

16. Question. But how did the Scetian fathers use the contradicting thought? Answer. Such a practice is also great and excellent, but it has labor and is not reliably good for all.

17. Question. How not for all? Answer. When a thought comes upon the soul, and it, after long struggle, expels it, another comes and occupies it, and thus, contradicting thoughts, it is not freed even for a minute for the contemplation of God.

18. Question. By what art, then, does the thought flee to God? Answer. When the thought of fornication comes, immediately shake off the mind, raise it up with diligence, and do not delay at all, for delay is akin to consent.

19. Question. If the thought of vainglory comes, saying that you have fulfilled a virtue, should one not contradict this thought also? Answer. As soon as anyone begins to contradict it, it immediately becomes stronger and fiercer, for it finds more of your devices for contradiction. Moreover, the Holy Spirit will no longer defend you so much, for He finds you being high-minded, thinking: I myself can also fight with thoughts. As one who has a spiritual father entrusts everything to the father and himself remains without care, so also one who

delivers himself to God should not at all be concerned about a thought or contradict it, even if it enters. If it does enter, take it above, to the Father, and say to it: I have nothing to do with this. Behold my Father! He knows. And while you are still bringing it up, in the middle of the way it will leave you and flee, for it cannot come with you to God or stand before His face. There is no practice higher than this, nor any commandment more free from care than this in the Church.

20. Question. How then did the Scetians please God, contradicting thoughts? Answer. Since they are doers in simplicity and with the fear of God, God also defended them, and afterward the same practice of contemplation came to them also, by the good pleasure of God, for their labors and love of God. At this, the one who taught this related the following: being once in Scetis, I came to a certain Scetian who had been living there a very long time. He kissed me, sat down, and said nothing to me. I sat, giving myself to contemplation, while he worked on a basket and did not once raise himself up to look at me, forgetting even about food. Thus for six days he remained without food, weaving a whole day. On the following day, around the tenth hour, he said to me: Brother! From where do you have such a practice? I asked: And how did you find it? We, from our spiritual childhood, have been taught this practice by our fathers. The Scetian said to me: I did not receive this practice from my fathers, but as you see me now, so I have remained all my time, with little handwork, with little meditation, with as much purification of my thought as I could manage, and with contradicting the thoughts that came upon me. And thus the spirit of contemplation came to me, while I did not know about it, nor did I know whether anyone has such a practice. I answered him: But I was taught it from childhood.

21. Question. In what manner should such a one attend to contemplation? Answer. As the divine Scripture teaches us: Daniel contemplated the Ancient of Days; Ezekiel, the cherubic chariot; Isaiah, the throne high and lifted up; Moses, *as seeing Him who is invisible, endured* (Hebrews 11:27).

22. Question. How can the mind contemplate that which it has never seen? Answer. You have never seen a king sitting, as we see on icons.

23. Question. But should the mind depict the Divinity? Answer. There is nothing better than to depict and not consent to impure thoughts.

24. Question. Will this not be reckoned as sin? Answer. Hold for now to what the prophets saw historically, and afterward the perfect itself will also come, as the Apostle also says: *For now we see in a mirror, dimly, but then face to face* (1 Corinthians 13:12). "Then," means when the thought is perfected, then it will behold with boldness.

25. Question. Will this not lead to ecstasy of the mind? Answer. It will not at all, if one struggles in truth. And one said at this: the whole day and the whole week I did not once remember a person. And another said: I was once going on a journey, and two Angels of God were walking with me, one on one side and the other on the other, but I did not pay attention to them.

26. Question. Why did you not pay attention? Answer. Because it is written that neither angel nor spirit can separate us from the love of Christ.

27. Question. Can the mind always contemplate? Answer. If not always, yet when the thought becomes entangled by passions, let it immediately flee to God in contemplative prayer, for if the thought succeeds in this, it would be easier to move a mountain than to bring it down from there. As a condemned man, confined in a dark prison, after he is released and sees the light, does not even want to remember that darkness, so also the thought, when it begins to behold its own light. Thus one of the fathers said: once, wishing to test my thought, whether it would wander if I let it out into the world, I let it go, but it stood in one place, not knowing where to go, until I took it up again above, for it knew that I would torment it if it went to wander. What corrects such practice is stillness with humility and prayer, for frequent prayer with humility quickly brings the mind to correctness.

28. Question. How can one pray unceasingly, for the body is weak for such service? Answer. Not only when we stand at prayer is it called prayer, but also what is done always and everywhere.

29. Question. How always? Answer. Whether you eat, drink, go on a journey, or sit at work, do not depart from prayer.

30. Question. But if you are speaking with someone, how can you fulfill the rule of unceasing prayer? Answer. For this reason the Apostle said: *with all prayer and supplication* (Ephesians 6:18). So if you cannot be free for prayer while conversing with another, pray with supplication.

31. Question. With what prayer should one pray? Answer. *Our Father who art in heaven...* and the rest.

32. Question. What measure should prayer have? Answer. No measure is shown, for the words "always" and *pray without ceasing* (1 Thessalonians 5:17) exclude all measure. And at this he said that whoever wishes to correct this must see all people as one and refrain from judging.

33. Question. Why can I not live with the brethren? Answer. Because you do not fear God, for if you remembered the testimony of Scripture, that Lot was saved among the Sodomites, judging no one, you would agree to live even among wild beasts.

34. Question. What is the sin of judging? Answer. The sin of judging will not allow a person to come before the face of God, for it is written: *The one who secretly slanders his neighbor, him I will destroy* (Psalm 101:5).

35. Question. Why is my thought not freed when I stand at prayer? Answer. The devil, who in the beginning did not wish to worship the God of all, was cast down from heaven and became a stranger to the kingdom of God, and therefore he strives to scatter our prayer, so that he might subject us also to the same condemnation.

36. Question. How can a person cut off the assault of the demon? Answer. A fish cannot prevent a fisherman from casting his hook into the sea, but if, understanding the danger of

the bait, it withdraws, then it is saved, and the labor of the fisherman remains fruitless. So should a person also do.

37. Question. Does remembrance make a person guilty of sin? Answer. Waves do not harm a stone, so also an assault not brought to action does not harm a person, as it is also said that sin not committed is not sin.

38. Question. What does the word of Scripture mean: *if you have faith as a mustard seed* (Matthew 17:20)? Answer. When a farmer, having plowed and cleared the earth, sows seeds, then the seed, finding room in the earth, puts roots down into the depths and shoots up above, so that the birds of heaven dwell on them, so also a person, if he cleanses his heart, receives the word of God, and it takes root in the heart and produces good thoughts, so that all the commandments of God dwell in him.

39. Question. Is it good to dwell in the desert? Answer. The sons of Israel, when they departed from the vanities of Egypt and dwelt in tents, then it was given them to know how one must fear God; similarly, ships, when they are carried by waves in the midst of the sea, remain fruitless, but when they enter the harbor, then their owners make trade and receive profit. So also a person, if he does not remain with patience in one place, will not receive the knowledge of the truth. And stillness God chose above all virtues, for it is written: *On this one will I look: on him who is poor and of a contrite spirit, and who trembles at My word* (Isaiah 66:2).

40. Question. Why does the devil so strongly draw me to distraction and away from handwork? Answer. Since the devil knows that from handwork comes the fruit-bearing of almsgiving, he draws us to distraction, so that, having removed us from handwork, he might cut off almsgiving.

41. Question. Is it good not to like the quarrels of the brethren? Answer. Flee from them, for it is written: *Stop your ears from hearing of bloodshed, and shut your eyes from seeing evil* (Isaiah 33:15).

42. Question. How can a person live alone? Answer. A wrestler, if he does not remain among people, cannot learn the art of conquering, so that he might afterward be able to enter into single combat with the opponent; so also a monk can only resist thoughts while living alone if before that, while living among the brethren, he learns the art of conquering thoughts.

43. Question. If it happens that necessity arises to enter into conversation with a woman, how should one conduct it? Answer. This necessity is from the devil, and he has many other pretexts of necessity. But if it happens that you enter into conversation with a woman, do not allow her to speak unnecessarily, and you yourself, finishing the conversation in a short time, dismiss her quickly, but if you delay in conversation, know that her foul odor will defile your thought.

44. Question. What thought can turn a person away from judging? Answer. As one who receives fire into his bosom is burned, so also one who receives the conversations of people will not be clean from judging.

45. Question. What is the meaning of the nocturnal fantasies of the devil? Answer. As during the day he occupies us with extraneous thoughts to turn us from prayer, so at night he gives wings to the mind with fantasies to take away the purity of our sleep.

46. Question. What should a person do when a temptation of the flesh comes upon him in sleep? Answer. As one who finds his adversary sleeping and strikes him cannot boast of victory, because this is shameful, so also a temptation occurring in sleep is of no account.

47. Question. How can a person receive the gift of loving God? Answer. When someone, seeing a brother in sin, cries out to God for help for him, then he will receive the knowledge of how one must love God.

48. Question. By the fulfillment of which commandments can a person be saved? Answer. Four virtues stand before a person: fasting, prayer, handwork, and chastity of body. Having risen up against these virtues, the devil drove Adam out of paradise, for having beguiled him with food and put him to shame, he drove him to hide himself and not go before the face of God to ask forgiveness for his sin; and when Adam was driven out of paradise, the devil wanted by idleness to cast him down into another sin, that of despair. Therefore the man-loving Master, seeing the malice of the devil, gave Adam work, saying: work the earth from which you were taken, so that he, being occupied with work, might cut off the evil suggestions of the devil. So also now the devil rises up against fasting, prayer, and handwork, which destroys all his schemes, as well as against chastity. Whoever acquires these four virtues will also possess all the virtues.

49. Question. What should one do to receive the gift of these virtues? Answer. Whoever wishes to learn any art leaves every other care and humbles himself, and through humility acquires the art. So, when a monk leaves every human care and abases himself below every person, not thinking that he is better than or equal to anyone, then the virtues, noticing his practice, come to him of their own accord, for it is said: *You shall cry, and He will say, "Here I am"* (Isaiah 58:9).

50. Question. How can a person know that his prayer is pleasing to God? Answer. If he keeps himself from offending his neighbor in any matter whatsoever, then he may be emboldened in thought that his prayer is pleasing to God; but if he offends his neighbor in anything, either bodily or spiritually, then his prayer is unpleasing and abhorrent, for the sighing of the offended one does not allow the prayer of the one who offended to enter before God. Moreover, if he does not hasten to be reconciled with his neighbor, he will never be cleansed from his sins, for it is written: *whatever you bind on earth will be bound in heaven* (Matthew 18:18).

51. Question. Is it good to learn the Holy Scripture by heart? Answer. A shepherd drives sheep to good grass, but as they walk through the wilderness, they also come upon bitter herbs. When this herb begins to burn, the sheep regurgitates the good grass and sweetens its taste. So also for a person, it is good to study the divine Scriptures against the assaults of demons, for as soon as one stands at psalm-singing and perfumes his mouth with crying out to God, the demons, not enduring the praise sent up to God, immediately leave the singers.

Chapter XXIII.
A Conversation of Twelve Anchorites

Twelve anchorites once gathered together, men holy, wise, and spiritual, and asked one another to tell what each had corrected in his cell and with what spiritual struggle he had struggled.

The first, the eldest among them, said: I, brethren, from the time I began to practice stillness, have crucified myself entirely to outward things, remembering what is written: *"Let us break Their bonds in pieces and cast away Their cords from us"* (Psalm 2:3), and, having set up as it were a wall between my soul and bodily things, I said in my mind: as one who is behind a wall does not see him who stands outside, so must you never look upon outward things, but attend to yourself, laying hold each day upon the hope of God. Evil desires I consider a serpent and the brood of vipers, and when I sense that they are being born in my heart, with wrath and fury I dry them up and do not cease being angry at my body and my soul, so that they may do nothing evil.

The second said: from the time I renounced the world, I said to myself: today you have been reborn, so begin now to order your heart as if you were sitting within as a stranger and tomorrow were to depart. This I continually impressed upon myself.

The third said: in the morning I depart to my Lord and worship Him, casting myself upon my face and confessing my sins; then I descend to His Angels and worship them, asking them to pray to God for me and for all God's creation; having done this, I descend into the abyss, and as the Jews do when they come to Jerusalem, that is, they rend their garments, weep and wail over the calamity of their fathers, so do I: I pass through the places of torment and weep with those who weep, seeing myself as if tormented with them.

The fourth said: I beheld myself as if sitting on the Mount of Olives with the Lord and His Angels, and said to myself: henceforth know no one according to the flesh, but always abide with these alone, seeking them and imitating their good life. Sit as Mary at the feet of the Lord and listen to His word, which He speaks: *"you shall be holy, for I am holy"* (Leviticus 11:44; 1 Peter 1:16), and *"be merciful"* and *"perfect, just as your Father in heaven is perfect"* (Matthew 5:48; Luke 6:36), and *"learn from Me, for I am gentle and lowly in heart"* (Matthew 11:29).

The fifth said: I behold the Angels ascending and descending every hour to summon souls, and, continually awaiting the end, I say: *"My heart is steadfast, O God, my heart is steadfast"* (Psalm 108:1).

The sixth said: every day I suppose that I hear these words from the Lord: labor for Me, and I will give you rest; struggle a little longer, and I will show you My salvation and My glory; if you love Me, then since you are My children, be ashamed before your Father who calls you; if you are My brethren, be ashamed before Me who suffered so much for you; if you are My sheep, then follow the footsteps of your Master.

The seventh said: three things I always keep in mind and continually impress upon myself: faith, hope, and love, so that by faith I may rejoice, by love never offend anyone, and by hope be strengthened.

The eighth said: I always behold the devil, *seeking whom he may devour* (1 Peter 5:8), and wherever I go, I behold with inner eyes my Master and God, and I pray to Him against the devil, that he may have no success and may have no power to do anything to those who fear Him.

The ninth said: each day I behold the church of the noetic Powers and the Lord of glory in its midst, brighter than all. When I grow fainthearted, I ascend to the heavens, behold the wondrous beauties of the Angels, attend to the hymns which they send up to God and their melodies, I am gladdened by their brightness and their singing, remembering what is written: *"The heavens declare the glory of God"* (Psalm 19:1), and I consider all things on earth as dust and smoke.

The tenth said: I always behold the Angel standing near me and I guard myself, remembering what is written: *"I have set the Lord always before me; because He is at my right hand I shall not be moved"* (Psalm 16:8), therefore I fear him who watches over my ways, for he ascends every day to God and reports to Him my words and deeds.

The eleventh said: attending to the virtues, to self-control, chastity, long-suffering, and love, I drew them to myself and surrounded myself with them, and wherever I go, I say to myself: where are your guides? Do not be fainthearted and do not despond, having them always near you, and whichever one you seek will stand before you. They intercede much for you before God because they have found rest in you.

The twelfth said: you, having received wings from heaven, have acquired a heavenly life, and it is no wonder, for I see that you are exalted in your deeds and mind heavenly things, and that you will be translated with glory from the earth, having wholly estranged yourselves from its affairs. But what shall I say to you, earthly angels and heavenly men? Counting myself unworthy even of life, I behold my sins before me always, wherever I go, and wherever I turn, I see that they go everywhere before me. Therefore I have condemned myself to the netherworld, saying: I shall be with those with whom I am worthy to be; in a little while I too shall be numbered among them. But seeing there the torments and the tears, unceasing and unutterable, the gnashing of teeth and the trembling of the whole body, I cast myself upon my face and entreat God that I may not experience those sorrows. Seeing the fiery sea, seething, whose waves reach to the heavens, and the fearsome angels casting into it a countless multitude of people who have turned away from themselves the mercy of God by their sins, who from the unbearable burning utter terrible cries, intolerable to any mortal, I weep for the human race, that in blindness it dares to give itself over to sins or earthly things, when such torments await them for this. With these thoughts I hold weeping in my heart, counting myself unworthy of heaven and earth and fulfilling the word of Scripture: *"My tears have been my food day and night"* (Psalm 42:3).

Such are the deeds of the wise and holy fathers. Grant, O Lord, that we too may take up a life worthy of remembrance, that, having become blameless, we may give thanks to our Master and God.

Chapter XXIV.
An Instructive Word of a Certain Great Elder to His Disciple. Read with Diligence and Seek Not Many Words, for Even One Word Can Rouse to Salvation

1. Upon arising from sleep, before any other word, glorify God and say: I thank Thee, O Lord, that Thou hast overlooked my iniquities and hast not given me over to death, but in Thy love for mankind hast raised me from my bed. Grant me the grace and strength always to glorify Thy most holy name and bless me at this hour to begin songs and psalms to Thee. For what the mind receives into itself in the morning, that, like a millstone, it will grind all day long, whether it be the wheat of good thoughts or the chaff of wicked thoughts. And when going to sleep, remember the grave, saying to yourself: shall I arise tomorrow? And pray diligently before sleep.

2. If you see images of women in a dream, pray that the Lord would deliver you from the remembrance of them during the day, for this is the death and destruction of the soul.

3. Attend to yourself and do not hold anything impure in your thoughts, whether standing or sitting, and do not remember any woman, even if she be a saint, but rather be zealous that Jesus Christ and the remembrance of death may always abide in your heart, and this will preserve you from every satanic fantasy.

4. When a thought tells you, by day or by night, "arise, pray," know that your guardian Angel is speaking to you. If you arise, he will stand with you and pray together, driving away from you the demons, who will gnash their teeth at you for it. But if you do not heed him and are too lazy to arise, he will withdraw from you, and you will fall into the hands of your enemies.

5. When you do any work together with the brethren, do not show them that you are working more than they, even if it be so, for otherwise you will destroy your reward.

6. When you are sitting at your handwork and the hour of your prayer comes, do not say: I will finish this little bit and then arise, but arise promptly at each hour and render to God the debt of your prayer, otherwise, little by little, you will grow accustomed to being negligent of prayer, and your soul will become empty because of it.

7. If evil thoughts trouble you, do not conceal them, but immediately speak them out and expose them, for the longer a man conceals his thoughts, the more they multiply and grow strong. Just as a serpent, driven out of its hole, hastens to escape in flight from the gaze of its pursuers, so also evil thoughts, when they are confessed and revealed, immediately vanish from the heart and memory, and just as a worm hiding inside a tree gnaws at it, so an evil thought consumes the heart as long as it is concealed in it. He who reveals his thoughts is healed at once, but he who conceals them is possessed by pride.

8. When going to confess your thoughts to your father or to ask him about something, first pray in your heart and say: Lord, what is pleasing to Thee, put this in my father's mouth, that he may say it to me, for I receive his word as if from Thy mouth. Establish him, O Lord, in Thy truth, that I may always hear from him Thy holy will. And afterward keep faithfully and with fear that which he tells you.

9. If someone asks you to pray for him, say thus: God, through the prayers of our holy fathers, have mercy on you, brother, and on me, as is pleasing to Him.

10. If someone comes to you of whom you have heard that he has reviled and slandered you, do not show him that you have learned of it, but be kindly disposed toward him and address him with a cheerful countenance, that you yourself may have boldness before God in prayer.

11. If it happens that you have burdened yourself with food, take up some bodily labor and do not lie down to sleep, lest you be defiled by impure fantasies. Be a good fighter against the devil and, from whatever side he attacks you, from that side answer him, that is, if he defeats you by overeating, you fight him by vigil; if he combats you with sleep, you press him with bodily labor.

12. If vainglory combats you, do before people some disreputable but not sinful deed or assume some doubtful appearance, so that they will speak of you without honor, for know that nothing so crushes the devil as when someone seeks humility and abasement with all his heart.

13. When you walk through the city, lower your eyes to the ground and cover them with your cowl.

14. When you are away and they do not receive you, do not be sorrowful, but rather say: if I were worthy, then God would have given me rest. For know that whether sorrow or some dishonor, it comes to a man from none other than God, either for his testing or for the cleansing of sins. He who does not believe this does not know that throughout all the earth are the judgments of God.

15. If a thought of arrogance attacks you, say to the demon suggesting it: The Lord said, *everyone who exalts himself will be humbled* (Luke 18:14). When you cease telling me that I am good, then I shall be assured that I am good, because I shall have humility; but in telling me that I

am good, by that very fact you certify to me that I am an enemy of God, for *the Lord resists the proud* (Proverbs 3:34).

16. Also, you must say the following: woe to me, woe to me! In outward appearance I am a monk and live in a monastery, but in deed I am a worldling, and my soul is dragged through the world. People honor me as a saint, thinking that I keep the rules of asceticism of the holy fathers, but I eat and drink intemperately, I sleep and am lazy, I am gripped by every negligence each day and am shameless in evil thoughts.

17. If you live with a certain brother, take care to command him nothing with authority, lest your heart be exalted, and in outward demeanor maintain lack of boldness, while in your soul consider yourself the servant of your brother.

18. If having fallen into sin, you arise and come to contrition and repentance, do not cease to be contrite and to sigh before God until the very day of your death, otherwise you will soon fall again into the same pit.

19. When you see that the Lord is showing you mercy and granting contrition to your heart, then you yourself also constrain yourself to keep stillness, fasting, and prayer, for then Satan will suggest to you supposedly necessary and urgent matters, so that, by undertaking them, you will lose your contrition. But do not listen to him and, leaving everything, even that which is truly necessary, kindle only contrition, until it accomplishes its work, for great is its value. If you do thus, soon expect also temptation and warfare, either from people or from demons, since Satan rises up mightily against a man when the man is coming out from under his power. But anger above all destroys the humility and contrition of the soul.

20. When you are sitting and demons surround you like bees with various thoughts, disturbing the three parts of your soul, immediately arise and pray, condemn yourself, reproach yourself, and weep, and they will be scattered.

21. If you desire to have weeping, love humility and poverty, have no fine garments and nothing superfluous in your cell, for when the soul desires something and does not find it in the cell, it will sigh and humble itself, and for this God will comfort it and grant it compunction. But when the soul tastes of the sweetness of God, then it will hate all that is worldly, even the clothing it wears and its very body, for I say to you, my son, if a man does not hate his body as an enemy and adversary, he will not be freed from the snares of the devil.

22. Abba Isaiah said: do not take anyone by the hand, do not touch another's body, except for the necessity of great infirmity, and even then with caution and fear. Likewise, do not allow another's hand to approach you or touch you. All your life, do not lie down to sleep close to another. Do not give a kiss to a youth who has no beard and do not laugh with him, lest you destroy your soul; do not go and do not sit near him; in general, never draw close to one another, for one who is truly reverent is ashamed even of himself. Many, through negligence in this, as in a minor and trifling matter, have fallen into the great pit of destruction. Remember that every evil begins with something small and then reaches something great.

23. If you love Christ and desire the consolation that comes from the weeping of those who seek Him, in all things and always choose that which is sorrowful for the flesh, for the Lord's sake, Who suffered for us. Thus, if white bread comes to you, save it for the case of a sick person, and yourself partake of black bread, for Christ's sake; if it happens that there is good wine, mix with it a little vinegar, for the sake of Christ, Who drank vinegar for you. When you eat vegetables, do not be satisfied, but leave a little, saying: here is Christ's portion; and if you find a soft pillow, leave it and place a stone under yourself, for Christ's sake; if you become chilled during sleep, endure, saying that others do not sleep at all; if they revile you, be silent, for Christ's sake, saying that He also was reviled for me; if you prepare a cooked dish for yourself, spoil it a little, saying: others, who are worthy, do not even partake of bread, so how can I, unworthy, eat a good cooked dish, when I should be nourished on dust and ashes. Thus, in general, in every matter, mix in a little that is bitter and unpleasant for the flesh, whether you eat or drink, sleep or work, and pass all the time of your life in hardship and humility, remembering how the saints lived, so that, when the hour of your departure comes, it may find you in sorrow and hardship, and then, without doubt, you will find rest in the land of the living.

24. Do not keep in your cell clothing or anything else that is unnecessary and superfluous to you, for this is death for you. Others, more righteous than you, are cold, while you, a sinner, have what is superfluous.

25. Do not store up money all your life, for otherwise God will no longer care for you, but when you happen to have some, then, if you have need of clothing or food, buy it at once, but if you have no need, give it away. And do not let it remain with you in your cell even for one night, all your life.

26. If a thought tells you: prepare more dishes for the feast, do not listen to it, otherwise you will be keeping the feast like the Jews. They usually prepare them, but for monks the adornment of the feast is weeping and tears.

27. If you hear that someone is slandering or reviling you, send him a small blessing according to your ability, so that in prayer you may say with boldness: *forgive us, O Master, our debts, as we forgive our debtors* (Matthew 6:12).

28. If you have a cell, even such a one as only covers your stature, by no means seek another in the desire to have spaciousness and room in it.

29. When you sell or buy something, it is better to bear a small loss to yourself and not to bargain for long, lest, wishing to obtain the proper price, you fall into contentiousness.

30. If you come somewhere and notice that your weeping and contrition are weakening, return quickly to your cell and resume your former disposition, lest you drive them away from yourself altogether.

31. If brethren are coming to you, then, as soon as you see them from afar, stand to prayer and say: Lord, deliver us from slander and condemnation. Then receive them in peace and see them off.

32. If you desire to acquire true weeping and humility, make it so that all the things you need are poor, as for the beggars who sit in the marketplace and ask for alms.

33. Do not keep in your cell even books and icons that are costly and superfluous.

34. Let not your hands search for or touch in your cell anything of silver or gold, even the smallest thing.

35. Let no new clothing come upon your body, nor a cowl, if it is attractive in appearance.

36. Do not have a soft cloth and do not hang it on your belt, for all such things drive away weeping.

37. When you see a fine thing belonging to your brother, do not desire it, lest you fall into great evil, for he who desires what is small will also desire what is great and will sin.

38. If you have some vessel, or knife, or anything else and feel attachment to it, cast it far from yourself, so as to teach your thought to love absolutely nothing except God alone.

39. If at night you are too lazy to rise for your rule, do not give yourself food that day, for the Apostle says: *if anyone will not work, neither shall he eat* (2 Thessalonians 3:10). Think of it this way, that if there is in the world a thief or some other criminal, so also is he who does not rise before God at the proper time for prayer, without extreme infirmity and sickness. However, even from the sick, God requires the prayer of the heart, which even without bodily standing can be raised up to God.

40. If you condemn a certain brother and he learns of it, go bow down to him and say: forgive me, brother, for I have condemned you. But if he does not learn of it, do not say anything to him, lest you disturb him, but confess it to God and to your father, reproaching yourself and resolving henceforth not to be mocked in like manner.

41. Hearing of the great ascetic labors of the fathers, try yourself to undertake one of them, calling upon the name of our Lord Jesus Christ, that He may strengthen you. If you are able to accomplish the deed, give thanks to God; if you are not able, reproach your weakness, recognize your impotence, and humble your thought until your very departure. Accuse your soul always, that it has begun and not finished.

42. When you fall into carnal sins, do not remember how you committed them, lest you again defile your soul thereby, but rather pray to God, saying: Lord, Thou knowest my vile and immeasurable sins! Blot them out Thyself, as Thou wilt. But I dare not remember them, lest by that I anger Thee even more.

43. If lust agitates your body and heart, search out the cause from which this warfare has arisen and remove it. It has arisen, surely, either from excessive food, or from immoderate sleep, or from arrogance, or from the fact that you have considered yourself better than

others, or have condemned someone, as though he does not serve God as he ought, or lives badly, or his deeds are not pleasing to God, while you have considered yourself as serving Him diligently, living well, and your deeds as pleasing to God, for without these causes a man is not subject to the assault of the passion of fornication.

44. Approaching any deed, say to yourself with attention: what will happen if the Lord visits me at this hour? And look at what the thought answers you. If it condemns you, immediately abandon that deed and take up another, for a worker must be ready at every hour for his journey. Whether you are sitting at handwork, or are on the road, or are visiting someone, or are partaking of food, always say to yourself: what will happen if God calls me now? Look at what your conscience answers you, and do as it tells you.

45. If you have taken upon yourself an ascetic labor and have fallen away from it, take it up again and do not cease to do this until your very death, for in whatever state death finds you, in that state you will go there, whether in negligence or in ascetic struggle.

46. Every month, year, week, and day, examine yourself, whether you have shown any progress, that is, whether you have become established in vigil, prayer, fasting, or obedience, and above all in humility, for it is the sign of true progress of the soul. This may be known from whether you consider yourself last among all and whether you sincerely say in your heart: every man is better than I, for without such a thought, even if a man works signs, even if he raises the dead, he is far from God.

47. When you come to some elder and, after prayers, he invites you to sit, say to him: Father! Say to me a word of life, how I may find God, and pray for me, for I have many sins. But apart from this, say nothing unless you are asked.

48. If one brother reveals a secret to you and another adjures you to tell him of it, do not fear the adjuration and do not betray the secret of your brother, for this oath will fall on the head of the one adjuring.

49. If you do not have contrition, know that you are possessed by vainglory, or gluttony, or bodily comfort, that is, sleep and idleness, for all these things hinder the soul from coming to contrition.

50. If someone of his own accord gives you something as a gift of love and you have need of it, take it, for this means that God has sent him. But if you have no need of it, by no means take it, for it may be that Satan is tempting you to take something beyond your need.

51. If any person praises you to your face, immediately remember your sins and ask him: for God's sake, do not praise me, brother, for I am weak and cannot bear it. But if this is someone among the great, then pray to God, saying: Lord! Cover me and deliver me from the praise and contempt of men.

52. Set a seal upon your eyes and do not look at beautiful faces, whether of women or of men. He who does not restrain his eyes is also unrestrained in his thoughts, and the mind of such a one is a captive of the passions.

53. While you are young, keep your body and your face in a certain neglect, for this is profitable for you.

54. When weeping comes to you, do not think that something special has happened to you, since you weep. Blessed is he who has no need of weeping. But humble yourself, otherwise, when God sees that you are becoming proud because of the grace of tears, He will take them from you, and then your heart will become hard as stone, incapable of any good deed.

55. If your soul desires various foods, deprive yourself for a time even of bread. Having grown hungry, you will desire to be satisfied with bread alone.

56. When you ask respected elders about something, receive their word with faith and strive to fulfill what they have told you. If, having grown lazy, you sometimes do not fulfill it, nevertheless do not cease to ask them again, condemning and humbling yourself. And never forget this good deed: perhaps the Lord will at last give some elder such a word as will inflame your inner being and turn your whole heart entirely to God.

57. If you fall into a carnal sin and the person with whom you have sinned is near you, withdraw from that place, for otherwise it will hardly be possible for you to depart from the sin.

58. If you see with your eyes a brother sinning and a thought tells you: condemn him, open up this thought and say to it: anathema to you, Satan! You are to blame, but what has my brother done? And establish your heart not to judge the brother, for otherwise the mercy of God will depart from you.

59. If a brother condemns a brother before you, take care not to irritate him further by saying: yes, this is so. But either be silent, or say to him: I myself am condemned and cannot judge another, and thereby you will save both yourself and him.

60. When you walk, keep your hands at your belt and do not swing them, as is customary for worldly people.

61. When in bodily infirmity you ask something of someone and he does not give it to you, do not be sorrowful at him, but rather say: if this were profitable for my soul, or if I were worthy to receive it, then God would have moved my brother to give it to me.

62. May our Lord Jesus Christ, O child, establish you in fear of Him, may He strengthen you to do His all-holy will and may He deem you worthy of His kingdom, that you may not hear the fearful sentence: *I do not know you, depart from Me, all you despisers of My commandments* (Psalm 6:8; Matthew 7:23; Luke 13:27).

Chapter XXV.
Instructions of Stephen the Sabaite to Those Who Have Renounced the World

1. First, have no association with women, lest you be consumed in their fire; nor with young boys, lest you fall into their snares.

2. Do not make acquaintance with persons of authority.

3. Do not love going to the city, lest you fall into fornication in heart and so keep your eye pure.

4. Do not eat a second time during the day without necessity, lest your body become fattened, and with it the passions.

5. Do not close your door to the stranger, lest the Lord close His door to you.

6. Care for the sick, that the Lord may also care for you.

7. Do not sleep much, and unceasingly ask help of God, that He may deliver you from temptations as a bird from the snare.

8. Do not be given to many words, lest you fall into lying.

9. Frequent the house of God for the giving of praise, for the Lord says: *"those who honor Me I will honor"* (1 Samuel 2:30).

10. Abide in purity, that you may quickly receive all that you ask.

11. Flee vanities and worldly cares.

12. Do not acquire for yourself things beyond necessity, but live temperately.

13. Work, so that you may have something to give to those in need in Christ Jesus our Lord, to Whom be glory unto the ages. Amen.

Chapter XXVI.
A Word of Holy Patriarch Luke:
How a Monk Ought to Conduct Himself in His Cell

1. In a day and night, perform 2,000 prayers—not all standing and not all sitting, but when you are able, stand, and when you cannot, sit. Three hundred prostrations—not all at once, but as you are able.

2. On Monday, Wednesday, and Friday, partake once of dry food and drink water.

3. Into your cell let not even the memory of a woman ever enter.

4. When brethren come to you in your cell, receive them and give them rest, yet do not yourself depart from your order and rule—unless perchance there be some brother, honorable and reverent, and moreover the hour for partaking of food should arrive; then partake with him, yet moderately and reverently.

5. Outside your cell, permit yourself no consolation, unless perchance you should happen upon some honorable and reverent house; but even there, allow yourself no more than three cups.

6. Each week, read through one Gospel from the Four Gospels.

7. When Christians permit themselves on Wednesday and Friday, permit yourself also. On the Lord's feasts, act according to the rule.

8. The services that Christians have, fulfill also yourself—namely: the midnight office, matins, the hours, vespers, and compline.

9. Read the Patericon and the lives of the saints, and have handiwork, as much as you can and as much as is needful.

Chapter XXVII.
Lessons of Our Holy Fathers and Teachers

1. Keep your mind always before God, whether you sleep or are awake, whether you take food or converse, whether you are occupied with handwork or do anything else, according to the word of Scripture: *I have set the Lord always before me* (Psalm 15:8), but at the same time consider yourself more sinful than any man. The unceasing remembrance of God illumines the mind like a ray, and the more you abide in it with all attention and sober thought, with labor and tears, the more your mind will be purified; the more it is purified, the more it will be enlightened; the more it is enlightened, the more it will become godlike, shining and discerning good from evil. However, brother, great labor and the help of God are needed for this remembrance to dwell in your soul and enlighten it, as the moon enlightens the darkness of night.

2. One must attend to the suggestions of thoughts of vainglory and self-conceit, so as not to condemn anyone, even if he does something unbecoming, for the demons, seeing that the soul through the indwelling of grace and its peaceful state has rejected vanities and passions, usually attack it with such suggestions: this is not help from the Lord.

3. Weep day and night and know no satiety in tears. See that you do not lose your inner consolation and contrition by imagining that you have them from your own labor and not from the grace of God. As soon as you imagine so, they will be taken from you, and afterward you will search much for them in your soul and not find them, until you realize that you have lost this gift by claiming as your own what belonged to another. But, O Lord! May we not be deprived of Thy grace! However, brother, if something should happen to you, cast your weakness upon the Lord and, rising up, stretch out your hands to Him and pray to Him, speaking thus: Lord! Have mercy on me, a sinner, and send me Thy grace and do not suffer me to be tempted beyond what I am able. Behold, O Lord, into what weakening and what darkness of thoughts my sins have cast me! If I say that I have suffered from demons, being deprived of Thy consolation, I lie, for Thou knowest, O Lord, that those who diligently fulfill Thy will in all things resist them with courage. But I, fulfilling their will in all things, how can I say that I am tempted by them? Therefore, do not abandon prayer even for one hour while there is breath in you, and it will soon restore you through the assistance of the grace of God.

BASED BOOKS

Based-Books.com